Project Management
A Managerial Approach
Fourth Edition

Selected Chapters

Jack R. Meredith
Samuel J. Mantel, Jr.

Prepared for

ESI International
Arlington, VA

WILEY

Printed in the United States of America.

ISBN 0-471-39359-2

FOURTH EDITION

PROJECT MANAGEMENT
A MANAGERIAL APPROACH

Jack R. Meredith
Broyhill Distinguished Scholar and Chair in Operations
Babcock Graduate School of Management
Wake Forest University

Samuel J. Mantel, Jr.
Joseph S. Stern Professor Emeritus of Operations Management
University of Cincinnati

JOHN WILEY & SONS
New York ▪ Chichester ▪ Weinheim ▪ Brisbane ▪ Toronto ▪ Singapore

ACQUISITIONS EDITOR   Beth Golub
MARKETING MANAGER   Peter Rytell
SENIOR PRODUCTION EDITOR   Patricia McFadden
DESIGNER   Karin Gerdes Kincheloe
ILLUSTRATION EDITOR   Anna Melhorn
PRODUCTION MANAGEMENT   Ingrao Associates
COVER PHOTO   Will McIntyre/Photo Researchers

This book was set in 10.5/12 Goudy by The PRD Group, Inc. and printed and bound by Quebecor Printing.
The cover was printed by Lehigh Press, Inc.

This book is printed on acid-free paper. ∞

ISBN 0-471-29829-8

Printed in the United States of America

10 9 8 7 6 5 4 3 2 1

Contents

PART I PROJECT INITIATION

2 Project Selection, 39
2.1 Criteria for Project Selection Models, 40
2.2 The Nature of Project Selection Models, 42
2.3 Types of Project Selection Models, 45
2.4 Analysis Under Uncertainty—The Management of Risk, 62
2.5 Comments on the Information Base for Selection, 66
2.6 Project Proposals, 68
    PROJECT MANAGEMENT IN PRACTICE: Project Selection for Spent Nuclear Fuel Cleanup, 52
    PROJECT MANAGEMENT IN PRACTICE: Selecting a Composting Project at Larry's Markets, 61
    PROJECT MANAGEMENT IN PRACTICE: The Military Mobile Communication System— A Procurement Innovation, 71
    DIRECTED READING: Automotive Builders, Inc.: The Stanhope Project, 79

5 Project Planning, 182
5.1 Initial Project Coordination, 184
5.2 Systems Integration, 192
5.3 Sorting Out the Project, 193
5.4 The Work Breakdown Structure and Linear Responsibility Charts, 203
5.5 Interface Coordination through Integration Management, 209
    PROJECT MANAGEMENT IN PRACTICE: Extensive Project Planning for Kodak's New Photographic System, 190

PROJECT MANAGEMENT IN PRACTICE: Disaster Project Planning in Iceland, 202
DIRECTED READING: Planning for Crisis in Project Management, 217

6 Conflict and Negotiation, 226
6.1 The Nature of Negotiation, 229
6.2 Partnering, Chartering, and Change, 230
6.3 Conflict and the Project Life Cycle, 234
6.4 Some Requirements and Principles of Negotiation, 243
6.5 Negotiation in Action—The Quad Sensor Project, 246
    PROJECT MANAGEMENT IN PRACTICE: Selling New Area Codes to Consumers Who Don't Want Them, 228
    PROJECT MANAGEMENT IN PRACTICE: A Consensus Feasibility Study for Montreal's Archipel Dam, 242
    DIRECTED READING: Methods of Resolving Interpersonal Conflict, 252

PART II PROJECT IMPLEMENTATION

7 Budgeting and Cost Estimation, 261
7.1 Estimating Project Budgets, 264
7.2 Improving the Process of Cost Estimation, 276
    PROJECT MANAGEMENT IN PRACTICE: Pathfinder Mission to Mars—on a Shoestring, 263

CONTENTS

PROJECT MANAGEMENT IN PRACTICE: Completing the Limerick Nuclear Facility Under Budget, 274
PROJECT MANAGEMENT IN PRACTICE: Managing Costs at Massachusetts' Neighborhood Health Plan, 290
DIRECTED READING: Three Perceptions of Project Cost, 295

8 Scheduling, 302
8.1 Background, 302
8.2 Network Techniques: PERT and CPM, 307
8.3 Gantt Charts, 332
8.4 Extensions and Applications, 339
PROJECT MANAGEMENT IN PRACTICE: Replacing the Atigun Section of the Trans Alaska Pipeline, 304
PROJECT MANAGEMENT IN PRACTICE: Hosting the Annual Project Management Institute Symposium, 336
DIRECTED READING: The Sharon Construction Corporation, 359

9 Resource Allocation, 361
9.1 Critical Path Method—Crashing a Project, 363
9.2 The Resource Allocation Problem, 371
9.3 Resource Loading, 372
9.4 Resource Leveling, 375
9.5 Constrained Resource Scheduling, 378
9.6 Multiproject Scheduling and Resource Allocation, 388
PROJECT MANAGEMENT IN PRACTICE: Expediting Los Angeles Freeway Repairs After the Earthquake, 362
PROJECT MANAGEMENT IN PRACTICE: Benefits of Resource Constraining at Pennsylvania Electric, 387
PROJECT MANAGEMENT IN PRACTICE: Minnesota DOT Ties Projects to Resources and Constraints, 399
DIRECTED READING: D. U. Singer Hospital Products Corp., 407

10 Monitoring and Information Systems, 410
10.1 The Planning-Monitoring-Controlling Cycle, 412
10.2 Information Needs and the Reporting Process, 422
10.3 Computerized PMIS (Project Management Information Systems), 437
PROJECT MANAGEMENT IN PRACTICE: Using Project Management Software to Schedule the Olympic Games, 411
PROJECT MANAGEMENT IN PRACTICE: Tracking Scope Creep: A Project Manager Responds, 421
PROJECT MANAGEMENT IN PRACTICE: Success Through Earned Value at Texas Instruments, 433
DIRECTED READING: Survey of Project Management Tools, 453

11 Project Control, 462
11.1 The Fundamental Purposes of Control, 464
11.2 Three Types of Control Processes, 468
11.3 Comments on the Design of Control Systems, 476
11.4 Control as a Function of Management, 482
11.5 Balance in a Control System, 487
11.6 Control of Creative Activities, 490
11.7 Control of Change and Scope Creep, 491
PROJECT MANAGEMENT IN PRACTICE: Extensive Controls for San Francisco's Metro Turnback Project, 466
PROJECT MANAGEMENT IN PRACTICE: Schedule and Cost Control for Australia's New Parliament House, 483
PROJECT MANAGEMENT IN PRACTICE: Better Control of Development Projects at Johnson Controls, 494
DIRECTED READING: Controlling Projects According to Plan, 500

CONTENTS

PART III PROJECT TERMINATION

13 Project Termination, 539

13.1 The Varieties of Project Termination, 540

13.2 When to Terminate a Project, 545

13.3 The Termination Process, 551

13.4 The Final Report—A Project History, 557

PROJECT MANAGEMENT IN PRACTICE: Nucor's Approach to Termination by Addition, 542

PROJECT MANAGEMENT IN PRACTICE: Terminating the Superconducting Super Collider Project, 550

DIRECTED READING: Knowing When to Pull the Plug, 563

Photo Credits, 593

Author Index, 595

Subject Index, 605

2

Project Selection

Project selection is the process of evaluating individual projects or groups of projects, and then choosing to implement some set of them so that the objectives of the parent organization will be achieved. This same systematic process can be applied to any area of the organization's business in which choices must be made between competing alternatives. For example, a manufacturing firm can use evaluation/selection techniques to choose which machine to adopt in a part-fabrication process; a TV station can select which of several syndicated comedy shows to rerun in its 7:30 PM weekday time-slot; a construction firm can select the best subset of a large group of potential projects on which to bid; or a hospital can find the best mix of psychiatric, orthopedic, obstetric, and other beds for a new wing.

In this chapter we look at the procedures firms use to decide which creative idea to support, which new technology to develop, which repair to authorize. Each project will have different costs, benefits, and risks. Rarely are these known with certainty. In the face of such differences, the selection of one project out of a set is a difficult task. Choosing a number of different projects, a *portfolio*, is even more complex.

This chapter covers a subject not customarily covered in books on project management. Though the PM often enters the picture at the stage of the project life cycle following selection, in many situations the PM is the person who has worked and lobbied for the selection of this specific project, particularly if a Request For Proposal (RFP) was involved. Moreover, though project evaluation and selection is usually a task for senior management, this is an important part of the project life cycle because project success is judged by the degree to which the project meets its goals. Since project selection is based on a direct statement of those goals, the PM needs to know them in order to perform effectively.

In this chapter we discuss several techniques that can be used to help senior managers select projects. Project selection is only one of many decisions associated with project management. To deal with all of these problems, we use *decision-aiding models*. We need such models because they abstract the relevant issues about a problem from the plethora of detail in which the problem is embedded. Realists cannot solve problems, only idealists can do that. Reality is far too complex to deal with in its entirety. An "idealist" is needed to strip away almost all the reality from a problem, leaving only the aspects of the "real" situation with which he or she wishes to deal. This process of carving away the unwanted reality from the bones of a problem is called *modeling the problem*. The idealized version of the problem that results is called a a *model*.

The model represents the problem's *structure*, its form. Every problem has a form, though often we may not understand a problem well enough to describe its structure. We will use many models in this book—graphs, analogies, diagrams, as well as *flow graph* and *network* models to help solve scheduling problems, and *symbolic* (mathematical) models for a number of purposes.

Models may be quite simple to understand, or they may be extremely complex. In general, introducing more reality into a model tends to make the model more difficult to manipulate. If the input data for a model are not known precisely, we often use probabilistic information; that is, the model is said to be *stochastic* rather than *deterministic*. Again, in general, stochastic models are more difficult to manipulate. (Readers who are not familiar with the fundamentals of decision making might find a book such as *The New Science of Management Decisions* [36] or *Fundamentals of Management Science* [40] useful.)

This chapter relies heavily on the use of models for project evaluation and selection. First, we examine fundamental types of project selection models and the characteristics that make any model more or less acceptable. Next we consider the limitations, strengths, and weaknesses of project selection models, including some suggestions of factors to consider when making a decision about which, if any, of the project selection models to use (see also the end of Section 2.3). We then discuss the problem of selecting projects when high levels of uncertainty about outcomes, costs, schedules, or technology are present, as well as some ways of managing the risks associated with the uncertainties. Finally, we comment on some special aspects of the information base required for project selection.

One might argue that we should discuss the *project proposal*, its contents and construction, before considering project selection models. It is, however, useful to understand how an idea will be evaluated before deciding on how best to present the idea. Further, we set aside the issue of where ideas come from and how they are introduced into the process that, sooner or later, results in a proposal. The subject is certainly of consequence, but PMs are rarely directly involved. As noted, project proposals are discussed later in this chapter. We finish the chapter with a guess about the future of project selection models.

2.1 CRITERIA FOR PROJECT SELECTION MODELS

We live in the midst of what has been called the "knowledge explosion." We frequently hear comments such as "90 percent of all we know about physics has been discovered since Albert Einstein published his original work on special relativity"; and

"80 percent of what we know about the human body has been discovered in the past 50 years." In addition, evidence is cited to show that knowledge is growing exponentially. Such statements emphasize the importance of the *management of change*. To survive, firms must develop strategies for assessing and reassessing the use of their resources. Every allocation of resources is an investment in the future. Because of the complex nature of most strategies, many of these investments are in projects.

To cite one of many possible examples, special visual effects accomplished through computer animation are common in the movies and television shows we watch daily. A few years ago they were unknown. When the capability was in its idea stage, computer companies as well as the firms producing movies and TV shows faced the decision whether or not to invest in the development of these techniques. Obviously valuable as the idea seems today, the choice was not quite so clear a decade ago when an entertainment company compared investment in computer animation to alternative investments in a new star, a new rock group, or a new theme park.

The proper choice of investment projects is crucial to the long-run survival of every firm. Daily we witness the results of both good and bad investment choices. In our daily newspapers we read of Cisco System's decision to purchase firms that have developed valuable communication network software rather than to develop its own software. We read of Procter and Gamble's decision to invest heavily in marketing its products on the Internet; British Airways' decision to purchase passenger planes from Airbus instead of from its traditional supplier, Boeing; or problems faced by school systems when they update student computer labs—should they invest in Windows®-based systems or stick with their traditional choice, Apple®. But can such important choices be made rationally? Once made, do they ever change, and if so, how? These questions reflect the need for effective selection models.

Within the limits of their capabilities, such models can be used to increase profits, select investments for limited capital resources, or improve the competitive position of the organization. They can be used for ongoing evaluation as well as initial selection, and thus are a key to the allocation and reallocation of the organization's scarce resources.

When a firm chooses a project selection model, the following criteria, based on Souder [37], are most important.

1. *Realism* The model should reflect the reality of the manager's decision situation, including the multiple objectives of both the firm and its managers. Without a common measurement system, direct comparison of different projects is impossible. For example, Project A may strengthen a firm's market share by extending its facilities, and Project B might improve its competitive position by strengthening its technical staff. Other things being equal, which is better? The model should take into account the realities of the firm's limitations on facilities, capital, personnel, etc. The model should also include factors that reflect project risks, including the technical risks of performance, cost, and time as well as the market risks of customer rejection and other implementation risks.

2. *Capability* The model should be sophisticated enough to deal with multiple time periods, simulate various situations both internal and external to the project (e.g., strikes, interest rate changes, etc.), and optimize the decision. An optimizing model will make the comparisons that management deems important, consider

major risks and constraints on the projects, and then select the best overall project or set of projects.

3. *Flexibility*   The model should give valid results within the range of conditions that the firm might experience. It should have the ability to be easily modified, or to be self-adjusting in response to changes in the firm's environment; for example, tax laws change, new technological advancements alter risk levels, and, above all, the organization's goals change.

4. *Ease of Use*   The model should be reasonably convenient, not take a long time to execute, and be easy to use and understand. It should not require special interpretation, data that are difficult to acquire, excessive personnel, or unavailable equipment. The model's variables should also relate one-to-one with those real-world parameters the managers believe significant to the project. Finally, it should be easy to simulate the expected outcomes associated with investments in different project portfolios.

5. *Cost*   Data-gathering and modeling costs should be low relative to the cost of the project and must surely be less than the potential benefits of the project. All costs should be considered, including the costs of data management and of running the model.

We would add a sixth criterion:

6. *Easy Computerization*   It must be easy and convenient to gather and store the information in a computer data base, and to manipulate data in the model through use of a widely available, standard computer package such as Lotus 1-2-3®, Quattro Pro®, Excel®, and like programs. The same ease and convenience should apply to transferring the information to any of the standard decision support systems.

2.2 THE NATURE OF PROJECT SELECTION MODELS

There are two basic types of project selection models, numeric and nonnumeric. Both are widely used. Many organizations use both at the same time, or they use models that are combinations of the two. Nonnumeric models, as the name implies, do not use numbers as inputs. Numeric models do, but the criteria being measured may be either objective or subjective. It is important to remember that the *qualities* of a project may be represented by numbers, and that *subjective* measures are not necessarily less useful or reliable than so-called *objective* measures. (We will discuss these matters in more detail in Section 2.5.)

Before examining specific kinds of models within the two basic types, let us consider just what we wish the model to do for us, never forgetting two critically important, but often overlooked, facts.

- Models do not make decisions; people do. The manager, not the model, bears responsibility for the decision. The manager may "delegate" the task of making the decision to a model, but the responsibility cannot be abdicated.

- All models, however sophisticated, are only partial representations of the reality they are meant to reflect. Reality is far too complex for us to capture more than a small fraction of it in any model. Therefore, no model can yield an optimal decision except within its own, possibly inadequate, framework.

We seek a model to assist us in making project selection decisions. This model should possess the characteristics discussed previously and, above all, it must evaluate potential projects by the degree to which they will meet the firm's objectives. To construct a selection/evaluation model, therefore, it is necessary to develop a list of the firm's objectives.

A list of objectives should be generated by the organization's top management. It is a direct expression of organizational philosophy and policy. The list should go beyond the typical clichés about "survival" and "maximizing profits," which are certainly real goals but are just as certainly not the only goals of the firm. Other objectives might include maintenance of share of specific markets, development of an improved image with specific clients or competitors, expansion into a new line of business, decrease in sensitivity to business cycles, maintenance of employment for specific categories of workers, and maintenance of system loading at or above some percent of capacity, just to mention a few.

A model of some sort is implied by any conscious decision. The choice between two or more alternative courses of action requires reference to some objective(s), and the choice is thus made in accord with some, possibly subjective, "model."

Since the development of computers and the establishment of operations research as an academic subject in the mid-1950s, the use of formal, numeric models to assist in decision making has expanded. Many of these models use financial metrics such as profits and/or cash flow to measure the "correctness" of a managerial decision. Project selection decisions are no exception, being based primarily on the degree to which the financial goals of the organization are met. As we will see later, this stress on financial goals, largely to the exclusion of other criteria, raises some serious problems for the firm, irrespective of whether the firm is for-profit or not-for-profit.

When the list of objectives has been developed, an additional refinement is recommended. The elements in the list should be *weighted*. Each item is added to the list because it represents a contribution to the success of the organization, but each item does not make an equal contribution. The weights reflect different degrees of contribution each element makes in accomplishing a set of goals.

Once the list of goals has been developed, one more task remains. The probable contribution of each project to each of the goals must be estimated. A project is selected or rejected because it is predicted to have certain outcomes if implemented. These outcomes are expected to contribute to goal achievement. If the estimated level of goal achievement is sufficiently large, the project is selected. If not, it is rejected. The relationship between the project's expected results and the organization's goals must be understood. In general, the kinds of information required to evaluate a project can be listed under production, marketing, financial, personnel, administrative, and other such categories.

Table 2-1 is a list of factors that contribute, positively or negatively, to these categories. In order to give focus to this list, we assume that the projects in question involve the possible substitution of a new production process for an existing one. The list is meant to be illustrative. It certainly is not exhaustive.

Some factors in this list have a one-time impact and some recur. Some are difficult to estimate and may be subject to considerable error. For these, it is helpful to identify a *range of uncertainty*. In addition, the factors may occur at different times. And some factors may have *thresholds*, critical values above or below which we might wish to reject the project. We will deal in more detail with these issues later in this chapter.

Clearly, no single project decision need include all these factors. Moreover, not only is the list incomplete, also it contains redundant items. Perhaps more important, the factors are not at the same level of generality: *profitability* and *impact on orga-*

Table 2-1. Project Evaluation Factors

Production Factors
1. Time until ready to install
2. Length of disruption during installation
3. Learning curve—time until operating as desired
4. Effects on waste and rejects
5. Energy requirements
6. Facility and other equipment requirements
7. Safety of process
8. Other applications of technology
9. Change in cost to produce a unit output
10. Change in raw material usage
11. Availability of raw materials
12. Required development time and cost
13. Impact on current suppliers
14. Change in quality of output

Marketing Factors
1. Size of potential market for output
2. Probable market share of output
3. Time until market share is acquired
4. Impact on current product line
5. Consumer acceptance
6. Impact on consumer safety
7. Estimated life of output
8. Spin-off project possibilities

Financial Factors
1. Profitability, net present value of the investment
2. Impact on cash flows

3. Payout period
4. Cash requirements
5. Time until break-even
6. Size of investment required
7. Impact on seasonal and cyclical fluctuations

Personnel Factors
1. Training requirements
2. Labor skill requirements
3. Availability of required labor skills
4. Level of resistance from current work force
5. Change in size of labor force
6. Inter- and intra-group communication requirements
7. Impact on working conditions

Administrative and Miscellaneous Factors
1. Meet government safety standards
2. Meet government environmental standards
3. Impact on information system
4. Reaction of stockholders and securities markets
5. Patent and trade secret protection
6. Impact on image with customers, suppliers, and competitors
7. Degree to which we understand new technology
8. Managerial capacity to direct and control new process

nizational image both affect the overall organization, but *impact on working conditions* is more oriented to the production system. Nor are all elements of equal importance. *Change in production cost* is usually considered more important than *impact on current suppliers*. Shortly, we will consider the problem of generating an acceptable list of factors and measuring their relative importance. At that time we will discuss the creation of a Decision Support System (DSS) for project evaluation and selection. The same subject will arise once more in Chapters 12 and 13 when we consider project auditing, evaluation, and termination.

Although the process of evaluating a potential project is time-consuming and difficult, its importance cannot be overstated. A major consulting firm has argued [21] that the primary cause for the failure of R & D projects is insufficient care in evaluating the proposal before the expenditure of funds. What is true for R & D projects also appears to be true for other kinds of projects, and it is clear that product development projects are more successful if they incorporate user needs and satisfaction in the design process [24]. Careful analysis of a potential project is a *sine qua non* for profitability in the construction business. There are many horror stories [25] about firms that undertook projects for the installation of a computer information system without sufficient analysis of the time, cost, and disruption involved.

Later in this chapter we will consider the problem of conducting an evaluation under conditions of uncertainty about the outcomes associated with a project. Before dealing with this problem, however, it helps to examine several different evaluation/selection models and consider their strengths and weaknesses. Recall that the problem of choosing the project selection model itself will also be discussed later.

2.3 TYPES OF PROJECT SELECTION MODELS

Of the two basic types of selection models, numeric and nonnumeric, nonnumeric models are older and simpler and have only a few subtypes to consider. We examine them first.

Nonnumeric Models

The Sacred Cow In this case the project is suggested by a senior and powerful official in the organization. Often the project is initiated with a simple comment such as, "If you have a chance, why don't you look into . . . ," and there follows an undeveloped idea for a new product, for the development of a new market, for the design and adoption of a global data base and information system, or for some other project requiring an investment of the firm's resources. The immediate result of this bland statement is the creation of a "project" to investigate whatever the boss has suggested. The project is "sacred" in the sense that it will be maintained until successfully concluded, or until the boss, personally, recognizes the idea as a failure and terminates it.

The Operating Necessity If a flood is threatening the plant, a project to build a protective dike does not require much formal evaluation, in an example of this scenario. Republic Steel Corporation (now a part of LTV Corp.) has used this criterion (and the following criterion also) in evaluating potential projects. If the project is required in order to keep the system operating, the primary question becomes: Is the system worth saving at the estimated cost of the project? If the answer is yes, project costs will be examined to make sure they are kept as low as is consistent with project success, but the project will be funded.

The Competitive Necessity Using this criterion, Republic Steel undertook a major plant rebuilding project in the late 1960s in its steel-bar-manufacturing facilities near Chicago. It had become apparent to Republic's management that the company's bar mill needed modernization if the firm was to maintain its competitive position in the Chicago market area. Although the planning process for the project was quite sophisticated, the decision to undertake the project was based on a desire to maintain the company's competitive position in that market.

In a similar manner, many business schools are restructuring their undergraduate and MBA programs to stay competitive with the more forward-looking schools. In large part, this action is driven by declining numbers of tuition-paying students and the stronger competition to attract them.

Investment in an *operating necessity* project takes precedence over a *competitive necessity* project, but both types of projects may bypass the more careful numeric analysis used for projects deemed to be less urgent or less important to the survival of the firm.

The Product Line Extension In this case, a project to develop and distribute new products would be judged on the degree to which it fits the firm's existing product line, fills a gap, strengthens a weak link, or extends the line in a new, desirable direction. Sometimes careful calculations of profitability are not required. Decision makers can act on their beliefs about what will be the likely impact on the total system performance if the new product is added to the line.

Comparative Benefit Model For this situation, assume that an organization has many projects to consider, perhaps several dozen. Senior management would like to select a subset of the projects that would most benefit the firm, but the projects do not seem to be easily comparable. For example, some projects concern potential new products, some concern changes in production methods, others concern computerization of certain records, and still others cover a variety of subjects not easily categorized (e.g., a proposal to create a daycare center for employees with small children). The organization has no formal method of selecting projects, but members of the Selection Committee think that some projects will benefit the firm more than others, even if they have no precise way to define or measure "benefit."

The concept of comparative benefits, if not a formal model, is widely adopted for selection decisions on all sorts of projects. Most United Way organizations use the concept to make decisions about which of several social programs to fund. Senior management of the funding organization then examines all projects with positive recommendations and attempts to construct a portfolio that best fits the organization's aims and its budget.

Of the several techniques for ordering projects, the Q-Sort [10] is one of the most straightforward. First, the projects are divided into three groups—*good, fair,* and *poor*—according to their relative merits. If any group has more than eight members, it is subdivided into two categories, such as *fair-plus* and *fair-minus*. When all categories have eight or fewer members, the projects within each category are ordered from best to worst. Again, the order is determined on the basis of relative merit. The rater may use specific criteria to rank each project, or may simply use general overall judgment. (See Figure 2-1 for an example of a Q-Sort.)

The process described may be carried out by one person who is responsible for evaluation and selection, or it may be performed by a committee charged with the responsibility. If a committee handles the task, the individual rankings can be developed anonymously, and the set of anonymous rankings can be examined by the committee itself for consensus. It is common for such rankings to differ somewhat from rater to rater, but they do not often vary strikingly because the individuals chosen for such committees rarely differ widely on what they feel to be appropriate for the parent organization. Projects can then be selected in the order of preference, though they are usually evaluated financially before final selection.

There are other, similar nonnumeric models for accepting or rejecting projects. Although it is easy to dismiss such models as unscientific, they should not be discounted casually. These models are clearly goal-oriented and directly reflect the primary concerns of the organization. The sacred cow model, in particular, has an added

Steps	Results at Each Step
1. For each participant in the exercise, assemble a deck of cards, with the name and description of one project on each card. 2. Instruct each participant to divide the deck into two piles, one representing a high priority, the other a low-priority level. (The piles need not be equal.) 3. Instruct each participant to select cards from each pile to form a third pile representing the medium-priority level. 4. Instruct each participant to select cards from the high-level pile to yield another pile representing the very high level of priority; select cards from the low-level pile representing the very low level of priority. 5. Finally, instruct each participant to survey the selections and shift any cards that seem out of place until the classifications are satisfactory.	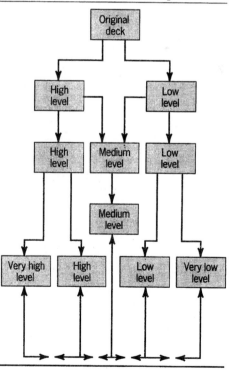

Figure 2-1 The Q-sort method. *Source:* [38]

feature; sacred cow projects are visibly supported by "the powers that be." Full support by top management is certainly an important contributor to project success [25]. Without such support, the probability of project success is sharply lowered.

Numeric Models: Profit/Profitability

As noted earlier, a large majority of all firms using project evaluation and selection models use profit/profitability as the sole measure of acceptability. We will consider these models first, and then discuss models that surpass the profit test for acceptance.

Payback Period The payback period for a project is the initial fixed investment in the project divided by the estimated annual cash inflows from the project. The ratio of these quantities is the number of years required for the project to repay its initial fixed investment. For example, assume a project costs $100,000 to implement and has annual net cash inflows of $25,000. Then

$$\text{Payback period} = \$100,000/\$25,000 = 4 \text{ years}$$

This method assumes that the cash inflows will persist at least long enough to pay back the investment, and it ignores any cash inflows beyond the payback period. The method also serves as an inadequate proxy for risk. The faster the investment is recovered, the less the risk to which the firm is exposed.

Average Rate of Return Often mistaken as the reciprocal of the payback period, the average rate of return is the ratio of the average annual profit (either before or after taxes) to the initial or average investment in the project. Because average annual profits are usually not equivalent to net cash inflows, the average rate of return does not usually equal the reciprocal of the payback period. Assume, in the example just given, that the average annual profits are $15,000:

$$\text{Average rate of return} = \$15,000/\$100,000 = 0.15$$

Neither of these evaluation methods is recommended for project selection, though payback period is widely used and does have a legitimate value for cash budgeting decisions. The major advantage of these models is their simplicity, but neither takes into account the time-value of money. Unless interest rates are extremely low and the rate of inflation is nil, the failure to reduce future cash flows or profits to their present value will result in serious evaluation errors.

Discounted Cash Flow Also referred to as the net present value method, the discounted cash flow method determines the net present value of all cash flows by discounting them by the required rate of return (also known as the *hurdle rate*, *cutoff rate*, and similar terms) as follows:

$$\text{NPV (project)} = A_0 + \sum_{t=1}^{n} \frac{F_t}{(1 + k)^t}$$

where

  F_t = the net cash flow in period t,
  k = the required rate of return, and
  A_0 = initial cash investment (because this is an outflow, it will be negative).

To include the impact of inflation (or deflation) where p_t is the predicted rate of inflation during period t, we have

$$\text{NPV (project)} = A_0 + \sum_{t=1}^{n} \frac{F_t}{(1 + k + p_t)^t}$$

Early in the life of a project, net cash flow is likely to be negative, the major outflow being the initial investment in the project, A_0. If the project is successful, however, cash flows will become positive. The project is *acceptable* if the sum of the net present values of all estimated cash flows over the life of the project is positive. A simple example will suffice. Using our $100,000 investment with a net cash inflow of $25,000 per year for a period of eight years, a required rate of return of 15 percent, and an inflation rate of 3 percent per year, we have

$$\text{NPV (project)} = -\$100,000 + \sum_{t=1}^{8} \frac{\$25,000}{(1 + 0.15 + 0.03)^t}$$

$$= \$1939$$

Because the present value of the inflows is greater than the present value of the outflow—that is, the net present value is positive—the project is deemed acceptable.

PsychoCeramic Sciences, Inc.

PsychoCeramic Sciences, Inc. (PSI), a large producer of cracked pots and other cracked items, is considering the installation of a new manufacturing line that will, it is hoped, allow more precise quality control on the size, shape, and location of the cracks in its pots as well as in vases designed to hold artificial flowers.

The plant engineering department has submitted a project proposal that estimates the investment requirements as follows: an initial investment of $125,000 to be paid up- front to the Pocketa-Pocketa Machine Corporation; an additional investment of $100,000 to install the machines; and another $90,000 to add new material handling systems and integrate the new equipment into the overall production system. Delivery and installation is estimated to take one year; integrating the entire system should require an additional year. Thereafter, the engineers predict that scheduled machine overhauls will require further expenditures of about $15,000 every second year, beginning in the fourth year. They will not, however, overhaul the machinery in the last year of its life.

The project schedule calls for production to begin in the third year, and to be up-to-speed by the end of that year. Projected manufacturing cost savings and added profits resulting from higher quality are estimated to be $50,000 in the first year of operation and are expected to peak at $120,000 in the second year of operation, and then to follow the gradually declining pattern shown in the table at the end of this box.

Project life is expected to be 10 years from project inception, at which time the proposed system will be obsolete and will have to be replaced. It is estimated that the machinery will have a salvage value of $35,000.

PSI has a 12 percent hurdle rate for capital investments and expects the rate of inflation to be about 3 percent over the life of the project. Assuming that the initial expenditure occurs at the beginning of the year and that all other receipts and expenditures occur as lump sums at the end of the year, we can prepare the Net Present Value analysis for the project as shown in the table below.

The Net Present Value of the project is positive and, thus, the project can be accepted. (The project would have been rejected if the hurdle rate were 14 percent.)

Just for the intellectual exercise, note that the total inflow for the project is $759,000,

or $75,900 per year on average for the 10 year project. The required investment is $315,000 (ignoring the biennial overhaul charges). Assuming 10 year, straight line depreciation or $31,500 per year, the payback period would be:

$$PB = \frac{\$315,000}{\$75,900 + 31,500} = 2.9 \text{ years}$$

A project with this payback period would probably be considered quite desirable.

Year A	Inflow B	Outflow C	Net Flow D = (B − C)	Discount Factor $1/(1 + k + p)^t$	Net Present Value D (Disc. Fact.)
1996*	$ 0	$125,000	$−125,000	1.0000	$−125,000
1996	0	100,000	−100,000	0.8696	− 86,960
1997	0	90,000	− 90,000	0.7561	− 68,049
1998	50,000	0	50,000	0.6575	32,875
1999	120,000	15,000	105,000	0.5718	60,039
2000	115,000	0	115,000	0.4972	57,178
2001	105,000	15,000	90,000	0.4323	38,907
2002	97,000	0	97,000	0.3759	36,462
2003	90,000	15,000	75,000	0.3269	24,518
2004	82,000	0	82,000	0.2843	23,313
2005	65,000	0	65,000	0.2472	16,068
2005	35,000		35,000	0.2472	8,652
Total	$759,000	$360,000	$ 399,000		$ 18,003

*$t = 0$ at the beginning of 1996

Internal Rate of Return   If we have a set of expected cash inflows and cash outflows, the internal rate of return is the discount rate that equates the present values of the two sets of flows. If A_t is an expected cash outflow in the period t and R_t is the expected inflow for the period t, the internal rate of return is the value of k that satisfies the following equation (note that the A_0 will be positive in this formulation of the problem):

$$A_0 + A_1/(1 + k) + A_2/(1 + k)^2 + \ldots + A_n/(1 + k)^n = R_1/(1 + k) + R_2/(1 + k)^2 + \ldots + R_n/(1 + k)^n \quad t = 1,2,3 \ldots ,n$$

The value of k is found by trial and error.

Profitability Index   Also known as the benefit–cost ratio, the profitability index is the net present value of all future expected cash flows divided by the initial cash investment. (Some firms do not discount the cash flows in making this calculation.) If this ratio is greater than 1.0, the project may be accepted.

Other Profitability Models There are a great many variations of the models just described. These variations fall into three general categories: (1) those that subdivide net cash flow into the elements that comprise the net flow; (2) those that include specific terms to introduce risk (or uncertainty, which is treated as risk) into the evaluation; and (3) those that extend the analysis to consider effects that the project might have on other projects or activities in the organization.

Several comments are in order about all the profit-profitability numeric models. First, let us consider their advantages:

1. The undiscounted models are simple to use and understand.
2. All use readily available accounting data to determine the cash flows.
3. Model output is in terms familiar to business decision makers.
4. With a few exceptions, model output is on an "absolute" profit/profitability scale and allows "absolute" go/no-go decisions.
5. Some profit models account for project risk.

The disadvantages of these models are the following:

1. These models ignore all nonmonetary factors except risk.
2. Models that do not include discounting ignore the timing of the cash flows and the time–value of money.
3. Models that reduce cash flows to their present value are strongly biased toward the short run.
4. Payback-type models ignore cash flows beyond the payback period.
5. The internal rate of return model can result in multiple solutions.
6. All are sensitive to errors in the input data for the early years of the project.
7. All discounting models are nonlinear, and the effects of changes (or errors) in the variables or parameters are generally not obvious to most decision makers.
8. All these models depend for input on a determination of cash flows, but it is not clear exactly how the concept of cash flow is properly defined for the purpose of evaluating projects.

A complete discussion of profit/profitability models can be found in any standard work on financial management—see [26, 32], for example. In general, the net present value models are preferred to the internal rate of return models. Despite wide use, financial models rarely include non-financial outcomes in their benefits and costs. In a discussion of the financial value of adopting project management (that is, selecting a project for adopting project management) in a firm, Githens notes that traditional financial models "simply cannot capture the complexity and value-added of today's process-oriented firm" [8].

In our experience, the payback period model, occasionally using discounted cash flows, is one of the most commonly used models for evaluating projects and other investment opportunities. Managers generally feel that insistence on short payout periods tends to minimize the uncertainties associated with the passage of time. While this is certainly logical, we prefer evaluation methods that discount cash flows and deal with uncertainty more directly by considering specific risks. Using the payout period as a cash-budgeting tool aside, *its only virtue is simplicity*, a dubious virtue at best.

Project Management in Practice
Project Selection for Spent Nuclear Fuel Cleanup

In 1994, Westinghouse Hanford Co., on contract to the Department of Energy's Hanford Nuclear Fuel Site, reorganized for "projectization" to help Hanford with facility shutdown, decommissioning, and site cleanup. The major project in this overall task was the site cleanup of 2,100 metric tons of degraded spent nuclear fuel slugs submerged beneath 16 feet of water (as a radiation shield) in two rectangular, 25 foot deep, half-football field–sized basins. Of the over 105,000 slugs, about 6,000 were severely damaged or corroded and leaking radiation into the basin water. The 40-year old basins, located only 400 yards from Washington State's pristine Columbia River, had an original 20-year design life and were in

very poor condition, experiencing major leaks in the late 1970s and again in 1993. Operating and attempting to maintain these "accidents waiting to happen" cost $100,000 a day.

To address this problem, Westinghouse Hanford went to the site's stakeholders—the media, activists, regulators, oversight groups, three Indian tribes, government leaders, Congress, and Hanford employees—to determine acceptable options for dealing with this immense problem. It required five months of public discussion for the stakeholders to understand the issues and regain their trust in Hanford. Another two months were required to develop four project options as follows:

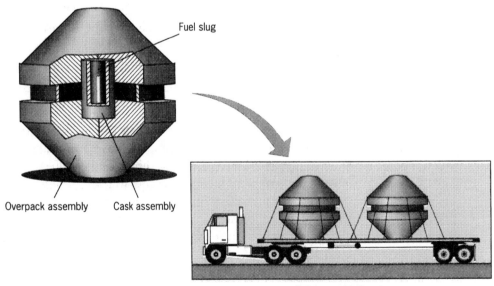

Fuel slug packaging system developed to transport and store fuel capsules.

1. Better encapsulate the fuel and leave it in the basins.
2. Place the fuel in wet storage elsewhere at Hanford.
3. Place the fuel in dry storage at Hanford.
4. Ship the fuel overseas for reprocessing.

Source: J.C. Fulton, "Complex Problem . . . Simple Concepts . . . Transformed Organization," *PM Network,* July 1996, pp. 15–21.

Following three months of evaluation, the third option was selected and an environmental impact statement (EIS) begun, which required eleven more months to complete (yet half the normal EIS completion time). The project is now underway and is expected to be complete by December 1999, three years ahead of the original schedule and thereby saving taxpayers $350 million. Also, the cost of maintaining the fuel is expected to drop to only $3,000 per day.

Numeric Models: Scoring

In an attempt to overcome some of the disadvantages of profitability models, particularly their focus on a single decision criterion, a number of evaluation/selection models that use multiple criteria to evaluate a project have been developed. Such models vary widely in their complexity and information requirements. The examples discussed illustrate some of the different types of numeric scoring models.

Unweighted 0–1 Factor Model A set of relevant factors is selected by management and then usually listed in a preprinted form. One or more raters score the project on each factor, depending on whether or not it qualifies for an individual criterion. The raters are chosen by senior managers, for the most part from the rolls of senior management. The criteria for choice are (1) a clear understanding of organizational goals and (2) a good knowledge of the firm's potential project *portfolio.* Figure 2-2 shows an example of the rating sheet for an unweighted, 0–1 factor model.

The columns of Figure 2-2 are summed and those projects with a sufficient number of qualifying factors may be selected. The main advantage of such a model is that it uses several criteria in the decision process. The major disadvantages are that it assumes all criteria are of equal importance and it allows for no gradation of the degree to which a specific project meets the various criteria.

Unweighted Factor Scoring Model The second disadvantage of the 0–1 factor model can be dealt with by constructing a simple linear measure of the degree to which the project being evaluated meets each of the criteria contained in the list. The x marks in Figure 2-2 would be replaced by numbers. Often a five-point scale is used, where 5 is very good, 4 is good, 3 is fair, 2 is poor, 1 is very poor. (Three-, seven-, and 10-point scales are also common.) The second column of Figure 2-2 would not be needed. The column of scores is summed, and those projects with a total score exceeding some critical value are selected. A variant of this selection process might choose the highest-scoring projects (still assuming they are all above some critical score) until the estimated costs of the set of projects equaled the resource limit. However, the criticism that the criteria are all assumed to be of equal importance still holds.

The use of a discrete numeric scale to represent the degree to which a criterion is satisfied is widely accepted. To construct such measures for project evaluation, we proceed in the following manner. Select a criterion, say, "estimated annual profits

Project _____

Rater _____ Date _____

	Qualifies	Does Not Qualify
No increase in energy requirements	x	
Potential market size, dollars	x	
Potential market share, percent	x	
No new facility required	x	
No new technical expertise required		x
No decrease in quality of final product	x	
Ability to manage project with current personnel		x
No requirement for reorganization	x	
Impact on work force safety	x	
Impact on environmental standards	x	
Profitability		
Rate of return more than 15% after tax	x	
Estimated annual profits more than $250,000	x	
Time to break-even less than 3 years	x	
Need for external consultants		x
Consistency with current line of business		x
Inpact on company image		
With customers	x	
With our industry		x
Totals	12	5

Figure 2-2 Sample project evaluation form.

in dollars." For this criterion, determine five ranges of performance so that a typical project, chosen at random, would have a roughly equal chance of being in any one of the five performance ranges. (Another way of describing this condition is: Take a large number of projects that were selected for support in the past, regardless of whether they were actually successful or not, and create five levels of predicted performance so that about one-fifth of the projects fall into each level.) This procedure will usually create unequal ranges, which may offend our sense of symmetry but need not concern us otherwise. It ensures that each criterion performance measure utilizes the full scale of possible values, a desirable characteristic for performance measures.

Consider the following two simple examples. Using the criterion just mentioned, "estimated annual profits in dollars," we might construct the following scale:

Score	Performance Level
5	Above $1,100,000
4	$750,001 to $1,100,000
3	$500,001 to $750,000
2	$200,000 to $500,000
1	Less than $200,000

As suggested, these ranges might have been chosen so that about 20 percent of the projects considered for funding would fall into each of the five ranges.

The criterion "no decrease in quality of the final product" would have to be restated to be scored on a five-point scale, perhaps as follows:

Score	Performance Level
	The quality of the final product is:
5	significantly and visibly improved
4	significantly improved, but not visible to buyer
3	not significantly changed
2	significantly lowered, but not visible to buyer
1	significantly and visibly lowered

This scale is an example of scoring cells that represent opinion rather than objective (even if "estimated") fact, as was the case in the profit scale.

Weighted Factor Scoring Model   When numeric weights reflecting the relative importance of each individual factor are added, we have a weighted factor scoring model. In general, it takes the form

$$S_i = \sum_{j=1}^{n} s_{ij} w_j$$

where

S_i = the total score of the ith project,

s_{ij} = the score of the ith project on the jth criterion, and

w_j = the weight of the jth criterion.

The weights, w_j, may be generated by any technique that is acceptable to the organization's policy makers. There are several techniques available to generate such numbers, but the most effective and most widely used is the Delphi technique. The Delphi technique was developed by Brown and Dalkey of the RAND Corporation during the 1950s and 1960s [5]. It is a technique for developing numeric values that are equivalent to subjective, verbal measures of relative value. The method of successive comparisons (or pairwise comparisons) may also be used for the same purpose [4].

Another popular and quite similar approach is the Analytic Hierarchy Process, developed by Saaty, see [33]. For an extensive example involving finance, sales, and purchasing, see pages 306–316 of Turban and Meredith [40]. This example also illustrates the use of Expert Choice®, a software package to facilitate the application of the Analytic Hierarchy Process.

When numeric weights have been generated, it is helpful (but not necessary) to scale the weights so that

$$0 \leq w_j \leq 1 \qquad j = 1,2,3, \ldots , n$$

$$\sum_{j=1}^{n} w_j = 1$$

The weight of each criterion can be interpreted as the "percent of the total weight accorded to that particular criterion."

A special caveat is in order. It is quite possible with this type of model to include a large number of criteria. It is not particularly difficult to develop scoring scales and weights, and the ease of gathering and processing the required information makes it tempting to include marginally relevant criteria along with the obviously important items. Resist this temptation! After the important factors have been weighted, there usually is little residual weight to be distributed among the remaining elements. The result is that the evaluation is simply insensitive to major differences in the scores on trivial criteria. A good rule of thumb is to discard elements with weights less than 0.02 or 0.03. (If elements are discarded, and if you wish $\sum w_j = 1$, the weights must be rescaled to 1.0.) As with any linear model, the user should be aware that the elements in the model are assumed to be independent. This presents no particular problems for these scoring models because they are used to make estimates in a "steady–state" system, and we are not concerned with transitions between states.

It is useful to note that if one uses a weighted scoring model to aid in project selection, the model can also serve as an aid to project *improvement*. For any given criterion, the difference between the criterion's score and the highest possible score on that criterion, multiplied by the weight of the criterion, is a measure of the potential improvement in the project score that would result were the project's performance on that criterion sufficiently improved. It may be that such improvement is not feasible, or is more costly than the improvement warrants. On the other hand, such an analysis of each project yields a valuable statement of the comparative benefits of project improvements. Viewing a project in this way is a type of sensitivity analysis. We examine the degree to which a project's score is sensitive to attempts to improve it—usually by adding resources. We will use sensitivity analysis several times in this book. It is a powerful managerial technique.

It is not particularly difficult to computerize a weighted scoring model by creating a template on Excel or one of the other standard computer spreadsheets. In Chapter 13, Section 13.3 we discuss an example of a computerized scoring model used for the project termination decision. The model is, in fact, a project selection model. The logic of using a "selection" model for the termination decision is straightforward: Given the time and resources required to take a project from its current state to completion, should we make the investment? A "Yes" answer to that question "selects" for funding the partially completed project from the set of all partially finished and not-yet-started projects.

Gettin' Wheels

Rather than using an example in which actual projects are selected for funding with a weighted factor scoring model (hereafter "scoring model") that would require tediously long descriptions of the projects, we can demonstrate the use of the model in a simple, common problem that many readers will have faced—the choice of an automobile for purchase. This problem is nicely suited to use of the scoring model because the purchaser is trying to satisfy multiple objectives in making the purchase and is typically faced with several different cars from which to choose.

Our model must have the following elements:

1. A set of criteria on which to judge the value of any alternative;

2. A numeric estimate of the relative importance (i.e., the "weight") of each criterion in the set; and

3. Scales by which to measure or score the performance or contribution–to–value of each alternative on each criterion.

The criteria weights and measures of performance must be numeric in form, but this does not mean that they must be either "objective" or "quantitative." (If you find this confusing, look ahead in this chapter and read the subsection entitled "Comments on Measurement" in Section 2.5.) Criteria weights, obviously, are subjective by their nature, being an expression of what the decision maker thinks is important. The development of performance scales is more easily dealt with in the context of our example, and we will develop them shortly.

Assume that we have chosen the criteria and weights shown in Table A to be used in our evaluations.* The weights represent the relative importance of the criteria measured on a 10-point scale. The numbers in parentheses show the proportion of the total weight carried by each criterion. (They add to only .99 due to rounding.) Raw weights work just as well for decision making as their percentage counterparts, but the latter are usually preferred because they are a constant reminder to the decision maker of the impact of each of the criteria.

Prior to consideration of performance standards and sources of information for the criteria we have chosen, we must ask, "Are there any characteristics that must be present (or absent) in a candidate automobile for it to be accept-

*The criteria and weights were picked arbitrarily for this example. Because this is typically an individual or family decision, techniques like Delphi or successive comparisons are not required.

Table A. Criteria and Weights for Automobile Purchase

Appearance	4	(.10)
Braking	3	(.07)
Comfort	7	(.17)
Cost, operating	5	(.12)
Cost, original	10	(.24)
Handling	7	(.17)
Reliability	5	(.12)
Total	41	.99

able?" Assume, for this example, that to be acceptable, an alternative must not be green, must have air conditioning, must be able to carry at least four adults, must have at least 10 cubic feet of luggage space, and must be priced less than $34,000. If an alternative violates any of these conditions, it is immediately rejected.

For each criterion, we need some way of measuring the estimated performance of each alternative. In this case, we might adopt the measures shown in Table B. Our purpose is to transform a

Table B. Automobile Selection Criteria, Measures and Data Sources

Appearance	Subjective judgment, personal
Braking	Distance in feet, 60–0 mph, automotive magazine[a]
Comfort	Subjective judgment, 30 min. road test
Cost, operating	Annual insurance cost plus fuel cost[b]
Cost, original	Dealer cost, auto-cost service[c]
Handling	Average speed through standard slalom, automotive magazine[a]
Reliability	Score on Consumer Reports, "Frequency-of-Repair" data (average of 2 previous years)

[a] Many automotive periodicals conduct standardized performance tests of new cars.

[b] Annual fuel cost is calculated as (17,500 mi/DOE ave. mpg) × $1.25/gal.

[c] There are several sources for dealer-cost data (e.g., AAA, which provides a stable data base on which to estimate the price of each alternative).

Criteria	Scores				
	1	*2*	*3*	*4*	*5*
Appearance	Ugh	Poor	Adequate	Good	WOW
Braking	>165	165–150	150–140	140–130	<130
Comfort	Bad	Poor	Adequate	Good	Excellent
Cost, operating*	>$2.5	$2.1–2.5	$1.9–2.1	$1.6–1.9	<$1.6
Cost, original*	>$32.5	$26–32.5	$21–26	$17–21	<$17
Handling	<45	45–49.5	49.5–55	55–59	>59
Reliability	Worst	Poor	Adequate	Good	Excellent

*Cost data in $1000s

Figure A   Performance measures and equivalent scores for selection of an automobile.

measure of the degree to which an alternative meets a criterion into a score, the s_{ij}, that is a general measure of the utility or value of the alternative with respect to that criterion. Note that this requires us to define the criterion precisely, as well as to specify a source for the information.

Figure A shows the scores for each criterion transformed to a 5-point scale, which will suffice for our ratings.

Using the performance scores shown in Figure A, we can evaluate the cars we have identified as our alternatives: the Leviathan 8, the Nuevo-Econ, the Maxivan, the Sporticar 100, and the Ritzy 300. Each car is scored on each criterion according to the categories shown in Figure A.

Then each score is multiplied by the criterion weight and the result is entered into the appropriate box in Figure B. Last, the results for each alternative are summed to represent the weighted score.

According to this set of measures, we prefer the Ritzy 300, but while it is a clear winner over the Leviathan 8 and the Maxivan, and scores about 8 percent better than the Sporticar, it rates only about 0.13 points or 4 percent above the NuevoEcon. Note that if we overrated the Ritzy by one point on comfort or handling, or if we underrated the NuevoEcon by one point on either of these criteria, the result would have been reversed. (We assume that the original cost data are

Alternatives	Criteria and Weights							
	Appearance (0.10)	**Braking (0.07)**	**Comfort (0.17)**	**Cost, operating (0.12)**	**Cost, original (0.24)**	**Handling (0.17)**	**Reliability (0.12)**	$\Sigma s_{ij}w_i$
Leviathan 8	3 × 0.1 = 0.30	1 × 0.07 = 0.07	4 × 0.17 = 0.68	2 × 0.12 = 0.24	1 × 0.24 = 0.24	2 × 0.17 = 0.34	3 × 0.12 = 0.36	2.23
NuevoEcon	3 × 0.1 = 0.30	3 × 0.07 = .21	2 × 0.17 = 0.34	5 × 0.12 = 0.60	4 × 0.24 = 0.96	2 × 0.17 = 0.34	4 × 0.12 = 0.48	3.23
Maxivan	2 × 0.1 = 0.20	1 × 0.07 = 0.07	4 × 0.17 = 0.68	4 × 0.12 = 0.48	3 × 0.24 = 0.72	1 × 0.17 = 0.17	3 × 0.12 = 0.36	2.68
Sporticar 100	5 × 0.1 = 0.50	4 × 0.07 = 0.28	3 × 0.17 = 0.51	2 × 0.12 = 0.24	2 × 0.24 = 0.48	5 × 0.17 = 0.85	2 × 0.12 = 0.24	3.10
Ritzy 300	4 × 0.1 = 0.40	5 × 0.07 = 0.35	5 × 0.17 = 0.85	2 × 0.12 = 0.24	1 × 0.24 = 0.24	4 × 0.17 = 0.68	5 × 0.12 = 0.60	3.36

Figure B   Scores for alternative cars on selection criteria.

accurate.) With the scores this close, we might want to evaluate these two cars by additional criteria (e.g., ease of carrying children, status, safety features like dual airbags or ABS, etc.) prior to making a firm decision.

All in all, if the decision maker has well delineated objectives, and can determine how specific kinds of performance contribute to those criteria, and finally, can measure those kinds of performance for each of the alternative courses of action, then the scoring model is a powerful and flexible tool. To the extent that criteria are not carefully defined, performance is not well linked to the criteria, and is carelessly or wrongly measured, the scoring model rests on a faulty foundation and is merely a convenient path to error.

Constrained Weighted Factor Scoring Model The temptation to include marginal criteria can be partially overcome by allowing additional criteria to enter the model as constraints rather than weighted factors. These constraints represent project characteristics that must be present or absent in order for the project to be acceptable. In our example concerning a product, we might have specified that we would not undertake any project that would significantly lower the quality of the final product (visible to the buyer or not).

We would amend the weighted scoring model to take the form:

$$S_i = \sum_{j=1}^{n} s_{ij} w_j \prod_{k=1}^{v} c_{ik}$$

where $c_{ik} = 1$ if the ith project satisfies the kth of r constraints, and 0 if it does not. Other elements in the model are as defined earlier.

Although this model is analytically tidy, in practice we would not bother to evaluate projects that are so unsuitable in some ways that we would not consider supporting them regardless of their expected performance against other criteria. For example, except under extraordinary circumstances, Procter & Gamble would not consider a project to add a new consumer product or product line:

- that cannot be marketed nationally;
- that cannot be distributed through mass outlets (grocery stores, drugstores);
- that will not generate gross revenues in excess of $ — million;
- for which Procter & Gamble's potential market share is not at least 50 percent; and
- that does not utilize Procter & Gamble's scientific expertise, manufacturing expertise, advertising expertise, or packaging and distribution expertise.

Again, a caveat is in order. Exercise care when adopting constraints. It may seem obvious that we should not consider a project if it has no reasonable assurance of long-run profitability. Such a constraint, however, can force us to overlook a project that, though unprofitable itself, might have a strong, positive impact on the profitability of other potential projects.

Other Scoring Models Goal programming is a variation of the general linear programming method that can optimize an objective function with multiple objectives. A detailed discussion of goal programming is beyond the scope of this book. The interested reader should consult any modern text on management science, for example, [40]. As was the case with profitability models, scoring models have their own characteristic advantages and disadvantages. The advantages are:

1. These models allow multiple criteria to be used for evaluation and decision making, including profit/profitability models and both tangible and intangible criteria.
2. They are structurally simple and therefore easy to understand and use.
3. They are a direct reflection of managerial policy.
4. They are easily altered to accommodate changes in the environment or managerial policy.
5. Weighted scoring models allow for the fact that some criteria are more important than others.
6. These models allow easy sensitivity analysis. The trade-offs between the several criteria are readily observable.

   The disadvantages are the following:

1. The output of a scoring model is strictly a relative measure. Project scores do not represent the value or "utility" associated with a project and thus do not directly indicate whether or not the project should be supported.
2. In general, scoring models are linear in form and the elements of such models are assumed to be independent.
3. The ease of use of these models is conducive to the inclusion of a large number of criteria, most of which have such small weights that they have little impact on the total project score.
4. Unweighted scoring models assume all criteria are of equal importance, which is almost certainly contrary to fact.
5. To the extent that profit/profitability is included as an element in the scoring model, this element has the advantages and disadvantages noted earlier for the profitability models themselves.

An interesting alternative to scoring models is an iterative rating process developed by Raz [29]. His method starts with a set of attributes that can be used to rank potential projects. He then removes all attributes that do not differentiate between the alternatives and all projects that are dominated by others. If a choice can then be made, it is made. If not, the process is repeated. In another paper, Pascale, *et al.* compare a weighted scoring model with an unweighted scoring model for the evaluation of innovations. They conclude that the former works well with incremental change, and the latter works better when the innovation is a "new idea" [27]. They also investigate the impact of the evaluation methods on idea generation.

Choosing a Project Selection Model

Selecting the type of model to aid the evaluation/selection process depends on the philosophy and wishes of management. Liberatore and Titus [20] conducted a survey of 40 high-level staff persons from 29 *Fortune 500* firms. Eighty percent of their respondents report the use of one or more financial models for R & D project decision making. Although their sample is small and nonrandom, their findings are quite consistent with the present authors' experience. None of the respondent firms used mathematical programming techniques for project selection or resource allocation.

We strongly favor weighted scoring models for three fundamental reasons. First, they allow the multiple objectives of all organizations to be reflected in the important decision about which projects will be supported and which will be rejected. Second, scoring models are easily adapted to changes in managerial philosophy or changes in the environment. Third, they do not suffer from the bias toward the short run that is inherent in profitability models that discount future cash flows. This is not a prejudice against discounting and most certainly does not argue against the inclusion of profits/profitability as an important factor in selection, but rather *it is an argument against the exclusion of nonfinancial factors* that may require a longer-run view of the costs and benefits of a project. For a powerful statement of this point, see [9].

It is also interesting to note that Liberatore and Titus found that firms with a significant amount of contract research funded from outside the organization used scoring models for project screening much more frequently than firms with negligible levels of outside funding. It was also found that firms with significant levels of outside funding were much less likely to use a payback period [20, p. 969].

The structure of a weighted scoring model is quite straightforward. Its virtues are many. Nonetheless, the actual use of scoring models is not as easy as it might seem. Decision makers are forced to make difficult choices and they are not always comfortable doing so. They are forced to reduce often vague feelings to quite specific words or numbers. Multiattribute, multiperson decision making is not simple. (For an interesting discussion of this process, see [13].)

Project Management in Practice
Selecting a Composting Project at Larry's Markets

In 1991, Larry's Markets of Seattle, Washington adopted a comprehensive environmental program that included recycling, waste reduction, energy conservation, water management, environmental landscaping, environmental product evaluation, community project support, and other environmental initiatives. One of the possible initiatives was a project to recover all of the produce and floral department's by-products

Source: B. Rogers, "Food Waste Composting at Larry's Markets," *PM Network*, February 1995, pp. 32–33.

through a regular, daily process of composting. Not only did this project promise to reduce the company's impact on the local natural environment but also appeared to offer potential cost savings.

A 1991 waste audit revealed that the company's five stores produced 3000 tons of waste by-products consisting of garbage, cardboard, food waste, plastics, glass, and so on. Of this, over 700 tons, most of which were produced by the produce and floral departments, were estimated to be compostable. Due to its high local visibility and potential cost savings, this project was selected for implementation with a goal of completion by late 1993.

In 1991, before composting, fully 69 percent of Larry's Markets by-product stream was going to landfill. When full-scale composting began in 1992 with 350 tons composted, this figure dropped to 47 percent. Continuing their efforts, in 1993 Larry's Markets composted almost 700 tons which further reduced the landfill percentage to 36, exceeding the county's 1995 goal of 50 percent and the state's 2000 goal of 40 percent. The project also saved the company over $20,000 a year in garbage fees, gave the employees and customers a sense of pride, and fostered community goodwill as represented by numerous letters, customer comments, and local government and environmental group awards.

■ 2.4 ANALYSIS UNDER UNCERTAINTY— THE MANAGEMENT OF RISK

During the past several years, increasing attention has been paid to the subject of managing some of the risks inherent in most projects. The subject first appeared in PMI's 1987 edition of *A Guide to the Project Management Body of Knowledge* [28]. For the most part, risk has been interpreted as being unsure about project task durations and/or costs, but uncertainty plagues all aspects of the work on projects and is present in all stages of project life cycles. In this section, we will consider uncertainty as it affects the selection process. The impact of imperfect knowledge on the way a project is organized and on its budget and schedule will be discussed in the chapters devoted to those subjects.

Before proceeding, it is useful to discuss briefly the distinction between two words, "risk," and "uncertainty." The outcome of any decision depends on two things: 1) what the decision maker does; and 2) what nature does—"nature" being the set of exogenous factors that interact with the decision maker's course of action to produce an outcome. If the decision maker knows the probability of each and every state of nature and thus of each and every outcome, she can find the *expected value* of each alternative course of action she has. The expected value of an action is the sum of the values of each outcome associated with the action times the probability that it will occur. She can select the course of action associated with the best of these expected outcomes. This is decision making under conditions of *risk*.

If the decision maker's information is not so complete and she does not know and cannot collect sufficient data to determine the probability of occurrence for some states of nature, she cannot find the expected value for each of her alternative actions. This is decision making under conditions of *uncertainty*. There is no way to solve problems under uncertainty without altering the nature of the problem. One can estimate, guess, or call "Psychic Friend" to assume some probability for each known state of nature and then deal with the problem as if it were one of risk. If the decision maker elects to ignore all states of nature except the one she thinks most likely, she then assumes there is one and only one possible outcome—which is decision making under conditions of *certainty*. Finally, the decision maker could assume that an opponent controls the state of nature and try to use *game theory* to solve her problem of decision making under conditions of conflict.

In the real world of project management, it has been common to deal with estimates of task durations, costs, etc. as if the information were known with certainty. On occasion, project task workers inflated times and costs and deflated specifications on the grounds that the boss would arbitrarily cut the project budget and duration and add to the specifications, thereby treating the problem as a decision under conflict with the boss as an opponent.

In fact, a great majority of all decisions made in the course of managing a project are actually made under conditions of uncertainty. In general, we will adopt the view that it is usually best to act as if decisions were made under conditions of risk. This will force us to make some estimates about the probability of various outcomes. If we use appropriate methods for doing this, we can apply what knowledge we have to solving project decision problems. We will not always be correct, but we will be doing the best we can. Such estimates are called "subjective probabilities," and are dealt with in most elementary courses on probability and statistics. While such probabilities are no more than guesses, they can be processed just as empirically determined probabilities are. [35] is a brief, basic description of the use of subjective probability in decision-making problems. In the world of project management, some knowledge is almost always better than none. Now we can examine some of the effects of uncertainty on project selection.

At times an organization may wish to evaluate a project about which there is little information. R & D projects sometimes fall into this general class. But even in the comparative mysteries of R & D activities, the level of uncertainty about the outcomes of R & D is not beyond analysis. As we noted earlier, there is actually not much uncertainty about whether a product, process, or service can be developed, but there can be considerable uncertainty about *when* it will be developed and at *what* cost.

As they are with R & D projects, time and cost are also often uncertain in other types of projects. When the organization undertakes projects in which it has little or no recent experience—for example, the installation of a computer network, investment in an unfamiliar business, engaging in international trade, and a myriad of other projects common enough to organizations, in general, but uncommon to any single organization—there are three distinct areas of uncertainty. First, there is uncertainty about the timing of the project and the cash flows it is expected to generate. Second, though not as common as generally believed, there may be uncertainty about the direct outcomes of the project—that is, what it will accomplish. Third, there is uncertainty about the side effects of the project—its unforeseen consequences.

Typically, we try to reduce such uncertainty by the preparation of *pro forma* documents. *Pro forma* profit and loss statements and break-even charts are examples of such documents. The results, however, are not very satisfactory unless the amount of uncertainty is reflected in the data that go into the documents. When relationships between inputs and outputs in the projects are complex, Monte Carlo simulation [19, 40] can handle such uncertainty by exposing the many possible consequences of embarking on a project. *Risk analysis* is a method based on such a procedure. With the great availability of microcomputers and user-friendly software (e.g., @Risk®, Risk+®, CrystalBall®), these procedures are becoming very common.

Risk Analysis

The principal contribution of risk analysis is to focus the decision maker's attention on understanding the nature and extent of the uncertainty associated with some variables used in a decision-making process. Although the method can be used with almost any kind of variable and decision-making problem, risk analysis is usually understood to use financial measures in determining the desirability of an investment project [11]. Instead of point estimates of the variables, probability distributions are determined or subjectively estimated for each of the "uncertain" variables. With such inputs, the probability distribution for the rate of return (or net present value) is then usually found by simulation. The decision maker not only has probabilistic information about the rate of return and future cash flows, but also gains knowledge about the variability of such estimates as measured by the standard deviation of the financial returns. Both the expectation and its variability are important decision-making criteria in the evaluation of the project.

This approach is useful for a wide range of project-related decisions. For example, simulation risk analysis was used to select the best method of moving a computer to a new facility [39]. The major task elements and their required sequences were identified. Cost and time distributions were then programmed for analysis and a computer run of 2,000 trials made, simulating various failures and variations in cost and time for each of three methods of moving the computer. A cost-probability distribution was constructed (see Figure 2-3) to help identify the lowest-cost alternative and also the alternative with the lowest risk of a high cost, alternatives that are often not the same. As seen in the illustration, alternative 3 had the lowest expected cost (of 9) but also had the highest likelihood for a cost of 20 or more.

General Simulation Analysis

Simulation combined with sensitivity analysis is also useful for evaluating R & D projects while they are still in the conceptual stage. Using the net present value approach, for example, we would support an R & D project if the net present value of the cash flows (including the initial cash investment) is positive and represents the best available alternative use of the funds. When these flows are estimated for purposes of analysis, it is well to avoid the *full-cost* philosophy that is usually adopted.

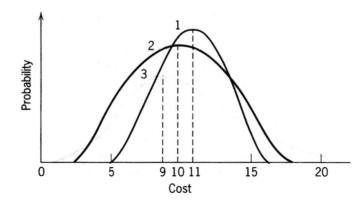

Figure 2-3 Probability density for three alternatives. *Note:* Alternative 3 has the lowest mean, but alternative 1 has a smaller variance and thus less risk.

The full-cost approach to estimating cash flows necessitates the inclusion of arbitrarily determined overheads in the calculation—overheads which, by definition, are not affected by change in product or process and, thus, are not relevant to the decision. The only relevant costs are those that will be changed by the implementation of the new process or product.

The determination of such costs is not simple. If the concept being considered involves a new process, it is necessary to go to the detailed *route sheet,* or *operations sequence sheet,* describing the operation in which the new process would be used. Proceeding systematically through the operating sequence step-by-step, one asks whether the present time and cost required for this step are likely to be altered if the new process concept is installed. If, and only if, the answer is yes, three estimates (optimistic, most likely, and pessimistic) are made of the size of the expected change. These individual estimated changes in production cost and time, together with upstream- or downstream-time and cost changes that might also result (e.g., a production method change on a part might also alter the cost of inspecting the final product), are used to generate the required cash flow information—presuming that the time savings have been properly costed. This estimation process will be explained in detail in Chapter 8.

The analysis gives a picture of the proposed change in terms of the costs and times that will be affected. The uncertainty associated with each individual element of the process is included. Simulation runs will then indicate the likelihood of achieving various levels of savings. Note also that investigation of the simulation model will expose the major sources of uncertainty in the final cost distributions.

Those without considerable experience in simulation should use this tool with caution. Simulation software is indifferent to assumptions-contrary-to-fact, and cares not a wit that the experimenter specifies a statistical distribution that implies a universe that never was nor ever will be. In such cases, the results of the simulation—often taken by the unwary as an estimate of reality—are apt to mislead.

Window-of-Opportunity Analysis

In the early stages of new product development, one may know little more than the fact that the potential product seems technically feasible. That one can achieve a new technology does not necessarily imply that the new technology is worthwhile. Fundamentally, the decision to invest in the development of a new process or product depends on an estimate of cash flows and other benefits expected to result if the innovation is successful—a difficult problem at best. The traditional approach has been to build the item in question and then test it in its predetermined application to see if it qualifies as useful and economic. This is a wasteful process because it assumes the innovation will meet the tests of economic feasibility—a condition not always met in practice.

Given some idea for a new product or process, we can invert the traditional approach by attempting to determine the cost and performance specifications that must be met by the new technology before any R & D is undertaken. We delineate the *window-of-opportunity* for the innovation. The method for conducting such an analysis is straightforward. Given a potential production process, for example, the current production process is analyzed in detail and, any element of that process that might be affected by the innovation, is noted. Baseline data on the current process is collected and performance of the innovation is estimated as a fraction or multiple of the baseline system. Having estimated in advance the economic impact of an innovation, the decision whether to undertake the development project is much simpler. For an example of such an approach see [6] and [23].

2.5 COMMENTS ON THE INFORMATION BASE FOR SELECTION

Our bias in favor of weighted scoring models is quite clear, but irrespective of which model is chosen for project selection, a data base must be created and maintained to furnish input data for the model. Directions for the actual construction of the data base go beyond the scope of this book, but some comments about the task are in order.

The use of any project selection model assumes that the decision-making procedure takes place in a reasonably rational organizational environment. Such is not always the case. In some organizations, project selection seems to be the result of a political process, and sometimes involves questionable ethics, complete with winners and losers [2]. In others, the organization is so rigid in its approach to decision making that it attempts to reduce all decisions to an algorithmic proceeding in which predetermined programs make choices so that humans have minimal involvement—and responsibility. Here too, Saaty's Analytic Hierarchy Process can lend rationality to a sometimes irrational process [33]. In an interesting paper, Huber examines the impact that the organizational environment has on the design of decision support systems [12].

The remainder of this section deals with three special problems affecting the data used in project selection models.

Comments on Accounting Data

Whether managers are familiar with accounting systems or not, they can find it useful to reflect on the methods and assumptions used in the preparation of accounting data. Among the most crucial are the following:

1. Accountants live in a linear world. With few exceptions, cost and revenue data are assumed to vary linearly with associated changes in inputs and outputs.

2. The accounting system often provides cost-revenue information that is derived from standard cost analyses and equally standardized assumptions regarding revenues. These standards may or may not be accurate representations of the cost-revenue structure of the physical system they purport to represent.

3. As noted in the previous section, the data furnished by the accounting system may or may not include overhead costs. In most cases, the decision maker is concerned solely with cost-revenue elements that will be changed as a result of the project under consideration. Incremental analysis is called for, and great care must be exercised when using *pro forma* data in decision problems. Remember that the as-

signment of overhead cost is always arbitrary. The accounting system is the richest source of information in the organization, and it should be used—but with great care and understanding.

Comments on Measurements

It is common for those who oppose a project, for whatever reason, to complain that information supporting the project is "subjective." This epithet appears to mean that the data are biased and therefore untrustworthy.

To use the scoring methods discussed or to practice risk management in project selection, we need to *represent* though not necessarily *collect* expected project performance for each criterion in numeric form. If a performance characteristic cannot be measured directly as a number, it may be useful to characterize performance verbally and then, through a word/number equivalency scale, use the numeric equivalents of verbal characterizations as model inputs.

Subjective versus Objective The distinction between subjective and objective is generally misunderstood. All too often the word *objective* is held to be synonymous with *fact* and *subjective* is taken to be a synonym for *opinion*—where fact = true and opinion = false. The distinction in measurement theory is quite different, referring to the location of the standard for measurement. A measurement taken by reference to an external standard is said to be "objective." Reference to a standard that is internal to the system is said to be "subjective." A yardstick, incorrectly divided into 100 divisions and labeled "meter," would be an objective but inaccurate measure. The eye of an experienced judge is a subjective measure that may be quite accurate.

Quantitative versus Qualitative The distinction between quantitative and qualitative is also misunderstood. It is not the same as numeric and nonnumeric. Both quantity and quality may be measured numerically. The number of words on this page is a quantity. The color of a red rose is a quality, but it is also a wavelength that can be measured numerically, in terms of microns. The true distinction is that one may apply the law of addition to quantities but not to qualities [41]. Water, for example, has a volumetric measure and a density measure. The former is quantitative and the latter qualitative. Two one-gallon containers of water poured into one larger container give us two gallons, but the density of the water, before and after joining the two gallons, is still 1.0.

Reliable versus Unreliable A data source is said to be reliable if repetitions of a measurement produce results that vary from one another by less than a prespecified amount. The distinction is important when we consider the use of statistical data in our selection models.

Valid versus Invalid Validity measures the extent to which a piece of information actually means what we believe it to mean. A measure may be reliable but not valid. Consider our mismarked 36 inch yardstick pretending to be a meter. It performs consistently, so it is reliable. It does not, however, match up accurately with other meter rules, so it would not be judged valid.

To be satisfactory when used in the previous project selection models, the measures may be either subjective or objective, quantitative or qualitative, but they must be numeric, reliable, and valid. Avoiding information merely because it is subjective or qualitative is an error and weakens decisions. On the other hand, including information of questionable reliability or validity in selection models, even though it may be numeric, is dangerous. It is doubly dangerous if decision makers are comfortable dealing with the selection model but are unaware of the doubtful character of some input data. A condition a colleague has referred to as GIGO—garbage in, *gospel* out—may prevail.

Comments on Technological Shock

If the parent organization is not experienced in the type of project being considered for selection, performance measures such as time to installation, time to achieve 80 percent efficiency, cost to install, and the like are often underestimated. It is interesting to observe that an almost certain, immediate result of installing a new, cost-saving technology is that costs rise. Sometimes we blame the cost increases on resistance to change, but a more sensible explanation is that when we alter a system, we disturb it and it reacts in ways we did not predict. A steelmaker recalling the installation of the then new technology for manufacturing tinplate by electrolysis remarked: "We discovered and installed the world's first electrolytic method for making scrap. It took a year before we had that line running the way it was designed."

Of course, if the organization is experienced, underestimation is not likely to be a serious problem. The Reliance Electric Company undertook several "18-month" plant construction projects that they predicted, accurately, would require 36 months to build from decision to the point when the plant was capable of operating at or above three-fourths capacity. (Note the potential for ethical problems here.)

To the extent possible, past knowledge of system actions and reactions should be built into estimates of future project performance.

2.6 PROJECT PROPOSALS

Now that project selection methods have been discussed, it is appropriate to consider what documentation is needed to evaluate a project that is being considered. The set of documents submitted for evaluation is called the *project proposal*, whether it is brief (a page or two) or extensive, and regardless of the formality with which it is presented. Several issues face firms preparing proposals, particularly firms in the aerospace, construction, defense, and consulting industries. These are:

1. Which projects should be bid on?
2. How should the proposal-preparation process be organized and staffed?
3. How much should be spent on preparing proposals for bids?
4. How should the bid prices be set? What is the bidding strategy? Is it ethical?

Generally, these decisions are made on the basis of their overall expected values, perhaps as reflected in a scoring model. In-house proposals submitted by a firm's personnel to that firm's top management do not usually require the extensive treatment given to proposals submitted to outside clients or agencies such as the Department of Defense. For the Department of Defense, a proposal must be precisely structured to meet the requirements contained in the official Request for Proposal (RFP) or Request for Quotation (RFQ)—more specifically, in the Technical Proposal Requirements (TPR) that is part of the RFP or RFQ. The construction and preparation of a proposal to be submitted to the government or other outside funder is beyond the scope of this book. However, the subject has been well treated by Knutson in a three-part paper that begins with a discussion of the decision whether or not to seek some particular business. The series then covers the composition of a team to write the proposal and Knutson's view of how to structure, price, and submit the proposal [16, 17, 18]. The interested reader is also referred to [30] and [31]. Finally, it should be noted that customs, practices, rules, and laws concerning proposals vary from nation to nation (e.g., see [14]).

All proposals should begin with a short summary statement (an "Executive Summary") covering the fundamental nature of the proposal in *minimally technical language*, as well as the general benefits that are expected. All proposals should be accompanied by a "cover letter." Roman [30, pp. 67–68] emphasizes that the cover letter is a key marketing document and is worthy of careful attention. In addition to the Executive Summary and the cover letter, every proposal should deal with four distinct issues: (1) the nature of the technical problem and how it is to be approached; (2) the plan for implementing the project once it has been accepted; (3) the plan for logistic support and administration of the project; and (4) a description of the group proposing to do the work, plus its past experience in similar work.

The precise way in which the contents of a proposal are organized usually follows the directions found in the TPR or RFP, the stated requirements of a specific potential funder, the traditional form used by the organization issuing the proposal, or, occasionally, the whim of the writer. As is the case with most products, the highest probability of acceptance will occur when the proposal meets the expectations of the "buyer," as to form and contents. At times there is a tendency to feel that so-called "nontechnical" projects (by which is usually meant projects that are not concerned with the physical sciences or a physical product) are somehow exempt from the need to describe how the problem will be approached and how the project will be implemented—including details such as milestones, schedules, and budgets. To deal with nontechnical projects casually is folly and casts considerable doubt on the proposer's ability to deliver on promises. (It is all too common for projects concerned with the development of art, music, drama, and computer software, among other "nontechnical" areas, to be quite vague as to deliverables, deadlines, and costs.) On the other hand, when the proposal is aimed at another division or department of the same parent organization, the technical requirements of the proposal may be greatly relaxed, but the technical approach and implementation plan are still required—even if their form is quite informal.

The Technical Approach

The proposal begins with a general description of the problem to be addressed or project to be undertaken. If the problem is complex, the major subsystems of the problem or project are noted, together with the organization's approach to each. The presentation is in sufficient detail that a knowledgeable reader can understand what the proposer intends to do. The general method of resolving critical problems is outlined. If there are several subsystems, the proposed methods for interfacing them are covered.

In addition, any special client requirements are listed along with proposed ways of meeting them. All test and inspection procedures to assure performance, quality, reliability, and compliance with specifications are noted.

The Implementation Plan

The implementation plan for the project contains estimates of the time required, the cost, and the materials used. Each major subsystem of the project is listed along with estimates of its cost. These costs are aggregated for the whole project, and totals are shown for each cost category. Hours of work and quantities of material used are shown (along with the wage rates and unit material costs). A list of all equipment costs is added, as is a list of all overhead and administrative costs.

Depending on the wishes of the parent organization and the needs of the project, time charts, Program Evaluation and Review Technique (PERT)/Critical Path Method (CPM), or Gantt charts are given for each subsystem and for the system as a whole. (See chapter 8 for more about PERT/CPM and Gantt charts.) Personnel, equipment, and resource usages are estimated on a period-by-period basis in order to ensure that resource constraints are not violated. Major milestones are indicated on the time charts. Contingency plans are specifically noted. For any facility that might be critical, load charts are prepared to make sure that the facility will be available when needed.

The Plan for Logistic Support and Administration

The proposal includes a description of the ability of the proposer to supply the routine facilities, equipment, and skills needed during any project. Having the means to furnish artist's renderings, special signs, meeting rooms, stenographic assistance, reproduction of oversized documents, computer graphics, word processing, video teleconferencing, and many other occasionally required capabilities provides a "touch of class." Indeed, their unavailability can be irritating. Attention to detail in all aspects of project planning increases the probability of success for the project—and impresses the potential funder.

It is important that the proposal contain a section explaining how the project will be administered. Of particular interest will be an explanation of how control over subcontractors will be administered, including an explanation of how proper subcontractor performance is to be insured and evaluated. The nature and timing of all progress reports, budgetary reports, audits, and evaluations are covered, together with a description of the final documentation to be prepared for users of the proposed deliverables. Termination procedures are described, clearly indicating the disposition of project personnel, materials, and equipment at project end.

A critical issue, often overlooked, that should be addressed in the administrative section of the proposal is a reasonably detailed description of how *change orders* will be handled and how their costs will be estimated. Change orders are a significant source of friction (and lawsuits) between the organization doing the project and the client. The client rarely understands the chaos that can be created in a project by the introduction of a seemingly simple change. To make matters worse, the group proposing the project seems to have a penchant for misleading the potential client about the ease with which "minor" changes can be adopted during the process of implementing the project. Control of change orders is covered in Chapter 11.

Past Experience

All proposals are strengthened by including a section that describes the past experience of the proposing group. It contains a list of key project personnel together with their titles and qualifications. For outside clients, a full résumé for each principal should be attached to the proposal. When preparing this and the other sections of a proposal, the proposing group should remember that the basic purpose of the document is to convince a potential funder that the group and the project are worthy of support. The proposal should be written accordingly.

Project Management in Practice
The Military Mobile Communications System— A Procurement Innovation

---

In 1981, the U.S. military was using a hodge-podge of communication equipment that largely didn't intercommunicate. Different services used different vendors, each with their own protocol, and equipment for voice communication was completely different than that for data, facsimile, or e-mail. James Ambrose, then Undersecretary of the Army, thus initiated a $4.2 billion project to completely revamp the entire Army communications system, the largest communications program ever placed by the Army. His conception of the need included six unique acquisition guidelines that led to an extremely successful project:

1. The contractor is responsible for all aspects of systems acquisition, production, integration, fielding, training, logistics, and maintenance.

2. The contractor will satisfy 19 required design and functional features and as many of 82 desired features as possible.

3. The contractor will provide only fully developed, working equipment; there is to be virtually no engineering development.

4. Delivery of the system will start after 22 months and be completed 60 months after basic operations.

5. The contractor will buy every piece of equipment needed for each system, even if that equipment is already in use.

6. The contract is firm fixed price with the contractor accepting all cost risks.

In 1985, GTE won the bidding with a proposal $3 billion lower than the next competitor's. GTE has developed and refined their program management capabilities over a period of 35 years. A project team was assembled consisting of 32 subcontractors and 700 vendors to supply over 8,000 mobile radios, 1,400 telephone switching centers, and 25,000 telephones. This system can send and receive calls, electronic mail, data, and facsimiles to mobile units without interruption over an area of 37,500 square kilometers, even while the connective elements of the system are on the move.

The system interconnects with the existing U.S. Army communications equipment, as well as that of the other military services, NATO, and commercial satellite and landline telephone networks around the world. The system was tested in late 1985 for 10 slushy days during winter in eastern France. Mobile units crossed fields and roads, reconnecting between coverage areas, while switching centers jumped from location to location, simulating a regular Army corps during combat.

Source: A.A. Dettbarn, et al., "Excellence in Cost, Schedule, and Quality Performance," *PM Network,* January 1992.

The final system met the requirement of 19 necessary features and 69 of the 82 desired features. The project also met the strict delivery deadlines and realized $21.7 million in cost savings as well. In 1991, the system was very successfully employed in the Persian Gulf for Operation Desert Shield/Storm. During the war period, the system operated for two straight weeks with only 45 minutes of downtime. It also was able to be set up and taken down in just the 30 minutes specified (completed in five minutes in one instance). It truly achieved the goal of "Effective communications from the foxhole to the theater commander to the President." This outstanding performance has been honored in four separate U.S. Army awards, including the Department of Defense (DoD) Value Engineering Contractor of the Year Award.

SUMMARY

This chapter initiated our discussion of the project management process by describing procedures for evaluating and selecting projects. We first outlined some criteria for project selection models and then discussed the general nature of these models. From this basic overview, the chapter then described the types of models in use and their advantages and disadvantages. Considering the degree of uncertainty associated with many projects, a section was devoted to selection models concerned with risk and uncertainty. Concluding the discussion, some general comments were made about data requirements and the use of these models. The final section discussed the documentation of the evaluation/selection process via project proposals.

The following specific points were made in the chapter:

- Primary model selection criteria are realism, capability, flexibility, ease of use, and cost.
- Preparatory steps in using a model include: 1) identifying the firm's objectives; 2) weighting them relative to each other; and 3) determining the probable impacts of the project on the firm's competitive abilities.
- Project selection models can generally be classified as either numeric or nonnumeric; numeric models are further subdivided into profitability and scoring categories.
- Nonnumeric models include: 1) the sacred cow; 2) the operating necessity; 3) the competitive necessity; and 4) comparative benefit.

- Profitability models include standard forms such as: 1) payback period; 2) average rate of return; 3) discounted cash flow; 4) internal rate of return; and 5) profitability index.
- Scoring models—the authors' preference—include: 1) the unweighted 0-1 factor model; 2) the unweighted factor scoring model; 3) the weighted factor scoring model; and 4) the constrained weighted factor scoring model.
- For handling uncertainty: 1) pro forma documents; 2) risk analysis; 3) and simulation with sensitivity analyses are all helpful.
- Special care should be taken with the data used in project selection models. Of concern are data taken from an accounting data base, how data are measured and conceived, and the effect of technological shock.
- Project proposals generally consist of a number of sections: 1) the technical approach; 2) the implementation plan; 3) the plan for logistic support and administration; and 4) past experience.

In the next chapter we consider the selection of the appropriate manager for a project and what characteristics are most helpful for such a position. We also address the issue of the project manager's special role, and the demands and responsibilities of this critical position.

GLOSSARY

Decision Support System A computer package and data base to aid managers in making decisions. It may include simulation programs, mathematical programming routines, and decision rules.

Delphi A formalized method of group decision making that facilitates drawing on the knowledge of experts in the group.

Deterministic Predetermined, with no possibility of an alternate outcome. Compare with stochastic.

Expert System A computer package that captures the knowledge of recognized experts in an area and can make inferences about a problem based on decision rules and data input to the package.

Model A way of looking at reality, usually for the purpose of abstracting and simplifying it, to make it understandable in a particular context.

Network A group of items connected by some common mechanism.

Portfolio A group or set of projects with varying characteristics.

Pro Forma Projected or anticipated, usually applied to financial data such as balance sheets and income statements.

Programming An algorithmic methodology for solving a particular type of complex problem, usually conducted on a computer.

Sensitivity Analysis Investigation of the effect on the outcome of changing some parameters or data in the procedure or model.

Simulation A technique for emulating a process, usually conducted a considerable number of times to understand the process better and measure its outcomes under different policies.

Stochastic Probabilistic, or not deterministic.

 QUESTIONS

Material Review Questions

1. What are the four parts of a technical proposal?

2. By what criteria do you think managers judge selection models? What criteria *should* they use?

3. Contrast the competitive necessity model with the operating necessity model. What are the advantages and disadvantages of each?

4. What is a sacred cow? Give some examples.

5. Give an example of a Q-Sort process for project selection.

6. What are some of the limitations of project selection models?

7. What is the distinction between a qualitative and a quantitative measure?

8. How does the discounted cash flow method answer some of the criticisms of the payback period and average rate of return methods?

9. What are some advantages and disadvantages of the profit/profitability numeric models?

10. How is sensitivity analysis used in project selection?

11. Contrast risk with uncertainty. Describe the window-of-opportunity approach.

Class Discussion Questions

12. What is the real difference between profitability and scoring models? Describe a model that could fit both categories.

13. Can risk analysis be used for nonproject business decision making? Explain how.

14. Discuss how the following project selection models are used in real-world applications.
    (a) Capital investment with discounted cash flow.
    (b) Simulation models.

15. Why do you think managers underutilize project selection models?

16. Would uncertainty models be classified as profitability models, scoring models, or some other type of model?

17. Contrast validity with reliability. What aspects, if any, are the same?

18. Contrast subjective and objective measures. Give examples of the proper use of each type of measure when evaluating competing projects.

19. Can a measure be reliable, yet invalid? Explain.

20. What are some possible extensions of project evaluation models for the future?

21. Are there certain types of projects that are better suited for nonnumeric selection methods as opposed to numeric ones?

22. Identify some of the ethical issues that can arise in a bid response to an RFP.

Questions for Project Management in Practice

Project Selection for Spent Nuclear Fuel Cleanup

23. Why did it take five months to explain the problem to the stakeholders?

24. Why do you think the stakeholders no longer trusted the authorities?

25. What might have been the problems with options 1, 2, and 4?

26. How is option 3 a solution?

Selecting a Composting Project at Larry's Markets

27. Why do you think this particular project was selected?

28. If 69 percent of their waste byproducts were going to landfill in 1991, where were the rest going?

29. Of the numeric models, which would probably be most appropriate for selection among these types of projects?

The Military Mobile Communications System

30. What was apparently different about this acquisition project than previous ones?

31. Was the $3 billion lower proposal a significant portion of the total project cost?

32. What does Guideline #3 indicate about how previous contracting was done?

▮ PROBLEMS

1. Two new Internet site projects are proposed to a young start-up company. Project A will cost $250,000 to implement and is expected to have annual cash flows of $75,000. Project B will cost $150,000 to implement and should generate annual cash flows of $52,000. The company is very concerned about their cash flow. Using the payback period, which project is better, from a cash flow standpoint?

2. Sean, a new graduate at a telecommunications firm, faces the following problem his first day at the firm: What is the average rate of return for a project that costs $200,000 to implement and has an average annual profit of $30,000?

3. A four-year financial project has net cash flows of $20,000; $25,000; $30,000 and $50,000 in the next four years. It will cost $75,000 to implement the project. If the required rate of return is 0.2, conduct a discounted cash flow calculation to determine the NPV.

4. What would happen to the NPV of the above project if the inflation rate was expected to be 4 percent in each of the next four years?

5. Calculate the profitability index for Problem 3. For Problem 4.

6. Use a weighted score model to choose between three locations (A, B, C) for setting up a factory.

The relative wieghts for each criterion are shown in the following table. A score of 1 represents unfavorable, 2 satisfactory, and 3 favorable.

Category	Weight	Location A	B	C
Labor costs	20	1	2	3
Labor productivity	20	2	3	1
Labor supply	10	2	1	3
Union relations	10	3	3	2
Material supply	10	2	1	1
Transport costs	25	1	2	3
Infrastructure	10	2	2	2

7. Develop a spreadsheet for Problem 6.
   a. What would your recommendation be if the weight for the transport cost went down to 10 and the weight of union relations went up to 25?
   b. Suppose location A received a score of 3 for transport cost and location C received a score of 2 for transport cost. Would your recommendation change under these circumstances?
   c. The vice president of finance has looked at your scoring model and feels that tax considerations should be included in the model with

a weight of 15. In addition, the VP has scored the locations on tax considerations as follows: location A received a score of 3, location B received a score of 2, and location C received a score of 1. How would this additional information affect your recommendation?

8. Nina is trying to decide in which of four shopping centers to locate her new boutique. Some cater to a higher class of clientele than others, some are in an indoor mall, some have a much greater volume than others, and, of course, rent varies considerably. Because of the nature of her store, she has decided that the class of clientele is the most important consideration. Following this, however, she must pay attention to her expenses and rent is a major item, probably 90 percent as important as clientele. An indoor, temperature-controlled mall is a big help, however, for stores such as hers where 70 percent of sales are from passersby slowly strolling and window shopping. Thus, she rates this as about 95 percent as important as rent. Last, a higher volume of shoppers means more potential sales; she thus rates this factor as 80 percent as important as rent.

As an aid in visualizing her location alternatives, she has constructed the following table. A "good" is scored as 3, "fair" as 2, and "poor" as 1. Use a weighted score model to help Nina come to a decision.

	Location			
	1	**2**	**3**	**4**
Class of clientele	Fair	Good	Poor	Good
Rent	Good	Fair	Poor	Good
Indoor mall	Good	Poor	Good	Poor
Volume	Good	Fair	Good	Poor

9. Referring to Problem 8, develop a spreadsheet to help Nina select a location for her boutique. Suppose Nina is able to negotiate a lower rent at location 3 and thus raise its ranking to "good." How does this affect the overall rankings of the four locations?

 INCIDENTS FOR DISCUSSION

Multiplex Company

Multiplex Company is in its third year of using a rather complex and comprehensive strategic planning process. Shannon Chase, CEO of Multiplex, is very pleased with the output of the planning process. Plans are logical, organized, and pertinent to the firm's business environment. However, implementation of the plans leaves something to be desired. Shannon is convinced that her managers do a poor job of estimating the amount of resources and time required to complete the strategic projects associated with the plan.

This fiscal year, eleven new strategic projects were identified. There were six major types of projects: new products, modifications of existing products, research and development, new applications studies, manufacturing process improvements, and reorganization of the sales department. Each project is sponsored by one of the functional department managers, who is required to prepare a simple cost-benefit analysis and a Gantt chart (see Chapter 8, Section 8.3) showing the aggregate time required to finish a project. This sponsor usually, but not always, winds up being assigned as the PM.

Tomorrow is the final day of the current year's strategic planning session. Ms. Chase plans to make a strong pitch to her managers to prioritize the strategic projects to ensure that those most important to the company get done. In the past, it seemed as though all the projects lagged behind when resource problems arose. In the future, she wants a consensus from the managers about which projects will go on the back burner and which will proceed on schedule when problems are encountered.

Questions: Ms. Chase is not sure how to go about ranking the projects. Will the managers be able to achieve consensus? Should they use the cost-benefit analysis done by the project sponsor? Perhaps the planning group could use their collective experience to rank the projects subjectively. What method would you recommend to Ms. Chase? Support your recommendation.

L & M Power

In the next two years, a large municipal gas company must begin constructing new gas storage facilities to accommodate the Federal Energy Regulatory Commission's Order 636 deregulating the gas industry. The vice-president in charge of the new project believes there are two options. One option is an underground deep storage facility (UDSF) and the other is a liquified natural gas facility (LNGF). The vice-president has developed a project selection model and will use it in presenting the project to the president. For the models she has gathered the following information:

	Initial Cost	Operating Cost/Cu.Ft.	Expected Life	Salvage Value
UDSF	$10,000,000	$0.004	20 years	10%
LGNF	25,000,000	$0.002	15 years	5%

Since the vice-president's background is in finance, she believes the best model to use is a financial one, net present value analysis.

Questions: Would you use this model? Why or why not? Base your answer on the five criteria developed by Souder and evaluate this model in terms of the criteria.

BIBLIOGRAPHY

1. ARCHIBALD, R. D. *Managing High Technology Programs and Projects.* New York: Wiley, 1992.

2. BAKER, B., and R. MENON. "Politics and Project Performance: The Fourth Dimension of Project Management." *PM Network,* November 1995.

3. BEALE, P., and M. FREEMAN. "Successful Project Execution: A Model," *Project Management Journal,* December 1991.

4. CHURCHMAN, C. W., R. L. ACKOFF, and E. L. ARNOFF. *Introduction to Operations Research.* New York: Wiley, 1957.

5. DALKEY, N. C. *The Delphi Method: An Experimental Study of Group Opinion* (RM-5888-PR). Santa Monica, CA: The RAND Corporation, June 1969.

6. EVANS, J. R., and S. J. MANTEL, JR. "A New Approach to the Evaluation of Process Innovations." *Technovation,* October 1985.

7. GARCIA, A., and W. COWDREY. "Information Systems: A Long Way from Wall-Carvings to CRTs." *Industrial Engineering,* April 1978.

8. GITHENS, G. "Finanical Models, Right Questions, Good Decision." *PM Network,* July 1998.

9. HAYES, R., and W. J. ABERNATHY. "Managing Our Way to Economic Decline." *Harvard Business Review,* July–August 1980.

10. HELIN, A. F., and W. E. SOUDER. "Experimental Test of a Q-Sort Procedure for Prioritizing R & D Projects." *IEEE Transactions on Engineering Management,* November 1974.

11. HERTZ, D. B., and H. THOMAS. *Risk Analysis and Its Applications.* New York: Wiley, 1983.

12. HUBER, G. P. "The Nature of Organizational Decision Making and the Design of Decision Support Systems," *MIS Quarterly,* June 1981.

13. IRVING, R. H., and D. W. CONRATH. "The Social Context of Multiperson, Multiattribute Decision-making," *IEEE Transactions on Systems, Man, and Cybernetics,* May–June 1988.

14. JERGEAS, G. F., and V. G. COOKE. "Law of Tender Applied to Request for Proposal Process." *Project Management Journal,* December 1997.

15. KHORRAMSHAHGOL, R., H. AZANI, and Y. GOUSTY. "An Integrated Approach to Project Evaluation and Selection," *IEEE Transactions on Engineering Management,* November 1988.

16. KNUTSON, J. "Proposal Management: Analyzing Business Opportunities." *PM Network,* January. 1996.

17. KNUTSON, J. "Proposal Management: Generating Winning Proposals, Part 1." *PM Network,* February 1996.

18. KNUTSON, J. "Proposal Management: Generating Winning Proposals, Part 2." *PM Network,* March 1996.

19. LAW, A. M., and W. KELTON. *Simulation Modeling and Analysis,* 2nd ed. New York: McGraw-Hill, 1990.

20. LIBERATORE, M. J., and G. J. TITUS. "The Practice of Management Science in R & D Project Management." *Management Science*, August 1983.

21. *Management of New Products*. New York: Booz, Allen, and Hamilton, Inc., 1966.

22. MANN, G. A. "VERT: A Risk Analysis Tool for Program Management." *Defense Management*, May–June 1979.

23. MANTEL, S. J., JR., J. R. EVANS, and V. A. TIPNIS. "Decision Analysis for New Process Technology," in B. V. Dean, ed., *Project Management: Methods and Studies*. Amsterdam: North-Holland, 1985.

24. MATZLER, K., and H. H. HINTERHUBER. "How to make product development projects more successful by integrating Kano's model of customer satisfaction into quality function deployment." *Technovation*, January 1998.

25. MEREDITH, J. "The Implementation of Computer Based Systems." *Journal of Operations Management*, October 1981.

26. MOYER, R. C., J. R. McGUIGAN, and W. J. KRETLOW. *Contemporary Financial Management*, 7th ed., Cincinnati: South-Western, 1998.

27. PASCALE, S., CARLAND, J. W., and J. C. CARLAND. "A Comparative Analysis of Two Concept Evaluation Methods for New Product Development Projects." *Project Management Journal*, December 1997.

28. PMI Standards Committee. *A Guide to the Project Management Body of Knowledge*. Upper Darby, PA: Project Management Institute, 1996.

29. RAZ, T. "An Iterative Screening Methodology for Selecting Project Alternatives." *Project Management Journal*, December 1997.

30. ROMAN, D. D. *Managing Projects: A Systems Approach*. New York: Elsevier,1986.

31. ROSENAU, M. D., JR. *Successful Project Management*, 2nd ed. New York: Van Nostrand Reinhold, 1991.

32. ROSS, S. A., R. W. WESTERFIELD, and B. D. JORDAN. *Fundamentals of Corporate Finance*, 3rd ed., Homewood, IL: Irwin, 1995.

33. SAATY, T. S. *Decision for Leaders: The Analytic Hierarchy Process*. Pittsburgh: University of Pittsburgh, 1990.

34. SCHMIDT, R. L. "A Model for R & D Project Selection with Combined Benefit, Outcome and Resource Interactions," *IEEE Transactions on Engineering Management*, November 1993.

35. SCHUYLER, J. R. "Decision Analysis in Projects: Judgments and Biases." *PM Network*, January 1995.

36. SIMON, H. *The New Science of Management Decisions*, rev. ed. Englewood Cliffs, NJ: Prentice Hall, 1977.

37. SOUDER, W. E. "Utility and Perceived Acceptability of R & D Project Selection Models." *Management Science*, August 1973.

38. SOUDER, W. E. "Project Evaluation and Selection," in D. I. Cleland, and W. R. King, eds., *Project Management Handbook*. New York: Van Nostrand Reinhold, 1983.

39. TOWNSEND, H. W. R., and G. E. WHITEHOUSE. "We Used Risk Analysis to Move Our Computer." *Industrial Engineering*, May 1977.

40. TURBAN, E., and J. R. MEREDITH. *Fundamentals of Management Science*, 6th ed. Homewood, IL: Irwin, 1994.

41. VAN GIGCH, J. P. *Applied General Systems Theory*, 2nd ed. New York: Harper & Row, 1978.

 The following reading, and the answers to the questions at the end, describe the stringent criteria this disguised, but well-known, firm uses to select among projects that offer major profit opportunities for the firm. In addition, the firm intentionally ties the criteria to their strategic goals so that each adopted project moves the organization further in the competitive direction they have chosen by adding to their core competencies. The reading also illustrates how the firm integrates their marketing, operations, engineering, and finance functions to forge a competitive advantage for the firm in the marketplace.

DIRECTED READING

AUTOMOTIVE BUILDERS, INC.: THE STANHOPE PROJECT
Jack Meredith

It was a cold, gray October day as Jim Wickes pulled his car into ABI's corporate offices parking lot in suburban Detroit. The leaves, in yellows and browns, swirled around his feet as he walked into the wind toward the lobby. "Good morning, Mr. Wickes," said his secretary as he came into the office. "That proposal on the Stanhope project just arrived a minute ago. It's on your desk." "Good morning, Debbie. Thanks. I've been anxious to see it."

This was the day Jim had scheduled to review the 1986 supplemental capital request and he didn't want any interruptions as he scrutinized the details of the flexible manufacturing project planned for Stanhope, Iowa. The Stanhope proposal, compiled by Ann Williamson, PM and managerial "champion" of this effort, looked like just the type of project to fit ABI's new strategic plan, but there was a large element of risk in the project. Before recommending the project to Steve White, executive vice president of ABI, Jim wanted to review all the details one more time.

History of ABI

ABI started operations as the Farm Equipment Company just after the First World War. Employing new technology to produce diesel engine parts for tractors, the firm flourished with the growth of farming and became a multimillion dollar company by 1940.

During the Second World War, the firm switched to producing tank and truck parts in volume for the military. At the war's end, the firm converted its equipment to the production of automotive parts for the expanding automobile industry. To reflect this major change in their product line, the company was renamed Automotive Builders, Inc. (ABI), though they remained a major supplier to the farm equipment market.

A Major Capital Project

The farm equipment industry in the 1970s had been doing well, but there were some disturbing trends.

Japanese manufacturers had entered the industry and were beginning to take a significant share of the domestic market. More significantly, domestic labor costs were significantly higher than overseas and resulted in price disadvantages that couldn't be ignored any longer. And perhaps most important of all, quality differences between American and Japanese farm equipment, including tractors, were becoming quite noticeable.

To improve the quality and costs of their incoming materials, many of the domestic tractor manufacturers were beginning to single-source a number of their tractor components. This allowed them better control over both quality and cost, and made it easier to coordinate delivery schedules at the same time.

In this vein, one of the major tractor engine manufacturers, code-named "Big Red" within ABI, let its suppliers know that it was interested in negotiating a contract for a possible 100 percent sourcing of 17 versions of special piston heads destined for a new line of high-efficiency tractor engines expected to replace the current conventional engines in both new and existing tractors. These were all six-cylinder diesel engines and thus would require six pistons each.

This put ABI in an interesting situation. If they failed to bid on this contract, they would be inviting competition into their very successful and profitable diesel engine parts business. Thus, to protect their existing successful business, and to pursue more such business, ABI seemed required to bid on this contract. Should ABI be successful in their bid, this would result in 100 percent sourcing in both the original equipment market (OEM) as well as the replacement market with its high margins. Furthermore, the high investment required to produce these special pistons at ABI's costs would virtually rule out future competition.

ABI had two plants producing diesel engine components for other manufacturers and believed they had a competitive edge in engineering of this type. These plants, however, could not accommodate the volume Big Red expected for the new engine. Big Red insisted at their negotiations that a 100 percent supplier be able to meet peak capacity at their assembly plant for this new line.

As Jim reviewed the proposal, he decided to refer back to the memos that restated their business strategy and started them thinking about a new Iowa plant located in the heart of the farm equipment industry for this project. In addition, Steve White had asked the following basic, yet rather difficult questions about the proposal at their last meeting and Jim wanted to be sure he had them clearly in mind as he reviewed the files.

- ABI is already achieving an excellent return on investment (ROI). Won't these investments simply tend to dilute it?

- Will the cost in new equipment be returned by an equivalent reduction in labor? Where's the payoff?

- What asset protection is there? This proposal requires an investment in new facilities before knowing whether a long-term contract will be procured to reimburse us for our investment.

- Does this proposal maximize ROI, sales potential, or total profit?

To address these questions adequately, Jim decided to recheck the expected after-tax profits and average rate of return (based on sales of 70,000 engines per year) when he reached the financial portion of the proposals. These figures should give a clear indication of the "quality" of the investment. There were, however, other aspects of capital resource allocation to consider besides the financial elements. One of these was the new business strategy of the firm, as recently articulated by ABI's executive committee.

The Business Strategy

A number of elements of ABI's business strategy were directly relevant to this proposal. Jim took out a note pad to jot each of them down and assign them a priority as follows:

1. Bid only on good margin products that have the potential for maintaining their margins over a long term.

2. Pursue only new products whose design or production process is of a proprietary nature and that exist

in areas where our technical abilities enable us to maintain a long-term position.

3. Employ, if at all possible, the most advanced technology in new projects that is either within our experience or requires the next step up in experience.

4. Foster the "project champion" approach to innovation and creativity. The idea is to encourage entrepreneurship by approving projects to which individual managers are committed and that they have adopted as personal "causes" based on their belief that the idea, product, or process is in our best interest.

5. Maintain small plants of no more than 480 employees. These have been found to be the most efficient and enjoy the best labor relations.

With these in mind, Jim reopened the proposal and started reading critical sections.

Demand Forecasts and Scenarios

For this proposal, three scenarios were analyzed in terms of future demand and financial impacts. The baseline "Scenario I" assumed the new line would be successful. "Scenario II" assumed the Japanese would soon follow and compete successfully with Big Red in this line. "Scenario III" assumed the new line was a failure. The sales volume forecasts under these three scenarios are shown in Table 1.

There was, however, little confidence in any of these forecasts. In the preceding few years Japan had become a formidable competitor, not only in price but also in more difficult areas of competition, such as quality and reliability. Furthermore, the economic situation in 1986 was taking a severe toll on American farmers and economic forecasts indicated there was no relief in sight. Thus, as stated in the proposal:

Table 1 Demand Forecasts (000s engines)*

Year	Baseline I	Scenario II	Scenario III
1987	69	69	69
1988	73	72	72
1989	90	81	77
1990	113	95	68
1991	125	87	62
1992	145	74	47

*Each engine requires six pistons.

The U.S. farm market will be a difficult battleground for world farm equipment manufacturers and any forecast of a particular engine's potential in this market must be considered as particularly risky. How much risk do we want to accept? Every effort should be made to minimize our exposure on this investment and maximize our flexibility.

Manufacturing Plan

The proposal stressed two primary aspects of the manufacturing process. First, a learning curve was employed in calculating production during the 1000-unit ramp-up implementation period in order to not be overly optimistic. A learning rate of 80 percent was assumed. Second, an advanced technology process using a flexible manufacturing system, based largely on turning centers, was recommended since it came in at $1 million less than conventional equipment and met the strategy guidelines of using sophisticated technology when appropriate.

Since ABI had closely monitored Big Red's progress in the engine market, the request for bids had been foreseen. In preparation for this, Jim had authorized a special manufacturing-process study to determine more efficient and effective ways of producing piston heads. The study considered product design, process selection, quality considerations, productivity, and manufacturing system planning. Three piston manufacturing methods were considered in the study: 1) batch manufacture via computer numerically controlled (CNC) equipment; 2) a flexible manufacturing system (FMS); and 3) a high volume, low-unit-cost transfer machine.

The resulting recommendation was to install a carefully designed FMS, if it appeared that additional flexibility might be required in the future for other versions, or even other manufacturers. Though such a system would be expensive, the volume of production over the FMS's longer lifetime would offset that expense. Four preferred machine builders were contacted for equipment specifications and bids. It was ABI's plan to work closely with the selected vendor in designing and installing the equipment, thus building quality and reliability into both the product and the process and learning about the equipment at the same time.

To add further flexibility for the expensive machinery, all design features that would facilitate retool or changeover to other products were incorporated. For example, the machining centers would also be capable of machining other metals, such as aluminum or nodular iron, and would be fitted with variable feed and speed motors, feed-force monitors, pressure-controlled clamping of workpieces, and air-leveling pallets. Also, fully interchangeable chucks, spindles, pallets, tooling, and risers would be purchased to minimize the spare parts inventories.

Plant Operation and Organization

As stated in the proposal, many innovative practices were to be employed at the new plant, such as.

- Machine operators will be trained to do almost all of their own machine maintenance.
- All employees will conduct their own statistical process control and piston heads will be subject to 100 percent inspection.
- There will only be four skill classes in the plant. Every employee in each of those classes will be trained to do any work within that class.
- There will not be any time clocks in the plant.

The organizational structure for the 11 salaried workers in the new plant is shown in Figure 1 and the complete labor summary is illustrated in Figure 2, including the shift breakdown. As can be seen, the plant will be relatively small, with 65 employees in the ratio of 1:5 salaried to hourly. The eight month acquisition of the employees during the ramp-up is illustrated in Figure 3, with full employment occurring by March 1987.

Financial Considerations

Financial aspects of new proposals at ABI were considered from a number of perspectives, in part because of the interdependent nature of many proposals. The results of not investing in a proposal are normally compared with the results of investing and the differences noted. Variations on the investment assumptions are also tested, including errors in the forecast sales volumes, learning rates, productivities, selling prices, and cancellations of both current and future orders for existing and potential business.

For the Stanhope proposal, the site investment required is $3,012,000. The details of this investment are shown in Table 2. The total investment required amounts to $7,108,000 (plus required working capital of $1,380,000). The equipment is depreciated over an eight-year life. ABI, under the revised tax laws, is in the 34 percent tax bracket. The price of the piston

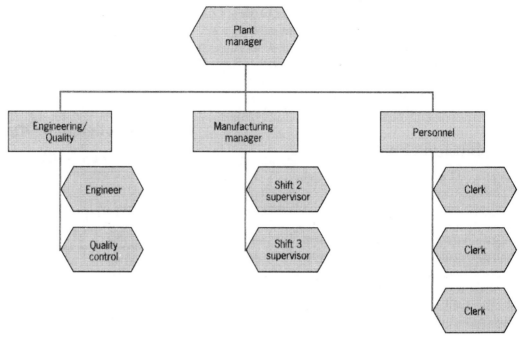

Figure 1 Stanhope organization.

Salaried Labor

plant manager	1
manufacturing managers (3 shifts)	3
quality control manager	1
engineering	2
personnel manager	1
clerical	3
	11

Hourly Labor

	Days	Afternoons	Nights
direct	14	14	10
inspection	1	1	1
maintenance	2	1	1
tooling	2	2	1
rec./shp./mtl.	2	1	1
Total	21	19	14

Summary

salary	11
hourly	54
Total	65

Figure 2 Stanhope labor summary.

heads has been tentatively set at $25.45 apiece. ABI's expected costs are shown in Table 3.

Some Concerns

Jim had spoken with some of his colleagues about the FMS concept after the preliminary financial results had been tabulated. Their concerns were what now interested him. For example, he remembered one manager asking: "Suppose Big Red's sales only reach 70 percent of our projections in the 1989-90 time period, or say, perhaps as much as 150 percent; how would this affect the project? Does the FMS still apply or would you consider some other form of manufacturing equipment, possibly conventional or CNC with potential after-market application in the former case or a transfer machine in the latter case?"

Another manager wrote his thoughts down as a memo to forward to Jim. He had two major concerns:

- "Scenario II" analysis assumes the loss of substantial volume to competition. This seems rather unlikely.

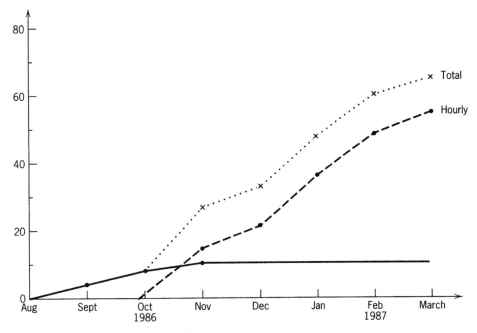

Figure 3 Stanhope labor buildup.

Table 2 Stanhope Site Capital Costs

Land and Site Preparation

land	$246,000
access roads/parking lot	124,000
landscaping	22,000

Building Costs

building (67,000 sq. ft.)	1,560,000
air conditioning	226,000
power	205,000
employee services	177,000
legal fees and permits	26,000

Auxiliary Equipment

ABI company sign	25,000
containers, racks, etc.	33,000
flume	148,000
coolant disposal	97,000
furnishings	51,000
fork lift trucks	72,000
Total	3,012,000

- After-tax margins seem unreasonably high. Can we get such margins on a sole-source contract?

Jim wondered what these changes in their assumptions would do to the ROI of the proposal and its overall profitability.

Table 3 Piston Head Cost Summary

material	$8.47
labor	1.06
variable overhead	2.23
fixed overhead	2.44
freight	0.31
Total factory cost	14.51
general & admin.	1.43
scrap	0.82
testing	0.39
Total cost	17.15

Conclusion

Jim had concerns about the project also. He wondered how realistic the demand forecasts were, given the weak economy and what the Japanese might do. If the demand didn't materialize, ABI might be sorry they had invested in such an expensive piece of equipment as an FMS.

Strategically, it seemed like ABI had to make this investment to protect its profitable position in the diesel engine business, but how far should this argument be carried? Were they letting their past investments color their judgment on new ones? He was also concerned about the memo questioning the high profit margins. They did seem high in the midst of a sluggish economy.

Questions

1. What project selection method described in the chapter will ABI probably employ for this proposal?

2. What are the answers to Steve White's questions?

3. What other factors are relevant to this issue?

4. How do the changes in assumptions mentioned by the other managers affect the proposal?

5. What position should Jim take? Why?

CHAPTER

5

Project Planning

In the Reader's Digest (March 1998, p. 49) Peter Drucker is quoted on planning: "Plans are only good intentions unless they immediately degenerate into hard work." To make such a transformation possible is no easy task. Inadequate planning is a cliché in project management. Periodically, articles appear in project management periodicals attesting to the value of good planning. Project managers pay little attention. PMs say, or are told, that planning "takes too much time," "customers don't know what they want," "if we commit we will be held accountable," and a number of similar weak excuses [7, p. 15]. Tom Peters, well-known seeker of business excellence, was quoted in the *Cincinnati Post:* "Businesses [believe] a lot of dumb things. . . . The more time you spend planning, the less time you'll need to spend on implementation. Almost never the case! Ready. Fire. Aim. That's the approach taken by businesses I most respect." We strongly disagree and, as we will report below (and in Chapter 13), there is a great deal of research supporting the view that careful planning is solidly associated with project success—and none, to our knowledge, supporting the opposite position. On the other hand, sensible planners do not kill the plan with overanalysis. This leads to a well-known "analysis by paralysis." In an excellent article, Langley finds a path in between the two extremes [20]. It is now time to consider how to plan the work of the project in such a way that it may be translated into "hard work" that actually leads to a successful completion of the project.

There are several reasons why we must use considerable care when planning projects. The primary purpose of planning, of course, is to establish a set of directions in sufficient detail to tell the project team exactly what must be done, when it must be done, and what resources to use in order to produce the deliverables of the project successfully. As we noted in Chapter 1, the deliverables (or scope, or specifications, or objectives) of a project are more than mere descriptions of the goods and/or services we promise to deliver to the client at a quality level that will meet client expectations. They also include the time and cost required to complete the project to the client's satisfaction. The plan must be designed in such a way that the project outcome also meets the objectives of the parent firm, as reflected by whatever selection process was used to approve the project. Because the plan is only an estimate of what must be done, it is always carried out in an environment of uncertainty. Therefore, the plan must include allowances for risk and features that allow it to be *adaptive*, i.e., to be responsive to things that might disrupt it while it is being carried out. One such thing—"scope creep"—is particularly common in software projects and will be discussed further in Chapter 11. Finally, the plan must also contain methods to ensure its integrity, which is to say it must include means of controlling the work it prescribes.

There is an extensive literature on project planning. Some of it is concerned with the strategic aspects of planning, being focused on the choice of projects that are consistent with the organization's goals (e.g., [3, 10, 23, and 38]). Another group of works is aimed at the process of planning individual projects, given that they have been chosen as strategically acceptable (e.g., [6, 30, 33, and 40]). Laufer [21], in particular, offers an interesting discussion on the theory of planning that includes some practical implications. Most fields have their own accepted set of project planning processes, though they are all similar, as we shall soon see. For example, in the field of Information Systems they refer to the standard "systems development cycle" for software projects, consisting of four or six or seven "phases," depending on which author is being consulted (e.g., see [34]). For a different view of the software planning process, see [9]. Prentis [33] breaks the general planning process into seven steps, while Roman [35] describes it as a set of six planning sequences.

The purpose of planning is to facilitate later accomplishment. The world is full of plans that never become deeds. The planning techniques covered here are intended to smooth the path from idea to accomplishment. It is a complicated process to manage a project, and plans act as a map of this process. The map must have sufficient detail to determine what must be done next but be simple enough that workers are not lost in a welter of minutiae.

In the pages that follow we discuss a somewhat formal method for the development of a project plan. Almost all project planning techniques lead to plans that contain the same basic elements. They differ only in the ways they approach the process of planning. We have adopted an approach that we think makes the planning process straightforward and fairly systematic, but it is never as systematic and straightforward as planning theorists would like. At its best, planning is tortuous. It is an iterative process yielding better plans from not-so-good plans, and the iterative process of improvement seems to take place in fits and starts. The process may be described formally, but it does not occur formally. Bits and pieces of plans are developed by individuals, by informal group meetings, or by formalized planning teams [29], and then improved by other individuals, groups, or teams, and improved again, and again. Both the plans themselves and the process of planning should start simple and then become more complex.

If the appropriate end product is kept firmly in mind, this untidy process yields a *project plan*. In this chapter we focus on designing the physical aspects of the project, defining what it is the project is supposed to accomplish, and who will have to do what for the project's desired output to be achieved. The project's budget and schedule are major parts of the master plan, but we delay discussion of them until Chapters 7 and 8. Indeed, what must be done to test and approve project outputs at both interim and final stages, and what records must be kept are both parts of the master plan and these are covered in later chapters, as is the part of the plan that covers ending the project. There is nothing sacrosanct about this sequence. It is simply in the order that these parts of the project plan tend to develop naturally.

Project plans may take many forms and in the coming pages we will mention several of these. A *project plan* should include the elements described in the next section. As we will see later, it should also include a record of all changes and adjustments that were made to the project during its life because it can then serve as the primary document of project termination, the *project history* (see Chapter 13). The master plan will include a complete set of schedules together with the associated resources and personnel needed to perform all of the tasks required to complete the project. If these are prepared in the tabular form we describe in Section 5.3, the result is an *action plan*, but even action plans may take other forms if desired. The focus of an action plan, however, is on the schedule/resource/personnel elements of the activities and/or events required by the project.

In Section 5.4 we describe the *project work breakdown structure* (WBS) that is another, and usually specialized way of viewing the action plan. Often, the WBS consists of a simple list of all project activities with major activities broken down into sub-activities, and these broken down still further. Schedules may be shown, and resources, budget account numbers, and other specific aspects of the project may be displayed. The WBS and the project action plan might be identical. The *project linear responsibility chart* or *table* is another specialized view of the action plan and focuses on who has what responsibility (e.g., performing, approving, communicating, supporting) associated with each project task. Many different forms may be used for both the WBS and responsibility charts,

It is appropriate to ask, "Why so many different ways of showing similar types of information?" As is true of so many things, tradition is probably the major reason. The master plan is usually a large and complex document. PMs need fast and simple ways of communicating specific kinds of information about their projects. Action plans, WBSs, and responsibility charts are simple and highly flexible ways of doing this.

5.1 INITIAL PROJECT COORDINATION

It is crucial that the project's objectives be clearly tied to the overall mission of the firm. Senior management should define the firm's intent in undertaking the project, outline the scope of the project, and describe the project's desired results. Without a clear beginning, project planning can easily go astray. It is also vital that a senior manager call and be present at the *project launch meeting*, an initial coordinating meeting, as a visible symbol of top management's commitment to the project.

The individual leading the launch meeting is first to define the scope of the project. The success of the project launch meeting is absolutely dependent on the existence of a well-defined set of objectives. Unless all parties to the planning process have a clear understanding of precisely what it is the project is expected to deliver, planning is sure to be inadequate. The precise nature of the scope statement depends on the nature of the project itself, and because of this, it reflects the fact that all projects are, to some extent, unique. For some useful comments on the scope statement, see [12]. We will have more to say about project scope and its management in Chapters 6 and 11.

At the launch meeting, the project is discussed in sufficient detail that potential contributors develop a general understanding of what is needed. If the project is one of many similar projects, the meeting will be short and routine, a sort of "touching base" with other interested units. If the project is unique in most of its aspects, extensive discussion may be required.

While various authors have somewhat different expectations for the project launch meeting [e.g., see 19, 26], we feel it is important not to allow plans, schedules, and budgets to go beyond the most aggregated level (Level 1), possibly Level 2 if the project deliverables are fairly simple and do not require much interdepartmental coordination. To fix plans in more detail at this initial meeting will tend to prevent team members from integrating the new project into their ongoing activities and from developing creative ways of coordinating activities that involve two or more organizational units. Worse still, departmental representatives will be asked to make "a ballpark estimate of the budget and time required" to carry out this first-blush plan. Everyone who has ever worked on a project is aware of the extraordinary propensity of preliminary estimates to metamorphose instantaneously into firm budgets and schedules. Remember that this is only one of a series of meetings that will be required to plan projects of more than minimal complexity. It is critical to the future success of the project to take the time required to do a technically and politically careful job of planning. "If this means many meetings and extensive use of participatory decision making, then it is well worth the effort [13, p. 316]".

Whatever the process, the outcome must be that: (1) technical scope is established (though perhaps not "cast in concrete"), (2) basic areas of performance responsibility are accepted by the participants, and (3) some tentative overall schedules and budgets are spelled out. Each individual/unit accepting responsibility for a portion of the project should agree to deliver, by the next project meeting, a preliminary but detailed plan about how that responsibility will be accomplished. Such plans should contain descriptions of the required tasks, and estimates of the budgets and schedules.

These plans are then scrutinized by the group and combined into a composite project plan. The composite plan, still not completely firm, is approved by each participating group, by the project manager, and then by senior organizational management. Each subsequent approval hardens the plan somewhat, and when senior management has endorsed it, any further changes in the project's scope must be made by processing a formal *change order*. If the project is not large or complex, informal written memoranda can substitute for the change order. The main point is that no *significant* changes in the project are made, without written notice, following top management's approval. The definition of "significant" depends on the specific situation and the people involved.

Source: DILBERT reprinted by permission of United Feature Syndicate, Inc.

The PM generally takes responsibility for gathering the necessary approvals and assuring that any changes incorporated into the plan at higher levels are communicated to, and approved by, the units that have already signed off on the plan. Nothing is as sure to enrage functional unit managers as to find that they have been committed by someone else to alterations in their carefully considered plans without being informed. Violation of this procedure is considered a betrayal of trust. Several incidents of this kind occurred in a firm during a project to design a line of children's clothing. The anger at this *change without communication* was so great that two chief designers resigned and took jobs with a competitor.

Because senior managers are almost certain to exercise their prerogative to change the plan, the PM should always return to the contributing units for consideration and reapproval of the plan as modified. The final, approved result of this procedure is the project plan, also sometimes known as the *master*, or *baseline plan*. When the planning phase of the project is completed, it is valuable to hold one additional meeting, a post-planning review [27]. This meeting should be chaired by an experienced project manager who is not connected with the project [2]. The major purpose of the post-planning review is to make sure that all necessary elements of a project plan have been properly developed and communicated.

Outside Clients

When the project is to deliver a product/service to an outside client, the fundamental planning process is unchanged except for the fact that the specifications cannot be altered without the *client's* permission. A common "planning" problem in these cases is that marketing has promised deliverables that engineering may not know how to produce on a schedule that manufacturing may be unable to meet. This sort of problem usually results when the various functional areas are not involved in the planning process at the time the original proposal is made to the potential client. We cannot overstate the importance of a carefully determined set of *deliverables*, accepted by both project team and client [25].

Two objections to such early participation by engineering and manufacturing are likely to be raised by marketing. First, the sales arm of the organization is trained to sell and is expected to be fully conversant with all technical aspects of the firm's products/services. Further, salespeople are expected to be knowledgeable about design and manufacturing lead times and schedules. On the other hand, it is widely assumed by marketing (with some justice on occasion) that manufacturing and design engineers do not understand sales techniques, will be argumentative and/or pessimistic about client needs in the presence of the client, and are generally not "housebroken" when customers are nearby. Second, it is expensive to involve so much technical talent so early in the sales process—typically, prior to issuing a proposal. It can easily cost a firm more than $10,000 to send five technical specialists on a trip to consider a potential client's needs. The willingness to accept higher sales costs puts even more emphasis on the selection process.

The rejoinder to such objections is simple. It is usually cheaper, faster, and easier to do things right the first time than to redo them. When the product/service is a complex system that must be installed in a larger, more complex system, it is appropriate to treat the sale like a project, which deserves the same kind of planning. A great many firms that consistently operate in an atmosphere typified by design and manufacturing crises have created their own panics. (Software producers and computer system salespeople take note!) In fairness, it is appropriate to urge that anyone meeting customers face to face should receive some training in the tactics of selling.

A potential remedy for these problems is the use of multifunctional teams, also known in this context as *concurrent engineering*. This latter term, born in the 1980s, has been applied to product/service development "where, typically, a product design and its manufacturing process are developed simultaneously, cross-functional groups are used to accomplish integration, and the voice of the customer is included in the product development process [37, p. 67]". Multifunctional teaming may also be applied to the software design and development process. In software projects it is critically important to keep the customer involved in the process of developing software requirements from the start of the project. Clients often ask such questions as "While you're at it, can you fix it so the software will also . . . ?" Software writers tend to focus on technical feasibility when dealing with these questions and not uncommonly fail to note the additional time and cost required. More will be said about multifunctional teaming later in this chapter.

Project Plan Elements

Given the project plan, approvals really amount to a series of authorizations. The PM is authorized to direct activities, spend monies (usually within preset limits) request resources and personnel, and start the project on its way. Senior management's approval not only signals its willingness to fund and support the project, but also notifies subunits in the organization that they may commit resources to the project.

The process of developing the project plan varies from organization to organization, but any project plan must contain the following elements:

- *Overview* This is a short summary of the objectives and scope of the project. It is directed to top management and contains a statement of the goals of the project, a brief explanation of their relationship to the firm's objectives, a description of the managerial structure that will be used for the project, and a list of the major milestones in the project schedule.

- *Objectives* This contains a more detailed statement of the general goals noted in the overview section. The statement should include profit and competitive aims as well as technical goals.

- *General Approach* This section describes both the managerial and the technical approaches to the work. The technical discussion describes the relationship of the project to available technologies. For example, it might note that this project is an extension of work done by the company for an earlier project. The subsection on the managerial approach takes note of any deviation from routine procedure—for instance, the use of subcontractors for some parts of the work.

- *Contractual Aspects* This critical section of the plan includes a complete list and description of all reporting requirements, customer-supplied resources, liaison arrangements, advisory committees, project review and cancellation procedures, proprietary requirements, any specific management agreements (e.g., use of subcontractors), as well as the technical deliverables and their specifications, delivery schedules, and a specific procedure for changing any of the above. (Project change orders will be discussed in Chapter 11.) Completeness is a necessity in this section. If in doubt about whether an item should be included or not, the wise planner will include it.

- *Schedules* This section outlines the various schedules and lists all milestone events. Each task is listed, and the estimated time for each task should be obtained from those who will do the work. The project master schedule is constructed from these inputs. The responsible person or department head should sign off on the final, agreed-on schedule.

- *Resources* There are two primary aspects to this section. The first is the budget. Both capital and expense requirements are detailed by task, which makes this a *project budget* (discussed further in Chapter 7). One-time costs are separated from recurring project costs. Second, cost monitoring and control procedures should be described. In addition to the usual routine elements, the monitoring and control procedures must be designed to cover special resource requirements for the project, such as special machines, test equipment, laboratory usage or construction, logistics, field facilities, and special materials.

- *Personnel* This section lists the expected personnel requirements of the project. Special skills, types of training needed, possible recruiting problems, legal or policy restrictions on work force composition, and any other special requirements, such as security clearances, should be noted here. (This reference to "security" includes the need to protect trade secrets and research targets from competitors as well as the need to protect the national security.) It is helpful to time-phase personnel needs to the project schedule. This makes clear when the various types of contributors are needed and in what numbers. These projections are an important element of the budget, so the personnel, schedule, and resources sections can be cross-checked with one another to ensure consistency.

- *Evaluation Methods*   Every project should be evaluated against standards and by methods established at the project's inception. This section contains a brief description of the procedure to be followed in monitoring, collecting, storing, and evaluating the history of the project.

- *Potential Problems*   Sometimes it is difficult to convince planners to make a serious attempt to anticipate potential difficulties. One or more such possible disasters such as subcontractor default, technical failure, strikes, bad weather, sudden required breakthroughs, critical sequences of tasks, tight deadlines, resource limitations, complex coordination requirements, insufficient authority in some areas, and new, complex, or unfamiliar tasks are certain to occur. The only uncertainties are which ones will occur and when. In fact, the timing of these disasters is not random. There are times, conditions, and events in the life of every project when progress depends on subcontractors, or the weather, or coordination, or resource availability, and plans to deal with unfavorable contingencies should be developed early in the project's life cycle. Some PMs disdain this section of the plan on the grounds that crises cannot be predicted. Further, they claim to be very effective firefighters. It is quite possible that when one finds such a PM, one has discovered an arsonist. No amount of current planning can solve the current crisis, but pre-planning may avert some.

These are the elements that constitute the project plan and are the basis for a more detailed planning of the budgets, schedules, work plan, and general management of the project. Once this basic plan is fully developed and approved, it is disseminated to all interested parties. The document is also known as the "project charter." Because the project charter is generated through negotiations involving the many parties-at-interest in the project (usually under the leadership of the PM), we discuss the charter in Chapter 6.

Before proceeding, we should make explicit that this formal planning process is required for relatively large projects that cannot be classified as "routine" for the organization. The time, effort, and cost of the planning process we have described is not justified for routine projects, for example, most plant or machine maintenance projects. Admittedly, no two routine maintenance projects are identical, but they do tend to be quite similar. It is useful to have a complete plan for such projects, but it is meant to serve as a template that can easily be modified to fit the specific maintenance project at hand. The template also can serve as a benchmark in a continuous improvement program.

Project Management in Practice
Extensive Project Planning for Kodak's New Photographic System

After five years of secret planning involving five major worldwide film and camera companies, the Kodak System Developing Companies announced the new *Advantix* photographic system on February 1, 1996. The project, code-named Orion, was among the most ambitious new product development projects ever undertaken by Kodak. The initial brainstorming of concepts began in the mid-1980s and the search for partners in the late 1980s. By November 1991, an agreement had been reached on how Kodak, Fuji, Canon, Minolta, and Nikon—the System Developing Companies—would work together to develop this new system.

The main project plan consisted of a four-stage, eight-gate process as illustrated below.

- **Stage 1: Define and Refine Value Proposition**
  - Gate 0: Project Inception
  - Gate 1: Project Assessment

- **Stage 2: Product and Market Launch Design**
  - Gate 2: Project Commitment
  - Gate 3: Design Readiness

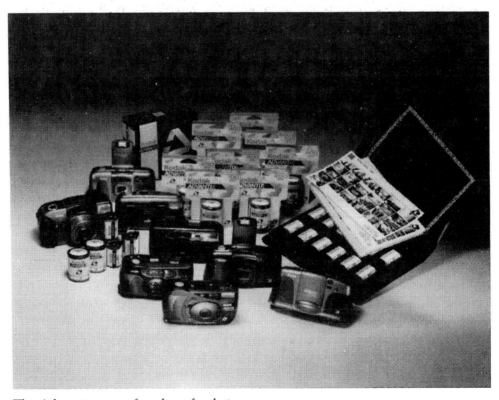

The Advantix array of products for their system.

- **Stage 3: Marketing and Manufacturing Implementation**
    Gate 4: Project Verification
    Gate 5: Launch Readiness
- **Stage 4: Production and Sales**
    Gate 6: Manufacturing Readiness
    Gate 7: Marketing and Manufacturing Re-Review

As an example of the elements of the project plan, a 25 page "Concept Document" was a deliverable at Gate 0 by December 1992. The doc-

Source: C. Adams, "A Kodak Moment: *Advantix* Named 1997 International Project of the Year," PM *Network,* January 1998, pp. 21–27.

ument included the identified consumer needs, benefits to Kodak and the industry, strategies, requirements, product descriptions, technology and manufacturing approaches, business case, schedule, and key risk areas. With significant changes occurring later on in the project, the Concept Document was modified and re-approved in mid-1994. The Gates represented major project milestones and always involved a major, top management review for verifying status and discussing upcoming issues.

Eleven months after announcement, *Business Week* selected the Advanced Photo System as one of the best new products on the market. *Consumers Digest* selected the Kodak Advantix 3700ix camera as a best buy in its 1997 annual buying guide.

Project Planning in Action

Project plans are usually constructed by listing the sequence of activities required to carry the project from start to completion. This is not only a natural way to think about a project; it also helps the planner decide the necessary sequence of things—a necessary consideration for determining the project schedule and duration. In a fascinating paper, Aaron and his colleagues describe the planning process used at a telecommunications firm [1].

Using a planning process oriented around the life-cycle events common for software and hardware product developers, they divide the project into nine segments:

- Concept evaluation
- Requirements identification
- Design
- Implementation
- Test
- Integration
- Validation
- Customer test and evaluation
- Operations and maintenance

Each segment is made up of activities and milestones (significant events). As the project passes through each of the segments, it is subjected to a series of "quality gates" that must be successfully passed before proceeding to the next segment. Note that the planning process must pass through the quality gates as must the physical output of the project itself. For example, the requirements identification segment must meet the appropriate quality standards before the design segment can be started, just as design must be approved before implementation can be commenced.

Beginning in Chapter 1, we have argued that quality should be an inherent part of the project's specification/deliverables. The approach taken by Aaron, et al. is a direct embodiment of our position. Indeed, it "goes us one better," by applying quality standards to the process of managing the project as well as to the project's deliverables.

5.2 SYSTEMS INTEGRATION

Systems integration (sometimes called *systems engineering*) is one part of *integration management*, discussed further in Section 5.5, and plays a crucial role in the performance aspect of the project. We are using this phrase to include any technical specialist in the science or art of the project who is capable of integrating the technical disciplines to achieve the customer's objectives, and/or integrating the project into the customer's system. As such, systems integration is concerned with three major objectives.

1. *Performance*   Performance is what a system does. It includes system design, reliability, quality, maintainability, and repairability. Obviously, these are not separate, independent elements of the system, but are highly interrelated qualities. Any of these system performance characteristics is subject to overdesign as well as underdesign but must fall within the design parameters established by the client. If the client approves, we may give the client more than the specifications require simply because we have already designed to some capability, and giving the client an overdesigned system is faster and less expensive than delivering precisely to specification. At times, the esthetic qualities of a system may be specified, typically through a requirement that the appearance of the system must be acceptable to the client.

2. *Effectiveness*   The objective is to design the individual components of a system to achieve the desired performance in an optimal manner. This is accomplished through the following guidelines:

   - Require no component performance specifications unless necessary to meet one or more systems requirements.
   - Every component requirement should be traceable to one or more systems requirements.
   - Design components to optimize system performance, not the performance of subsystems.

   It is not unusual for clients or project teams to violate any or all of these seemingly logical dicta. Tolerances specified to far closer limits than any possible system requirement, superfluous "bells and whistles," and "off the shelf" components that do not work well with the rest of the system are so common they seem to be taken for granted by both client and vendor. The causes of these strange occurrences are probably associated with some combination of inherent distrust between buyer and seller, the desire to overspecify in order "to be sure," and the feeling that "this part will do just as well." As we will see in Chapter 6, these attitudes can be softened and replaced with others that are more helpful to the process of systems integration.

3. *Cost* Systems integration considers cost to be a design parameter, and costs can be accumulated in several areas. Added design cost may lead to decreased component cost, leaving performance and effectiveness otherwise unchanged. Added design cost may yield decreased production costs, and production cost may be traded off against unit cost for materials. *Value engineering* (or *value analysis*) examines all these cost trade-offs and is an important aspect of systems integration [28]. It can be used in any project where the relevant cost tradeoffs can be estimated. It is simply the consistent and thorough use of cost/effectiveness analysis.

Multifunctional teaming (see Section 5.5) is a way of achieving systems integration and, as such, may play a major role in the success or failure of any complex project. If a risky approach is taken by systems integration, it may delay the project. If the approach is too conservative, we forego opportunities for enhanced project capabilities or advantageous project economics. A good design will take all these trade-offs into account in the initial stages of the technical approach. A good design will also avoid locking the project into a rigid solution with little flexibility or adaptability in case problems occur later or changes in the environment demand changes in project performance or effectiveness.

Multifunctional teams are also valuable for assessing and mitigating risk in the project. The management of risk was already discussed in Section 2.4 but it applies in project planning as well, particularly in anticipating crises during the execution of the project (refer to the Directed Reading: "Planning for Crises in Project Management" at the end of this chapter). The application of risk analysis (see Section 2.4) is particularly useful in risk management. For an example, see again the Directed Reading at the end of this chapter.

The details of systems integration are beyond the scope of this book. The interested reader is referred to [4, 8]. In any case, the ability to do systems integration/engineering depends on at least a minimal level of technical knowledge about most parts of the project. It is one of the reasons project managers are expected to have some understanding of the technology of the projects they head.

5.3 SORTING OUT THE PROJECT

In this and the following sections of this chapter, and in Chapters 7 and 8 on budgeting and scheduling, we move into a consideration of the details of the project. We need to know exactly what is to be done, by whom, and when. All activities required to complete the project must be precisely delineated and coordinated. The necessary resources must be available when and where they are needed, and in the correct amounts. Some activities must be done sequentially, but some may be done simultaneously. If a large project is to come in on time and within cost, a great many things must happen when and how they are supposed to happen. In this section, we propose a conceptually simple method to assist in sorting out and planning all this detail. It is a *hierarchial planning system*. We have also named it the "*even planning process.*"

To accomplish any specific project, a number of major activities must be undertaken and completed. Make a list of these activities in the general order in which they would occur. This is Level 1. A reasonable number of activities at this level might be anywhere between 2 and 20. (There is nothing sacred about these limits. Two is the minimum possible breakdown and 20 is about the largest number of interrelated items that can be comfortably sorted and scheduled at a given level of aggregation.) Now break each of these Level 1 items into 2 to 20 tasks. This is Level 2. In the same way, break each Level 2 task into 2 to 20 subtasks. This is Level 3. Proceed in this way until the detailed tasks at a level are so well understood that there is no reason to continue with the work breakdown.

It is important to be sure that all items in the list are at roughly the same level of task generality. In writing a book, for example, the various chapters tend to be at the same level of generality, but individual chapters are divided into finer detail. Indeed, subdivisions of a chapter may be divided into finer detail still. It is difficult to overstate the significance of this simple dictum. It is central to the preparation of most of the planning documents that will be described in this chapter and those that follow.

The logic behind this simple rule is persuasive. We have observed both students and professionals in the process of planning. We noted that people who lack experience in planning tend to write down what they perceive to be the first activity in a sequence of activities, begin to break it down into components, take the first of these, break it further, until they have reached a level of detail they feel is sufficient. They then take the second step and proceed similarly. If they have a good understanding of a basic activity, the breakdown into detail is handled well. If they are not expert, the breakdown lacks detail and tends to be inadequate. Further, we noted that integration of the various basic activities was poor. An artist of our acquaintance explained. When creating a drawing, the artist sketches in the main lines of a scene, and then builds up the detail little by little over the entire drawing. In this way, the drawing has a "unity." One cannot achieve this unity by drawing one part of the scene in high detail, then moving to another part of the scene and detailing it. He asked a young student to make a pen-and-ink sketch of a fellow student. Her progress at three successive stages of her drawing is shown in Figure 5-1.

This illustrates the "even planning process." The PM will probably generate the most basic level (Level 1) and possibly the next level as well. Unless the project is quite small, the generation of additional levels will be delegated to the individuals or groups who have responsibility for doing the work. Maintaining the "even planning" discipline will help keep the plan focused on the project's deliverables rather than on the work at a subsystem level.

Sometimes a problem arises because some managers tend to think of outcomes (events) when planning and others think of specific tasks (activities). Many mix the two. The problem is to develop a list of both activities and outcomes that represents an exhaustive, nonredundant set of results to be accomplished (outcomes) and the work to be done (activities) in order to complete the project.

In this hierarchical planning system, the objectives are taken from the project master plan. This aids the planner in identifying the set of required activities for the objectives to be met, the project's *action plan*. Each activity has an outcome (event)

Figure 5-1   The "even planning process"

associated with it, and these activities and events are decomposed into subactivities and subevents, which, in turn, are subdivided again.

Assume, for example, that we have a project whose purpose is to acquire and install a large machining center in an existing plant. In the hierarchy of work to be accomplished for the installation part of the project, we might find such tasks as "Develop a plan for preparation of the floor site" and "Develop a plan to maintain plant output during the installation and test period." These tasks are two of a larger set of jobs to be done. The task " . . . preparation of the floor site" is subdivided into its elemental parts, including such items as "Get specifics on machine center mounting points," "Check construction specifications on plant floor," and "Present final plan for floor preparation for approval." A form that may help to organize this information is shown in Figure 5-2. (Additional information about each element of the project will be added to the form later when budgeting and scheduling are discussed.) Figure 5-3 shows an action plan for a college "Career Day." (Clearly, Figure 5-3 is not complete. For example, the list of activities does not show such items as "setting and decorating the tables." In the interest of simplicity and in order to avoid doubling the

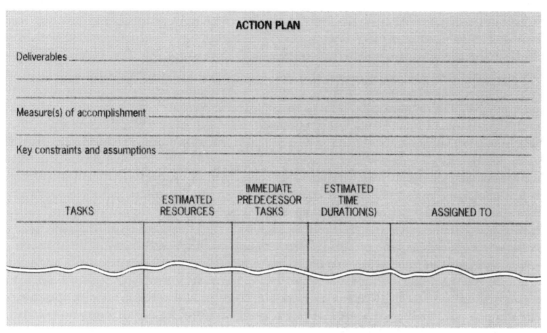

Figure 5-2   A form to assist hierarchical planning.

length—and cost—of this book, the examples shown in this and following chapters are meant to be indicative, not exhaustive.)

A short digression is in order before continuing this discussion on action plans. The actual form the action plan takes is not sacrosanct. As we will show in this and the coming chapters, not even all elements of the action plan shown in Figure 5-2 are necessary in all cases. In some cases, for example, the amounts of specific resources required may not be relevant. In others, "due dates" may be substituted for activity durations. The appearance of action plans differs in different organizations, and may even differ between departments or divisions of the same organization (though standardization of format is usual, and probably desirable in any given firm). In some plans, numbers are used to identify activities; in others, letters. In still others, combinations of letters and numbers are used. In this chapter, we will illustrate several different forms of action plans drawn from "real life." Our purpose is not to confuse the reader, but to focus the reader's attention on the *content* of the plan, not its *form*.

A tree diagram can be used to represent a hierarchical plan as in Figure 5-4. Professor Andrew Vazsonyi has called this type of diagram a *Gozinto chart* after the famous Italian mathematician, Prof. Zepartzat Gozinto, of Vazsonyi's invention. Readers familiar with the Bill of Materials in a Materials Requirements Planning (MRP) system will recognize the parallel to nested hierarchical planning.

If the project does not involve capital equipment and special materials, estimates may not be necessary. Some projects require a long chain of tasks that are mostly sequential—for example, the real estate syndication of an apartment complex or the development and licensing of a new drug. Other projects require the coordination of

ACTION PLAN

Objective Career Day				
Steps	Responsibility	Time (weeks)	Prec.	Resources
1. Contact Organizations				
a. Print forms	Secretary	6	–	Print shop
b. Contact organizations	Program manager	15	1.a	Word processing
c. Collect display information	Office manager	4	1.b	
d. Gather college particulars	Secretary	4	1.b	
e. Print programs	Secretary	6	1.d	Print shop
f. Print participants' certificates	Graduate Assistant	8	–	Print Shop
2. Banquet and Refreshments				
a. Select guest speaker	Program manager	14	–	
b. Organize food	Program manager	3	1.b	Caterer
c. Organize liquor	Director	10	1.b	Dept. of Liquor Control
d. Organize refreshments	Graduate Assistant	7	1.b	Purchasing
3. Publicity and Promotion				
a. Send invitations	Graduate Assistant	2	–	Word processing
b. Organize gift certificates	Graduate Assistant	5.5	–	
c. Arrange banner	Graduate Assistant	5	1.d	Print shop
d. Contact faculty	Program manager	1.5	1.d	Word processing
e. Advertise in college paper	Secretary	5	1.d	Newspaper
f. Class announcements	Graduate Assistant	1	3.d	Registrar's office
g. Organize posters	Secretary	4.5	1.d	Print shop
4. Facilities				
a. Arrange facility for event	Program manager	2.5	1.c	
b. Transport materials	Office manager	.5	4.a	Movers

Figure 5-3   Partial action plan for college "Career Day."

many concurrent tasks that finally come together—for example, the design and manufacture of an aircraft engine or the construction of a house. Still others have the characteristics of both. An example of a plan to acquire a subsidiary is illustrated in Figures 5-5a and 5-5b. A verbal "action plan" was written in the form of a memorandum, Figure 5-5a, and was followed by the more common, tabular plan shown in Figure 5-5b. Only one page of a five-page plan is shown. The individuals and groups

Figure 5-4   Gozinto chart for a toy bus. *Source* [14]

mentioned developed similar plans at a greater level of detail. (Names have been changed at the request of the firm.)

As we have noted several times, the importance of careful planning can scarcely be overemphasized. Pinto and Slevin [31, 32] developed a list of ten factors that should be associated with success in implementation projects. The factors were split into strategic and tactical clusters. Of interest here are the strategic factors:

1. *Project mission.*   It is important to spell out clearly defined and agreed-upon objectives in the project plan.

2. *Top management support.*   It is necessary for top managers to get behind the project at the outset and make clear to all personnel involved that they support successful completion.

3. *Project's action plan.*   A detailed plan of the required steps in the implementation process needs to be developed, including all resource requirements (money, raw materials, staff, and so forth).

Extensive empirical testing showed these factors to be required for implementation project success. (Tactical factors are also necessary for success, but they are not a consideration here.)

At this point, it might be helpful to sum up this section with a description of how the planning process actually works in many organizations. Assume that you, the PM,

MEMO

To allow Ajax to operate like a department of Instat by April 1, 1996, we must do the following by the dates indicated.

September 24

Ajax Management to be advised of coming under Instat operation. The Instat sales department will begin selling Ajax Consumer Division production effective Jan. 1, 1996. There will be two sales groups: (1) Instat, (2) Ajax Builder Group.

October 15

Instat Regional Managers advised—Instat sales department to assume sales responsibility for Ajax products to distribution channels, Jan. 1, 1996.

October 15

Ajax regional managers advised of sales changes effective Jan. 1, 1996.

October 15

Instat Management, Bob Carl, Van Baker, and Val Walters visit Ajax management and plant. Discuss how operations will merge into Instat.

October 22

Ajax regional managers advise Ajax sales personnel and agents of change effective Jan. 1, 1996.

October 24

Brent Sharp and Ken Roadway visit Instat to coordinate changeover.

October 29

Instat regional managers begin interviewing Ajax sales personnel for possible positions in Instat's sales organization.

November 5

Instat regional managers at Ajax for sales training session.

November 26

Walters visits Ajax to obtain more information.

November 30

Data Processing (Morrie Reddish) and Mfg. Engineering (Sam Newfield): Request DP tapes from Bob Cawley, Ajax, for conversion of Ajax to Instat eng. records: master inventory file, structure file, bill of materials file, where-used file, cross-reference Instat to Ajax part numbers, etc.

Allow maximum two weeks until December 14, 1995, for tapes to be at Instat.

December 3

ADMINISTRATIVE (Val Walters): Offer Norwood warehouse for sublease.

December 3

SALES (Abbott and Crutchfield): Week of sales meeting . . . Instruction of salespeople in Ajax line . . . including procedure in writing Ajax orders on separate forms from Instat orders . . . temporarily, adding weight and shipping information, and procedure below:

Crutchfield to write procedure regarding transmission of orders to Instat, credit check, and transmission of order information to shipping point, whether Norwood, San Francisco, or, later, Instat Cincinnati.

Figure 5-5a   Action plan for merger of Ajax Hardware into Instat Corp (page 1 of 5).

ACTION PLAN

Objective: Merger of Ajax Hardware into Instat Corp. by April 1, 1996			
Steps	**Due Date**	**Responsibility**	**Precedent**
1. Ajax management advised of changes	September 24	Bob Carl, Van Baker	—
2. Begin preparing Instat sales dept. to sell Ajax Consumer Division products effective 1/1/96	September 24	Bob Carl	1
3. Prepare to create two sales groups: (1) Instat, (2) Ajax Builder Group effective 1/1/96	September 24	Bob Carl	1
4. Advise Instat regional managers of sales division changes	October 15	Bob Carl	2,3
5. Advise Ajax regional managers of sales division changes	October 15	Van Baker	2,3
6. Visit Ajax management and plan to discuss merger of operations	October 15	Bob Carl, Van Baker, Val Walters	4,5
7. Advise Ajax sales personnel and agents	October 22	Van Baker	6
8. Visit Instat to coordinate changeover	October 24	Brent Sharp, Ken Roadway	6
9. Interview Ajax sales personnel for possible position	October 29	Instat regional managers	7
10. Sales training sessions for Ajax products	November 5	Instat regional managers	9
11. Visit Ajax again	November 26	Val Walters	8,10
12. Request DP tapes from Bob Cawley for conversion	November 30	Morrie Reddish, Sam Newman	6
13. Offer Norwood warehouse for sublease	December 3	Val Walters	11
14. Write order procedures	December 3	Doug Crutchfield	10
15. Sales meeting (instruction—product line and procedures)	December 3	Fred Abbott, Doug Crutchfield	14
16. DP tapes due for master inventory file, bill of materials, structure file	December 14	Bob Cawley	12
. . .			
. . .			
. . .			

Figure 5-5b   Tabular action plan for Ajax-instat merger based on Figure 5-4a.

have been given responsibility for developing the computer software required to transmit a medical X-ray from one location to another over a telephone line. There are several problems that must be solved to accomplish this task. First, the X-ray image must be translated into computer language. Second, the computerized image must be transmitted and received. Third, the image must be displayed (or printed) in a way that makes it intelligible to the person who must interpret it. You have a team of four programmers and a couple of assistant programmers assigned to you. You also have a specialist in radiology assigned part-time as a medical advisor.

Your first action is to meet with the programmers and medical advisor in order to arrive at the technical requirements for the project. From these requirements, the project mission statement and detailed specifications will be derived. (Note that the original statement of your "responsibility" is too vague to act as an acceptable mission statement.) The basic actions needed to achieve the technical requirements for the project are then developed by the team. For example, one technical requirement would be to develop a method of measuring the density of the image at every point on the X-ray and to represent this measurement as a numerical input for the computer. This is the first level of the project's action plan.

Responsibility for accomplishing the first level tasks is delegated to the project team members who are asked to develop their own action plans for each of the first level tasks. These are the second level action plans. The individual tasks listed in the second level plans are then divided further into third level action plans detailing how each second level task will be accomplished. The process continues until the lowest level tasks are perceived as "units" or "packages" of work.

Early in this section, we advised the planner to keep all items in an action plan at the same level of "generality" or detail. One reason for this is now evident. The tasks at any level of the action plan are usually monitored and controlled by the level just above. If senior managers attempt to monitor and control the highly detailed work packages several levels down, we have a classic case of micromanagement. Another reason for keeping all items in an action plan at the same level of detail is that planners have an unfortunate tendency to plan in great detail all activities they understand well, and to be dreadfully vague in planning activities they do not understand well. The result is that the detailed parts of the plan are apt to be carried out and the vague parts of the plan are apt to be given short shrift.

In practice, this process is iterative. Members of the project team who are assigned responsibility for working out a second, third, or lower-level action plan generate a tentative list of tasks, resource requirements, task durations, predecessors, etc., and bring it to the delegator for discussion, amendment, and approval. This may require several amendments and take several meetings before agreement is reached. The result is that delegator and delegatee both have the same idea about what is to be done, when, and at what cost. Not uncommonly, the individuals and groups that make commitments during the process of developing the action plan actually *sign-off* on their commitments. The whole process involves negotiation and will be further developed in the chapters to follow. Of course, like any managers, delegators can micromanage their delegatees, but micromanagement cannot be mistaken for negotiation—especially by the delegatee.

Natural hazards abound in the remote island nation of Iceland. Not only is it one of the most volcanically active countries in the world but its remote and exposed location in the North Atlantic Ocean leaves it vulnerable to gales, landslides, snow avalanches, and other such natural disasters.

There are three phases of a natural disaster: the disaster itself, the response in terms of planning for the future, and the actual rebuilding project phase. Based on previous disasters such as the 1995 avalanche in Suodavik which claimed 15 lives, it has been proposed that the response phase be moved up in terms of contingency planning so the rebuilding phase can begin immediately after the disaster.

The normal stakeholders in an Icelandic disaster typically include the population experienc-

Source: G. Torfason, "Lessons from a Harsh Land: Project Management and Disaster Preparedness in Iceland," PM Network, February 1998, pp. 39–42.

ing the disaster, the local government, the insurance bodies, Iceland Catastrophe Insurance, the Landslide and Avalanche Fund, and the consulting and contracting repair organizations. In the past, these bodies have not been coordinated so every natural disaster had a delayed response to the event until all the political issues could be resolved, which often took months.

The proposal for reorganizing the response phase includes such items as:

- Documenting the response plans in a compulsory project handbook
- Charging the financing bodies with directing the actual rebuilding process
- Identifying an appropriate coordinating body for each disaster type and location
- Identifying a process for the appointment of a project manager independent, both financially and emotionally, of all the main stakeholders.

A house, half-buried in a lava flow, on the Icelandic island of Heimacy.

5.4 THE WORK BREAKDOWN STRUCTURE AND LINEAR RESPONSIBILITY CHARTS

As was the case with project action plans and contrary to popular notion, the Work Breakdown Structure (WBS) is not one thing. It can take a wide variety of forms that, in turn, serve a wide variety of purposes. The WBS often appears as an outline with the Level 1 tasks on the left and successive levels appropriately indented. The WBS may also picture a project subdivided into hierarchical units of tasks, subtasks, work packages, etc. as a type of Gozinto chart or tree constructed directly from the project's action plans. Most current project management software will generate a WBS on command. Microsoft's Project 98®, for example, links the indented activity levels with a Gantt chart (see Chapter 10, Fig 10-16 for example) that visually shows the activity durations at any level.

Another type of WBS shows the organizational elements associated with specific categories of tasks. Figure 5-6 is such a WBS. The project is to build a robot. The control group of the Electronics Department of the organization has responsibility for developing control systems for the robot. Five different control functions are shown, each of which is presumably broken down into more detailed tasks. In this case, the account numbers for each task are shown so that proper charges can be assigned for each piece of work done on the project.

Some writers recommend using the WBS as the fundamental tool for planning [16, for instance]. We find nothing logically wrong with this approach, but it seems overly structured when compared to the way that firms noted for high-quality planning actually proceed. If this approach is used, the PM is well advised to adopt the general philosophy of building the WBS that was used when building the action plan (see Section 5.3). Other writers pay scant attention to the WBS, giving the subject little more than a mention [4 and 24, among others]. We do not find this a fatal error as long as the planning activity is otherwise carried out to an appropriate level of detail.

In general, the WBS is an important document and can be tailored for use in a number of different ways. It may illustrate how each piece of the project contributes to the whole in terms of performance, responsibility, budget, and schedule. It may, if the PM wishes, list the vendors or subcontractors associated with specific tasks. It may be used to document that all parties have signed-off on their various commitments to the project. It may note detailed specifications for any work package, establish account numbers, specify hardware/software to be used, and identify resource needs. It may serve as the basis for making cost estimates (see Chapter 7) or estimates of task duration (see Chapter 8). Its uses are limited only by the needs of the project and the imagination of the PM. No one version of the WBS will suit all needs, so the WBS is not *a* document, but any given WBS is simply one of many possible documents.

The following general steps explain the procedure for designing and using the WBS. For small or moderate-size projects, and depending on the use for which the WBS is designed, some of the following steps might be skipped, combined, extended, and handled less formally than our explanation indicates, particularly if the project is of a type familiar to the organization.

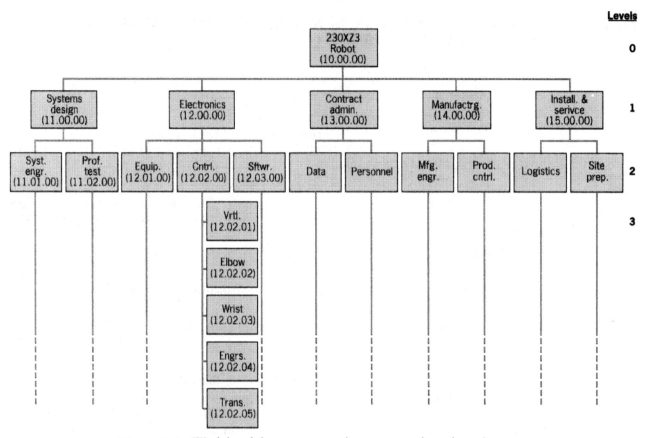

Figure 5-6   Work breakdown structure (account numbers shown).

1. Using information from the action plan, list the task breakdown in successively finer levels of detail. Continue until all meaningful tasks or work packages have been identified and each task can be individually planned, budgeted, scheduled, monitored, and controlled.

2. For each such work package, identify the data relevant to the WBS (e.g., vendors, durations, equipment, materials, special specifications, etc.). List the personnel and organizations responsible for each task. It is helpful to construct a *linear responsibility chart* (sometimes called a *responsibility matrix*) to show who is responsible for what. This chart also shows critical interfaces between units that may require special managerial coordination. With it, the PM can keep track of who must approve what and who must report to whom. Such a chart is illustrated in Figure 5-7. If the project is not too complex, the responsibility chart can be simplified (see Figure 5-8). Figure 5-9 shows one page of a verbal responsibility chart developed by a firm to reorganize its distribution system. In this case, the chart takes the form of a 30-page document covering 116 major activities.

3. All work package information should be reviewed with the individuals or organizations who have responsibility for doing or supporting the work in order to verify

WBS Responsibility		Project Office				Field Oper.	
Subproject	Task	Project Manager	Contract Admin.	Project Eng.	Industrial Eng.	Field Manager	
Determine	A1	o		●	▲		
need	A2	■	o	▲	●		
Solicit quotations	B1	o	■	▲		●	
Write approp. request.	C1	■	▲	o	●		
	C2		●	o	▲		
	C3	●	■	▲		■	
"	"						
"	"						
"	"						

Legend:
▲ Responsible
● Support
■ Notification
o Approval

Figure 5-7 Linear responsibility chart.

the WBS's accuracy. Resource requirements, schedules, and subtask relationships can now be aggregated to form the next higher level of the WBS, continuing on to each succeeding level of the hierarchy. At the uppermost level, we have a summary of the project, its budget, and an estimate of the duration of each work element.

4. For the purpose of pricing a proposal, or determining profit and loss, the total project budget should consist of four elements: direct budgets from each task as just described; an indirect cost budget for the project, which includes general and administrative overhead costs (G&A), marketing costs, potential penalty charges, and other expenses not attributable to particular tasks; a project "contingency" reserve for unexpected emergencies; and any residual, which includes the profit derived from the project, which may, on occasion, be intentionally negative. In Chapter 7 we argue that the budget used for pricing or calculation of profit should not be the same budget that the PM uses to control the project.

5. Similarly, schedule information and milestone (significant) events can be aggregated into a *project master schedule*. The master schedule integrates the many different schedules relevant to the various parts of the project. It is comprehensive and may include contractual commitments, key interfaces and sequencing, mile-

	Vice-president	General manager	Project manager	Manager engineering	Manager software	Manager manufacturing	Manager marketing	Subprogram manager manufacturing	Subprogram manager software	Subprogram manager hardware	Subprogram manager services
Establish project plan	6	2	1	3	3	3	3	4	4	4	4
Define WBS		5	1	3	3	3	3	3	3	3	3
Establish hardware specs		2	3	1	4	4	4				
Establish software specs		2	3	4	1		4				
Establish interface specs		2	3	1	4	4	4				
Establish manufacturing specs		2	3	4	4	1	4				
Define documentation		2	1	4	4	4	4				
Establish market plan	5	3	5	4	4	4	1				
Prepare labor estimate			3	1	1	1		4	4	4	4
Prepare equipment cost estimate		3	1	1	1			4	4	4	4
Prepare material costs			3	1	1	1		4	4	4	4
Make program assignments			3	1	1	1		4	4	4	4
Establish time schedules		5	3	1	1	1	3	4	4	4	4

1 Actual responsibility   4 May be consulted
2 General supervision   5 Must be notified
3 Must be consulted   6 Final approval

Figure 5-8   Simplified linear responsibility chart.

stone events, and progress reports. In addition, a time contingency reserve for unforeseeable delays might be included. A graphic example of a master schedule is shown in Figure 5-10.

Listed items 1 to 5 focus on the WBS as a planning tool. It may also be used as an aid in monitoring and controlling projects. Again, it is important to remember that no single WBS contains all of the elements described and any given WBS should be designed with specific uses in mind.

6. As the project is carried out, step by step, the PM can continually examine actual resource use, by work element, work package, task, and so on up to the full project level. By comparing actual against planned resource usage at a given time, the PM can identify problems, harden the estimates of final cost, and make sure that relevant corrective actions have been designed and are ready to implement if needed. It is necessary to examine resource usage in relation to results

Activities	Responsible Individuals		
	Initiate Action	Work with	Clear Action with
Distribution System and Its Administration			
1. Recommend distribution system to be used.	Mktg Officers	ILI & IHI LOB MCs M-A Cttee VP & Agcy Dir	Sr VP Mktg
	Mktg Officers	Group LOB MC M-A Cttee VP & Agcy Dir	Sr VP Mktg
	Mktg Officers	IA LOB MC M-A Cttee VP & Agcy Dir	Sr VP Mktg
Compensation			
2. Determine provisions of sales compensation programs (e.g., commissions, subsidies, fringes).	Compensation Task Force	Mktg, S&S & Eqty Prod Offrs	President
	Compensation Task Force	Mktg, S&S & Eqty Prod Offrs	
	Compensation Task Force	Mktg, S&S & Eqty Prod Offrs	President
3. Ensure cost-effectiveness testing of sales compensation programs.	Compensation Task Force	Mktg, S&S & Eqty Prod Offrs	President
Territory			
4. Establish territorial strategy for our primary distribution system.	VP & Agcy Dir	Dir MP&R M-A Cttee	Sr VP Mktg
5. Determine territories for agency locations and establish priorities for starting new agencies.	VP & Agcy Dir	Dir MP&R M-A Cttee	Sr VP Mktg
6. Determining agencies in which advanced sales personnel are to operate.	Dir Ret Plnng Sls Dir Adv Sls	VP S & S	Sr VP Mktg

Legend: IA, ILI, IHI: Product lines
LOB: Line of business
MC: Management committee
M-A Cttee: Marketing administration committee
S&S: Sales and service
MP&R: Marketing planning and research

Figure 5-9   Verbal responsibility chart.

Subproject		Task	Responsible Dept.	Dependent Dept.	J	F	M	A	M	J	J	A	S	O	N	D	J	F	M	A	M	J	J	A	S	O	N	D
								19X4												**19X5**								
Determine need	A1	Find operations that benefit most	Industrial				△▲																						
	A2	Approx. size and type needed	Project Eng.	I.E.				△	▲																				
Solicit quotations	B1	Contact vendors & review quotes	P.E.	Fin., I.E., Purch.							○	●	△○	▲	□													
Write appropriation request	C1	Determine tooling costs	Tool Design	I.E.								○		●		△												
	C2	Determine labor savings	I.E.	I.E.										△▲														
	C3	Actual writing	P.E.	Tool dsgn. Fin., I.E.														△○										
Purchase machine tooling, and gauges	D1	Order robot	Purchasing	P.E.																△								
	D2	Design and order or manufacture tooling	Tool design	Purch., Tooling																				△				
	D3	Specify needed gauges and order or mfg.	Q.C.	Tool dsgn., Purch.																				△○				
Installation and Startup	E1	Install robot	Plant Layout	Mill-wrights																					△			
	E2	Train employees	Personnel	P.E. Mfg.																					△			
	E3	Runoff	Mfg.	Q.C.																								△□

∧ Status date (as of Jan. 31, 19X5) * Project completion

Note: As of Jan. 31, 19X5, the project is one month behind schedule. This is due mainly to the delay in task C1, which was caused by the late completion of A2.

Legend:
* Project completion
□ Contractual commitment
△ Planned completion
▲ Actual completion
∧ Status date
○ Milestone planned
● Milestone achieved
--- Planned progrss
— Actual progress

Figure 5-10 Project master schedule.

achieved because, while the project may be over budget, the results may be farther along than expected. Similarly, the expenses may be exactly as planned, or even lower, but actual progress may be much less than planned. Control charts showing these *earned values* are described in more detail in Chapter 10. In Chapters 7 and 8, we will discuss how to include risk in the budget and in the schedule.

7. Finally, the project schedule may be subjected to the same comparisons as the project budget. Actual progress is compared to scheduled progress by work element, package, task, and complete project, to identify problems and take corrective action. Additional resources may be brought to those tasks behind schedule to expedite them. These added funds may come out of the budget reserve or from other tasks that are ahead of schedule. This topic is discussed further in Chapter 9.

5.5 INTERFACE COORDINATION THROUGH INTEGRATION MANAGEMENT

The most difficult aspect of implementing a project plan is the coordination and integration of the various elements of the project so that they meet their joint goals of performance, schedule, and budget in such a way that the total project meets its goals. When the project is complex, involving input and work from several departments or groups and possibly also contributions from several outside contractors, the intricate process of coordinating the work and timing of these inputs is called *integration management*. The term *interface coordination* is used to denote the process of managing this work across multiple groups. The linear responsibility chart discussed above is a useful aid to the PM in carrying out this task. It displays the many ways the members of the project team (which, as usual, includes all of the actors involved, not forgetting the client and outside vendors) must interact and what the rights, duties, and responsibilities of each will be.

An early approach to this problem was developed by Benningson [6]. Called TREND (Transformed Relationships Evolved from Network Data), the analysis was designed to illustrate important linkages and dependencies between work groups. The aim was to alert the PM to potential problems associated with cross-functional interfaces and to aid in the design of effective ways to avoid or deal with potential interface problems. Benningson added interdependence, uncertainty, and prestige to the mix. The precise way in which these elements were attached to the relationships delineated in the project master plan is best seen by reference to [6]. (A brief explanation of TREND also appeared in the third edition of this work, pp. 221–24.) A key point is that mapping all dependencies in the project can show a complete description of project interfaces.

Recent work on managing the interface focuses on the use of multifunctional teams (MT) to plan the project as well as design the products/services the project is intended to produce. There is general agreement that MT has a favorable impact on product/service design and delivery. As we noted in Chapter 4, Section 4.3, the Chrysler Corporation's use of concurrent engineering (CE), one form of MT, not only resulted in excellent design, it also produced major economic benefits by shortening the design cycle. Work by Hauptman and Hirji shows that CE has had a "favorable impact . . . on attainment of project budget goals, but achieves this without any adverse impact on quality, cost or schedule" [15, p. 161. Note: this entire issue of *IEEE Transactions on Engineering Management* is devoted to CE.] The process also was associated with higher levels of team job satisfaction.

The use of MT in product development and planning is not without its difficulties. Successfully involving cross-functional teams in project planning requires that some structure be imposed on the planning process. The most common structure is simply to define the task of the group as having the responsibility to generate a plan to accomplish whatever is defined as the project scope. There is considerable evidence that this is not sufficient for complex projects. Using MT creates what Kalu [17] has defined as a virtual project. In Section 4.3 of the previous chapter, we noted the high level of conflict in many virtual projects [cf. 11]. It follows that MT tends to involve conflict.

In an interesting attempt to give structure to the product design and planning problem and to make creative use of the conflict inherent in MT, Tan, Hayes, and Shaw [38] proposed a planning model with four components: (1) an integrated base of information about the product plus design and production constraints, both technical and human; (2) software to aid the process of detecting conflicts in the information base, and to aid in the process of resolving those conflicts; (3) software that, given a product design, could generate a production plan and could also simulate changes in the plan suggested by design changes resulting from resolving conflicts; and (4) a model incorporating the knowledge base of the autonomous project team members and a network linking them, their intelligent-agents (computerized assistants), and their computers. The components all use an electronic blackboard for communication so the participants do not need to be in a common location.

With these parts, the design/planning process is conceptually straightforward. Team members with different technical backgrounds will view the product design task differently. Therefore, initial design ideas will be in conflict. Conflict resolution will result in design improvement, which alters the production plans that are simulated to test manufacturing feasibility. At base, the approach suggested by Tan and her colleagues uses MT to generate conflicts on the design of a product, and uses the resolution of the conflicts to suggest feasible design improvements.

Bailetti et al. make a different attack on the problem of interface management [5]. They define and map all interdependencies between various members of the project team. The concept of mapping interdependencies recalls TREND, but TREND maps interfaces on the firm's organization chart while Bailetti et al. map the interdependencies directly. Because the nature of these interfaces may differ during different phases of the product/service design/production process, they map each major phase separately. Figure 5-11 shows the mapping for the design of a silicon chip.

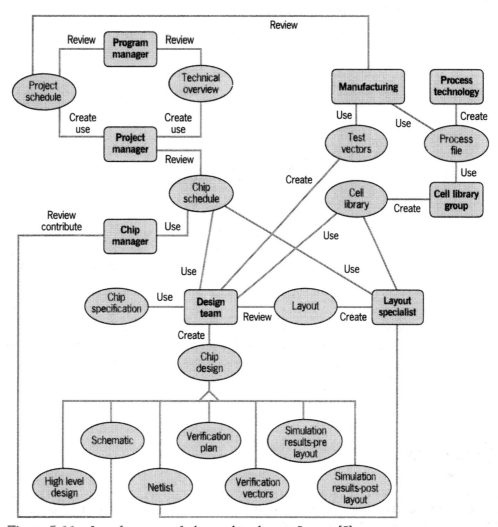

Figure 5-11   Interface map of silicon chip design. *Source:* [5]

The logic of this approach to structuring MT is strong. The WBS and linear responsibility charts are a good initial source of information on interfaces, but they do not reflect the uncertainty associated with tasks on large, complex projects. Further, they implicitly assume that interfaces are stable within and across project phases—an assumption often contrary to fact. This does not ignore the value of the WBS, PERT/CPM networks, and similar tools of long-standing use and proven value in project management. It simply uses interface maps as a source of the coordination requirement to manage the interdependencies. The fundamental structure of this approach to interface management is shown in Figure 5-12.

None of these approaches to interface management is sufficient to the task. They do not tell the manager what to do. They do, however, point out locations that have a high potential for trouble. Among the three described here, and there are

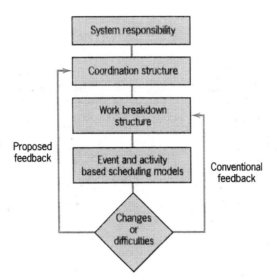

Figure 5-12   Coordination structure model of project management. *Source:* [5]

others, we feel that the method of Bailetti and his colleagues is probably most helpful. It is the simplest of the three, is conceptually consistent with traditional project management philosophy, and fits neatly into standard project management methodologies.

SUMMARY

In this chapter we initiated planning for the project in terms of identifying and addressing the tasks required for project completion. We emphasized the importance of initial coordination of all parties involved and the smooth integration of the various systems required to achieve the project objectives. Last, we described some tools such as the Work Breakdown Structure (WBS), the linear responsibility chart, the action plan, TREND, and the Gozinto chart to aid in the planning process.

Specific points made in the chapter were these:

- The preliminary work plans are important because they serve as the basis for personnel selection, budgeting, scheduling, and control.

- Top management should be represented in the initial coordinating meeting where technical objectives are established, participant responsibility is accepted, and preliminary budgets and schedules are defined.

- The approval and change processes are complex and should be handled by the project manager.

- Common elements of the project plan are the overview, statement of objectives, general approach, contractual requirements, schedules, budget, cost control procedures, evaluation procedures, and potential problems.

- Systems integration concerns the smooth coordination of project systems in terms of cost, performance, and effectiveness.

- The hierarchical approach (even planning process) to project planning is most appropriate and can be aided by a tree diagram of project subsets, called a Gozinto chart, and a Work Breakdown Structure (WBS). The WBS relates the details of each subtask to its task and provides the final basis for the project budget, schedule, personnel, and control.

- A linear responsibility chart is often helpful to illustrate the relationship of personnel to project tasks and to identify where coordination is necessary.
- When multifunctional terms are used to plan complex projects, their work must be integrated and coordinated. Interface maps are a useful way of identifying the interdependencies that must be managed.

Based on the now-established project plan and WBS, we can consider the task of negotiating for the resources to implement the project. This topic completes Part I of the text.

GLOSSARY

Baseline Plan The nominal plan to which deviations will be compared.

Bill of Materials The set of physical elements required to build a product.

Control Chart A graph showing how a statistic is changing over time compared to its average and extreme values.

Deliverables The physical items to be delivered from a project. This typically includes reports and plans as well as physical objects.

Earned Value A measure of project progress, frequently related to tasks accomplished and milestones achieved.

Effectiveness Achieving the objectives set beforehand; to be distinguished from efficiency, which is measured by the output realized for the input used.

Engineering Change Orders Product improvements that engineering has designed after the initial product design was released.

Gozinto Chart A pictorial representation of a product that shows how the elements required to build a product fit together.

Hierarchical Planning A planning approach that breaks the planning task down into the activities that must be done at each managerial level. Typically, the upper level sets the objectives for the next lower level.

Interface Management Managing the problems that tend to occur between departments and disciplines, rather than within individual departments.

Material Requirements Planning (MRP) A planning and material ordering approach based on the known or forecast final demand requirements, lead times for each fabricated or purchased item, and existing inventories of all items.

Systems Engineering The engineering tasks involved in the complete system concerning the project and the integration of all the subsystems into the overall system.

Value Engineering An approach that examines each element of a product or system to determine if there is a better or cheaper way of achieving the same function.

Work Statement A description of a task that defines all the work required to accomplish it, including inputs and desired outputs.

QUESTIONS

Material Review Questions

1. List the nine component planning sequences of software project planning.
2. Any successful project plan must contain nine key elements. List these items and briefly describe the composition of each.
3. What are the basic guidelines for systems design which assure that individual components of the system are designed in an optimal manner?
4. What are the general steps for managing each work package within a specific project?

5. Describe the "even planning process" and explain why it is helpful.

6. What is shown on a linear responsibility chart? How is it useful to a PM?

7. What should be accomplished at the initial coordination meeting?

8. Why is it important for the functional areas to be involved in the project from the time of the original proposal?

9. What are the three major objectives of systems integration?

10. What are the basic steps to design and use the Work Breakdown Structure?

11. What is the objective of interface management?

Class Discussion Questions

12. What percentage of the total project effort do you think should be devoted to planning? Why?

13. Why do you suppose that the coordination of the various elements of the project is considered the most difficult aspect of project implementation?

14. What kinds of problem areas might be included in the project plan?

15. What is the role of systems integration in project management? What are the three major objectives of systems integration?

16. In what ways may the WBS be used as a key document to monitor and control a project?

17. Describe the process of subdivision of activities and events that composes the tree diagram known as the Work Breakdown Structure or Gozinto chart. Why is the input of responsible managers and workers so important an aspect of this process?

18. Why is project planning so important?

19. What are the pros and cons concerning the early participation of the various functional areas in the project plan?

20. What trade-offs might exist among the three objectives of system integration?

21. Task 5-C is the critical, pacing task of a rush project. Fred always nitpicks anything that comes his way, slowing it down, driving up its costs, and irritating everyone concerned. Normally, Fred would be listed as "Notify" for task 5-C on the responsibility matrix but the PM is considering "forgetting" to make that notation on the chart. Is this unethical, political, or just smart management?

Questions for Project Management in Practice

Extensive Project Planning for Kodak's New Photographic System

22. Compare and contrast Kodak's project plan with the description in the chapter.

23. How do you think Kodak kept a project of this magnitude and involving so many major photographic firms a secret for over a decade?

24. How is this "photographic system" different from another advanced camera?

Disaster Project Planning in Iceland

25. The United States emergency body FEMA (Federal Emergency Management Act) was formed for much the same reasons as Iceland's disasters. How do the two approaches appear to differ?

26. Given a nation so prone to disasters, why do you think it took so long to formulate a contingency disaster plan?

27. The directed reading at the end of this chapter describes four tools for crises in projects. Might any of these be useful to Iceland in their planning?

■ INCIDENTS FOR DISCUSSION

Ringold's Pool and Patio Supply

John Ringold, Jr., just graduated from a local university with a degree in industrial management and joined his father's company as executive vice-president of operations. Dad wants to break John in slowly and has decided to see how he can do on a project that John Sr. has never had time to investigate. Twenty percent of the company's sales are derived from the sale of above-ground swimming pool kits. Ringold's does not install the pools. John Sr. has asked John Jr. to determine whether or not they should get into that business. John Jr. has decided that the easiest way to impress Dad and get the project done is personally to estimate the cost to the company of setting up a pool and then call some competitors and see how much they charge. That will show whether or not it is profitable.

John Jr. remembered a method called the work breakdown structure (WBS) that he thought might serve as a useful tool to estimate costs. Also, the use of such a tool could be passed along to the site supervisor to help evaluate the performance of work crews. John Jr.'s WBS is shown in Table 5-2. The total cost John Jr. calculated was $185.00, based on 12.33 labor-hours at $15.00/labor-hour. John Jr. found that, on average, Ringold's competitors charged $229.00 to install a similar pool. John Jr. thought he had a winner. He called his father and made an appointment to present his findings the next morning. Since he had never assembled a pool himself, he decided to increase the budget by 10 percent, "just in case."

Questions: Is John Jr.'s WBS projection reasonable? What aspects of the decision will John Sr. consider?

Better-Built

Better-Built Tape Recorder Company of Cleveland, Ohio, is planning to manufacture a new line of mini-digital tape recorders to compete with the small digital

Table 5-2. Pool Installation WBS

Works Tasks		Labor-hours (estimated)
Prepare ground surface		2.67
Clear	1	
Rake	$\frac{1}{3}$	
Level	1	
Sand bottom	$\frac{1}{3}$	
Lay out pool frame		2.50
Bottom ring	1	
Side panels	$\frac{1}{2}$	
Top ring	1	
Add plastic liner		0.50
Assemble pool		1.66
Build wooden support		3.00
Layout	1	
Assemble	2	
Fill and test		2.00
Total		12.33

pocket recorders made by competitors. The company currently manufactures about 10,000 regular size digital recorders per year and hopes to be manufacturing 5000 of the smaller version beginning in two years. The new recorder will require a 25 percent enlargement of the existing facility. The company has already selected the project manager and the project team. The project manager is ready to get the project under way. The three aspects she is most concerned about are schedules, resources, and personnel.

Questions: If you were the project manager, which project planning tools would you start with to resolve your concerns? Do these tools relate to each other? Explain.

BIBLIOGRAPHY

1. Aaron, J. M., C. P. Bratta, and D. P. Smith. "Achieving Total Project Control Using the Quality Gate Method." *Proceedings of the Annual Symposium of the Project Management Institute*, San Diego, Oct. 4, 1993.

2. Antonioni, D. "Post-Planning Review Prevents Poor Project Performance." *PM Network*, October 1997.

3. Archibald, R. D. "Projects: Vehicles for Strategic Growth." *Project Management Journal*, September 1988.

4. Badiru, A. B. *Project Management in Manufacturing and High Technology Operations*. New York: Wiley, 1988.

5. Bailetti, A. J., J. R. Callahan, and P. Di-Pietro. "A Coordination Structure Approach

to the Management of Projects." *IEEE Transactions on Engineering Management,* November 1994.

6. BENNINGSON, L. A. "TREND: A Project Management Tool." *Proceedings of the Project Management Conference,* Philadelphia, October 1972.

7. BIGELOW, D. "Planning Is Important—Why Don't We Do More of It?" *PM Network,* July 1998.

8. BLANCHARD, B. S., and W. FABRYCKY. *Systems Engineering and Analysis, 2nd ed.* Englewood Cliffs, NJ: Prentice Hall, 1990.

9. BOEHM, B. W. "A Spiral Model of Software Development and Enhancement." *IEEE Engineering Management Review,* Winter 1995, reprinted from *Computer,* May 1988.

10. CLELAND, D. I., and R. K. KIMBALL. "The Strategic Context of Projects." *Project Management Journal,* August 1987.

11. DE LAAT, P. B. "Matrix Management of Projects and Power Struggles: A Case Study of an R & D Laboratory." *IEEE Engineering Management Review,* Winter 1995, reprinted from *Human Relations,* Vol. 47, No. 9, 1994.

12. DUNCAN, W. R. "Scoping Out A Scope Statement." *PM Network,* December 1994.

13. FORD, R. C., and F. S. McLAUGHLIN. "Successful Project Teams: A Study of MIS Managers." *IEEE Transactions on Engineering Management,* November 1992.

14. HARRIS, R. D., and R. F. GONZALEZ. *The Operations Manager.* St. Paul: West, 1981.

15. HAUPTMAN, O., and K. K. HIRJI. "The Influence of Process Concurrency on Project Outcomes in Product Development: An Empirical Study of Cross-Functional Teams." *IEEE Transactions on Engineering Management,* May 1996.

16. HUBBARD, D. G. "Work Structuring," in P. C. Dinsmore, ed., *The AMA Handbook of Project Management.* New York: AMACOM, 1993.

17. KALU, T. CH. U. "A Framework for the Management of Projects in Complex Organizations." *IEEE Transactions on Engineering Management,* May 1993.

18. KERZNER, H. *Project Management: A Systems Approach to Planning, Scheduling, and Controlling,* 6th ed. New York: Wiley, 1998.

19. KNUTSON, J. "How to Manage a Project Launch Meeting." *PM Network,* July 1995.

20. LANGLEY, A. "Between 'Paralysis by Analysis' and 'Extinction by Instinct.'" *IEEE Engineering Management Review,* Fall 1995, reprinted from *Sloan Management Review,* Spring 1995.

21. LAUFER, A. "Project Planning: Timing Issues and Path of Progress." *Project Management Journal,* June 1991.

22. LAVOLD, G. D. "Developing and Using the Work Breakdown Structure," in Cleland, D. I., and W. R. King, *Project Management Handbook.* New York: Van Nostrand Reinhold, 1983.

23. LIBERATORE, M. J. "A Decision Support System Linking Research and Development Project Selection with Business Strategy." *Project Management Journal,* November, 1988.

24. LOVE, S. F. *Achieving Problem Free Project Management.* New York: Wiley, 1989.

25. MARTIN, M. G. "Statement of Work: The Foundation for Delivering Successful Service Projects." *PM Network,* October 1998.

26. MARTIN, P. K., and K. TATE. "Kick Off the Smart Way." *PM Network,* October 1998.

27. MARTINEZ, E. V. "Executives to Project Manager: Get a Plan." *PM Network,* October 1994.

28. MORRIS, W. T. *Implementation Strategies for Industrial Engineers.* Columbus, OH: Grid, 1979.

29. PALEY, A. I. "Value Engineering and Project Management: Achieving Cost Optimization," in P. C. Dinsmore, ed., *The AMA Handbook of Project Management.* New York: AMACOM, 1993.

30. PELLS, D. L. "Project Management Plans: An Approach to Comprehensive Planning for Complex Projects," in P. C. Dinsmore, ed., *The AMA Handbook of Project Management.* New York: AMACOM, 1993.

31. PINTO, J. K., and D. P. SLEVIN. "Critical Factors in Successful Project Implementation." *IEEE Transactions on Engineering Management,* February 1987.

32. PINTO, J. K., and D. P. SLEVIN. "Project Success: Definitions and Measurement Techniques." *Project Management Journal,* February 1988.

33. PRENTIS, E. L. "Master Project Planning: Scope, Time and Cost." *Project Management Journal,* March 1989.

34. RAKOS, J. J. *Software Project Management*. Englewood Cliffs, NJ: Prentice Hall, 1990.

35. ROMAN, D. *R & D Management*. New York: Appleton-Century-Crofts, 1968.

36. SCHULTZ, R. L., D. P. SLEVIN, and J. K. PINTO. "Strategy and Tactics in a Process Model of Project Implementation." *Interfaces*, May–June 1987.

37. SMITH, R. P. "The Historical Roots of Concurrent Engineering Fundamentals." *IEEE Transactions on Engineering Management*, February 1997.

38. TAN, G. W., C. C. HAYES, and M. SHAW. "An Intelligent-Agent Framework for Concurrent Product Design and Planning." *IEEE Transactions on Engineering Management*, August 1996.

39. WEBSTER, J. L., W. E. REIF, and J. S. BRACKER. "The Manager's Guide to Strategic Planning Tools and Techniques." *Planning Review*, November/December 1989, reprinted in *Engineering Management Review*, December 1990.

40. WESTNEY, R. E. "Paradigms for Planning Productive Projects," in P. C. Dinsmore, ed., *The AMA Handbook of Project Management*. New York: AMACOM, 1993.

The following reading applies the planning tools from emergency management to projects with their inevitable crises. The application of risk analysis, contingency plans, logic charts, and tabletop exercises is discussed in terms of both planning for and managing crises when they actually occur. Examples such as the 1996 Atlanta Olympic Games are used to illustrate the effectiveness of crisis planning tools.

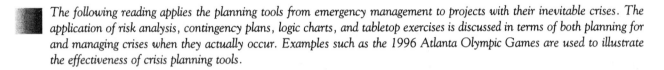

DIRECTED READING

PLANNING FOR CRISES IN PROJECT MANAGEMENT

L. M. Mallak, H. A. Kurstedt, Jr., G. A. Patzak: Planning for Crises in Project Management. *Project Management Journal*, June 1997. ©1997 by the Project Management Institute. Reprinted by permission.

Project managers can't always foresee every contingency when planning and managing their projects. Many supurious events affecting project milestones and resource allocations can surface once the project is under way. Experienced project managers find crises, miscommunications, mistakes, oversights, and disasters must be managed as part of successful project management. Project managers need effective tools to plan for and anticipate these crises. These are tools project managers may not use everyday, yet they need these tools to serve them in time of emergency. The ideas and information in this paper will help project managers identify the appropriate crisis planning tools and how to use them. The project manager's experience, training, and skills should allow the understanding and use of these emergency management tools to support quicker and better decision making. In a crisis the worst decision is no decision and the second worst

decision is a late one (Sawle, 1991). Managing crises better means mitigating and preparing for crises so we can reduce their occurrence and manage the consequences better if crises do occur. Based on the authors' experience in emergency management for the public and private sectors and several experiences shared in the literature, we recommend ways of planning for crises in projects.

We offer a brief list of emergency management planning tools and skills for project managers: risk analyses, contingency plans, logic charts, and tabletop exercises. These tools have different uses in different types of crises, whether they are natural, chemical/technological, or security types of crises. They also require different kinds of support—police, fire, medical, rescue, etc.

Crises are analyzed from the project management perspective, identifying the similarities and differences between crises in project management and crises in general. We discuss crisis planning strategies and tools by looking at the tools used for emergency management and investigating how we can modify them or design new tools for crisis management in projects.

Framing the Crisis

Many crises become projects once the deleterious effects are gone. A commercial airline crash, such as TWA 800 in summer 1996, where all passengers and crew died, is managed as a project once the threat of explosion and other immediate dangers diminish. However, we're concerned with crises occurring within an existing project, rather than a crisis or emergency that becomes a project.

In many of emergency management's phases and types, the primary skills required are project management skills we're already familiar with. When we're in an emergency situation and we're in the mitigation, preparedness, or recovery phase in a chronic, long-term emergency, we can readily apply our project management skills. The focus of this paper is the use of emergency management tools to aid in anticipating and planning for crises in projects. Project managers need additional tools to respond to acute emergencies—here is where emergency management tools become paramount.

The scope of application for emergency management tools will vary based on the size of the project. The tools can be quite elaborate, such as volumes for a risk analysis or reserved space for an emergency operations center (EOC) with many dedicated phone lines. The tools can also be quite simple, such as a one- to two-page list of risks in priority order or a designated office or conference room (to function as a mini-EOC) with the ability to bring in portable phones. All the tools should be used, even if just in simple form. In a small project, using one hour of a staff meeting to assign roles in the event of a crisis may suffice for more elaborate means in a larger project. The elaborateness of tools should be balanced with the cost and time required for preparation.

Typical project management requires attention to issues of cost, schedule, and quality. As the customer demands for quality increase, either the cost or the schedule must yield to balance these new demands. But at what point do increased demands reach a crisis point? Increased demands may lead to a perplexity. A perplexity is "an event with an unknown start and an unknown end." An example of a perplexity is an earthquake centered around the New Madrid (Mo.) fault line—we don't know when the earthquake will occur, for how long, nor what the extent of damage will be. In fact, the earthquake may not occur in our lifetime. The opposite of a perplexity is a process, an event with a known start and a known end and the cycle is constantly repeated (as in a manufacturing process). The concept of perplexity helps in understanding the amount and level of uncertainty faced in emergency planning for projects.

In this paper, a crisis could be externally generated, as in an earthquake, deregulation, loss of key executives through accidental death (airplane or automobile crash), or internally generated, as in a plant explosion or a strike. We use Lagadec's (1993) definition of a crisis as being an incident that upsets normal conditions, creating a disturbance that cannot be brought back to normal using existing or specialized emergency functions. A crisis, according to Lagadec, can occur when the incident passes a certain level or when the system is unstable or close to the breaking point before the incident took place. Consequently, crises considered in this paper disrupt project activities to the point where new (and typically unanticipated) decisions must be made to continue the project.

Projects have characteristics that make the design and preparation of elaborate tools difficult. First, many projects lack the permanence of a large plant, mine, or government installation. Second, emergencies in smaller projects tend to be more constrained to the site, while larger projects must deal with emergencies of greater scope and impact, such as chemical and radiological releases. Third, in a plant, a large number of people are affected by an emergency—especially the public as opposed to the workers. When the public or a large number of workers are involved, the organization's confidence in safe operations has a heavy influence, and this begets elaborateness. A simple tool can afford us most of the protection we need (for example, 70% of maximum), while a more elaborate tool will buy us more confidence and protection (perhaps up to 99% of maximum). The more elaborate tool is worth the investment when confidence is at stake.

Tools to Help Project Managers Plan for Crises

We've chosen four types of tools used primarily in emergency management to help project managers plan for crises better. We'll describe and show how to apply risk analyses, contingency plans, logic charts, and tabletop exercises.

Risk Analysis. An essential crisis planning tool is risk analysis. Risk analysis helps us find out what can go wrong, what's most probable, and what has the greatest impact. The combination of an event's probability of occurrence and severity of consequences (e.g., catastrophic failure) determines priorities. Incident analysis can also help us understand the lessons learned in an actual crisis and develop plans to mitigate the effects of similar incidents in the future.

The 1996 Olympic Games in Atlanta presented many potential disruptions to area businesses (Bradford, 1996). Comprehensive contingency plans were needed to increase the potential for business continuity. Atlanta-based BellSouth Business Systems' Director of Business Continuity Services John Copenhaver stated, "If you plan for a medium-case scenario and a worst-case scenario happens, it's like having no plans at all." BellSouth's plan attempted to minimize disruptions during the Olympics through special arrangements for deliveries, telecommuting, and increased modem pools so employees could work from home. BellSouth conducted a vulnerability assessment and then put systems into place to avoid interruptions to service or minimize the impact of interruptions.

Another Bell company, BellSouth Advertising and Publishing Co. (BAPCO), saw the need to develop a plan to deal with the human side of crises (traumatic stress), because those could disable a firm just as well as interruption of normal business operations (e.g., phone, equipment, facilities) (Kruse, 1993). BAPCO brought in a consultant team to deliver a one-day crisis management training session. The training was given to members of a human resources crisis team and other members of management who wanted to participate. Through counseling, housing, "BellMart," rental cars, and other support mechanisms, BAPCO weathered Hurricane Andrew much better than most South Florida organizations. BellMart was a stocked warehouse of essentials that BAPCO employees (and even their non-BAPCO neighbors) were invited to visit to take whatever they needed. Eighty-five percent of BAPCO employees were affected by the hurricane, although none were killed by the hurricane. The company pointed to several initiatives that were taken to reduce traumatic stress so that people could return to work sooner and with fewer worries. These initiatives included a rapid deployment system to immediately attend to their employees' needs, determining those needs in advance, heading off traumatic stress with constant information (daily bulletin, people sought out on phone, foot, car, etc.), bringing in BAPCO volunteers from other areas, making cash available immediately, and giving employees time off from work to get their personal lives together.

Sometimes nature surprises us and sometimes nature just tests us. The Virginia Department of Transportation (VDOT) had an opportunity to test its emergency preparedness in a potential disaster that never materialized (Slack, 1996). Hurricane Bertha threatened to slam into Virginia as a full-force hurricane, but then weakened into a tropical gale with heavy winds and rain—not the widespread destruction of a hurricane. Bertha served as a drill for VDOT's Emergency Operations Center (EOC), which used a new computer system designed to keep various safety agencies up to date with the latest information during a crisis. One of the problems VDOT faced during many natural disasters was conflicting information among VDOT, state police, local police, and other state agencies involved in emergency response. All parties now have the same information via a real-time connection, rather than each agency gathering its own information.

The availability of accurate, real-time information is not enough to mitigate crises in project management. Good implementation of risk analysis helps to plan and properly prepare for crises in projects and take steps to reduce the occurrences of crises. Engineering analyses support this process of risk analysis and make up the quantitative portion of mitigation. Cause-and-effect analyses make up the qualitative portion of mitigation and help us assess the systematic effects both forward and backward.

In emergency management, we use risk analysis to find out the risks beforehand. The use of risk analysis in this paper should be differentiated from a probabilistic risk analysis. Establishing consequences of accidents or incidents by deterministic or risk analysis provides effective tools in emergency management. In project management, we concentrate on planning and sequencing activities to maximize our efficiencies and effectively schedule resources.

Illinois Power (IP) has a risk analysis process, called the Risk Register, that was developed and implemented in 1988 and serves as a comprehensive risk assessment system. "The Risk Register is a formal process that identifies, quantifies, and categorizes the risks facing Illinois Power, develops cost-effective methods to control them, and positions the company to achieve its stated goals" (Leonard, 1995). The system continually assesses new risks, generates information for decision-making and supports employees at all levels.

IP's Risk Register process has five phases: risk analysis, mitigation development, mitigation selection, implementation, and monitoring. In conjunction with the Risk Register, IP has a Corporate Disaster Recovery Plan. This plan is designed to "obtain information on levels of damage, resource availability, and the status of restoration activities; provide timely and accurate information to the media, government officials, regulatory authorities, employees, and the general public; give guidance on restoration activities; coordinate acquisition and allocation of resources and coordinate operations with city, county, state and federal emergency-service operations" (Leonard, 1995).

For each identified risk, IP decides on a post-loss goal—in other words, the minimum acceptable capabilities following an event. The post-loss goal sets the target for what the crisis management tool should help IP achieve and helps reduce uncertainty during and after an event.

Contingency Plans. Once the risk analysis is performed, project managers must translate those risks into contingency plans. Project managers need to sit down and ask, "What can go wrong with my project?" Once identified, the project manager has a list of risks associated with a particular project—the output of a risk analysis. Then they should ask, "Which of these risks is most likely to happen?" and "Which of these will have the greatest impact?" "On what or whom?" This last question implies the vulnerability of the organization to the identified risks. Project managers should develop plans that use the data from a risk analysis to prepare them and their organizations for the broadest range of emergencies.

Appointing a person to be in charge of crisis planning puts responsibility and resources together, thereby reducing the need to overload already busy executives with planning for a low-probability event. Nestle U.S.A., Inc.'s headquarters are in Glendale, California, a suburb of Los Angeles. To support its contingency

planning efforts, Nestle has appointed a director of business interruption planning (Ceniceros, 1995). As part of its contingency plan, Nestle has a contract with the Stouffer Renaissance Esmeralda, a resort hotel in the desert near Palm Springs, stipulating that the hotel has three days to empty out its ballroom if Nestle needs the space to resume business. The hotel was selected because it is already set up to provide comfort, food, and beverages—and that relieves the demands on Nestle managers and counselors, so they can get back into serving their customers more rapidly and effectively. "Concern for personnel in planning for business resumption is just as important as facilities or data recovery" (Ceniceros, 1995). Nestle has contracts with work-area-recovery vendors that have 72 hours to deliver office materials to the hotel. The hotel is accessible from an airport in Palm Springs, which expands access from Phoenix, should supplies need to come from elsewhere.

Nestle's contingency plan was tested with good results: "With the help of two furniture installation specialists and some hotel staff, the ballroom can quickly convert into 300 workstations complete with copy machines, computers, telecommunication cables, double-circuited power distribution panels, and everything else workers usually take for granted, such as sound barriers so business can be conducted with minimal distractions. . . . At our last exercise, we pulled together 100 workstations in 20 clock hours" (Ceniceros, 1995).

Risk analyses support planning by helping project managers pick the most probable and most severe events combined with a vulnerability assessment to see who or what is vulnerable and what will be affected. Therefore, when the crisis occurs, the project manager has thought about the crisis and what can be affected. Plans incorporating this thinking help the project manager be ready when the crisis occurs and do what is necessary to fix it. If a manager is responsible for a project, he or she should require that someone conduct a risk analysis. The risk analysis improves early recognition of warning signs; the vulnerability assessment helps identify whom to notify and how to start support to them early.

Logic Charts. Logic charts employ project flow logic to show the project flow with all dependencies in an extremely flexible, time-scale-independent diagram.

Logic charts are a form of expert system because they embody the decision-making knowledge of the expert in a system that can be followed procedurally. Project flow logic is the basis for any personal computer-assisted project management tool. Project managers are skilled at charting. But, in times of crisis, different types of charts are needed.

When a crisis occurs, people need procedures to follow. Logic charts from the basis for writing these procedures. In project management, the most commonly used charts are Gantt charts for looking at activities against time and networks for looking at precedence. Emergency logic charts depend heavily on logic because of branching due to chained contingencies (e.g., "if event A and event B happened, then event C is likely").

Logic charts provide an overview of principal emergency response events and recovery operations. The charts also depict decisions, notifications, support requests, and public information actions. Use of properly prepared charts take the affected site personnel through event discovery, event assessment, identification of emergency classification level, and to the activation of on-site response actions.

Logic charts force project managers to think through the critical decisions necessary in a crisis. Project managers won't have time to go through the logic chart when the actual emergency occurs—the project manager must learn from the preparation and thinking required to construct a logic chart and feed this into or reinforce it through a tabletop exercise. When the crisis occurs, the project manager isn't thinking as clearly as usual, and the more that has been done before the crisis occurs, the better action the project manager can take.

The Oak Ridge Office (ORO) of the U.S. Department of Energy (DOE) used logic charts in its emergency response and recovery operations. ORO's logic charts offered specific steps to take based on the type of event. The first step was event discovery, where provisions for an initial response were depicted. This resulted in an event assessment leading to an initial emergency classification. Four levels of emergency classification followed, each evoking a particular response: a hazardous materials Usual Event (non-radiological), a hazardous materials Alert, a Site Emergency, and a General Emergency. A logic chart corresponding to the event discovery and initial response logic is shown in Figure 1.

Tabletop Exercises. Tabletops and other exercises use the information from the risk analysis in the mitigation phase to simulate the decision-making and action-taking occurring in an actual crisis. A tabletop exercise involves assembling the people who will be responding to a crisis and acting out possible scenarios in advance, usually in a conference room or similar space. There, without the pressure of time or the actual crisis, people have the freedom to discuss alternatives and decide on the best courses of action in a given situation. Tabletops also provide the opportunity to rehearse the steps to take in a potential crisis. These same techniques can help project managers prepare for possible crises that may occur in their projects.

The events or crises occurring to project managers won't be the things being tracked. What we don't track is what will go wrong. The need for tracking illustrates the use of a structured management process to catch the small problems through a thorough, systematic, and frequent review of relevant indicators (Kurstedt, Mallak & Pacifici, 1992).

Gershanov (1995) offers a five-stage process for holding tabletop exercises. Stage 1 is to identify significant policy issues surrounding disasters in the organization. This identification may be done using an assessment tool, reviewing documents on responses to previous disasters, researching competitors' experiences, and reviewing debriefings of past exercises. Stage 2 examines these issues and isolates appropriate discussion questions. These discussion questions must be appropriate to the participants' level of responsibility in the organization. Discussion questions should address policy-level rather than operations-level concerns. Stage 3 is the tabletop exercise itself. According to Gershanov, one realistic scenario that encompasses the essential issues and problems should drive the exercise. A written version of the scenario should be available for the participants to refer to during the exercise. An outside facilitator with experience in emergency preparedness planning should run the exercise. Stage 4 is the debriefing of the exercise, providing a basis for further action and bringing a sense of closure to the exercise. Stage 5, follow-up planning, concerns how the outcomes of the debriefing will be handled and getting commitment to developing plans based on the tabletop exercise.

Tabletop exercises were used in planning for security for the 1996 Democratic National Convention (DNC) in Chicago (O'Connor, 1996). The Federal

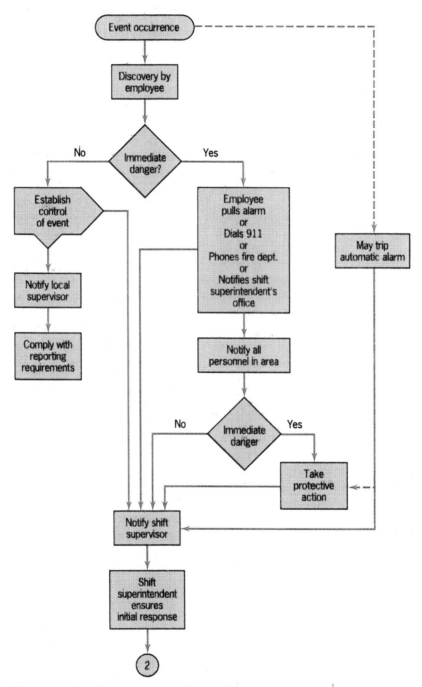

Figure 1 Event Discovery and Initial Response Logic Chart.

Emergency Management Agency (FEMA) facilitated tabletop exercises with members of the Chicago Police Department, the FBI, and the Secret Service to examine various scenarios and work out what would be done. Chicago Police also observed training and security practices for the 1996 Atlanta Olympic Games for lessons they could bring back to the DNC in Chicago.

Tabletop exercises are generally used in the beginning of crisis planning and focus on managerial information flows—who we talk to, what we do, who needs what information, and so forth. Issues surface in tabletops. Tabletops are a training device used to elicit understanding by carefully guiding the participants through a simulated emergency requiring a response. Although tabletop exercises are typically less expensive to conduct than drills or field exercises, they cannot substitute for the simulation of actual emergency events available through drills and field exercises.

Tabletop exercises should be conducted every quarter to keep emergency plans, procedures, and necessary thinking fresh in project managers' minds. Thinking through the decisions beforehand in an evaluative session such as a tabletop pays off when a real crisis occurs.

Tabletop exercises force managers to think through the decisions made during a crisis in advance, thereby reducing the need for decision-making during the crisis and reducing the time needed to make those decisions. "A tabletop is accomplished in controlled phases to allow discrete, individual answers, which focuses group attention on each point and thereby promotes a common understanding of roles and responsibilities and the entire response sequence by all participants" (Walker & Middleman, 1988). The tabletop exercise is a versatile tool that can be applied to all phases of project management. The overarching benefit of tabletops is they require people and systems to pay attention both during development and as the system evolves (Walker & Middleman).

One essential element to have in place for effective crisis management is a notification system. An effective notification system not only provides for contacting emergency response units, authorities, and key decision-makers, but also provides for accounting for personnel whereabouts and disposition.

After the 1996 Atlanta Olympics bombing, a plan to track the whereabouts of U.S. athletes and officials was deployed within 15 minutes of the blast (Lloyd,

Table 1. Summary of Crisis Planning Tools

Tool	Output
Risk analysis	Identification of risks
Contingency plan	Steps to take based on identified risks
Logic chart	Specific steps to take in a crisis
Tabletop exercise	Rehearse, discuss, and solidify a specific emergency response

1996). Dick Schultz, executive director of the U.S. Olympic Committee, stated: "In a two-hour time span, we not only determined the location of everybody, we had them secured. We had put together a crisis management plan for as many situations as we needed to" (Lloyd, 1996). Each U.S. Athlete was issued a pager, the first time that this was ever done in an Olympics. The ability to account for all athletes and their whereabouts provides evidence for the effectiveness of their crisis plan.

Risk analysis, contingency planning, logic charts, and tabletop exercises represent several of the more common tools to help plan for crises in projects. Table 1 summarizes these tools by output. Project managers should think through their projects, in consultation with other project personnel, to select and use the tools judged to be most effective for the specific project. Once selected, these tools should be developed and tested to ensure people understand how to use them and what types of outcomes will result. Most certainly, any test of the tools results in refinement of the tools and learning on participants' behalf.

Recommendations for Project Managers

While we don't have a closed set of comprehensive strategies to offer other project managers to better plan for crises, we do have several recommendations to offer based on experience in emergency management. Considering the uncertainty involved in crisis management, we would be wary of any closed set of strategies. Crisis management, by definition, is perplexing, constantly changing, full of uncertainties, and challenging to any manager, especially the project manager. Crisis planning logically parallels the uncertain nature of crisis management. Although there is no simple solution to the complex problems posed by crises, here are our recommendations:

- Even for small projects, assign the job of developing at least a two-page risk analysis and contingency plan before the project begins. This is similar to a company appointing a manager of business interruption planning.

- Assign the job of producing a notification sequence.

- Use logic charts to design procedures that won't go awry during a crisis.

- Use tabletop exercises, because few people will look at a logic chart or even a procedure when a crisis occurs. Project managers will depend on what they've practiced, and this underscores the need and value of tabletops.

- Conduct these tabletop exercises quarterly to ensure readiness and to update procedures and responsibilities.

- Establish authority for crisis management before the crisis. The project manager isn't always the best emergency manager, so choose the person who has greatest knowledge of the operational issues associated with the crisis.

- Use emergency planning processes in projects, including risk analysis and contingency planning.

- Design effective, accurate, and timely feedback systems to provide early warning signs of failure and impending crises. A structured management process can help in focusing attention on regular tracking of relevant and critical indicators to surface the little problems before they become big ones. Become sensitive to indicators of impending project failure. Pay special attention to untracked indicators, because these are the most likely to cause trouble. Develop antennae and know when the project is going wrong.

- Choose a project manager indigenous to the country where the project is being conducted. An indigenous project manager will be sensitive to the social and political aspects of the project and its peripheral issues and will catch more problems while they're small or otherwise undetectable to the outsider.

- Be mindful of the social and political consequences of crises or events. Critics, or stakeholders, bear significant influence on project success regardless of what the indicators of cost, schedule, and quality show. Learn how to satisfy stakeholders (Mallak, Patzak & Kurstedt,1991). Identify one spokesperson as a liaison with the public and prepare a procedure for quick dissemination of information to all affected parties.

- Adopt a systems view and separate the crisis from the origin of the crisis. Consider the basic performance principles and problem analysis techniques popularized in total quality management programs. Look forward and backward to access the potential overall effects of the crisis.

These tools, recommendations, and strategies should help project managers to manage their crises better and perhaps to avoid some crises altogether. Making time and resources available to those in charge of crisis planning is essential; otherwise these critical tasks will be subordinated to the day-to-day activities, a vicious circle that can increase the likelihood for a larger crisis going undetected until it's too late. The regular and proper use and testing of risk analyses, contingency plans, logic charts, and tabletop exercises should surface the information, discussion of decisions and actions, and mitigation techniques that may reduce the occurrence and impact of crises in projects.

Acknowledgments

The preparation of this paper was partially funded by U.S. Department of Energy (DOE) Grant No. DE-FG05-86DP70033.

References

Bradford, M. (1996, Feb. 2). Firms may be caught in a five-ring circus: With games on, planning will pay off. *Business Insurance*, P. 3.

Ceniceros, R. (1995, Oct. 23). Nestle resorts to crisis. *Business Insurance*, p. 83.

Gershanov, K. M. (1995). Emergency preparedness in five easy steps. *Occupational Health and Safety*, 64 (3), 51–53.

Kruse, C. (1993, June). Disaster plan stands test of hurricane. *Personnel Journal*, 36–43.

Kurstedt, H. A., Jr., Mallak, L. A., & Pacifici, L. C. (1992). Expand quality management into the customer's environment to establish effective measures and standards. *Proceedings of the 1st International Symposium on Productivity and Quality Improvement*, February 1992, 478–485.

Lagadec, P. (1993). *Preventing chaos in a crisis.* London: McGraw-Hill.

Leonard, J. B. (1995). Assessing risk systematically: Illinois Power's risk assessment system. *Risk Management, 42*:1, p. 12.

Lloyd, J. (1996, July 28). U.S. official says athletes were safe—and feel safe. *USA Today*, p. 3C.

Mallak, L. A., Patzak, G. R., & Kurstedt, Jr., H. A. (1991). Satisfying stakeholders for successful project management. *Computers and Industrial Engineering, 21,* 429–433.

O'Connor, P. J. (1996, May 23). Security practice for convention called a success. *Chicago Sun-Times*, p. 23.

Sawle, W. S. (1991). Concerns of project managers: Crisis project management. *PM Network*, 5(1), 25–29.

Slack, C. (1996, July 15). Bertha gives VDOT center real-life situation to test computer system. *Richmond Times Dispatch*, p. D–13.

Walker, J. A., & Middleman, L. I. (1988). Tabletop exercise programs complement any emergency management system. *Proceedings of the ANS Topical Meeting on Emergency Response—Planning, Technologies, and Implementation*. Charleston, SC.

Questions

1. Planning for inevitable crises seems to be quite logical, yet is rarely done in projects. Why?

2. Would some of these tools have been of value to Iceland in the Project Management in Practice example?

3. Scenario analysis—the brainstorming of possible crises and anticipation of their outcomes—seems like another useful tool here. How does this approach compare to the tools described?

4. Which of the four tools would have the most value? Which would be easiest to implement?

5. In their recommendations to project managers regarding implementing these tools, which recommendations are most important?

6

Conflict and Negotiation

As we noted in Chapter 5, the process of planning a project usually requires inputs from many people. Even when the project is relatively small and simple, planning involves the interaction of almost every functional and staff operation in the organization. It is virtually impossible for these interactions to take place without conflict, and when a conflict arises, it is helpful if there are acceptable methods to reduce or resolve it.

This chapter thus represents somewhat of an aside in our progress through the project management life cycle, the organizational principle of this book. Planning would normally be followed by budgeting and scheduling but during the planning process the need for some rational means of addressing interpersonal/intergroup conflicts arises. The matters discussed in this chapter all impact on the plan and the planning process, and do so in ways that are not obvious until both the planning process and the output of that process are well understood.

Conflict has been defined as "the process which begins when one party perceives that the other has frustrated, or is about to frustrate, some concern of his" [36, p. 891]. While conflict can arise over issues of belief or feelings or behavior, our concern in this chapter is focused for the most part on goal conflicts that occur when an individual or group pursues goals different from those of other individuals or groups [30, Chapter 12]. A party to the conflict will be satisfied when the level of frustration has been lowered to the point where no action, present or future, against the other party is contemplated. When all parties to the conflict are satisfied to this point, the conflict is said to be resolved.

There are, of course, many ways to resolve conflict. Brute force is a time-honored method, as is the absolute rule of the monarch, but the rule of law is the method of choice for modern societies—in spite of occasional lapses. Conflict resolution is the ultimate purpose of law.

Organizations establish elaborate and complex sets of rules and regulations to settle disputes between the organization itself and the individuals and groups with whom it interacts. Contracts between a firm and its suppliers, its trade unions, and its customers are written to govern the settlement of potential conflicts. But the various parties-at-interest (stakeholders) do not always agree about the meaning of a law or a provision in a contract. No agreement, however detailed, can cover all the circumstances that might arise in the extensive relationships between the buyer and the seller of complicated industrial equipment, between the user and the supplier of engineering consulting services, between the producer and user of computer programs—the list of potential conflicts is endless. Our overcrowded courts are witness to the extent and variety of conflict. According to the web page of the New York State Bar Association, there are approximately 850,000 lawyers in the United States. The great majority of this group that numbers between 25 and 35 percent of the world's supply of lawyers are employed in helping conflicting parties to adjudicate or settle their differences.

In this chapter we examine the nature of negotiation as a means of reducing or resolving the kinds of conflict that typically occur within projects. But before we begin the discussion, it must be made quite clear that *this chapter is not a primer on how to negotiate*; a course in negotiation is beyond the scope of this book and beyond our expertise (for such information, the reader is referred to the bibliography). Rather, this chapter focuses on the roles and applications of negotiation in the management of projects. Note also that we have excluded negotiations between the organization and outside vendors. In our experience, this type of negotiation is conducted sometimes by the project manager, sometimes by the project engineer, but most often by members of the organization's purchasing department. In any case, negotiations between buyer and seller are admirably covered by [16 and 30].

As we noted in the previous chapter, conflict can play a creative role in the planning process. Debate over the proper technical approach to a problem often generates a collaborative solution that is superior to any solution originally proposed. Conflict often educates individuals and groups about the goals/objectives of other individuals and groups in the organization, thereby satisfying a precondition for valuable win-win negotiations (see Section 6.3). Indeed, the act of engaging in win-win negotiations serves as an example of the positive outcomes that can result from such an approach to conflict resolution.

In Chapter 3 we noted that negotiation was a critical skill required of the project manager. In this chapter, we describe typical areas of project management where this skill is mandatory. In addition, we will cover some of the appropriate and inappropriate approaches to negotiation, as well as a few of the characteristics of successful negotiation suggested by experts in the field or indicated by our experience. We will also note some ethical issues regarding negotiation. There are probably more opportunities for ethical missteps in handling conflicts and negotiations than in any other aspect of project management. Unlike other chapters, we will use comparatively few illustrative examples. Successful negotiation tends to be idiosyncratic to the actual situation, and most brief examples do little to help transform theory into practice. We have, however, included a vignette at the end of the chapter. This vignette was adapted from "real life"; the names were changed to protect innocent and guilty alike.

No project manager should attempt to practice his or her trade without explicit training in negotiation. We are appalled that the subject is rarely mentioned in books on project management, excepting [16] on buyer-seller negotiations.

Project Management in Practice
Selling New Area Codes to Consumers Who Don't Want Them

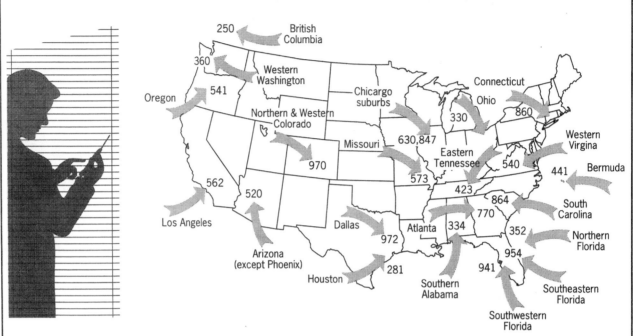

British Columbia — 250
Western Washington — 360
Oregon — 541
Northern & Western Colorado — 970
Los Angeles — 562
Arizona (except Phoenix) — 520
Chicago suburbs
Missouri — 630,847
Ohio — 330
Connecticut — 860
Western Virgina — 540
Bermuda — 441
Eastern Tennessee — 573
423
864
770
South Carolina
Dallas — 972
Atlanta — 334
Northern Florida — 352
954
Houston — 281
Southern Alabama — 941
Southeastern Florida
Southwestern Florida

This map reflects the large number of new area codes introduced in 1995–96 alone.

After analyzing the area code problem for some time, BellSouth received permission from all regulatory and organizational authorities in December 1994 to proceed with splitting South Carolina into two area codes and install the new code, 864, in the upper northwest region of the state. The project task was massive, yet the conversion of all equipment, databases, and associated systems had to be completed before the existing prefixes ran out in 12–18 months.

However, in spite of the demanding technical challenges, one of the most difficult tasks facing the project team was confronting the dilemma that this conversion was a product that South Carolina's phone customers absolutely did not want! Nevertheless, the exploding demand for fax machines, cellular telephones, pagers, additional residential phone lines, internet service,

and other such recent technological innovations required additional area codes to make them operative. Here was a basic conflict: "selling" a populace on the need to change their area code so they can use the new innovations they are purchasing.

The problem was exacerbated by the lack of time to involve the populace in the decision-making process and options available: changing the area code boundaries, using multiple area codes in the same region, splitting an area code region and adding a new code, and a few others. BellSouth thus adopted a variety of measures to communicate the need for the new area code to their customers:

- Developing a regional advertising campaign
- Sending out promotional brochures

- Putting inserts into customer bills
- Contract with an inbound telemarketing company to handle calls and provide information

Source: M.W. Strickland, "'Mission Possible': Managing an Area Code Relief Project," *PM Network*, March 1997, pp. 39–46.

- Informing all employees who had customer contact about how to explain the need
- Establishing a "South Carolina Area Code Assistance Hotline"

As the new system went live on May 1, 1996, the changeover was smooth and uneventful, a tribute not only to the technical ability of the project team but also their marketing prowess.

6.1 THE NATURE OF NEGOTIATION

The favored technique for resolving conflict is *negotiation*. What is negotiation? Wall [38, Preface] defines negotiation as "the process through which two or more parties seek an acceptable rate of exchange for items they own or control." Dissatisfied with this definition, he spends part of a chapter extending and discussing the concept [38, Chapter 1], without a great deal of improvement. Cohen [9, p. 15] says that "Negotiation is a field of knowledge and endeavor that focuses on gaining the favor of people from whom we want things." Other authors define negotiation differently, but do not appreciably extend Cohen's definition. Even if no single definition neatly fits all the activities we label "negotiation," we do recognize that such terms as "mediate," "conciliate," "make peace," "bring to agreement," "settle differences," "moderate," "arbitrate," "adjust differences," "compromise," "bargain," "dicker," and "haggle," [33] are synonyms for "negotiate" in some instances.

Most of the conflicts that involve the organization and outsiders have to do with property rights and contractual obligations. In these cases, the parties to negotiation see themselves as opponents. Conflicts arising inside the organization may also appear to involve property rights and obligations, but they typically differ from conflicts with outsiders in one important way: As far as the firm is concerned, they are conflicts between allies, not opponents. Wall makes this point neatly:

> Organizations, like groups, consist of interdependent parts that have their own values, interests, perceptions, and goals. Each unit seeks to fulfill its particular goal . . . and the effectiveness of the organization depends on the success of each unit's fulfillment of its specialized task. Just as important as the fulfillment of the separate tasks is the integration of the unit activities such that each unit's activities aid or at least do not conflict with those of the others. [38, pp. 149–50]

One of the ways in which organizations facilitate this integration is to establish "*lateral relations* [which] allow decisions to be made horizontally across lines of authority" [38, p. 150]. Because each unit will have its own goals, integrating the activities of two or more units is certain to produce the conflicts that Wall says should not take place. The conflicts may, however, be resolved by negotiating a solution, if one exists, that produces gains (or minimizes losses) for all parties. Raiffa [30, p. 139] defines a Pareto-optimal solution to the two-party conflict and discusses the nature of the bargaining process required to reach optimality, a difficult and time-consuming process. While it is not likely that the conflicting parties will know and understand the complex tradeoffs in a real world, project management, many-persons/many-issues conflict [see 30, Chapters 17–23], the general objective is to find a solution such that no party can be made better off without making another party worse off by the same amount or more—i.e., a Pareto-optimal solution.

The concept of a Pareto-optimal solution is important. Approaching intraproject conflicts with a desire to win a victory over other parties is inappropriate. The PM must remember that she will be negotiating with project stakeholders many times in the future. If she conducts a win-lose negotiation and the other party loses, from then on she will face a determined adversary who seeks to defeat her. This is not helpful. The proper outcome of this type of negotiation should be to optimize the outcome in terms of overall organizational goals. Although it is not always obvious how to do this, negotiation is clearly the correct approach.

During the negotiation process, an ethical situation often arises that is worth mentioning. Consider the situation where a firm requests an outside contractor to develop a software package to achieve some function. When the firm asks for a specific objective to be accomplished, it frequently does not know if that is a major job or a trivial task because it lacks technical competence in that area. Thus, the contractor has the opportunity to misrepresent the task to its customer, either inflating the cost for a trivial task or minimizing the impact of a significant task in order to acquire the contract and then boosting the cost later. The ethics of the situation require that each party in the negotiation be honest with the other, even in situations where it is clear there will not be further work between the two.

6.2 PARTNERING, CHARTERING, AND CHANGE

Projects provide ample opportunity for the project manager (PM) to utilize her or his skills at negotiation. There are, however, three situations commonly arising during projects that call for the highest level of negotiating skill the PM can muster: the use of subcontractors, the use of input from two or more functional units to design and develop the project's mission, and the management of changes ordered in the project's deliverables and/or priorities after the project is underway [11, 18, 35]. The former probably accounts for more litigation than all other aspects of the project combined. The latter two are, in the authors' experience, by far the most common and most troublesome issues project managers report facing.

Partnering

In recent years there has been a steady growth in the frequency of outsourcing parts of projects [34]. External suppliers, increasingly, are delivering parts of projects, including tangible products and services as well as intangible knowledge and skills. There are many reasons beyond avoidance of litigation that firms enter partnering arrangements with each other, for example, diversification of technical risk, avoidance of capital investment, reducing political risk on multinational projects, shortening the duration of the project, and pooling of complementary knowledge, among others [5, p. 192].

Generally, relations between the organization carrying out a project and a subcontractor working on the project are best characterized as adversarial. The parent organization's objectives are to get the deliverable at the lowest possible cost, as soon as possible. The subcontractor's objectives are to produce the deliverable at the highest possible profit with the least effort. These conflicting interests tend to lead both parties to work in an atmosphere of mutual suspicion and antagonism. Indeed, it is almost axiomatic that the two parties will have significantly different ideas about the exact nature of the deliverable, itself. The concept of "partnering" has been developed to replace this atmosphere with one of cooperation and mutual helpfulness, but the basically adversarial relationship makes cooperation difficult in the best of cases [20].

Cowan, Gray, and Larson define partnering as follows:

> *Project partnering is a method of transforming contractual relationships into a cohesive, cooperative project team with a single set of goals and established procedures for resolving disputes in a timely and effective manner.* [10, p. 5, italics in original]

They present a multistep process for building partnered projects. First, the parent firm must make a commitment to partnering, select subcontractors who will also make such a commitment, engage in joint team-building exercises, and develop a "charter" for the project. (See the next subsection for a description of such a charter.) Second, both parties must implement the partnering process with a four-part agreement on: (1) "joint evaluation" of the project's progress, (2) a method for resolving any problems or disagreements, (3) acceptance of a goal for continuous improvement (also known as TQM) for the joint project, and (4) continuous support for the process of partnering from senior management of both parties. Finally, the parties commit to a joint review of "project execution" when the project is completed. Beecham and Cordey-Hayes note several things that can "doom" partnering agreements and they develop several "propositions" that lead to success [5, p. 194ff; see also 39].

Clearly, each step in this process must be accompanied by negotiation, and just as clearly, the negotiations must be nonadversarial. The entire concept is firmly rooted in the assumption of mutual trust between the partners, and this assumption, too, requires nonadversarial negotiation. Finally, these articles focus on partnering when the partners are members of different organizations. We think the issue is no less relevant when the partners are from different divisions or departments of the same parent organization. Identical assumptions hold, identical steps must be taken, and interparty agreements must be reached for partnering to succeed. (Also see [4].)

There can be no doubt that those who have not had much experience with partnering underrate its difficulty. Partnering requires strong support from senior management of both firms, and it requires continuous support of project objectives and partnering agreements [24]. Above all, and most difficult of all, it requires open and honest communication between the partners. With all of its problems, however, partnering yields benefits great enough to be worth the efforts required to make it work correctly [3, 21].

Chartering

A project charter is simply a written agreement between the PM, senior management, and the functional managers who are committing resources and/or people to the project [23]. Like planning documents, WBSs, and responsibility charts, the charter may take many different forms. Typically, it details the expected project deliverables, often including the project's schedule and budget. It attests to the fact that senior management, functional managers, and the PM are "on the same page," agreeing about what is to be done, when, and at what cost. Note that if there is such an agreement, there is also an implication that none of the parties will change the agreement unilaterally, or, at least, without prior consultation with the other parties. Most projects do not have charters, which is one reason for observing that most projects are not completed on specification, on time, and on budget. Also note the additional fact that project managers are among the most frustrated people in American industry.

In the previous chapter, we described an iterative process for developing project action plans wherein individuals responsible for a task or subtask provided an action plan for completing it. We noted that it is not uncommon for the individuals or groups who make commitments during the process of developing the project's action plan to sign-off on their commitments. The signed-off project master plan or set of action plans might constitute a project charter, particularly if senior management has signed-off on the overall mission statement, *and if it is recognized as a charter by all parties to the plan.*

A somewhat less specific charter appears in [10], in which the various members of the partnering team sign a commitment to

- Meet design intent
- Complete contract without need for litigation
- Finish project on schedule:
    - Timely resolution of issues
    - Manage joint schedule
- Keep cost growth to less than 2 percent . . . etc. [10, Figure 2, p. 8]

Of course, even this charter assumes some agreement on the "design intent," the schedule, and costs.

Scope Change

No matter how carefully a project is planned, it is almost certain to be changed before completion. There are three basic causes for change in projects. Some changes result because planners erred in their initial assessment about how to achieve a given end or erred in their choice of the proper goal for the project. Technological uncertainty is the fundamental causal factor for either error. The foundation for a building must be changed because a preliminary geological study did not reveal a weakness in the structure of the ground on which the building will stand. An R & D project must be altered because metallurgical test results indicate another approach should be adopted. The project team becomes aware of a recent innovation that allows a faster, cheaper solution to the conformation of a new computer.

Other changes result because the client/user or project team learns more about the nature of the project deliverable or about the setting in which it is to be used. An increase in user or team knowledge or sophistication is the primary factor leading to change. A computer program must be extended or rewritten because the user thinks of new uses for the software. Physicians request that intensive care units in a hospital be equipped with laminar air-flow control in order to accommodate patients highly subject to infection who might otherwise not be admissible in an ICU. The fledgling audio-addict upgrades the specifications for a system to include very high frequencies so that his or her dog can enjoy the music, too.

A third source of change is the mandate. This is a change in the environment in which the project is being conducted. As such, it cannot be controlled by the PM. A new law is passed. A government regulatory unit articulates a new policy. A trade association sets a new standard. The parent organization of the user applies a new criterion for its purchases. In other words, the rules of conduct for the project are altered. A state-approved pollution control system must be adopted for each chemical refinery project. The state government requires all new insurance policies to conform to a revised law specifying that certain information must be given to potential purchasers. At times, mandates affect only priorities. The mandate in question might move a very important customer to the "head of the line" for some scarce resource or service.

To some extent, risk management techniques can be applied to scope change. Technological uncertainty can be mitigated by careful analysis of the technologies involved, including the use of technological forecasting. Risk of scope change caused by increased user knowledge can only be managed by improving the up-front communication with the client and then establishing a formal process to handle change. See Chapter 11 for more about this. Finally, mandates are, for the most part, unpredictable. These can be "managed" only by having some flexibility built into the budget and schedule of the project. Ways of doing this sensibly will be discussed in the following two chapters.

As Greek philosopher Heraclitus said, "Nothing endures but change." It is thus with projects, but whatever the nature of the change, specifications of the deliverables must be altered, and the schedule and budget recalculated. Obviously, negotiation will be required to develop new agreements between the parties-at-interest to the project. These negotiations are difficult because most of the stakeholders will have a strong interest in maintaining the status quo. If the proposed change benefits the client and increases the cost of the project, the producer will try to sequester some of the user's potential benefit in the form of added charges to offset the added cost. The client will, of course, resist. All parties must, once again, seek a Pareto-optimal solution—always a difficult task.

Change by mandate raises an additional problem. Not only are the project's deliverables, budget, and schedule usually changed, the *priorities* of other projects are typically changed too, if only temporarily while the mandate receives the system's full attention. Suddenly, a PM loses access to key resources, because they are urgently required elsewhere. Key contributors to a project miss meetings or are unable to keep promised task-delivery dates. All too often, the PM's response to this state of affairs is anger and/or discouragement. Neither is appropriate.

> This project is so important, we can't let things that are more important interfere with it.

After discussing priorities with both PMs and senior managers, it has become clear to us that most firms actually have only three levels of priority (no matter how ornate the procedure for setting project priorities might seem to be). First, there are the high-priority projects, that is the "set" of projects currently being supported. Second, there are the lower-priority projects, the projects "we would like to do when we have the time and money." Third, occasionally, there are urgent projects, mandates, that must be done immediately. "Customer A's project must be finished by the end of the month." "The state's mandate must be met by June 30." Everything else is delayed to ensure that mandates are met. As noted above, we will have more to say on this subject in Chapter 11.

While project charters and partnerships would certainly help the PM deal with conflicts that naturally arise during a project, the use of charters and partnering is growing slowly—though outsourcing is growing rapidly. It is understandably difficult to convince senior managers to make the firm commitments implied in a project charter in the face of a highly uncertain future. Functional managers are loath to make firm commitments for precisely the same reason. So, too, the client, aware of her or his own ignorance about the degree to which the project output will meet his or her needs, is cautious about commitment—even when a procedure for negotiating change exists.

Partnering is a recently developed concept, and in our litigious society any system for conflict resolution that asks parties to forego lawsuits is viewed with considerable suspicion. Indeed, we find that a great many organizations preach "team building," "TQM," and "employee involvement," but many fail to practice what they preach. For each participative manager you find, we can show you a dozen micromanagers. For each team player ready to share responsibility, we can show you a dozen "blame placers." The era of project charters and partnering is approaching, but it is not yet here.

6.3 CONFLICT AND THE PROJECT LIFE CYCLE

In this section, following a brief discussion of the project life cycle, we will categorize the types of conflicts that frequently occur in the project environment, and then amplify the nature of these conflicts. Finally, we will link the project life cycle with the fundamental conflict categories and discover that certain patterns of conflict are associated with the different periods in the life of a project. With this knowledge, the PM can do a faster and more accurate job of diagnosing the nature of the conflicts he or she is facing, thereby reducing the likelihood of escalating the conflict by dealing with it ineffectually.

More on the Project Life Cycle

Various authors define the stages of the project life cycle (see Figures 1-3, 1-4, and 1-5 in Chapter 1) in different ways. Two of the most commonly cited definitions are those of Thamhain and Wilemon [36] and Adams and Barndt [1]. The former use a four-stage model with project formation, buildup, main program, and phaseout identified as the stages of the life cycle. Adams and Barndt also break the project life cycle into four stages: conceptualization, planning, execution, and termination.

For our purposes, these two views of the cycle are not significantly different. During the first stage, senior management tentatively, sometimes unofficially, approves preliminary planning for a project. Often, this management recognition is preceded by some strictly unofficial "bootleg" work to test the feasibility of an idea. Initial planning is undertaken, basic objectives are often adopted, and the project may be "scoped out." The second stage is typified by detailed planning, budgeting, scheduling, and the aggregation of resources. In the third stage, the lion's share of the actual work on the project is accomplished. During the final stage of the life cycle, work is completed and products are turned over to the client or user. This stage also includes disposition of the project's assets and personnel. It may even include preparation for the initial stage of another related project to follow.

Categories of Conflict

All stages of the project life cycle appear to be typified by conflict. In Chapter 4, we discussed some of the human factors that require the PM to be skilled at reducing interpersonal tensions. In that chapter we also introduced the work of Thamhain and Wilemon [36, 37] on conflict in the project. These conflicts center on such matters as schedules, priorities, staff and labor requirements, technical factors, administrative procedures, cost estimates, and, of course, personality conflicts. Thamhain and Wilemon collected data on the frequency and magnitude of conflicts of each type during each stage of the project life cycle. Multiplying frequency by a measure of conflict magnitude and adjusting for the proportion of PMs who reported each specific type of conflict, they derived an estimate of the "intensity" of the conflicts (see Tables 4-1 and 4-2). Figure 4-8 illustrates these conflicts and is repeated here as Figure 6-1 for the reader's convenience.

On examination of the data, it appears that the conflicts fall into three fundamentally different categories:

1. Groups working on the project may have different goals and expectations.
2. There is considerable uncertainty about who has the authority to make decisions.
3. There are interpersonal conflicts between people who are parties-at-interest in the project.

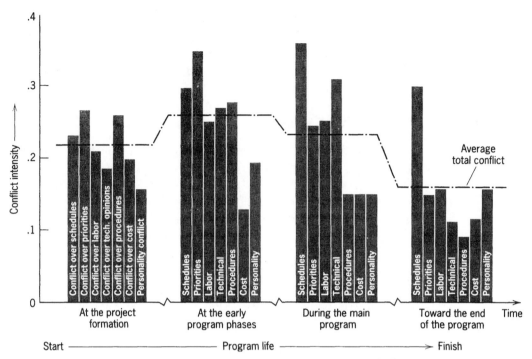

Figure 6-1   Conflict intensity over the project life cycle. *Source:* [36]

Some conflicts reflect the fact that the day-to-day work on projects is usually carried out by many different units of the organization, units that often differ in their objectives and technical judgments. The result is that these units have different expectations about the project, its costs and rewards, its relative importance, and its timing. Conflicts about schedules, intra-and interproject priorities, cost estimates, and staff time tend to fall into this category. At base, they arise because the project manager and the functional managers have very different goals. The PM's concern is the project. The primary interest of the functional manager is the daily operation of the functional department.

Other conflicts reflect the fact that both technical and administrative procedures are important aspects of project management. Uncertainty about who has the authority to make decisions on resource allocation, on administrative procedures, on communication, on technological choices, and on all the other matters affecting the project produces conflict between the PM and the other parties. It is simple enough (and correct) to state that in a matrix organization, the functional manager controls who works on the project and makes technical decisions, while the project manager controls the schedule and flow of work. In practice, in the commonly hectic environment of the project, amid the day's countless little crises faced by project and functional manager alike, the distinction is rarely clear.

Finally, some conflicts reflect the fact that human beings are an integral part of all projects. In an environment that depends on the cooperation of many persons, it seems inevitable that some personalities will clash. Also, in conflicts between the project and the client, or between senior management and the project, it is the project manager who personifies the project and thus is generally a party to the conflict.

We can categorize these conflicts as conflict over differing goals, over uncertainty about the locus of authority, and between personalities. For the entire array of conflict types and parties-at-interest, see Table 6-1.

The three types of conflict seem to involve the parties-at-interest to the project in identifiable ways. the different goals and objectives of the project manager, senior management, and functional managers are a major and constant source of conflict. For example, senior management (at times, arbitrarily) is apt to fix all three parameters of the project—time, cost, and performance—and then to assume that the PM will be able to achieve all the preset targets. As we will see in Chapter 7 on budgeting, underestimation of cost and time is a natural consequence of this practice, and it leads directly to conflict between the PM, as a representative of the project team, and senior management. A second consequence is that the PM tries to pass the stringent cost and time estimates along to functional managers whose units are expected to perform certain work on the project. More conflict arises when the functional managers complain that they cannot meet the time and cost restrictions. All this tends to build failure into the job of managing a project, another source of conflict between the PM and senior management.

Functional managers also may not see eye-to-eye with the PM on such issues as the project's priority or the desirability of assigning a specifically named individual to work on the project, or even the applicability of a given technical approach to the project. In addition, the client's priorities and schedule, whether an inside or outside client, may differ radically from those of senior management and the project team. Finally, the project team has its own ideas about the appropriateness of the schedule or level of project staffing. The Thamhain and Wilemon data show that these goal-type conflicts occur in all stages of the project's life cycle, though they are particulary serious in the early stages (see Figure 6-1). Regardless of the timing, in many cases it is not certain just whose priorities are ruling.

There are, of course, a number of methods for settling conflicts about priorities between projects, as well as intraproject conflicts. Often, the project selection model used to approve projects for funding will generate a set of projects ranked by some measure of value. It is also common for senior management to determine interproject

Table 6-1. Project Conflicts by Category and Parties-at-Interest

Parties-at-Interest	Categories of Conflict		
	Goals	Authority	Interpersonal
Project team	Schedules Priorities	Technical	Personality
Client	Schedules Priorities	Technical	
Functional and senior management	Schedules Priorities Labor Cost	Technical Administrative	Personality

priorities. The relative importance of the various tasks in an individual project is set by the project manager, who allocates scarce resources depending on the requirements of schedule, task difficulty, resource availability, and similar considerations. The existence of these methods for resolving priority conflicts is all too often irrelevant, because there is a powerful tendency for both project and functional managers to optimize their individual interests, with little regard for the total organization.

In matrix organizations, the center of authority is particularly unclear. Locus-of-authority conflicts are endemic to matrix-organized projects. The project team and the client tend to focus on the technical procedures, debating the proper approach to the project, or perhaps how to solve individual problems that can occur at any stage. Senior management has other fish to fry. Not only do they insist that the project manager adopt and maintain a set of administrative procedures that conform to organizational and legal standards, but they also are quite concerned with who reports to whom and whose permission is required to take what action. The astute reader will note that such concerns are not entirely appropriate for matrix-organized projects. Our discussions with senior managers lead us to the obvious conclusion that it is common for senior management to want the efficiency and other advantages of matrix management but simultaneously to attempt to maintain the managerial comforts of traditional hierarchical structures—a sure source of conflict.

The conflict-resolution potential of partnering and project charters should be quite clear. Neither technique will stop conflicts from arising, but they will sharply lower the intensity of the conflicts as well as provide a framework for resolving conflict. They will even allow an environment in which the PM and functional managers can take positions that support the total organization rather than suboptimizing the project or the function.

Project managers will often find themselves arguing for scheduling or resource priorities from functional managers who outrank them by several levels. Neither the functional nor the project managers are quite sure about who has what authority. (The reader will recall that the pure project form of organization has a tendency to breed deviant administrative behaviors, and that matrix organization is characterized by superior-subordinate confusion.) A constant complaint of project managers is "I have to take the responsibility, but I have no authority at all."

People problems arise, for the most part, within the project team, though functional managers may clash with PMs—the former accusing the latter of being "pushy," and the latter accusing the former of "foot dragging." In our experience, most personality clashes on the project team result from differences in technical approach or philosophy of problem solving, and in the methods used to implement the project results. Of course, it is quite possible that a personality conflict causes a technical conflict. It is also possible that any type of conflict will appear, at first blush, to be a personality clash.

Next we put these conflicts into the chronological perspective of the project life cycle.

Project Formation

In the initial stage of the project life cycle, most of the conflict centers around the inherent confusion of setting up a project in the environment of matrix management. Almost nothing about the project or its governance has been decided. Even the project's technical objectives, not clearly defined or established, are apt to be understood only in the most general sense. Moving from this state of semi-chaos to the relatively ordered world of the buildup stage is difficult. To make this transition, four fundamental issues must be handled, although not necessarily in the order presented here.

First, the technical objectives of the project must be specified to a degree that will allow the detailed planning of the buildup stage to be accomplished. Second, commitment of resources to the project must be forthcoming from senior management and from functional managers. Third, the priority of the project, relative to the priorities of the parent organization's other projects, must be set and communicated. (Our comments about priorities at the end of Section 6.2 notwithstanding, we feel the project's priority must be set as early as possible in the life of the project. While it will probably not save the project from delay in the event of a mandate, it stands as an important political signal to functional managers about which projects take precedence in case of resource conflicts.) Fourth, the organizational structure of the project must be established to an extent sufficient for the WBS and a linear responsibility chart, or its equivalent, to be prepared during the next stage of the life cycle.

These conditions are not sufficient, but they are most certainly necessary if the conflicts typical of the formation stage are to be resolved—at least at a reasonable level—and not simply carried forward to the buildup stage in an exacerbated state.

The project manager who practices conflict avoidance in this stage is inviting disaster in the next. The four fundamental issues above underlie such critical but down-to-earth matters as these: Which of the functional areas will be needed to accomplish project tasks? What will be the required level of involvement of each of the functional areas? How will conflicts over resources/facility usage between this and other projects be settled? What about those resource/facility conflicts between the project and the routine work of the functions? *Who* has the authority to decide the technical, scheduling, personnel, and cost questions that will arise? Most important, how will changes in the parent organization's priorities be communicated to everyone involved?

Note that three of the four fundamental issues—delimiting the technical objectives, getting management commitment, and setting the project's relative priority— must be resolved irrespective of what organizational form is selected for the project. It should also be noted that the organizational structure selected will have a major impact on the ways in which the conflicts are handled. The stronger the matrix, having the pure project as its limit, the more authoritative the role played by the PM. The weaker the matrix, having functional organization as its limit, the more authority is embedded in the functional managers. Lack of clarity about the relative power/influence/authority of the PM and the functional managers is a major component of all conflicts involving technical decisions, resource allocation, and scheduling.

Project Buildup

Thamhain and Wilemon note that conflict occurring in the buildup stage "over project priorities, schedules, and administrative procedures . . . appears as an extension from the previous program phase" [36, pp. 39]. This is the period during which the project moves (or should move) from a general concept to a highly detailed set of plans. If the project's organizational format is a strong matrix, the PM seeks a commitment of *people* from the functional departments. If the project is organized as a weak matrix, the PM seeks a commitment of *work* from the functional departments. In either case, the PM seeks commitment from functional managers who are under pressure to deliver support to other projects, in addition to the routine, everyday demands made on their departments.

As the project's plans become detailed, conflicts over technical issues build— again, conflicts between the PM and the functional areas tend to predominate. Usually, the functional departments can claim more technical expertise than the PM, who is a "generalist." On occasion, however, the PM is also a specialist. In such situations, discussions between the functional manager and the project manager about the best technical approach often result in conflict. The total level of conflict is at its highest in this transition period.

Main Program

Schedules are still a major source of conflict in the main program phase of the project life cycle, though the proximate cause of schedule-related conflict is usually different than in the earlier stages. Project plans have been developed and approved by everyone involved (although, perhaps, grudgingly), and the actual work is under way. Let us make an assumption that is certain to be correct; let us assume that some activity runs into difficulty and is late in being completed. Every task that is dependent on this late activity will also be delayed. Some of these subsequent activities will, if sufficiently late and if the late work is not made up, delay the entire project.

In order to prevent this consequence, the PM must try to get the schedule back on track. But catching up is considerably more difficult than falling behind. Catching up requires extra resources that the functional groups who are doing the "catching up" will demand, but which the PM may not have.

The more complex the project, the more difficult it is to trace and estimate the impact of all the delays, and the more resources that must be consumed to get things back on schedule. Throughout this book we have referred to the PM's job of managing time/cost/performance trade-offs. Maintaining the project schedule is precisely an exercise in managing trade-offs, but adding to the project's cost or scaling down the project's technical capabilities in order to save time are trade-offs the PM will not take if there is any viable alternative. The PM's ability to make trade-offs is often constrained by contract, company policy, and ethical considerations. In reality, trade-off decisions are extremely difficult.

Like schedule conflicts, technical conflicts are frequent and serious during the main program stage. Also like schedule conflicts, the source of technical conflict is somewhat different than in earlier stages. Just as a computer and a printer must be correctly linked together in order to perform properly, so must the many parts of a project. These linkages are known as *interfaces*. The number of interfaces increases rapidly as the project gets larger, which is to say that the system gets more complex. The need to manage these interfaces and to correct incompatibilities is the key to the technical conflicts in the main program phase.

Project Phaseout

As in the main program stage, schedule is the major source of conflict during project phaseout. If schedule slippage has occurred in the main program stage (and it probably has), the consequences will surely be felt in this final stage. During phaseout, projects with firm deadlines develop an environment best described as hectic. The PM, project team, and functional groups often band together to do what is necessary to complete the project on time and to specification. Cost overruns, if not outrageously high, are tolerated—though they may not be forgiven and they will certainly be remembered.

Technical problems are comparatively rare during phaseout because most have been solved or bypassed earlier. Similarly, working interfaces have been developed and put in place. If the project involves implementing a technology in an outside client's system, technical conflicts will probably arise, but they are usually less intense.

Thamhain and Wilemon [37, p. 41] note that personality conflicts are the second-ranked source of conflict during phaseout. They ascribe these conflicts to interpersonal stress caused by the pressure to complete the project, and to individuals' natural anxiety about leaving the project either to be assigned to another, or be returned to a functional unit. In addition, we have observed conflict, sometimes quite bitter, focused on the distribution of the project's capital equipment and supplies when the project is completed. Conflict also arises between projects phasing out and those just starting, particularly if the latter need resources or personnel with scarce talents being used by the former.

The way in which Thamhain and Wilemon have defined conflict as having its source in differences about goals/expectations, uncertainty about authority, and interpersonal problems, precludes identifying conflict as occurring between discipline-oriented and problem-oriented team members. Recall our discussions of Hughes [18], de Laat [11], and Pill [28] among several others. We do not argue that Thamhain and Wilemon are in error, but merely that their classification does not specifically include a type of conflict we feel is both frequent and important. Much of the conflict identified during our discussion of planning in Chapter 5, it seems to us, is due to discipline/problem-orientation differences. A clear example comes from an interview recorded during Pelled and Adler's research on conflict in multifunctional design teams [27]. One team member speaking of another said, "He will do whatever he thinks is right to get his [own] job done, whether or not it's good for [the company] or anyone else" [27, p.23]. In context, it is clear that this conflict was between a problem-oriented individual and one who was discipline-oriented.

The upshot is simple. As we noted in the first section of Chapter 1, conflict is an inherent characteristic of projects, and the project manager is constantly beset by conflict. The ability to reduce and resolve conflict in ways that support achievement of the project's goals is a prime requisite for success as a PM. The primary tool to accomplish conflict resolution and reduction is negotiation, and the method of handling conflict established in the project formation stage will set the pattern for the entire project. Therefore, the style of negotiation adopted by the PM is critical.

Much has been written on conflict resolution. Burke's classic paper on the confrontation-problem solving method of resolving conflicts is offered as a "Reading" at the end of this chapter. The similarities between the confrontation-problem solving technique for conflict resolution and win-win negotiation covered in the following section are quite striking. Pinto and Kharbanda also approach conflict resolution in the spirit of win-win negotiation [29]. Dyer [13] writes of resolving conflicts, focusing on conflict between members of a team, and [2] is a general work on the subject.

Project Management in Practice
A Consensus Feasibility Study for Montreal's Archipel Dam

To assess the desirability of a feasibility study evaluating the costs and benefits of constructing a dam for watershed development within the St. Lawrence river basin in the Montreal metropolitan area, Quebec initiated an interdepartmental evaluation. The evaluation concluded that a feasibility study that considered the hydroelectric power generated, the flood control possible, and the shoreline restoration for recreation for the 3 million local area residents was justified. It was recommended that a central authority act as project manager for the study and that arbitration procedures be instituted for the interests of all affected parties.

Thus, a new body called "Secretariat Archipel" was created to directly supervise the feasibility study. Secretariat Archipel, however, rejected the recommendations of the prior evaluation and chose to use a more democratic "consensus" approach between all involved agencies rather than a central authority approach. Doing so avoided the need for arbitration procedures as well. In addition, a matrix structure was put in place to guarantee a veto right to each of the ten governmental departments involved in the process. It was believed that this consensus approach would lead to a solution acceptable to all, while protecting the jurisdictional responsibilities of all departments.

Although this approach apparently avoided difficult conflicts, and the concomitant need to arbitrate them, a post-study evaluation of the process concluded that it was neither effective nor efficient. By discarding the recommendation

for a central authority body, a leadership gap arose in the decision framework and veto rights were abused by many of the participants. The leadership gap led, for example, to no one identifying incompatible objectives, rules for making decisions, or common priorities.

In terms of effectiveness, the recommendations of the study are questionable: that the dam be postponed until the year 2015 while only $35 million—less than the cost of the feasibility study—be spent on recreational facilities. Considering efficiency, it was found that many of the expensive support studies authorized by the Secretariat did not add significantly to the feasibility process. Also, the study appeared to take one to two years longer than necessary, with a correspondingly higher cost.

The evaluation proposed three probable causes of the lack of decisiveness in this study process:

1. Fear of litigation between the governmental departments and municipalities,
2. Difficulty comparing positive and negative impacts due to a lack of decision rules, and
3. Long delays and unavoidable sacrifices through a failure of the consensus process.

In retrospect, the consensus approach appeared to have been selected to protect the fields of jurisdiction of each governmental department rather than for defining the best project for the community. Since many of the goals were incompatible to start with, a consensual decision process with veto override would simply have to reject any recommendation—no matter how appropriate for the community—that was incompatible with another goal or disliked by any of the ten departments involved in the study. Although consensus is a highly desirable goal for public studies, leadership cannot be abandoned in the process. Attempting to avoid conflict through mandated consensus simply defeats the purpose of any study in the first place, except a study to determine what everyone commonly agrees upon.

Source: R. Desbiens, R. Houde, and P. Normandeau, "Archipel Feasibility Study: A Questionable Consensus Approach," *Project Management Journal,* March 1989.

6.4 SOME REQUIREMENTS AND PRINCIPLES OF NEGOTIATION

The word "negotiation" evokes many images: the United States President and Congress on the annual federal budget, the "Uruguay Round" of the GATT talks, a player's agent and the owner of an NFL team, the buyer and seller of an apartment complex, attorneys for husband and wife in a divorce settlement, union and management working out a collective bargaining agreement, tourist and peddler haggling over a rug in an Ankara market. But as we noted in the introduction to this chapter, none of these images is strictly appropriate for the project manager who must resolve the sorts of conflicts we have considered in the previous section.

The key to understanding the nature of negotiation as it applies to project management is the realization that few of the conflicts arising in projects have to do with *whether* or not a task will be undertaken or a deliverable produced. Instead, they have to do with the precise *design* of the deliverable and/or *how* the design will be achieved, by *whom, when,* and at *what cost.* The implication is clear: *The work of the project will be done.* If conflicts between any of the parties to the project escalate to the point where negotiations break down and work comes to a halt, everyone loses. *One requirement* for the conflict reduction/resolution methods used by the PM is that *they must allow the conflict to be settled without irreparable harm to the project's objectives.*

A closer consideration of the attorneys negotiating the divorce settlement makes clear a second requirement for the PM negotiating conflicts between parties-at-interest to the project. While the husband and wife (or the rug peddler and tourist) may employ unethical tactics during the negotiation process and, if not found out, profit from them at the expense of the other party, it is much less likely for the attorneys representing the husband and wife to do so—particularly if they practice law in the same community. The lawyers know they will have to negotiate on other matters in the future. Any behavior that breeds mistrust will make future negotiations extremely difficult, perhaps impossible. The rug peddler assumes no further contact with the tourist, so conscience is the sole governor of his or her ethics. A *second requirement* for the conflict resolution/reduction methods used by the PM is that *they allow (and foster) honesty between the negotiators.*

The conflicting parties-at-interest to a project are not enemies or competitors, but rather allies—members of an alliance with strong common interests. It is a *requirement of all conflicting parties to seek solutions to the conflict that not only satisfy their own individual needs, but also satisfy the needs of other parties to the conflict, as well as the needs of the parent organization.* In the language of negotiation, this is called a win-win solution. Negotiating to a win–win solution is the key to conflict resolution in project management.

Fisher and Ury [14] have developed a negotiation technique that tends to maintain these three requirements. They call it "principled negotiation." The method is straightforward; it is defined by four points [14, p. 11].

1. *Separate the people from the problem.* The conflicting parties are often highly emotional. They perceive things differently and feel strongly about the differences. Emotions and objective fact get confused to the point where it is not clear which is which. Conflicting parties tend to attack one another rather than the problem. to minimize the likelihood that the conflict will become strictly interpersonal, the substantive problem should be carefully defined. Then everyone can work on it rather than each other.

2. *Focus on interests, not positions.* Positional bargaining occurs when the PM says to a functional manager: "I need this subassembly by November 15." The functional manager responds: "My group can't possibly start on it this year. We might be able to deliver it by February 1." These are the opening lines in a dialogue that sounds suspiciously like the haggling of the tourist and the rug peddler. A simple "Let's talk about the schedule for this subassembly" would be sufficient to open the discussion. Otherwise each party develops a high level of ego involvement in his or her position and the negotiation never focuses on the real interests and concerns of the conflicting parties—the central issues of the conflict. The exchange deteriorates into a series of positional compromises that do not satisfy either party and leave both feeling that they have lost something important.

   In positional negotiation, the "positions" are statements of immediate wants and assume that the environment is static. Consider these positional statements: "I won't pay more than $250,000 for that property." Or, as above, "We might be able to deliver it by February 1." The first position assumes that the bidder's estimates of future property values are accurate, and the second assumes that the group's current workload (or a shortage of required materials) will not change. When negotiation focuses on interests, the negotiator must determine the underlying concern of the other party. The real concerns or interests of the individuals stating the positions quoted above might be to earn a certain return on the investment in a property, or to not commit to delivery of work if delivery on the due date cannot be guaranteed. Knowledge of the other party's interests allows a negotiator to suggest solutions that satisfy the other party's interests without agreeing with the other's position.

3. *Before trying to reach agreement, invent options for mutual gain.* The parties-in-conflict usually enter negotiations knowing the outcome they would like. As a result, they are blind to other outcomes and are not particulary creative. Nonetheless, as soon as the substantive problems are spelled out, some effort should be devoted to finding a wide variety of possible solutions—or elements thereof—that advance the mutual interests of the conflicting parties. Success at finding options

that produce mutual gain positively reinforces win-win negotiations. Cohen [9] reports on a conflict between a couple in which "he" wanted to go to the mountains and "she" wanted to go to the shore. A creative win-win solution sent them both to Lake Tahoe.

4. *Insist on using objective criteria.* Rather than bargaining on positions, attention should be given to finding standards (e.g., market value, expert opinion, law, company policy) that can be used to determine the quality of an outcome. Doing this tends to make the negotiation less a contest of wills or exercise in stubbornness. If a functional manager wants to use an expensive process to test a part, it is acceptable for the PM to ask if such a process is required to ensure that the parts meet specified quality standards.

Fisher and Ury [14] have had some success with their approach, "principled negotiation," in the Harvard (Graduate School of Business) Negotiation Project. Use of their methods increases the chance of finding win-win solutions.

There are many books on negotiation, some of which are listed in the bibliography of this chapter. Most of these works are oriented toward negotiation between opponents, not an appropriate mindset for the project manager, but all of them contain useful, tactical advice for the project manager. Wall's book [38] is an excellent academic treatment of the subject. Fisher and Ury [14] is a clear presentation of principled negotiation, and contains much that is relevant to the PM. In addition, Herb Cohen's *You Can Negotiate Anything* [9] is an outstanding guide to win-win negotiation. The importance of negotiation is beginning to be recognized by the project management profession [12, 15, 22, 32], but the subject has not yet found its way into the Project Management Body of Knowledge.

Among the tactical issues covered by most books on negotiation are things the project manager, as a beginning negotiator, needs to know. For example, what should a negotiator who wishes to develop a win-win solution do if the other party to the conflict adopts a win-lose approach? What do you do if the other party tries to put you under psychological pressure by seating you so that a bright light shines in your eyes? What do you do if the other party refuses to negotiate in order to put you under extreme time pressure to accept whatever solution he or she offers? How do you settle what you perceive to be purely technical disputes? How should you handle threats? What should be your course of action if a functional manager, with whom you are trying to reach agreement about the timing and technology of a task, goes over your head and attempts to enlist the aid of your boss to get you to accept a solution you feel is less than satisfactory? How can you deal with a person you suspect dislikes you?

Almost every writer on negotiation emphasizes the importance of understanding the interests of the person with whom you are negotiating. As we noted above, the positions taken by negotiators are not truly understandable without first understanding the interests and concerns that prompt those positions. The statement that a test requested for May 15 cannot be run until June 2 may simply mean that the necessary test supplies will not be delivered until the latter date. If the PM can get the supplies from another source in time for the May 15 deadline, the test can be run on schedule. But the ability to do this depends on knowing *why* the test was to be delayed. If the negotiation remains a debate on positions, the PM will never find out that the test could have been run on time. *The key to finding a negotiator's interests and concerns is to ask "Why?" when he or she states a position.* The following vignette demonstrates the maintenance of a nonpositional negotiating style. This vignette is based on an actual event and was described to the authors by an "actor" in the case.

6.5 NEGOTIATION IN ACTION—THE QUAD SENSOR PROJECT

Dave Dogers, an experienced project manager, was assigned the project of designing and setting up a production system for an industrial instrument. The instrument would undoubtedly be quite delicate, so the design and fabrication methods for the shipping container were included in the project. Production of containers capable of meeting the specifications in this case were outside the experience of the firm, but one engineer in the container group had worked with this type of package in a previous job. This engineer, Jeff Gamm, was widely recognized as the top design engineer in the container group.

During the initial meetings on the project, which was organized as a weak matrix, Dogers asked Tab Baturi, manager of the Container Group, to assign Gamm to the project because of his unique background. Baturi said he thought they could work it out, and estimated that the design, fabrication of prototypes, and testing would require about four weeks. The package design could not start until several shape parameters of the instrument had been set and allowable shock loadings for the internal mechanisms had been determined. The R&D group responsible for instrument design thought it would require about nine months of work before they could complete specifications for the container. In addition to the actual design, construction, and test work, Gamm would have to meet periodically with the instrument design team to keep track of the project and to consult on design options from the container viewpoint. It was estimated that the entire project would require about 18 months.

Seven months into the project, at a meeting with Dave Dogers, the senior instrument design engineer, Richard Money casually remarked: "Say, Dave, I thought Jeff Gamm was going to do the package for the Quad Sensor."

"He is, why?" Dogers replied.

"Well," said the engineer, "Gamm hasn't been coming to the design team meetings. He did come a couple of times at the start of the project, but then young McCutcheon showed up saying that he would substitute for Gamm and would keep him informed. I don't know if that will work. That package is going to be pretty tricky to make."

Dogers was somewhat worried by the news the engineer had given him. He went to Gamm's office, as if by chance, and asked, "How are things coming along?"

"I'm up to my neck, Dave," Gamm responded. "We've had half a dozen major changes ordered from Baker's office (V.P. Marketing) and Tab has given me the three toughest ones. I'm behind, getting behinder, and Baker is yelling for the new container designs. I can't possibly do the Quad Sensor package unless I get some help—quick. It's an interesting problem and I'd like to tackle it, but I just can't. I asked Tab to put McCutcheon on it. He hasn't much experience, but he seems bright."

"I see," said Dogers. "Well, the Quad Sensor package may be a bit much for a new man. Do you mind if I talk to Tab? Maybe I can get you out from under some of the pressure."

"Be my guest!" said Gamm.

The next day Dogers met with Tab Baturi to discuss the problem. Baturi seemed depressed. "I don't know what we're supposed to do. No sooner do I get a package design set and tested than I get a call changing things. On the Evans order, we even had production schedules set, had ordered the material, and had all the setups figured out. I'm amazed they didn't wait till we had completed the run to tell us to change everything."

Baturi continued with several more examples of changed priorities and assignments. He complained that he had lost two designers and was falling further and further behind. He concluded: "Dave, I know I said you could use Gamm for the Quad Sensor job, but I simply can't cut him loose. He's my most productive person, and if anyone can get us out from under this mess, he can. I know McCutcheon is just out of school, but he's bright. He's the only person I can spare, and I can only spare him because I haven't got the time to train him on how we operate around here—if you can call this 'operating.' "

The two men talked briefly about the poor communications and the inability of senior management to make up its collective mind. Then Dogers suggested, "Look, Tab, Quad Sensor is no more screwed up than usual for this stage of the project. How about this? I can let you borrow Charlotte Setter for three or four weeks. She's an excellent designer and she's working on a low-priority job that's not critical at the moment. Say, I'll bet I can talk Anderson into letting you borrow Levy, too, maybe half time for a month. Anderson owes me a favor."

"Great, Dave, that will help a lot, and I appreciate the aid. I know you understand my problem and you know that I understand yours." Baturi paused and then added, "You realize that this won't take much pressure off Jeff Gamm. If you can get him the designing help he needs he can get more done, but I can't release him for the amount of time you've got allocated for the Quad Sensor."

They sat quietly for a while, then Dogers said, "Hey, I've got an idea. Container design is the hard problem. The production setup and test design isn't all that tough. Let me have Gamm for the container design. I'll use McCutcheon for the rest of the project and get him trained for you. I can get Carol Mattson to show him how to set up the shock tests and he can get the word on the production setup from my senior engineer, Dick Money.

Baturi thought a moment. "Yeah, that ought to work," he said. "But Gamm will have to meet with your people to get back up to speed on the project. I think he will clean up Baker's biggest job by Wednesday. Could he meet with your people on Thursday?"

"Sure, I can arrange that," Dogers said.

Baturi continued. "This will mean putting two people on the package design. McCutcheon will have to work with Gamm if he is to learn anything. Can your budget stand it?"

"I'm not sure," Dogers said, "I don't really have any slack in that account, but . . ."

"Never mind," interrupted Baturi, "I can bury the added charge somewhere. I think I'll add it to Baker's charges. He deserves it. After all, he caused our problem."

SUMMARY

This chapter addressed the need for negotiation as a tool to resolve project conflicts. We discussed the nature of negotiation and its purpose in the organization. We also described various categories of conflict and related them to the project life cycle. We followed this by identifying a number of requirements and principles of negotiation. Finally, we presented a short vignette illustrating an actual negotiation situation.

Specific points made in the chapter were these:

- Negotiation within the firm should be directed at obtaining the best outcome for the organization, not winning.

- There are three traditional categories of conflict: goal-oriented, authority-based, and interpersonal.

- There are also three traditional sources of conflict. They are the project team itself, the client, and functional and senior management. We added the problem/discipline-orentation of people working on the project.

- Critical issues to handle in the project formation stages are delimiting technical objectives,

getting management commitment, setting the project's relative priority, and selecting the project organizational structure.

- The total level of conflict is highest during the project buildup stage.

- Scheduling and technical conflicts are most frequent and serious in the project buildup and main program stages, and scheduling conflicts in particular during the phaseout stage.

- Project negotiation requirements are that conflicts must be settled without permanent damage, the methodology must foster honesty, and the solution must satisfy both individuals' and the organization's needs.

- One promising approach to meeting the requirements of project negotiation is called principled negotiation.

This chapter concludes the subject of project initiation. In the next part of the text, we address project implementation, starting with the subject of budgeting. We look at various budgeting methods. The chapter also addresses the issue of cost estimation and its difficulty.

 GLOSSARY

Interfaces The boundaries between departments or functions.

Lateral Relations Communications across lines of equivalent authority.

Pareto-Optimal Solution A solution such that no party can be made better off without making another party worse off by the same amount or more.

Positional Negotiation Stating immediate wants on the assumption that the environment is static.

Principled Negotiation A process of negotiation that aims to achieve a win-win result.

Parties-at-interest Those who have a vested interest in the outcome of the negotiations.

Win-win When both parties are better off in the outcome.

 QUESTIONS

Material Review Questions

1. Review and justify the placement of the seven types of conflicts into the nine cells of Table 6-1.

2. Discuss each of the four fundamental issues for potential conflict during the project formation stage.

3. Identify the types of likely conflicts during the project buildup, main program, and phaseout stages.

4. What are the three main requirements of project negotiation?

5. Describe the four points of principled negotiation.

6. What is the objective of negotiation?

7. What are the four categories of conflict?

8. What is "principled negotiation"?

Class Discussion Questions

9. Summarize the vignette in the chapter in terms of the negotiation skill used. Comment on the appropriateness and ethical aspects related to "burying" the cost.

10. What will be the likely result of a win-win style manager negotiating with a win-lose style manager? What if they are both win-lose styled?

11. Reallocate the placement of the seven types of conflicts into the nine cells of Table 6-1 according to your own logic.

12. How does the type of project organization affect each of the types of conflicts that occur over the project life cycle?

13. Project managers are primarily concerned with project interfaces. At what rate do these interfaces increase with increasing project size?

14. The critical term in the concept of principled negotiation is "position." Elaborate on the multiple meanings of this term relative to negotiation. Can you think of a better term?

15. Give an example of a Pareto-optimal solution in a conflict.

16. Given that many conflicts are the result of different parties having different interests, is it possible to achieve a win-win situation?

17. The chairman of Cadbury Schweppes PLC, G.A.H. Cadbury, suggests [8] the following test for an ethical action: Would you be embarrassed to have it described in the newspaper? Is this a sufficient test for ethics? Can you think of any others?

Questions for Project Management in Practice

Selling New Area Codes to Consumers Who Don't Want Them

18. Did BellSouth's customers want new area codes or not? What was the true nature of the problem here?

19. Why did BellSouth have to change all the area codes instead of simply using the new codes for the new devices?

20. BellSouth employed a number of measures to communicate the need for change. In the end, what was probably the main reason their customers accepted the change?

A Consensus Feasibility Study for Montreal's Archipel Dam

21. Given the results of the study, did the consensus approach indeed lead to a solution acceptable to all? Why wasn't everyone happy with this outcome?

22. Based on this case situation, does the consensus approach lead to what is best for the overall community? Why (not)?

23. What approach should have been adopted to determine what was best for the overall community?

 INCIDENTS FOR DISCUSSION

Pritchard Soap Co.

Samantha ("Sam") Calderon is manager of a project that will completely alter the method of adding perfume to Pritchard Soap's "Queen Elizabeth" gift soap line. The new process will greatly extend the number of available scents and should result in a significant increase in sales. The project had been proceeding reasonably well, but fell several weeks behind when the perfume supplier, the Stephen Marcus Parfumissary, was unable to meet its delivery deadline because of a wildcat strike.

Under normal circumstances this would not have caused problems, but the project had been subject to a particularly long evaluation study and now was in danger of not being ready for the Christmas season. The major scheduling problem concerned Pritchard's toxicity lab. Kyle Lee, lab manager, had been most cooperative in scheduling the Queen Elizabeth perfumes for toxicity testing. He had gone out of his way to rearrange his own schedule to accommodate Sam's project. Because of the strike at Marcus, however, Sam cannot have the perfumes ready for test as scheduled, and the new test date Lee has given Sam will not allow her to make the new line available by Christmas. Sam suspects that the project might not have been approved if senior management had known that they would miss this year's Christmas season.

Questions: What are Sam's alternatives? What should she do?

Sutton Electronics

Eric Frank was still basking in the glory of his promotion to project manager for Sutton Electronics Corporation, manufacturer of fire alarm systems for motels, offices, and other large-scale installations. Eric's first project involved the development of an alarm system based on sophisticated circuitry that would detect and identify a large number of dangerous gases as well as smoke and very high temperatures. The device was the brainchild of Ira Magoo, vice-president of research and the technical wizard responsible for many of Sutton's most successful products

It was unusual for so young and relatively inexperienced an employee as Eric to be given control of such a potentially important project, but he had shown skill in handling several complex, though routine, jobs. In addition, he had the necessary scientific background to allow him to understand the nature of Magoo's proposed gas detection system.

Four weeks into the project, Eric was getting quite worried. He had tried to set up an organizational and basic planning meeting several times. No matter when he scheduled the meeting, the manager of the marketing department, Jaki Benken, was unable to attend. Finally, Eric agreed that marketing could be represented by young Bill Powell, a Benken protégé who had just graduated from college and joined Sutton Electronics. Eric was doubtful that Powell could contribute much to the project.

Eric's worry increased when Powell missed the first planning meeting completely and did not appear at the second meeting until it was almost over. Powell seemed apologetic and indicated that departmental crises had kept him away from both meetings. The project was now seven weeks old, and Eric was almost five weeks late with the master plan. He was thinking about asking Ira Magoo for help.

Questions: Do you think that Eric should involve Magoo at this point? If so, what outcome would you expect? If not, what should he do?

BIBLIOGRAPHY

1. ADAMS, J. R., and S. E. BARNDT. "Behavorial Implications of the Project Life Cycle." In D. I. Cleland, and W.R. King, eds., *Project Management Handbook.* New York: Van Nostrand Reinhold, 1983.

2. AFZALUR, R. M. *Managing Conflict in Organizations.* Westport, Ct: Praeger, 1992.

3. BAKER, K. R. "Measuring the Benefits of Partnering." *PM Network,* June 1996.

4. BAKER, S. T. "Partnering: Contracting for The Future." *Cost Engineering,* April 1990.

5. BEECHAM, M. A., and M. CORDEY-HAYES. "Partnering and knowledge transfer in the U.K. motor industry." *Technovation,* March 1998.

6. BROCKS, E., and G. S. ODIORNE. *Managing by Negotiation.* Melbourne, Fl: Krieger 1990.

7. BURTON, J. *Conflict Resolution and Prevention.* New York: St. Martins, 1990.

8. CADBURY, G. A. H. "Ethical Managers Make Their Own Rules." *Harvard Business Review,* September–October 1987.

9. COHEN, H. *You Can Negotiate Anything.* Secaucus, N.J.: Lyle Stuart Inc., 1980.

10. COWEN, C., C. GRAY, and E. W. LARSON. "Project Partnering." *Project Management Journal,* December 1992.

11. DE LAAT, P. B. "Matrix Management of Projects and Power Struggles: A Case Study of an R&D Laboratory." *IEEE Engineering Management Review,* Winter 1995, reprinted from *Human Relations,* vol. 47, no. 9, 1994.

12. DODSON, W. R. "Virtually International." *PM Network,* April 1998.

13. Dyer, W. G. *Team Building*, 2nd ed. Reading, MA: Addison-Wesley, 1987.

14. Fisher, R., and W. Ury. *Getting to Yes*. Harmondsworth, Middlesex, G.B.: Penguin Books, 1983.

15. Grossman, J. "Resolve Conflicts So Everybody Wins." *PM Network*, September 1995.

16. Hajek, V. G. *Management of Engineering Projects*, 3rd ed. New York: McGraw Hill, 1984.

17. Helpern, A. *Negotiating Skills*. Holmes Beach, FL: W. W. Gaunt, 1992.

18. Hughes, T. P. *Rescuing Prometheus*, New York: Pantheon, 1998.

19. Jandt, F. E. *Win-Win Negotiating*. New York: Wiley, 1987.

20. Larson, E. W., and J. A. Drexler, Jr. "Barriers to Project Partnering: Reports from the Firing Line." *Project Management Journal*, March 1997.

21. Larson, E. W. "Partnering on Construction Projects: A Study of the Relationship between Partnering Activities and Project Success." *IEEE Transactions on Engineering Management*, May 1997.

22. Long, A. "Negotiating the Right Decision." *PM Network*, December 1997.

23. Love, S. F. *Achieving Problem Free Project Management*. New York: Wiley, 1989.

24. Moore, C. C., J. D. Maes, and R. A. Shearer. "Recognizing and Responding to the Vulnerabilities of Partnering." *PM Network*, September 1995.

25. Nierenberg, G. I. *Fundamentals of Negotiating*. New York: HarperCollins, 1987.

26. Obrodovitch, M. M., and S. E. Stephenou. *Project Management: Risks and Productivity* (see Chapter 11, "Ethics"). Bend, OR: Daniel Spencer Pub., 1990.

27. Pelled, L. H., and P. S. Adler. "Antecedents of Intergroup Conflict in Multifunctional Product Development Teams: A Conceptual Model." *IEEE Transactions on Engineering Management*, February 1994.

28. Pill, J. *Technical Management and Control of Large Scale Urban Studies: A Comparative Analysis of Two Cases*. Ph.D. dissertation, Cleveland: Case Western Reserve University, 1971.

29. Pinto, J. K., and O. P. Kharbanda. "Project Management and Conflict Resolution." *Project Management Journal*, December 1995.

30. Raiffa, H. *The Art and Science of Negotiation*. Cambridge: Belknap/Harvard Press, 1982.

31. Reck, R., and B. G. Long. *The Win-Win Negotiator: How to Negotiate Favorable Agreements that Last*. Portage, MI: Spartan, 1987.

32. Robinson, T. "When Talking Makes Things Worse!" *PM Network*, March 1997.

33. *Roget's International Thesaurus*. New York: Thomas Y. Crowell, 1993.

34. Smith, M. B. "Financial Constraints on Service and Outsourcing Projects." *PM Network*, October 1998.

35. Tan, G. W., C. C. Hayes, and M. Shaw. "A Intelligent-Agent Framework for Concurrent Product Design and Planning." *IEEE Transactions on Engineering Management*, August 1996.

36. Thamhain, H. J., and D. L. Wilemon. "Conflict Management in Project Life Cycles." *Sloan Management Review*, Summer 1975.

37. Thamhain, H. J., and D. L. Wilemon. "Diagnosing Conflict Determinants in Project Management." *IEEE Transactions on Engineering Management*, February 1975.

38. Wall, J. A., Jr. *Negotiation: Theory and Practice*. Glenview, IL: Scott, Foresman, 1985.

39. Walles, T. K. "Enhancing Supplier Relationships." *PM Network*, October 1998.

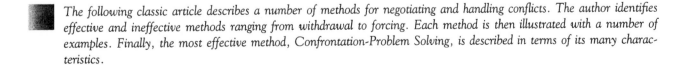

The following classic article describes a number of methods for negotiating and handling conflicts. The author identifies effective and ineffective methods ranging from withdrawal to forcing. Each method is then illustrated with a number of examples. Finally, the most effective method, Confrontation-Problem Solving, is described in terms of its many characteristics.

D I R E C T E D   R E A D I N G

METHODS OF RESOLVING INTERPERSONAL CONFLICT

R. J. Burke: Methods of Resolving Interpersonal Conflict. *Personnel Administration,* July–August 1969. ©1969 by the International Personnel Management Association. Reprinted by permission.

The management of conflict in creative and useful ways, rather than its containment or abolition, has been proposed by many writers. Various strategies for dealing with conflict at different levels and for managing disagreements have also been proposed. Most of these methods have not been experimentally evaluated. Given the central and inevitable role of conflict in human affairs, a high priority of importance is to be placed on learning the most effective way to resolve it.

Purpose of This Study

In a previous investigation, Burke (1969a) collected questionnaire data from 74 managers, in which they described the way they and their superiors dealt with conflict between them. It was possible to relate five different methods of conflict resolution originally proposed by Blake and Mouton (1964)—Withdrawing, Smoothing, Compromising, Forcing, and Confrontation or Problem Solving—to two major areas of the superior-subordinate relationship. These were (1) constructive use of differences and disagreements, and (2) several aspects of the superior-subordinate relationship in planning job targets and evaluating accomplishments.

In general, the results showed that Withdrawing and Forcing behaviors were consistently negatively related to these two areas. Compromising was not related to these two areas. Use of Smoothing was inconsistently related, sometimes positive and sometimes negative. Only Confrontation-Problem Solving was always related positively to both. That is, use of Confrontation was associated with constructive use of differences and high scores on various measures of the superior-subordinate relationship.

This study has the dual purpose of attempting to specify more precisely the characteristics of the Confrontation-Problem Solving method of conflict resolution, and replicating the earlier study (Burke, 1969a) using different methodology.

Method

Subjects: The respondents were managers from various organizations who were enrolled in a university course emphasizing behavioral science concepts relevant to the functions of management. Their organizational experience ranged from one year to over 30 years.

Procedure: Each respondent was asked to describe a time when he felt particularly GOOD (or BAD) about the way in which an interpersonal conflict was resolved. The specific instructions stated:

"Think of a time when you felt especially GOOD (or BAD) about the way an interpersonal conflict or disagreement (e.g., boss-subordinate, peer-peer, etc.) in which you were involved was resolved. It may have been on your present job, or any other job, or away from the work situation.

"Now describe it in enough detail so a reader would understand the way the conflict or differences were handled."

This statement appeared at the top of a blank sheet of paper.

Approximately half the respondents were first to describe the instance when they felt particularly good, followed by the instance when they felt particularly bad. The remaining respondents described the instances in the reverse order. No apparent effects were observed from the change in order, so the data from both groups will be considered together in this report.

Results

Fifty-three descriptions of effective resolution of conflict (felt especially GOOD) and 53 descriptions of ineffective resolutions of conflict (felt especially BAD) were obtained. These were provided by 57 different individuals. Some individuals provided only one example. The response rate was about 70 percent of the total available population.

The written descriptions were then coded into one of the five methods of conflict resolution proposed by Blake and Mouton (1964).

1. *Withdrawing*—easier to refrain than to retreat from an argument; silence is golden. "See no evil, hear no evil, speak no evil."

2. *Smoothing*—play down the differences and emphasize common interests; issues that might cause divisions or hurt feelings are not discussed.

3. *Compromising*—splitting the difference, bargaining, search for an intermediate position. Better half a loaf than none at all; no one loses but no one wins.

4. *Forcing*—a win-lose situation; participants are antagonists, competitors, not collaborators. Fixed positions, polarization. Creates a victor and a vanquished.

5. *Confrontation-Problem Solving*—open exchange of information about the conflict or problem as each sees it, and a working through of their differences to reach a solution that is optimal to both. Both can win.

Table 1 presents the method of conflict resolution associated with effective resolution (left half of Table 1) and ineffective resolution (right half of Table 1). Considering the left half of the table, Confrontation-Problem Solving was the most common method for effective resolution (58.5%), followed by Forcing

Table 1 Methods Associated with Effective and Ineffective Conflict Resolution

	Effective Resolution (N = 53)		Ineffective Resolution (N = 53)	
	N	%	N	%
Withdrawal	0	0.0*	5	9.4*
Smoothing	0	0.0	1	1.9
Compromise	6	11.3	3	5.7
Forcing	13	24.5*	42	79.2*
Confrontation-problem solving	31	58.5*	0	0.0*
Other (still unresolved; unable to determine how resolved; irrelevant to assignment; etc.)	3	5.7	2	3.8

*Percentage difference between groups is significant at the .05 level of confidence.

(24.5%), and Compromise (11.3%). The prominence of Confrontation as an effective method is consistent with the earlier study (Burke, 1969a) but the value for Forcing was higher than expected. When these 13 cases are considered as a group, 11 of them are similar in that the party providing the written description benefited as a result of the Forcing. That is, Forcing was perceived as an effective method of resolving conflict by the victor, but not by the vanquished.

Moving to the right half of Table 1, Forcing was the most commonly used method for ineffective resolution, followed in second place by Withdrawal with only 9.4 percent. The vast majority of individuals providing written descriptions of Forcing methods were victims or "losers" as a result of Forcing behavior.

In summary, the major differences in methods of conflict resolution found to distinguish effective versus ineffective examples were: (1) significantly greater use of Confrontation in the effective examples (58.5% vs. 0.0%); (2) significantly less use of Forcing in the effective examples (24.5% vs. 79.2%); and (3) significantly less use of Withdrawing in the effective examples (0.0% vs. 9.4%).

When Forcing was seen to be effective, the authors of the examples were "winners" of a win-lose conflict; when Forcing was seen to be ineffective, the authors of the examples were "losers" of a win-lose conflict. Whether the resolution of conflict via Forcing would actually be perceived to be effective by members of the organization outside the conflict (i.e., objectively seen as effective), as it was perceived to be effective by the "winners," remains to be determined by future research.

Effective Conflict Resolution

A few of the examples of effective conflict resolution are provided to highlight specific features of Confrontation. These were taken verbatim from the written descriptions.

1. *This example highlights the presentation of a problem of mutual interest—meeting deadlines more often at the earliest opportunity (when the problem is observed). Superior is open-minded and asking for help.*

"I once was given the responsibility for managing a small group of technicians engaged in turning out critical path schedules. I spent some time trying to get organized and involved with the group, but I sensed a hostile atmosphere, accompanied by offhand sarcastic remarks. At the end of the day very little work had been accomplished.

"The next day when I came in, I called the group together and told them that we were falling behind, and asked them to help me find a solution. After the initial distrust had been dissipated, the group produced some good ideas on work reallocation, office arrangement, priorities and techniques. I told the group that all of their agreed-upon suggestions would be implemented at once, and their reply was that the backlog would be cleared in three days and would not build up again.

"Within three days the backlog was gone, the group worked together better, and for the six months I was in charge, schedules were always ready before they were required."

2. *This example highlights emphasis on facts in determining the best resolution of conflict. Both had strong convictions but one willingly moved to the other's position when facts indicated that this position was best.*

"The project engineer and I disagreed about the method of estimating the cost of alternative schemes in a highway interchange. Neither of us could agree on the other's method. Eventually I was able to satisfy him using algebra. We were both happy with the result."

3. *Like Example 2, this one highlights an emphasis on facts and the conviction that by digging and digging, the truth will be discovered. Although the superior had a vested interest in the "old" system (a product of his thinking), the discussion was never personalized. That is, it did not involve "me" versus "you," but rather a comparison of two systems, two concepts or two ideas.*

"About a year ago I developed a new system for processing the accounting of the inventory of obsolete material on hand in our plant. It was my estimation that it would prove to be an easier system to operate and control and would also involve a considerable monetary saving for the company.

"When I approached my boss with the system, he immediately turned it down as he had developed the present system and was sure it was the best possible system. As I was sure my new system was superior to the present one, I then convinced him to join me in analyzing a comparison of the two systems, pointing out the strengths and weaknesses of the two. After a period of evaluation involving many differences of opinion, we were able to resolve that my system had definite merit and should be brought into operation."

4. *This example highlights the fact that through problem solving both parties can benefit. Instead of compromising, the issues are discussed until a solution completely satisfactory to both is found. Often this is superior to the ones initially favored by the separate parties.*

"In the—Board of Education, there were eight inspectors of Public Schools and four superintendents. Last February the inspectors were given the assignment of developing an in-service plan for the training of teachers for the school year 1968–69. The inspectors gave the assignment to a group of three of their number who were to bring a report to the next inspectors' meeting. I was not a member of the in-service committee but in conversations with the committee members I discovered that they contemplated having an in-service program for two teachers from each school (there are about 85 schools) once a month for the entire year in mathematics. I felt that this would be a very thin coverage of our 2000 or so teachers.

"Consequently I worked on a plan whereby utilizing two Thursday mornings a month and the specialized teaching help available in—, every teacher would have the opportunity to become involved in an in-service training session in a subject of his or her choice once during the year. At the inspectors' meeting the subcommittee presented its report and after some procedural wrangling I was permitted to present my plan. The two were diametrically opposed and it looked as if my plan would be voted down except the chairman suggested that both plans be presented to the superintendents.

"At the meeting of the superintendents, the subcommittee made its report and I presented my plan. As the meeting progressed there was some give and take and instead of one or the other being discarded both plans were adopted. For this school year mathematics is stressed for the first eight Thursday mornings (their plan in a rather concentrated form); then for the next eight months on the second and fourth Thursday my plan is used. We came out of this meeting with a combination of the two plans which was better than either one individually."

Ineffective Conflict Resolution

Examples 5, 6, and 7 illustrate Forcing methods of conflict resolution. A win-lose situation is set up, and usually the superior wins. The individual with the greater power triumphs (a personalized disagreement) rather than the one whose position is supported by the most factual evidence.

5. "In a previous job, I worked for a major management consulting group as a consultant. One assignment, lasting four months, was to use a simulation technique to evaluate the most preferable investment decision using defined quantitative criteria. At the end of the job two alternatives were shown to be marginally better than the other. However, later sensitivity tests also showed that the analytical technique could not rate one to be substantially better than the other.

"Therefore, I wrote a 'technically honest' report stating that our analysis could not provide the one best alternative. My manager, feeling that we were hired to recommend a 'one best' alternative, wanted to cover up the limitations of our methodology.

"We disagreed and I was overruled. The manager wrote a 'technically dishonest' version of the report and the revised report was sent to the client indicating the 'one best' alternative."

6. "Recently in my firm, management had sprung a secrecy agreement contract upon all of the technical people. No word of introduction or explanation was given. It was simply handed out and we were asked to sign it. Most of us found objection in several clauses in the agreement. However, management officials stated that the agreement would probably not stand up in a court of law. They further stated that it was something that was sent from corporate in the United States and was not their idea. The employees continued to show reluctance.

"The vice-president called on everyone individually and stated that there would be no room for advancement for anyone who did not sign the contract. As a result everyone signed."

7. "I was assigned a project by my boss to determine the optimum way, using predetermined times, to lay out an assembly line. It would have to provide optimum efficiency with the following variables: (a) different hourly production rates (e.g., 100/hr. Mon., 200/hr. Tues.) which would mean different numbers of operators on the line; (b) different models of the product (electric motors). The group was on group incentive.

"After much research and discussion, the system was installed utilizing the floating system of assembly (operators could move from station to station in order to keep out of the bottleneck operation). This system was working out well. However, at this time I was informed by my boss that he and the foreman of the area decided that they wished to use the 'paced' system of assembly. This would mean the conveyor belt would be run at set speeds and that the stripes would be printed on the belt indicating that one device would have to be placed on each mark and operators would not float.

"I was dead against this since I had considered it and rejected it in favor of the implemented method. I was,

however, given the order to use their proposed system or else. There was no opportunity for discussion or justification of the method."

8. *This example is a classic description of Withdrawal as a mode of conflict resolution. Clearly the problem is not resolved.*

"On the successful completion of a project which involved considerable time and effort, I was praised and thanked for a job well done by my immediate supervisor and his supervisor, the vice-president in charge of manufacturing. They promised me that on my next salary review I would receive a substantial increase.

"The next salary review came up and my immediate supervisor submitted an amount that he and I felt was a good increase. The amount I received was one-third of this figure. I felt insulted, cheated, and hurt that the company considered I was worth this 'token' amount.

"I had a personal interview with the vice-president where I argued that I felt I should receive more. He agreed in sort of an offhanded way—he felt the whole salary schedule should be reviewed and that my area of responsibility should be increased. He said the company wants people to 'prove themselves' before they give them increases; and he suggested a salary review. I felt I had just done this in my last project—I felt I was being put off, but agreed to the salary review.

"One month passed and nothing happened. I became frustrated—I purposely slowed down the amount of work I turned out.

"Another month passed and still no action. I became disillusioned with the company and resolved at this point to look for another position. Several months later with still no action, I resigned and accepted another position."

Inability to Resolve Conflict

These descriptions of ineffective resolution of conflict indicate that an impressive number of respondents included termination or change of employment of one member in the situation (19 of 53, 26%). These cases tended to be of two types.

The first is represented by Example 8. Here an employee decides to quit because he felt the problem was not resolved in a satisfactory manner. Forcing is likely to be associated with instances of voluntary termination.

The second centered around an inability to resolve the conflict. Then the "problem employee" (a visible symptom of the conflict) was dismissed.

9. *The following example illustrates this:*

"This concerned a young girl about 18 years old who was a typist in our office. This girl lacked a little maturity, but was not really all that bad. She was tuned to all the latest fashions in both dress and manners.

"I felt and still feel that this girl was a potentially good employee. But it was decided that she should be let go. The argument used was that she was not a good worker and lacked the proper attitude for office work. Rather than spend a little time and effort to understand the girl and perhaps develop her into a good employee, the easy way was taken and the girl was fired."

There were two other clear cases of "effective" conflict resolution resulting in voluntary employee terminations. In both instances a Forcing mode was employed and the "loser" resigned from the organization soon after. Our finding is that these were given as examples of effective conflict resolution by the "winner." In another effective example of Forcing, the "loser" was dismissed.

Conclusions

The results of this investigation are consistent with an earlier study (Burke, 1969a), and the data of Lawrence and Lorsch (1967a, 1967b) in showing the value of Confrontation-Problem Solving as a method of conflict resolution. About 60 percent of the examples of effective conflict resolution involved use of the method, while no examples of ineffective conflict resolution did. The poorest method of conflict resolution was Forcing. This method accounted for 80 percent of the examples of ineffective conflict resolution and only 24 percent of the examples of effective conflict resolution.

The latter conclusion is somewhat at odds with Lawrence and Lorsch's findings that Forcing was an effective backup method to Confrontation, from an organizational effectiveness standpoint. In fact, the earlier study (Burke, 1969a) found that the use of these methods tended to be negatively correlated. Managers high in use of one of them tended to be low in use of the other.

Characteristics of Problem Solving

Let us now consider more specific features of Confrontation, the most effective method of resolving interpersonal conflict. Insights from the present investigation and the writings of others (e.g., Blake, Shepard and Mouton, 1964; Maier, 1963; Maier and Hoffman, 1965) becomes relevant. The following then are characteristics of Confrontation as a method of managing conflict:

(1) Both people have a vested interest in the outcome. (Examples 1, 2, 3, and 4).

(2) There is a belief on the part of the people involved that they have the potential to resolve the conflict and to achieve a better solution through collaboration.

(3) There is a recognition that the conflict or the problem is mainly in the relationship between the individuals and not in each person separately. If the conflict is in the relationship, it must be defined by those who have the relationship. In addition, if solutions are to be developed, the solutions have to be generated by those who share the responsibility for assuring that the solution will work and for making the relationship last.

(4) The goal is to solve the problem, not to accommodate different points of view. This process identifies the causes of reservation, doubt, and misunderstanding between the people confronted with conflict and disagreement. Alternative ways of approaching conflict resolution are explored and tested (Examples 2 and 3).

(5) The people involved are problem-minded instead of solution-minded; "fluid" instead of "fixed" positions. Both parties jointly search out the issues that separate them. Through joint effort, the problems that demand solutions are identified, and later solved.

(6) There is a realization that both aspects of a controversy have potential strengths and potential weaknesses. Rarely is one position completely right and the other completely wrong. (Example 4).

(7) There is an effort to understand the conflict or problem from the other person's point of view, and from the standpoint of the "real" or legitimate needs that must be recognized and met before problem solving can occur. Full acceptance of the other is essential.

(8) The importance of looking at the conflict objectively rather than in a personalized sort of way is recognized. (Example 3).

(9) An examination of one's own attitudes (hostilities, antagonisms) is needed before interpersonal contact on a less effective basis has a chance to occur.

(10) An understanding of the less effective methods of conflict resolution (e.g., win-lose, bargaining, etc.) is essential.

(11) One needs to present "face-saving" situations. Allow people to "give" so that a change in one's viewpoint does not suggest weakness or capitulation.

(12) There is need to minimize effects of status differences, defensiveness, and other barriers which prevent people from working together effectively.

(13) It is important to be aware of the limitations of arguing or presenting evidence in favor of your own position while downgrading the opponent's position. This behavior often stimulates the opponent to find even greater support for his position (increased polarization). In addition, it leads to selective listening for weaknesses in the opponent's position rather than listening to understand his or her position.

Attitude, Skill, and Creativity

Two related themes run through these characteristics, one dealing with attitudes, and the other with skills (interpersonal, problem solving) of the individuals involved. As the research of Maier and his associates has shown, differences and disagreements need not lead to dissatisfaction and unpleasant experiences but rather can lead to innovation and creativity. One of the critical variables was found to be the leader's attitudes toward disagreement. The person with different ideas, especially if he or she is a subordinate, can be seen as a problem employee and troublemaker or as an innovator, depending on the leader's attitude.

There are some people that go through life attempting to sell their ideas, to get others to do things they do not want to do. They set up a series of win-lose situations, and attempt to emerge victorious. Many of these people are able to accomplish their ends. There are others who are more concerned with the quality and effectiveness of their operations, and who, with creative solutions to problems, are genuinely open-minded and able and willing to learn from others (and to teach others), in a collaborative relationship.

The interpersonal skills are related to the development of a "helping relationship" and include among other things, mutual trust and respect, candid communication, and awareness of the needs of others. The problem solving skills center around locating and stating the problem, seeking alternatives, exploring and testing alternatives, and selecting the best alternative. Knowledge and insight gained through experience with the benefits of problem solving and the dysfunctional effects of other strategies would be valuable in developing interpersonal skills.

Further Research Needed

Two additional areas need immediate research consideration. The first needs to explore the notions of conflict resolution from the organizational as well as the individual viewpoint. Lawrence and Lorsch report that Forcing was an effective back-up mode to Confrontation from the organization's standpoint, because at least things were being done. Our data in two separate investigations indicate that this mode of conflict resolution is very unsatisfactory from the standpoint of the one forced, the "loser," and may also have dysfunctional consequences.

The second research area concerns the application of these principles of effective conflict resolution (Confrontation-Problem Solving, with their more specific attitudinal and skill components) in an attempt to arrive at more constructive use of disagreement. Preliminary results from an experiment simulating conflict situations using role playing suggest that knowledge of these principles and some limited practice in their use increases one's ability to use differences constructively in obtaining a quality solution, and decreases the tendency to engage in "limited war" (Burke, 1969b).

References

BLAKE, R. R., and J. S., MOUTON. *The Managerial Grid*, Houston: Gulf Publishing Company, 1964.

BLAKE, R. R., H. A. SHEPARD, and J. S MOUTON. *Managing Intergroup Conflict in Industry*, Houston: Gulf Publishing Company, 1964.

BOULDING, K. "A pure theory of conflict applied to organization." In R. I. Kahn and E. Boulding (eds.), *Power and Conflict in Organizations*. New York: Basic Books, Inc., 1964, pp. 136–145.

BURKE, R. J. "Methods of managing superior-subordinate conflict: Their effectiveness and consequences." Unpublished manuscript, 1969a.

BURKE, R. J. "Effects of limited training on conflict resolution effectiveness." Unpublished manuscript, 1969b.

KATA, D. "Approaches to managing conflict." In R. L. Kahn and E. Boulding (eds.), *Power and Conflict in Organizations*. New York: Basic Books, Inc., 1964, pp. 105–114.

LAWRENCE, P. R., and J. W. LORSCH. "Differentiation and intergration in complex organizations." *Administrative Science Quarterly*, 1967a, 12, 1–47.

LAWRENCE, P. R., and J. W LORSCH. *Organization and Environment*, Boston: Division of Research, Harvard Business School, Harvard University, 1967b.

MAIER, N. R. F. *Problem-Solving Discussions and Conferences.* New York: McGraw-Hill, 1963.

MAIER, N. R. F., and L. R. HOFFMAN. "Acceptance and quality of solutions as related to leaders' attitudes toward disagreement in group problem-solving." *Journal of Applied Behavioral Science*, 1965, 1, pp. 373–386.

McGREGOR, D. *The Professional Manager.* New York: McGraw-Hill, 1967.

SHEPARD, H. A. "Responses to situations of competition and conflict." In R. L. Kahn and E. Boulding (eds.), *Power and Conflict in Organizations.* New York: Basic Books, Inc., 1964, pp. 127–135.

Questions

1. In Table 1, what was the second best resolution technique? What was the worst resolution technique? What do you conclude from this?

2. Which of the four examples of conflict resolution is the best example, in your opinion, of effective resolution? Why?

3. Of the ineffective resolution examples, which was the worst, in your opinion? Why?

4. Summarize or condense the 13 characteristics of Confrontation as a conflict-resolving method.

5. The article concludes on the note that conflict need not be a bad thing. Compare this view with that in the chapter concerning the win-win approach to negotiation.

7

Budgeting and Cost Estimation

In Chapter 5 we reviewed the planning process, gave some guidelines for designing the project plan, and in Chapter 6 we discussed the conflicts arising around the project plan and its implementation. We proposed win-win negotiation and other conflict resolution techniques to deal with these conflicts.

We are now ready to begin implementation. First priority is, of course, obtaining resources with which to do the work. Senior management approval of the project budget does exactly that. A budget is a plan for allocating resources. Thus, the act of budgeting is the allocation of scarce resources to the various endeavors of an organization. The outcomes of the allocation process often do not satisfy managers of the organization who must live and work under budget constraints. It is, however, precisely the pattern of constraints in a budget that embodies organizational policy. The degree to which the different activities of an organization are fully supported by an allocation of resources is one measure of the importance placed on the outcome of the activity. Most of the senior managers we know try hard to be even-handed in the budgetary process, funding each planned activity at the "right" level—neither overfunding, which produces waste and encourages slack management, nor underfunding, which inhibits accomplishment and frustrates the committed. (This is not to suggest that subordinate managers necessarily agree with our assessment.)

The budget is not simply one facet of a plan, nor is it merely an expression of organizational policy; it is also a control mechanism. The budget serves as a standard for comparison, a baseline from which to measure the difference between the actual and planned uses of resources. As the manager directs the deployment of resources to accomplish some desired objective, resource usage should be monitored carefully. This allows deviations from planned usage to be checked against the progress of the project, and exception reports can be generated if resource expenditures are not consistent with accomplishments. Indeed, the pattern of deviations (variances) can be examined to see if it is possible, or reasonable, to forecast significant departures from budget. With sufficient warning, it is sometimes possible to implement corrective actions. In any event, such forecasting helps to decrease the number of undesirable surprises for senior management.

Budgets play an important role in the entire process of management. It is clear that budgeting procedures must associate resource use with the achievement of organizational goals or the planning/control process becomes useless. If budgets are not tied to achievement, management may ignore situations where funds are being spent far in advance of accomplishment but are within budget when viewed by time period. Similarly, management may misinterpret the true state of affairs when the budget is overspent for a given time period but outlays are appropriate for the level of task completion. Data must be collected and reported in a timely manner, or the value of the budget in identifying and reporting current problems or anticipating upcoming problems will be lost. The reporting process must be carefully designed and controlled. It is of no value if the data are sent to the wrong person or the reports take an inordinately long time to be processed through the system. For example, one manager of a large computer company complained that, based on third-quarter reports, he was instructed to act so as to alter the fourth-quarter results. However, he did not receive the instructions until the first quarter of the following year.

In Chapter 5 we described a planning process that integrated the planning done at different levels of the project. At the top level is the overall project plan, which is then divided and divided again and, perhaps, still again into a "nest" of plans. Project plans were shown to be the verbal equivalents of the WBS. If we cost the WBS, step by step, we develop a project budget. If we cost project plans, we achieve exactly the same end. Viewed in this way, *the budget is simply the project plan in another form.*

Let us now consider some of the various budgeting methods used in organizations. These are described in general first, then with respect to projects. We also address some problems of cost estimation, with attention to the details and pitfalls. We consider some of the special demands and concerns with budgeting for projects. Throughout the chapter attention is paid to dealing with budgetary risk, although the methods of handling risk will be covered in greater detail in Chapter 8. Finally, we present a method for improving one's skills at budget estimation, or estimation and forecasting of any kind. Printouts of project budgets from PM software packages will be shown in Chapter 10 where we cover project management information systems.

Project Management in Practice
Pathfinder Mission to Mars—on a Shoestring

The Pathfinder Rover explores Martian terrain.

In 1976, NASA's two Viking Mars-lander missions took six years and $3 billion (in 1992 dollars) to develop. Twenty-one years later, on July 4, 1997, Mars Pathfinder and Sojourner Rover landed on Mars once again, but at a development cost of only $175 million, representing a whopping 94 percent cost reduction over the earlier mission. This amazing cost reduction was achieved through a variety of means but the most important was perhaps the philosophical one that this was a design-to-cost project rather than a design-to-performance project. Given this philosophy, the scope of the mission was intentionally limited and "scope-creep" was never an issue:

- to achieve a successful landing
- return of engineering telemetry
- acquisition and transmission of a *single*, partial panoramic image
- successful rover deployment and 7 sol (Martian day) operation on the surface
- completion of a 30 sol lander mission meeting all engineering, science, and technology objectives
- *one* successful alpha proton X-ray spectrometer measurement of a Martian rock and soil sample.

The means of limiting the cost of the mission were multiple and creative:

- development was cost-capped, with no opportunity for more funds
- identifying a set of "de-scope" options which could be implemented in case the cost grew beyond the fixed budget
- mission, flight, and ground systems designs were driven by existing hardware and system capability
- a project cash reserve of 27 percent of the total budget was held back and carefully planned for time-phased release throughout the duration of the project
- mission designers/builders transitioned into the testers/operators to save documentation, time, labor cost, and chance of error
- existing NASA mission infrastructure was used rather than designing new systems

Source: C. Sholes and N. Chalfin, "Mars Pathfinder Mission," *PM Network*, January 1999, pp. 30–35.

- instituting time-phased "what if" and lien lists for real or potential current and anticipated items of cost growth during the project
- choosing to use a "single-string" but higher risk design and offsetting the risk by using more reliable parts
- 70 percent of major procurements contracts were fixed-price rather than cost-plus
- creative procurement, such as existing equipment spares, and accounting, such as lower burden rate personnel

On July 5, the Mars Sojourner Rover rolled down its deployment ramp and the resulting pictures made the headlines on newspapers around the world. The mission continued for almost three months and returned 2.6 gigabites of scientific and engineering data, 16,000 lander camera images, 550 rover camera images, 8.5 million environmental measurements, and the results of 16 chemical rock/soil experiments and 10 technology rover experiments.

7.1 ESTIMATING PROJECT BUDGETS

In order to develop a budget, we must forecast what resources the project will require, the required quantity of each, when they will be needed, and how much they will cost—including the effects of potential price inflation. Uncertainty is involved in any forecast, though some forecasts have less uncertainty than others. An experienced cost estimator can forecast the number of bricks that will be used to construct a brick wall of known dimensions within 1 to 2 percent. (The estimator knows almost exactly how many bricks are needed to build the wall and must simply add a small allowance for broken or discolored bricks being delivered to the job, plus a few more for bricks broken during construction work.) On the other hand, the errors are apt to be much larger for an estimate of the number of programmer hours or lines of code that will be required to produce a specific piece of software (see Section 7.2). While the field of software science makes such estimations quite possible, the level of uncertainty is considerably higher and the typical error size is much larger.

In many fields, cost estimation methods are well codified. The office walls of organizational purchasing departments are lined with catalogues detailing what materials, services, and machines are available, from whom, and at what prices. Also on the bookshelves are volumes devoted to the techniques of estimating the quantities of materials and labor required to accomplish specific jobs. Every business has its own rules of thumb for cost estimation. These usually distill the collective experience gained by many estimators over many years. An experienced producer of books, for example, can leaf through a manuscript and, after asking a few questions about the number and type of illustrations and the quality of paper to be used, can make a fairly accurate estimate of what it will cost to produce a book.

At times, the job of cost estimation for entire complex projects may be relatively simple because experience has shown that some formula gives a good *first approximation* of the project's cost. For example, the Goodyear Aircraft Company makes an initial estimate of the cost of building a blimp by multiplying the estimated weight of the blimp by a specific dollar factor. (The weight is estimated in pounds, presumably prior to the blimp's inflation with helium.) The cost of buildings is commonly estimated as dollars per square foot times the square feet of floor area. Obviously these approximations must be adjusted for any special characteristics associated with each individual project, but this adjustment is far easier than making an estimate from scratch.

We will have more to say about gathering data shortly. Before doing so, however, and before discussing budget construction and presentation, it is helpful to understand that developing project budgets is much more difficult than developing budgets for more permanent organizational activities. The influence of history is strong in the budget of an ongoing activity, and many entries may ultimately become just "last year's figure plus X percent," where X is any number the budgeter feels "can be lived with" and is probably acceptable to the person or group who approves the budgets. No single item in the budget for an ongoing activity is apt to be crucial, because over the course of years the budget has gained sufficient slack that internal adjustments will probably take care of minor shortages in the key accounts.

But the project budgeter cannot depend on tradition. At project inception, there may be no past budgets to use as a base. At times, the budgeter may have budgets and audit reports for similar projects to serve as guides, but these are rough guides at best. In any case, all projects are unique and all project budgets are based on *forecasts* of resource usage and the associated costs. Thus estimating costs for any project involves risk. Tradition, however, has another impact on budgeting, this time a helpful one. In the special case of R & D projects, it has been found [15] that project budgets are stable over time when measured as a percent of the total allocation to R & D from the parent firm, though within the project the budget may be reallocated among activities. There is no reason to believe that the situation is different for other kinds of projects, and we have some evidence that shows stability similar to R & D projects.

For multiyear projects, another problem is raised. The plans and schedules for such projects are set at the beginning of project life, but over the years, the forecast resource usage may be altered by the availability of alternate or new materials, machinery, or personnel—available at different costs than were estimated. The longer the project life, the less the PM can trust that traditional methods and costs will be relevant. As if that were not enough, the degree of executive oversight and review is usually much higher for projects than for ongoing operations, so the budgeter must expect to defend any and all budget entries.

Tradition has still another impact on project budgeting. Every organization has its idiosyncrasies. One firm charges the project's R & D budget with the cost of training sales representatives on the technical aspects of a new product. Another adopts special property accounting practices for contracts with the government. Unless the PM understands the organizational accounting system, there is no way to exercise budgetary control over the project. The methods for project budgeting described below are intended to avoid these problems as much as possible, but complete avoidance is out of the question. Further, it is not politically feasible for the PM to plead a special case with the accountants, who have their own problems. The PM simply must be familiar with the organization's accounting system!

One aspect of cost estimation and budgeting that is not often discussed has to do with the *actual* use of resources as opposed to the accounting department's assumptions about how and when the resources will be used. For instance, presume that you have estimated that $5000 of a given resource will be used in accomplishing a task that is estimated to require five weeks. The actual use of the resource may be none in the first week, $3000 worth in the second week, none in the third week, $1500 in the fourth week, and the remaining $500 in the last week. Unless this pattern of expenditure is detailed in the plan, the accounting department, which takes a linear view of the world, will spread the expenditure equally over the five-week period. This may not affect the project's budget, but it most certainly affects the project's cash flow. The PM must be aware of both the resource requirements and the specific time pattern of resource usage. The subject will be mentioned again in Chapter 9.

Another aspect of preparing budgets is especially important for project budgeting. Every expenditure (or receipt) must be identified with a specific project task (and with its associated milestone, as we will see in the next chapter). Referring back to Figure 5-6, we see that each element in the WBS has a unique account number to which charges are accrued as work is done. These identifiers are needed for the PM to exercise budgetary control.

With these things in mind, the issue of how to gather input data for the budget becomes a matter of some concern. There are two fundamentally different strategies for data gathering, top-down and bottom-up.

Top-Down Budgeting

This strategy is based on collecting the judgments and experiences of top and middle managers, and available past data concerning similar activities. These managers estimate overall project cost as well as the costs of the major subprojects that comprise it. These cost estimates are then given to lower-level managers, who are expected to continue the breakdown into budget estimates for the specific tasks and work packages that comprise the subprojects. This process continues to the lowest level.

The process parallels the hierarchical planning process described in the last chapter. The budget, like the project, is broken down into successively finer detail, starting from the top, or most aggregated level following the WBS. It is presumed that lower-level managers will argue for more funds if the budget allocation they have been granted is, in their judgment, insufficient for the tasks assigned. This presumption is, however, often incorrect. Instead of reasoned debate, argument sometimes ensues, or simply sullen silence. When senior managers insist on maintaining their budgetary positions—based on "considerable past experience"—junior managers feel forced to accept what they perceive to be insufficient allocations to achieve the objectives to which they must commit.

Discussions between the authors and a large number of managers support the contention that lower-level managers often treat the entire budgeting process as if it were a zero-sum game, a game in which any individual's gain is another individual's loss. Competition among junior managers is often quite intense.

The advantage of this top-down process is that aggregate budgets can often be developed quite accurately, though a few individual elements may be significantly in error. Not only are budgets stable as a percent of total allocation, the statistical distribution of the budgets is also stable, making for high predictability [15]. Another advantage of the top-down process is that small yet costly tasks need not be individually identified, nor need it be feared that some small but important aspect has been overlooked. The experience and judgment of the executive is presumed automatically to factor all such elements into the overall estimate.

Bottom-Up Budgeting

In this method, elemental tasks, their schedules, and their individual budgets are constructed, again following the WBS. The people doing the work are consulted regarding times and budgets for the tasks to ensure the best level of accuracy. Initially, estimates are made in terms of resources, such as labor hours and materials. These are later converted to dollar equivalents. Standard analytic tools such as learning curve analysis (discussed in the next section) and work sampling are employed where appropriate to improve the estimates. Differences of opinion are resolved by the usual discussions between senior and junior managers. If necessary, the project manager and the functional manager(s) may enter the discussion in order to ensure the accuracy of the estimates. The resulting task budgets are aggregated to give the total direct costs of the project. The PM adds such indirect costs as general and administrative (G&A), possibly a project reserve for contingencies, and then a profit figure to arrive at the final project budget.

Bottom-up budgets should be, and usually are, more accurate in the detailed tasks, but it is critical that all elements be included. It is far more difficult to develop a complete list of tasks when constructing that list from the bottom up than from the top down. Just as the top-down method may lead to budgetary game playing, the bottom-up process has its unique managerial budget games. For example, individuals overstate their resource needs because they suspect that higher management will probably cut all budgets. Their suspicion is, of course, quite justified, as Gagnon [17, 18] and others have shown. Managers who are particularly persuasive sometimes win, but those who are consistently honest and have high credibility win more often.

The advantages of the bottom-up process are those generally associated with participative management. Individuals closer to the work are apt to have a more accurate idea of resource requirements than their superiors or others not personally involved. In addition, the direct involvement of low-level managers in budget preparation increases the likelihood that they will accept the result with a minimum of grumbling. Involvement also is a good managerial training technique, giving junior managers valuable experience in budget preparation as well as the knowledge of the operations required to generate a budget.

While top-down budgeting is common, true bottom-up budgets are rare. Senior managers see the bottom-up process as risky. They tend not to be particularly trusting of ambitious subordinates who may overstate resource requirements in an attempt to ensure success and build empires. Besides, as senior managers note with some justification, the budget is the most important tool for control of the organization. They are understandably reluctant to hand over that control to subordinates whose experience and motives are questionable. This attitude is carried to an extreme in one large corporation that conducts several dozen projects simultaneously, each of which may last five to eight years and cost millions of dollars. Project managers do not participate in the budgeting process in this company, nor do they have access to project budgets during their tenure as PMs. (In the past few years, the firm has decided to give PMs access to project budgets, but they are still not allowed to participate in the budgetary process.)

Work Element Costing

The actual process of building a project budget—either top-down or bottom-up or, as we will suggest, a combination of both—tends to be a straightforward but tedious process. Each work element in the action plan or WBS is evaluated for its resource requirements, and the cost of each resource is estimated.

Suppose a work element is estimated to require 25 hours of labor by a technician. The specific technician assigned to this job is paid $17.50/hr. Overhead changes to the project are 84 percent of direct labor charges. The appropriate cost appears to be

$$25 \text{ hr} \times \$17.50 \times 1.84 = \$805.00$$

but the accuracy of this calculation depends on the precise assumptions behind the 25-hr estimate. Industrial engineers have noted that during a normal eight hour day, no one actually works for all eight hours. Even on an assembly line, workers need breaks called "personal time." This covers such activities as visiting the water cooler, the toilet, having a cigarette, blowing one's nose, and all the other time consuming activities engaged in by normal people in a normal workplace. A typical allowance for personal time is 12% of total work time. If personal time was not included in the 25 hr estimate, then the cost calculation becomes

$$1.12 \times 25 \text{ hr} \times \$17.50 \times 1.84 = \$901.60*$$

Direct costs for resources and machinery are charged directly to the project, and are not usually subject to overhead charges. If a specific machine is needed by the project and is the property of a functional department, the project may "pay" for it by transferring funds from the project budget to the functional department's budget. The charge for such machines will be an operating cost ($/hr or $/operating cycle), plus a depreciation charge based on either time or number of operating cycles. Use of general office equipment, e.g., copy machines, drafting equipment, and coffeemakers, is often included in the general overhead charge.

In addition to these charges, there is also the *General and Administrative (G&A)* charge. This is composed of the cost of senior management, the various staff functions, and any other expenses not included in overhead. G&A charges are a fixed percent of either the direct costs or the total of all direct and indirect costs.

Thus, a fully costed work element would include direct costs (labor, resources, and

---

*In a weak matrix project, the Technical Assistance Group (TAG) would submit a lump-sum charge to the project, calculated in much the same way. The charge would, of course, include the costs noted in the rest of this section.

special machinery) plus overhead and G&A charges. We advise the PM to prepare two budgets, one with overheads and G&A charges, and one without. The full cost budget is used by the accounting group to estimate the profit earned by the project. The budget that contains only direct costs gives the PM the information required to manage the project without being confounded with costs over which the PM has no control. Let us now consider a combination of top-down and bottom-up budgeting.

An Iterative Budgeting Process—Negotiation-in-Action

In Chapter 5, we recommended an iterative planning process with subordinates* developing action plans for the tasks for which they were responsible. Superiors review these plans, perhaps suggesting amendments. (See also the latter part of Section 5.3.) The strength of this planning technique is that primary responsibility for the design of a task is delegated to the individual accountable for its completion, and thus it utilizes participative management (or "employee involvement"). If done correctly, estimated resource usage and schedules are a normal part of the planning process at all planning levels. Therefore, the individual concocting an action plan at the highest level would estimate resource requirements and durations for each of the steps in the highest level action plan. Let us refer to these as r_i and t_i, the resource level and task time requirements for the ith task, respectively. Similarly, the subordinate estimates the resource and time requirements for each step of the lower-level action plan. Let us denote the *aggregate* resource and time requirements for the lower level action plan as r_i' and t_i', respectively.

In a perfect world, r_i would equal r_i'. (As regards t_i and t_i', our argument holds for duration estimates as well as resource estimates.) We do not, however, live in a perfect world. As a matter of fact, the probable relationship between the original estimates made at the different levels is $r_i \ll r_i'$. This is true for several reasons, three of which are practically universal. First, as Gagnon has found [17], the farther one moves up the organizational chart away from immediate responsibility for doing the work, the easier, faster, and cheaper the job looks to the superior than to the one who has to do it. This is because the superior either does not know the details of the task, or has conveniently forgotten the details, as well as how long the job takes and how many problems can arise. Second, wishful thinking leads the superior to underestimate cost (and time), because the superior has a stake in representing the project to senior management as a profitable venture. Third, the subordinate is led to build-in some level of protection against failure by adding an allowance for "Murphy's Law" onto a budget that already has a healthy contingency allowance.

Assuming that the superior and subordinate are reasonably honest with one another (any other assumption leads to a failure in win-win negotiations), the two parties meet and review the subordinate's action plan. Usually, the initial step toward reducing the difference in cost estimates is made by the superior who is "educated" by

---

*We use the terms "superior" and "subordinate" here for the sole purpose of identifying individuals working on different relative levels of a project's set of action plans. We recognize that in a matrix organization it is not uncommon for PMs ("superiors") to delegate work to individuals ("subordinates") who do not report to the PM and who may be senior to the PM on the parent firm's organizational chart.

the subordinate in the realities of the job. The result is that r_i rises. The next step is typically made by the subordinate. Encouraged by the boss's positive response to reason, the subordinate surrenders some of protection provided for by the budgetary "slop," and r_i' falls. The subordinate's cost estimate is still greater than the superior's, but the difference is considerably decreased.

The pair now turn their attention to the technology of the task at hand. They carefully inspect the subordinate's work plan, trying to find a more efficient way to accomplish the desired end; that is, they practice total quality management (TQM) and/or value engineering. It may be that a major change can be made that allows a lower resource commitment than either originally imagined. It may be that little or no further improvement is possible. Let us assume that moderate improvement is made, but that r_i' is still somewhat greater than r_i, although both have been altered by the negotiations thus far. What should the superior do, accept the subordinate's estimate or insist that the subordinate make do with r_i? In order to answer this question, we must digress and reconsider the concept of the project life cycle.

In Chapter 1, we presented the usual view of the project life cycle in Figure 1-3, shown here as Figure 7-1 for convenience. This view of the life cycle shows decreasing returns to inputs as the project nears completion. Figure 1-5 is also shown here as Figure 7-2 for convenience. In this case, the project shows increasing return to inputs as the project nears completion. In order to decide whether to adopt the subordinate's resource estimate, r_i', or the superior's, r_i, we need to know which picture of the life cycle is representative of the task under consideration. Note that we are treating the subordinate's action plan as if it were a project, which is perfectly all right because it has the characteristics of a project that were described in Chapter 1. Also note that we do not need to know the shape of the life cycle with any precision, merely if its last stage is concave or convex to the horizontal axis.

Remember that the superior's and subordinate's resource estimates are not very

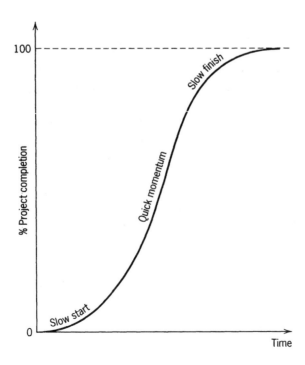

Figure 7-1 The project life cycle (Figure 1-3 reproduced).

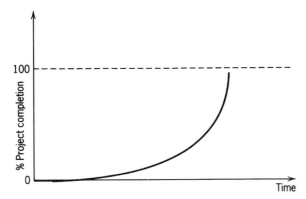

Figure 7-2   Another possible project life cycle (Figure 1-5 reproduced).

far apart as a result of the negotiations preceding this decision. If the latter part of the life-cycle curve is concave (as in Figure 7-1), showing diminishing marginal returns, we opt for the superior's estimate because of the small impact on completion that results from withholding a small amount of resources. The superior might say to the subordinate, "Jeremy, what can you get me for r_i? We will have to live with that." If, on the other hand, the life cycle curve is convex, showing increasing marginal returns as in Figure 7-2, the subordinate's estimate should be chosen because of the potentially drastic effect a resource shortage would have on project completion. In this event, the superior might say, "OK, Brandon, we have got to be sure of this job. We'll go with your numbers." If the disagreement had concerned schedule (duration) instead of resources, the negotiation process and underlying logic would be unaltered.

This is a time-consuming process. At the same time the PM is negotiating with the several subordinates responsible for the pieces of the PM's action plan, each of the subordinates are negotiating with their subordinates, and so on. This multilevel process is messy and not particularly efficient, but it allows a free-flow of ideas up and down the system at all levels.

It is worth noting that ethics is just as important in negotiations within an organization as in negotiations between an organization and an outside party. In this case, the superior and subordinate have the responsibility to be honest with each other. For one thing, they must continue to work together in the future under the conditions of mutual trust. Second, it is ethically necessary to be honest in such negotiations.

Comments on the Budget Request Process

The budget process often begins with an invitation from top management for each division to submit a *budget request* for the coming year. Division heads pass the invitation along to departments, sections, and subsections, each of which presumably collects requests from below, aggregates them, and passes the result back up the organizational ladder.

This sounds like bottom-up budgeting, but there is an important difference between this procedure and a true bottom-up system. Along with the formal invitation for submission of a budget request, in the iterative system another message is passed down—a much less formal message that carries the following kinds of information: the percent by which the wage bill of the organization will be allowed to be increased, organizational policy on adding to the work force, the general attitude toward capital expenditures, knowledge about which projects and activities are considered to be high priority and which are not, and a number of other matters that, in effect, prescribe a set of limits on lower-level managers. As the budget requests are passed back up the organization, they are carefully inspected for conformity to guidelines. If they do not conform, they are "adjusted," often with little or no consultation with the originating units.

The less autocratic the organization (and the less pressured it is by current financial exigencies), the greater the probability that this process will allow dialogue and some compromise between managerial levels. Even the most *participative* firms, however, will not long tolerate lower-level managers who are not sensitive to messages relating to budget limitations. It makes little difference whether budget policy is passed down the system by means of formal, written policy statements or as a haphazard set of oral comments informally transmitted by some senior managers and practically neglected by others; the PM's budget request is expected to conform to policy. Ignorance of the policy is no excuse. Repeated failure to conform will be rewarded with a ticket to "corporate Siberia." It is the budget originator's responsibility to find out about budget policy. Again we see the importance of political sensitivity. The PM's channels of communication must be sensitive enough to receive policy signals even in the event that a noncommunicative superior blocks those signals.

Category/Activity Budgeting vs. Program Budgeting

Thus far we have discussed one facet of an organization's philosophy of budgeting. Another facet has to do with the degree to which a budget is category/activity-oriented or program-oriented, a distinction we have mentioned before. The traditional organizational budget is either category-oriented or activity-oriented, often based upon historical data accumulated through an accounting system such as *activity-based costing* [13, 33]. Individual expenses are classified and assigned to basic budget *lines* such as phone, materials, personnel-clerical, utilities, direct labor, etc. or to production centers or processes [6]. These expense lines are gathered into more inclusive categories, and are reported by organizational unit—for example, by section, department, and division. In other words, the budget can be overlaid on the organizational chart. Table 7-1 shows one page of a typical, activity-oriented monthly budget report for a real estate project.

With the advent of project organization, it became necessary to organize the budget in ways that conformed more closely to the actual pattern of fiscal responsibility. Under traditional budgeting methods, the budget for a project could be split up among many different organizational units, which diffused control so widely that it was frequently nonexistent. It was often almost impossible to determine the actual size of major expenditure categories in a project's budget. In light of this problem, ways were sought to alter the budgeting process so that budgets could be associated directly with the projects that used them. This need gave rise to *program budgeting*. Table 7-2 shows a program-oriented project budget divided by task and expected time of expenditure. In an interesting paper, Brimson [6] critiques both systems separately, and then combines them.

Program budgeting aggregates income and expenditures across programs (projects). In most cases, aggregation by program is in addition to, not instead of, aggregation by organizational unit. The project has its own budget. The physical arrangement

Table 7-1. Typical Monthly Budget for a Real Estate Project (Page 1 of 6)

	Current			
	Actual	**Budget**	**Variance**	**Pct.**
Corporate—Income Statement				
Revenue				
8430 Management fees				
8491 Prtnsp reimb—property mgmt	7,410.00	6,222.00	1,188.00	119.0
8492 Prtnsp reimb—owner acquisition	.00	3,750.00	3,750.00−	.0
8493 Prtnsp reimb—rehab	.00	.00	.00	.0
8494 Other income	.00	.00	.00	.0
8495 Reimbursements—others	.00	.00	.00	.0
Total revenue	7,410.00	9,972.00	2,562.00−	74.3
Operating expenses				
Payroll & P/R benefits				
8511 Salaries	29,425.75	34,583.00	5,157.25	85.0
8512 Payroll taxes	1,789.88	3,458.00	1,668.12	51.7
8513 Group ins & med reimb	1,407.45	1,040.00	387.45−	135.3
8515 Workmens compensation	43.04	43.00	.04−	100.0
8516 Staff apartments	.00	.00	.00	.0
8517 Bonus	.00	.00	.00	.0
Total payroll & P/R benefits	32,668.12	39,124.00	6,457.88	83.5
Travel & entertainment expenses				
8512 Travel	456.65	300.00	156.65−	152.2
8522 Promotion, entertainment & gift	69.52	500.00	430.48	13.9
8523 Auto	1,295.90	1,729.00	433.10	75.0
Total travel & entertainment exp	1,822.07	2,529.00	706.93	72.1
Professional fees				
8531 Legal fees	419.00	50.00	369.00−	838.0
8532 Accounting fees	289.00	.00	289.00−	.0
8534 Temporary help	234.58	200.00	34.58−	117.2

of such budget reports varies widely, but usually takes the form of a spreadsheet with the standard budget categories listed down the left-hand side of the sheet and category totals disaggregated into "regular operations" and charges to the various projects. For example, the columns shown in Table 7-1 would be repeated for each project.

The estimation of capital costs raises special problems. Accounting systems in different industries handle capital costs differently. Further, estimation requires highly specialized knowledge because the prices of some durable goods, e.g., machine tools, rise and fall in response to much different forces than affect the prices of other equipment, e.g., computer systems or aircraft. In an interesting two-part article, Sigurdsen notes that capital costs are variant with quantity of output and compares two methods of making capital cost estimates [29, 30]. We will have more to say about Sigurdsen's risk analysis methods in Chapter 8.

Table 7-2. Project Budget by Task and Month

Task	I	J	Estimate	Monthly Budget (£)							
				1	2	3	4	5	6	7	8
A	1	2	7000	5600	1400						
B	2	3	9000		3857	5143					
C	2	4	10000		3750	5000	1250				
D	2	5	6000		3600	2400					
E	3	7	12000				4800	4800	2400		
F	4	7	3000				3000				
G	5	6	9000			2571	5143	1286			
H	6	7	5000					3750	1250		
I	7	8	8000						2667	5333	
J	8	9	6000								6000
			75000	5600	12607	15114	14193	9836	6317	5333	6000

Source: ([20])

Project Management in Practice
Completing the Limerick Nuclear Facility Under Budget

On January 8, 1990, the Limerick nuclear power generating facility in Pennsylvania began commercial operation, thereby setting a construction record for nuclear facilities. In an era when it is common to hear of nuclear plants that massively overrun their budgets and completion schedules, Limerick was completed eight months ahead of its 49-month schedule and came in $400 million under its $3.2 billion budget. Limerick has truly set a standard for the industry.

It was no accident that Limerick was completed ahead of schedule and under budget. When construction started in February 1986, a project goal was to complete the project eight months ahead of the planned completion, which would help keep the costs under the budget limit as well. To achieve this early target, a series of innovative approaches were taken. Two of the major ones were to accelerate ramp-up staffing and to use an extensive, fully-supported second shift. The momentum of the speedy start-up set the fast pace for the remainder of the project. The second shift earned a very favorable premium, as well as having a full complement of managers and engineers to work with the manual workers. In this fashion, the second shift productivity was equal to, if not higher than, the first shift's.

Other decisions and actions further helped either the cost or the schedule. For example, it was decided that overtime would not be worked since a second shift was being used. And as a condition of the project approval, a project labor agreement with the local unions (rather than the national) had to be developed that would eliminate strikes, lockouts, and delays and provide for peaceful resolution of disputes. Also, an incentive fee contract with the building contractor was signed whereby the contractor would share

Limerick Nuclear Facility contractor logos and lost-time clock

equally in cost/schedule overruns or underruns, with limits set.

Source: T. P. Gotzis, "Limerick Generating Station No. 2," PM *Network*, January 1991.

With such attention to the goal of an early and underbudget completion, the team, numbering almost 3000 workers by June 1987, worked diligently and with high morale, meeting the goal in January 1990.

■ 7.2 IMPROVING THE PROCESS OF COST ESTIMATION

The cooperation of several people is required to prepare cost estimates for a project. If the firm is in a business that routinely requires bids to be submitted to its customers, it will have "professional" cost estimators on its staff. In these cases, it is the job of the PM to generate a description of the work to be done on the project in sufficient detail that the estimator can know what cost data must be collected. Frequently, the project will be too complex for the PM to generate such a description without considerable help from experts in the functional areas.

Even with the finest of experts working to estimate resource usage, the one thing that is certain is that things will not go precisely as planned. There are two fundamentally different ways to manage the risks associated with the chance events that occur on every project. The simpler and far more common way is to make an allowance for contingencies—usually 5 or 10 percent of the estimated cost. Just why these numbers are chosen in preference to $6\frac{7}{8}$ or $9\frac{1}{4}$ for instance, we do not know. We strongly prefer another method in which the forecaster selects "most likely, optimistic, and pessimistic" estimates. This method is described in detail in Chapter 8 when we cover the issue of estimating the duration of elements in the action plan. The method described in Chapter 8 is applicable, unchanged, to the estimation of resource requirements and costs.

Turning now to the problem of estimating direct costs,* project managers often find it helpful to collect direct cost estimates on a form that not only lists the level of resource needs, but also indicates when each resource will be needed, and notes if it is available (or will be available at the appropriate time). Figure 7-3 shows such a form. It also has a column for identifying the person to contact in order to get specific resources. This table can be used for collating the resource requirements for each task element in a project, or for aggregating the information from a series of tasks onto a single form.

Note that Figure 7-3 contains no information on overhead costs. The matter of what overhead costs are to be added and in what amounts is unique to the firm, beyond the PM's control, and generally a source of annoyance and frustration to one and all. The allocation of overhead is arbitrary by its nature, and when the addition of overhead cost causes an otherwise attractive project to fail to meet the organization's economic objectives, the project's supporters are apt to complain bitterly about the "unfairness" of overhead cost allocation.

At times, firms fund projects that show a significant incremental profit over direct costs but are not profitable when fully costed. Such decisions can be justified for a number of reasons, such as:

---

*Our emphasis on estimating direct costs and on focusing on resources that are "direct costed" in the action plan is based on our belief that the PM should be concerned with only those items over which he or she has some control—which certainly excludes overheads. The PM, however, may wish to add some nonchargable items to the resource column of the action plan simply to "reserve" that item for use at a specific time.

- To develop knowledge of a technology
- To get the organization's "foot in the door"
- To obtain the parts or service portion of the work
- To be in a good position for a follow-on contract
- To improve a competitive position
- To broaden a product line or a line of business.

Project Name _____
Date _____
Task Number _____

RESOURCES NEEDED

Resources	Person to Contact	How Many/ Much Needed	When Needed	Check (✓) If Available
People: Managers, Supervisors				
Professional & Technical				
Nontechnical				
Money				
Materials: Facilities				
Equipment				
Tools				
Power				
Space				
Special Services: Research & Test				
Typing/clerical				
Reproduction				
Others				

Figure 7-3   Form for gathering data on project resource needs.

All of these are adequate reasons to fund projects that, in the short term, may lose money but provide the organization with the impetus for future growth and profitability. It is up to senior management to decide if such reasons are worth it.

Learning Curves

If the project being costed is one of many similar projects, the estimation of each cost element is fairly routine. If the project involves work in which the firm has little experience, cost estimation is more difficult, particularly for direct labor costs. For example, consider a project that requires 25 units of a complex electronic device to be assembled. The firm is experienced in building electronic equipment but has never before made this specific device, which differs significantly from the items routinely assembled.

Experience might indicate that if the firm were to build many such devices, it would use about seventy hours of direct labor per unit. If labor is paid a wage of $12 per hour, and if benefits equal 28 percent of the wage rate, the estimated labor cost for the 25 units is

$$(1.28)(\$12/\text{hr})(25 \text{ units})(70 \text{ hr/unit}) = \$26,880$$

In fact, this would be an underestimate of the actual labor cost because more time per unit output is used early in the production process. Studies have shown that human performance usually improves when a task is repeated. In general, performance improves by a fixed percent each time production doubles. More specifically, *each time the output doubles, the worker hours per unit decrease to a fixed percentage of their previous value*. That percentage is called the *learning rate*. If an individual requires 10 minutes to accomplish a certain task the first time it is attempted and only 8 minutes the second time, that person is said to have an 80 percent learning rate. If output is doubled again from two to four, we would expect the fourth item to be produced in

$$8(0.8) = 6.4 \text{ min}$$

Similarly, the eighth unit of output should require

$$6.4(0.8) = 5.12 \text{ min}$$

and so on. The time required to produce a unit of output follows a well-known formula:

$$T_n = T_1 n^r$$

where

T_n = the time required for the *n*th unit of output,
T_1 = the time required for the initial unit of output,
n = the number of units to be produced, and
r = log decimal learning rate/log 2.

The total time required for all units of a production run of size N is

$$\text{total time} = T_1 \sum_{n=1}^{N} n^r$$

Tables are widely available with both unit and total values for the learning curves, and have been calculated for many different improvement ratios (learning rates—e.g., see [28]).

In the example of the electronic device just given, assume that after producing the twentieth unit, there is no significant further improvement (i.e., assembly time has reached a steady state at 70 hours). Further assume that previous study established that the usual learning rate for assemblers in this plant is about 85 percent. We can estimate the time required for the first unit by letting $T_n = 70$ hours by the unit $n = 20$. Then

$$r = \log 0.85/\log 2$$
$$= -0.1626/0.693$$
$$= -0.235$$

and

$$70 = T_1(20)^r$$
$$T_1 = 141.3 \text{ hr}$$

Now we know the time for the initial unit. Using a table that shows the total time multipler (see [28, pp. 343–346], for example), we can find the appropriate total time multiplier for this example—the multiplier for 20 units given a learning rate of 85 percent. With this multiplier, 12.40, we can calculate the total time required to build all 20 units. It is

$$(12.40)(141.3 \text{ hr}) = 1752.12 \text{ hr}$$

The last five units are produced in the steady-state time of 70 hours each. Thus the total assembly time is

$$1752.12 + 5(70 \text{ hr}) = 2102.12 \text{ hr}$$

We can now refigure the direct labor cost.

$$2102.12(\$12)(1.28) = \$32,288.56$$

Our first estimate, which ignored learning effects, understated the cost by

$$\$32,288.56 - \$26,880 = \$5,408.56$$

or about 17 percent. Figure 7-4 illustrates this source of the error.

In recent years, learning curves have received increasing interest from project managers, particularly in the construction industry. Methods have been developed for the approximation of composite learning curves for entire projects [2], and for the approximation of total cost from the unit learning curve [8]. Badiru has included learning curve effects in his critical resource diagramming, which is discussed in Chapter 8 [3].

The conclusion is simple. For any task where labor is a significant cost factor and the production run is reasonably short, the PM should take the learning curve into account when estimating costs.

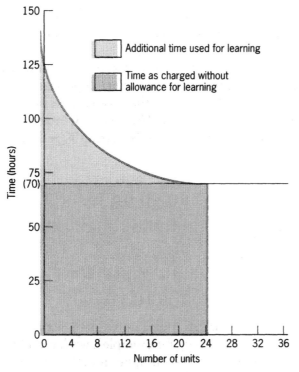

Figure 7-4   Effects of ignoring learning curve.

The implications of this conclusion should not be overlooked. We do not often think of projects as "production," but they are. While the construction, electronics, and aircraft assembly industries have used learning curves for many years, other industrial areas have been slow to follow. For example, research [18] has shown that the learning curve effect is important to decisions about the role of engineering consultants on computer-assisted design (CAD) projects. The failure to consider performance improvement is a significant cause of project cost underestimation.

A Special Case of Learning—Technological Shock

If the parent organization is not experienced in the type of project being considered for selection, performance measures such as time to installation, time to achieve 80 percent efficiency, cost to install, and the like are often underestimated. It is interesting to observe that an almost certain, immediate result of installing a new, cost-saving technology is that costs rise. Sometimes we blame the cost increases on resistance to change, but a more sensible explanation is that when we alter a system, we disturb it and it reacts in unpredictable ways. A steelmaker recalling the installation of the then new technology for manufacturing tinplate by electrolysis remarked, "We discovered and installed the world's first electrolytic method for making scrap. It took a year before we had that line running the way it was designed." Of course, if the organization is experienced, underestimation is not likely to be a serious problem. The

Reliance Electric Company undertook several "18-month" plant construction projects that they predicted, accurately, would require 36 months to build from decision to the point when the plant was capable of operating at or above three-fourths capacity. (Note the potential for ethical problems here.) To the extent possible, past knowledge of system actions and reactions should be built into estimates of future project performance.

Other Factors

Depending on the reference, anywhere from about three-fifths to five-sixths of projects fail to meet their time, cost, and/or specification objectives. (See, for example, [16].) The record of IS projects is particularly poor, according to article after article in the journals of the Project Management Institute. Possibly the problem is that Dilbert's pointy-haired boss sets arbitrary and impossible goals. Possibly scope-creep impacts all projects (though cost overruns are not necessarily associated with changing scope [12]). Possibly PMs use wildly optimistic estimates in order to influence the project selection process. Or maybe they are simply unaware of good cost (or time) estimating practices. For example, there are at least 45 estimating models available for IS projects, but few IS project managers use any of them [21, 24]. Possibly all of these things, and even others, act together to produce this unenviable track record.

While the number of things that can produce errors in cost estimates is almost without limit, some problems occur with particularly high frequency. Changes in resource prices is one of these. The most commonly used solution to this problem is to increase all cost estimates by some fixed percentage. A more useful approach is to identify each input that accounts for a significant portion of project cost and estimate the direction and rate of price change for each.

The determination of which inputs account for a "significant" portion of project cost is not difficult, although it may be somewhat arbitrary. Suppose, for example, that our initial, rough cost estimate (with no provision for future price changes) for a project is $1 million and is to be spent over a three-year period in approximately equal amounts per year. If we think personnel costs will comprise about 40 percent of that total, also spread equally over time, the wage/salary bill will be about $400,000. Split into three equal amounts, we have expenditures of $133,333 per year. If we estimate that wage/salary rates will increase by 6 percent per year, our expense for the second year rises to $141,333 (an increase of $8,000), and to $149,813 in the third year (an increase of $8,480). Failure to account for wage/salary inflation would result in an underestimate of project cost of about $16,500. This is an error of slightly more than 4 percent of the personnel cost and almost 2 percent of the total project budget.

Further improvements can be made by taking into account the fact that the prices of different inputs often change at very different rates. A quick examination of the Bureau of Labor Statistics (BLS) wage and price indices, which cover a very large number of specific commodities and wage rates, will reveal that even in periods of stable prices, the prices of some things rise while others fall and still others do not change appreciably. Thus, the PM may wish to use different *inflators/deflators* for each of several different classes of labor or types of commodities. While most PMs are concerned only with price increases, any industry submitting competitive bids on projects must remember that failure to be aware of falling prices will lead to cost overestimation and uncompetitive bids.

The proper level of breakdown in estimating the impact of price changes simply depends on the organization's willingness to tolerate error. Assume that management is willing to accept a 5 percent difference between actual and estimated cost for each major cost category. In the example above, expected increases in wage/salary costs will use more than four-fifths of that allowance. That leaves less than 1 percent (about $3,500) of allowable error, and the need to add one part-time clerk to the project for a single year would more than use the remaining allowance.

Other elements that need to be factored into the estimated project cost include an allowance for waste and spoilage. No sane builder would order "just enough" lumber to build a house. Also, personnel costs can be significantly increased by the loss and subsequent replacement of project professionals. Not only must new people go through a learning period—which, as we have seen, will have a negative effect on production—but professional starting salaries often rise faster than the general rate of annual salary increases. Thus, it may well cost more to replace a person who leaves the project with a newcomer who has approximately the same level of experience.

We have already mentioned the inclination PMs have toward understating the costs of a project in order to make it appear more profitable to senior managers, as well as the proclivity of lower-level project workers to overestimate costs in order to protect themselves. If the project is in its initial planning stage as a response to an RFP from an outside organization, over- and underestimation of cost can have a serious impact on the probability of winning the contract—or on the level of profit, if a win occurs.

Serious ethical problems may arise during the process of estimating costs and submission of bids in response to a Request for Proposal (RFP). If the job is to be paid on a cost-plus basis, or even if it is a fixed-fee project, with fee increases allowed for special circumstances, some bidders may "low ball" a contract (submit underestimated costs). By doing this, they hope to win the bid, counting on the opportunity to increase costs or to plead special circumstances once the job is underway. At times, clients have been known to give favored bidders a "last look" at supposedly sealed bids so that the favored bidder can submit a winning bid, often with an unwritten agreement to allow some cost escalation at a later date. There is considerable opportunity for unethical behavior during cost estimation and bidding. Further, estimation and bidding practices vary widely from industry to industry.

Finally, there is plain bad luck. Delays occur for reasons that cannot be predicted. Machinery with the reliability of a railroad spike suddenly breaks down. That which has never failed fails. Every project needs an "allowance for contingencies."

Some writers and instructors differentiate four bases for estimating costs: experience, quantitative (statistical) methods, constraints, and worksheets. They discuss the advantages and disadvantages of each and then, typically, decide that one or another gives the best results. We feel strongly that all four are useful and that no single approach to cost estimation should be accepted as the best or rejected out of hand. The best estimators seem to employ an eclectic approach that uses, as one said, "anything that works." The wise PM takes into account as many known influences on the project budget as can be predicted. What cannot be predicted must then, by experience, simply be "allowed for." There are two other factors, particularly common to projects involving intangible outputs such as software programming, that need to be mentioned relating to cost-estimation and the schedule. These two factors have been identified in a classic and highly readable work—*The Mythical Man-Month*—by Brooks [7].

First, most projects involve a tangible medium that tends not to be under our control—the wood splits, the paint smears—and thus we blame implementation problems of our "good" ideas on these physical elements. So, when we are working with a purely intellectual medium that has no physical elements, such as computer code, we are highly optimistic and foolishly assume that all will go well. However, when any project consisting of a series of components can only be successful if all of the components are successful, and each component has a small probability of failing, the chances of the overall project being successful are in fact very poor. Consider, for example, a software program consisting of 1000 lines of code, each of which is 99.9 percent reliable. The chance of the program itself working is only about 36 percent! Brooks' experience has led him to the following rule of thumb for software projects. As a fraction of the total time of the project, planning consumes about $\frac{1}{3}$, coding consumes $\frac{1}{6}$, component test consumes $\frac{1}{4}$, and system test consumes $\frac{1}{4}$. Thus, if a project estimate is made based on the expected coding time (the main element for which we can derive an estimate), this in reality will usually represent only about 17 percent of the entire project time rather than the 80 to 90 percent commonly assumed.

The second factor is what Brooks calls "the mythical man month" and relates to our tendency to assume that workers and time are interchangeable. Thus, when a schedule slips, the traditional response is to add labor which is like trying to douse a fire with gasoline. Our assumption that workers and time are interchangeable is correct only when a task can be partitioned such that there is no communication needed between the workers, such as in picking cotton by hand. Most projects, however, especially computer programming, are not set up that way and the more workers that are added require even more workers to train, as well as lines of communication to coordinate their efforts. Thus, three workers require three times as much pairwise intercommunication as two, and four require six times as much, etc. This result is captured in Brooks' law: *Adding manpower to a late software project makes it later.*

The Emanon Aircraft Corporation

Emanon Aircraft is a major manufacturer of aircraft parts, specializing in landing gear parts and assemblies. They are located in a highly industrialized midwestern state. The local area suffers from somewhat higher than average unemployment, partly because Emanon has experienced a downturn in business. In the past three years, they have lost out on a number of landing gear contracts, being underbid by competitors from other areas of the country. Senior management studied the problem, but has come to no conclusion about what can be done. They have hired a consulting team from a nearby university to study the situation and make a recommendation.

Business in the aircraft industry is not significantly different than in many other industries specializing in the building of complex machines. Aircraft builders are primarily assembly operations. They build planes from subassemblies and parts manufactured by themselves or by subcontractors who, in turn, specialize in specific subassemblies; for example, landing gear, avionics, passenger seats, heating and air conditioning, etc. When an order is received to build some number of a given type of plane, the builder (prime contractor) requests bids for the proper number of a certain part or subassembly from appropriate subcontractors. All relevant specifications for the part or subassembly are included in the RFP. The subcontractors who wish to participate in the project submit proposals that include a complete description of the proposed subassembly together with price information, delivery dates, and any other pertinent conditions of sale.

The university consulting team studied three aspects of Emanon's landing gear operation: the manufacturing process, the cost structure, and the bidding behavior and profit structure on landing gear bids. They determined that the manufacturing process was reasonably efficient and not significantly different from Emanon's competitors.

Second, they found that all competitors were using approximately the same level of mark-up when determining their cost-plus price. When examining the cost structure, however, they noted that in the past three years, the firm consistently ran negative cost variances in material accounts. That is, the amount of material actually used in the construction of landing gears was approximately 10 percent less than the plan indicated. The team was unsure of this finding because there were only a few winning contracts for landing gears during the past three years.

An investigation was conducted on the estimation and purchase of materials for this department. It exposed the following facts. Three and one-half years ago, Emanon was late making a delivery of landing gear parts. The firm paid a large penalty and was threatened with loss of further business with the prime contractor. The late delivery resulted when Emanon ordered an insufficient quantity of a special steel alloy used in landing gear struts, and was unable to purchase any on the open market. The steel company required a manufacturing lead time of more than 90 days, so Emanon's delivery was late.

As a result, the purchasing official who had responsibility for this contract was demoted. The new purchasing official handled the problem in a straightforward fashion by inflating the material estimates by approximately 10 percent. The cost of material is about half of the total cost of landing gear production, which resulted in bids that were approximately 5 percent above the competition.

On Making Better Estimates

Let us begin with the assumption that budget estimation errors are not the result of deliberate dishonesty, but derive from honest errors on the part of the PM, project cost estimators, or anyone else involved. We have already noted that there are many reasons why "honest" errors occur—that projects look easier, faster, and cheaper to senior managers than to those who must do the work—that nonexpert estimators tend to overlook details required to do a complete job—that everyone seems to assume that Murphy's law has been repealed for their personal project. But these things should be learned by experience. Why do experienced managers err on their budget and schedule estimates?

Ambrose Bierce, in *The Devil's Dictionary*, defined "experience" as "The wisdom that enables us to recognize as an undesirable old acquaintance the folly that we have already embraced." It is axiomatic that we should learn through experience. It is a truism that we do not. Nowhere is this more evident than in project management, and yet it is not difficult to improve one's estimation/forecasting skills.

Recall that there are two generic types of estimation error. First, there is random error in which overestimates and underestimates are equally likely. Second, there is bias, which is systematic error. For biased estimates, the chance of over- and underestimates are not equally likely. Using the ubiquitous Excel® we can construct a spreadsheet that captures the essence of a person's performance as an estimator. Two simple statistical measures are used: the mean absolute deviation (MAD), and the tracking signal (TS). The printout* of such a spreadsheet is shown in Figure 7-5. Appendix C and references [10 and 28] include information on probability, statistics, and forecasting.

Figure 7-5 assumes that for each period (Column A) someone has made an estimate of a variable (Column B), and that the actual value of that variable is, sooner or later, known (Column C). (It should be noted that Column A need not be time periods. This column simply counts the number of estimates made and links estimates with their respective actuals.) Column D calculates the difference between the actual value, $A(t)$, and the estimate or forecast for that period, $F(t)$. Column E contains the absolute value of that difference. We can now calculate a statistic known as the *mean absolute deviation* (MAD).

As the information in Row 3 of the spreadsheet shows,

$$MAD = \sum(|A(t) - F(t)|)/n$$

where n is the number of differences. The MAD is therefore the arithmetic average of the absolute values of the differences—the mean absolute deviation.

Students of statistics may note that the MAD has certain logical similarities to the standard deviation. Assuming that the forecast errors are normally distributed, the MAD is approximately 80 percent of a standard deviation (see [10] and elsewhere). Thus, if the MAD is a sizable fraction of the variable being estimated, the average error is large and the forecast or estimate is not very accurate.

Now, consider Column D. The sum of the entries in this column for any number of periods is the sum of the forecast errors, often referred to as the "running sum of the forecast errors" (RSFE). If the estimator's errors are truly random, their sum should approach zero; that is, the RSFE should be a small number because positive errors should be offset by negative errors. If either positive or negative errors are more numerous or consistently larger than the other, the estimation process is said to be biased and the errors are not random. In Figure 7-5, RSFE = 133, so the forecast is quite positively biased.

---

*Any of the common spreadsheet programs can easily handle all of the calculations shown in this chapter and will accept formulas and calculations from any of the others.

	A	B	C	D	E	F	G
1	This is a template for improving one's estimating skills						
2							
3	MAD = SUM (|A(t) − F (t)|)/n The Average Absolute Error						
4	Tracking Signal = SUM (A(t) − F(t))/MAD A Measure of Bias						
5							Tracking
6	Period	Estimate	Actual	A(t)−F(t)	|A(t)−F(t)|	MAD	Signal
7	======	========	========	========	========	========	========
8							
9	1	155	163	8	8		
10	2	242	240	−2	2	5.00	1.20
11	3	46	67	21	21	10.33	2.61
12	4	69	78	9	9	10.00	3.60
13	5	75	71	−4	4	8.80	3.64
14	6	344	423	79	79	20.50	5.41
15	7	56	49	−7	7	18.57	5.60
16	8	128	157	29	29	19.88	6.69
17							
18				133	159		

Figure 7-5   Excel ® template for cost estimation.

The tracking signal measures the estimator's bias. It is easily found:

$$TS = RSFE/MAD$$

Note that it calculates the number of MADs in the RSFE (see column G in Figure 7-5, and recall the similarity between MAD and standard deviation). If the RSFE is small, approaching zero, the TS will also approach zero. As the RSFE grows, the TS will grow, indicating bias. Division of the RSFE by the MAD creates a sort of "index number," the TS, that is independent of the size of the variables being considered. We cannot say just how much bias is acceptable in an estimator/forecaster. We feel that a $TS \geq 3$ is too high unless the estimator is a rank beginner. Certainly, an experienced estimator should have a much lower TS. (It should be obvious that the TS may be either negative or positive. Our comment actually refers to the absolute value of the TS.) Perhaps more important than worrying about an acceptable limit on the size of the tracking signal is the practice of tracking it and analyzing why the estimator's bias, if there is one, exists. Similarly, the estimator should consider how to reduce the MAD, the average estimation error. Such analysis is the embodiment of "learning by experience." The Excel® template makes the analysis simple to conduct, and should result in decreasing the size of both the MAD and the TS. (The formulae used in Figure 7-5 are shown in Figure 7-6. Similar formulae can be used in other popular spreadsheets.)

	A	B	C	D	E	F	G
1							
2							
3							
4							
5							Tracking
6	Period	Estimate	Actual	A(t)−F(t)	|A(t)−F(t)|	MAD	Signal
7	======	=======	=======	==========	============	================	=============
8							
9	1	155	163	=C9−B9	=ABS(C9−B9)		
10	2	242	240	=C10−B10	=ABS(C10−B10)	=(SUM($E$9:E10))/A10	=(SUM($D$9:D10))/F10
11	3	46	67	=C11−B11	=ABS(C11−B11)	=(SUM($E$9:E11))/A11	=(SUM($D$9:D11))/F11
12	4	69	78	=C12−B12	=ABS(C12−B12)	=(SUM($E$9:E12))/A12	=(SUM($D$9:D12))/F12
13	5	75	71	=C13−B13	=ABS(C13−B13)	=(SUM($E$9:E13))/A13	=(SUM($D$9:D13))/F13
14	6	344	423	=C14−B14	=ABS(C14−B14)	=(SUM($E$9:E14))/A14	=(SUM($D$9:D14))/F14
15	7	56	49	=C15−B15	=ABS(C15−B15)	=(SUM($E$9:E15))/A15	=(SUM($D$9:D15))/F15
16	8	128	157	=C16−B16	=ABS(C16−B16)	=(SUM($E$9:E16))/A16	=(SUM($D$9:D16))/F16
17							
18				= SUM(D9:D17)	= SUM(E9:E17)		

Figure 7-6 Excel ® formulas for Figure 7-5.

Some estimators would like to speed up the process of improving their estimation skills by grouping forecasts of different resources to generate more data points when calculating their MADs and TSs. Use of the tracking signal requires that the input data, estimates (forecasts) and actuals, be collected and processed separately for each variable being estimated. Cost estimates and actuals for different resources, for instance, would be used to find the MAD and TS for each individual resource. The reason for this inconvenience is that resources come in different units and the traditional caution about adding apples and oranges applies. (Even if all resources are measured in dollars, we still have scale problems when we mix resource costs of very different sizes.) Fortunately, there is a way around the problem.

Instead of defining the estimation error as the *difference* between actual and forecast, we can define it as the *ratio* of actual to forecast. Therefore, the new error for the first forecast (Period 1) in Figure 7-5 is not eight units, but rather is

$$A(t)/F(t) = 163/155 = 1.052$$

or a 5.2 percent error. In order to produce measures similar in nature and concept to the MAD and TS, we will subtract 1 from the ratio. Thus, when the actual is greater than the forecast, the measure (i.e., the error ratio minus 1) will be positive, and if

	A	B	C	D	E	F	G
1	This is a template for improving one's estimating skills						
2							
3	MAR = SUM {|(A(t) / F (t)) −1|} /n						
4	Tracking Signal = SUM {(A(t) / F (t)) − 1}/MAR						
5							Tracking
6	Period	Estimate	Actual	A(t)F(t))−1	|(A(t)/F(t))−1|	MAR	Signal
7	====	=======	=======	========	==========	========	========
8							
9	1	155	163	0.052	0.052		
10	2	242	240	−0.008	0.008	0.030	1.448
11	3	46	67	0.457	0.457	0.172	2.904
12	4	69	78	0.130	0.130	0.162	3.898
13	5	75	71	−0.053	0.053	0.140	4.120
14	6	344	423	0.230	0.230	0.155	5.205
15	7	56	49	−0.125	0.125	0.151	4.523
16	8	128	157	0.227	0.227	0.160	5.670
17							
18				0.908	1.281		

Figure 7-7   Estimation template using ratios.

	A	B	C	D	E	F	G
1							
2							
3							
4							
5							Tracking
6	Period	Estimate	Actual	(A(t)/F(t))−1	|(A(t)/F(t))−1|	MAR	Signal
7	======	=======	=======	========	==========	========	========
8							
9	1	155	163	=(C9/B9)−1	=ABS((C9/B9)−1)		
10	2	242	240	=(C10/B10)−1	=ABS((C10/B10)−1)	=(SUM($E$9:E10))/A10	=(SUM($D$9:D10))/F10
11	3	46	67	=(C11/B11)−1	=ABS((C11/B11)−1)	=(SUM($E$9:E11))/A11	=(SUM($D$9:D11))/F11
12	4	69	78	=(C12/B12)−1	=ABS((C12/B12)−1)	=(SUM($E$9:E12))/A12	=(SUM($D$9:D12))/F12
13	5	75	71	=(C13/B13)−1	=ABS((C13/B13)−1)	=(SUM($E$9:E13))/A13	=(SUM($D$9:D13))/F13
14	6	344	423	=(C14/B14)−1	=ABS((C14/B14)−1)	=(SUM($E$9:E14))/A14	=(SUM($D$9:D14))/F14
15	7	56	49	=(C15/B15)−1	=ABS((C15/B15)−1)	=(SUM($E$9:E15))/A15	=(SUM($D$9:D15))/F15
16	8	128	157	=(C16/B16)−1	=ABS((C16/B16)−1)	=(SUM($E$9:E16))/A16	=(SUM($D$9:D16))/F16
17							
18				=SUM(D9:D16)	=SUM(E9:E16)		

Figure 7-8 Formulas for Figure 7-7.

the actual is *less* than the forecast, the measure will be negative. Figure 7-7 shows the calculations of {A(t)/F(t) − 1} for the data used in Figure 7-5. The formulas are shown in Figure 7-8. Column E shows the absolute value of column D, and column F lists the MAR (mean absolute ratio). The tracking signal is calculated as usual by dividing the "running sum of the forecast ratios" (RSFR) by the MAR,

$$TS = RSFR/MAR$$

Notice that this calculation does not suffer from unit or scale effects because the ratio of actual to forecast is a dimensionless number and we are finding the percent error rather than the "real" error.

One caution remains. While this technique will allow one to aggregate dissimilar data and, thereby, measure the degree of random error and bias faster than when using differences, care must be exercised to aggregate only data for which there is good reason to believe that the amount of bias and uncertainty is roughly the same for all resource estimations.

At the beginning of this discussion, we made the assumption that estimation errors were "honest." That assumption is not necessary. If a manager suspects that costs are purposely being under- or overestimated, it is usually not difficult to collect appropriate data and calculate the tracking signal for an individual estimator—or even for an entire project team. If it is known that such information is being collected, one likely result is that the most purposeful bias will be sharply reduced.

A *final note:* In the next chapter, we discuss a method for managing schedule and budget risk. We also briefly describe some software used for risk management. Most of the useful methods require that the forecaster specify the mode and range of the variable being forecast. These models tacitly assume that the data supplied represent unbiased estimates. As we noted previously, if the input estimates are biased, the output will incorporate that error and the danger is not "Garbage in, garbage out" but "Garbage in, gospel out."

Project Management in Practice
Managing Costs at Massachusetts' Neighborhood Health Plan

Between 1994 and 1996, Medicaid reduced its rate of reimbursement by 20 percent while the State of Massachusetts imposed higher eligibility requirements for health subscribers, thereby significantly reducing Neighborhood Health Plan's (NHP) revenues and threatening its viability. In the past, NHP had controlled costs by controlling hospital bed utilization and increasing preventive medicine. However, no matter how low hospital utilization is, if hospital contract rates are expensive the cost to NHP will be high. Thus, in November 1995, NHP chartered a project team to help it manage costs through better selection and management of hospital contracts.

More specifically, the team's charter was to develop a method to examine hospital contracts to assure that proposed rates were financially viable to NHP but high-quality care would be available when needed.

The team first selected the top 10 to 20 hospitals based on total annual payments from NHP for analysis. From these they determined that to control costs effectively, NHP's contracting philosophy would have to change from the current

Source: J. H. Hertenstein and K. A. Vallancourt, "Contract Management = Cost Management," *PM Network,* July 1997, pp. 31–34.

95 percent of all line items per episode to a fixed cost per episode or per day per type of stay. The team then constructed a spreadsheet that allowed cost comparisons to be made across hospitals which allowed management to bargain for lower rates or, if hospitals were inflexible, suggest to health centers what alternative hospitals to refer patients to. This and later developments by the team significantly enhanced management's ability to contain their costs while guaranteeing that quality care would be available when needed. It also allowed management to examine and respond to contracts and proposed contract changes in a timely and informed manner.

 SUMMARY

This chapter initiated the subject of project implementation by focusing on the project budget, which authorizes the project manager to obtain the resources needed to begin work. Different methods of budgeting were described along with their impacts on project management. Then, a number of issues concerning cost estimation were discussed, particularly the effect of learning on the cost of repetitive tasks and how to use the concept of the learning curve. Finally, methods for improving cost estimation skills were described.

Specific points made in the chapter were these:

- The intent of a budget is to communicate organizational policy concerning the organization's goals and priorities.

- There are a number of common budgeting methods: top-down, bottom-up, the program budget.

- A form identifying the level of resource need, when it will be needed, who the contact is, and its availability is especially helpful in estimating costs.

- It is common for organizations to fund projects whose returns cover direct but not full costs in order to achieve long-run strategic goals of the organization.

- If projects include repetitive tasks with significant human input, the learning phenomenon should be taken into consideration when preparing cost estimates.

- The learning curve is based on the observation that the amount of time required to produce one unit decreases a constant percentage every time the cumulative output doubles.

- A method for determining whether or not cost estimates are biased is described. The method can be used to improve any estimation/forecasting process.

- Other major factors, in addition to learning, that should be considered when making project cost estimates are inflation, differential changes in the cost factors, waste and spoilage, personnel replacement costs, and contingencies for unexpected difficulties.

In the next chapter, we address the subject of task scheduling, a topic of major importance in project management. More research and investigation has probably been conducted on the subject of scheduling than any other element of project management.

GLOSSARY

Bottom-up Budgeting A budgeting method that begins with those who will be doing the tasks estimating the resources needed. The advantage is more accurate estimates.

Learning Rate The percentage of the previous worker hours per unit required for doubling the output.

Program Budgeting Aggregating income and expenditures by project or program, often in addition to aggregation by organizational unit or activity.

Top-Down Budgeting A budgeting method that begins with top managers' estimates of the resources needed for a project. Its primary advantage is that the aggregate budget is typically quite accurate because no element has been left out. Individual elements, however, may be quite inaccurate.

Variances The pattern of deviations in costs and usage used for exception reporting to management.

 QUESTIONS

Material Review Questions

1. What are the advantages of top-down budgeting? Of bottom-up budgeting? What is the most important task for top management to do in bottom-up budgeting?

2. In preparing a budget, what indirect costs should be considered?

3. Describe the purpose and use of a tracking signal.

4. Describe the top-down budgeting process.

5. What is a variance?

6. Describe the learning curve phenomenon.

7. How might you determine if cost estimates are biased?

8. What is "program budgeting"?

9. What is the difference between activity- and program-oriented budgets?

Class Discussion Questions

10. Discuss ways in which to keep budget planning from becoming a game.

11. List some of the pitfalls in cost estimating. What steps can a manager take to correct cost overruns?

12. Why do consulting firms frequently subsidize some projects? Is this ethical?

13. What steps can be taken to make controlling costs easier? Can these steps also be used to control other project parameters, such as performance?

14. Which budgeting method is likely to be used with which type of organizational structure?

15. What are some potential problems with the top-

down and bottom-up budgeting processes? What are some ways of dealing with these potential problems?

16. How is the budget planning process like a game?

17. Would any of the conflict resolution methods described in the previous chapter be useful in the budget planning process? Which?

18 How does the fact that capital costs vary with different factors complicate the budgeting process?

19. Why is learning curve analysis important to project management?

20. Why is it "ethically necessary to be honest" in negotiations between a superior and subordinate?

Questions for Project Management

Pathfinder Mission to Mars—On a Shoestring

21. How did a change in philosophy make such a drastic difference in project cost?

22. Why was the mission scope so limited? Why even spend the money to go to Mars with such limited objectives?

23. Describe their "de-scope," "lien list," and "cash reserve" approaches.

24. What do you think a "single string" design means?

Completing the Limerick Nuclear Facility Under Budget

25. What "trick" did the construction firm use to come in ahead of schedule and under budget?

26. What extra expenses did the contractor incur in order to finish ahead of schedule? How can one tell whether they are spending too much to finish early, thereby saving not only time but also overhead costs?

Managing Costs at Massachusetts' Neighborhood Health Plan

27. Wouldn't higher eligibility requirements for subscribers cut NHP's health care costs? Why did this exacerbate NHP's situation?

28. Explain the tradeoff between hospital utilization and contract rates.

29. How did changing from a line item pay plan to an episode plan allow comparisons and save costs?

 # INCIDENTS FOR DISCUSSION

Preferred Sensor Company

Sean Cole has been appointed project manager of the Preferred Sensor Company's new sensor manufacturing process project. Sensors are extremely price-sensitive, and Preferred has done a great deal of quantitative work so it can accurately forecast changes in sales volume relative to changes in pricing.

The company president, "Dude" Sensor, has considerable faith in the firm's sensitivity model and insists that all projects that affect the manufacturing cost of sensors be run against the sensitivity model in order to generate data to calculate the return on investment. The net result is that project managers, like Sean, are under a great deal of pressure to submit realistic budgets so go/no-go project decisions can be made quickly. Dude has canceled several projects that appeared marginal during their feasibility stages and recently fired a project manager for overestimating project costs on a new model sensor. The project was killed very early in the design stage and six months later a competitor introduced a similar sensor that proved to be highly successful.

Sean's dilemma is how to go about constructing a budget that accurately reflects the cost of the proposed new manufacturing process. Sean is an experienced executive and feels comfortable with his ability to come close to estimating the cost of the project. However, the recent firing of his colleague has made him a bit gun-shy. Only one stage out of the traditional four-stage sensor manufacturing process is being changed, so he has detailed cost information about a good percentage of the process. Unfortunately, the tasks involved in the process stage being modified are unclear at this point. Sean also believes that the new modification will cause some minor changes in the other three stages, but these changes have not been clearly identified. The stage being addressed by the project represents almost 50 percent of the manufacturing cost.

Questions: Under these circumstances, would Sean be wise to pursue a top-down or a bottom-up budgeting approach? Why? What factors are most relevant here?

General Ship Company

General Ship Company has been building nuclear destroyers for the Navy for the last 20 years. It has recently completed the design of a new class of nuclear destroyer and will be preparing a detailed budget to be followed during construction of the first destroyer.

The total budget for this first destroyer is $90 million. The controller feels the initial project cost estimate prepared by the planning department was too low because the waste and spoilage allowance was underestimated. Thus, she is concerned that there may be a large cost overrun on the project and wants to work closely with the project manager to control the costs.

Question: How would you monitor the costs of this project?

BIBLIOGRAPHY

1. AGGARWAL, R. *Capital Budgeting Under Uncertainty.* Englewood Cliffs, NJ: Prentice-Hall, 1993.

2. AMOR, J. P. and C. J. TEPLITZ. "An Efficient Approximation for Project Composite Learning Curves." *Project Management Journal,* September 1998.

3. BADIRU, A. B. "Incorporating Learning Curve Effects Into Critical Resource Diagramming." *Project Management Journal,* June 1995.

4. BIERMAN, H. *The Capital Budgeting Decision: Economic Analysis of Investment Projects,* 7th ed. New York: Macmillan, 1988.

5. BOQUIST, J. A. "How do you win the capital allocation game?" *Sloan Management Review,* Winter 1998.

6. BRIMSON, J. A. "Activity Product Cost." *IEEE Engineering Management Review,* Spring 1993.

7. BROOKS, F. P. *The Mythical Man-Month.* Reading, MA: Addison-Wesley, 1975.

8. CAMM, J. D., J. R. EVANS, and N. K. WOMER. "The Unit Learning Curve Approximation of Total Cost." *Computers in Industrial Engineering.* Vol. 12, No. 3, 1987.

9. CASE, J. "Opening the books." *Harvard Business Review,* March/April 1997.

10. CHASE, R. B., and N. J. AQUILANO. *Production and Operations Management,* 5th ed. Homewood, IL: Irwin, 1989.

11. CHILDS, P. D., S. H. OTT, and A. J. TRIANTIS. "Capital Budgeting for Interrelated Projects: A Real Options Approach." *Journal of Financial and Quantitative Analysis,* September 1998.

12. CHRISTENSEN, D. S., and GORDON, J. A. "Does a Rubber Baseline Guarantee Cost Overruns on Defense Acquisition Contracts?" *Project Management Journal,* September 1998.

13. COBURN, S. "How Activity Based Costing was used in Capital Budgeting." *Management Accounting,* May 1997.

14. COOPER, R. "The Promise—and the Peril—of Integrated Cost Systems." *Harvard Business Review,* July/August 1998.

15. DEAN, B. V., S. J. MANTEL, JR., and L. A. ROEPCKE. "Research Project Cost Distributions and Budget Forecasting." *IEEE Transactions on Engineering Management,* November 1969.

16. FRAME, J. D. "Risk Assessment Groups: Key Component of Project Offices." *PM Network,* March 1998.

17. GAGNON, R. J. *An Exploratory Analysis of the Relevant Cost Structure of Internal and External Engineering Consulting,* Ph.D. dissertation. Cincinnati: University of Cincinnati, 1982.

18. GAGNON, R. J., and S. J. MANTEL, JR. "Strategies and Performance Improvement for Computer-Assisted Design." *IEEE Transactions on Engineering Management,* November 1987.

19. GLASS, G. W. *Assessing the Effectiveness of Milestone Budgeting.* Washington, DC: U.S. Congress, 1987.

20. HARRISON, F. L. *Advanced Project Management.* Hants, Eng: Gower, 1983.

21. LAWRENCE, A. O. "Using Automated Estimating Tools to Improve Project Estimating." *PM Network,* December. 1994.

22. LAYARD, P. R. G. *Cost-Benefit Analysis.* Cambridge, England: Cambridge University Press, 1994.

23. LUEHRMAN, T. A. "Investment Opportunities as Real Options: Getting Started on the Numbers." *Harvard Business Review,* July/August 1998.

24. MARTIN, J. E. "Selecting an Automated Estimating Tool for IS Development Projects." *PM Network,* December 1994.

25. MOOLMAN, G. C. "A Capital Budgeting Model Based on the Project Portfolio Approach: Avoiding Cash Flows per Project." *The Engineering Economist,* Winter 1997.

26. RAY, A. *Cost-Benefit Analysis: Issues and Methodologies.* Baltimore, MD: Johns Hopkins Press, 1984.

27. REIMUS, B. "The IT System that Couldn't Deliver." *Harvard Business Review,* May/June 1997.

28. SHAFER, S. M., and J. R. MEREDITH. *Operations Management: A Process Approach with Spreadsheets.* New York: Wiley, 1998.

29. SIGURDSEN, A. "Principal Errors in Capital Cost Estimating Work, Part 1: Appreciate the Relevance of the Quantity-Dependent Estimating Norms." *Project Management Journal,* September 1996.

30. SIGURDSEN, A. "Principal Errors in Capital Cost Estimating, Part 2: Appreciate the Relevance of the Objective Cost Risk Analysis Method." *Project Management Journal*, December 1996.

31. TOWN, C. "Project Control and Earned Value Management." *Management Accounting*, September 1998.

32. UMAPATHY, S. *Current Budgeting Practices in U.S. Industry: The State of the Art.* New York: Quorum Books, 1987.

33. VANDAMENT, W. F. and D. P. JONES. *Financial Management: Progress and Challenges.* San Francisco: Jossey-Bass, 1993.

This article clearly describes the importance and impact of cost-related issues on a project. These issues can significantly alter the profitability and even success of a project. Costs are discussed from three viewpoints: that of the project manager, the accountant, and the controller. Not only are the amounts of expenditures and encumbrances important, but their timing is critical also. Perhaps most important is having a project cost system that accurately reports costs and variances in a way that can be useful for managerial decisions.

DIRECTED READING

THREE PERCEPTIONS OF PROJECT COST

D. H. Hamburger: Three Perceptions of Project Cost—Cost is More Than a Four Letter Word. *Project Management Journal*, June 1986. ©1987 by the Project Management Institute. Reprinted by permission.

Project cost seems to be a relatively simple expression, but "cost" is more than a four letter word. Different elements of the organization perceive cost differently, as the timing of project cost identification affects their particular organizational function. The project manager charged with on-time, on-cost, on-spec execution of a project views the "on cost" component of his responsibility as a requirement to stay within the allocated budget, while satisfying a given set of specified conditions (scope of work), within a required time frame (schedule). To most project managers this simply means a commitment to project funds in accordance with a prescribed plan (time based budget). Others in the organization are less concerned with the commitment of funds. The accounting department addresses expense recognition related to a project or an organizational profit and loss statement. The accountant's ultimate goal is reporting profitability, while positively influencing the firm's tax liability. The comptroller (finance department) is primarily concerned with the organization's cash flow. It is that person's responsibility to provide the funds for paying the bills, and putting the unused or available money to work for the company.

To be an effective project manager, one must understand each cost, and also realize that the timing of cost identification can affect both project and corporate financial performance. The project manager must be aware of the different cost perceptions and the manner in which they are reported. With this knowledge, the project manager can control more than the project's cost of goods sold (a function often viewed as the project manager's sole financial responsibility). The project manager can also influence the timing of cost to improve cash flow and the cost of financing the work, in addition to affecting revenue and expense reporting in the P&L statement.

Three Perceptions of Cost

To understand the three perceptions of cost—commitments, expenses, and cash flow—consider the purchase of a major project component. Assume that a $120,000 compressor with delivery quoted at six months was purchased. Figure 1 depicts the order execution cycle. At time 0 an order is placed. Six months later the vendor makes two shipments, a large box containing the compressor and a small envelope

Figure 1 Three perceptions of project cost.

containing an invoice. The received invoice is processed immediately, but payment is usually delayed to comply with corporate payment policy (30, 60, 90, or more days may pass before a check is actually mailed to the vendor). In this example, payment was made 60 days after receipt of the invoice or 8 months after the order for the compressor was given to the vendor.

Commitments—The Project Manager's Concern Placement of the purchase order represents a *commitment* to pay the vendor $120,000 following satisfactory delivery of the compressor. As far as the project manager is concerned, once this commitment is made to the vendor, the available funds in the project budget are reduced by that amount. When planning and reporting project costs the project manager deals with commitments. Unfortunately, many accounting systems are not structured to support project cost reporting needs and do not identify commitments. In fact, the value of a purchase order may not be recorded until an invoice is received. This plays havoc with the project manager's fiscal control process, as he cannot get a "handle" on the exact budget status at a particular time. In the absence of a suitable information system, a conscientious project manager will maintain personal (manual or computer) records to track his project's commitments.

Expenses—The Accountant's Concern Preparation of the project's financial report requires identification of the project's revenues (when applicable) and all project *expenses*. In most conventional accounting systems, expenses for financial reporting purposes are recognized upon receipt of an invoice for a purchased item (not when the payment is made—a common miscon-

ception). Thus, the compressor would be treated as an expense in the sixth month.

In a conventional accounting system, revenue is recorded when the project is completed. This can create serious problems in a long-term project in which expenses are accrued during each reporting period with no attendant revenue, and the revenue is reported in the final period with little or no associated expenses shown. The project runs at an apparent loss in each of the early periods and records an inordinately large profit at the time revenue is ultimately reported—the final reporting period. This can be seriously misleading in a long-term project which runs over a multi-year period.

To avoid such confusion, most long-term project P&L statements report revenue and expenses based on a "percentage of completion" formulation. The general intent is to "take down" an equitable percentage of the total project revenue (approximately equal to the proportion of the project work completed) during each accounting period, assigning an appropriate level of expense to arrive at an acceptable period gross margin. At the end of each accounting year and at the end of the project, adjustments are made to the recorded expenses to account for the differences between actual expenses incurred and the theoretical expenses recorded in the P&L statement. This can be a complex procedure. The misinformed or uninformed project manager can place the firm in an untenable position by erroneously misrepresenting the project's P&L status; and the rare unscrupulous project manager can use an arbitrary assessment of the project's percentage of completion to manipulate the firm's P&L statement.

There are several ways by which the project's percentage of completion can be assessed to avoid these risks. A typical method, which removes subjective judgments and the potential for manipulation by relying on strict accounting procedures is to be described. In this process a theoretical period expense is determined, which is divided by the total estimated project expense budget to compute the percentage of total budget expense for the period. This becomes the project's percentage of completion which is then used to determine the revenue to be "taken down" for the period. In this process, long delivery purchased items are not expensed on receipt of an invoice, but have the value of their purchase order prorated over the term of order execution. Figure 2 shows the $120,000 compressor in the example being expensed over the six-month delivery period at the rate of $20,000 per month.

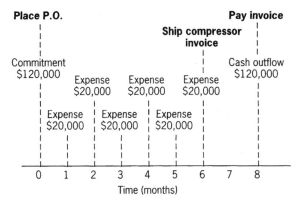

Figure 2 Percentage of completion expensing.

Cash Flow—The Comptroller's Concern The comptroller and the finance department are responsible for managing the organization's funds, and also assuring the availability of the appropriate amount of cash for payment of the project's bills. Unused funds are put to work for the organization in interest-bearing accounts or in other ventures. The finance department's primary concern is in knowing when funds will be needed for invoice payment in order to minimize the time that these funds are not being used productively. Therefore, the comptroller really views project cost as a *cash outflow*. Placement of a purchase order merely identifies a future cash outflow to the comptroller, requiring no action on his part. Receipt of the invoice generates a little more interest, as the comptroller now knows that a finite amount of cash will be required for a particular payment at the end of a fixed period. Once a payment becomes due, the comptroller provides the funds, payment is made, and the actual cash outflow is recorded.

It should be noted that the compressor example is a simplistic representation of an actual procurement cycle, as vendor progress payments for portions of the work (i.e., engineering, material, and delivery) may be included in the purchase order. In this case, commitment timing will not change, but the timing of the expenses and cash outflow will be consistent with the agreed-upon terms of payment.

The example describes the procurement aspect of project cost, but other project cost types are treated similarly. In the case of project labor, little time elapses between actual work execution (a commitment), the recording of the labor hours on a time sheet (an expense), and the payment of wages (cash outflow). Therefore, the three perceptions of cost are treated as if they each occur simultaneously. Subcontracts are treated in a manner similar to equipment purchases. A commitment is recorded when the subcontract is placed and cash outflow occurs when the monthly invoice for the work is paid. Expenses are treated in a slightly different manner. Instead of prorating the subcontract sum over the performance period, the individual invoices for the actual work performed are used to determine the expense for the period covered by each invoice.

Thus the three different perceptions of cost can result in three different time-based cost curves for a given project budget. Figure 3 shows a typical relationship between commitments, expenses, and cash outflow. The commitment curve leads and the cash outflow curve lags, with the expense curve falling in the middle. The actual shape and the degree of lag/lead between the curves are a function of several factors, including: the project's labor, material, and subcontract mix; the firm's invoice payment policy; the delivery period for major equipment items; subcontract performance period and the schedule of its work; and the effect of the project schedule on when and how labor will be expended in relation to equipment procurement.

The conscientious project manager must understand these different perceptions of cost and should be prepared to plan and report on any and all approaches required by management. The project manager should also be aware of the manner in which the accounting department collects and reports "costs." Since the project manager's primary concern is in the commitments, he or she should insist on an accounting system which is compatible with the project's reporting needs. Why must a project manager resort to a manual control system when the appropriate data can be made avail-

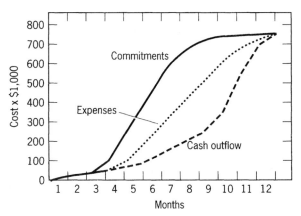

Figure 3 Three perceptions of cost.

able through an adjustment in the accounting department's data processing system?

Putting Your Understanding of Cost to Work

Most project managers believe that their total contribution to the firm's profitability is restricted by the ability to limit and control project cost, but they can do much more. Once the different perceptions of cost have been recognized, the project manager's effectiveness is greatly enhanced. The manner in which the project manager plans and executes the project can improve company profitability through influence on financing expenses, cash flow, and the reporting of revenue and expenses. To be a completely effective project manager one must be totally versed in the cost accounting practices which affect the firm's project cost reporting.

Examination of the typical project profit & loss statement (see Table 1) shows how a project sold for profit is subjected to costs other than the project's costs (cost of goods sold). The project manager also influences other areas of cost as well, addressing all aspects of the P&L to influence project profitability positively.

Specific areas of cost with examples of what a project manager can do to influence cost of goods sold, interest expense, tax expense, and profit are given next.

Cost of Goods Sold (Project Cost)

- Evaluation of alternate design concepts and the use of "trade-off" studies during the development phase of a project can result in a lower

Table 1 Typical Project Profit & Loss Statement

Revenue (project sell price)	$1,000,000
(less) cost of goods sold (project costs)	($ 750,000)
Gross margin	$ 250,000
(less) selling, general & administrative expenses	($ 180,000)
Profit before interest and taxes	$ 70,000
(less) financial expense	($ 30,000)
Profit before taxes	$ 40,000
(less) taxes	($ 20,000)
Net profit	$ 20,000

project cost, without sacrificing the technical quality of the project's output. The application of value engineering principles during the initial design period will also reduce cost. A directed and controlled investment in the evaluation of alternative design concepts can result in significant savings of project cost.

- Excessive safety factors employed to ensure "on-spec" performance should be avoided. Too frequently the functional members of the project team will apply large safety factors in their effort to meet or exceed the technical specifications. The project team must realize that such excesses increase the project's cost. The functional staff should be prepared to justify an incremental investment which was made to gain additional performance insurance. Arbitrary and excessive conservatism must be avoided.

- Execution of the project work must be controlled. The functional groups should not be allowed to stretch out the project for the sake of improvement, refinement, or the investigation of the most remote potential risk. When a functional task has been completed to the project manager's satisfaction (meeting the task's objectives), cut off further spending to prevent accumulation of "miscellaneous" charges.

- The project manager is usually responsible for controlling the project's contingency budget. This budget represents money that one expects to expend during the term of the project for specific requirements not identified at the project onset. Therefore, these funds must be carefully monitored to prevent indiscriminate spending. A functional group's need for a portion of the contingency budget must be justified and disbursement of these funds should only be made after the functional group has exhibited an effort to avoid or limit its use. It is imperative that the contingency budget be held for its intended purpose. Unexpected problems will ultimately arise, at which time the funds will be needed. Use of this budget to finance a scope change is neither advantageous to the project manager nor to management. The contingency budget represents the project manager's authority in dealing with corrections to the project work. Management must be made aware of the true cost of a change so that financing the change will be based on its true value (cost-benefit relationship).

- In the procurement of equipment, material and subcontract services, the specified requirements should be identified and the lowest priced, qualified supplier found. Adequate time for price "shopping" should be built into the project schedule. The Mercury project proved to be safe and successful even though John Glenn, perched in the Mercury capsule atop the Atlas rocket prior to America's first earth orbiting flight, expressed his now famous concern that "all this hardware was built by the low bidder." The project manager should ensure that the initial project budget is commensurate with the project's required level of reliability. The project manager should not be put in the position of having to buy project reliability with unavailable funds.

- Procurement of material and services based on partially completed drawings and specifications should be avoided. The time necessary for preparing a complete documentation package before soliciting bids should be considered in the preparation of the project schedule. Should an order be awarded based on incomplete data and the vendor then asked to alter the original scope of supply, the project will be controlled by the vendor. In executing a "fast track" project, the project manager should make certain that the budget contains an adequate contingency for the change orders which will follow release of a partially defined work scope.

- Changes should not be incorporated in the project scope without client and/or management approval and the allocation of the requisite funds. Making changes without approval will erode the existing budget and reduce project profitability; meeting the project manager's "on-cost" commitment will become extremely difficult, if not impossible.

- During periods of inflation, the project manager must effectively deal with the influence of the economy on the project budget. This is best accomplished during the planning or estimating stage of the work, and entails recognition of planning in an inflationary environment for its effect by estimating the potential cost of two distinct factors. First, a "price protection" contingency budget is needed to cover the cost increases that will occur between the time a vendor provides a firm quotation for a limited period and the actual date the order will be placed. (Vendor quotations used to prepare an estimate usually expire long before the material is actually purchased.) Second, components containing certain price-volatile materials (e.g., gold, silver, etc.) may not be quoted firm, but will be offered by the supplier as "price in effect at time of delivery." In this case an "escalation" contingency budget is needed to cover the added expense that will accrue between order placement and material delivery. Once the project manager has established these inflation related contingency budgets, the PM's role becomes one of ensuring controlled use.

Financial Expense

- The project's financial cost (interest expense) can be minimized by the project manager through the timing of order placement. Schedule slack time can be used to defer the placement of a purchase order so that the material is not available too early and the related cash outflow is not premature. There are several risks associated with this concept. Delaying an order too long could backfire if the desired material is unavailable when needed. Allowing a reasonable margin for error in the delivery cycle, saving some of the available slack time for potential delivery problems, will reduce this risk. Waiting too long to place a purchase order could result in a price increase which can more than offset the interest savings. It is possible to "lock-up" a vendor's price without committing to a required delivery date, but this has its limitations. If vendor drawings are a project requirement, an "engineering only" order can be placed to be followed by hardware release at the appropriate time. Deferred procurement which takes advantage of available slack time should be considered in the execution of all projects, especially during periods when the cost of money is excessively high.

- Vendors are frequently used to help "finance the project" by placing purchase orders which contain extended payment terms. Financially astute vendors will build the cost of financing the project into their sell price, but only to the extent of remaining competitive. A vendor's pricing structure should be checked to determine if progress payments would result in a reduced price and a net project benefit. A discount for prompt payment should be taken if the discount exceeds the interest savings that could result from deferring payment.

- Although frequently beyond the project manager's control, properly structured progress payment terms can serve to negate most or all project financial expenses. The intent is simple. A client's progress payment terms can be structured to provide scheduled cash inflows which offset the project's actual cash outflow. In other words, maintenance of a zero net cash position throughout the period of project execution will minimize the project's financial expense. In fact, a positive net cash position resulting from favorable payment terms can actually result in a project which creates interest income rather than one that incurs an interest expense. Invoices to the client should be processed quickly, to minimize the lost interest resulting from a delay in receiving payment.

- Similarly, the project manager can influence receipt of withheld funds (retention) and the project's final payment to improve the project's rate of cash inflow. A reduction in retention should be pursued as the project nears completion. Allowing a project's schedule to indiscriminately slip delays project acceptance, thereby delaying final payment. Incurring an additional expense to resolve a questionable problem should be considered whenever the expense will result in rapid project acceptance and a favorable interest expense reduction.

- On internally funded projects, where retention, progress payments, and other client related financial considerations are not a factor, management expects to achieve payback in the shortest reasonable time. In this case, project spending is a continuous cash outflow process which cannot be reversed until the project is completed and its anticipated financial benefits begin to accrue from the completed work. Unnecessary project delays, schedule slippages, and long-term investigations extend system startup and defer the start of payback. Early completion will result in an early start of the investment payback process. Therefore, management's payback goal should be considered when planning and controlling project work, and additional expenditures in the execution of the work should be considered if a shortened schedule will adequately hasten the start of payback.

Tax Expense and Profit

- On occasion, management will demand project completion by a given date to ensure inclusion of the project's revenue and profit within a particular accounting period. This demand usually results from a need to fulfill a prior financial performance forecast. Delayed project completion by only a few days could shift the project's entire revenue and profit from one accounting period to the next. The volatile nature of this situation, large sums of revenue and profit shifting from one period to the next, results in erratic financial performance which negatively reflects on management's ability to plan and execute their efforts.

- To avoid the stigma of erratic financial performance, management has been known to suddenly redirect a carefully planned, cost-effective project team effort to a short-term, usually costly, crash exercise, directed toward a project completion date, artificially necessitated by a corporate financial reporting need. Unfortunately, a project schedule driven by influences external to the project's fundamental objectives usually results in additional cost and reduces profitability.

- In this particular case, the solution is simple if a percentage of completion accounting process can be applied. Partial revenue and margin take-down during each of the project's accounting periods, resulting from this procedure (rather than lump sum take down in a single period at the end of the project, as occurs using conventional accounting methods) will mitigate the undesirable wild swings in reported revenue and profit. Two specific benefits will result. First, management's revenue/profit forecast will be more accurate and less sensitive to project schedule changes. Each project's contribution to the overall forecast will be spread over several accounting periods and any individual performance change will cause the shift of a significantly smaller sum from one accounting period to the next. Second, a project nearing completion will have had 90–95 percent of its revenue/profit taken down in earlier periods which will lessen or completely eliminate management pressure to complete the work to satisfy a financial reporting demand. Inordinate, unnecessary spending to meet such unnatural demands can thereby be avoided.

- An Investment Tax Credit,* a net reduction in corporate taxes gained from a capital investment project (a fixed percentage of the project's installed cost), can be earned when the project actually provides its intended benefit to the owner. The project manager should consider this factor in scheduling the project work, recognizing that it is not necessary to complete the entire project to obtain this tax benefit as early as possible. Failure to substantiate beneficial use within a tax year can shift this savings into the next tax year. The project manager should consider this factor in establishing the project's objectives, diligently working toward attainment by scheduling the related tasks to meet the tax deadline. Consideration should also be given to expenditures (to the extent they do not offset the potential tax savings) to reach this milestone by the desired date.

- In managing the corporate P&L statement, the need to shift revenue, expenses, and profit from one tax period to the next often exists. By managing the project schedule (expediting or delaying major component procurements or shifting expensive activities) the project manager can support this requirement. Each individual project affords a limited benefit, but this can be maximized if the project manager is given adequate notice regarding the necessary scheduling adjustments.

- Revenue/profit accrual based on percentage of completion can create a financial problem if actual expenses greatly exceed the project budget. In this case the project's percentage of completion will accumulate more quickly than justified and the project will approach a theoretical 100 percent completion before all work is done. This will "front load" revenue/profit take down

and will ultimately require a profit reversal at project completion. Some managers may find this desirable, since profits are being shifted into earlier periods, but most reputable firms do not wish to overstate profits in an early period which will have to be reversed at a later time. Therefore, the project manager should be aware of cost overruns and, when necessary, reforecast the project's "cost on completion" (increasing the projected cost and reducing the expected profit) to reduce the level of profit taken down in the early periods to a realistic level.

Conclusion

Cost is not a four letter word to be viewed with disdain by the project manager. It is a necessary element of the project management process which the project manager must comprehend despite the apparent mysteries of the accounting systems employed to report cost. The concept of cost is more than the expenses incurred in the execution of the project work: the manner in which cost is treated by the organization's functional elements can affect project performance, interest expenses and profitability. Therefore, the conscientious project manager must develop a complete understanding of project cost and the accounting systems used to record and report costs. The project manager should also recognize the effect of the timing of project cost, and the differences between commitments, expenses, and cash flow. The project manager should insist on the accounting system modifications needed to accommodate project cost reporting and control requirements. Once an appreciation for these concepts has been gained, the project manager can apply this knowledge towards positively influencing project and organizational profitability in all areas of cost through control of the project schedule and the execution of the project's work.

Questions

1. What is the major point of the article?
2. How does the accountant view project costs?
3. How does the controller view project costs?
4. How does the project manager view project costs?
5. What other costs does the project manager need to be cognizant of? What actions should the PM take concerning these other costs?

---

*The proposed tax law revisions under consideration in Congress at the time this article was written include a provision which eliminates the Investment Tax Credit.

8

Scheduling

The previous chapter initiated our discussion of project implementation. In this and the following three chapters, we continue with the implementation of the project plans we made in Chapter 5. In this chapter we examine some scheduling techniques that have been found to be useful in project management. We cover the Program Evaluation and Review Technique (PERT), the Critical Path Method (CPM), Gantt charts, and briefly discuss Precedence Diagramming, the Graphical Evaluation and Review Technique (GERT), Critical Resource Diagramming, Goldratt's "critical chain" [16], and report-based methods. Risk analysis and management will be considered as an inherent feature of all scheduling methods.

In Chapter 9, we consider the special problems of scheduling when resource limitations force conflicts between concurrent projects, or even between two or more tasks in a single project. We also look at ways of expediting activities by adding resources. Following a discussion of the monitoring and information system function in Chapter 10, we discuss the overall topic of project control in Chapter 11.

8.1 BACKGROUND

A schedule is the conversion of a project action plan into an operating timetable. As such, it serves as the basis for monitoring and controlling project activity and, taken together with the plan and budget, is probably the major tool for the management of projects. In a project environment, the scheduling function is more important than it would be in an ongoing operation because projects lack the continuity of day-to-day operations and often present much more complex problems of coordination. Indeed, project scheduling is so important that a detailed schedule is sometimes a customer-

Source: By permission of Johnny Hart and Creators Syndicate, Inc.

specified requirement. In later chapters we discuss the fact that a properly designed, detailed schedule can also serve as a key input in establishing the monitoring and control systems for the project.

Not all project activities need to be scheduled at the same level of detail. In fact, there may be several schedules (e.g., the master schedule, the development and testing schedule, the assembly schedule). These schedules are typically based on the previously determined action plan and/or work breakdown structure (WBS), and it is good practice to create a schedule for each major task level in the WBS that will cover the work packages. It is rarely necessary, however, to list all work packages. One can focus mainly on those that need to be monitored for maintaining adequate control over the project. Such packages are usually difficult, expensive, or have a relatively short time frame for their accomplishment.

The basic approach of all scheduling techniques is to form a network of activity and event relationships that graphically portrays the sequential relations between the tasks in a project. Tasks that must precede or follow other tasks are then clearly identified, in time as well as function. Such a network is a powerful tool for planning and controlling a project, and has the following benefits:

- It is a consistent framework for planning, scheduling, monitoring, and controlling the project.

- It illustrates the interdependence of all tasks, work packages, and work elements.

Project Management in Practice
Replacing the Atigun Section of the TransAlaska Pipeline

In June of 1977, the TransAlaska Pipeline was put into service as the successful conclusion of one of the most difficult projects in history. As part of the maintenance of the 48-inch diameter pipeline, instrumented "pigs" are run along the pipeline every year to detect both internal and external corrosion. In the fall of 1988, data from the pig run indicated that excessive external corrosion had occurred in an 8.5 mile section of the pipeline located in the Atigun River flood plain, 135 miles north of the Arctic Circle (see map). Thus, in the spring of 1989 a project team was formed to take total responsibility for replacing this portion of the buried pipeline with another buried pipe that had much better external corrosion protection, fusion bonded epoxy covered

with 1.25 inches of concrete, an articulated concrete mat, and then five to fifteen feet of dirt. As part of the project objectives, the oil flow of two million barrels per day at pressures exceeding 800 psi was *not* to be interrupted, and there could be absolutely no oil spills!

This meant that a bypass system had to be constructed while the pipe was being replaced, all in a very hostile work environment. The site is subject to flooding, rockslides, avalanches, mudslides, temperatures that reach −60°F in the winter (tires break like glass and gasoline turns to jelly at that temperature), and as little as three hours of sunshine in which to work during the winter months. To minimize exposure to the springtime avalanches, they worked in another

Polar bears at construction site—Atigun Section of TransAlaska Pipeline.

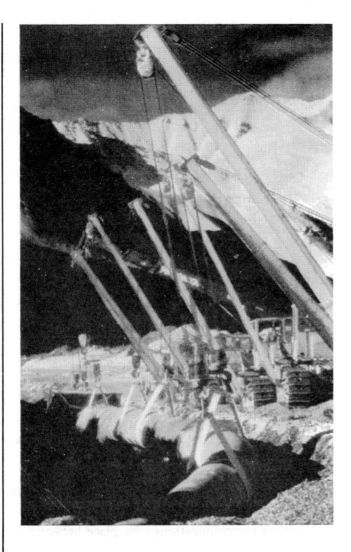

Sidebooms lower new pipe into ditch at −50°F temperatures.

area first and then used explosives to trigger potential avalanches and unstable snow deposits. Also, a full-time avalanche control and forecasting expert was present during construction in the danger area. Blasting was also used to dig the ditch, ironically, to protect the existing pipeline which was only 30 feet away. Another ironic aspect of the project was the constant curiosity of the wildlife in the area: "What impressed me most was completing this project right there in the middle of all these animals, and seeing that we didn't affect them at all—that was gratifying."

Source: Project Team, "Atigun Mainline Reroute Project," *PM Network*, January 1993.

The project began in September of 1989 and was completed in December 1991, a 27-month duration. Scheduling was a major facet of the project, not just due to the limited hours of sunshine, but also in obtaining facilities and materials for the project. For example, some elements of the replacement pipeline had to be shipped to Saudi Arabia for corrosion treatment and then shipped back, all just prior to the Persian Gulf war. Yet, the project met or exceeded all expectations, without one oil spill. More surprisingly, the project was completed 34 percent under budget through careful analysis of the financial and physical risks and assignment to the most appropriate contractor.

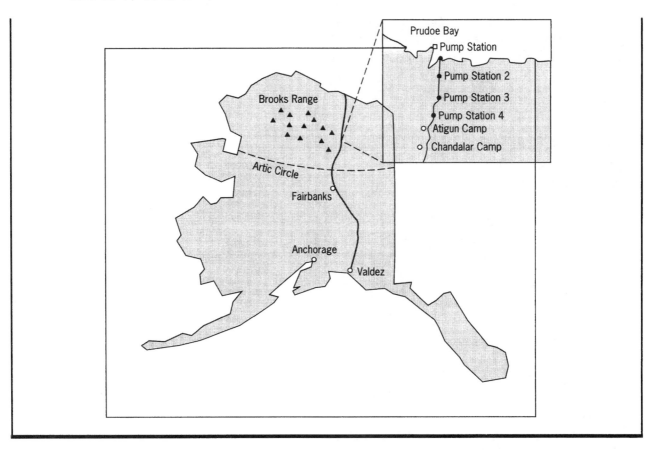

- It denotes the times when specific individuals must be available for work on a given task.

- It aids in ensuring that the proper communications take place between departments and functions.

- It determines an expected project completion date.

- It identifies so-called critical activities that, if delayed, will delay the project completion time.

- It also identifies activities with slack that can be delayed for specified periods without penalty, or from which resources may be temporarily borrowed without harm.

- It determines the dates on which tasks may be started—or must be started if the project is to stay on schedule.

- It illustrates which tasks must be coordinated to avoid resource or timing conflicts.

- It also illustrates which tasks may be run, or must be run, in parallel to achieve the predetermined project completion date.

- It relieves some interpersonal conflict by clearly showing task dependencies.

- It may, depending on the information used, allow an estimate of the probability of project completion by various dates, or the date corresponding to a particular a priori probability.

8.2 NETWORK TECHNIQUES: PERT AND CPM

With the exception of Gantt charts, to be discussed below, the most common approach to project scheduling is the use of network techniques such as PERT and CPM. The Program Evaluation and Review Technique was developed by the U.S. Navy in cooperation with Booz-Allen Hamilton and the Lockheed Corporation for the Polaris missile/submarine project in 1958. The Critical Path Method was developed by DuPont, Inc., during the same time period.

In application, PERT has primarily been used for R&D projects, the type of projects for which it was developed, though its use is more common on the "development" side of R&D than it is on the "research" side. CPM was designed for construction projects and has been generally embraced by the construction industry. (There are many exceptions to these generalities. The Eli Lilly Company, for example, uses CPM for its research projects.)

The two methods are quite similar and are often combined for educational presentation. Throughout most of this chapter we will not distinguish between them except where the differences are of direct interest to us. We will write "PERT/CPM" whenever the distinction is not important. Originally, however, PERT was strictly oriented to the time element of projects and used probabilistic activity time estimates to aid in determining the probability that a project could be completed by some given date. CPM, on the other hand, used deterministic activity time estimates and was designed to control both the time and cost aspects of a project, in particular, time/cost trade-offs. In CPM, activities can be "crashed" (expedited) at extra cost to speed up the completion time. Both techniques identified a project *critical path* whose activities could not be delayed, and also indicated activities with *slack* (or *float*) that could be somewhat delayed without lengthening the project completion time. Some writers insist on a strict differentiation between PERT and CPM. This strikes us as unnecessary. One can estimate probabalistic CPM times, and can "crash" PERT networks.

We might note in passing that the *critical* activities in real-world projects typically constitute less than 10 percent of the total activities. In our examples and simplified problems in this chapter, the critical activities constitute a much greater proportion of the total because we use smaller networks to illustrate the techniques.

Before explaining the mechanics of these methods, we must note that their value in use was not totally accepted by everyone. Research on the use of PERT/CPM conducted in the 1960s and early 1970s (e.g., [8]) found that there was no significant difference in the technological performance on projects where PERT/CPM was used and where it was not. This research found, however, that there was a significantly lower probability of cost and schedule overruns when PERT/CPM was used. In our experience, the use of network scheduling techniques has increased markedly in recent years, particularly with the proliferation of project management software packages that are inexpensive and reasonably friendly to PMs who are familiar with the fundamental concepts of PERT/CPM, and who are also sensible enough to avoid trying to construct complex networks by hand.

Research [4] finds that a greater use of "project management techniques" (PERT/CPM among a number of others) occurs on R&D type projects, on projects with greater levels of complexity, and on projects with resource limitations, than on other types of projects or those with lower levels of complexity and fewer resource limitations. Unfortunately, this otherwise excellent research did not investigate whether or not the use of project management software influenced the number of project management techniques used. The use of project management software for scheduling projects will be discussed and illustrated in Chapter 10.

Terminology

Let us now define some terms used in our discussion of networks.

Activity A specific task or set of tasks that are required by the project, use up resources, and take time to complete.

Event The result of completing one or more activities. An identifiable end state occurring at a particular time. Events use no resources.

Network The combination of all activities (often drawn as *arcs*) and events (often drawn as *nodes* at the beginning and end of each arc) defines the project and the activity precedence relationships. Networks are usually drawn starting on the left and proceeding to the right. Arrowheads placed on the arcs are used to indicate the direction of flow—that is, to show the proper precedences. Before an event can be *realized*—that is, achieved—all activities that immediately precede it must be completed. These are called its *predecessors*. Thus, an event represents an instant in time when each and every predecessor activity has been finished. They are merely points on the network, conditions of the system that can be recognized.

Path The series of connected activities (or intermediate events) between any two events in a network.

Critical Activities, events, or paths which, if delayed, will delay the completion of the project. A project's *critical path* is understood to mean that sequence of critical activities (and critical events) that connect the project's start event to its finish event.

To transform a project plan into a network, one must know what activities comprise the project and, for each activity, what its predecessors (and/or successors) are.

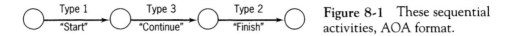

Figure 8-1 These sequential activities, AOA format.

An activity can be in any of these conditions: (1) it may have a successor(s) but no predecessor(s), (2) it may have a predecessor(s) but no successor(s), and (3) it may have both predecessor(s) and successor(s). The first of these is an activity that starts a network. The second ends a network. The third is in the middle. Figure 8-1 shows each of the three types of activities. Arrows are labeled with the appropriate type numbers. More than one arrow can start a network, end a network, or be in the middle. Any number of arrows can end at a node or depart from a node, as in Figure 8-2.

The interconnections depend on the technological relationships described in the action plan. For example, when one paints a room, filling small holes and cracks in the wall and masking windows and woodwork are predecessors to painting the walls. Similarly, removing curtains and blinds, as well as pictures and picture hooks from the wall are predecessors to spackling and masking. It is the nature of the work to be done that determines predecessor-successor relationships.

> As of tomorrow, employees will only be able to access the building using individual security cards. Pictures will be taken next Wednesday, and employees will receive their cards in two weeks.

In the examples above, arrows represent activities while nodes stand for events. This is an AOA (activity-on-arrow) network. Another format for drawing networks is AON (activity-on-node). In this case, activities are represented by nodes (usually shown as rectangles) with arrows to show the precedence relationships. In AON notation, when there are multiple activities with no predecessors, it is usual to show them all emanating from a single node called "start." Similarly, when multiple activities have no successors, it is usual to show them connected to a node called "end," as in Figure 8-3.

Figure 8-2 Activity network, AOA format

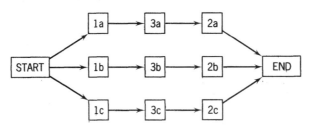

Figure 8-3   Activity network, AON format.

The choice between AOA and AON representation is largely a matter of personal preference. Our impression is that users of PERT favor AOA and users of CPM favor AON, but both approaches appear in the educational literature. Both are also used in commercially available computer packages, though AON is typically used in the most popular PC-based software. AOA networks are slightly harder to draw, but they identify events (milestones) clearly. AON networks do not require the use of *dummy* activities (defined below) and are easier to draw. Throughout most of this chapter we adopt the AOA format of PERT, but following the calculation of network time and activity slack, we will show equivalent calculations for an AON network. In this way, the reader can become familiar with both types of networks. This chapter is intended as an introduction to project scheduling at a level sufficient for the PM who wishes to use most commercial computerized project scheduling packages. For a deeper understanding of PERT/CPM, we refer the reader to [9, 33, 34, 52].

Recall the planning documents we developed in Chapter 5. In particular, the action plan contains the information we need. It is a list of all activities that must be undertaken in order to complete a specified task, the time each activity is expected to take, any nonroutine resources that will be used by the activity, and the predecessor activities for each activity. For example, we might have an action plan like that shown in Figure 8-4.

ACTION PLAN

Objective: To complete . . . .

Measures of Performance . . . .

Constraints . . . .

Tasks	Precedence	Time	Cost	Who Does
a	—	5 days	—	—
b	—	4 days	—	—
c	a	6 days	—	—
d	b	2 days	—	—
e	b	5 days	—	—
f	c,d	8 days	—	—

Figure 8-4   Sample action plan.

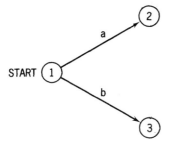

Figure 8-5   Sample of network construction.

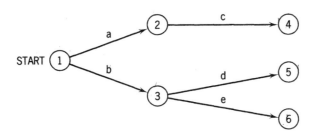

Figure 8-6   Sample of network construction.

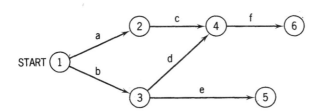

Figure 8-7   Sample of network construction.

Constructing the Network

Let us start by assuming the node numbered 1 denotes the event called "START." Activities **a** and **b** have no predecessors, so we assume their source is at START (node 1) and their destination at nodes we will number 2 and 3, respectively (Figure 8-5). As explained above, the arrowheads show the direction of flow.

Activity **c** follows **a**, activity **d** follows **b**, and activity **e** also follows **b**. Let's add these to our network in Figure 8-6. Note that we number the event nodes sequentially from left to right as we construct the network. No great damage occurs if we do not use this convention, but it is convenient.

Now note that activity **f** must follow both **c** and **d**, but *any given activity must have its source in one, and only one node.* Therefore, it is clear that **c** and **d**, both of which must precede **f**, must conclude in the same node from which **f** originates. We can now redraw the network, collapsing nodes 4 and 5 (and renumbering them) as in Figure 8-7.

The action plan does not indicate any further activity is required to complete the task, so we have reached the end of this particular plan. Once again, we can redraw

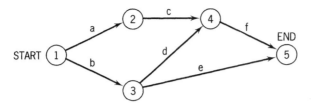

Figure 8-8 Sample of network construction.

the network to show that the final activities (those with no successors) end in a single node, Figure 8-8.

This process of drawing and redrawing the network may seem a bit awkward, and is. If the list of activities associated with a project is long, with complicated interrelationships, this way of constructing the network would be too time-consuming to be practical. Many of the project management software packages will generate these networks on request.

Construction of a network may not be straightforward in some cases. For instance, there may be a need for a dummy activity to aid in indicating a particular precedence, via a dashed arc. A dummy activity has no duration and uses no resources. Its sole purpose is to indicate a technological relationship.

Figure 8-9 illustrates the proper way to use a dummy activity if two activities occur between the same *two* events. Figure 8-9 also shows why dummy activities may be needed for AOA networks. An activity is identified by its starting and ending nodes as well as its "name." For example, activities **a** and **b** both start from node 1 and end at node 2. Many computer programs that are widely used for finding the critical path and time for networks require the nodes to identify which activity is which. In our example, **a** and **b** would appear to be the same, both starting at node 1 and ending at node 2.

Figure 8-10 illustrates how to use a dummy activity when activities **a, b,** and **c** must precede activity **d,** but only **a** and **b** must precede activity **e.** Last, Figure 8-11 illustrates the use of dummy activities in a more complex setting.

Let us now consider a small project with ten activities in order to illustrate the network technique. Table 8-1 lists the activities, their most likely completion times, and the activities that must precede them. The table also includes optimistic and pessimistic estimates of completion time for each activity in the list. Actual activity time is expected rarely to be less than the optimistic time or more than the pessimistic time. (More on this matter shortly.)

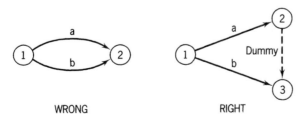

WRONG   RIGHT

Figure 8-9 Networking concurrent activities.

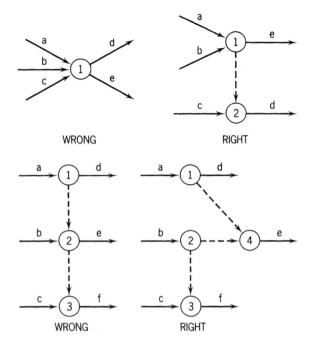

Figure 8-10   Activity **c** not required for **e.**

Figure 8-11   **a** precedes **d; a** and **b** precede **e; b** and **c** precede **f** (**a** does not precede **f**).

As described earlier, we start the network by finding those activities that have no predecessors. In the table activities **a, b,** and **c** meet the test. Therefore, they can all be drawn emerging from our starting node.

Next, we look for activities that only require **a, b,** or **c,** or some combination of **a, b,** and **c,** to precede them. Activity **d** requires that **a** be completed, and **e, f,** and **g** all require that **b** and **c** be completed. Note that a dummy will be necessary unless we begin the network from separate nodes for **b** and **c.** Last, **h** requires only that **c** be completed. To this point, the network might look like Figure 8-12.

Table 8-1.   Project Activity Times and Precedences

Activity	Optimistic Time	Most Likely Time	Pessimistic Time	Immediate Predecessor Activities
a	10	22	22	—
b	20	20	20	—
c	4	10	16	—
d	2	14	32	a
e	8	8	20	b,c
f	8	14	20	b,c
g	4	4	4	b,c
h	2	12	16	c
i	6	16	38	g,h
j	2	8	14	d,e

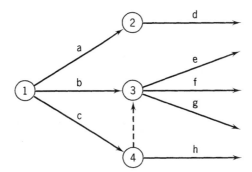

Figure 8-12   Partial network.

The last two activities, **i** and **j,** are drawn in the same manner. Activity **i** requires that both **g** and **h** be completed, so **g** and **h** are directed to a single node (node 5). Similarly, activity **j** requires the completion of both **d** and **e,** which are directed to node 6. Since no activities require that **f, i,** or **j** precede them, these activities are directed to the project completion node, 7. The complete project network is shown in Figure 8-13.

Calculating Activity Times

The next step is to calculate expected activity completion times from the data in Table 8-1. These expected completion times are found by using the three time estimates (optimistic, pessimistic, and most likely) in the table. Remember that these estimates are an expression of the risk associated with the time required for each activity and this begins the process of *risk management*. (The optimistic, pessimistic, and most likely estimates made for activity times are equally applicable to the estimates of resource usage made in Chapter 7, as are the calculations that follow.)

Once again, a short digression is helpful. Precisely what is meant by "optimistic," "pessimistic," and "most likely"? Assume that all possible times for some specific activity might be represented by a statistical distribution (e.g., the asymmetrical distribution in Figure 8-14). The "most likely" time, m, for the activity is the mode of this distribution. In theory, the "optimistic" and "pessimistic" times are selected in the following way. The PM, or whoever is attempting to estimate a and b, is asked to select

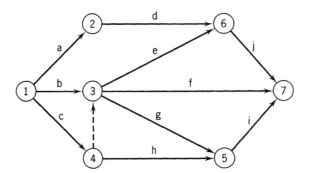

Figure 8-13   The complete network from Table 8-1.

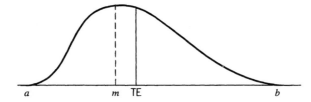

Figure 8-14   Distribution of all possible activity times for an activity.

a such that the actual time required by the activity will be a or greater about 99 percent of the time. Similarly, b is estimated such that about 99 percent of the time the activity will have a duration of b or less. (We know of no project managers or workers who are comfortable making estimates at this level of precision, but we will delay dealing with this problem for the moment.)

The expected time, TE, is found by

$$TE = (a + 4m + b)/6$$

where

a = optimistic time estimate,

b = pessimistic time estimate

m = most likely time estimate, the mode.

Note in Table 8-1 that some activity durations are known with certainty, which is to say that a, b, and m are the same (see activity **g**, for instance). Note further that the most likely time may be the same as the optimistic time ($a = m$) as in activity **e,** or that the most likely time may be identical to the pessimistic time ($m = b$) as in activity **a.** The range about m may be symmetric where

$$m - a = b - m$$

as in activity **c,** or may be quite asymmetric, as in activities **h** and **i.**

The above formula for calculating expected times is usually said to be based on the beta statistical distribution.* This distribution is used rather than the more common normal distribution because it is highly flexible in form and can take into account such extremes as where $a = m$ or $b = m$.

TE is an estimate of the mean of the distribution. It is a weighted average of a, m, and b with weights of 1-4-1, respectively. Again, we emphasize that this *same method can be applied to finding the expected level of resource usage given the appropriate estimates of the modal resource level as well as optimistic and pessimistic estimates.*

This process of estimating activity times comes occasionally under criticism. In general, critics argue that when activity times are set, these come to be considered as targets, leading to a comparison with Management by Objectives (MBO) [28]. This argument maintains that PERT/CPM success is due to the process of estimating times rather than to the estimates themselves. Although this assumes that MBO is still an operational concept in turn-of-the-century industry, the estimates are said to become self-

*We remind readers who wish a short refresher on elementary statistics and probability that one is available in Appendix B at the end of this book.

fulfilling prophecies. An additional argument [54] is that actual activity times are rarely less than the estimate of the mode, and are often greater, accounting for the right skew of the distribution. The cause is attributed to Parkinson's law—that work expands to fill the allotted time. If problems occur, the activity may require more time, but it will almost never require less. While no one, to the best of our knowledge, had proven this empirically, there is some anecdotal evidence that supports this notion. There is, however, also anecdotal evidence that supports the traditional assumption, that PERT/CPM estimates are the "best guesses" of people who have experience in similar activities. In any event, our purpose here is to estimate the range of time required for each activity rather than argue with the underlying logic of the estimation process.

> "Doing it right is no excuse for not meeting the schedule. No one will believe you solved this problem in one day! Now, go act busy for a few weeks and I'll let you know when it's time to tell them."

Sasieni noted [43] that writers (including himself) have been using the formula used here to estimate TE. He pointed out that it could not be derived from the formula for the beta distribution without several assumptions that were not necessarily reasonable, and he wondered about the original source of the formula. Fortunately, for two generations of writers on the subject, Littlefield and Randolph [28] cited a U.S. Navy paper that derives the approximations used here and states the not unreasonable assumptions on which they are based. Gallagher [14] makes a second derivation of the formula using a slightly different set of assumptions.

The results of the expected value calculations are shown in Table 8-2 and are included on Figure 8-15 as well. Also included in the table and on the network are

Table 8-2. Expected Activity Times (TE), Variances (σ^2), and Standard Deviations (σ)

Activity	Expected Time, TE	Variance σ^2	Standard Deviation, σ
a	20	4	2
b	20	0	0
c	10	4	2
d	15	25	5
e	10	4	2
f	14	4	2
g	4	0	0
h	11	5.4	2.32
i	18	28.4	5.33
j	8	4	2

measures of the uncertainty for the duration of each activity, the *variance*, σ^2, that is,

$$\sigma^2 = ((b - a)/6)^2$$

and the *standard deviation*, σ, which is given by

$$\sigma = \sqrt{\sigma^2}$$

This calculation of σ is based on the assumption that the standard deviation of a beta distribution is approximately one-sixth of its range, $(b - a)/6$.

Sasieni's inquiry [43] caused a flurry of research on the estimation of activity times for PERT analysis. For example, Keefer and Verdini report on the error associated with several different ways of approximating the mean and variance of activity times [23]. Kamburowski validates the methods used here [22]. (Both [22] and [23] have excellent bibliographies for anyone interested in investigating or pursuing the debate.) Later in this chapter, we will argue for an amendment to the estimation procedure for the variance of activity times if the estimates of a and b are not made at the 99 percent level.

Critical Path and Time

Consider the hypothetical project shown in Figure 8-15. Assume, for convenience, that the time units involved are days. How long will it take to complete the project? (Below each arrow, the expected activity time and its variance are shown in parentheses. For the moment we will treat the expected times as if they were certain.) If we start the project on day zero, we can begin simultaneously working on activities **a, b,** and **c,** each of which have no predecessor activities. We will reach event 2 in 20 days, event 3 in 20 days, and event 4 in ten days. We have shown these times just above or below their respective nodes. They are labeled EOT, earliest occurrence time, (or EFT, earliest finish time) because they represent the earliest times that the event can occur. Activity **d,** for example, cannot begin before event 2 has occurred, which means that all activities that precede event 2 must be completed. In this case, of course, activity **a** is the only predecessor of event 2.

Note that event 3 not only requires the completion of activity **b,** but also requires the completion of activity **c,** as shown by the dummy activity. (Refer to Figure 8-9 for

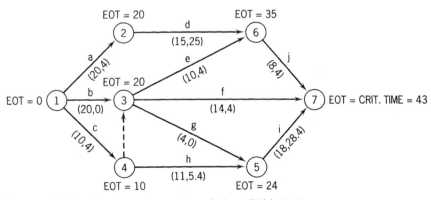

Figure 8-15   The complete network from Table 8-2.

a refresher.) The dummy requires neither time nor resources, so it does not affect the network time in any way. Event 3 does not occur until all paths leading to it have been completed. Therefore, the EOT for event 3 is equal to the time required by the *longest* path leading to it. The path from event 1 to event 3 requires the completion of activity **b** (20 days) *and* the completion of activities **c** and **dummy** (ten + zero days). Because the two paths may be followed simultaneously, we can reach event 3 in 20 days. Therefore, the earliest starting time (EST) for any activity emanating from event 3 is 20 days.

Proceeding similarly, we see that event 6 has two predecessor activities, **d** and **e.** Activity **d** cannot start until day 20, (EST = 20) and it requires 15 days to complete. Thus, its contribution to event 6 will require a total of 35 days from the start of the project. Activity **e** may also start after 20 days, the EOT for event 3, but it requires only ten days, a total of 30 days from the project start. Because event 6 requires the completion of both activities **d** and **e,** the EOT for event 6 is 35 days, the longest of the paths to it. Event 5 has an EOT of 24 days, the longest of the two paths leading to it, and event 7, the completion event of the network, has a time of 43 days. The EOTs are shown in Figure 8-15.

There are eight activity paths leading to event 7. They are

a-d-j = 20 + 15 + 8 = 43 days   **c-dummy-e-j** = 10 + 0 + 10 + 8 = 28 days

b-e-j = 20 + 10 + 8 = 38 days   **c-dummy-f**   = 10 + 0 + 14   = 24 days

 b-f = 20 + 14   = 34 days   **c-dummy-g-i** = 10 + 0 + 4 + 18 = 32 days

b-g-i = 20 + 4 + 18 = 42 days

c-h-i = 10 + 11 + 18 = 39 days

The longest of these paths is **a-d-j** using 43 days, which means that 43 days is the shortest time in which the entire network can be completed. This is called the *critical time* of the network, and **a-d-j** is the *critical path*, usually shown as a heavy line.

In a simple network such as our example, it is easy to find and evaluate every path between start and finish. Many real networks are considerably more complex, and finding all paths can be taxing. Using the method illustrated above, there is no need to worry about the problem. Every node is characterized by the fact that one or more activities lead to it. Each of these activities has an expected duration and originates in an earlier node. As we proceed to calculate the EOT of each node, beginning at the start, we are *actually finding the critical path and time to each of the nodes* in the network. Note that event 5 has an EOT (critical time) of 24 days, and its critical path is **b-g** rather than **c-h** which requires 21 days, or **c-dummy-g** which takes 14 days.

The number of activities directly entering an event tells us the number of paths we must evaluate to find the EOT for that event. Here, *path* is defined as originating at immediate predecessor events, not at the network origin. With event 5, that number is two, so we find the EOT and activity times for the two immediate predecessors. For event 7, we have three evaluations to do, the EOT of event 6 plus the duration of activity **j** (43 days), the EOT of event 3 plus the duration of **f** (34 days), and the EOT of event 5 plus the duration of **i** (42 days). There is, therefore, no need to find, list, and evaluate all possible start-to-finish paths in the network.

Although we will assume throughout this chapter that we always employ the "as-soon-as-possible" approach to scheduling tasks ("early start"), there are situations where other approaches are sometimes used. One example is the simultaneous start, where all resources are launched at the beginning. Another is the simultaneous finish, where a facility can be moved to its next location once all the tasks are finished. Of course, delay early on in a project runs the risk of delaying the overall project if some other activities inadvertently become delayed. One important reason for using an "as-late-as-possible" approach is that it delays the use of resources as much as possible, thereby optimizing the cash flow of the project, but again at some risk of delay.

Slack

Thus far in this discussion we have focused mostly on the events in the network. We found the EOTs for the project milestones (significant, identifiable events). It is now helpful to focus on the activities by finding their earliest starting times (EST) and latest possible starting times (LST). As noted in the previous section, the EST for an activity is equal to the EOT for the event from which the activity emanates. Activity i cannot start until event 5 has occurred. Event 5 has an EOT of 24 days, and so activity i has an EST of 24 days. An important question for the PM is this: What is the latest time (LST) activity i could start without making the entire project late?

Refer again to Figure 8-15. The project has a critical time of 43 days. Activity i requires 18 days to be accomplished. Therefore, i must be started no later than day 25 ($43 - 18 = 25$) if the project is to be complete on day 43. The LST for activity i is day 25. Because i cannot begin until event 5 has occurred, the latest occurrence time (LOT) for event 5 is also day 25. The difference between the LST and the EST for an activity is called its *slack* or *float*. In the case of activity i, it must be started no later than day 25, but *could* be started as early as day 24, so it has one day of slack. It should be immediately obvious that all activities on the critical path have zero slack. They cannot be delayed without making the project late.

For another example, consider activity f. Its EST is day 20, which is equal to the EOT for event 3 from which it emanates. The LST for activity f is $43 - 14 = 29$. If f is started later than day 29, it will delay the entire project. Activity f has slack of $LST - EST = 29 - 20 = 9$ days.

To find the slack for any activity or the LOT for any event, we make a backward pass (right to left) through the network just as we made a forward pass (left to right) to find the critical path and time and the EOTs for all events (which are also the ESTs for successor activities). There is one simple convention we must adopt: *When there are two or more noncritical activities on a path, it is conventional to calculate the slack for each activity as if it were the only activity in the path.* Thus, when finding the slack for activity i, for example, we assume that none of i's predecessors are delayed, and that event 5 occurred on its EOT of day 24. Of course, if some activity, x, had six days of slack (given a specific EOT for the immediate preceding event), and if an earlier activity was late, causing the event to be delayed say two days, then activity x would have only four days of slack, having lost two days to the earlier delay.

It is simple to calculate slack for activities that are immediate predecessors of the final node. As we move to earlier activities, it is just a bit more complicated. Consider activity **g.** Remembering our assumption that the other activities in the same path use none of the available slack, we see that activity **i** must follow **g,** and that **g** emanates from event 3. Starting with the network's critical time of 43 days, we subtract 18 days for activity **i** and four more days for **g** ($43 - 18 - 4 = 21$). Thus **g** can begin no later than day 21 without delaying the network. The EST for **g** (EOT for event 3) is day 20, so **g** has one day of slack.

To find the LOT for event 3, we must investigate each path that emanates from it. We have already investigated two paths, one with activity **g** and one with activity **f.** Recall that **f** could start as late as day 29. For **f** not to delay the network, event 3 would have to be complete not later than day 29. But activity **g** must start no later than day 21, so event 3 must be complete by day 21 or the **g-i** path will cause a delay. Now consider activity **e,** the only remaining activity starting from event 3. Activity **e** must be completed by day 35 or event 6 will be late and the network will be delayed. (Note that we do not have to work backward from the end of the network to find the slack for any activity that ends at a node on the critical path. All events and activities on the critical path have zero slack, so any activity ending on this path must arrive at event 6 not later than day 35.) The LST for **e** is $35 - 10 = 25$. Its EST is day 20, so activity **e** has five days of slack.

We now can see that the LOT for event 3 is day 21, the most restrictive (earliest) time required, so that no activity emanating from it will cause the network to be late. Table 8-3 shows the LST, EST, and slack for all activities, and the LOT, EOT, and slack for all events.

Table 8-3. Times and Slacks for Network In Figure 8-15

Event	LOT	EOT	Slack
1	0	0	0
2	20	20	0
3	21	20	1
4	14	10	4
5	25	24	1
6	35	35	0
7	43	43	0

Activity	LST	EST	Slack
a	0	0	0
b	1	0	1
c	4	0	4
d	20	20	0
e	25	20	5
f	29	20	9
g	21	20	1
h	14	10	4
i	25	24	1
j	35	35	0

On occasion, the PM may negotiate an acceptable completion date for a project which allows for some slack in the entire network. If, in our example, an acceptable date was 50 working days after the project start, then the network would have a total of $50 - 43 = 7$ days of slack. This is the latest occurrence time minus the earliest occurrence time for the ending node, 7, of the network.

There is another interesting, manual method for finding the critical time and path for a network as well a calculating activity slack for all activities in the network [55]. Just as construction of the network and the calculations shown just above require an ordered listed of all activities, their precedences, and times (either expected or deterministic), so does this optional method. Rather than construct a network, however, the optional method requires construction of a from-to matrix for all activities. Calculation of the critical path, time, and slack is straightforward and simple.*

Uncertainty of Project Completion Time

When discussing project completion dates with senior management, the PM should try to determine the probability that a project will be completed by the suggested deadline—or find the completion time associated with a predetermined level of risk. With the information in Table 8-2, this is not difficult.

If we assume that the activities are statistically independent of each other, then the variance of a set of activities is equal to the sum of the variances of the individual activities comprising the set. Those who have taken a course in statistics will recall that the variance of a population is a measure of the population's dispersion and is equal to the square of the population's standard deviation. The variances in which we are interested are the variances of the activities on the critical path.

The critical path of our example includes activities **a, d,** and **j.** From Table 8-2 we find that the variances of these activities are 4, 25, and 4, respectively; and the variance for the critical path is the sum of these numbers, 33 days. Assume, as above, that the PM has promised to complete the project in 50 days. What are the chances of meeting that deadline? We find the answer by calculating Z, where

$$Z = (D - \mu)/\sqrt{\sigma_\mu^2}$$

and

D = the desired project completion time

μ = the critical time of the project, the sum of the TEs for activities on the critical path

σ_μ^2 = the variance of the critical path, the sum of the variances of activities on the critical path

Z = the number of standard deviations of a normal distribution (the *standard normal deviate*)

---

*Recognizing that the primary purpose of solving these problems manually is to teach PERT/CPM to students or neophyte project managers, we note this optional method for use when a non-network approach might be an aid to understanding.

Z, as calculated above, can be used to find the probability of completing the project on time.

Using the numbers in our example, D = 50, μ = 43, and σ_μ^2 = 33 (the square root of σ_μ^2 is 5.745), we have

$$Z = (50 - 43)/5.745$$
$$= 1.22 \text{ standard deviations}$$

We turn now to Table 8-4, which shows the probabilities associated with various levels of Z. (Table 8-4 also appears as Appendix A. It is shown here for the reader's convenience.) We go down the left column until we find Z =1.2, and then across to column .02 to find Z = 1.22. The probability value of Z = 1.22 shown in the table is .8888, which is the likelihood that we will complete the critical path of our sample project within 50 days of the time it is started. Figure 8-16 shows the resulting probability distribution of the project completion times.*

We can work the problem backward, too. What deadline is consistent with a .95 probability of on-time completion? First, we go to Table 8-4 and look through the table until we find .95. The Z value associated with .95 is 1.645. (The values in the table are not strictly linear, so our interpolation is only approximate.) We know that μ is 43 days, and that $\sqrt{\sigma_\mu^2}$ is 5.745. Solving the equation for D, we have

$$D = \mu + 5.745(1.645)$$
$$= 43 + 9.45$$
$$= 52.45 \text{ days.}$$

Thus, there is a 95 percent chance of finishing the project by 52.45 days.

Note that as D approaches μ, Z gets smaller, approaching zero. Table 8-4 shows that for Z = 0, the chance of on-time completion is 50–50. The managerial implications are all too clear. If the PM wants a reasonable chance of meeting a project deadline, there must be some slack in the project schedule. When preparing a project budget, it is quite proper to include some allowance for contingencies. The same principle holds for preparing a project schedule. The allowance for contingencies in a schedule is *network slack*, and the wise PM will insist on some.

Finally, to illustrate an interesting point, let's examine a noncritical path, activi-

Figure 8-16 Probability distribution of project completion times.

---

* Our use of the normal distribution is allowed by the Central Limit Theorem which attests to the fact that the sum of independent activity times is normally distributed if the number of activities is large.

Table 8-4. Cumulative (Single Tail) Probabilities of the Normal Probability Distribution (Areas under the Normal Curve from $-\infty$ to Z)

Example: the area to the left of $Z = 1.34$ is found by following the left Z column down to 1.3 and moving right to the .04 column. At the intersection read .9099. The area to the right of $Z = 1.34$ is $1 - .9099 = .0901$. The area between the mean (dashed line) and $Z = 1.34 = .9099 - .5 = .4099$.

z	.00	.01	.02	.03	.04	.05	.06	.07	.08	.09
.0	.5000	.5040	.5080	.5120	.5160	.5199	.5239	.5279	.5319	.5359
.1	.5398	.5438	.5478	.5517	.5557	.5596	.5636	.5675	.5714	.5753
.2	.5793	.5832	.5871	.5910	.5948	.5987	.6026	.6064	.6103	.6141
.3	.6179	.6217	.6255	.6293	.6331	.6368	.6406	.6443	.6480	.6517
.4	.6554	.6591	.6628	.6664	.6700	.6736	.6772	.6808	.6844	.6879
.5	.6915	.6950	.6985	.7019	.7054	.7088	.7123	.7157	.7190	.7224
.6	.7257	.7291	.7324	.7357	.7389	.7422	.7454	.7486	.7517	.7549
.7	.7580	.7611	.7642	.7673	.7704	.7734	.7764	.7794	.7823	.7852
.8	.7881	.7910	.7939	.7967	.7995	.8023	.8051	.8078	.8106	.8133
.9	.8159	.8186	.8212	.8238	.8264	.8289	.8315	.8340	.8365	.8389
1.0	.8413	.8438	.8461	.8485	.8508	.8531	.8554	.8577	.8599	.8621
1.1	.8643	.8665	.8686	.8708	.8729	.8749	.8770	.8790	.8810	.8880
1.2	.8849	.8869	.8888	.8907	.8925	.8944	.8962	.8980	.8997	.9015
1.3	.9032	.9049	.9066	.9082	.9099	.9115	.9131	.9147	.9162	.9177
1.4	.9192	.9207	.9222	.9236	.9251	.9265	.9279	.9292	.9306	.9319
1.5	.9332	.9345	.9357	.9370	.9382	.9394	.9406	.9418	.9429	.9441
1.6	.9452	.9463	.9474	.9484	.9495	.9505	.9515	.9525	.9535	.9545
1.7	.9554	.9564	.9573	.9582	.9591	.9599	.9608	.9616	.9625	.9633
1.8	.9641	.9649	.9656	.9664	.9671	.9678	.9686	.9693	.9699	.9706
1.9	.9713	.9719	.9726	.9732	.9738	.9744	.9750	.9756	.9761	.9767
2.0	.9772	.9778	.9783	.9788	.9793	.9798	.9803	.9808	.9812	.9817
2.1	.9821	.9826	.9830	.9834	.9838	.9842	.9846	.9850	.9854	.9857
2.2	.9861	.9864	.9868	.9871	.9875	.9878	.9881	.9884	.9887	.9890
2.3	.9893	.9896	.9898	.9901	.9904	.9906	.9909	.9911	.9913	.9916
2.4	.9918	.9920	.9932	.9925	.9927	.9929	.9931	.9932	.9934	.9936
2.5	.9938	.9940	.9941	.9943	.9945	.9946	.9948	.9949	.9951	.9952
2.6	.9953	.9955	.9956	.9957	.9959	.9960	.9961	.9962	.9963	.9964
2.7	.9965	.9966	.9967	.9968	.9969	.9970	.9971	.9972	.9973	.9974
2.8	.9974	.9975	.9976	.9977	.9977	.9978	.9979	.9979	.9980	.9981
2.9	.9981	.9982	.9982	.9983	.9984	.9984	.9985	.9985	.9986	.9986
3.0	.9987	.9987	.9987	.9988	.9988	.9989	.9989	.9989	.9990	.9990
3.1	.9990	.9991	.9991	.9991	.9992	.9992	.9992	.9992	.9993	.9993
3.2	.9993	.9993	.9994	.9994	.9994	.9994	.9994	.9995	.9995	.9995
3.3	.9995	.9995	.9995	.9996	.9996	.9996	.9996	.9996	.9996	.9997
3.4	.9997	.9997	.9997	.9997	.9997	.9997	.9997	.9997	.9997	.9998

ties **b-g-i**. The variance of this path (from Figure 8-15) is $0 + 0 + 28.4 = 28.4$, which is slightly less than the variance of the critical path. The path time is 42 days. The numerator of the fraction $(D - \mu)/\sqrt{\sigma_\mu^2}$ is larger, and in this case the denominator is smaller. Therefore, Z will be larger, and the probability of this path delaying project completion is less than for the critical path. But consider the noncritical path **c-h-i** with a time of $10 + 11 + 18 = 39$ days, and a total variance of 37.8. (Remember, we are trying to find the probability that this noncritical path with its higher variance but shorter completion time will make us late, given that the critical path is 43 days.)

$$Z = (50 - 39)/6.15$$
$$Z = 1.79$$

The result is that we have a 96 percent chance for this noncritical path to allow the project to be on time.

If the desired time for the network equaled the critical time, 43 days, we have seen that the critical path has a 50–50 chance of being late. What are the chances that the noncritical path **c-h-i,** will make the project late? D is now 43 days, so we have

$$Z = \frac{(43 - 39)}{6.15}$$
$$= .65$$

$Z = .65$ is associated with a probability of .74 of being on time, or $1 - .74 = .26$ of being late.

Assuming that these two paths (**a-d-j** and **c-h-i**) are independent, the probability that *both* paths will be completed on time is the product of the individual probabilities, $(.50)(.74) = .37$, which is considerably less than the 50–50 we thought the chances were. (If the paths are not independent, the calculations become more complicated.) Therefore, it is a good idea to consider noncritical paths that have activities with large variances and/or path times that are close to critical in duration (i.e., those with little slack).

This leads us to what is often referred to as *merge bias* [20]. Any time two or more paths of a network come together or merge we have the case noted just above, the probability of both paths being on time is the product of the probabilities for the individual paths. If one of the paths is critical and the others have a reasonable amount of slack (and/or low path variance compared to the critical path), the problem of merge bias is rarely serious. If, however, a second path has low slack and significant path variance, we cannot ignore it. If the merged path leads to another path merger later in the network, the likelihood of that merger being on time is, once again, the product of the probabilities of the two paths. While this is not conceptually hard to handle, in a large network the problem can make for considerable arithmetic. If one wishes to avoid the arithmetic, we can use simulation.

Simulation is an obvious way to check the nature and impacts of interactions between probabilistic paths in a network. While this used to be difficult and time consuming, software has now been developed which simplifies matters greatly. There are several excellent software packages that link directly many of the popular project management application packages, for instance, Risk+®, @Risk®, and Crystal Ball®. All the above allow easy simulation of network interactions and yield data that show the probability of completing the networks in specific times [26]. These simulations, of course, include the possible results of path mergers. As we have stated earlier, the methods noted here can also be applied to risk analysis for resources. If resource usage is related to the time required by an activity, then the uncertainty about time means that there is also uncertainty about resource use. If the relationship between activity time and resource use is known or can be assumed to be roughly linear, it is not difficult to estimate the resource equivalents of the simulation. The likelihood of a strictly linear relationship is very low unless one gets the data from the accounting department. Hulett [20] mentions integrated cost/schedule risk, and notes that most software does not deal with this issue.

If one does not have easy access to such software as Risk+® or some similar type of application software, it is quite possible to use Excel® to conduct a simulation. The method for using Excel® for simulation of PERT networks is clearly explained in Shafer and Meredith [45, pp. 716–720]. It is important to note that if the optimistic and pessimistic time (or resource) estimates are made at the 95 or 90 percent levels (rather than the traditional but impossible 99 percent level, as we will advise in the next section), care must be taken to calculate the variance or standard deviation correctly. Fortunately, it is simple to enter the appropriate method of calculation in Excel®.

Toward Realistic Time Estimates

The calculations of expected network times, and the uncertainty associated with those time estimates performed in the preceding sections are based, as we noted, on estimating optimistic and pessimistic times at the .99 level. That is, a is estimated such that the actual time required for an activity will be a or higher 99 percent of the time and will be b or lower 99 percent of the time. We then noted, parenthetically, that no project managers of our acquaintance are comfortable making estimates at that level of precision.

Fortunately, in practice it is not necessary to make estimates at the one-in-a-hundred level. Unless the underlying distribution is very asymmetric, no great error is introduced in finding TE if the pessimistic and optimistic estimates are made at the 95 percent, or even at the 90 percent levels; that is to say, only once in 20 times (or ten times for the 90 percent level) will the actual activity time be greater than or less than the pessimistic or optimistic estimates, respectively. *The formula for calculating the variance of an activity, however, must be modified.*

Recall that the calculation of variance is based on the assumption that the standard deviation of a beta distribution is approximately one-sixth of its range. Another way of putting this assumption is that a and b are estimated at the -3σ and $+3\sigma$ limits respectively—roughly at the 99+ percent levels. Let the 95 percent estimates be represented by a' and b' and 90 percent estimates by a'' and b''. If we use a 95 or 90

Consider the following project (times given in days).

Activity	a	m	b	Predecessors
a	1	4	7	—
b	2	2	2	—
c	2	5	8	a
d	3	4	5	a
e	4	6	8	c,b
f	0	0	6	c,b
g	3	6	9	d,e

Find:

1. The network.
2. All expected activity times, variances, and slacks.
3. The critical path and expected completion time.
4. The probability the project will be done in 23 days.
5. The completion time corresponding to 95% probability

2.

Activity	TE	σ^2	Slack
a	4	1.00	0
b	2	0	7
c	5	1.00	0
d	4	0.11	7
e	6	0.44	0
f	1	1	11
g	6	1	0

3. Critical path is a-c-e-g for a time of 21 days.
4. $z = (23 - 21)/\sqrt{3.44} = 1.078$ for a probability of 85.9%.
5. $P = 0.95$ corresponds to $z = 1.65 = (T - 21)/1.855$, or $T = 24.06$ days.

Answer

1.

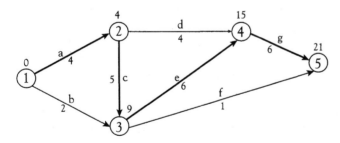

percent estimation level, we are actually moving both a and b in from the distribution's tails so that the range will no longer represent $\pm 3\sigma$. See Figure 8-17.

It is simple to correct the calculation of variance for this error. Consider the 95 percent estimates. Referring to Table 8-4 we can find the Z associated with .95 of the area under the curve from a' to ∞. For .95, Z is approximately -1.65. (Of course, this applies to the normal distribution rather than to the beta distribution, but this heuristic appears to work quite well in practice.) Similarly, $Z = 1.65$ for the area under the curve from $-\infty$ to b'.

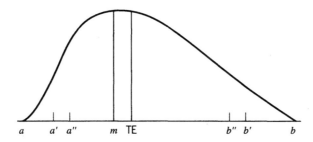

Figure 8-17 a, m, and b estimates at the 99, 95, and 90 percent levels.

The range between b' and a' represents $2(1.65)\sigma = 3.3\sigma$, rather than the 6σ used in the traditional estimation of the variance. Therefore when estimating a' and b' at the 95 percent level, we should change the variance calculation formula to read

$$\sigma^2 = ((b' - a')/3.3)^2$$

For estimations at the 90 percent level (a'' and b'' in Figure 8-17), Z is approximately 1.3 and the variance calculation becomes

$$\sigma^2 = ((b'' - a'')/2.6)^2$$

In order to verify that this modification of the traditional estimator for the variance of a beta distribution gave good estimates of the true variance, we ran a series of trials using Statistical Analysis Systems (SAS) PROC IML for beta distributions of different shapes and estimated a and b at the 95 and 90 percent levels. We then compared these estimates of a and b with the true variance of the distribution and found the differences to be quite small, consistently under five percent.

It is important to repeat that we have never met a PM who was comfortable attempting to estimate the optimistic and pessimistic levels for an activity time or resource level at the one-in-a-hundred level. Few have any real confidence in such estimates. Estimates at the 90 or 95 percent levels are quite a different matter. If estimates are made at these levels, however, use of the traditional calculation for variance ($\{[b - a]/6\}^2$) will result in a serious underestimation of path variances and introduce considerable error into estimates of the probabilities of completing projects by specific dates. (A similar warning holds when one uses a triangular distribution as shown in [39, p.116] and [20, pp.22ff]) Some writers recommend the use of contingency allowances. While we applaud Eichhorn's approach [12] that clearly identifies such allowances by introducing them as activities that show up on networks or Gantt charts, we think that such allowances are not particularly helpful. They simple codify the "padding" that is typical in organizations in which workers avoid measurement of work, largely because they distrust their managers.

Once again, we caution readers. Neither statistical analysis [e.g., 41 and 18] nor simulation [e.g., 36 and 26], nor contingency allowances [12] will help the PM manage risk if the input data are biased or carelessly developed. One suggestion made by several writers is to use specialized teams to assess risk and make estimates [13, 30]. Another writer suggests a "10-step mini-process" for estimating [10]. Still another recommends a group of experts who will use the Delphi process [6]. Any of these may help increase care and reduce bias when making estimates.

An alternate method for approximating the mean and variance of a beta distribution when a and b are estimated at the 95 percent level is given in the last section of Appendix B. For the full exposition of the method, see reference 5 of Appendix B.

Another Excel® File

Just as we did in Chapter 7 on budgeting, we can construct an Excel® template to do the calculations for finding the expected times, variances, and standard deviations associated with a series of three-time estimates for PERT/CPM networks. Figure 8-18 shows the file itself and Figure 8-19 shows the formulas used. Remember that the formula for calculation of variance must be modified according to the previous section unless a and b are estimated at the 99+ percent levels.

Most of the project management software packages will not accept three-time estimates or do the necessary calculations to use such estimates, but a large majority of such software packages will routinely exchange information with Lotus 1-2-3®, Excel®, and similar spreadsheet software. It is therefore quite simple to enter the three-time estimates into an Excel® file and enter the expected activity times, TEs, into a project management scheduling package where they can be used as if they were deterministic times in finding a project's critical path and time. Calculations of the probability of completing a project on or before some elapsed time can easily be done by hand.

Activity-On-Node (AON) Notation

As we stated above, the more popular PC-based project management software programs display AON networks. Consider Table 8-1 again. We can easily construct an AON network. Beginning with a node named START, connect the three activities with no predecessors, (a, b, and c), to the Start node as in Figure 8-20. Activity **d** has a predecessor of **a,** and thus it follows **a.** Activities **e, f,** and **g** all must follow both **b** and **c** as predecessors. Activity **h** follows **c.** Activity **j** follows both **d** and **e.** Activity **i** follows **g** and **h.** Because there are no more activities, we must be at the end of the network. Add a node labeled "End" and connect any nodes without successor activities, in this case, **j, f,** and **i,** reading from top to bottom. As was the case with AOA networks, always show the direction of a connection with an arrowhead. For a more complex AON network, see Figure 8-30, toward the end of the chapter. This was easily drawn by hand, but an AOA network of this size would be difficult to draw by hand.

Given knowledge of the AOA network and the calculations of critical time, critical path, and activity slack, we can now easily find the same items in the AON network. Figure 8-21 shows the same network as in Figure 8-20 based on the information in Table 8-1. In addition, the expected times tabulated in Table 8-2 have been entered on Figure 8-21 in the appropriate nodes. (We will pretend that the activity times are deterministic to simplify this example.) The "a 20" entered in the upper left-hand node means that this is Activity **a** with a duration of 20 days—similarly for all other nodes. We can now make the left-to-right pass through the network, just as we did in the AOA examples.

The numbers appearing just above each node in Figure 8-21 are the earliest start time on the left and the earliest finish time on the right. (Most software does not au-

	A	B	C	D	E	F	G	H
1	This is a template for three-time PERT schedule estimates							
2								
3	a = optimistic time estimate							
4	b = pessimistic time estimate							
5	m = typical (modal) time estimate							
6								
7	Activity		a	m	b	TE	Variance	Std. Dev.
8	=======	========	=======	========	=======	========	=========	========
9								
10	a		5	6	8	6.17	0.250	0.500
11	b		4	7	8	6.67	0.444	0.667
12	c		6	8	12	8.33	1.000	1.000
13	d		7	7	7	7.00	0.000	0.000
14	e		6	7	8	7.00	0.111	0.333
15	f		4	5	12	6.00	1.778	1.333
16	g		4	6	9	6.17	0.694	0.833
17								

Figure 8-18   A spreadsheet template for PERT schedules.

	A	B	C	D	E	F	G
1							
2							
3							
4							
5							
6							
7	Activity	a	m	b	TE	Variance*	Std. Dev.
8	----	----	----	----	----	----	----
9							
10	a	5	6	8	=(B10+(4*C10)+D10)/6	=(((D10−B10)/6)^2)	=(F10^0.5)
11	b	4	7	8	=(B11+(4*C11)+D11)/6	=(((D11−B11)/6)^2)	=(F11^0.5)
12	c	6	8	12	=(B12+(4*C12)+D12)/6	=(((D12−B12)/6)^2)	=(F12^0.5)
13	d	7	7	7	=(B13+(4*C13)+D13)/6	=(((D13−B13)/6)^2)	=(F13^0.5)
14	e	6	7	8	=(B14+(4*C14)+D14)/6	=(((D14−B14)/6)^2)	=(F14^0.5)
15	f	4	5	12	=(B15+(4*C15)+D15)/6	=(((D15−B15)/6)^2)	=(F15^0.5)
16	g	4	6	9	=(B16+(4*C16)+D16)/6	=(((D16−B16)/6)^2)	=(F16^0.5)
17							

*Adjust variance formula for level of precision (99+, 95, or 90).

Figure 8-19 Template formulas for PERT spreadsheet.

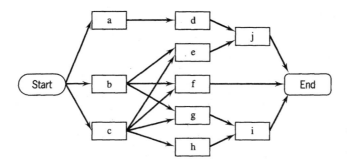

Figure 8-20 An AON network from Table 8-1.

tomatically list the start and finish times on the activity nodes, but rather, given a project start date, the start and finish dates are listed in columns, as illustrated in Chapter 10. On request, however, activity start and finish dates can be displayed in the nodes.) Activities **a, b,** and **c** all start at time 0 and have early finish times equal to their activity times. Activity **d** cannot start until **a** has been completed, day 20 in this case. Its duration is 15 days, so its early finish time is 35 days. Just as in the AOA case, activities **e, f,** and **g** cannot begin until both **b** and **c** are complete so their early start times are 20 days which is equal to the longest duration of their predecessor activities. Proceeding through the rest of the network, we find that the critical path is **a, d, j** and the critical time is 43 days just as it was in the AOA calculation.

The calculation of slack is equally easy. We make a right-to-left pass through the network. The numbers just below each node are the latest start time on the left and the latest finish time on the right. Consider node **i.** It might be completed in as early as 42 days, but it must be finished by day 43 or the project will be late. Because it has a duration of 18 days, it cannot start later than day 25, or it will not be completed in time to finish the project on day 43. Slack is defined exactly as in the AOA case, LST-

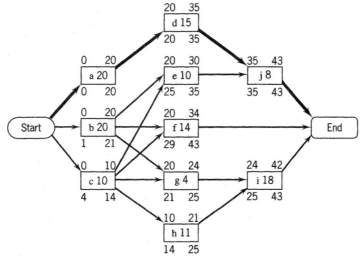

Figure 8-21 The AON network from Table 8-1, showing activity durations and earliest and latest start and finish times for each activity.

EST = slack (or LFT-EFT = slack), in this case $25 - 24 = 1$ days (or $43 - 42 = 1$ days). Note also that if activity **i** must start no later than day 25, that means that its predecessors, **g** and **h**, must be finished no later than day 25. Given their durations, **g** can start no later than day 21 and **h** no later than day 14—again, similarly for all other nodes.

We used single-time estimates in this example for simplicity. We could easily have used three-time estimates. The duration of each activity would be expressed in the optimistic, mode, pessimistic format, with the expected time shown in the node itself along with the activity variance. All of the probability calculations are done the same way regardless of the format of the network. The distinction between PERT (usually AOA and three-time) and CPM (usually AON and single-time) is meaningless. Anything that can be done in one format can be done in the other.

8.3 GANTT CHARTS

One of the oldest and still one of the most useful methods of presenting schedule information is the Gantt chart, developed around 1917 by Henry L. Gantt, a pioneer in the field of scientific management. The Gantt chart shows planned and actual progress for a number of tasks displayed against a horizontal time scale. It is a particularly effective and easy-to-read method of indicating the actual current status for each of a set of tasks compared to the planned progress for each item of the set. As a result, the Gantt chart can be helpful in expediting, sequencing, and reallocating resources among tasks, as well as in the valuable but mundane job of keeping track of how things are going. In addition, the charts usually contain a number of special symbols to designate or highlight items of special concern to the situation being charted.

There are several advantages to the use of Gantt charts. First, even though they may contain a great deal of information, they are easily understood. While they do require frequent updating (as does any scheduling/control device), they are easy to maintain *as long as task requirements are not changed or major alterations of the schedule are not made*. Gantt charts provide a clear picture of the current state of a project.

Another significant advantage of Gantt charts is that they are easy to construct. While they may be constructed without first drawing a PERT diagram, there is a close relationship between the PERT/CPM network and the Gantt chart. We use the example in the previous section to illustrate this relationship and, at the same time, demonstrate how to construct such a chart.

First, the PERT/CPM network of Figure 8-15 is redrawn so that the lengths of all arcs are in proportion to their respective task times. In essence, we redraw the network along a horizontal time scale. This modified network is shown in Figure 8-22. The heavy line, **a-d-j** is the critical path, and the horizontal dashed line segments indicate slack times. The vertical dashed line segments are dummy activities (as between events 4 and 3), or merely connectors (as elsewhere in the drawing). Note that to transform the network in this manner requires that we "explode" single nodes into multiple nodes when multiple activities emanate from the single node. In this modified network, each activity must originate from an individual node, although several activities still can have a common destination node.

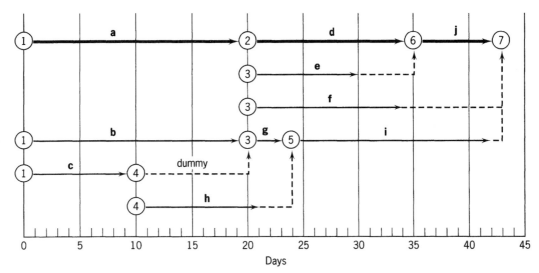

Figure 8-22 Gantt chart style representation of PERT/CPM network in Figure 8-15.

The nodes of Figure 8-15 are placed at their EOTs (the early start times for ensuing activities), and the slack is shown *after* the activity duration. (We have used an arrowhead to separate the activity duration from its slack.) To draw the modified diagram only requires that the nodes be placed at their EOTs listed on the PERT/CPM network and the activity durations drawn out from them as solid lines. Precedence is shown by connecting the duration lines with dashed line segments, showing each specific connection to the appropriate nodes.

The Gantt chart can be drawn directly from the modified PERT/CPM diagram. A list is made of all activities required to complete the project. Activities are usually listed in alphanumeric order—which is most often the order in which they were listed in the action plan or whatever source document was originally used. As Figure 8-23 shows, activity times are superimposed on a linear calendar, much as in Figure 8-22. Precedence relationships are preserved by not allowing the activity line or bar for a successor activity to begin until its predecessors are complete. Scheduled activity times are drawn as light lines or hollow bars. A heavy line or a filled-in bar indicates actual progress. Often, a bold bar is used to show the critical path. Color is sometimes used for easy visibility. The PM's ability to customize Gantt charts is limited only by the PM's imagination and the software being used.

Figure 8-23 transforms the modified PERT/CPM network into a Gantt chart. Note that three milestones are shown as diamonds below the baseline. These are the events that occur along the critical path. While there is no particular rule mandating the use of critical path events as project milestones, it is common for them to be chosen in this way. (If there are many critical events, some may be ignored and only the particularly noteworthy critical events are selected as milestones.) We can also see that while all precedence relationships must be preserved, it is not possible to distinguish easily their technical relationships simply by observing the chart itself. For example, activities **a** and **b** both have a duration of 20 days. Activities **d, e, f,** and **g** begin on the twentieth day. Using the Gantt chart, however, it is not possible to

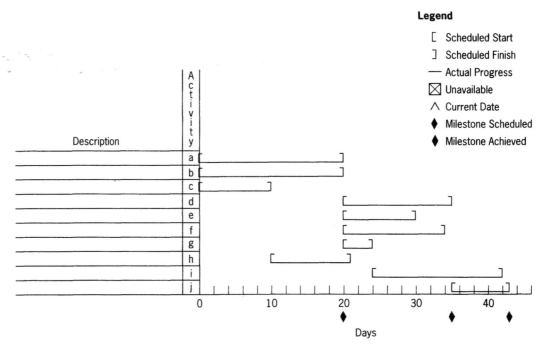

Figure 8-23 Gantt project chart from Figure 8-15.

determine which, **a** or **b,** is predecessor to which of **d, e, f,** or **g.** If a single activity is completed at some time, it is reasonable to assume that other activities starting at that point are dependent on the first one; but if two or more activities end at the same time, the relationships between them and subsequent activities are unclear. Gantt charts, therefore, are generally inadequate for showing technological dependencies.*

Figure 8-24 pictures the project as it might appear on its twenty-second day. Actual progress is shown as a heavy line added just below the scheduled progress line. Activity **a** started and finished on time, while **b** started on time but was completed one day late. Activity **c** was begun two days late and finished three days late, which delayed the start of **h.** (In this case, the predecessor relationship of **c** to **h** is clear.) Activity **d** is under way and was started on time. Activities **e, f,** and **g** were all started one day late. Even with some activities starting late, nothing has happened to delay the actual critical path. While it is not clear from the Gantt chart, the network (Figure 8-15) shows that the delay in **b** means that the **b-g-i** path has gone critical.

This example illustrates both the strength and weakness of the Gantt chart. Its major strength is that it is easy to read. All popular project management software will prepare Gantt charts, and most have some options available for customization. Gantt charts are often mounted on the wall of the project office and updated frequently.

---

*Actually, precedence relationships can be shown on Gantt charts, but the charts may become cluttered and difficult to read.

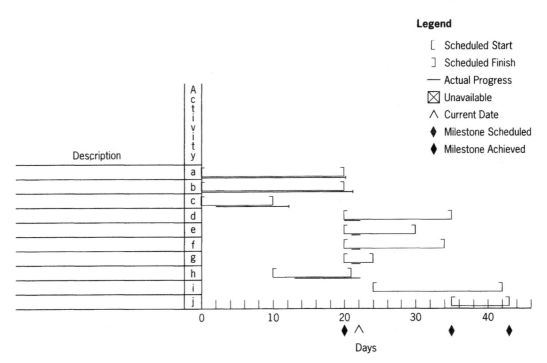

Figure 8-24   Gantt chart showing progress of project on Day 22.

Anyone interested in the project can see the state of progress easily, even if the interested party knows little about the actual nature of the work being done. The weakness of the Gantt chart is simply that one needs the PERT/CPM network (or the WBS) to interpret what appears on the Gantt chart beyond a cursory level—or to plan how to compensate for lateness.

Another advantage is the ease of construction of the chart. In our example, we converted the PERT/CPM network in Figure 8-15 to a Gantt chart by modifying the network as in Figure 8-22. In practice, this intermediate stage is not necessary, and one can easily go from network to chart in a single step. On balance, ease of construction and ease of use have made the Gantt chart the most popular method for displaying a project schedule. Nonetheless, a PERT/CPM network is still needed for the PM to exercise control over the schedule, and the viewer may be misled if the Gantt chart is not read carefully or if it does not contain all appropriate information [53].

In many ways, the Gantt chart is similar to the project master schedule described in Chapter 5. Both are types of bar charts and are used similarly. The major difference is that the Gantt chart is intended to monitor the detailed progress of work, whereas the master schedule contains only major tasks and is oriented toward overall project management rather than precise control of the detailed aspects of the project.

While PERT/CPM and Gantt charts are both scheduling techniques, they are not merely different ways of achieving the same ends; they are complementary rather than competitive. The budget can be directly related to the Gantt chart, as shown in Figure 8-25.

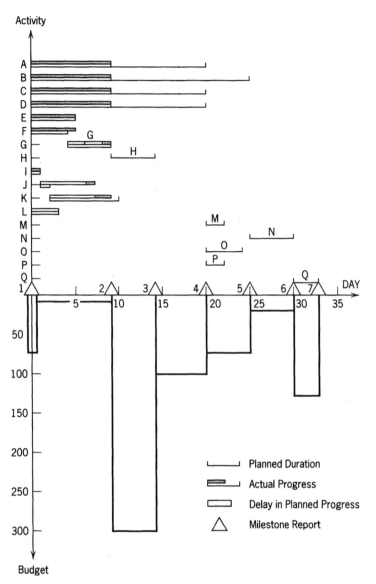

Figure 8-25   Relating the budget to the Gantt chart schedule.

Project Management in Practice
Hosting the Annual Project Management Institute Symposium

Planning and implementing a national conference for a society that will draw about 1000 attendees is a major project. The tasks involved in hosting such an event are considerable and involve selecting a program committee, choosing a theme, con-

tacting exhibitors, making local arrangements, planning the program, and on and on.

Pittsburgh was selected as host city/chapter for the 1992 Project Management Institute's annual September seminar/symposium. The objectives for the event were three: (1) to deliver a high-quality, value-added program that would be useful and last for years to come, (2) to offer a social and guest program that would reflect well on the host city, and (3) to meet strict financial criteria. The first task after selecting the city and hotel facilities was to put together the project team and chairperson. This included managers in charge of each of the tracks, the social program, the local arrangements, and all the other details. The project team was organized using a functional approach. Pittsburgh PMI Chapter officers had most of the primary responsibilities, with members from nine other chapters assisting in other duties.

Next was the development of the work breakdown structure, shown in Figure A, and the Gantt chart of activity schedules, shown in Figure B. As seen in the Gantt chart, scheduling all the work for a major conference such as this is an overwhelming effort. In the WBS, the major task was the development of the technical program. For PMI '92, the technical program offered 22 workshops composed of 70 technical papers,

WORK BREAKDOWN STRUCTURE AND TASKS

S/S Project Management
Recruit Project Team
Establish Organizational
    Procedures
Establish CAO Support Levels
    and Budget
Issue Reports to VP-Tech and
    Board of Directors
Develop S/S Goals and
    Objectives
Assemble and Issue Post-S/S
    Report

Technical Program
Develop S/S Theme
Strategize Tracks and SIGs
Recruit Technical Program Team
Develop Selection Process
    Procedures
Interface with Education
    Committee on Workshops
Plan and Issue Call for
    Papers/Panel Discussion
Recruit Invited Papers/Panel
    Discussions
Recruit Moderators
Develop and Issue Master
    Schedule for Presentations
Select Printer
Plan and Issue Abstract Books
    and Proceedings
Organize Awards for Speakers'
    Breakfasts

Identify Audio/Visual
    Requirements
Develop and Issue Post-S/S
    Technical Report

Social Guest Program
Establish Objectives
Identify Available Activities
Analyze Cost-Benefit
Identify Recommendations
Complete Contracts
Recruit Staff

Speakers
Identify Candidates and Related
    Benefits and Costs
Make Recommendations and
    Obtain Approval
Complete Contracts
Maintain Periodic Contact
Host Speakers

Publicity/Promotion
Theme Establishment and
    Approval
Logo Development and
    Approval
Video Production
Promotional Materials
    Identification and Approval
Advertising: PMI, Public and
    Trade Media Releases
Regional Newsletter Articles

Finance
Initiate Code of Accounts
Develop Procedures of Financial
    Operation
Develop Independent Auditing
    Procedure
Initiate Separate Banking
    Account
Develop Cash Flow Estimates/
    Projections
Develop and Issue Standard
    Reports
Interact with CAO on
    Account Reconciliation
Develop and Issue Post-S/S
    Financial Report

Corporate Sponsorship
Establish Participation
    Philosophy
Target Prime Corporations
Solicit Participation
Recognition

Facilities Vendor/COA Support
Contract with Host and
    Backup Hotels
Staff Recruiting
(Details to be Identified and
    Scheduled with PMI Exective
    Director and Events Manager)

Figure A   The work breakdown structure.

Figure B Gantt chart.

special panel discussions, and case studies. The technical tracks included engineering and construction, pharmaceuticals, utilities, software, automotive, R&D, defense, education, and manufacturing. The workshops included sessions on preparing for the PMI certification examinations, learning about Taguchi concepts of statistical quality control, and future practice in project management. All of these also required careful scheduling.

The vendor program included exhibits by dozens of vendors and a large number of showcase sessions for in-depth demonstrations of their wares. The social program included a golf

Pittsburgh—host city for the PMI Annual Symposium.

tournament, numerous social activities to meet with colleagues, tours of Pittsburgh's attractions, and a wide variety of entertainment opportunities.

Source: PMI Staff, "Catch the Spirit . . . at Pittsburgh," *PM Network*, May 1992.

All in all, a conference such as PMI's is as difficult a project as many firms face in their competitive markets.

8.4 EXTENSIONS AND APPLICATIONS

There have been a large number of extensions to the basic ideas of PERT and CPM. These extensions are often oriented toward handling rather specific problem situations through additional program flexibility, computerizing some of the specific problems, fine-tuning some of the concepts for special environments, and combining various management approaches with the PERT/CPM concepts.

One interesting extension deals with the case when it is very difficult to estimate activity times because no one has experience with the activity, or because the activity is ill-defined. In this case, the concepts of fuzzy-set theory are applied [31]. In this section we discuss some of these extensions and look at the utility of network scheduling models in general. However, we delay our coverage of extensions aimed primarily at resource allocation and formal applications of CPM until Chapter 9. Specifically, we will briefly discuss Critical Resource Diagramming [2 and 3], Goldratt's "critical chain" [16], and resource constrained scheduling [50] in Chapter 9.

Precedence Diagramming

One shortcoming of the PERT/CPM network method is that it does not allow for leads and lags between two activities without greatly increasing the number of subactivities to account for this. In construction projects, in particular, it is extremely common for the following restrictions to occur.

- Activity B must not start before activity A has been in progress for at least two days (Figure 8-26a).
- Activity A must be complete at least three days before activity B can be finished (Figure 8-26b).
- Activity B cannot begin before four days after the completion of A (Figure 8-26c).
- Activity B cannot be completed before eight days from the start of A (Figure 8-26d).

Precedence diagramming is an AON network method that allows for these leads and lags within the network. Node designations are illustrated in Figure 8-26e. Because of the increased flexibility regarding required lead and lag times, it must be known whether each activity can be split or not. Splitting allows easier satisfaction of the lead and lag restrictions. If splitting is not allowed, the project may be significantly delayed.

Some anomalies tend to occur in precedence diagramming that are not encountered in PERT/CPM. For example, because of the lead and lag requirements, activities may appear to have slack when they really do not. Also, the critical path of the network will frequently go backward through an activity, with the result that increasing the activity time may actually decrease the project completion time. Such an activity is called *reverse critical*. This happens when the critical path enters the completion of an activity through a finish constraint (Figure 8-26b or d), continues backward through the activity, and leaves through a start constraint (Figure 8-26a or d).

Network node times are calculated in a manner similar to PERT/CPM times. Because of the lead and lag restrictions, it is often helpful to lay out a Gantt chart to see what is actually happening.

Precedence diagramming seems to be gaining in popularity. The richer set of precedence relationships it allows is pertinent for a variety of projects, particularly construction projects. For more details on this technique, see [1, 9 (Chapters 6 and 17), and 33]. Most current project management software will allow leads, lags, delays, and other constraints in the context of their standard AON network and Gantt chart programs.

GERT

The Graphical Evaluation and Review Technique (GERT) is a network model developed to deal with more complex modeling situations than can be handled by

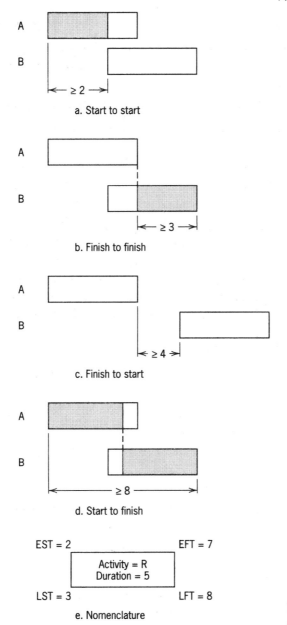

Figure 8-26 Precedence diagramming conventions.

PERT/CPM. GERT combines signal flowgraph theory, probabilistic networks, PERT/CPM, and decision trees all in a single framework. Its components consist of *logical nodes* (defined below) and *directed arcs* (or branches) with two parameters; the probability that a given arc is taken (or "realized") and the distribution function describing the time required by the activity. Evaluation of a GERT network yields the probability of each node being realized and the elapsed time between all nodes.

At this point, it may be useful to compare GERT and PERT/CPM in order to focus on what is different about GERT.

GERT	PERT/CPM
Branching from a node is probabilistic	Branching from a node is deterministic.
Various possible probability distributions for time estimates.	Only the beta distribution for time estimates.
Flexibility in node realization.	No flexibility in node realization.
Looping back to earlier events is acceptable.	Looping back is not allowed.
Difficult to use as a control tool.	Easy to use for control.
Arcs may represent time, cost, reliability, etc.	Arcs represent time only.

While there are computer programs that optimize PERT/CPM problems, GERT and its various enhancements are computer simulations. Most of the programs (and the enhancements) are the result of work conducted by Pritsker [38]. His modeling package called Q-GERT simulates queues, or waiting lines, in the network. (There are other extensions of PERT that have some features similar to GERT and Q-GERT—VERT, for example—but GERT seems to be the most widely used extension.)

The steps employed in using GERT are these:

1. Convert the qualitative description of the project action plan into a network, just as in the use of PERT/CPM.

2. Collect the necessary data to describe the arcs of the network, focusing not only on the specific activity being modeled, but also on such characteristics of the activity as the likelihood it will be realized, the chance it might fail, any alternative activities that exist, and the like.

3. Determine the *equivalent function* of the network.

4. Convert the equivalent function of the network into the following two performance measures:

    The probability that specific nodes are realized.

    The *moment generating function* of the arc times.

5. Analyze the results and make inferences about the system.

It is not appropriate to deal here with the complex solution techniques employed for GERT networks. They make use of topology equations, equivalent functions, moment generating functions, and extensive calculation. The interested reader is urged to consult the papers of Pritsker and others [1, 38, 46] for formal descriptions of the methods involved in formulating and solving GERT networks. Instead, we will describe how to construct a GERT network of a simple situation.

The list of common GERT symbols, together with a few examples, is given in Figure 8-27. This figure describes the left, or input side of the nodes first, and then the right-hand output side next. All combinations of input and output symbols are feasible, as shown in the examples.

Now let us describe a manufacturing project situation developed by Pritsker and portray it through the GERT approach. This situation concerns the initiation of a

Symbol	Name	Explanation
		INPUT
K	Exclusive—or	Any branch leading into the node causes the node to be realized, but only one branch can occur.
<	Inclusive—or	Any branch causes the node to be realized and at the time of the earliest branch.
(	And	The node is realized only after ALL branches have occurred.
		OUTPUT
)	Deterministic	All branches out must occur if the node is realized.
>	Probabilistic	Only one of the branches may occur if the node is realized.
		EXAMPLES
		Beginning node with branches that must occur.
		Ending node that occurs whenever **a** or **b** occurs.
		Intermediate node that occurs if **a** occurs with either **b** or **c** following.
		Intermediate node that occurs when all **a, b,** and **c** occur with either **d** or **e** following.

Figure 8-27   GERT symbols.

new production process developed by manufacturing engineering for an electronic component. The resulting GERT model could just as well describe an R & D project, a government project, or a Girl Scout project.

Sample Problem, Modeled with GERT

A part is manufactured on a production line in four hours. Following manufacture, parts are inspected. There is a 25 percent failure rate, and failed parts must be reworked. Inspection time is a stochastic variable, exponentially distributed, with a mean of 1 hour. Rework takes 3 hours, and 30 percent of the reworked parts fail the next inspection and must be scrapped. Parts that pass their original inspection or pass inspection after rework are sent to finishing, a process that requires 10 hours 60 percent of the time and 14 hours otherwise. A final inspection rejects 5 percent of the finished parts, which are then scrapped.

We can now model this situation as a GERT network so that it can be solved for the expected percentage of good parts and the expected time required to produce a good part. This GERT network is illustrated in Figure 8-28.

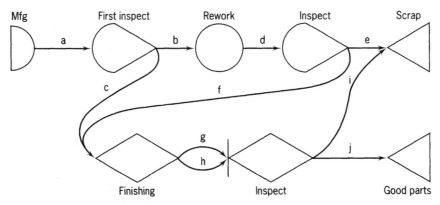

Figure 8-28 Sample GERT network.

Activity **a** represents the output of the four-hour manufacturing process. The outputs enter an inspection from which 75 percent are passed, **c,** and 25 percent fail, **b.** The latter go to rework, with flow **d** emerging. Another inspection takes place—**e** (30 percent of 25 percent = 7.5%) flows to scrap, while the successfully reworked parts (70 percent of 25 percent = 17.5 percent), represented by **f,** go with the other good parts, **c,** to the finishing process. Sixty percent of this input requires 10 hours of work, **g,** and the remainder (40 percent) needs 14 hours, **h.** The final inspection process discards 5 percent of the output, **i** which goes to scrap, and the remainder (which is 87.875 percent of the original input) is sent to "good parts," **j.**

The time for an "average" part to proceed through the network can be found in much the same way as we calculated the output. The result of the entire analysis is therefore considerably richer than the simpler PERT/CPM. It should, however, be obvious that the input information requirements for GERT are more extensive and the computational requirements are far more extensive than for PERT/CPM, particularly for large networks. As always, the PM should adopt the simplest scheduling technique consistent with the needs of the project.

Other Methods

Two straightforward methods for project scheduling that do not use networks or Gantt charts are employed by some agencies of the U.S. government. The Goddard Space Flight Center develops its project schedules in three phases. Phase I is advanced schedule planning, where the basic project schedule is developed directly from the work breakdown structure. Phase I lists all major elements of the project. This is used for presenting the proposed project to NASA and to the congress and its many committees.

Phase II consists of the preparation of the operational schedule. This is the equivalent of the project master schedule. Phase III is schedule administration. In this last phase, the project is monitored and the master schedule is updated through the use of biweekly reports. Any necessary corrections and alterations to the project master schedule are made as a result of this process.

The Department of General Services uses a project scheduling system that provides planning, scheduling, and control in three distinct but closely related stages.

Activity scheduling is the initial stage. At this point the planner attempts to develop optimum timing for the start and completion of all tasks associated with the project. Labor-hour and progress scheduling is carried out in the second stage. This identifies the labor (and other resources) required to initiate project activities on time and to sustain the necessary rate of progress to keep the project on schedule. Progress reporting takes place in the final stage. In this third stage, the project is monitored and a more or less constant stream of reports is filed so that appropriate action can be taken to keep the project on schedule. The information reported to senior management shows the project status relative to activity milestones and actual progress relative to planned progress. The value of the progress achieved as well as the estimated value of progress remaining is used to calculate (forecast) the labor-hours required to complete the remaining work on schedule.

Note that these methods parallel the basic concept of the project action plan with its specific steps to be taken, its estimate of resource requirements, times, and precedences, and most important, with each step in the higher-level plans broken down into lower-level action plans.

Using These Tools

We have heard differing opinions on the value of each of the tools we have described, including many of the computerized project management information systems (PMISs). We have been told, "No one uses PERT/CPM/Precedence diagramming," "No one uses three-time PERT," and "No one uses____computer package." But we have first-hand knowledge of PERT users, of CPM users, and of precedence diagram users. We know PMs who collect and use three-time PERT. For example, refer to the boxed Apartment Complex example (Figure 8-29).

Figure 8-29 is a portion of a 48-step action plan for the syndication of an apartment complex. Note that several of the steps are obvious composites of multistep action plans designed for a lower level (e.g., see 1-4). Figure 8-30 is an AON network of Figure 8-29. The firm also has a Gantt chart version of the network that is used for tracking each project. Figure 8-29 also contains three time estimates of the "calendar" time used for each step (in days) and of the "resource" time used for each step (in hours). The time estimate 2(10) is read, "2 days, 10 labor-hours." The duplicate data are useful for scheduling workloads.

We are reluctant to give advice about which tools to use. If the PM indulges in a bit of experimentation with the major systems, their relative advantages and disadvantages in a given application will become evident. We have noted Bubshait and Selen's work [4] on the use of project management techniques. Digman and Green [11] have also developed an interesting and useful framework for evaluating the various planning and control techniques. More recently, interest has been growing in the development of a model for measuring the "maturity level" of an organization's practice of project management [for example, 5, 7, 40 and 44] and to develop benchmarks of "best practice" in the field [17, 21, 47, 49]. In one particularly well-developed model, Ibbs and Kwak measured and published scores of the level of project management maturity in 38 firms representing several industries [21].

There are several forces driving this effort. First, and most obvious, is the desire of professionals in the field to develop standards by which practice of the art can be

Task	a (days,hours)	m	b	TE (days)	σ² (days)	TE (hr)	σ² (hr)
1. Product package received by Secy. in Real Estate (R.E.) Dept.	n/a	(.3)	(.4)				
2. Secy. checks for duplicates, and forwards all packages in Atlanta region (but not addressed to R.E staff member) to Atl. via fast mail. Atl. office sends copy of submittal log to L.A. office on weekly basis.	n/a	(.2)	(.3)				
3. Secy, date stamps, logs, checks for duplication, makes new file, checks for contact source, adds to card file all new packages. Sends criteria letter to new source. Send duplication letter. Forwards package to Admin. Asst. (AA).	(.7)	(.7)	(.9)				
4. AA reviews package, completes Property Summary Form, forwards to L.A. Reg. Acquisit. Director (RAD) officer or to R.E. staff member to whom package is addressed.	(.5)	(.5)	(.7)				
Total 1–4	1(1.7)	1(1.7)	3(2.3)	1.3	0.11	1.8	0.01
5. Person to whom package forwarded determines action. (May refer to other or retain for further review.) "Passes" sent to Secy. for files. "Possibles" retained by RAD for further review.	1(.5)	1(.5)	1(1)	1.0		.58	0.01
6. RAD gets add'l data as needed, gets demographic and comparables. Rough numbers run. Looks for the "opportunities." If viable, continue.	4(3)	5(3)	3(2.3)	5.5	0.69	3.83	0.69
•	•	•	•		•		
•	•	•	•		•		
•	•	•	•		•		
45. Prop. Mgt./Fin. prepares for closing and take-over. At closing, prorations of taxes, rents, service contracts.	3(4)	5(8)	10(24)	5.5	1.36	10.0	11.11
46. PM final inspect. On-site at close.	1(4)	1(8)	2(12)	1.2	0.03	8.0	1.78
47. Legal closes.	2(8)	2(14)	4(25)	2.3	0.11	14.83	8.03
48. Legal issues Post Closing Memorandum.	2(5)	5(8)	10(10)	5.3	1.78	7.83	0.69

Figure 8-29 Action plan for syndication of an apartment complex.

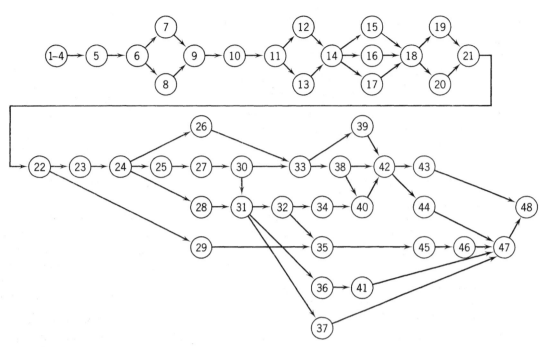

Figure 8-30   Apartment complex network.

measured. Second, senior management, considering investment in project management, has a need to know what level of competency they are buying. Third, the Software Engineering Institute developed a Capability Maturity Model that served as an indication that the development of such a model was feasible. Fourth, it was generally felt that such models would allow individual firms to document a level of excellence in project management that would be attractive to potential customers. Fifth, some consulting firms felt that such models would be saleable. While the logic of some of the reasons for developing a maturity model may seem questionable [5, p.54], the work is well underway. Several consulting firms claim to have developed models (see [21] for one example) and the Project Management Institute's Standards Committee has established a " working group" [7, p.21] to pursue the matter.

Although the effort is still in its infancy, so are the several efforts to measure the return on investment (ROI) assignable to investing in project management [e.g., 25]. (Those trying to measure the ROI from project management would do well to review efforts in the 1950s and 1960s to determine the ROI from investments in R&D.) Until generally acceptable standards for maturity and methods for calculating the ROI from project management are developed, the PM should opt for the simplest method sufficient to the needs of the project and its parent firm.

SUMMARY

In this chapter the scheduling aspect of project implementation was addressed. Following a description of the benefits of using a network for planning and controlling a project, the PERT/CPM approach was described. Next, Gantt charts were described and their relation to the PERT/CPM diagram was illustrated. Finally, precedence diagramming, GERT, and a few other extensions were discussed.

Specific points covered in the chapter were these:

- Scheduling is particularly important to projects because of complex coordination problems.

- The network approach to scheduling offers a number of specific advantages of special value for projects.

- Critical project tasks typically constitute fewer than 10 percent of all the project tasks.

- Although research indicates technological performance is not significantly affected by the use of PERT/CPM, there did seem to be a significantly lower probability of cost and schedule overruns.

- Network techniques can adopt either an activity-on-node or activity-on-arc framework without significantly altering the analysis.

- Networks are usually constructed from left to right, indicating activity precedence and event times as the network is constructed. Through use of the network, critical activities and events are identified, early and late activity start times are found, available slacks for each activity are determined, and probabilities of project completion by various times are calculated.

- Gantt charts, a monitoring technique, are closely related to network diagrams, but are more easily understood and provide a clearer picture of the current state of the project. However, while offering some advantages, they also have some drawbacks, such as not clearly indicating task precedence and dependencies.

- GERT is one of the more common extensions of PERT/CPM and allows: probabilistic branching from nodes, various probability distributions for the activity times, looping in the network, and representation of project elements other than time, such as cost or reliability.

In the next chapter we investigate the scheduling problem further when multiple projects require a set of common resources to be shared. Again, a number of techniques are useful for resource allocation and activity expediting under such circumstances.

GLOSSARY

Activity   A specific project task that requires resources and time to complete.

Activity-On-Arc (Node)   The two ways of illustrating a network: placing the activities on the arcs or on the nodes.

Arc   The line connecting two nodes.

Crash   In CPM, an activity can be conducted at a normal pace or at an expedited pace, known as crashing, at a greater cost.

Critical   An activity or event that, if delayed, will delay project completion.

Event   An end state for one or more activities that occurs at a specific point in time.

Gantt Chart   A manner of illustrating multiple, time-based activities on a horizontal time scale.

Milestone   A clearly identifiable point in a project or set of activities that commonly denotes a reporting requirement or completion of a large or important set of activities.

Network   A combination of interrelated activities and events depicted with arcs and nodes.

Node   An intersection of two or more lines or arrows, commonly used for depicting an event or activity.

Path   A sequence of lines and nodes in a network.

Project Management Information System (PMIS)   The systems, activities, and data that allow information flow in a project, frequently computerized but not always.

Trade-off   The amount of one factor that must be sacrificed in order to achieve more or less of another factor.

■ QUESTIONS

Material Review Questions

1. Define *activity, event,* and *path* as used in network construction. What is a dummy activity?

2. What characteristic of the critical path times makes them critical?

3. What two factors are compared by Gantt charting? How does the Gantt chart differ in purpose from the project master schedule?

4. How is the GERT technique different from the PERT technique?

5. When is each scheduling technique appropriate to use?

6. What is the difference between activity-on-node and activity-on-arrow diagrams?

7. What does it mean to "crash" an event?

8. Briefly summarize how a network is drawn.

9. Define "late start time" and "early start time."

10. How is the critical path determined?

11. What is "slack"?

Class Discussion Questions

12. How do you think the network technique could be used to estimate costs for manufacturing?

13. What are some benefits of the network approach to project planning? What are some drawbacks?

14. What is your position on the statements in the Using These Tools section?

15. Why is PERT of significant value to the project manager?

16. How is uncertainty in project scheduling dealt with?

17. Are there any drawbacks to using GERT?

18. How are activity times estimated?

19. Should the critical path activities be managed differently from noncritical path activities? Explain.

Questions for Project Management in Practice

Replacing the Atigun Section of the TransAlaska Pipeline

20. How do you imagine the polar bear got on top of the pipe?

21. One requirement of the project was to keep the oil flowing while replacing the pipeline section. How do you think they managed to do this?

22. Did the project team always have to work in 3-hour segments? What would you expect their longest shifts ran?

Hosting the Annual Project Management Institute Symposium

23. Elaborate on the uniqueness of this work breakdown structure.

24. Based on the Gantt chart, when did the symposium actually occur?

25. Why are there activities scheduled after the symposium? When is the project finally done?

PROBLEMS

1. Given the following information, drawn the PERT/CPM diagram:

Activity	Immediate Predecessor
1	—
2	—
3	1,4
4	2
5	2
6	3,5

2. Convert the AON diagram below to an AOA diagram.

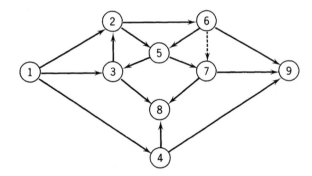

3. Find three errors in the diagram below.

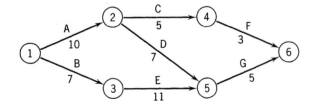

4. Given the diagram below, find:
   (a) The critical path.
   (b) How long it will take to complete the project.

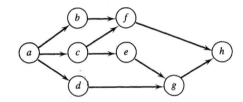

5. Convert the AOA diagram in Problem 4 to an AON diagram. How would the AON diagram change if there had been a dummy from node 2 to node 3 in Problem 4?

6. Convert each of the following AOA diagrams into AON diagrams.

a.

b.

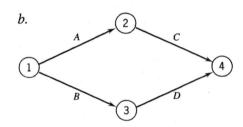

7. Given the following activities and precedences, draw a PERT/CPM diagram:

Activity	Immediate Predecessor
A	—
B	—
C	A
D	A,B
E	A,B
F	C
G	D,F
H	E,G

8. Given the following network:
   (a) What is the critical path?
   (b) How long will it take to complete this project?
   (c) Can activity **B** be delayed without delaying the completion of the project? If so, how many days?

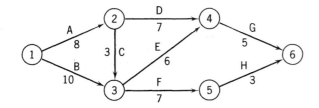

Find

(a) the critical path;
(b) all event slacks;
(c) critical path to event D;
(d) probability of completion in 14 days;
(e) the effect if CD slips to 6 days; to 7 days; to 8 days.

9. Given the estimated activity times below and the network in Problem 8 above:

Activity	a	m	b
A	6	7	14
B	8	10	12
C	2	3	4
D	6	7	8
E	5	5.5	9
F	5	7	9
G	4	6	8
H	2.5	3	3.5

What is the probability that the project will be completed within:
(a) 21 days?
(b) 22 days?
(c) 25 days?

10.

Activity*	a	m	b
AB	3	6	9
AC	1	4	7
CB	0	3	6
CD	3	3	3
CE	2	2	8
BD	0	0	6
BE	2	5	8
DF	4	4	10
DE	1	1	1
EF	1	4	7

---

* The nomenclature AB means the activity *between* events A and B.

11.

Activity*	TE
AB	1
AC	2
AD	3
DC	4
CB	3
DE	8
CF	2
BF	4
IJ	2
CE	6
EF	5
FG	10
FH	11
EH	1
GH	9
EJ	3
GI	8
HJ	6

(a) Draw the PERT diagram.
(b) Find the critical path.
(c) Find the completion time.

12. The Denver Iron & Steel Company is expanding its operations to include a new drive-in weigh station. The weigh station will be a heated/air-conditioned building with a large floor and small office. The large room will have the scales, a 15-foot counter, and several display cases for its equipment.

Before erection of the building, the project manager evaluated the project using PERT/CPM analysis. The activities with their corresponding times were recorded in Table A:

Using PERT/CPM analysis, find the critical path, the slack times, and the expected completion time.

Table A

#	Activity	Times			Preceding Tasks
		Optimistic	Most Likely	Pessimistic	
1	Lay foundation	8	10	13	—
2	Dig hole for scale	5	6	8	—
3	Insert scale bases	13	15	21	2
4	Erect frame	10	12	14	1,3
5	Complete building	11	20	30	4
6	Insert scales	4	5	8	5
7	Insert display cases	2	3	4	5
8	Put in office equipment	4	6	10	7
9	Finishing touches	2	3	4	8,6

13. Dockside Shipbuilding Company has received a contract from the government to build the prototype of a new U.S. Navy destroyer. The destroyer is to be nuclear-powered, include advanced weapon systems, and have a small crew. Dockside Shipbuilding Company has assigned to the task a project manager who, in turn, has delegated minor subprojects to subordinate managers.

The project was evaluated using PERT/CPM analysis. Due to the extensive length of the project, many activities were combined: The following is the result.

Activity*	Time (months)
AB	3
BC	6
BD	2
BF	5
BE	4
CD	9
DG	20
FG	6
EH	11
EI	19
GJ	1
HK	3
IL	9
LM	12
KN	7

*See nomenclature note in Problem 10.

Activity*	Time (months)
JO	4
MN	15
NP	13
OP	10

Find the critical path and expected completion date.

14. The following PERT chart was prepared at the beginning of a small construction project. The project begins with two activities: Actuate (A) and Build (B).

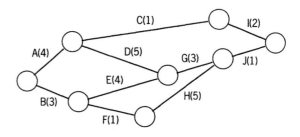

The duration, in days, follows the letter of each activity. What is the critical path? Which activities should be monitored most closely?

At the end of the first week of construction, it was noted that activity **A** was completed in 2.5 days, but activity **B** required 4.5 days. What impact does this have on the project? Are the same activities critical?

15. Given the following advertising project being

considered by a media firm, find the probability of completion by 17 weeks. By 24 weeks. By what date is management 90 percent sure completion will occur?

Times (weeks)

Activity*	Optimistic	Most Likely	Pessimistic
1–2	5	11	11
1–3	10	10	10
1–4	2	5	8
2–6	1	7	13
3–6	4	4	10
3–7	4	7	10
3–5	2	2	2
4–5	0	6	6
5–7	2	8	14
6–7	1	4	7

If the media firm can complete the project for the customer within 18 weeks it will receive a bonus of $10,000. But if the project delays beyond 22 weeks it must pay a penalty of $5000 due to lost customer impact. If the firm can choose whether or not to bid on this project, what should its decision be if the project is only a breakeven one normally?

16. Given an auditing project with the following activities:

Activity	Standard Deviation	Critical?	Duration
a, add	2	yes	2
b, balance	1		3
c, count	0	yes	4
d, deduct	3		2
e, edit	1	yes	1
f, finance	2		6
g, group	2	yes	4
h, hold	0	yes	2

Find:
(a) The probability of completing this project in 12 weeks (or less), as the client desires.
(b) The probability of completing this project in 13 weeks (or less).

*See nomenclature note in Problem 10.

(c) The probability of completing this project in 16 weeks (or less), the client's drop-dead date.
(d) The number of weeks required to assure a 92.5 percent chance of completion, as guaranteed by the auditing firm.

17. The following PERT network is a compressed representation of the prospectus of a start-up firm that plans to develop a new, bio-electronic computer chip.

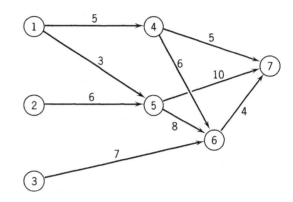

Note that three activities, the biological elements, can start immediately.

Find:
(a) The critical path.
(b) The earliest time to complete the project.
(c) The slack on activities **4-6, 5-6,** and **4-7.**
(d) Draw the network on a Gantt chart.

18. The events of the project below are designated as 1, 2, and so on.
(a) Draw the PERT network and the Gantt chart.
(b) Find the critical path.
(c) Find the slacks on all the events and activities

Activity	Prec. Evt.	Suc. Evt.	TE (weeks)	Prec. Activ.
a	1	2	3	none
b	1	3	6	none
c	1	4	8	none
d	2	5	7	a
e	3	5	5	b
f	4	5	10	c

Activity	Prec. Evt.	Suc. Evt.	TE (weeks)	Prec. Activ.
g	4	6	4	c
h	5	7	5	d,e,f
i	6	7	6	g

19. Given the following PERT network (times are in weeks):

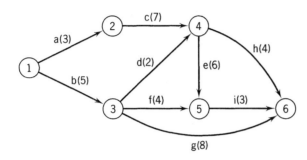

Determine:
(a) The EOT and LOT for each event.
(b) The slacks on all events and activities.
(c) The critical activities and path.

20. Given the schedule in Table B for a liability work package done as part of an accounting audit in a corporation, find:
(a) The critical path.
(b) The slack time on "process confirmations."
(c) The slack time on "test pension plan."
(d) The slack time on "verify debt restriction compliance."

Table B

Activity	Duration (days)	Preceding Activities
a. Obtain schedule of liabilities	3	none
b. Mail confirmation	15	a
c. Test pension plan	5	a
d. Vouch selected liabilities	60	a
e. Test accruals and amortization	6	d
f. Process confirmations	40	b
g. Reconcile interest expense to debt	10	c,e

Activity	Duration (days)	Preceding Activities
h. Verify debt restriction compliance	7	f
i. Investigate debit balances	6	g
j. Review subsequent payments	12	h,i

21. In the website development project network shown in the figure below, the number alongside each activity designates the activity duration (TE) in weeks.

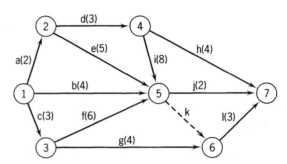

Determine:
(a) The EOT and LOT for each event.
(b) The earliest time that the website can be completed.
(c) The slack on all events and activities.
(d) The critical events and activities.
(e) The critical path.

22. Given the following information regarding a project concerning an initial public offering (IPO):

Activity	TE (weeks)	Preceding Activities
a	3	none
b	1	none
c	3	a
d	4	a
e	4	b
f	5	b
g	2	c,e
h	3	f

(a) Draw the PERT network and the Gantt chart.
(b) What is the critical path?
(c) What will the offering be available (completion of the project)?
(d) What is the critical path to event 4 (legal documents, end of activities c and e)? What is the earliest time that this event can be reached?
(e) What is the effect on the project if activity e (approvals) takes an extra week? Two extra weeks? Three extra weeks?

23. Construct a network for the aerospace launch project below and find its critical path.

Activity	TE (weeks)	Preceding Activities
a	3	none
b	5	a
c	3	a
d	1	c
e	3	b
f	4	b,d
g	2	c
h	3	g,f
i	1	e,h

24. Construct a network for the following training and development project:

Activity	TE (weeks)	Preceding Activities
a	3	none
b	5	none
c	14	a
d	5	a
e	4	b
f	7	b
g	8	d,e
h	5	g,f

(a) Draw the PERT network and the Gantt chart.
(b) Find the critical path.
(c) Assume activity a (hire trainers) took five weeks. Replan the project.

(d) From where would you suggest transferring resources, and to what activities, so that the original target training date may be maintained?

25. Resolve part (d) of problem 10 assuming the values of a and b are given at the 95 percent level. Repeat, assuming the values are given at the 90 percent level.

26. Using the landscaping information below, draw an AOA network. Find the critical path and compute the number of days you would be 95% sure the garden would be completed. Calculate the slack, earliest start, and latest start times for each activity and show in table form. Does any path come close to causing a problem in determining the probability of project completion based on the critical path alone?

Activity	Time (Days) a	m	b
1-2	6	8	10
1-3	5	6	7
1-4	6	6	6
2-6	0	0	0
2-7	10	11	12
3-6	12	14	16
4-5	5	8	11
4-9	7	9	11
5-6	8	10	12
5-9	0	0	0
6-7	14	15	16
6-8	10	12	14
7-10	9	12	15
8-10	0	4	14
9-11	5	5	5
10-11	7	8	9

27. Given the following information about staging a community play on Independence Day.
(a) Construct an AON diagram.
(b) Determine the earliest completion time for advertising the play and the critical path.
(c) What completion date are you 80% confident of achieving? 40% confident?
(d) Will a one-day delay in this project be serious?

Activity	Predecessor	Time (Days)		
		a	m	b
1	—	2	4	6
2	—	5	5	5
3	2	3	5	7
4	1	7	10	13
5	1	11	12	13
6	2, 4	5	6	7
7	3	9	10	11
8	3, 6	5	7	9
9	4	7	9	11
10	5	3	3	3
11	7	15	17	19
12	8	6	8	10
13	9, 10	7	8	15
14	7	12	14	16
15	12, 13	16	17	18

28. Draw an AON network using the following data and find the probability of completing the critical path of the pharmaceutical project in 44 days, the official release date.

Activity	Predecessor	Time (Days)		
		a	m	b
1	—	6	10	14
2	1	0	1	2
3	1	16	20	30
4	2	3	5	7
5	4	2	3	4
6	3	7	10	13
7	4	1	2	3
8	7	0	2	4
9	3, 7	2	2	2
10	9	2	3	4
11	8	0	1	2
12	10, 11	1	2	3

INCIDENTS FOR DISCUSSION

Yankee Chair Company

The Yankee Chair Company was anxious to get a new model rocking chair onto the market. Past efforts to introduce new models had resulted in frustrating failures. Bret Ricks, president of Yankee Chair, was determined that it would not happen again with the newest model. He had no confidence in his current management team, so he hired Jan Dymore, a local consultant, to organize and manage this project. He assigned a Yankee Chair manager, Tom Gort, to work with Dymore to start developing some talent for project management within the company. Dymore decided to set up a PERT network and guided Gort through the process of listing activities, assigning precedence, and estimating completion times. She also explained the critical path concept to Gort, who by this time had a reasonable grasp of the project direction. At the first review session with Mr. Ricks, the PERT approach was accepted enthusiastically, but toward the end of the review Dymore made some critical remarks about the product design and was subsequently released from the project.

Ricks then asked Gort if he could carry on the PERT approach by himself. Gort jumped at the chance, but later in his office he began to question whether or not he really could use the PERT network effectively. Dymore had made a guess at what the critical path would be and how long the project would take, but she had also told Gort that several other calculations had to be made in order to calculate the exact time estimates for each activity and the variances of those activity times. Gort really did not understand the mathematics involved and certainly did not want to look bad in Ricks' eyes, so he decided to take Dymore's guess at the critical path and get the best possible estimates of those activity times. By concentrating his attention on the critical path activities and ignoring the variance issues, he figured he could bring the project in on time.

Questions: Will Gort's approach work? How much more of a gamble is Gort taking than any project manager normally takes? What should Gort watch out for?

Cincinnati Equipment Company

Cincinnati Equipment Company, which specializes in the manufacture of modern construction equipment, will be building a facility to house a new foundry. The company has selected a project manager and team to follow the project through to completion. The project team is very interested in selecting an appropriate scheduling technique for the project. The project manager has thus set the following guidelines for the selec-tion process: simple; able to show durations of events, the flow of work, and the relative sequence of events; able to indicate planning and actual flow, which items may proceed at the same time, and how far they are from completion. The assistant project manager favors the Gantt chart, the finance representative likes PERT, and the construction supervisor prefers CPM.

Questions: If you were the project manager, which method would you use, and why?

BIBLIOGRAPHY

1. AL-HAMMED, A., and S. ASSAF. "A Survey of Cost Reduction Techniques Used by Construction Firms in Saudi Arabia."*American Association of Cost Engineers Transactions*, 1988.

2. BADIRU, A. B. "Incorporating Learning Curve Effects Into Critical Resource Diagramming." *Project Management Journal*, June 1995.

3. BADIRU, A. B. "Activity-Resource Assignments Using Critical Resource Diagramming." *Project Management Journal*, September 1993.

4. BUBSHAIT, K. A., and W. J. SELEN. "Project Characteristics That Influence The Implementation of Project Management Techniques: A Survey." *Project Management Journal*, June 1992.

5. CABANIS, J. "Show Me the Money." *PM Network*, September 1998.

6. CAMPANIS, N. A. "Delphi: Not the Greek Oracle, but Close." *PM Network*, February. 1997.

7. COMBE, M. W. "Standards Committee Tackles Project Management Maturity Models." *PM Network*, August 1998.

8. DAVIS, E. W. "Networks: Resource Allocation." *Industrial Engineering*, April 1974.

9. DEAN, B. V. *Project Management: Methods and Studies*. New York: Elsevier, 1985.

10. DEYOUNG-CURREY, J. "Want Better Estimates? Let's Get to Work." *PM Network*, December 1998.

11. DIGMAN, L. A., and G. I. GREEN. "A Framework of Evaluating Network Planning and Control Techniques." *Research Management*, January 1981.

12. EICHHORN, B. R. "Manage Contingencies, Reduce Risk: The PCA Technique." *PM Network*, October 1997.

13 FRAME, J. D. "Risk Assessment Groups: Key Component of Project Offices." *PM Network*, March 1998.

14. GALLAGHER, C. "A Note on Pert Assumptions." *Management Science*, October 1987.

15. GIDO, J. *Successful Project Management*, Cincinnati, OH: South-Western, 1999.

16. GOLDRATT, E. M. *Critical Chain*, Great Barrington, MA, North River, 1997.

17. GUPTA, V. K., and D. J. GRAHAM. "A Customer-Driven Quality Improvement and Management Project at Diamond Offshore Drilling." *Project Management Journal*, September 1997.

18. HARE, L. B., R. W. HOERL, J. D. HROMI, and R. D. SNEE. "The Role of Statistical Thinking in Management." *IEEE Engineering Management Review*, Fall 1998, reprinted with permission of the American Society for Quality (1995).

19. HULETT, D. T. "Schedule Risk Analysis Simplified." *PM Network*, July 1996.

20. HULETT, D. T. "Project Schedule Risk Assessment." *Project Management Journal*, March 1995.

21. IBBS, C. W., and Y.-H. KWAK. "Benchmarking, Project Management Organizations." *PM Network*, February 1998.

22 KAMBUROWSKI, J. "New Validations of PERT Times." *Omega, International Journal of Management Science*, Vol. 25, No. 3, 1997.

23. KEEFER, D. L., and W. A. VERDINI. "Better Estimation of PERT Activity Time Parameters." *Management Science*, September 1993.

24. KERZNER, H. *Project Management: A Systems Approach to Planning, Scheduling, and Controlling*, 6th ed. New York: Wiley, 1998.

25. Knutson, J. "From Making Sense to Making Cents: Measuring Project Management ROI—Part 1." *PM Network*, January 1999.

26. Levine, H. A. "Risk Management for Dummies, Part 2." *PM Network*, April 1996.

27. Liberatore, M. J., and G. J. Titus. "The Practice of Management Science in R & D Project Management." *Management Science*, August 1983.

28. Littlefield, T. K., Jr., and P. H. Randolph. "An Answer to Sasieni's Question on PERT Times." *Management Science*, October 1987.

29. Mallon, J. C. "Verifying Cost and Schedule During Design." *Project Management Journal*, March 1992.

30. Martin, P., and K. Tate. "Team-Based Risk Assessment." *PM Network*, February 1998.

31. McCahon, C. S. "Using PERT as an Approximation of Fuzzy Project-Network Analysis." *IEEE Transactions on Engineering Management*, May 1993.

32. Mills, N. L. "The Development of a University Sports Complex: A Project Management Application." *Computers and Industrial Engineering*, 17:149–153, 1989.

33. Moder, J. J., C. R. Phillips, and E. W. Davis. *Project Management with CPM, PERT, and Precedence Diagramming*, 3rd ed. New York: Van Nostrand Reinhold, 1983.

34. Naik, B. *Project Management: Scheduling and Monitoring by PERT/CPM*. Advent Books, 1984.

35. Orczyk, J. J., and L. Chang. "Parametric Regression Model for Project Scheduling." *Project Management Journal*, December 1991.

36. Pascale, S., J. Carland, and C. Lorenz. "Risk Analysis: Making the Right Call, Part 2." *PM Network*, March 1998.

37. Powers, J. R. "A Structured Approach to Schedule Development and Use." *Project Management Journal*, November 1988.

38. Pritsker, A. A. B. "GERT Networks." *The Production Engineer*, October 1968.

39. Project Management Institute Standards Committee *A Guide to the Project Management Body of Knowledge*. Upper Darby, PA: Project Management Institute, 1996.

40. Remy, R. "Adding Focus to Improvement Efforts with PM^3." *PM Network*, July 1997.

41. Robinson, P. B. "The Performance Measurement Baseline—A Statistical View." *Project Management Journal*, June 1997.

42. Santell, M. P., J. R. Jung, and J. C. Warner. "Optimization in Project Coordination Scheduling through Application of Taguchi Methods." *Project Management Journal*, September 1992.

43. Sasieni, M. W. "A Note on PERT Times." *Management Science*, December 1986.

44. Schlicter, J. An Organizational PM Maturity Model. *PM Network*, February 1999.

45. Shafer, S. M., and J. R. Meredith. *Operations Management: A Process Approach with Spreadsheets*, New York: Wiley, 1998.

46. Silverberg, E. C. "Predicting Project Completion." *Research-Technology Management*, May–June 1991.

47. Thamhain, H. J. "Best Practices for Controlling Technology-Based Projects." *Project Management Journal*, December 1996.

48. Toelle, R. A., and J. Witherspoon. "From 'Managing the Critical Path' to 'Managing Critical Activities.'" *Project Management Journal*, December 1990.

49. Toney, F. "What the Fortune 500 Know about PM Best Practices." *PM Network*, February 1997.

50. Tukel, O. I. "Scheduling Resource-Constrained Projects When Non-conformities Exist." *Project Management Journal*, September 1996.

51. Vazsonyi, A. "L'Histoire de Grandeur et la Decadence de la Methode PERT." *Management Science*, April 1979.

52. Weist, J. D., and F. K. Levy. A *Management Guide to PERT/CPM*, 2nd ed. Englewood Cliffs, NJ: Prentice Hall, 1977.

53. Wilkens, T. T. "Are You Being Misled by Your Progress Gantt Chart?" *PM Network*, August 1997.

54. Williams, T. M. "What are PERT Estimates?" *Journal of the Operational Research Society*, Vol. 44, No. 12, 1995.

55. Zhu, Z., and R. B. Heady. "A Simplified Method of Evaluating PERT/CPM Network Parameters." *IEEE Transactions on Engineering Management*, November 1994.

The following reading presents a realistic situation facing a construction firm that has just won a competitive contract. The realistic conditions complicating the project are described in detail, as are the alternatives offered by the staff for dealing with these complexities.

D I R E C T E D R E A D I N G

THE SHARON CONSTRUCTION CORPORATION
E. Turban and J. R. Meredith

The Sharon Construction Corporation has been awarded a contract for the construction of a 20,000-seat stadium. The construction must start by February 15 and be completed within one year. A penalty clause of $15,000 per week of delay beyond February 15 of next year is written into the contract.

Jim Brown, the president of the company, called a planning meeting. In the meeting he expressed great satisfaction at obtaining the contract and revealed that the company could net as much as $300,000 on the project. He was confident that the project could be completed on time with an allowance made for the usual delays anticipated in such a large project.

Bonnie Green, the director of personnel, agreed that in a normal year only slight delays might develop due to a shortage of labor. However, she reminded the president that for such a large project, the company would have to use unionized employees and that the construction industry labor agreements were to expire on November 30. Past experience indicated a fifty–fifty chance of a strike.

Jim Brown agreed that a strike might cause a problem. Unfortunately, there was no way to change the contract. He inquired about the prospective length of a strike. Bonnie figured that such a strike would last either eight weeks (70 percent chance) or possibly 12 weeks (30 percent chance).

Jim was not pleased with these prospects. However, before he had a chance to discuss contingency plans he was interrupted by Jack White, the vice-president for engineering. Jack commented that a colder December than had been assumed was now being predicted. This factor had not been taken into consideration during earlier estimates since previous forecasts called for milder weather. Concrete pouring in December might thus require in one out of every three cases (depending on the temperature) special heating that cost $500 per week.

This additional information did not please Jim at all. The chances for delay were mounting. And an overhead expense of $500 per week would be incurred in case of any delay. The technical details of the project are given in the appendix to this case.

The management team was asked to consider alternatives for coping with the situation. At the end of the week five proposals were submitted.

1. Expedite the pouring of seat gallery supports. This would cost $20,000 and cut the duration of the activity to six weeks.

2. The same as proposal 1, but in addition, put a double shift on the filling of the field. A cost of $10,000 would result in a five-week time reduction.

3. The roof is very important since it precedes several activities. The use of three shifts and some overtime could cut six weeks off the roofing at an additional cost of only $9000.

4. Do nothing special until December 1. Then, if December is indeed cold, defer the pouring of the seat gallery supports until the cold wave breaks, schedule permitting, and heat whenever necessary. If a strike occurs, wait until it is over (no other choice) and then expedite all remaining activities. In that case, the duration of any activity could be cut but to no less than one third of its normal duration. The additional cost per activity for any week which is cut would be $3000.

5. Do not take any special action; that is, hope and pray that no strike and no cold December occur (no cost).

Appendix: Technical Details of the Stadium

The stadium is an indoor structure with a seating capacity of 20,000. The project begins with clearing the site, an activity that lasts eight weeks. Once the site is clear, the work can start simultaneously on the structure itself and on the field.

The work in the field involves subsurface drainage which lasts eight weeks, followed by filling for the playing field and track. Only with the completion of the filling (14 weeks) can the installation of the artificial playing turf take place, an activity that consumes 12 weeks.

The work on the structure itself starts with excavation followed by the pouring of concrete footings. Each of these activities takes four weeks. Next comes the pouring of supports for seat galleries (12 weeks), followed by erecting pre-cast galleries (13 weeks). The seats can then be poured (4 weeks) and are ready for painting. However, the painting (3 weeks) cannot begin until the dressing rooms are completed (4 weeks). The dressing rooms can be completed only after the roof is erected (8 weeks). The roof must be erected on

a steel structure which takes 4 weeks to install. This activity can start only after the concrete footings are poured.

Once the roof is erected, work can start simultaneously on the lights (5 weeks) and on the scoreboard and other facilities (4 weeks). Assume there are 28 days in February and that February 15 falls on a Monday.

Questions

1. Analyze the five proposals and make recommendations based on expected costs.

2. What other basis might be used to make a decision besides expected costs? What then might the decision be?

3. What other factors might enter into the decision such as behavioral, organizational, and political?

4. What decision would you make as the president?

CHAPTER

9

Resource Allocation

In the previous chapter, we looked at a special type of resource allocation problem, that of allocating time among project tasks, better known as *scheduling*. Now we consider the allocation of physical resources as well. Also, we are concerned with using resources in both individual and in multiple, simultaneous projects. The subject relates directly to the topic of scheduling because altering schedules can alter the need for resources and—just as important—alter the timing of resource needs. At any given time, the firm may have a fixed level of various resources available for its projects. The fixed resources might include labor-hours of various types of special professional or technical services, machine-hours of various types of machinery or instrumentation, hours of computing time, and similar scarce resources needed for accomplishing project tasks. For example, if the need for some resource varies between 70 and 120 percent of resource capacity, then that resource will be under utilized (and wasted if no alternative use exists) at one point in the project and in insufficient supply at another. If the project schedule can be adjusted to smooth the use of the resource, it may be possible to avoid project delay and, at the same time, not saddle the project with the high cost of excess resources allocated "just to make sure."

This chapter addresses situations that involve resource problems. We discuss the trade-offs involved, the difference between allocation to one project and allocation between multiple projects, the relationship between resource loading and leveling, and some of the approaches employed to solve allocation problems, including the Critical Path Method (CPM), constrained resource diagramming and scheduling, Goldratt's "critical chain," and several other approaches to the problem of scheduling under conditions of resource scarcity. We begin with resource conflicts in a single project, and extend the discussion to the multiple project case. Although CPM is not actually a resource allocation method, we include it here because we view time as a resource, and trade-offs between time and other resources are a major problem in resource management. Finally, we note the major impact that current project management software has had on the PM's ability—and willingness—to deal with resource loading and leveling.

At 4:31 A.M. on January 17, 1994 a 6.8 magnitude earthquake hit Los Angeles and collapsed large sections of four major freeways, snarling one million commuters in daily gridlock for the indefinite future. Clearly, solutions to this crisis were of the highest priority. Caltrans, the California Department of Transportation, sprung into action with a three-pronged attack. First, they rushed into emergency response, fanning out to conduct visual inspections and close dangerous segments of the roads and freeways. Second, they initiated interim traffic management strategies for all closed segments, utilizing parallel streets and old bypass roads to expand their capacity, change their signage and striping, and redirect adjacent traffic including traffic signal timing. Last, they planned for speedy demolition and rebuilding of the damaged portions of the freeways.

Time was all-important and Caltrans used every tradeoff available to expedite the repairs which would normally take years to complete.

1. California's governor signed an Emergency Declaration allowing Caltrans to streamline its contracting procedures so that RFPs, bids, and evaluations that usually took four months could be completed in five days.

The earthquake leaves some commuters stranded.

2. Significant incentives/disincentives were built into the contracts, the incentive depending on the value of the construction under consideration. One firm spent heavily on overtime, extra equipment rentals, and bonuses to keep working 24 hours a day, rain or shine, and came in 74 days ahead of a contractual date of 140 days, thereby earning a $14.8 million bonus that became the talk of the town!

3. All resources of the Federal Highway Administration were made available to work with Caltrans.

Source: J. B. Baxter, "Responding to the Northridge Earthquake," *PM Network,* November 1994, pp. 13–22.

4. "Force Account" contracting was employed for immediate selection of sole-source contractors. The contractor then begins work immediately under the direction of a Caltrans Resident Engineer.

5. Major project management processes were initiated including disaster response and an earthquake recovery task force consisting of top executives in local and national governmental agencies.

6. Millions in additional funds were made available through Caltrans' Director, a declaration of a state of emergency by President Clinton, and eventually Congress.

9.1 CRITICAL PATH METHOD—CRASHING A PROJECT

In Chapter 8 we mentioned that CPM is similar to PERT. Originally, there was one important difference: CPM included a way of relating the project schedule to the level of physical resources allocated to the project. This allowed the PM to trade time for cost, or vice versa. In CPM, two activity times and two costs are specified, if appropriate, for each activity. The first time/cost combination is called *normal,* and the second set is referred to as *crash.* Normal times are "normal" in the same sense as the *m* time estimate of the three times used in PERT. Crash times result from an attempt to expedite the activity by the application of additional resources—for example, overtime, special equipment, and additional staff or material.

It is standard practice with PERT/CPM to estimate activity times under the assumption of resource loadings that are normal. To discuss a time requirement for any task without some assumption about the level of resources devoted to the task makes no real sense. At the same time, it does not make sense to insist on a full list of each and every resource that will be spent on each of the hundreds of activities that may comprise a PERT/CPM network. Clearly, there must have been some prior decision about what resources would be devoted to each task, but much of the decision making is, in practice, relegated to the common methods of standard practice and rules of thumb. The allocation problem requires more careful consideration if it is decided to speed up the accomplishment of tasks and/or the total project. We need to know what additional resources it will take to shorten completion times for the various activities making up the project.

While standard practice and rules of thumb are sufficient for estimating the resource needs for normal progress, careful planning is critical when attempting to expedite (crash) a project. Crash plans that appear feasible when considered activity by activity may incorporate impossible assumptions about resource availability. For example, we may need to crash some activities on the Wild Horse Dam Project. To do so, we have all the labor and materials required, but we will need a tractor-driven crawler crane on the project site not later than the eighth of next month. Unfortunately, our crane will be in Decatur, Illinois, on that date. No local contractor has a suitable crane for hire. Can we hire one in Decatur or Springfield and bring ours here? And so it goes. When we expedite a project, we tend to create problems; and the solution to one problem often creates several more problems that require solutions.

Difficulties notwithstanding, the wise PM adopts the Scout's motto: "Be prepared." If deterministic time estimates are used, and if project deadlines are firm, there is a high likelihood that it will be necessary to crash the last few activities of most projects. Use of the three probabilistic time estimates of PERT may reduce the chance that crashing will be needed because they include uncertainties that are sometimes forgotten or ignored when making deterministic time estimates. Even so, many things make crashing a way of life on some projects—things such as last-minute changes in client specifications, without permission to extend the project deadline by an appropriate increment, i.e., scope creep. An example of one of the problems that commonly result from the use of deterministic time estimates can be seen in the boxed example that follows.

Architectural Associates, Inc.

Architectural Associates, Inc. (AAI) specializes in large, industrial, retail, and public projects, including shopping malls, manufacturing complexes, convention centers, and the like. The firm is considered to be one of the region's most effective and creative design studios. Their design facility is located in a large, midwestern city and is housed on the second floor of an old building, originally used for light manufacturing. The offices are at one end of the floor, and about two-thirds of the floor space is occupied by the design staff and technicians. The entire space devoted to design is a single, open area and workstations are laid out in such a way as to encourage communication between individuals working on a common project.

A senior executive of AAI noticed that, for the past year or two, the chance of bringing design projects in on time and on budget had decreased to the point where the only uncertainty was how late and how much over budget a project would be. Architectural projects, like computer programming and a few other creative processes, seem to be typified by the need to crash projects at the last minute, but even with the usual crash, AAI was still late and, consequently, over budget.

An examination of the workplace disclosed a large, green felt, display board mounted on the wall where it was visible to the entire design staff. The board listed the names of individual designers and technicians vertically, and design contract numbers across the horizontal axis. The times allocated for work on each project by appropriate staff members were shown at the intersections of the rows and columns. The time estimates were made by senior managers, themselves architects, based on their experience. The individuals with direct responsibility for design work generally felt that the time estimates were reasonable.

The work process was studied and the following problem was revealed. If the design of the electrical systems involved in a plan was estimated to take five days, for example, the individual(s) responsible for the work planned it in such a way that it used the five days allowed. If a problem occurred on the first day, the worker(s) simply stayed late or speeded up work the next day in order to get back on schedule. Problems on the second day, and even on the third and fourth days were handled in the same way, by crashing the work. Problems occurring on the fifth day, however, could not be handled so easily and this part of the project would be late. Because most of the different systems (the mechanicals, landscape, etc.) were designed simultaneously and staffed to require about the same number of days (rather than being sequential), and because problems were very likely to arise late in the design process of at least one of the systems, the overall design project, which required all tasks to be completed on time, was almost invariably late.

In an attempt to solve the problem, a simple check-mark to show job assignments was substituted for time allocations on the green board. Additionally, senior management made normal, optimistic, and pessimistic time estimates for each task and calculated "TE," also used to help estimate project cost. These estimates were not given to the design staff who were simply told to do the work involved as efficiently and effectively as they could. The result was that the range of task times increased slightly, but the average time required for the various tasks fell somewhat since they were now designed for efficiency rather than X days. Roughly the same number of tasks were accomplished in less than the expected time as tasks that took more than the expected time.

Consider the data in Table 9-1. First, we compute a cost/time slope for each activity that can be expedited (crashed). Slope is defined as follows:

$$\text{slope} = \frac{\text{crash cost} - \text{normal cost}}{\text{crash time} - \text{normal time}}$$

that is, the cost per day of crashing a project. The slope is negative, indicating that as the time required for a project or task is decreased, the cost is increased. Note that activity **c** cannot be expedited. Table 9-2 shows the time/cost slopes for our example.

An implication of this calculation is that activities can be crashed in increments of one day (or one period). Often, this is not true. A given activity may have only two or three technically feasible durations. The "dollars per day" slope of such activities is relevant only if the whole crash increment is useful. For example, if an activity can be carried out in either eight days or four days, with no feasible intermediate times, and if an uncrashable parallel path goes critical when the first activity is reduced from eight down to six days, then the last two days (to four days) of time reduction are useless. (Of course, there are times when the PM may expedite activities that have little

Table 9-1. An Example of Two-Time CPM

Activity	Precedence	Duration, Days (normal, crash)	Cost (normal, crash)
a	—	3,2	$ 40,80
b	a	2,1	20,80
c	a	2,2	20,20
d*	a	4,1	30,120
e**	b	3,1	10,80

*Partial crashing allowed
**Partial crashing *not* allowed

Table 9-2. Activity Slopes—Cost per Period for Crashing

Activity	Slope ($/day)
a	40/–1 = –40
b	60/–1 = –60
c	—
d	90/–3 = –30
e	–70 (2 days)

or no impact on the network's critical time, such as when the resources used must be made available to another project.)

One must remember that crashing a project results in a change of the technology with which something is done. In the language of economics, it is a change in the "production function." At times, crashing may involve a relatively simple decision to increase groups of resources already being used. If the project, for instance, is to dig a ditch of a certain length and depth, we might add units of labor-shovel to shorten the time required. On the other hand, we might replace labor-shovel units with a Ditch Witch. Technological discontinuities in outcomes usually result. Different amounts of labor-shovel input may result in a job that takes anywhere from one to three days. Use of the Ditch Witch may require three hours. There may be no sensible combination of resources that would complete the job in, say, six hours. In some cases, technology cannot be changed, and task duration is fixed. A 30-day toxicity test for a new drug requires 30 days—no more, no less.

Not only do changes in technology tend to produce discontinuities in outcomes, they also tend to produce discontinuities in cost. As the technology is changed to speed a project, the relationship of input cost to activity duration is apt to jump as we move from less to more sophisticated production systems. For an extended treatment of this subject, see [27, Chapter 13].

With CPM, our first task is to develop a table or graph of the cost of a project as a function of the project's various possible completion dates. Starting with the normal schedule for all project activities, crash selected activities, one at a time, to decrease project duration at the minimum additional cost. To crash a project, follow two simple principles: First, focus on the critical path(s) when trying to shorten the duration of a project, with the exception we noted above when a resource used by an activity not on the critical path is needed for another project. Crashing a noncritical activity will not influence project duration. Second, when shortening a project's duration, select the least expensive way to do it.

Given these guides, consider the network shown in Figure 9-1a that was constructed from the data in Table 9-1. We use the AOA representation to illustrate that this procedure can be used with PERT as well as with CPM. Also, we use dummy activities in this case not to illustrate precedence but to show time durations on the time axis. As indicated in Tables 9-1 and 9-2, activity **d** can be partially crashed but activity **e** involves a technological discontinuity and must take either three days to complete at $10 or one day at $80. In general, the impact of

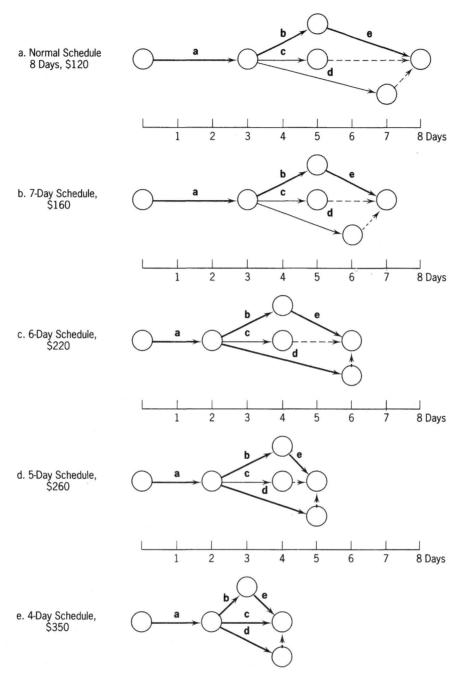

Figure 9-1   A CPM example.

having such a technological discontinuity is that the best solution for crashing n days might not be part of the best solution for crashing $n + 1$ days. Rather, it may be best to crash the activity with the technological discontinuity at $n + 1$ days and not crash another activity that could be crashed for n days. This situation is illustrated in the example that follows.

The network's critical path is **a-b-e,** the project duration is eight days, and the normal total cost is $120, as illustrated in the network of Figure 9-1a. The decision about which activities to crash depends on how much we need to reduce the duration of the project. To reduce the total network duration by one day, we must reduce the time required by one of the activities along the critical path. Inspecting Table 9-2 to see which critical activity can be reduced at the least cost, we find it is activity **a** which adds $40 to the project's current cost of $120. Activity **b** could be crashed at a cost of $60 or we could even crash **e** two days for a cost of $70. Of course, crashing **e** would only shorten the project duration by one day because when **e** is shortened, the path **a-d-dummy,** seven days long, becomes the critical path and does not allow the project to be shortened to six days. Of the three options, crashing **a** is the lowest cost and therefore preferable, see Figure 9-1b. Notice that crashing **a** also shortens **a-d-dummy** and **a-c-dummy** by a day.

Suppose the project must be crashed by two days. What are the options? Reconsidering Table 9-2 and Figure 9-1a, we see that we could crash activity **e** for two days ($70), but path **a-d-dummy** (7-days' duration) must also be crashed at least one day. We choose **d** ($30/day) because it is cheaper than **a** ($40). The cost of crashing is $100, and the total project cost is $120 + $100 = $220. Alternatively, we could crash **a** and **b,** also for a cost of $100 ($40 + $60). Arbitrarily, we choose the latter option (Figure 9-1c).

Now suppose we wanted to crash the project by three days, from the original eight days down to five days. Clearly **e** must be crashed by two days, costing $70, and **a** or **b** by a day. We choose **a,** the cheapest, for an additional $40. This leaves **d** to be crashed by one day for another $30 resulting in a total crashing cost of $140 and a project cost of $120 + $140 = $260 (Figure 9-1d). Note that we did not crash **b** this time, as we did for six days. This is due to the technological discontinuity in activity **e.**

Last, let us consider crashing the project by four days down to a project duration of four days. Since we crashed **e,** the technological discontinuity, to reach a five-day duration, all the remaining activities can be incrementally crashed. Thus, we can simply inspect Figure 9-1d to see what else needs incremental crashing to reduce the project by another day. Notice in Figure 9-1d that **a-b-e** and **a-d-dummy** are both critical paths. Only **b** and **d** can still be crashed so we crash each by one day for an additional cost beyond the five-day schedule of Figure 9-1d of $60 + $30 = $90 for a total project cost of $260 + $90 = $350 (Figure 9-1e). Note that **c** is now critical so *all* activities are critical. Since the critical paths **a-b-e** and **a-c** are at their full extent of crashing, the project duration cannot be further reduced, even though activity **d** could be crashed another day. Thus, Figure 9-1e is *not* the all-crash network, although it equals the all-crash time schedule of four days.

Another approach to CPM would have been starting with an all-crash schedule costing $380 and "relaxing" the activities one at a time. Of course, the activities relaxed first should be those that do not extend the completion date of the project. In our example, this is possible because **d** does not need to be at one day and so could be extended by one day at a cost saving of $30 without altering the project's completion date. This can be seen in Figure 9-1e, where activity **d** is shown taking two days with a project cost of $350. Continuing in this manner and relaxing the most expensive

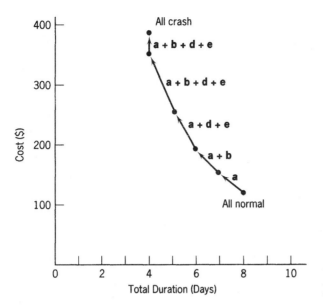

Figure 9-2   CPM cost-duration history.

activities first would eventually result in the all-normal schedule of eight days and a cost of $120, as shown in Figure 9-1a.

Whether or not all this crashing is worthwhile is another matter. On the cost side, Figure 9-2 shows the time/cost relationship of crashing the project. On the benefit side, some projects have penalty clauses that make the parent organization liable for late delivery—and sometimes bonuses for early delivery. Starting at the right (all-normal) side of Figure 9-2, note that it becomes increasingly costly to squeeze additional time out of the project. Charts such as the one shown in Figure 9-2 are useful to the PM in exercising control over project duration and cost. They are particularly helpful in dealing with senior managers who may argue for early project completion dates with little understanding of the costs involved. Similarly, such data are of great benefit when clients plead for early delivery. If the client is willing to pay the cost of crashing, or if the firm is willing to subsidize the client, the PM can afford to listen with a sympathetic ear. (While we advise the PM to ignore overhead cost over which he or she has no control, it should be noted that indirect costs are often altered when a project is crashed.)

Some organizations have more than one level of crashing. Table 9-3 illustrates such a case. In this example, the firm has two distinct levels of expediting a project, *rush* and *blitz*. The differences in the precedence relationships between tasks are noted in the table, as are differences in resource commitments. The last two rows of the table show the expected changes in cost and time if the project is expedited.

Fast-Tracking

Another way to expedite a project is known as "fast-tracking." This term has been applied mostly to construction projects, but the technique can be used in many other types of projects. It refers to overlapping the design and build phases of a project. Be-

Table 9-3. Official Pace of a Project

Title	Normal	Rush	Blitz
Approved Project Definition	Full	Some abbreviations from normal pace.	Only as necessary for major management decisions, purchasing and design engineering.
Study of Alternates	Reasonable	Quick study of major profitable items.	Only those not affecting schedule.
Engineering Design	Begins near end of Approved Project Definition.	Begins when Approved Project Definition 50–75% complete.	Concurrently with such approved Project Definition as is done.
Issue Engineering to Field	Allow adequate time for field to plan and purchase field items. Usually 1/2–2 months lead time between issue and field erection.	Little or no lead time between issue and field erection.	No lead time between issue and field erection.
Purchasing	Begins in latter stages of Approved Project Definition.	Done concurrently with Approved Project Definition. Rush purchase of all long delivery items. Many purchases on "advise price" basis.	Done concurrently with such Approved Project Definition as is done. Rush buy anything that will do job. Overorder and duplicate order to guarantee schedule.
Premium Payments	Negligible	Some to break specific bottlenecks.	As necessary to forestall any possible delays.
Field Crew Strength	Minimum practical or optimum cost.	Large crew with some spot overtime.	Large crew; overtime and/or extra shifts.
Probable Cost Difference Compared with Normal Pace, as a Result of:			
*Design and Development	Base	5–10% more	15% and up, more
*Engineering and Construction costs	Base	3–5% more	10% and up, more
Probable Time	Base	Up to10% less	Up to 50% less

cause design is usually completed before construction starts, overlapping the two activities will result in shortening the project duration. Beginning to build before design is completed might also, however, result in an increased number of change orders, subsequent loss of productivity, increased cost, and loss of time. Studies of construction projects revealed, however, that while there were more design changes in fast-tracked projects, the total number of project change orders was not significantly different than in similar projects that were not fast-tracked [16]. Fast-tracking seems to be a reasonable way to expedite construction projects, as well as other types of projects when the early "build" or "carry out" steps are fairly routine and well understood.

Solved Problem

Given the following network (time in days):

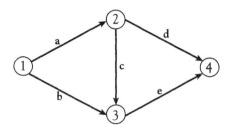

Activity	Crash Time, Normal Time, Cost	Partial Cost	Crashing?
a	3, $60	3, $60	No
b	6, 80	7, 30	Yes
c	2, 90	5, 50	No
d	5, 50	6, 30	No
e	2, 100	4, 40	Yes

Find the lowest cost to complete the project in 10 days.

Answer:
Current time and cost: 12 days and $210

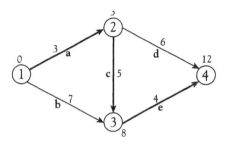

Since the critical path is **a-c-e,** we only initially need consider these three activities:

  a: cannot be crashed
  c: can cut 3 days at an extra cost of $40 but only results in project completion by day 11, due to **b.** To reach 10 days, cut **b** by one day, total extra cost $90.
  e: can cut **e** by 2 days for an extra cost of $60 and results in project completion by day 10.

Thus, cut **e** two days at a cost of $60.

9.2 THE RESOURCE ALLOCATION PROBLEM

A shortcoming of the scheduling procedures covered in the previous chapter is that they do not address the issues of resource utilization and availability. They focus on time rather than physical resources. Also, in the discussion that follows it will not be sufficient to refer to resource usage simply as "costs." Instead, we must refer to individual types of labor, specific facilities, kinds of materials, individual pieces of equipment, and other discrete inputs that are relevant to an individual project but are limited in availability. Last, we must not forget that time itself is always a critical resource in project management, one that is unique because it can neither be inventoried nor renewed.

The relationship between progress, time, and resource availability/usage is the major focus of this chapter. Schedules should be evaluated not merely in terms of meeting project milestones, but also in terms of the timing and use of scarce resources. A fundamental measure of the PM's success in project management is the skill with which the trade-offs among performance, time, and cost are managed. It is a continuous process of cost-benefit analysis: "I can shorten this project by a day at a cost of $400. Should I do it?" "If I buy 300 more hours of engineering time, I may be able to improve performance by 2 or 3 percent. Should I do it?"

Occasionally it is possible that some additional (useful) resources can be added at little or no cost to a project during a crisis period. At other times, some resources in abundant supply may be traded for scarce ones. Most of the time, however, these trades entail additional costs to the organization, so a primary responsibility for the PM is to make do with what is available.

The extreme points of the relationship between time use and resource use are these:

- **Time Limited:** The project must be finished by a certain time, using as few resources as possible. But it is time, not resource usage, that is critical.

- **Resource Limited:** The project must be finished as soon as possible, but without exceeding some specific level of resource usage or some general resource constraint.

The points between these two extremes represent time/resource-use trade-offs. As in Figure 9-2, they specify the times achievable at various resource levels. Equivalently, they specify the resources associated with various completion times. Clearly, the range of time or resource variability is limited.

Occasionally, both time and resources may be limited, but in this case, the specifications cannot also be fixed. If all three variables—time, cost, specifications—are fixed, the system is "overdetermined." The PM has lost all flexibility to perform the trade-offs that are so necessary to the successful completion of projects. Of course, it is possible that all three variables might be fixed at levels that allowed the PM plenty of maneuvering room, but this is most unlikely. Far more likely, our project manager acquaintances tell us, is the case in which senior management assigns budgets, schedules, and specifications without regard for the uncertainties of reality. It is the PM's responsibility, possibly with help from the project's champion, to warn senior management of the impropriety of such restrictions in spite of the chance that a senior manager might respond with "I'll get someone who can. . . !"

On occasion, it may be that one or more tasks in a project are *system-constrained*. A system-constrained task requires a fixed amount of time and known quantities of resources. Some industrial processes—heat treating, for instance—are system-constrained. The material must "cook" for a specified time to achieve the desired effect. More or less "cooking" will not help. When dealing with a system-constrained task or project, no trade-offs are possible. The only matter of interest in these cases is to make sure that the required resources are available when needed.

In the following sections we discuss approaches for understanding and using these relationships in various project situations.

9.3 RESOURCE LOADING

Resource loading describes the amounts of individual resources an existing schedule requires during specific time periods. Therefore, it is irrelevant whether we are considering a single work unit or several projects; the loads (requirements) of each resource type are simply listed as a function of time period. Resource loading gives a general understanding of the demands a project or set of projects will make on a firm's resources. It is an excellent guide for early, rough project planning. Obviously, it is also a first step in attempting to reduce excessive demands on certain resources, regardless of the specific technique used to reduce the demands. Again, we caution the PM to recognize that the use of resources on a project is often nonlinear. Much of the project management software does not recognize this fact [11].

Given an action plan, deriving a resource-loading document is not difficult. Figure 5-3 (Chapter 5, Section 5-3) shows part of an action plan for a "Career Day" at a college. The part of the plan shown lists the personnel resources needed for each activity. (The hours required are included in the plan, but were not printed in Figure 5-3.) Utilizing data in the plan, Microsoft Project 98® generated (Figure 9-3) the resource loading diagram. Each of the human resources used in the project is listed,

			May				June				July				
ID	Resource Name	Work	25	2	9	16	23	30	6	13	20	27	4	11	18	25
1	**Secretary**	**1,020 hrs**	24h	40h	40h	40h	88h	120h	102h	40h	40h	40h	40h	40h	40h	40h
	Print forms	240 hrs														
	Gather college particulars	160 hrs	24h	40h	40h	40h	16h									
	Print programs	240 hrs					24h	40h	40h	40h	40h	40h	16h			
	Advertise in college paper	200 hrs					24h	40h	36h	0h	0h	0h	24h	40h	36h	
	Organize posters	180 hrs					24h	40h	26h	0h	0h	0h	0h	0h	4h	40h
2	**Program Manager**	**1,440 hrs**	40h	40h	40h	16h	24h	40h	40h	40h	16h					
	Contact organizations	600 hrs	16h													
	Select guest speaker	560 hrs														
	Organize food	120 hrs	24h	40h	40h	16h										
	Contact faculty	60 hrs					24h	36h								
	Arrange facility for event	100 hrs						4h	40h	40h	16h					
3	**Office Manager**	**180 hrs**	24h	40h	40h	40h	16h				20h					
	Collect display information	160 hrs	24h	40h	40h	40h	16h									
	Transport materials	20 hrs									20h					
4	**Graduate Assistant**	**1,140 hrs**	24h	40h	40h	40h	64h	80h	80h	56h	40h	40h	16h			
	Print participants' certificates	320 hrs														
	Organize refreshments	280 hrs	24h	40h	40h	40h	40h	40h	40h	16h						
	Send invitations	80 hrs														
	Organize gift certificates	220 hrs														
	Arrange banner	200 hrs					24h	40h	40h	40h	40h	16h				
	Class announcements	40 hrs										24h	16h			
5	**Director**	**400 hrs**	24h	40h	40h	40h	40h	40h	40h	40h	40h	40h	16h			
	Organize liquor	400 hrs	24h	40h	40h	40h	40h	40h	40h	40h	40h	40h	16h			

Career Day Project
Resource Usage Calendar

Figure 9-3   Resource usage calendar for the Career Day Project.

followed by the name of the activities in which the resource is used. The total hours of work for each resource called for by the action plan are shown together with the amount planned for each activity. The schedule for resource loading is derived and the loading is then shown for each resource for each week (or day or month) of the project.

An examination of Figure 9-3 shows that the secretary is overloaded during late May and early June. Assuming that there is only one secretary, he or she must work 17+ hours per day of a 7-day week (or 24 hours per 5-day week). This is apt to try the patience of the most determined and loyal employee. Graduate assistants are certainly considered slaves by their faculty masters, but are usually indentured for only 20 hours per week of servitude. Unless there are four GAs, the project will have problems. It is the job of the PM to deal with these problems, either by adding people or by changing the schedule in such a way that the demand for resources does not exceed resource capacities.

Because the project action plan is the source of information on activity precedences, durations, and resources requirements, it is the primary input for both the project schedule and its budget. The action plan links the schedule directly to specific demands for resources. Thus, the PERT/CPM network technique can be modified to generate time-phased resource requirements. A Gantt chart could be adapted, but the PERT/CPM diagram, particularly if modified to illustrate slacks, will be helpful in the analysis used for resource leveling. Let us illustrate with the PERT/CPM network used as an example in the previous chapter. The network (Table 8-2) reappears as Figure 9-4, and resource usage is illustrated for two hypothetical resources, A and B, on the arcs. The expected activity time is shown above the arc and resource usage is shown in brackets just below the arc, with the use of A shown first and B second—e.g., [5, 3] would mean that five units of A and three units of B would be used on the activity represented by the arc. Figure 9-5 shows the "calendarized" PERT/CPM diagram, similar to the familiar Gantt chart. Resource demands can now be summed by time period across all activities.

The loading diagram for resource A is illustrated in Figure 9-6a, and that for resource B in Figure 9-6b. The loads are erratic and vary substantially over the duration of the project. Resource A, used in tasks **a, b,** and **c,** has a high initial demand that

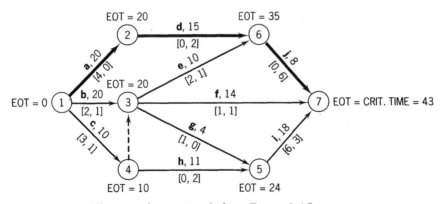

Figure 9-4 The complete network from Figure 8-15.

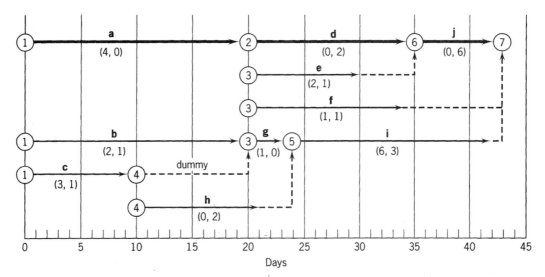

Figure 9-5 Modified PERT/CPM diagram showing resource usage (from Figure 9-3).

drops through the middle of the project and then climbs again. Resource B, on the other hand, has low initial use but increases as the project develops. The PM must be aware of the ebbs and flows of usage for each input resource throughout the life of the project. It is the PM's responsibility to ensure that the required resources, in the required amounts, are available when and where they are needed. In the next three sections, we will discuss how to meet this responsibility.

9.4 RESOURCE LEVELING

In the preceding example, we noted that the project began with the heavy use of resource A, used smaller amounts during the middle of the project, and then continued with rising usage during the project's latter stages. Usage of B started low and rose throughout the project's life. Large fluctuations in the required loads for various resources are a normal occurrence—and are undesirable from the PM's point of view. Resource leveling aims to minimize the period-by-period variations in resource loading *by shifting tasks within their slack allowances*. The purpose is to create a smoother distribution of resource usage.

There are several advantages to smoother resource usage. First, much less hands-on management is required if the use of a given resource is nearly constant over its period of use. The PM can arrange to have the resource available when needed, can have the supplier furnish constant amounts, and can arrange for a backup supplier if advisable. Moreover, the PM can do this with little error. Second, if resource usage is level, the PM may be able to use a "just-in-time" inventory policy without much worry that the quantity delivered will be wrong. If the resource being leveled is people, leveling improves morale and results in fewer problems in the personnel and payroll offices because of increasing and decreasing labor levels.

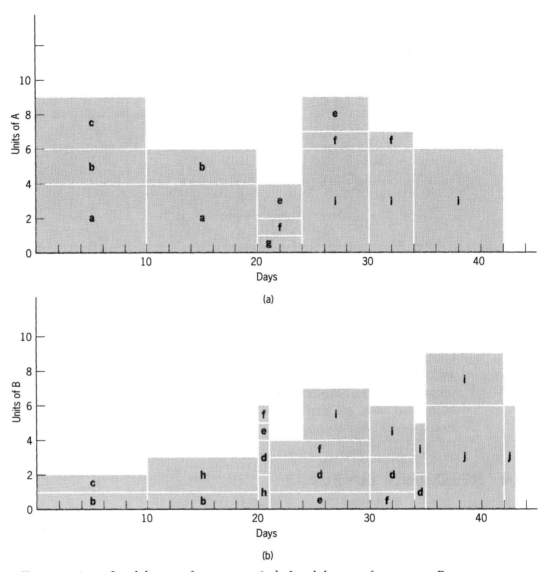

Figure 9-6   *a:* Load diagram for resource A. *b:* Load diagram for resource B.

Not only are there managerial implications to resource leveling, there are also important cost implications. When resources are leveled, the associated costs also tend to be leveled. If resource use increases as time goes by, and if resources are shifted closer to the present by leveling, costs will be shifted in the same way. The opposite is true, of course, if resource usage is shifted to the future. Perhaps most important from a cost perspective is leveling employment throughout a project or task. For most organizations, the costs of hiring and layoff are quite significant. It is often less expensive to level labor requirements in order to avoid hiring and layoff, even if it means some extra wages will be paid. In any case, the PM must be aware of the cash flows associated with the project and of the means of shifting them in ways that are useful to the parent firm.

The basic procedure for resource leveling is straightforward. For example, consider the simple network shown in Figure 9-7a. The activity time is shown above the arc, and resource usage (one resource, workers) is in brackets below the arc. Activities **a, b,** and **c** follow event 1, and all must precede event 4. Activity **a** requires two workers and takes two days, **b** requires two workers and takes three days, and **c** needs

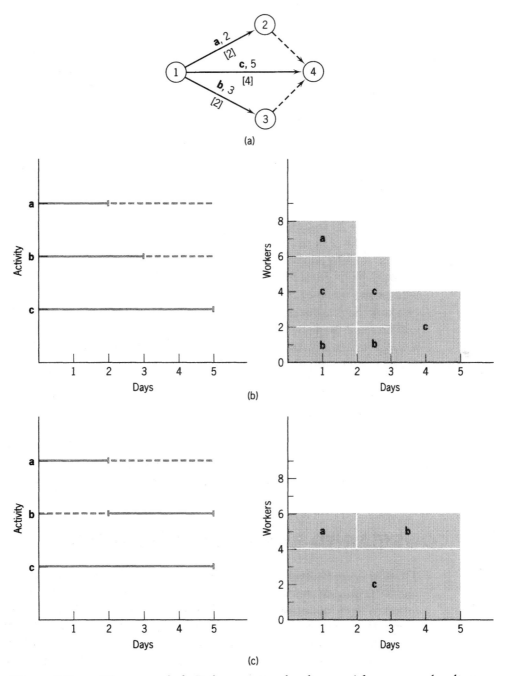

Figure 9-7   *a:* The network. *b:* Before resource leveling. *c:* After resource leveling.

four workers and five days. (We addressed the problem of trade-offs between labor and activity time in the first section of this chapter.) If all these tasks are begun on their early start dates, the resource loading diagram appears as shown in Figure 9-7b, steps of decreasing labor demand varying from eight workers to four workers. If, however, task **b** is delayed for two days, the full length of its slack in this particular case, the resource loading diagram is smoothed, as shown in Figure 9-7c. The same result would have occurred if **b** were started as early as possible and task **a** were delayed until day 3.

Resource leveling is a procedure that can be used for almost all projects, whether or not resources are constrained. If the network is not too large and there are only a few resources, the leveling process can be done manually. For larger networks and multiple resources, resource leveling becomes extremely complex, far beyond the power of manual solutions. Fortunately, a number of computer programs can handle most leveling problems efficiently (discussed in Chapter 10).

Reconsider the load diagrams of Figures 9-6a and b. Assume it is desired to smooth the loading of resource B, which is particularly jagged. both activities **e** and **f** can be delayed (**e** has five days of slack and **f** has nine). If we delay both for one day, we remove the peak on day 20 without increasing any of the other peaks (see Figure 9-8b). If we do this, however, it also alters the use of resource A and deepens the "valley" on day 20 (see Figure 9-8a). If we further delay **f** another seven days in order to level the use of A toward the end of the project, we would deepen the valley between days 20 and 24, and the resultant use of A would be as shown by the dotted lines on Figure 9-8a. Activity **f** would begin on day 28 (and would become critical). The effect on the usage of B is easy to see (Figure 9-8b). The change would lower usage by one unit beginning on day 21 (remember that we have already delayed **f** one day), and increase usage by one unit beginning on day 35, continuing to the end of the project. This action increases peak use of B from nine to ten units.

It is important to emphasize that if the network under consideration is more complex and the number of resources to be leveled is realistically large, a manual leveling process is out of the question. Computer-aided leveling is not only mandatory, it is also helpful because it allows the PM to experiment with various patterns of resource usage through simulation.

In the next section, we raise the most general problem of minimizing resource usage while still achieving various completion dates—or the inverse problem, minimizing completion times while operating with specified limits on resources.

9.5 CONSTRAINED RESOURCE SCHEDULING

There are two fundamental approaches to constrained allocation problems: heuristics and optimization models. Heuristic approaches employ rules of thumb that have been found to work reasonably well in similar situations. They seek better solutions. Optimization approaches seek the best solutions but are far more limited in their ability to handle complex situations and large problems. We will discuss each separately.

Most PC software designed for project management will level resources and solve the problems of overscheduling resources. They require priority rules to establish

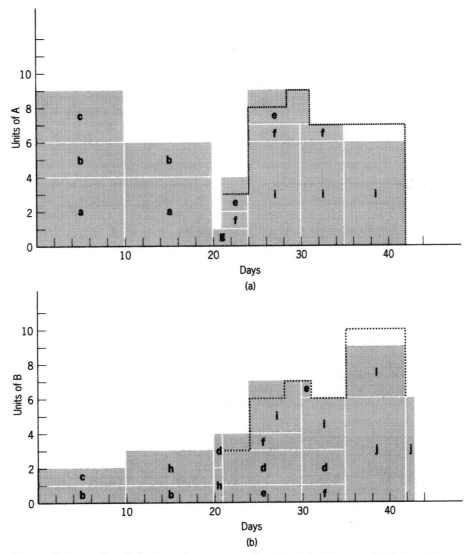

Figure 9-8   *a:* Load diagram for resource A with activities **e** and **f** delayed by one day each. *b:* Load diagram for resource B with activities **e** and **f** delayed by one day each.

which activities take precedence. The priority rules the programs use vary somewhat, but most packages offer a choice. Figures 9-9a and 9-9b show a resource conflict and the resource leveling solution. Note the changes in the scheduled finish dates for the leveled solution. (The example is from a project shown in Chapter 10.)

Heuristic Methods

Heuristic approaches to constrained resource scheduling problems are in wide, general use for a number of reasons. First, they are the only feasible methods of attacking the large, nonlinear, complex problems that tend to occur in the real world of project management. Second, while the schedules that heuristics generate may not be opti-

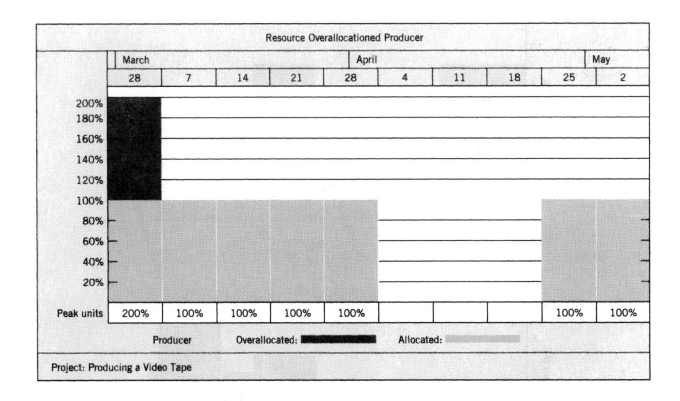

Figure 9-9a Resource conflict, producer used beyond capacity.

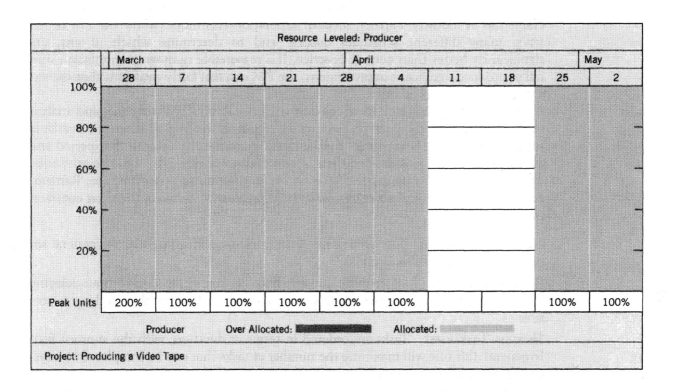

Figure 9-9b   Rescheduling to level resource usage without exceeding capacity.

mal, they are usually quite good—certainly good enough for most purposes. Commercially available computer programs handle large problems and have had considerable use in industry. Further, modern simulation techniques allow the PM to develop many different schedules quickly and to determine which, if any, are significantly better than current practice. If a reasonable number of simulation runs fail to produce significant improvement, the PM can feel fairly confident that the existing solution is a good one.

Most heuristic solution methods start with the PERT/CPM schedule and analyze resource usage period by period, resource by resource. In a period when the available supply of a resource is exceeded, the heuristic examines the tasks in that period and allocates the scarce resource to them sequentially, according to some priority rule. The major difference among the heuristics is in the priority rules they use. Remember that the *technological necessities always take precedence*. Some of the most common priority rules are:

As Soon as Possible   The default rule for scheduling. This provides the general solution for critical path and time.

As Late as Possible   all activities are scheduled as late as possible without delaying the project. The usual purpose of this heuristic is to defer cash outflows as long as possible.

Shortest Task First   Tasks are ordered in terms of duration, with the shortest first. In general, this rule will maximize the number of tasks that can be completed by a system during some time period.

Most Resources First   Activities are ordered by use of a specific resource, with the largest user heading the list. The assumption behind this rule is that more important tasks usually place a higher demand on scarce resources.

Minimum Slack First   This heuristic orders activities by the amount of slack, least slack going first. (It is common, when using this rule, to break ties by using the shortest-task-first rule.)

Most Critical Followers   Tasks are arranged by number of critical activities following them. The ones with the greatest number of critical followers go first.

Most Successors   This is the same as the previous rule, except that all followers, not merely critical ones, are counted.

Arbitrary   Priorities are assigned to activities according to some rule not associated with task length, slack, or resource requirements. Such rules might be that tasks on projects of higher value to the parent organization (or for the project of a favored customer) are taken before those of lower value.

There are many such priority rules employed in scheduling heuristics. From time to time researchers subject several of the more popular of the PC-based project management application programs to tests of their ability to handle such tasks as allocating constrained resources and resource leveling. They test several heuristics with each program and compare the results with optimal solutions. The results are published [e.g., 8 and 17] but are fairly short-lived, often not surviving later releases of the several software packages.

Most priority rules are simple adaptations and variations of the heuristics used for the traditional "job shop scheduling" problem of production/operations management, a problem that has much in common with multiproject scheduling and resource allocation. Also, most heuristics use a combination of rules—a primary rule, with a secondary rule used to break ties.

Several researchers [9, 19, 20] have conducted tests of the more commonly used schedule priority rules. Although their findings vary somewhat because of slightly different assumptions, the minimum slack rule was found to be best or near-best quite often and rarely caused poor performance. It usually resulted in the minimum amount of project schedule slippage, the best utilization of facilities, and the minimum total system occupancy time.

As the scheduling heuristic operates, one of two events will result. The routine runs out of activities (for the current period) before it runs out of the resources, or it runs out of resources before all activities have been scheduled. (While it is theoretically possible for the supply of resources to be precisely equal to the demand for such resources, even the most careful planning rarely produces such a tidy result.) If the former occurs, the excess resources are left idle, assigned elsewhere in the organization as needed during the current period, or applied to future tasks required by the project—always within the constraints imposed by the proper precedence relationships. If one or more resources are exhausted, however, activities requiring those resources are slowed or delayed until the next period when resources can be reallocated.

If the minimum slack rule is used, resources would be devoted to critical or nearly critical activities, delaying those with greater slack. Delay of an activity uses some of its slack, so the activity will have a better chance of receiving resources in the next allocation. Repeated delays move the activity higher and higher on the priority list. We consider later what to do in the potentially catastrophic event that we run out of resources before all critical activities have been scheduled.

The heuristic procedure just described is probably the most common. There are, however, other heuristic procedures that work in a similar manner. One works in reverse and schedules jobs from the end of the project instead of from its beginning. Activities that just precede the project finish are scheduled to be completed just barely within their latest finish times. Then, the next-to-last tasks are considered, and so on. The purpose of this approach is to leave as much flexibility as possible for activities that will be difficult to schedule in the middle and early portions of the project. This logic seems to rest on the idea that flexibility early in the project gives the best chance of completing early and middle activities on time and within budget, thereby improving the chances of being on time and within budget at the ending activities.

Other heuristics use the *branch and bound* approach. They generate a wide variety of solutions, discard those that are not feasible and others that are feasible but poor solutions. This is done by a *tree search* that prunes infeasible solutions and poor solutions when other feasible solutions dominate them. In this way, the heuristic narrows the region in which good, feasible solutions may be found. If the "tree" is not too large, this approach can locate optimal solutions, but more computer search time will be required. See [33] for further details.

These heuristics are usually embedded in a computer simulation package that describes what will happen to the project(s) if certain schedules or priority rules are followed. A number of different priority rules can be tried in the simulation in order to derive a set of possible solutions. Simulation is a powerful tool and can also handle unusual project situations. Consider, for example, the following problem in *resource contouring*.

Given the network and resource demands shown in Figure 9-10, find the best schedule using a constant crew size. Each day of delay beyond 15 days incurs a penalty of $1000. Workers cost $100 per day, and machines cost $50 per day. Workers are interchangeable, as are machines. Task completion times vary directly with the number of workers, and partial work days are acceptable. The critical time for the project is 15 days, given the resource usage shown in Figure 9-10. (There are other jobs in the system waiting to be done.)

Figure 9-10 lists the total worker-days and machines per day normally required by each activity (below the activity arc). Because activity times are proportional to worker demands, path **b-c-e-i** is most demanding and this path uses 149 worker-days.

The fact that completion times vary with the number of workers means that activity **a** could be completed in six days with ten workers or in 10 days with six workers. Applying some logic and trying to avoid the penalty, which is far in excess of the cost of additional resources, we can add up the total worker-days required on all activities, obtaining 319. Dividing this by the 15 days needed to complete the project results in a requirement of slightly more than 21 workers—say, 22. How should they be allocated to the activities? Figure 9-11 shows one way, arbitrarily determined. Workers are shown above the "days" axis and machines below. We have 22 workers at $100 per day for 15 days ($33,000) and 128.5 machine days at $50 per day ($6425). The total cost of this particular solution is $39,425.

The "critical path" illustrated in Figure 9-11 is **a-g-i**, which takes 15 days. However, inspecting Figure 9-10, activity **g** does not follow activity **a** so how can this be a true "critical path"? The reason is when resources are shared among activities, the resources for one activity may not be available because an earlier activity (though not necessarily a predecessor) is still using them. Thus, in theory, **g** (and **f** too) could have started at day 4 when **b** was completed but there were no workers available.

The availability of workers is indicated by the shaded regions in Figure 9-11. Thus, if we use the six idle workers shown between activities **f** and **h** (for 0.7 days,

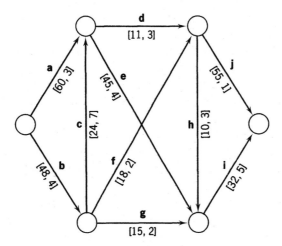

Figure 9-10   Network for resource load simulation. *Note:* The numbers on the arcs represent, respectively, worker-days, machines per day.

Figure 9-11   Load chart for a simulation problem.

thereby releasing 4.2 worker-days) to reduce the length of activity **g,** we could reduce it by 42/3 (workers) = 1.4 days, finishing now at 9.6 days. However, path **b-c-d-h** would then become critical at 10.8 days, resulting in only 0.2 days of overall project reduction. Using the 4.2 worker-days to reduce not only activity **g** but also activities **d** and **e,** would allow us to complete all of activities **e, h,** and **g** at day 10.32, thereby reducing the project time by 0.68 days. The idle labor following activity **j** could be used similarly to reduce activity **i.**

After all reallocations, it is important to recalculate the demand for machines since this will also change. Note that we have assumed that machine use depends only on time and is independent of the number of workers: if this is not the case, then a different set of calculations is required to determine the machine requirements. Finally, there may be limitations on the total number of workers or machines that are available at any one time and this can affect the solution. For example, how would the solution change if only 20 workers were available?

The purpose of reassignments is not to decrease labor cost in the project. This is fixed by the base technology implied by the worker/machine usage data. The reassignments do, however, shorten the project duration and make the resources available for other work sooner than expected. If the trade-offs are among resources, for instance, trading more labor for fewer machines or more machines for less material input, the problem is handled in the same way. Always, however, the technology itself constrains what is possible. The Chinese build roads in the mountains by using labor. In the United States machines are used. Both nations exercise an option because either labor-intensive or machine-intensive technology is feasible. The ancient Israelites, however, could not substitute labor for straw in making bricks: No straw, no bricks.

On small networks with simple interrelationships among the resources, it is not difficult to perform these resource trade-offs by hand. But for networks of a realistic size, a computer is clearly required. If the problem is programmed for computer solution, many different solutions and their associated costs can be calculated. But, as with heuristics, simulation does not guarantee an optimal, or even feasible, solution. It can only test those solutions fed into it.

Another heuristic procedure for leveling resource loads is based on the concept of minimizing the sum of the squares of the resource requirements in each period. That is, the smooth use of a resource over a set of periods will give a smaller sum of squares than the erratic use of the resource that averages out to the same amount as the smooth use. This approach, called *Burgess's method,* was applied by Woodworth and Willie [37] to a multiproject situation involving a number of resources. The method was applied to each resource sequentially, starting with the most critical resource.

In the past several years, a wide range of attacks have been made on the problems of resource allocation and scheduling when resources are constrained. Some of these depend on sophisticated mathematical and/or graphical tools and may be quite powerful in what they can do [e.g., 18]. Tukel found that the minimum slack rule and the longest path rule both worked well for scheduling resource constrained problems when some level of rework was required [32]. Morse et al. examined combinations of several heuristics for scheduling when there were some constrained resources [24]. Badiru's critical resource diagramming allows the construction of a network that shows the relationships of the various resources used on a project, e.g., if the use of resource 1 precedes the use of resource 2, an arrow connects the node representing resource 1 with the node representing resource 2. Given some resource availabilities, the critical resources can be found, together with project duration that depends on the availability of the critical resource(s) [3]. The effect of learning curves on resource usage has also been included [4]. Finally, simulation has been used to solve resource-constrained scheduling problems; see [10] for an interesting approach.

Next, we briefly discuss some optimizing approaches to the constrained resource scheduling problem.

Optimizing Methods

The methods to find an optimal solution to the constrained resource scheduling problem fall into two categories: mathematical programming (linear programming for the most part) and enumeration. In the 1960s, the power of LP improved from being able to handle three resources and 15 activities to four resources and 55 activities. But even with this capacity, LP is usually not feasible for reasonably large projects where there may be a dozen resources and thousands of activities. (See [7] for more detail.)

In the late 1960s and early 1970s, limited enumeration techniques were applied to the constrained resource problem with more success. Tree search and branch and bound methods [29] were devised to handle up to five resources and perhaps 200 activities. Advances in LP techniques now allow LP to be used on large constrained resource scheduling problems.

Other approaches have combined programming and enumeration methods. Patterson and Huber [28], for example, employ an integer programming approach combined with a minimum bounding procedure to reduce the computation time for minimizing project duration. Similarly, Talbot [30] uses integer programming and implicit enumeration to formulate and solve problems where the completion time is a function of the resources allocated to the project.

One problem with even the newer combination of approaches is that the characteristics of problems that can be usefully addressed with these methods is still largely unknown. Why various methods will work on one problem and not on a similar problem is still being researched.

Project Management in Practice
Benefits of Resource Constraining at Pennsylvania Electric

Pennsylvania Electric Company, headquartered in Johnstown, PA, operates generating facilities with a capacity of 6950 megawatts to serve 547,000 customers over an area of 17,600 square miles. The Generation Division Planning Group is responsible for planning all maintenance and capital projects. In the early 1980s, the group used a manual method of planning with hand-drawn charts. The planning process has now been computerized, which is faster, allows "what-if" analyses, and controls more than just the previously monitored critical path. In bringing the planning process in-house, the group also saved $100,000 a year in service fees from an outside engineering firm who was planning their construction activities.

A special feature of the computerized system is its resource constraining module which establishes labor requirements across all jobs. In the pilot program to test the new software, $300,000 was saved when it was discovered that a job could be done with 40 percent fewer mechanics than normally used and still complete the job on time. In another application, it was found that a turbine disassembly and inspection could be added to the task list without delaying the project or exceeding the project budget.

After worker-hours are input to the program by activity, actual progress is monitored (see figure) and schedule and cost deviations are highlighted for management attention. This allows management to make adjustments to recover the

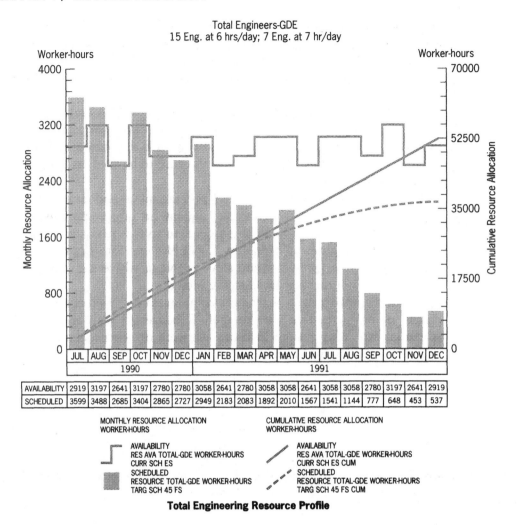

Total Engineers-GDE
15 Eng. at 6 hrs/day; 7 Eng. at 7 hr/day

	JUL	AUG	SEP	OCT	NOV	DEC	JAN	FEB	MAR	APR	MAY	JUN	JUL	AUG	SEP	OCT	NOV	DEC
AVAILABILITY	2919	3197	2641	3197	2780	2780	3058	2641	2780	3058	3058	2641	3058	3058	2780	3197	2641	2919
SCHEDULED	3599	3488	2685	3404	2865	2727	2949	2183	2083	1892	2010	1567	1541	1144	777	648	453	537

MONTHLY RESOURCE ALLOCATION
WORKER-HOURS

CUMULATIVE RESOURCE ALLOCATION
WORKER-HOURS

AVAILABILITY
RES AVA TOTAL-GDE WORKER-HOURS
CURR SCH ES

SCHEDULED
RESOURCE TOTAL-GDE WORKER-HOURS
TARG SCH 45 FS

AVAILABILITY
RES AVA TOTAL-GDE WORKER-HOURS
CURR SCH ES CUM

SCHEDULED
RESOURCE TOTAL-GDE WORKER-HOURS
TARG SCH 45 FS CUM

Total Engineering Resource Profile

schedule, slow the project down, or acquire more funds to get the project back on schedule. Obviously, there are always some emergencies outside the plan that must be handled on an exception basis. But with this software, management knows what effect different actions will have on the basic plan and can thereby make the best use of available resources to handle the emergency with minimal impact on the plan.

Source: A. J. Cantanese, "At Penelec, Project Management is a Way of Life," *Project Management Journal*, December 1990.

9.6 MULTIPROJECT SCHEDULING AND RESOURCE ALLOCATION

Scheduling and allocating resources to multiple projects is much more complicated than for the single-project case. The most common approach is to treat the several projects as if they were each elements of a single large project. (A more detailed explanation is given below when we consider a specific multiproject scheduling heuristic.) Another way of attacking the problem is to consider all projects as completely independent; see [19, 20], for example. As [19] shows, these two approaches lead to different scheduling and allocation outcomes. For either approach, the conceptual basis for scheduling and allocating resources is essentially the same.

There are several projects, each with its own set of activities, due dates, and resource requirements. In addition, the penalties for not meeting time, cost, and performance goals for the several projects may differ. Usually, the multiproject problem involves determining how to allocate resources to, and set a completion time for, a new project that is added to an existing set of ongoing projects. This requires the development of an efficient, dynamic multiproject scheduling system.

To describe such a system properly, standards are needed by which to measure scheduling effectiveness. Three important parameters affected by project scheduling are: (1) schedule slippage, (2) resource utilization, and (3) in-process inventory. The organization (or the PM) must select the criterion most appropriate for its situation.

Schedule slippage, often considered the most important of the criteria, is the time past a project's due date or delivery date when the project is completed. Slippage may well result in penalty costs that reduce profits. Further, slippage of one project may have a ripple effect, causing other projects to slip. Indeed, expediting a project in order to prevent slippage may, and usually does, disturb the overall organization to the point where slippage due to resource shortages may then be caused in other projects. The loss of goodwill when a project slips and deliveries are late is important to all producers. As is the case with many firms, Grumman Aircraft, purchased by the Northrup Corporation in 1994, jealously guards its reputation for on-time delivery. During a project to install a new machine control system on a production line, Grumman insisted that the project be designed to minimize disturbance to operations in the affected plant and avoid late shipments. This increased the cost of the project, but the firm maintained delivery schedules.

A second measure of effectiveness, *resource utilization*, is of particular concern to industrial firms because of the high cost of making resources available. A resource allocation system that smooths out the peaks and valleys of resource usage is ideal, but it is extremely difficult to attain while maintaining scheduled performance because all the projects in a multiproject organization are competing for the same scarce resources. In particular, it is expensive to change the size of the human resource pool on which the firm draws.

While it is relatively easy to measure the costs of excess resource usage required by less than optimal scheduling in an industrial firm, the costs of uncoordinated multiproject scheduling can be high in service-producing firms, too. In the real estate syndication firm used as an example of an AON network in Chapter 8 (see Figure 8-20), the scarce resource is executive judgment time. If two deals arrived at the same time, one would have to wait. This is undesirable because other potential buyers are seeking properties, and the process must move along without delay.

The third standard of effectiveness, the amount of *in-process inventory*, concerns the amount of work waiting to be processed because there is a shortage of some resource(s). Most industrial organizations have a large investment in in-process inventory, which may indicate a lack of efficiency and often represents a major source of expense for the firm. The remedy involves a trade-off between the cost of in-process inventory and the cost of the resources, usually capital equipment, needed to reduce the in-process inventory levels. It is almost axiomatic that the most time-consuming operation in any production system involving much machining of metals is an operation called "wait." If evidence is required, simply observe parts sitting on the plant floor or on pallets waiting for a machine, or for jigs, fixtures, and tools.

All these criteria cannot be optimized at the same time. As usual, trade-offs are involved. A firm must decide which criterion is most applicable in any given situation, and then use that criterion to evaluate its various scheduling and resource allocation options.

At times, the demands of the marketplace and the design of a production/distribution system may require long production runs and sizable levels of in-process inventory. This happens often when production is organized as a continuous system, but sales are organized as projects, each customized to a client order. Items may be produced continuously but held in a semifinished state and customized in batches.

A mattress manufacturing company organized to produce part of its output by the usual continuous process; but the rest of its production was sold in large batches to a few customers. Each large order was thought of as a project and was organized as one. The customization process began after the metal frames and springs were assembled. This required extensive in-process inventories of semi-finished mattresses.

As noted earlier, experiments by Fendley [9] revealed that the minimum-slack-first rule is the best overall priority rule, generally resulting in minimum project slippage, minimum resource idle time, and minimum system occupancy time (i.e., minimum in-process inventory) for the cases he studied. But the most commonly used priority rule is first come, first served—which has little to be said for it except that it fits the client's idea of what is "fair." In any case, individual firms may find a different rule more effective in their particular circumstances and should evaluate alternative rules by their own performance measures and system objectives.

Fendley found that when a new project is added to a multiproject system, the amount of slippage is related to the average resource load factor. The load factor is the average resource *requirement* during a set time period divided by resource *availability* for that time period. When the new project is added, the load factor for a resource increases and slippage rises. analysis of resource loads is an important element in determining the amount of slippage to expect when adding projects.

Manufacturing Process Models

The general approach implied by the previous discussion is adopted from the model of a job-shop manufacturing system. The criteria for measuring schedule effectiveness are those applied to job-shops, and several approaches to resource-constrained multiple project scheduling use the job shop model. A scarce resource required for several projects or by several different activities in one project acts like a bottleneck in a manufacturing system. The bottleneck acquires a waiting line or queue. A short digression into queuing theory is in order.

Assume a random arrival rate, λ, of jobs to be processed by a facility, and the facility's rate of servicing jobs is also random, denoted μ. The average number of jobs, J, waiting in line for service is $J = (\lambda/\mu)/(1 - \lambda/\mu)$. Clearly, as the arrival rate approaches the service rate, the queue length heads toward infinity. The result is that to avoid long waiting lines for projects or for activities within a project, the capacity of the scarce resource must be significantly greater than the demand for it, or else the arrival rate of jobs must be tightly controlled so that it is no longer random. Even if the arrival rate is controlled, it must still be at a level that is less than the service rate (which is still random).

Adler et al. [1] found that some highly successful firms had been applying work-process management to product development projects. Specifically, they found that projects are completed faster when the firm does fewer of them, that increasing bottleneck capacity pays large dividends to the investment, and that eliminating unnecessary workload and processes decreases the variation in service times [1, p.134]. Levy and Globerson also adopt queuing theory to deal with multiproduct management. They illustrate calculations for the "cost of waiting in line," the "cost of underutilizing" a facility with capacity greater than the demand for it, and "the cost of delayed projects [21]." They also discuss ways of reducing these costs.

Perhaps the best known attack on the resource-constrained scheduling problem is Goldratt's *Critical Chain* [14]. The way in which Goldratt deals with the constrained resource problem allows it to be applied to the multiple project case as well as to a single project with multiple uses of the scarce resource. The celebrated author of *The Goal* applies his Theory of Constraints to the problem. Random events occur that cause some project activities to be late. Introducing "activity buffers" (activity slack) does not solve the problem because Parkinson's Law applies. Instead, a "project buffer" is required. But another problem occurs, paths that feed into the critical path may be late, causing the critical path to be delayed. "Feeding buffers" help protect against this. Even this may not be sufficient, however, if a scarce resource is used by the critical path and by one or more of the feeding paths. The cure is a schedule that allocates the scarce resource by an equivalent to the minimum slack heuristic, except that the slack includes all relevant buffers. The sequence by which the scarce-resource using activities are processed is the "critical chain." In order to ensure that the scarce resource is not underutilized as a result of chance events, a feeding buffer is placed just prior to each activity on the critical chain. The critical resource, a bottleneck, is treated as it was in *The Goal*. The system is "subordinated" to the scarce resource and then the scarce resource is "exploited."

Given these observations, let us examine some examples of the various types of multiproject scheduling and resource allocation techniques. We begin with a short description of one optimization method, briefly cover several heuristics, and then discuss one heuristic in greater detail.

Mathematical Programming

Mathematical programming [6, 7, 33] can be used to obtain optimal solutions to certain types of multiproject scheduling problems. These procedures determine when an activity should be scheduled, given resource constraints. In the following discussion, it is important to remember that each of the techniques can be applied to the activities in a single project, or to the projects in a partially or wholly interdependent set of projects. Most models are based on integer programming that formulates the problem using 0–1 variables to indicate (depending on task early start times, due dates, sequencing relationships, etc.) whether or not an activity is scheduled in specific periods. The three most common objectives are these:

1. Minimum total throughput time (time in the shop) for all projects
2. Minimum total completion time for all projects
3. Minimum total lateness or lateness penalty for all projects

Constraint equations ensure that every schedule meets any or all of the following constraints, given that the set of constraints allow a feasible solution.

1. Limited resources
2. Precedence relationships among activities
3. Activity-splitting possibilities
4. Project and activity due dates
5. Substitution of resources to assign to specified activities
6. Concurrent and nonconcurrent activity performance requirements

In spite of its ability to generate optimal solutions, mathematical programming has some serious drawbacks when used for resource allocation and multiproject scheduling. As noted earlier, except for the case of small problems, this approach has proved to be extremely difficult and computationally expensive.

Heuristic Techniques

Because of the difficulties with the analytical formulation of realistic problems, major efforts in attacking the resource-constrained multiproject scheduling problem have focused on heuristics. We touched earlier on some of the common general criteria used for scheduling heuristics. Let us now return to that subject.

There are scores of different heuristic-based procedures in existence. A great many of the procedures have been published (see [7], for example), and descriptions of some are generally available in commercial computer programs.

The most commonly applied rules were discussed in Section 9.5. The logical basis for these rules predates PERT/CPM. They represent rather simple extensions of well-known approaches to job-shop scheduling. Some additional heuristics for resource allocation have been developed that draw directly on PERT/CPM. All these are commercially available for computers, and most are available from several different software vendors in slightly different versions.

Resource Scheduling Method In calculating activity priority, give precedence to that activity with the minimum value of d_{ij} where

d_{ij} = increase in project duration resulting when activity *j* follows activity *i*.

$\qquad$ = Max $[0; (EFT_i - LST_j)]$

where

$\qquad EFT_i$ = early finish time of activity *i*

$\qquad LST_j$ = latest start time of activity *j*

The comparison is made on a pairwise basis among all activities in the conflict set.

Minimum Late Finish Time   This rule assigns priorities to activities on the basis of activity finish times as determined by PERT/CPM. The earliest late finishers are scheduled first.

Greatest Resource Demand   This method assigns priorities on the basis of total resource requirements, with higher priorities given for greater demands on resources. Project or task priority is calculated as

$$\text{Priority} = d_j \sum_{i=1}^{m} r_{ij}$$

where

d_j = duration of activity j

r_{ij} = per period requirement of resource i by activity j

m = number of resource types

Resource requirements must be stated in common terms, usually dollars. This heuristic is based on an attempt to give priority to potential resource bottleneck activities.

Greatest Resource Utilization   This rule gives priority to that combination of activities that results in maximum resource utilization (or minimum idle resources) during each scheduling period. The rule is implemented by solving a 0-1 integer programming problem, as described earlier. This rule was found to be approximately as effective as the minimum slack rule for multiple project scheduling, where the criterion used was project slippage. Variations of this rule are found in commercial computer programs such as RAMPS (see [25]).

Most Possible Jobs   Here, priority is given to the set of activities that results in the greatest number of activities being scheduled in any period. This rule also requires the solution of a 0–1 integer program. It differs from the greatest-resource-utilization heuristic in that the determination of the greatest number of possible jobs is made purely with regard to resource feasibility (and not with regard to any measure of resource utilization).

Heuristic procedures for resource-constrained multiproject scheduling represent the only practical means for finding workable solutions to the large, complex multiproject problems normally found in the real world. Let us examine a multiproject heuristic in somewhat more detail.

A Multiproject Scheduling Heuristic

To attack this problem, recall the hierarchical approach to project planning we adopted in Chapter 5. A project plan is a nested set of plans, composed of a set of generalized tasks, each of which is decomposed into a more detailed set of work packages that are, in turn, decomposed further. The decomposition is continued until the work packages are simple enough to be considered "elemental." A PERT/CPM diagram of

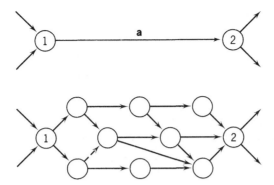

Figure 9-12   Task **a** decomposed into a network of subtasks.

a project might be drawn for any level of task aggregation. A single activity (arrow) at a high level of aggregation would represent an entire network of activities at a lower level (see Figure 9-12). Another level in the planning hierarchy is shown as a Gantt chart in Figure 9-13.

If an entire network is decomposed into subnetworks, we have the equivalent of the multiproject problem where each of the projects (subnetworks) is linked to predecessor and successor projects (other subnetworks). In this case, the predecessor/successor relationships depend on the technology of the parent project. In the true multiproject case, these relationships may still depend on technological relationships—for example, a real estate development project being dependent on the outcome of a land procurement project. The relationships may, however, be determined more or less arbitrarily, as when projects are sequenced on a first-come, first-served basis, or by any other priority-setting rule, or undertaken simultaneously in the hope that some synergistic side effects might occur. Or the relationship among the projects may simply be that they share a common pool of resources.

With this conceptual model, assume we have a set of projects. Each individual project is represented by a network of tasks. We can form a single network of these projects by connecting them with dummy activities (no resources, no duration) and/or pseudoactivities (no resources, some duration). Both dummy activities and pseudoactivities represent dependency relationships, but these dependencies, as noted above, may be technological or quite arbitrary.*

As usual, and excepting dummy and pseudoactivities, each task in each network requires time and resources. The amount of time required may or may not vary with the level of resources applied to it. The total amount of resources and/or amounts of individual resources are limited in successive scheduling periods. Our problem is to find a schedule that best satisfies the sequence and resource constraints and minimizes the overall duration of the entire network. The resulting schedule should indicate when to start any activity and at what level of resources it should be maintained while it is active.

---

*This exposition is based on Weist's work [35], and on Corwin's application of Weist's papers to resource allocation among multiple R & D projects [5].

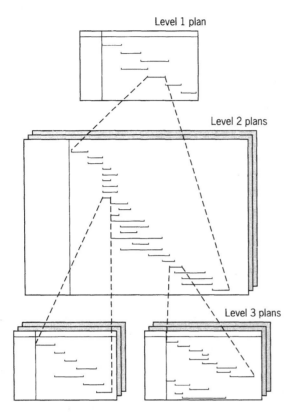

Level 1 plan

Level 2 plans

Level 3 plans

Figure 9-13   Hierarchy of Gantt charts.
Source: [15].

Before undertaking the allocation of resources, it is proper to consider the quantity of resources available for allocation. (For the moment, we consider "resources" as an undifferentiated pool of assets that can be used for any purpose.) At the beginning of any period (hour, day, week, month, etc.) we have available any resources in inventory, R_I, which is to say, left over as excess from the previous allocation process. Changes in the inventory can be made from within the system of projects or by importing or exporting inventory from the outside. Excluding activities that have been completed in previous periods, every activity planned by the project is in one of four states; ongoing, stopping, waiting and technologically able to start, or waiting and technologically unable to start.

Figure 9-14 illustrates these conditions. We label ongoing activities as "resource users." Those stopping are "resource contributors." Those waiting and able to start are "resource demanders." Those waiting and unable to start can be ignored for the present. The amount of resources available for allocation is, therefore, the amount in inventory plus the amount contributed, $R_I + R_C$. If the amount demanded is less than this sum, there will be a positive inventory to start the next period. If not, some demanders will go unfunded.

Weist's heuristic (SPAR-1, Scheduling Program for Allocation of Resources) allocates resources to activities in order of their early start times. In the first period, we would list all available tasks and order them by their slack, from least to most. (Calculation of slack is based on the assumption that activities will be supported at *normal* resource levels.) Activities are selected for support and scheduling one by one, in

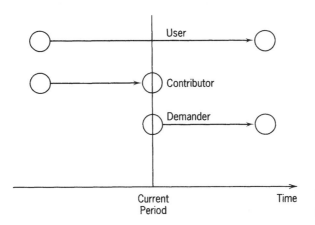

Current
Period   Time   Figure 9-14   Sources and uses of
                                   resources.

order. As activities at the top of the list are supported, the relevant resource stocks are debited. Tasks are scheduled sequentially until the list of available jobs is completed, or until the stock of one or more necessary resources is depleted. If we deplete resources before completing the task list, remaining tasks are delayed until the next period. Postponed activities lose slack and rise toward the top of the priority list.

The information requirements for this heuristic are straightforward. Each period, we need a period-by-period updating of the list of currently active tasks continued from the previous period, including the resource usage level for each active task, the current scheduled (or expected) completion date, and the current activity slack. We need to know the currently available stocks of each type of resource, less the amounts of each in use. We also need a list of all available tasks together with their slacks and normal resource requirements. As activities are completed, their resources are "credited" to the resource pool for future use.

Thus, resources are devoted to activities until the supply of available resources or activities is exhausted. If we use up the resources before all critical activities are scheduled, we can adopt one of two subheuristics. First, we may be able to borrow resources from currently active, but noncritical, tasks. Second, we may "deschedule" a currently active, noncritical task. The former presumably slows the progress of the work, and the latter stops it. In both cases, some resources will be released for use on critical tasks. Obviously, if a critical task is slowed, descheduled, or not supported, the duration of the associated project will be extended.

The decision about which of these courses of action to take, borrowing or descheduling, can be made by adopting the same logic used in Chapter 7 when we discussed the budget negotiations between subordinate and superior. The decision to borrow or deschedule depends on our estimate of the impact either action would have on the task under consideration, given its current state of completion. Figure 9-15 shows two different versions of the project or task life cycle discussed in Chapter 7. If the task is a Type 1, borrowing would minimize the damage to the task unless it is quite near completion and we are willing to accept the outcome in its current state, in which case we can deschedule. If the task is Type 2, borrowing is apt to have a catastrophic effect on the task and we should either deschedule it (and start it again later) or reject it as a source of resources.

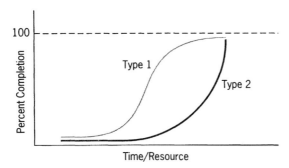

Figure 9-15   Project or task life cycles.

If the size of the resource pool is more than sufficient for the list of active and available tasks, the extra resources may be used to crash critical activities in order to put some slack in the critical path as insurance against project delays caused by last-minute crises. In fact, it is often possible to borrow resources from tasks with plenty of slack in order to crash critical items that are frequent causes of project delay.

As a result of this scheduling process, each task from the previous period, along with any tasks newly available for support, will be:

1. Continued as is, or newly funded at a normal level
2. Continued or funded at a higher level of resources as a result of criticality
3. Continued or funded at a lower-than-normal level as a result of borrowing
4. Delayed because of a resource shortage

If there is more than one scarce resource, a separate activity can be created for each type of scarce resource. These "created" activities must be constrained to start in the same period as the parent activity, and to have the same level of resource assignment (normal, crash, or minimal.) Figure 9-16 shows a flow diagram for SPAR-1.

As we have noted, many commercially available software packages have the ability to schedule constrained resources and deal with resource conflicts [12, 17, 34]. The journal *PM Network* published by the Project Management Institute is an excellent source of reviews on project management software. These reviews typically include a discussion of the package's capabilities. Many will allow the user to solve the problem either automatically, using the program's heuristics, or by hand in which case the user can adopt any method desired. If a set of projects is linked together by dummy activities so that it can be treated like a single project, the software will report resource usage conflicts; that is, cases in which the scheduled utilization of a resource is greater than the supply of that resource.

In one sense this chapter's emphasis on resource shortages is misleading. The common case of shortage applies not to resources in general, but to one or two highly specific resources. For example, an insurance firm specializing in casualty insurance has a typical kind of scarce resource, a "Walt." Walter A. is a specialist in certain types of casualty losses in the firm's commerical lines business. He is the only such specialist in the firm, and his personal knowledge is required when designing new policies in the field. His knowledge is based on years of experience and an excellent, analytical mind. It is common for projects involving the modification or creation of policies in

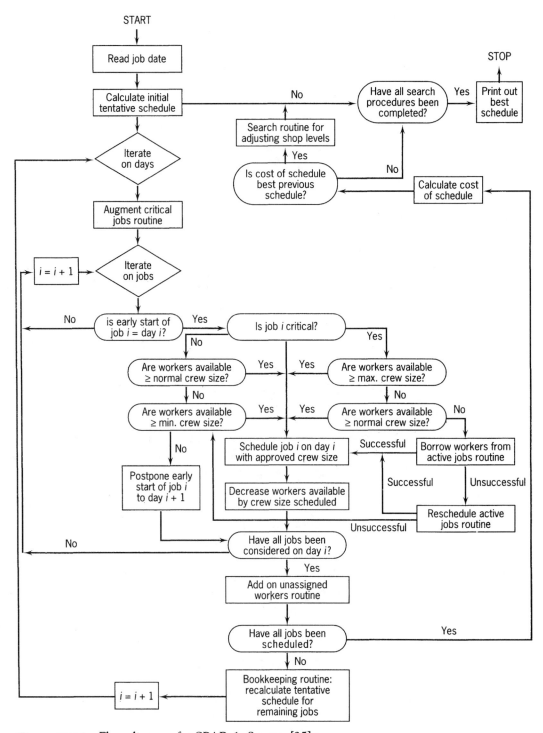

Figure 9-16 Flow diagram for SPAR-1. *Source:* [35]

the commercial lines area to have problems associated with the fact that the firm has one, and only one Walt. Walt-capacity cannot be hired, trained, or subcontracted within an appropriate time frame. The firm's ability to extend its Walt-capacity is not sufficient to satisfy its Walt-demand. Left with no alternative, some projects must be delayed so that others can proceed.

Project Management in Practice
Minnesota DOT Ties Projects to Resources and Constraints

The Minnesota Department of Transportation (DOT) is responsible for facility construction and maintenance for highways, bridges, airports, waterways, railroads, and even bicycle paths. At any given time, there will be approximately 1100 projects—typically, highway improvements—in

MINOR OR NON-PEAK DELAY ———— MAJOR DELAY

active development, with a turn-over of about 300 per year. These projects will range from $50,000 paint jobs to multimillion dollar freeway interchanges. The computerized Project Management and Scheduling System (PMSS) used to manage these projects is based on a work breakdown structure detailing about 100 activities involving 75 functional groups, 40 of which are in-house groups and the rest being consultants.

The PMSS encompasses three major areas: scheduling, funding, and human resource planning. It allows planning, coordination, and control of the work progress and resource requirements for multiple projects over a multiyear time span, since projects may continue for up to four years in some cases. This integration offers the capability to relate work plans to funding availability as well as human resource availability. Conversely, resource use can be planned according to the construction project schedule. Other constraints can also be included in the system and its reports, such as avoiding projects that might overly congest a high-traffic area (see figure) or properly sequencing subprojects such as grading, surfacing, and finishing.

The PMSS system gives management a "big picture" perspective of what is happening in terms of workflow over time and geography. It has also enhanced the department's ability to answer questions about activities, funding, labor, and equipment, and to present reports in a variety of configurations to satisfy the needs of many different parties.

Source: R. Pearson, "Project Management in the Minnesota Department of Transportation," *PM Network*, November 1988.

SUMMARY

In this chapter, we looked at the problem of allocating physical resources, both among the multiple activities of a project and among multiple projects. The continuous problem to the PM is finding the best trade-offs among resources, particularly time. We considered resource loading, allocation, and leveling, and presented methods and concepts to aid in all these tasks.

Specific points made in the chapter were these:

- The critical path method (CPM) is a network constructed in the same manner as PERT but considers the possibility of adding resources to tasks (called crashing) to shorten their duration, thereby expediting the project.

- The resource allocation problem is concerned with determining the best trade-offs between available resources, including time, throughout the duration of a project.

- Resource loading is the process of calculating the total load from project tasks on each resource for each time period of the project's duration.

- Resource leveling is concerned with evening out the demand for various resources required in a project by shifting tasks within their slack allowances. The aid of a computer is mandatory for realistic projects.

- There are two basic approaches to addressing the constrained resources allocation problem:

  –*Heuristic methods* are realistic approaches that may identify feasible solutions to the problem. They essentially use simple priority rules, such as shortest task first, to determine which task should receive resources and which task must wait.

  –*Optimizing methods*, such as linear programming, find the best allocation of resources to tasks but are limited in the size of problems they can efficiently solve.

- For multiproject scheduling, three important measures of effectiveness are schedule slippage, resource utilization, and level of in-process inventory.

- When a new project is added to a multiproject system, the amount of slippage is directly related to the average resource load.

- Mathematical programming models for multiproject scheduling aim either to minimize total throughput time for all projects, minimize the completion time for all projects, or minimize the total lateness (or lateness penalty) for all projects. These models are limited to small problems. There are a number of heuristic methods, such as the resource scheduling method, available for the multiproject scheduling problem.

In the next chapter, we move to the ongoing implementation of the project and consider the project information systems used for monitoring progress, costs, performance, and so on. The chapter also describes some available computer packages for this function.

 # GLOSSARY

Cost/Time Slope The ratio of the increased cost for expediting to the decreased amount of time for the activity.

Followers The tasks that logically follow a particular task in time.

Heuristic A formal process for solving a problem, like a rule of thumb, that results in an acceptable solution.

Mathematical Programming A general term for certain mathematical approaches to solving constrained optimization problems, including linear programming, integer programming, and so on.

Predecessors The tasks that logically precede a particular task in time.

Priority Rules Formal methods, such as ratios, that rank items to determine which one should be next.

Resource Leveling Approaches to even out the peaks and valleys of resource requirements so that a fixed amount of resources can be employed over time.

Resource Loading The amount of resources of each kind that are to be devoted to a specific activity in a certain time period.

Successors See followers.

Tree Search The evaluation of a number of alternatives that logically branch from each other like a tree with limbs.

QUESTIONS

Material Review Questions

1. Identify several resources that may need to be considered when scheduling projects.

2. What is resource loading? How does it differ from resource leveling?

3. What is an activity slope and what does it indicate?

4. Name four priority rules. What priority rule is best overall? How would a firm decide which priority rule to use?

5. Name three efficiency criteria that might be considered when choosing a multiproject scheduling system.

6. What is the average resource load factor? How is it used to determine project completion times?

7. What are two methods for addressing the constrained resources allocation problem?

8. What are three measures of effectiveness for multiproject scheduling?

9. What is a "system constrained" task?

10. How does the resource scheduling method heuristic work?

Class Discussion Questions

11. Why are large fluctuations in the demands for particular resources undesirable? What are the costs of resource leveling? How would a PM determine the "best" amount of leveling?

12. When might a firm choose to crash a project? What factors must be considered in making this decision?

13. Why is the impact of scheduling and resource allocation more significant in multiproject organizations?

14. How much should a manager know about a scheduling or resource allocation computer program to be able to use the output intelligently?

15. With the significantly increased power of today's computers, do you think the mathematical programming optimization approaches will become more popular?

16. What are some of the limitations of CPM?

17. Why is leveling of resources needed?

Questions for Project Management in Practice

Expediting Los Angeles Freeway Repairs After the Earthquake

21. Of the 6 constraints, which were cost tradeoffs and which were performance tradeoffs?

22. In what way were the performance tradeoffs made? That is, how did they affect performance.

23. What kinds of resource allocation approaches discussed in the chapter were used in this situation?

Benefits of Resource Constraining at Pennsylvania Electric

24. Why would the planning group use 40% more mechanics than necessary?

25. What does the availability in the chart represent? Why do the monthly values move up and down?

18. What are some implications of resource allocation when an organization is involved in several projects at once?

19. What are some of the indirect costs of crashing?

20. How might CPM be used for strategic planning purposes?

26. What does the scheduled amount represent? Why does it drop off in 1991? How can it exceed the availability?

Minnesota DOT Ties Projects to Resources and Constraints

27. Why are the three areas of scheduling, funding, and human resource planning needed in such a system? Why aren't equipment planning and materials requirements included?

28. How would the system facilitate planning? Coordination? Control?

29. What other big-picture issues might this system be useful for besides identifying when projects might overly congest an area?

PROBLEMS

1. Given the following network, determine the first activity to be crashed by the following priority rules:
   (a) Shortest task first
   (b) Minimum slack first
   (c) Most critical followers
   (d) Most successors.

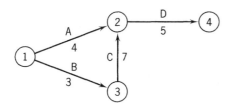

2. Using the network above and the additional information below, find;
   (a) The crash cost per day
   (b) Which activities should be crashed to meet a project deadline of 13 days at minimum cost. Assume partial crashing.

Activity	Crash Time	Crashed Cost (total)	Normal Time (days)	Normal Cost
A	3	$500	4	$300
B	1	325	3	250
C	4	550	7	400
D	3	250	5	150

3. Consider the following network for conducting a two-week (10 working days) computer training class:

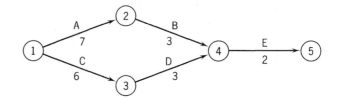

(a) Construct a schedule showing
ESTs for all activities
LSTs for all activities
EOTs for all events
LOTs for all events
Slacks for all activities and events
Critical path

(b) Given the following.

Activity	Crash Time	Crashed Cost (total)	Normal Time (days)	Normal Cost
A	4	$800	7	$500
B	2	350	3	200
C	4	900	6	500
D	1	500	3	200
E	1	550	2	300
		$3100		

1. Find the crash cost per day.
2. Which activities should be crashed to meet a project deadline of 10 days with a minimum cost? Assume partial crashing.
3. Find the new cost.
4. Is partial crashing an appropriate assumption in this kind of project?

4. Given the following highway rerouting project:

Activity	Immediate Predecessor	Activity Time (months)
A	—	4
B	—	6
C	A	2
D	B	6
E	C,B	3
F	C,B	3
G	D,E	5

(a) Draw the network.
(b) Find the ESTs, LSTs, EOTs, LOTs, and slacks.
(c) Find the critical path.
(d) If the project has a 1 1/2 year deadline for reopening, should we consider crashing some activities? Explain.

5. Given the following network for a video recording project with equipment resource demands, con-

struct a modified PERT chart with resources and a resource load diagram. Suggest how to level the equipment load if you can split operations.

Code: activity, time / resource units

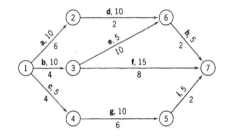

6. Reconsider Problem 18 in Chapter 8 under the constraint that the problem must be completed in 16 weeks. This time, however, activities c, f, h, and i may be crashed as follows. Assume partial crashing.

Activity	Crash Time (weeks)	Additional Cost per Week
c	7	$40
f	6	20
h	2	10
i	3	30

Find the best schedule and its cost.

7. The following data were obtained from a study of the times required to overhaul a chemical plant:

Activity	Crash Schedule Time	Crash Schedule Cost	Normal Schedule Time	Normal Schedule Cost
1–2	3	$6	5	$4
1–3	1	5	5	3
2–4	5	7	10	4
3–4	2	6	7	4
2–6	2	5	6	3
4–6	5	9	11	6
4–5	4	6	6	3
6–7	1	4	5	2
5–7	1	5	4	2

Note: Costs are given in thousands of dollars, time in weeks.

(a) Find the all-normal schedule and cost.
(b) Find the all-crash schedule and cost.

(c) Find the total cost required to expedite all activities from all-normal (case a) to all-crash (case b).

(d) Find the *least-cost* plan for the all-crash time schedule. Start from the all-crash problem (b). Assume partial crashing.

8. Given the data in Problem 7, determine the first activities to be crashed by the following priority rules:
   (a) Shortest task first.
   (b) Most resources first (use normal cost as the basis).
   (c) Minimum slack first.
   (d) Most critical followers.
   (e) Most successors.

9. Consider Problem 14 in Chapter 8 again. Suppose the duration of both activities **A** and **D** can be reduced to one day, at a cost of $15 per day of reduction. Also, activities **E, G,** and **H** can be reduced in duration by one day at a cost of $25 per day of reduction. What is the least cost approach to crash the project two days? What is the shortest "crashed" duration, the new critical path, and the cost of crashing?

10. Given a network for an engineering project with normal times and crash times (in parentheses), find the lowest cost time–cost plan. Assume indirect costs for facilities and equipment are $100 per day. The data are:

Activity	Time Reduction, Direct Cost per Day
1–2	$30 first, $50 second
2–3	$80
3–4	$25 first, $60 second
2–4	$30 first, $70 second, $90 third

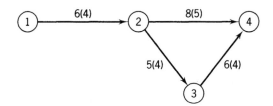

11. Reconsider Problem 2 assuming a fixed overhead cost of $30 per day but no project deadline. What is the least-cost crash program? If the overhead cost was $40? If it was $60?

12. The network for shooting a TV commercial as shown in the table has a fixed cost of $90 per day, but money can be saved by shortening the project duration. Find the least cost schedule.

Activity	Normal Time	Crash Time	Cost Increase (1st, 2nd, 3rd day)
1–2	7	4	$30, 50, 70
2–3	9	6	40, 45, 65
1–3	12	10	60, 60
2–4	11	9	35, 60
3–4	3	3	—

▮ INCIDENTS FOR DISCUSSION

Bryce Power Tool Company

Kevin Ertle is the director of engineering for the Bryce Power Tool Company. A decision was made recently to modernize Bryce's entire tool line. The president of Bryce has indicated that he expects the modernization program to result in a significant improvement in design technology. Ertle is concerned with the possibility that his department will not have adequate resources to support the modernization program. Kevin believes he has enough staff to handle the aggregate engineering requirements, but he is not too sure he will be able to supply engineering personnel at the times and quantities requested by the company's project managers.

To complicate matters further, the tool modernization program will be under the control of four different project managers. Each major market segment has been recognized as a separate business unit with the authority to modernize the key tools for that segment based on a schedule that makes sense for it.

Kevin knows a little bit about resource allocation techniques. He remembers that one of the most effective allocation techniques is to work first on the activity with the minimum slack, so he has instructed his staff to approach any tasks they are assigned as members of a project team on that basis.

Questions: Is this technique a reasonable way to schedule the engineering resources of Bryce? Why or why not? What complication is added by making this four separate projects?

Critical Care Hospital

Critical Care Hospital will be purchasing a CATSCAN (computerized axial tomography scanner) in the next six months. The CATSCAN equipment will be installed in the radiology department and will require a significant renovation for the area. The scanner will arrive in about five months, but the construction project cannot be started until the unit is set in place. This will result in a project length of approximately 12 months. The hospital estimates the equipment will generate an income of $25,000 per month and is therefore in a hurry to complete the project. The project manager feels she may be able to cut the time on some aspects of the project, but at an increased cost. She has decided, in an effort to make the best decision, to use a resource allocation version of CPM.

Questions: What information must the project manager gather to use this method properly? How should she use this version of CPM to reduce the project time?

BIBLIOGRAPHY

1. ADLER, P. S., A. MANDELBAUM, V. NGUYEN, and E. SCHWERER. "Getting the Most out of Your Product Development Process." *Harvard Business Review,* March–April 1996.
2. ANDERSON, D. R., D. J. SWEENEY, and T. A. WILLIAMS. *An Introduction to Management Science,* 6th ed. Minneapolis, MN: West Publishing, 1991.
3. BADIRU, A. B. "Critical Resource Diagram: A New Tool for Resource Management." *Industrial Engineering,* October 1992.
4. BADIRU, A. B. "Incorporating Learning Curve Effects Into Critical Resource Diagramming." *Project Management Journal,* June 1995.
5. CORWIN, B. D. "Multiple R and D Project Scheduling with Limited Resources." *Technical Memorandum No. 122,* Dept. of Operations Research, Cleveland: Case Western Reserve University, 1968.
6. DAVIS, E. W. *Project Management: Techniques, Applications, and Managerial Issues,* 2nd ed. Norcross, GA: Institute of Industrial Engineers, 1983.
7. DAVIS, E. W., and J. H. PATTERSON. "A Comparison of Heuristic and Optimum Solutions in Resource-Constrained Project Scheduling." *Management Science,* April 1975.
8. FARID, F., and S. MANOHARAN. "Comparative Analysis of Resource-Allocation Capabilities of Project Management Software Packages." *Project Management Journal,* June 1996.
9. FENDLEY, L. G. "Towards the Development of a Complete Multiproject Scheduling System." *Journal of Industrial Engineering,* October 1968.
10. GEMMILL, D. D., and Y. W. TSAI. "Using a Simulated Annealing Algorithm to Schedule Activities of Resource-Constrained Projects." *Project Management Journal,* December 1997.
11. GILYUTIN, I. "Using Project Management in a Nonlinear Environment." *Project Management Journal,* December 1993.
12. GLAUBER, L. W. "Project Planning With Scitor's PS5000." *Project Management Journal,* June 1985.
13. GOLDRATT, E. M., and J. COX. *The Goal.* Great Barrington, MA: North River, 1992.
14. GOLDRATT, E. M. *Critical Chain.* Great Barrington, MA: North River, 1997.
15. HARRISON, F. L. *Advanced Project Management.* Hants, GB: Gower, 1983.
16. IBBS, C. W., S. A. LEE, and M. I. LI. "Fast-Tracking's Impact on Project Change." *Project Management Journal,* December 1998.
17. JOHNSON, R. V. "Resource Constrained Scheduling Capabilities of Commercial Project Management Software." *Project Management Journal,* December 1992.

18. KUMAR, V. K., and L. S. GANESH. "Use of Petri Nets for Resource Allocation in Projects." *IEEE Transactions on Engineering Management*, February 1998.

19. KURTULUS, I., and E. W. DAVIS. "Multi-Project Scheduling: Categorization of Heuristic Rules Performance." *Management Science*, February 1982.

20. KURTULUS, I., and S. C. NARULA. "Multi-Project Scheduling: Analysis of Project Performance." *IEEE Transactions on Engineering Management*, March 1985.

21. LEVY, N. S., and S. GLOBERSON. "Improving Multiproject Management by Using a Queuing Theory Approach." *Project Management Journal*, December 1997.

22. MILLS, N. L. "The Development of a University Sports Complex: A Project Management Application." *Computers and Industrial Engineering*, 1989.

23. MODER, J. J., C. R. PHILLIPS, and E. W. DAVIS. *Project Management With CPM, PERT and Precedence Diagramming*, 3rd ed. New York: Van Nostrand Reinhold, 1983.

24. MORSE, L. C., J. O. McINTOSH, and G. E. WHITEHOUSE. "Using Combinations of Heuristics to Schedule Activities of Constrained Multiple Resource Projects." *Project Management Journal*, March 1996.

25. MOSHMAN, J., J. R. JOHNSON, and M. LARSEN. "RAMPS-A Technique for Resource Allocation and Multiproject Scheduling." *Proceedings*, Spring Joint Computer Conference, 1963.

26. NAVARRE, C., and J. SCHAAN. "Design of Project Management Systems from Top Management's Perspective," *Project Management Journal*, June 1990.

27. NICHOLAS, J. M. *Managing Business & Engineering Projects*. Englewood Cliffs, NJ: Prentice Hall, 1990.

28. PATTERSON, J. H., and W. D. HUBER. "A Horizon-Varying, Zero-One Approach to Project Scheduling." *Management Science*, February 1974.

29. STINSON, J. P., E. W. DAVIS, and B. KHUMAWALA. "Multiple Resource-Constrained Scheduling Using Branch and Bound." *AIIE Transactions*, September 1978.

30. TALBOT, F. B. "Project Scheduling with Resource-Duration Interactions: The Nonpreemptive Case." *Working paper No. 200*, Graduate School of Business Administration, Ann Arbor, MI: University of Michigan, January 1980.

31. TALBOT, F. B., and J. H. PATTERSON. "Optimal Methods for Scheduling Under Resource Constraints." *Project Management Quarterly*, December 1979.

32. TUKEL, O. I. "Scheduling Resource-Constrained Projects When Non-conformities Exist." *Project Management Journal*, September 1996.

33. TURBAN, E., and J. R. MEREDITH. *Fundamentals of Management Science*, 6th ed. Homewood, IL: Irwin, 1994.

34. WEAVER, J. "Mainframe ARTEMIS: More Than a Project Management Tool." *Project Management Journal*, April 1988.

35. WEIST, J. D. "A Heuristic Model for Scheduling Large Projects with Limited Resources." *Management Science*, February 1967.

36. WEIST, J. D. "Heuristic Programs for Decision Making." *Harvard Business Review*, September-October 1965.

37. WOODWORTH, B. M., and C. T. WILLIE. "A Heuristic Algorithm for Resource Levelling in Multi-Project, Multi-Resource Scheduling." *Decision Sciences*, 1975.

The following reading describes the evolution of a new product and the project devised to take it to market. As well as discussing the issues of developing a work breakdown structure, network diagram, schedule, and resource loading diagrams for each of the involved departments, the reading also brings up the issues of time–cost tradeoffs, cash flows, and resource leveling.

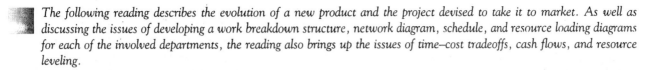

D. U. SINGER HOSPITAL PRODUCTS CORP.
Herbert F. Spirer
©1980 by Herbert F. Spirer. Reprinted by permission.

D. U. Singer Hospital Products Corp. has done sufficient new product development at the research and development level to estimate a high likelihood of technical success for a product of assured commercial success: A long-term antiseptic. Management has instructed Singer's Antiseptic Division to make a market entry at the earliest possible time; they have requested a complete plan up to the startup of production. Marketing and other plans following startup of production are to be prepared separately after this plan has been completed.

Project responsibility is assigned to the division's Research and Development Group; Mike Richards, the project scientist who developed the product, is assigned responsibility for project management. Assistance will be required from other parts of the company: Packaging Task Force, R & D Group; Corporate Engineering; Corporate Purchasing; Hospital Products Manufacturing Group; Packaged Products Manufacturing Group.

Mike was concerned about the scope of the project. He knew from his own experience that a final formula had yet to be developed, although such development was really a "routine" function. The remaining questions had to do with color, odor, and consistency additives rather than any performance-related modification. Fortunately, the major regulatory issues had been resolved and he believed that submission of regulatory documentation would be followed by rapid approval as they already had a letter of approval contingent on final documentation.

But there were also issues in packaging that had to be resolved; development of the packaging design was one of his primary concerns at this time. Ultimately, there will have to be manufacturing procedures in accordance with corporate policies and standards: capital equipment selection and procurement, installation of this equipment and startup.

Mike was concerned about defining the project unambiguously. To that end, he obtained an interview with S. L. Mander, the group vice-president.

When he asked Mander where his responsibility should end, the executive turned the question back to him. Mike had been prepared for this and said that he would like to regard his part of the project as done when the production process could be turned over to manufacturing. They agreed that according to Singer practice, this would be when the manufacturing operation could produce a 95 percent yield of product (fully packaged) at a level of 80 percent of the full production goal of 10 million liters per year.

"But I want you to remember," said Mander, "that you must meet all current FDA, EPA, and OSHA regulations and you must be in compliance with our internal specification—the one I've got is dated September and is RD78/965. And you know that manufacturing now—quite rightly, I feel—insists on full written manufacturing procedures."

After this discussion, Mike felt that he had enough information about this aspect to start to pin down what had to be done to achieve these results. His first step in this effort was to meet with P. H. Docent, the director of research.

"You are naive if you think that you can just start right in finalizing the formula," said Docent. "You must first develop a product rationale (a).* This is a formally defined process according to company policy. Marketing expects inputs at this stage, manufacturing expects their voice to be heard, and you will have to have ap-

---

*Tasks which must be accounted for in a network plan are identified by lower-case alphabetic symbols in parentheses. Refer to Exhibit 1.

provals from every unit of the company that is involved; all of this is reviewed by the Executive Committee. You should have no trouble if you do your homework, but expect to spend a good eight weeks to get this done."

"That certainly stretches things out," said Mike. "I expected to take 12 weeks to develop the ingredient formula (**b**) and you know that I can't start to establish product specifications (**c**) until the formula is complete. That's another three weeks."

"Yes, but while you are working on the product specifications you can get going on the regulatory documentation (**d**). Full internal specifications are not required for that work, but you can't start those documents until the formula is complete."

"Yes, and I find it hard to believe that we can push through both preparation of documents and getting approval in three weeks, but Environmental swears it can be done."

"Oh, it can be done in this case because of the preparatory work. Of course, I won't say that this estimate of three weeks is as certain as our other time estimates. All we need is a change of staff at the Agency and we are in trouble. But once you have both the specifications and the approval, you can immediately start on developing the production processing system (**g**)."

"Yes, and how I wish we could get a lead on that, but the designers say that there is too much uncertainty and they won't move until they have both specifications and regulatory documentation and approval. They are offering pretty fast response; six weeks from start to finish for the processing system."

"They are a good crew, Mike. And of course, you know that you don't have to delay on starting the packaging segment of this project. You can start developing the packaging concept (**e**) just as soon as the product rationale has been developed. If my experience is any judge, it will take a full eight weeks; you'll have to work to keep the process from running forever."

"But as soon as that is finished we can start on the design of the package and its materials (**f**) which usually takes about six weeks. Once that is done we can start developing the packaging system (**h**) which shouldn't take longer than eight weeks," concluded Mike. At this point he realized that although Docent would have general knowledge, he needed to talk directly to the Director of Manufacturing.

"The first step, which follows the completion of the development of processing and packaging systems," said the Director of Manufacturing, "is to do a complete study of the facilities requirements (**i**). You won't be able to get that done in less than four weeks. And that must precede the preparation of the capital equipment list (**j**) which should take about three-quarters as long. Of course, as soon as the development of both the process system and packaging system are completed, you could start on preparing the written manufacturing procedures (**q**)."

"But," said Mike, "Can I really finish the procedures before I have installed and constructed the facilities (**p**)?"

"No, quite right. What you can do is get the first phase done, but the last three of the ten weeks it will take to do that will have to wait for the installation and construction."

"Then this means that I really have two phases for the writing, that which can be completed without the installation and construction (**q**), and that which has to wait for those inputs (**q'**)."

"True. Now you realize that the last thing you have to do is to run the equipment in a pilot test (**r**) which will show that you have reached a satisfactory level?"

"Yes. Since that must include debugging, I've estimated a six-week period as adequate." The director of manufacturing assented. Mike continued, "What I'm not sure of is whether we can run all the installation tasks in parallel."

"You can let the purchase orders and carry out the procurement of process equipment (**k**), packaging equipment (**l**), and facilities (**m**) as soon as the capital equipment list is complete. The installation of each of these types of equipment and facilities can start as soon as the goods are on hand (**n,o,p**)."

"What do you estimate for the times to do these tasks?" asked Mike. The director of manufacturing estimated 18, 8, and 4 weeks for the purchasing phases for each of the subsystems in that order and four weeks for each of the installations. "Then I can regard my job as done with the delivery of the procedures and when I show my 95 percent yield," said Mike, and the director of manufacturing agreed, but reminded Mike that none of the purchasing cycles could start until the capital equipment list had been prepared and approved (**j**) which he saw as a three-week task.

The executive committee of D. U. Singer Hospital Products Corporation set a starting date for the project of March 10 and asked Mike to project a completion date with his submission of the plan. The committee's request implied that whatever date Mike came up with was acceptable, but Mike knew that he would be expected to show how to shorten the time to complete the project. However, his task in making the schedule was clear; he had to establish the resource requirements and deal with calendar constraints as best as he could.

Exhibit 1 Labor Requirements (Worker-weeks)

Activity	Packaging Task Force	R & D Group	Corp. Eng.	H-P Manuf.	Pack. Prod. Manuf.	Maint.	Purchasing	Material & Other Direct Charges
a—prod. rationale	1	12	1	1	2	0	0	$ 0
b—dev. formula	0	16	4	2	0	0	0	500
c—prod. spec.	1	6	3	1	1	0	1	0
d—reg. document	0	12	4	2	0	0	0	0
e—dev. pkg. conc.	12	8	4	2	8	0	2	4000
f—design pkg.	12	2	3	0	3	0	3	2000
g—dev. proc. sys.	0	18	12	12	0	0	0	0
h—dev. pkg. sys.	24	8	8	0	8	0	2	0
i—study fac. req.	0	4	16	2	2	0	0	0
j—cap. equip. list	0	1	3	0	0	0	1	0
k—procure proc. eqpt.	0	1	1	1	0	0	7	40,000
l—procure pkg. eqpt.	1	0	1	0	1	0	9	160,000
m—procure facil.	0	0	1	1	1	1	6	30,000
n—install proc. eqpt.	0	2	4	8	0	4	1	4000
o—install pkg. eqpt.	2	0	4	0	8	4	1	8000
p—install fac.	0	0	5	5	5	10	1	6000
q,q'—written procedures	5	5	5	10	15	10	0	5000
r—pilot test	3	6	6	6	6	6	0	0

To this end, Mike had to get an estimate of resources which he decided to do by making a list of the activities and asking each group involved what was their level of employee input. The results of this survey are shown in Exhibit 1.

For the purposes of overall planning, the accounting department told Mike that he could estimate a cost of $600 per week per employee. This would enable him to provide a cash flow forecast along with his plan, which the chief accountant said would be expected, something that Mike had not realized.

Mike knew that it was customary at D. U. Singer to provide the following as parts of a plan to be submitted to the executive committee:

1. Statement of Objectives.
2. Work Breakdown Structure.
3. An activity-on-node (PERT) network.
4. A determination of the critical path(s) and the duration along the path.
5. An activity list, early-start schedule, slack list, and master schedule. Assume every activity begins at its early start, regardless of resource constraints.

6. A period labor requirements table for each group and the project as a whole. Include bar graphs to illustrate the labor loads.
7. A cumulative labor requirements table for each group and the project as a whole. Include line graphs to illustrate the cumulative loads.
8. A schedule based on the best leveling of labor requirements that could be achieved without lengthening project duration by more than 14 percent in calendar days.
9. A cash flow requirements graph for the project when leveled, assuming that charges are uniformly distributed throughout the activity.

Questions

1. Construct the nine elements of the plan identified above.
2. Analyze the plan for potential problems.
3. Analyze the plan for opportunities.
4. Should the executive committee approve the plan? Why or why not?
5. What alternatives might the executive committee suggest for analysis?

10

Monitoring and Information Systems

In this chapter, perhaps more than in any other, it would be helpful if we could consider everything at once. How is it possible to discuss monitoring without specifying what is to be controlled? On the other hand, how is it possible to specify a control system without understanding what aspects of a project are subject to measurement and how the measurement is to be accomplished? As a matter of fact, one could just as easily argue that evaluation, the primary subject of Chapter 12, should precede both monitoring and control. The placement of these chapters is arbitrary, and readers may feel free to read them in any order. Irrespective of the order in which one considers these subjects, however, their interdependence is clear.

Our fundamental approach to evaluation and control of projects is that these activities are, at base, the opposite sides of project selection and planning. The logic of selection dictates the components to be evaluated, and the details of planning expose the elements to be controlled. The ability to measure is prerequisite to either.

Monitoring is collecting, recording, and reporting information concerning any and all aspects of project performance that the project manager or others in the organization wish to know. In our discussion it is important to remember that monitoring, as an activity, should be kept distinct from controlling (which uses the data supplied by monitoring to bring actual performance into approximate congruence with planned performance), as well as from evaluation (through which judgments are made about the quality and effectiveness of project performance).

First we expand on the nature of this link between planning and control, including a brief discussion of the various aspects of project performance that need to be monitored. We also examine some of the problems associated with monitoring a project. Finally, we report on several computer software packages that can greatly increase the speed and effectiveness of project monitoring.

This book is addressed to practicing PMs as well as students of project management. Students resist the idea that PMs do not have immediate access to accurate information on every aspect of the project. But PMs know it is not always easy to find out what's going on when working on a project. Records are frequently out of date, incomplete, in error, or "somewhere else" when needed. A hospital executive of our acquaintance carried out a project that was designed to generate a major improvement in profitability by altering the patient mix. The hospital's accounting system could not report on the results of the project until six months later.

Throughout the chapter, our primary concern is to ensure that all parties interested in the project have available, *on a timely basis*, the information needed to exercise effective control over the project. The other uses for monitoring (e.g., auditing, learning from past mistakes, or keeping senior management informed), important as they are, must be considered secondary to the control function when constructing the monitoring system. The key issue, then, is to create an information system that gives project managers the information they need to make informed, timely decisions that will keep project performance as close as possible to the project plan.

One final note: In this chapter, we frequently refer to a "project monitor," a " project controller," or even to the "group" responsible for monitoring. These individuals and groups do in fact exist on most large projects. On a small project, it is likely that the person in charge of monitoring is the same person as the project controller— and the same person as the PM. That is, when we refer to the project monitor and controller, we are referring to roles needed in project management, not necessarily to different individuals.

Project Management in Practice
Using Project Management Software to Schedule the Olympic Games

The XV Olympiad in Calgary involved nearly 2000 athletes from 57 countries in 129 competitive events, attracted over 1,500,000 spectators, was covered by over 5000 journalists, and was run by a staff of 600 professionals complemented by 10,000 volunteers. For those 600 responsible for organizing, planning, scheduling, coordinating, and handling the information requirements for the 16-day extravaganza, the task was overwhelming. The top managers of the organizing committee thus turned to a Computer Based Project Planning and Scheduling (CBPPS) system for scheduling and managing the 30,000 tasks organized into 50 projects.

The goal for the Calgary Games was to provide the best games ever, but within the budget. The philosophy employed was to let each project manager plan his/her own project but meet firm completion dates and budget limits. This made a lot of additional work for the upper managers since each project's reports and needs were different from every other project's. However, two major features of the project helped make this a success: (1) Knowing that the Games would happen on the scheduled date regardless of whether they were ready or not, and (2) Being such a high-visibility, challenging project that demands exceptional focus on the task.

To schedule the entire Winter Games, the 129-event, 16-day Olympics was broken down into 15-minute periods, except for short-track speed skating which was segmented into 1-minute intervals. There was a printout for every day by venue, minute by minute, and a complete set of drawings of every site, building, and room. Meticulous scheduling was necessary to ensure that the 2500 or so competitors, members of royalty, and government officials were at the right

Source: R. G. Holland, "The XV Olympic Winter Games: A Case Study in Project Management," *PM Network*, November 1989.

place at the right time. Support staff, including medical and security personnel, were also carefully scheduled for each event as crowds shifted from competition to competition. Transportation-600 buses—also had to be scheduled, oftentimes on short notice. The biggest concern was the weather, and sure enough, the Chinook winds forced the rescheduling of over 20 events, some of them twice!

Yet, the Calgary Games were the best yet, and organized better than ever before. Moreover, as compared to the budget overruns of many other cities, this Olympiad was completed under budget!

■ 10.1 THE PLANNING-MONITORING-CONTROLLING CYCLE

Throughout this book we have stressed the need to plan, check on progress, compare progress to the plan, and take corrective action if progress does not match the plan. The key things to be planned, monitored, and controlled are time (schedule), cost (budget), and performance (specifications). These, after all, encompass the fundamental objectives of the project.

There is no doubt that some organizations do not spend sufficient time and effort on planning and controlling projects. It is far easier to focus on doing, especially because it appears to be more effective to "stop all the talk and get on with the work." We could cite firm after firm that incurred great expense (and major losses) because the planning process was inadequate for the tasks undertaken.

- A major construction project ran over budget by 63 percent and over schedule by 48 percent because the PM decided that, since "he had managed similar projects several times before, he knew what to do without going into all that detail that no one looks at anyway."

- A large industrial equipment supplier "took a bath" on a project designed to develop a new area of business because they applied the same planning and control procedures to the new area that they had used (successfully) on previous, smaller, less complex jobs.

- A computer store won a competitive bid to supply a computer, five terminals, and associated software to the Kansas City office of a national firm. Admittedly insufficient planning made the installation significantly late. Performance of the software was not close to specified levels. This botched job prevented the firm from being invited to bid on more than 20 similar installations planned by the client.

The planning (budgeting and scheduling) methods we propose "put the hassles up front." They require a significantly greater investment of time and energy early in the life of the project, but they significantly reduce the extent and cost of poor performance and time/cost overruns. Note that this is no guarantee of a trouble-free project, merely a decline in the risk of failure.

It is useful to perceive the control process as a *closed loop* system, with revised plans and schedules (if warranted) following corrective actions. We delay a detailed discussion on control until the next chapter, but the planning-monitoring-controlling cycle is continuously in process until the project is completed. The information flows for such a cycle are illustrated in Figure 10-1. Note the direction of the flows, information flowing from the bottom toward the top and authority flowing from the top down.

It is also useful to construct this process as an internal part of the organizational structure of the project, not something external to and imposed on it or, worse, in conflict with it. Finally, experience tells us that it is also desirable, though not mandatory, that the planning-monitoring-controlling cycle be the normal way of life in the parent organization. What is good for the project is equally good for the parent firm. In any case, unless the PM has a smoothly operating monitoring/control system, it will be difficult to manage the project effectively.

	Planning and Scheduling			Reporting and Monitoring		
President and General Manager Director of Engineering Director of Research Director of Manufacturing		Project review and signature approval			Distribution to directors and managers Feeder copy	Review and action as required
Administration		Administration review, type, and prepare final copies	Initiate project records Distribute copies		Post to weekly project status report and project expenditure and control schedule chart	Prepare and forward management reports as required
Responsible Engineer	Rough draft of engineering project authorization and project expenditure and control schedule chart		Copy	Weekly time tickets milestone report	Feeder copy Distribution to responsible engineer	

Figure 10-1   Project authorization and expenditure control system information flow.
Source: [8]

Designing the Monitoring System

The first step in setting up any monitoring system is to identify the key factors to be controlled. Clearly, the PM wants to monitor performance, cost, and time but must define precisely which specific characteristics of performance, cost, and time should be controlled and then establish exact boundaries within which control should be maintained. There may also be other factors of importance worth noting, at least at milestones or review points in the life of the project. For example, the number of labor hours used, the number or extent of process or output changes, the level of customer satisfaction, and similar items may be worthy of note on individual projects.

But the best source of items to be monitored is the project action plan—actually, the set of action plans that describe what is being done, when, and the planned level of resource usage for each task, work package, and work element in the project. The monitoring system is a direct connection between planning and control. If it does not collect and report information on some significant element of the plan, control can be faulty or missing. The action plan furnishes the key items that must be measured and reported to the control system, but it is not sufficient. For example, the PM might want to know about changes in the client's attitudes toward the project. Information on the morale of the project team might be useful in preparing for organizational or personnel changes on the project. These two latter items may be quite important, but are not reflected in the project's action plans.

Unfortunately, it is common to focus monitoring activities on data that are easily gathered—rather than important—or to concentrate on "objective" measures that are easily defended at the expense of softer, more subjective data that may be more valuable for control. Above all, monitoring should concentrate primarily on measuring various facets of output rather than intensity of activity. It is crucial to remember that effective PMs are not primarily interested in how hard their project teams work. They are interested in achieving results.

The measurement of project performance usually poses the most difficult data gathering problem. There is a strong tendency to let project inputs serve as surrogate measures for output. If we have spent 50 percent of the budget (or of the scheduled time), we assume we have also completed 50 percent of the project or reached 50 percent of our performance goal. If the item being referenced is a small work unit, it does not make a significant difference if we are wrong. If, however, the reference is to a task or to the entire project, the assumption of input/output proportionality (hereafter, the "proportionality rule") is apt to be badly misleading.

One must also be aware of the fact that it is common to specify performance to a level of precision that is both unnecessary and unrealistic. For example, a communications software project specified that a telephone "information" system had to locate a phone number and respond to the querier in 5 seconds or less. Is 5.1 seconds a failure? Does the specification mean 5 seconds or less every time, or merely that response times should average 5 seconds or less? Is the specification satisfied if the response time is 5 seconds or less 90 percent of the time?

The monitoring systems we describe in this chapter, however, focus mainly on time and cost as measures of performance, not specifications. While we are most certainly concerned with keeping the project "on spec," and do consider some of the problems of monitoring output, the subject is not fully developed here because the software designed to monitor projects is not constructed to deal with the subject adequately. The matter will get more attention in Chapter 12 when auditing is discussed.

Given all this, performance criteria, standards, and data collection procedures must be established for each of the factors to be measured. The criteria and data collection procedures are usually set up for the life of the project. The standards themselves, however, may not be constant over the project's life. They may change as a result of altered capabilities within the parent organization or a technological breakthrough made by the project team; but, perhaps more often than not, standards and criteria change because of factors that are not under the control of the PM. For example, they may be changed by the client. One client who had ordered a special piece of audio equipment altered performance specifications significantly when electronic parts became available that could filter out random noises.

Standards may also be changed by the community as a response to some shift in public policy—witness the changes in the performance standards imposed on nuclear power installations or automotive exhaust systems. Shifts in the prime rate of interest or in unemployment levels often alter the standards that the PM must use for making project related decisions. The monitoring process is based on the criteria and standards because they dictate, or at least constrain, the set of relevant measures.

Next, the information to be collected must be identified. This may consist of accounting data, operating data, engineering test data, customer reactions, specification changes, and the like. The fundamental problem is to determine precisely which of all the available data should be collected. It is worth repeating that the typical determinant for collecting data too often seems to be simply the ease with which they can be gathered. Of course the nature of the required data is dictated by the project plan, as well as by the goals of the parent organization, the needs of the client, and by the fact that it is desirable to improve the process of managing projects.

Closely monitoring project work is often justified with the argument that keeping close track of progress will reduce the amount of crashing required near the end of the project. Partovi and Burton tested this argument and found that it was not strictly true. They examined five monitoring policies: no monitoring, monitoring at random times, equal interval monitoring, monitoring more frequently at the start of the project, and monitoring more frequently late in the project's life. They found that there was no significant difference in the amount of crashing effort expended whatever monitoring protocol was used, but that high frequency monitoring late in the project life was the best policy to prevent project lateness [40].

Perhaps the most common error made when monitoring data is to gather information that is clearly related to project performance but has little or no probability of changing significantly from one collection period to the next. Prior to its breakup, the American Telephone and Telegraph Company used to collect monthly statistics on a very large number of indicators of operating efficiency. The extent of the collection was such that it filled a telephone-book-sized volume known as "Ma Bell's Green Book." For a great many of the indicators, the likelihood of a significant change from one month to the next was extremely small. When asked about the matter, one official remarked that the mere collection of the data kept the operating companies "on their toes." We feel that there are other, more positive and less expensive ways of motivating project personnel. Certainly, "collect everything" is inappropriate as a monitoring policy.

Therefore, the first task is to examine the project plans in order to extract performance, time, and cost goals. These goals should relate in some fashion to each of the different levels of detail; that is, some should relate to the project, some to its tasks, some to the work packages, and so on. Data must be identified that measure achievement against these goals, and mechanisms designed that gather and store such data. If at least some of the data do not relate to the work unit level, no useful action is apt to be taken. In the end, it is the detailed work of the project that must be altered if any aspect of project performance is to be changed.

Similarly, the process of developing and managing projects should be considered and steps taken to ensure that information relevant to the diagnosis and treatment of the project's organizational infirmities and procedural problems are gathered and collected. A reading of the fascinating book *The Soul of a New Machine* [25] reveals the crucial roles that organizational factors, interpersonal relationships, and managerial style play in determining project success.

How to Collect Data

Given that we know *what type* of data we want to collect, the next question is *how* to collect this information. At this point in the construction of a monitoring system, it is necessary to define precisely what pieces of information should be gathered and when. In most cases, the PM has options. Questions arise. Should cost data be gathered before or after some specific event? Is it always mandatory to collect time and cost information at exactly the same point in the process? What do we do if a specific item is difficult to collect because the data source (human) fears reporting any information that might contribute to a negative performance evaluation? What do we do about the fact that some use of time is reported as "hours charged" to our project, and we are quite aware that our project has been charged for work done on another project (but for the same customer) that is over budget? Are special forms needed for data collection? Should we set up quality control procedures to ensure the integrity of data transference from its source to the project information system? Such questions merely indicate the broad range of knotty issues that must be handled.

A large proportion of all data collected take one of the following forms, each of which is suitable for some types of measures.

1. *Frequency counts* A simple tally of the occurrence of an event. This type of measure is often used for "complaints," "number of times a project report is late," "days without an accident," "bugs in a computer program," and similar items. The data are usually easy to collect and are often reported as events per unit time or events as a percent of a standard number.

2. *Raw numbers* Dates, dollars, hours, physical amounts of resources used, and specifications are usually reported in this way. These numbers are reported in a wide variety of ways, but often as direct comparisons with an expected or standard number. Also, "variances" are commonly reported either as the difference between actual and standard or as the ratio of actual to standard. Differences or ratios can also be plotted as a time series to show changes in system performance. When collecting raw project data, it is important to make sure that all data are collected from sources that operate on the same time intervals and with the same rules for data collection.

3. *Subjective numeric ratings* These numbers are subjective estimates, usually of a quality, made by knowledgeable individuals or groups. They can be reported in most of the same ways that objective raw numbers are, but care should be taken to make sure that the numbers are not manipulated in ways only suitable for quantitative measures. (See Chapter 2 for comments on measurements.) Ordinal rankings of performance are included in this category.

4. *Indicators* When the PM cannot measure some aspect of system performance directly, it may be possible to find an indirect measure or indicator. The speed with which change orders are processed and changes are incorporated into the project is often a good measure of team efficiency. Response to change may also be an indicator of the quality of communications on the project team. When using indicators to measure performance, the PM must make sure that the link between the indicator and the desired performance measure is as direct as possible.

5. *Verbal measures* Measures for such performance characteristics as "quality of team member cooperation," "morale of team members," or "quality of interaction with the client" frequently take the form of verbal characterizations. As long as the set of characterizations is limited and the meanings of the individual terms consistently understood by all, these data serve their purposes reasonably well.

Drug Counseling Program

A social service agency applied for and received funding for a special project to counsel male drug addicts between 18 and 24 years of age, and to secure full-time employment for each client (or part-time employment for clients who were still in school). To qualify for the program, the addicts must have been arrested for a crime, but not be classed as "repeat offenders." Further, the addict must be living with at least one member of his family who is a parent or guardian. Among other conditions placed on the grant, the agency was asked to develop a measure of effectiveness for the counseling program that was acceptable to the funding agency.

The primary measure of effectiveness adopted by most drug programs was "rate of recidivism." A recidivistic incident is defined as any rearrest for a drug-related crime, or any behavior that resulted in the individual reentering the social service system after completing the program and being discharged.

While a "re-arrest" is most surely recidivistic, there were several cases in which former clients contacted the agency and asked to be readmitted to the program. These voluntary readmissions resulted when a former client either began to use drugs again or was fearful that he would begin again. It seemed to the agency professionals that voluntary readmissions were successes, not failures.

A new measure of effectiveness was developed to replace "rate of recidivism." It was composed of scores on three different measures, combined with equal weighting.

1. Number of successive weeks of "clean urines."
2. Number of successive months of satisfactory employment (or schooling) experience.
3. Number of successive months of satisfactory behavior at home.

Scores on the second and third measures were based on interviews with employers, teachers, and parent(s).

After data collection has been completed, reports on project progress should be generated. These include project status reports, time/cost reports, and variance reports, among others. Causes and effects should be identified and trends noted. Plans, charts, and tables should be updated on a timely basis. Where known, "comparables" should be reported, as should statistical distributions of previous data if available. Both help the PM (and others) to interpret the data being monitored. Figures 10-2 and 10-3 illustrate the use of such data. Figure 10-2 shows the results of a count of "bugs" found during a series of tests run on a new piece of computer software. (Bugs found were fixed prior to subsequent tests.) Figure 10-3 shows the percent of the time a computer program retrieved data within a specified time limit. Each point represents a series of trials.

Figure 10-2   Number of bugs found during test of Datamix program.

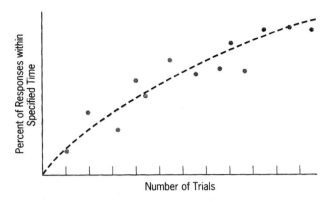

Figure 10-3 Percent of specified performance met during repeated trials.

The PM can fit a statistical function to the data shown in Figure 10-2 and make a rough estimate of the number of tests that will have to be run to find some predetermined number of additional bugs in the program. By fitting a curve (formally or "by eyeball") to the data in Figure 10-3, the PM can estimate the cost and time (the number of additional trials and adjustments) required to get system performance up to the specified level.

The nature of *timeliness* will be amplified next, but it is important that the PM make sure that the PERT/CPM and Gantt charts in the project war room (office) are frequently updated. Monitoring can serve to maintain high morale on the project team as well as to alert team members to problems that will have to be solved.

The purpose of the monitoring system is to gather and report data. The purpose of the control system is to act on the data. To aid the *project controller*, it is helpful for the *monitor* to carry out some data analysis. Significant differences from plan should be highlighted or "flagged" so that they cannot be overlooked by the controller. The methods of statistical quality control are very useful for determining what size variances are "significant" and sometimes even help in determining the probable cause(s) of variances. Where causation is known, it should be noted. Where it is not known, an investigation may be in order. The decisions about when an investigation should be conducted, by whom, and by what methods are the prerogative of the project controller, although the actual investigation may be conducted by the group responsible for monitoring.

The Emanon Aircraft Company example presented in Chapter 7 is a case in point. While the study team collected and analyzed a great deal of cost information during the process of finding the problem, the method used for the analysis was actually quite simple. The team compared forecast or estimated cost, $F(t)$, with actual cost, $A(t)$, for each batch of output from the manufacturing system. This analysis was done for each cost center. The ratio of actual cost to estimated cost was calculated and plotted as a time series, as in Figure 10-4.* Note that $A(t)/F(t) < 1$ when the cost forecast for a cost center is greater than actual. In this case, the cost involved was "material cost." Though careful statistical analysis was not necessary in this specific

---

* Actual data were not used in constructing Figure 10-4, but the figure reflects the consultants' findings.

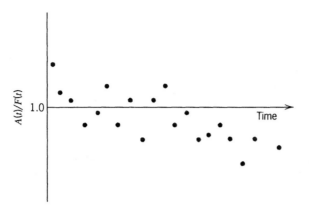

Figure 10-4 Ratio of actual material cost to estimated material cost. Emanon Aircraft Company.

case, standard quality control techniques have wide application to project management (see any book on statistical quality control, [9 or 13] for example). Time series analysis can often give the PM an early warning of problems.

At base, this provides a *management by exception* reporting system for the PM. But management by exception has its flaws as well as its strengths. It is essentially an "after-the-fact" approach to control. Variances occur, are investigated, and only then is action taken. The astute PM is far more interested in preventing problems than curing them. Therefore, the monitoring system should develop data streams that indicate variances yet to come. Obviously, such indicators are apt to be statistical in nature, hinting at the likelihood of a future problem rather than predicting it with certainty. An example would be a trend in the data showing a system heading out of control. Interested readers are referred to the "2-5-7 Rule" (see [48], quality chapters). The PM may waste time and effort trying to deal with trouble that will not actually occur. This may be frustrating, but the costs of dealing with some nonproblems is usually minor when compared to the costs of dealing with real problems too late.

In creating the monitoring system, some care should be devoted to the issues of honesty and bias. The former is dealt with by setting in place an internal audit. The audit serves the purpose of ensuring that the information gathered is honest. No audit, however, can prevent bias. All data are biased by those who report them, advertently or inadvertently. The controller must understand this fact of life. The first issue is to determine whether the possibility of bias in the data matters significantly. If not, nothing need be done. Bias finding and correcting activities (cf. Chapter 7) are worthwhile only if data with less or no bias are required.

The issue of creating an atmosphere that fosters honesty on a project is widely ignored, but it is of major importance. A set of instructions to the PM on how to do this is not beyond the scope of this book, but if such instructions exist, we do not know of them. We do, however, have some advice to offer. The PM can tolerate almost any kind of behavior except dishonesty. Projects are vulnerable to dishonesty, far more vulnerable than the ongoing operations of the parent organization. Standard operations are characterized by considerable knowledge about expected system performance. When the monitoring system reports information that deviates from expectations, it is visible, noteworthy, and tends to get attention. In the case of many projects, expectations are not so well known. Deviations are not recognized for what they are. The PM is often dependent on team members to call attention to problems. To get this cooperation, the PM must make sure that the bearer of bad news is not punished; nor is the admitter-to-error executed. On the other hand, the hider-of-mistakes may be shot with impunity—and then sent to Siberia.

There is some tendency for project monitoring systems to include an analysis directed at the assignment of blame. This practice has doubtful value. While the managerial dictum "rewards and punishments should be closely associated with performance" has the ring of good common sense, it is actually not good advice. Instead of motivating people to better performance, the practice is more apt to result in lower expectations. If achievement of goals is directly measured and directly rewarded, tremendous pressure will be put on people to understate goals and to generate plans that can be met or exceeded with minimal risk and effort.

Project Management in Practice
Tracking Scope Creep: A Project Manager Responds

Dear Editor:

The two-part *Scope Creep* article in the Winter and Spring issues of *Today's Engineer* presented an interesting case study. The engineering-only solution, however, misses the bigger issue—lack of a formal project management process. It is unfortunate that the need for formal project management is omitted from the article. A formal project management process is the cornerstone of on-time and on-schedule projects. Such a process includes:

- A formal project plan development process
- A tracking system capable of providing variance analysis data
- Managing project scope, schedule, and resource changes throughout the project life cycle.

This case study depicts an all-too-familiar scenario:

1. An engineer is selected as project manager—usually with no formal project management training.
2. The project team is composed of primarily engineers—marketing and other functional organizations are viewed as project outsiders, rather than team members, and do not participate in the planning process.
3. Project objectives and deliverables are poorly defined—usually by engineering—including only engineering deliverables.
4. A comprehensive work breakdown structure, task completion criteria, and network diagram are nonexistent—progress measurement is therefore somewhat arbitrary and difficult to ascertain.
5. Task duration estimates are probably determined by someone other than the task owner—making estimates invalid.
6. The project schedule is pasted together to look good and match target dates—missing the opportunity to use critical path method (CPM) to develop a credible schedule.
7. Resource requirements, including people and budget, are guesses—usually without the benefit of using a comprehensive CPM-developed preliminary schedule.
8. A risk management plan does not exist—most project risks are treated as surprises.

9. The project plan is not validated and base-lined by the project sponsor—missing the opportunity to obtain team and sponsor commitment prior to implementation.

10. A formal project tracking and change management system does not exist—impossible to track a project without a plan to measure progress against and to manage changes.

Project management, like engineering, is a discipline that must be learned. Project management is not for everyone. It requires a different skill set than, say, engineering or marketing.

Source: J. Sivak, "Scope Creep: A Project Manager Responds," ©1998 IEEE. Reprinted with permission from Today's Engineer, Vol. 1, No. 3 (Summer), p. 8, 1998.

—Jack Sivak
Project Rescue, LLC
Scottsdale, Arizona

10.2 INFORMATION NEEDS AND THE REPORTING PROCESS

Everyone concerned with the project should be appropriately tied into the project reporting system. The monitoring system ought to be constructed so that it addresses every level of management, but reports need not be of the same depth or at the same frequency for each level. Lower-level personnel have a need for detailed information about individual tasks and the factors affecting such tasks. Report frequency is usually high. For the senior management levels, overview reports describe progress in more aggregated terms with less individual task detail. Reports are issued less often. In both cases, the structure of the reports should reflect the WBS, with each managerial level receiving reports that allow the exercise of control at the relevant level. At times it may be necessary to move information between organizations, as illustrated in Figure 10-5, as well as between managerial levels.

The proliferation of electronic mechanisms along with a wide array of software has made the process of collecting and disseminating information much faster and less arduous than seemed possible when the first edition of this book was written [47]. (And, of course, it follows that a great deal more information is being collected, and sometimes used.) The globalization of industry has lead to a sharp increase in the number of projects that are carried out in places far from some of the project workers and even from management. These *virtual* projects can be managed from remote locations only because the virtual meetings involved in planning and controlling the projects are conducted through electronic media. Use of the Internet and Web sites for projects allows communication of (and response to) the most complex information. Even tracking and control of multiple projects through electronic systems is quite feasible.

In addition to its use for conducting the routines of project management, the Internet is a rich source of information, including building codes, databases on almost anything, the Yellow Pages for practically anywhere, patent information, and technical aid for managing projects, to mention only a small fraction of readily available information [23]. Many current project management software packages allow easy connection to the Internet and e-mail to transmit information, action plans, charts, networks, and reports practically anywhere. The material can be altered or updated

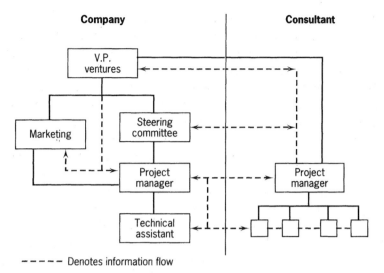

Figure 10-5 Reporting and information flows betwen organizations working on a common project.

and returned to the sender with minimal effort beyond that needed to move the information to the next cubicle.

> "E-mail is not to be used to pass on information or data. It should be used only for company business."

The relationship of project reports to the project action plan or WBS is the key to the determination of both report content and frequency. Reports must contain data relevant to the control of specific tasks that are being carried out according to a specific schedule. The frequency of reporting should be great enough to allow control to be exerted during or before the period in which the task is scheduled for completion. For example, efficacy tests of drugs do not produce rapid results in most cases. Thus, there is no reason for weekly (and perhaps not even monthly) reports on such tests. When test results begin to occur, more frequent reports and updates may be required.

In addition to the criterion that reports should be available in time to be used for project control, the timing of reports should generally correspond to the timing of project milestones. This means that project reports may not be issued periodically—excepting progress reports for senior management. There seems to be no logical reason, except for tradition, to issue weekly, monthly, quarterly, etc. reports. Few projects require attention so neatly consistent with the calendar. This must not be taken as advice to issue reports "every once in a while." Reports should be scheduled in the project plan. They should be issued on time. The report schedule, however, need not call for *periodic* reports.

Identification of project milestones depends on who is interested. For senior management, there may be only a few milestones, even in large projects. For the PM there may be many critical points in the project schedule at which major decisions must be made, large changes in the resource base must be initiated, or key technical results achieved. The milestones relevant to lower levels relate to finer detail and occur with higher frequency. Individual senior managers have widely varying preferences in the frequency and content of reports they wish to see. The PM is well advised to supply them. But irrespective of the senior manager's wishes the PM must make sure that relevant information about progress is always included—and reported in a way it cannot be overlooked. It is also counterproductive to delay reporting on a current or immediately potential crisis until the next routine report is due.

The nature of the monitoring reports should be consistent with the logic of the planning, budgeting, and scheduling systems. The primary purpose is, of course, to ensure achievement of the project plan through control. There is little reason to burden operating members of the project team with extensive reports on matters that are not subject to control—at least not by them. For example, overhead costs or the in-house rental cost of the project war room are simply not appropriate considerations for a team member who is supervising a research experiment in polymer chemistry or designing the advertising campaign for a new brand of coffee. The scheduling and resource usage columns of the project action plan will serve as the key to the design of project reports.

There are many benefits of detailed, timely reports delivered to the proper people. Among them are:

- Mutual understanding of the goals of the project
- Awareness of the progress of parallel activities and of the problems associated with coordination among activities
- More realistic planning for the needs of all groups and individuals working on the project
- Understanding the relationships of individual tasks to one another and to the overall project
- Early warning signals of potential problems and delays in the project
- Minimizing the confusion associated with change by reducing delays in communicating the change
- Faster management action in response to unacceptable or inappropriate work
- Higher visibility to top management, including attention directed to the immediate needs of the project
- Keeping the client and other interested outside parties up to date on project status, particularly regarding project costs, milestones, and deliverables.

Report Types

> "One day my boss asked me to submit a status report to him concerning a project I was working on. I asked him if tomorrow would be soon enough. He said, 'If I wanted it tomorrow, I would have waited until tomorrow to ask for it!' "

For the purposes of project management, we can consider three distinct types of reports: routine, exception, and special analysis. The routine reports are those issued on a regular basis; but, as we noted above, *regular* does not necessarily refer to the calendar. For senior management, the reports will usually be periodic, but for the PM and lower-level project personnel, milestones may be used to trigger routine reports. At times, it may be useful to issue routine reports on resource usage periodically, occasionally on a weekly or even daily basis.

Exception reports are useful in two cases. First, they are directly oriented to project management decision making and should be distributed to the team members who will have prime responsibility for decisions or who have a clear "need to know." Second, they may be issued when a decision is made on an exception basis and it is desirable to inform other managers as well as to document the decision—in other words, as part of a sensible procedure for protecting oneself. (PMs should be aware that overuse of exception reporting will be perceived by top management as sheep-like, overly cautious behavior.)

Special analysis reports are used to disseminate the results of special studies conducted as part of the project or as a response to special problems that arise during the project. Usually they cover matters that may be of interest to other PMs, or make use of analytic methods that might be helpful on other projects. Studies on the use of substitute materials, evaluation of alternative manufacturing processes, availability of external consultants, capabilities of new software, and descriptions of new governmental regulations are all typical of the kinds of subjects covered in special analysis reports. Distribution of these reports is usually made to anyone who might be interested.

Meetings

To celebrate his 50th birthday, columnist Dave Barry listed "25 things you will learn in 50 years of living." The sixteenth was "If you had to identify, in one word, the reason why the human race has not and never will achieve its full potential, that word would be 'meetings.'" For a large majority of project managers and workers, meetings are as welcome as bad checks or unmentionable diseases. Widespread rumors that meetings were invented by Torquemada to the contrary, there is no doubt that meetings of project teams are necessary and often helpful. The main complaints are that they are interminably long, come to no conclusions, and waste everyone's time. Indeed, a short commentary on how not to run a meeting is entitled, "Creative Time Wasting" [38].

Thus far, we have implicitly assumed that "reports" were written and disseminated by hard-copy, e-mail or by Internet. Far more often, however, all three types of reports are delivered in face-to-face meetings, and in telephone conference calls. Indeed, senior managers usually insist on face-to-face meetings for staying informed about project progress, and these meetings may touch on almost any subject relevant to the project. Project review meetings can be either highly structured (see [26], for instance) or deceptively casual, but they are always important.

A large majority of project meetings do not concern senior management. They are project team meetings, occasionally including the client, and concern the day-today problems met on all projects. There is no particular reason that these meetings need be conducted in a manner that is so dreaded by attendees. A few simple rules can remove most of the onus associated with project meetings.

- Use meetings for making group decisions or getting input for important problems. Avoid "show-and-tell" meetings, sometimes called "status and review meetings." If the latter type of meeting has been used to keep project team members informed about what others are doing on the project, insist that such information be communicated personally or electronically by the relevant individuals to the relevant individuals. Only when there is a clear need, such as informing senior management of the project's status, and it is difficult for team members to "get together" on their own, are status and review meetings appropriate.

- Have preset starting and stopping times as well as a written agenda. Stick with both, and above all, do not penalize those who show up on time by making them wait for those who are tardy.

- Make sure that you (and others) do their homework prior to the meeting. Be prepared!

- If you chair the meeting, take your own minutes. Reality (and the minutes become reality as soon as the meeting is over) is too important to be left to the most junior person present. Distribute the minutes as soon as possible after the meeting, not later than the next work day.

- Avoid attributing remarks or viewpoints to individuals in the minutes. Attribution makes people quite wary about what they say in meetings and damps creativity as well as controversy. Also, do not report votes on controversial matters. It is, for example, inappropriate to report in the minutes that the project team voted to send a "Get Well" card to the boss; 4 yea and 3 nay.

- Avoid overly formal rules of procedure. A project meeting is not a parliament and is not the place for Robert's Rules of Order, though courtesy is always in order.

- If a serious problem or crisis arises, call a meeting for the purpose of dealing with that issue only. The stopping time for such meetings may be "When the problem has been solved."

Some types of meetings should never be held at all. A large, diversified manufacturing firm holds monthly "status and review" meetings in each of its divisions at which the managers of all projects report to a Project Review Committee (PRC). The divisional PRCs are made up of senior managers. At least one, and we are told more than one, of the PRCs apparently models its meetings on "Hell Week" at a nearby university fraternity. Hazing and humiliating the project managers who must report to the committee is standard practice. The results are to be expected. Projects are managed defensively. Creativity is avoided. Project managers spend time printing and distributing résumés. The best PMs do not stay long.

In 1976, Antony Jay wrote a classic article on how to conduct a meeting [22]. We recommend it; it is still a classic.

Common Reporting Problems

There are three common difficulties in the design of project reports. First, there is usually too much detail, both in the reports themselves and in the input being solicited from workers. Unnecessary detail (or too frequent reporting) usually results in the reports not being read. Also, it prevents project team members from finding the information they need. Furthermore, the demand for large quantities of highly detailed input information often results in careless preparation of the data, thereby casting doubt on the validity of reports based on such data. Finally, the preparation and inclusion of unnecessary detail are costly, at the very least.

A second major problem is the poor interface between the project information system and the parent firm's information system. Data are rarely comparable, and interaction between the PM and the organization's accountants is often strained. In our experience, the PM may try to force a connection. It rarely works well. The parent organization's information system must serve as the definitional prototype for the project's information system. In effect, this means that the parent's accounting, engineering, marketing, finance, personnel, and production information systems should be used as the base on which the project's information system is built. Obviously, different types of reports must be constructed for managing the project, but they can be built by using standard data for the most part. The PM can feel free to add new kinds of data to the information base but cannot insist that costs, resource usage, and the like be reported in the project differently from how they are reported in the parent organization. (Clearly, this rule does not apply to information generated or requested by the PM for the purpose of project management.)

The project oriented firm or the organization that simultaneously conducts a large number of projects can justify a customized project database and report system specifically tailored to its special needs. In such cases, the interface between the project information system and the organization's overall information system must be carefully designed to insure that data are not lost or distorted when moving from one system to the other. It is also important to make sure that when cost/performance data are reported, the data represent appropriate time periods.

The third problem concerns a poor correspondence between the planning and the monitoring systems. If the monitoring system is not tracking information directly related to the project's plans, control is meaningless. This often happens when the firm's existing information system is used for monitoring without modifications specifically designed for project management. For example, an existing cost tracking system oriented to shop operations would be inappropriate for a project with major activities in the area of research and development. But as we just noted, the option of running the project from a different database is generally not viable. The PM's problem is to fit standard information into a reporting and tracking system that is appropriate for the project.

The real message carried by project reports is in the comparison of actual activity to plan and of actual output to desired output. Variances are reported by the monitoring system, and responsibility for action rests with the controller. Because the project plan is described in terms of performance, time, and cost, variances are reported for those same variables. Project variance reports usually follow the same format used by the accounting department, but at times they may be presented differently.

The Earned Value Chart

Thus far, our examples have covered monitoring for parts of projects. The monitoring of performance for the entire project is also crucial because performance is the *raison d'être* of the project. *Individual* task performance must be monitored carefully because the timing and coordination between individual tasks is important. But overall project performance is the crux of the matter and must not be overlooked. One way of measuring overall performance is by using an aggregate performance measure called *earned value*.

There is a considerable body of literature devoted to earned value. To note only a few of the available items, see [2, 5, 12–17, 20, 21, 42, and 49]. One must, however, exercise some care when reading any article on the subject. Various ratio index numbers have almost as many names (and hence, acronyms) as there are writers. Some authors take further license, see [5] for instance, and also see the subsequent *Project Management Journal's* Correspondence column, (September 1998, p. 53) for readers' reactions. We will adopt and stick to the PMBOK version of things, but will also note the names and acronyms used by Microsoft's Project 98®.* Any other names/acronyms will be identified with the author(s). A history of earned value from its origin in PERT/Cost to its culmination in C/SCSC (Cost/Schedule Control System Criteria) together with its techniques, advantages, and disadvantages is reported in a series in *PM Network* starting with [17].

A serious difficulty with comparing actual expenditures against budgeted or *baseline* expenditures for any given time period is that the comparison fails to take into account the amount of work accomplished relative to the cost incurred. The earned value of work performed (*value completed*) for those tasks in progress is found by multiplying the estimated percent completion for each task by the planned cost for that task. The result is the amount that should have been spent on the task thus far. This can then be compared with the actual amount spent.

Making an overall estimate of the percent completion of a project, without careful study of each of its tasks and work units, is not sensible—though some people make such estimates nonetheless. Instead, it is apparent that at any date during the life of a project the following general condition exists: some work units have been finished and they are 100 percent complete, some work units have not yet been started and they are 0 percent complete, other units are been started but are not yet finished, and for this latter group we may estimate a percent completion.

As we said, estimating the "percent completion" of each task (or work package) is nontrivial. If the task is to write a piece of software, percent completion can be estimated as the number of lines of code written divided by the total number of lines to be written—given that the latter has been estimated. But what if the task is to test the software? We have run a known number of tests, but how many remain to be run? There are several conventions used to aid in estimating percent completion. The most popular seems to be the 50–50 estimate. Fifty percent completion is assumed when the task is begun, and the remaining 50 percent when the work is complete.

---

*Earlier versions of Microsoft Project used different ways to calculate earned value variances.

Other conventions include the 0–100 percent rule which allows no credit for work until the task is complete, or assignment of credit according to the amount of a critical input that has been used. Also common is use of the proportionality rule that divides planned (or actual) time-to-date by total scheduled time, or budgeted (or actual) cost-to-date by total budgeted cost to calculate percent complete.

These rough guides to "percent completion" are not meant to be applied to the project as a whole, though sometimes they are, but rather to individual activities. For projects with few activities, rough measures can be misleading. For projects with a fairly large number of activities, however, the error caused by percent completion rules is such a small part of the total project time/cost that the errors are insignificant. More serious is the tendency to speak of an entire project as being "73 percent complete." In most cases this has no real meaning—certainly not what is implied by the overly exact number. Some authors assume that making estimates of percent completion is simple [5, p. 12, col. 2, for instance]. The estimation task is difficult and arbitrary at best, which is why the 50–50 and other rules have been adopted.

A graph such as that shown in Figure 10-6 can be constructed and provides a basis for evaluating cost and performance to date. If the total value of the work accomplished is in balance with the planned (baseline) cost (i.e., minimal scheduling variance), then top management has no particular need for a detailed analysis of individual tasks. Thus the concept of earned value combines cost reporting and aggregate performance reporting into one comprehensive chart.

We identify several variances on the earned value chart following two primary

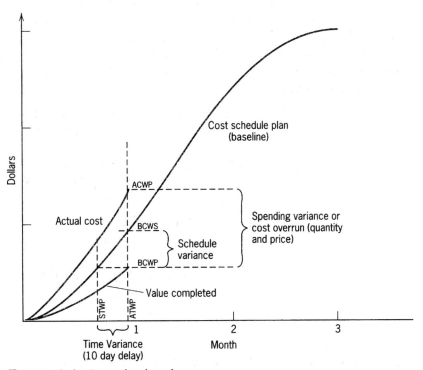

Figure 10-6 Earned value chart.

guidelines: 1) A negative variance is "bad," and 2) the cost variances are calculated as the earned value minus some other measure. Specifically, the *cost* or *spending variance* is the difference between the amount of money we budgeted for the work that has been performed to date (the budgeted cost of work performed or *earned value*, BCWP) and the actual cost of that work (ACWP). The *schedule variance* is the difference between the BCWP and the cost of the work we scheduled to be performed to date (BCWS). The *time variance* is the difference in the time scheduled for the work that has been performed (STWP) and the actual time used to perform it (ATWP).* In compact form,

$$\text{BCWP–ACWP} = \text{cost variance (CV, overrun is negative)}$$
$$\text{BCWP–BCWS} = \text{schedule variance (SV, behind is negative)}$$
$$\text{STWP–ATWP} = \text{time variance (TV, delay is negative)}$$

Typically, variances are defined in such a way that they will be negative when the project is behind schedule and/or over cost. As we have noted, however, this practice is not universal either in the literature or in practice.

The variances are also often formulated as ratios rather than differences so that the cost variance become the Cost Performance Index (CPI) = BCWP/ACWP, the schedule variance becomes the Schedule Performance Index (SPI) = BCWP/BCWS, and the time variance becomes the Time Performance Index (TPI) = STWP/ATWP. Use of ratios is particularly helpful when an organization wishes to compare the performance of several projects—or project managers. As we justed noted, however, the accuracy and usefulness of all these performance measures depend on the degree in which estimates of percent completion reflect reality.

Cost and schedule variances (or CPI and SPI) are very commonly used. A short example illustrates their application. Assume that operations on a work package were expected to cost $1500 to complete the package. They were originally scheduled to have been finished today. At this point, however, we have actually expended $1350, and we estimate that we have completed two-thirds of the work. What are the cost and schedule variances?

$$
\begin{aligned}
\text{cost variance} &= \text{BCWP} - \text{ACWP} \\
&= \$1500(2/3) - 1350 \\
&= -\$350 \\
\text{schedule variance} &= \text{BCWP} - \text{BCWS} \\
&= \$1500(2/3) - 1500 \\
&= -\$500 \\
\text{CPI} &= \text{BCWP} / \text{ACWP} \\
&= \$(1500\,(2/3)) / 1350 \\
&= .74 \\
\text{SPI} &= \text{BCWP} / \text{BCWS} \\
&= \$(1500\,(2/3)) / 1500 \\
&= .67
\end{aligned}
$$

---

*A fourth variance can be found. It is the difference between the cost the project budget says should have been expended to date (BCWS) and the actual cost, incurred to date by the project (ACWP), BCWS–ACWP is what we call the *resource flow variance*. (Note that the resource flow variance is not a "cash flow" variance.)

In other words, we are spending at a higher level than our budget plan indicates, and given what we have spent, we are not as far along as we should be (i.e., we have not completed as much work as we should have).

It is quite possible for one of the indicators to be favorable while the other is unfavorable. We might be ahead of schedule and behind in cost, or vice versa. Barr (and others) combines the two indexes, CPI and SPI, to make a type of "critical ratio" (described further in Chapter 11) called the Cost–Schedule Index [2, p. 32].

$$CSI = (CPI)(SPI)$$
$$= (BCWP/ACWP)(BCWP/BCWS)$$
$$= BCWP^2 / (ACWP)(BCWS)$$

In our case:

$$= \$(1500\,(2/3))^2 / (1350)(1500)$$
$$= \$1{,}000{,}000 / 2{,}025{,}000$$
$$= 0.49$$

As Barr writes, CSI < 1 is indicative of a problem.

One can continue the analysis to forecast the future of this work unit if no measures are taken to correct matters. (Note that Microsoft Project 98® calculates no final variances until the work unit is complete. See Figure 10-7, lines "Advertise in college paper" and "Organize posters" for example.) The cost to complete the work unit can be estimated as the budgeted cost of the entire unit, less the earned value to date, adjusted by the CPI to reflect the actual level of performance. The budget at completion (BAC) in our example is $1500. The budgeted cost of the work performed to date (BCWP) is $1,500 × 2/3 = $1000. The estimated cost to complete (ECT)—and we use Barr's term [2] rather than Microsoft's FAC or any of the many other names in the literature—is defined as

$$ECT = (BAC - BCWP)/CPI$$
$$= \$(1500 - 1000)/0.74$$
$$= \$676$$

The total cost of the work unit is the amount expended to date (ACWP) plus the estimated cost to complete (ECT)

$$Total\ work\ unit\ cost = ECT + ACWP$$
$$= \$676 + 1350$$
$$= \$2026$$

rather than the original estimate of $1500. For a complete description of this approach to estimating the total cost of a work unit, or a set of work units, see [2]. For similar approaches with different notation, see [14] and elsewhere.

Thus far, the focus has been on measuring performance on a work unit rather than on the project as a whole. Where dealing with a specific work unit, the estimates of costs and time can be fairly precise. Even the estimate of percent completion can be made without introducing too much error when using, as we did above, the proportionality rule. Given the relatively short time frame and relatively small cost compared to the whole project, errors are not apt to be significant. Random errors in estimating will tend to cancel out and we can aggregate the work unit data into larger elements, e.g., tasks or even the whole project. (Bias in estimating is, of course, a different matter.) Although the measurement error may be minimal, for most projects there is still no sound basis for estimating percent completion of the project as a whole.

Even if this aggregation is feasible, the use of earned value analysis for forecasting project schedules and costs does not mean that the forecasts will make it possible to correct malperformance. The case for remediation is not hopeful. In a study of more than 700 projects carried out under Department of Defense contracts, the chances of correcting a poorly performing project more than 15 percent complete were effectively nil [14]. The study concludes that if the beginning of the project was underestimated and took longer and cost more than the plan indicated, there was little or no chance that the rest of the project would be estimated more accurately [14, p. 13ff]. For relatively small deviations from plan, the PM may be able to do a lot a catching up.

If the earned value chart shows a cost overrun or performance underrun, the PM must figure out what to do to get the system back on target. Options include such things as borrowing resources from activities performing better than expected, or holding a meeting of project team members to see if anyone can suggest solutions to the problems, or perhaps notifying the client that the project may be late or over budget.

Name	BCWS	BCWP	ACWP	Sch. Variance	Cost Variance	BAC	FAC	Variance
Contact Organizations	$3,797.30	$3,980.00	$3,920.00	$182.00	$60.00	$3,980.00	$3,920.00	$60.00
Print forms	$645.00	$645.00	$645.00	$0.00	$0.00	$645.00	$645.00	$0.00
Contact organizations	$840.00	$840.00	$728.00	$0.00	$112.00	$840.00	$728.00	$112.00
Collect display information	$660.00	$660.00	$660.00	$0.00	$0.00	$660.00	$660.00	$0.00
Gather college particulars	$520.00	$520.00	$520.00	$0.00	$0.00	$520.00	$520.00	$0.00
Print programs	$687.00	$870.00	$922.00	$182.70	($52.00)	$870.00	$922.00	($52.00)
Print participants' certificates	$445.00	$445.00	$445.00	$0.00	$0.00	$445.00	$445.00	$0.00
Banquet and Refreshments	$1,220.00	$1,220.00	$1,200.00	$0.00	$20.00	$1,220.00	$1,200.00	$20.00
Select guest speaker	$500.00	$500.00	$500.00	$0.00	$0.00	$500.00	$500.00	$0.00
Organize food	$325.00	$325.00	$325.00	$0.00	$0.00	$325.00	$325.00	$0.00
Organize liquor	$100.00	$100.00	$100.00	$0.00	$0.00	$100.00	$100.00	$0.00
Organize refreshments	$295.00	$295.00	$275.00	$0.00	$20.00	$295.00	$275.00	$20.00
Publicity and Promotion	$2,732.55	$2,797.75	$2,039.00	($434.80)	$258.75	$3,010.00	$2,870.00	$140.00
Send invitations	$700.00	$700.00	$560.00	$0.00	$140.00	$700.00	$560.00	$140.00
Organize gift certificates	$330.00	$330.00	$330.00	$0.00	$0.00	$330.00	$330.00	$0.00
Arrange banner	$570.00	$570.00	$570.00	$0.00	$0.00	$570.00	$570.00	$0.00
Contact faculty	$280.00	$280.00	$280.00	$0.00	$0.00	$280.00	$280.00	$0.00
Advertise in college paper	$165.00	$82.50	$65.00	($82.50)	$17.50	$165.00	$165.00	$0.00
Class announcements	$99.00	$0.00	$0.00	($99.00)	$0.00	$220.00	$220.00	$0.00
Organize posters	$588.00	$325.25	$234.00	($253.30)	$101.25	$745.00	$745.00	$0.00
Facilities	$200.00	$0.00	$0.00	($200.00)	$0.00	$200.00	$200.00	$0.00
Arrange facility for event	$52.00	$0.00	$0.00	($52.00)	$0.00	$52.00	$52.00	$0.00
Transport materials	$148.00	$0.00	$0.00	($148.00)	$0.00	$148.00	$148.00	$0.00

Project: Career Day Date: 3/24/99 — Critical, Noncritical, Progress, Summary, Milestone, Rolled up

Figure 10-7 Microsoft Project 98® (corrected) budget sheet for career day project (cf. Chapter 5).

Figure 10-7 shows a budget for the Career Day project described in Chapter 5, Section 5.3. This budget was generated as a standard report from Microsoft Project 98® but we have corrected the signs on the cost and BAC-FAC variances to correspond to the standard Project Management Institute definitions in the *Project Management Body of Knowledge (PMBOK)*. (Similar reports are available through most

---

Project Management in Practice
Success Through Earned Value at Texas Instruments

When Texas Instruments, Inc. wanted an imaging system designed for their Accounts Receivable department that would interface with their mainframe accounts receivable system, they turned to ViewStar Corporation to design it. Several leading edge technologies were desired so ViewStar compiled the work breakdown structure from which to plan the budget and track actual spending. However, the planned budget exceeded the contract funds available so the budget for selected early-on tasks was arbitrarily reduced so the overall budget would match the contract

Source: T. Ingram, "Client/Server, Imaging and Earned Value: A Success Story," *PM Network*, December 1995, pp. 21–25.

funds because top management wanted to win this contract.

As the contract progressed, the underbudgeted items showed up quickly in the earned value chart, as illustrated below. Although funds were being expended at the planned rate, progress wasn't keeping up with the plan. However, with special attention to meeting *only* key requirements for later project tasks, earned value began to climb back toward plan. Near the very end of the project, the client asked for additional technology, which Viewstar easily provided in trade for Texas Instruments completing some of the high-earned-value production tasks themselves, thereby bringing the project in only one percent over budget.

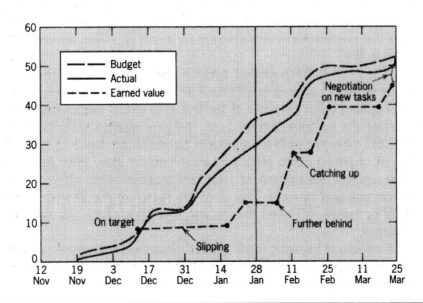

other PC project management software packages.) Note that the project is reported on at the work package level. The first two tasks, *Contact Organizations* and *Banquet and Refreshments* have been completed, and the third task, *Publicity and Promotion* is currently underway. The first four work packages under *Publicity and Promotion* have been completed, but the fifth and seventh are only partially finished. The sixth has not been started, nor has the fourth task, *Facilities*, been started. A compressed Gantt chart is shown on the right side.

The three columns of data on the right, BAC, FAC, and Variance, are "Budget at Completion," "Forecast at Completion" and the Variance or difference between BAC and FAC. For all activities that have been completed, BAC = BCWP and FAC = ACWP. The work packages that have not been completed, however, tell a different story. *Advertise in college paper* is 50 percent complete, and *Organize posters* is 45 percent complete. (The percent complete data are from another report.) *Class announcements* has not yet been started. Note that for *Advertise in the college paper*, the BCWP is 50 percent of the BCWS, which is to say that $82.50 is 50 percent of the BAC and FAC. Similarly for *Organize posters*, with $335.25 being 45 percent of BAC and FAC ($335.25/.45 = $745.00). When the two work packages are completed, however, and if there is still a cost variance, then BAC and FAC will no longer be equal. For a completed work package, the cost variance BCWP – ACWP = BAC – FAC.

Cost/Schedule Control System Criteria (C/SCSC)

C/SCSC was developed by the U.S. Department of Defense in the late 1960s and for many years was required for defense projects. While it is no longer a requirement for DOD projects, it is still requested by some project funders and used by some project vendors. Fundamentally, it is an extension of earned value analysis. C/SCSC, as its name implies, spelled out a number of standards of organization, accounting, budgeting, etc., that firms must meet if they are to be considered acceptable for government contracts. For an excellent extended discussion of C/SCSC together with the process for accomplishing it, see [27]. Also, an extensive bibliography is given in [6].

The need to keep project performance, cost, and schedule related when monitoring projects has been emphasized in this chapter. This emphasis will be reinforced in Chapter 11. For purposes of control, it is just as important to emphasize the need to relate the realities of time, cost, and performance with the project's master plan. C/SCSC takes just such an approach, but there is a major caveat that must be heeded: *The set of project action plans (the project master plan) must be kept up to date.* These plans contain descriptions of each task together with estimates of the time and resources required by each. The plans are therefore the primary source of the STWPs, BCWSs, and BCWPs and the framework within which the ATWPs and ACWPs are collected.

Differences between work scheduled and work planned can develop from several different causes—for example, official change orders in the work elements required to accomplish a task, informal alterations in the methods used to accomplish specific tasks, or official or unofficial changes in the tasks to be accomplished. Similarly, cost variances can result from any of the above as well as from changes in input factor prices, changes in the accounting methods used by the project, or changes in the mix of input factors needed to accomplish a given task. If the plan is not altered to reflect such changes, comparisons between plan and actual are not meaningful.

Milestone Reporting

We referred earlier to milestone reports. A typical example of such a report is shown in Figure 10-8a, b, and Fig. 10-9. In this illustration, a sample network with milestones is shown, followed by a routine milestone report form. A model top management project status report is illustrated in the next chapter. When filled out, these reports show project status at a specific time. They serve to keep all parties up to date on what has been accomplished. If accomplishments are inadequate or late, these reports serve as starting points for remedial planning.

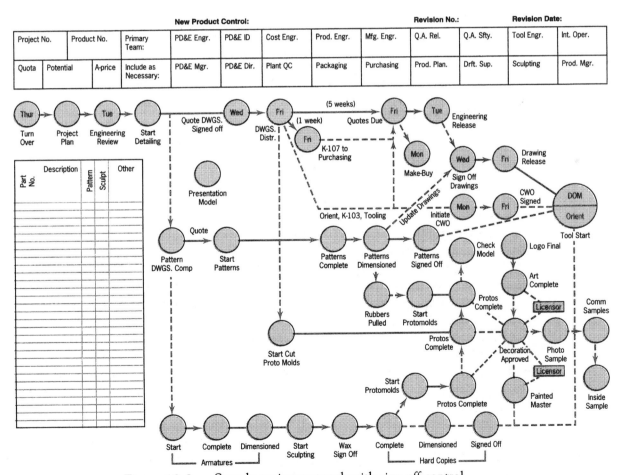

Figure 10-8a Sample project network with sign-off control.

Product Name _____ Project No. _____ Revision _____ Date _____

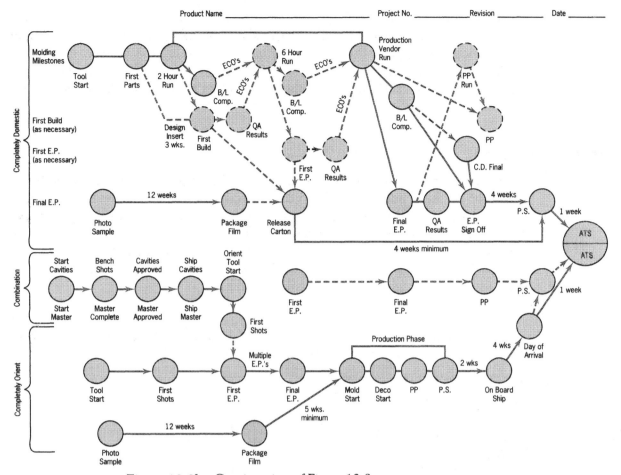

Figure 10-8b Continuation of Figure 10-8a.

Figures 10-8a and b show the network for a new product development project for a manufacturer. A steady flow of new products is an essential feature of this firm's business, and each new product is organized as a project as soon as its basic concept is approved by a project selection group. If we examine Figures 10-8a and b closely, we see that the sign-off control boxes at the top of the page correspond with sequences of events in the network. For example, look at the bottom line of the network in Figure 10-8a. The design of this product requires a sculpture that is formed on an armature. The armature must be constructed, and the sculpture of the product completed and signed off. Note that the sculpture is used as a form for making models that are, in turn, used to make the prototype product. The completion of the sculpture is signed off in the next-to-last box in the lower line of boxes at the top of the page.

A careful examination of Figure 10-8b reveals that it is a continuation of the previous page. Figure 10-8a is primarily concerned with product design and Figure 10-8b with production. The expected times for various activities are noted on the network, along with the various operations that must be performed. Figure 10-9 is a summary

NAME					PROJECT PLAN	ENGR. REVIEW	DESIGN REVIEW	QUOTE QUES.	PAT SCULP COMPL.	PAT SCULP COMPL	QUOTES DUE	MAKE BUY
PROJECT NO.	PRODUCT NO.	MFG SOURCE	TURNOVER	ORIGINAL								
A = PRICE	QUOTA	POTENTIAL		CURRENT								
				ACTUAL								

ENGR. RELEASE	PROJECT REVIEW	RELEASE DWGS.	TOOL START	PHOTO SAMPLES	INSIDE SAMPLES	PKG. FILM	INSTR. LAYOUT	INSTR. FILM ART	FINAL PARTS	FIRST EP	FINAL EP	EP SIGN-OFF	ORIENT PS	OBS	PROD. PILOT	PT SIGN-OFF	PROD. START	ATS

Figure 10-9   Milestone monitoring chart for Figures 10-8a and b.

milestone report. Each project has a series of steps that must be completed. Each has an original schedule that may be amended for use as a current schedule. Steps are completed in actual times. This form helps program managers coordinate several projects by trying to schedule the various steps to minimize the degree to which the projects interfere with one another by being scheduled for the same facilities at the same time.

The next section of this chapter, which discusses computerized project management information systems, contains several other examples of project reports.

10.3 COMPUTERIZED PMIS (PROJECT MANAGEMENT INFORMATION SYSTEMS)

The project examples used in Chapters 8 and 9 were small, so that the concepts could be demonstrated. But real projects are often extremely large, with hundreds of tasks and thousands of work units. Diagramming, scheduling, and tracking all these tasks is clearly a job for the computer, and computerized PMISs were one of the earlier business applications for computers. Initially, the focus was on simple scheduling packages, but this quickly extended to include costs, earned values, variances, management reports, and so on.

The earlier packages ran on large, expensive mainframe computers; thus, only the larger firms had access to them. Still, the use of these packages for managing projects on a day-to-day basis was not particularly successful. This was because of the inability of project managers to update plans in real time, mainframe computers typically being run in a batch rather than online mode. With the development and proliferation of microcomputers, and the corresponding availability of a wide variety of project management software, project managers use one or more PMISs.

These new microcomputer-based PMISs are considerably more sophisticated than earlier systems and use the microcomputer's graphics, color, and other features more extensively. Many systems can handle almost any size project, being limited only by the memory available in the computer. Many will handle multiple projects and link them together to detect resource over-allocation; e.g., Microsoft Project 98® can consolidate more than 1000 projects. The PMIS trend of the early 1990s has been to integrate the project management software with spreadsheets, databases, word processors, communication, graphics, and the other capabilities of Windows-based software packages. The current trend is to facilitate the global sharing of project information, including complete status reporting, through local networks as well as the Internet.

In this section, we will illustrate some output from one project management software package, Microsoft's Project 98® (MP98). A survey of project management tools recently published in *Project Management Journal* [19] polled 1000 members of the Project Management Institute and listed MP98 as being used by 48.4 percent of respondents. Primavera Project Planner®, a system designed for very large projects, used by 13.8 percent was second. The development of these and other powerful software systems was accompanied by the development of desktop computers with memory, power, and speed undreamed of a few years ago. With project files stored in large memory banks on anything from a mainframe machine, to a minicomputer, and more frequently to workstations, servers, and PC's the software and project files became available on LAN and WAN systems, as well as through the Internet.

This area is developing so rapidly that any information given must be considered dated by the time it reaches print. The reader interested in current capabilities would be wise to refer to recent annual or monthly software reviews such as those in the Project Management Institute's 1999 Software Survey [50], *PC Magazine* [43], and *Federal Computer News* [44]. Of additional interest are the comments frequently appearing in *PM Network,* especially Harvey Levine's "Software Forum" column. Reviews of software are also widely available on the Internet at such magazine-sponsored Web sites as "qualitymag.com" and "zdnet.com." or sites sponsored by the software producers.

Current Software

The explosive growth of project management software during the early 1990s saw the creation of more than 500 packages. This software came in a wide variety of capabilities and prices. Some packages cost less than $50, and a few cost more than $100,000. A large majority, however, fall in the $400–$5,000 bracket and many of these sell for around $500. The mainstream products have roughly similar capabilities, with each having its individual strengths and weaknesses. The simple fact that the lower cost programs generally do not have the ability to do everything an experienced project manager might want has led to the rapid growth of a different type of software, the "add-on." Add-on software is specially crafted to accomplish specific tasks and to be fully compatible, sometimes almost seamlessly so, with specific general project management packages. Microsoft's market dominance means that a lion's share of the add-on software is compatible with MP98.

Until recently, most project management software was unable to handle three-time PERT input, and even now the ability to deal with cost and shedule risk management problems is quite limited. The result is that there are risk management add-on programs available. (We noted several in our discussion of simulation in

DILBERT reprinted by permission of United Features Syndicate, Inc.

Chapter 8.) These add-ons can handle quite sophisticated stochastic problems and transport information easily between the add-on and the host program. With the ability to perform simulations on project schedules or resource usage, the PM can observe the probable results of many different assumptions about resource availability and schedule uncertainties.

The prevalence of multiple project firms as well as the increasing number of firms that are project-oriented have lead to the demand for software that will combine the data records for all projects into a single database. The purpose is to allow the PM to aggregate resource requirements, more easily spot resource and schedule conflicts, and to report on resource usage, personnel time charges, and the like to the firm's accounting system. These add-ons are often referred to as "consolidators" or "repositories" and "time capture" programs. (For an interesting description of such systems and the requirements they meet, see [29]). Additional add-ons deal with extensions to the earned value calculations, conformity with C/SCSC accounting and reporting rules, specialized cost management programs, responsibility charts, preparation of files for Internet use, e-mail systems, a variety of templates for project reports, LAN and WAN communication systems and workgroup capability, and so on. All this, of course, is useful if the basic project management software does not already have sufficient abilities—and if the PM needs them. While no single tool is a panacea, MP98 is a competent, easy-to-use software package and its popularity means that a large number of "add-ons" are available.

Finally, it is worth noting that these systems can very easily be misused or inappropriately applied—as can any tools. The most common error of this type is managing the PMIS rather than the project itself. This and other such errors are described by Thamhain [52] and listed below.

- *Computer paralysis.* Excessive computer involvement with computer activity replacing project management; loss of touch with the project and its realities.

- *PMIS verification.* PMIS reports may mask real project problems, be massaged to look good, or simply verify that real problems exist, yet are not acted upon.

- *Information overload.* Too many reports, too detailed, or the distribution of reports, charts, tables, data, and general information from the PMIS to too many people overwhelms managers and effectively hides problems.
- *Project isolation.* The PMIS reports replace useful and frequent communication between the project manager and top management, or even between the PM and the project team.
- *Computer dependence.* PM or top management wait for the computer reports/results to react to problems rather than being proactive and avoiding problems in the first place.
- *PMIS misdirection.* Due to the unequal coverage of the PMIS, certain project subareas are overmanaged and other areas receive inadequate attention; symptoms of problems are monitored and managed (budget overruns, schedule slippages), rather than the problems themselves.

We have also found that problems can result when someone other than the PM attempts to update projects without involving the PM in the changes.

Choosing Software

When choosing project management software, the potential user should read several software surveys conducted with project managers. We have included several in the bibliography to this chapter [for example, 1, 19, 29, and 43]. All of these are now last year's news and thus, obsolete, but they clearly indicate the sorts of capabilities that are important to most users. Avots [1] warns against reviews in computer magazines because software specialists who know little or nothing about project management often write them. We suspect that this warning is not as relevant today as it was a few years ago. We would, however, strongly warn against allowing the organization's software technicians from making the choice, unaided. Software that appeals to software specialists is not necessarily the optimal choice for the project manager.

The following characteristics of generally desirable attributes in project management software are based on a number of user surveys and the comments of experienced PMs.

- *Friendliness.* For the novice user, this includes clear and logical manuals, help screens, tutorials, a menu-driven structure, easy editing, and so on. For firms implementing project management, this means the existence of an organized training program on the use of the software conducted by trainers who have some understanding of project management.
- *Schedules.* Gantt charts are mandatory, as well as automatic recalculation with updates of times, costs, and resources. Plots of earliest start, scheduled start, slack/float, latest finish, planned finish, and actual finish times are desirable. The software should also be able to display PERT/CPM networks. The time units for schedule display (and resource usage) should vary from minutes to months. The ability to handle three-time schedule inputs is desirable.

- *Calendars.* Either a job shop and/or calendar dates are necessary, plus the ability to indicate working days, nonworking days, and holidays for each resource used.

- *Budgets.* The ability to include a budget for planning, monitoring, and control. Especially desirable is the ability to interface this with a spreadsheet program.

- *Reports.* Individualizing report formats is most desirable. Again, having the ability to interface the reports with a word processing package is highly desirable.

- *Graphics.* The ability to see the schedule and interactions is especially important. For Gantt charts, the software should be able to show the technical dependencies between work units or tasks.

- *Charts.* Charts for responsibility and histograms for resources were deemed particularly useful.

- *Migration.* The ability to transfer data to and from spreadsheets, word processors, database programs, graphics programs, and desired add-on programs. The ability to interface with telecommunication systems and the Internet is required for most applications.

- *Consolidation.* The ability to aggregate multiple projects into a single database for determination of total resource usage and detection of resource conflicts. The software must have the ability to recalculate all schedules and resource records when updated information is added.

It is heartening to note that many of the current project management software packages have available almost all of the characteristics noted above. It is important, however, to remember that no one package will meet all needs. Numerous trade-offs exist not only between price and capability but also between functional capability, ease of use, complexity, and speed. In general, there are five areas of PMIS internal capabilities, separate from the ability to migrate data and communicate externally, that should be considered. These are project planning, resource management, tracking/monitoring, report generation, and decision aiding.

The potential purchaser of a PMIS should consider the intended use of the package, the background and needs of all the potential users, and the organizational setting where the package is to be employed, including the needs and orientation of those who will be receiving the reports and graphics.

A general PMIS selection process roughly based on Levine's excellent work [31] is as follows:

1. Establish a comprehensive set of selection criteria, considering capabilities in project planning, resource management, tracking/monitoring, report generation, earned value/variance analysis, risk management.

2. Set priorities for the criteria, separating "must have" items from "nice to have" items and "not needed" items.

3. Conduct a preliminary evaluation of the software packages relative to the criteria using vendor-supplied data, product reviews, and software surveys.

4. Limit the candidate packages to three and obtain demos of each, evaluating the vendors at the same time in terms of interest, software maintenance, and support.

5. Evaluate each package with a standard project typical of your current and projected future needs. Make note of any weaknesses or strengths that are particularly relevant to your situation.

6. Negotiate on price, particularly if you are making a volume purchase or contemplating a site license. Include descriptions of vendor support, training, and product maintenance in the contract.

Typical Software Output

Figures 10-10 to 10-17 illustrate some typical outputs available from MP98. This package, along with several others, is a good product, not difficult to learn and use. Figure 10-10 is an action plan for a "software evaluation project" with three levels of tasks, task durations, and predecessors. From this information, MP98 produces a

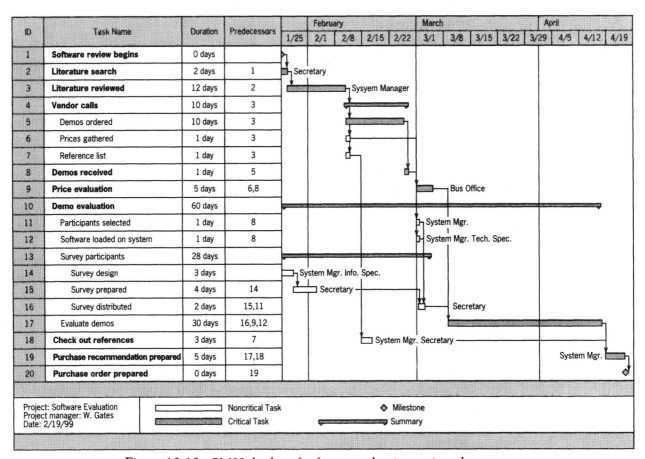

Figure 10-10 PM98 display of software evaluation action plan.

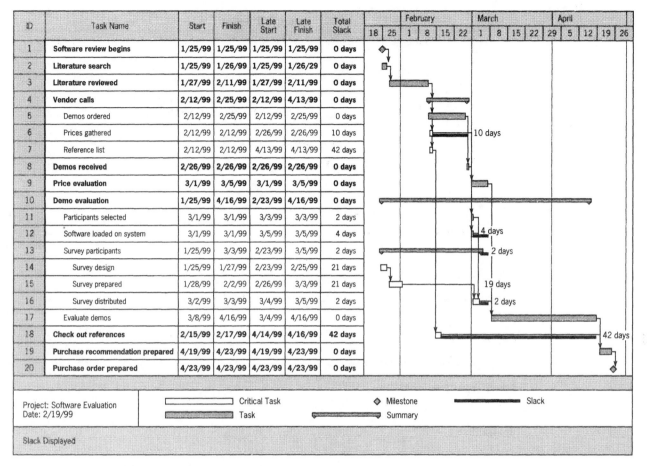

Figure 10-11 PM98 software evaluation plan with early and late start and finish dates and slack.

Gantt chart complete with arrows showing technological dependencies and listing the types of resources required for each activity. To illustrate the output flexibility, note Figure 10-11 that shows the same project, now with a starting date of January 25, 1999. Early and late starts and finishes are calculated and slack is determined for each activity—note that slack can be shown on the Gantt chart as well as in the data columns. The first column of both figures shows task numbers. A simple command will replace these with WBS numbers.

Figure 10-12 is the MP98 March 1999 calendar for a project designed to produce a video tape. Critical activities are shown with dark cross-hatching, and task duration as well as the appropriate resource(s) is noted for each activity. Lightly shaded days (Saturday and Sunday) are nonworkdays. Other holidays, or a fractional day schedule can be easily added to the calendar. A Gantt chart of this project is shown in Figure 10-13 with critical tasks highlighted, and resources noted for each activity. Figure 10-14 shows the AON network version of the video tape project. Notation in the nodes shows WBS numbers, task duration, and early start and finish times for each

		March 1999				
Sunday	Monday	Tuesday	Wednesday	Thursday	Friday	Saturday
	1	**2**	**3**	**4**	**5**	**6**
	Project approval / Begin scheduling	Script writing, 14 days, Script Writer / Propose shoots, 5 days, Producer, Client, Script Writer / Hire secretary, 12 days, Producer				
7	**8**	**9**	**10**	**11**	**12**	**13**
		Script writing, 14 days, Script Writer / Hire secretary, 12 days, Producer				
14	**15**	**16**	**17**	**18**	**19**	**20**
	Script writing, 14 days, Script Writer / Hire secretary, 12 days, Producer			Schedule shoots, 5 days, Secretary / Script approval, 8 days, Client, Producer		
21	**22**	**23**	**24**	**25**	**26**	**27**
	Schedule shoots, 5 days, Secretary / Scheduling complete / Script approval, 8 days, Client, Producer					
28	**29**	**30**	**31**			
	Script approval, 8 days, Client, Producer		Revise script, 5 days, Producer, Script Writer			

Project: Producing a Video Tape   Critical Tasks Highlighted

Figure 10-12   PM98 March calendar for video tape production project, critical path highlighted.

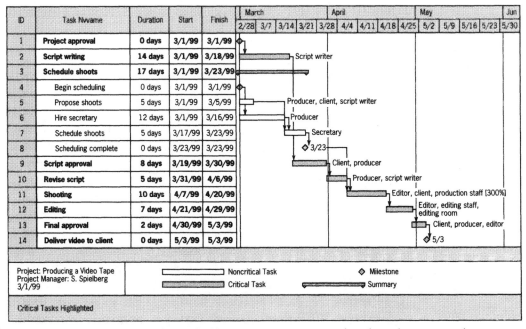

Figure 10-13   PM98 Gantt chart of video tape project, critical path and resources shown.

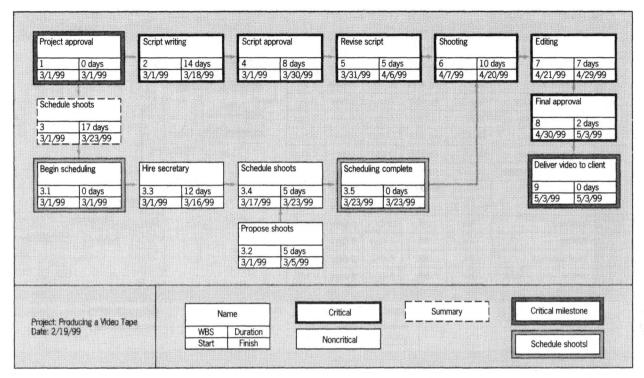

Figure 10-14   PM98 AON network with critical path, resources, dates, and WBS numbers.

activity. The critical path is shown in bold and milestones have a special frame. In Figure 10-15, the software evaluation project (see Figure 10-10) is shown as a network. This view shows the technological dependencies at all levels of the project together with activity WBS numbers.

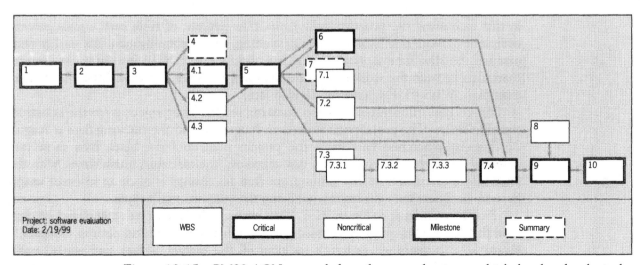

Figure 10-15   PM98 AON network for software evaluation, multiple-level technological connections shown.

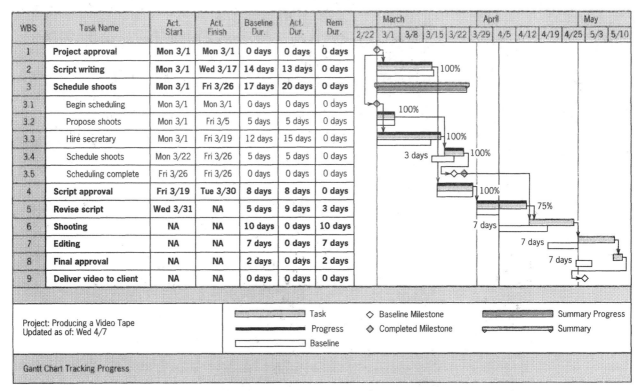

WBS	Task Name	Act. Start	Act. Finish	Baseline Dur.	Act. Dur.	Rem Dur.
1	Project approval	Mon 3/1	Mon 3/1	0 days	0 days	0 days
2	Script writing	Mon 3/1	Wed 3/17	14 days	13 days	0 days
3	Schedule shoots	Mon 3/1	Fri 3/26	17 days	20 days	0 days
3.1	Begin scheduling	Mon 3/1	Mon 3/1	0 days	0 days	0 days
3.2	Propose shoots	Mon 3/1	Fri 3/5	5 days	5 days	0 days
3.3	Hire secretary	Mon 3/1	Fri 3/19	12 days	15 days	0 days
3.4	Schedule shoots	Mon 3/22	Fri 3/26	5 days	5 days	0 days
3.5	Scheduling complete	Fri 3/26	Fri 3/26	0 days	0 days	0 days
4	Script approval	Fri 3/19	Tue 3/30	8 days	8 days	0 days
5	Revise script	Wed 3/31	NA	5 days	9 days	3 days
6	Shooting	NA	NA	10 days	0 days	10 days
7	Editing	NA	NA	7 days	0 days	7 days
8	Final approval	NA	NA	2 days	0 days	2 days
9	Deliver video to client	NA	NA	0 days	0 days	0 days

Project: Producing a Video Tape
Updated as of: Wed 4/7

Task — Baseline Milestone ◇ — Summary Progress
Progress — Completed Milestone ◇ — Summary
Baseline

Gantt Chart Tracking Progress

Figure 10-16   PM98 Gantt chart tracking progress of video tape project.

Displays of project progress are available, also. Figure 10-16 shows the status on April 7, 1999 for the video tape project which was started on March 1, 1999. The status date is shown with a vertical line on the display. Schedule slippage is shown on the Gantt chart, and the column data allow a comparison between planned and actual duration for each completed activity. The chart also shows percent completion, in this case using the proportionality rule that percent of time used equals percent completion. Note that WBS #2, Script writing, was accomplished a day earlier than planned, but the summary task, Schedule shoots (WBS #3) took three days longer than plan because the work unit, Hire secretary (WBS #3/3) took three days longer than plan. WBS #5, Revise script, is also late.

Figure 10-17 illustrates a project tracking report. The project is for the construction of a house. The project was started on August 2, and the tracking date is August 22. The cross-hatched bars show the project plan, and the black bars show task progress. The dates shown for each task represent the task start finish times, with the finish times calculated on the assumption that no change is made in resource usage. Percent complete data was estimated using the proportionality rule.

Finally, refer back to Figure 10-7. This earned value chart was calculated on data from the Career Day planning project used to illustrate an action plan in Chapter 5, Figure 5-2. As described earlier, it includes all the budget, actual, and earned value figures for each work package in the project, as well as projections at completion. Note again that we have corrected the software's error in signs on the cost variance and BAC-FAC variance.

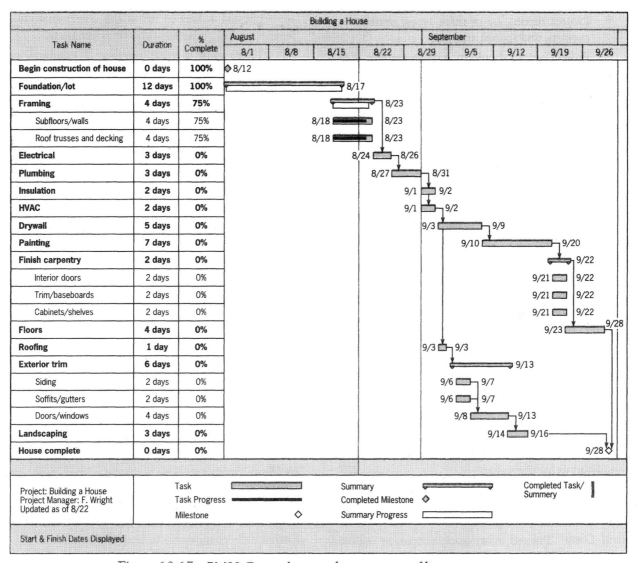

Figure 10-17   PM98 Gantt chart tracking progress of house construction project.

SUMMARY

In this chapter, we reviewed the monitoring function, relating it to project planning and control, and described its role in the project implementation process. The requirements for monitoring were discussed, in addition to data needs and reporting considerations. Last, some techniques for monitoring progress were illustrated and some computerized PMISs were described.

Specific points made in the chapter were these:

- It is important that the planning-monitoring-

controlling cycle be a closed loop cycle based on the same structure as the parent system.

- The first task in designing the monitoring system is to identify the key factors in the project action plan to be monitored and to devise standards for them. The factors should concern results, rather than activities.

- The data collected are usually either frequency counts, numbers, subjective numeric ratings, indicators, or verbal measures.

- Project reports are of three types: routine, exception, and special analysis.

- Project reports should include an amount of detail appropriate to the target level of management with a frequency appropriate to the need for control (i.e., probably not weekly or other such regular basis). More commonly, reports occur near milestone dates.

- Three common project reporting problems are too much detail, poor correspondence to the parent firm's reporting system, and a poor correspondence between the planning and monitoring systems.

- The earned value chart depicts scheduled progress, actual cost, and actual progress (earned value) to allow the determination of spending, schedule, and time variances.

- There exist a great number of computerized PMISs that are available for PMs, with software evaluations occurring regularly in various magazines.

- Project managers' preferred PMIS features were friendliness, schedules, calendars, budgets, reports, graphics, networks, charts, migration, and consolidation.

In the next chapter, we move into the final phase of project implementation, project control. We discuss the different types of control and describe some techniques useful to the PM in controlling the project.

 ## GLOSSARY

Computer Paralysis Excessive fascination or activity with the computer rather than the project itself such that the project suffers.

Cost Variance The budgeted cost of the work performed less the actual cost of the work performed.

Earned Value An approach for monitoring project progress that relies on the budgeted cost of activities completed to ascribe value.

Friendliness When applied to computer use, this term refers to how easy it is to learn and/or use a computer or software package.

Hard Copy Printed information output, as opposed to screen output.

Information Overload Having an excess of information so that the information desired is difficult to locate.

Migration The ability to move files and data between software packages.

Monitor To keep watch in order to take action when progress fails to match plans.

Schedule Variance The budgeted cost of work completed less the budgeted cost of work scheduled at this time.

Software The instructions for running a computer.

Spending Variance The budgeted cost of work completed less the actual cost at this time.

Spreadsheet A matrix of data used with a computer. As the data in particular cells are changed, the results of other cells change also to keep in accordance.

Time Variance The scheduled time for the work completed less the actual time.

Variance A deviation from plan or expectation.

Windowing A computer software feature that allows different functions to be conducted in a separate section of the screen, called a window.

QUESTIONS

Material Review Questions

1. Define *monitoring*. Are there any additional activities that should be part of the monitoring function?

2. Identify the key factors that need to be considered when setting up a monitoring system.

3. List some factors that would be difficult to monitor.

4. Describe routine reports and some problems with them.

5. What are the primary difficulties experienced in the design of project reports?

6. Describe the three variances of an earned value chart and explain their significance.

Class Discussion Questions

10. Discuss the benefits of timely, appropriate, detailed information. How can a value be assigned to these characteristics?

11. What are the advantages for a PM of having a computerized system over a manual one? The disadvantages?

12. A project is usually a one-time activity with a well-defined purpose. What is the justification of setting up a PMIS for such a project?

13. A more intensive, and extensive, monitoring system is needed in project management than in a functional organization. Why?

14. The earned value chart is an attempt to put the three-dimensional concept of Figure 1-1 (see

Questions for Project Management in Practice

Using Project Management Software to Schedule Olympic Games

21. Why did they need drawings of every site, building, and room?

22. How do you think they did planning for the bad weather?

23. Was scheduling the difficult aspect of planning the games or the logistics?

Tracking Scope Creep: A Project Manager Responds

24. Is the point of the letter to the editor about scope creep, or tracking? What is it about?

25. The author criticizes the selection of engineers for

7. Can you identify other symptoms of computer misuse besides those in section 10.3?

8. What types of measures do data come in?

9. What is "earned value"?

Chapter 1) into a two-dimensional format. Is it successful? What is missing?

15. How might a variance be traced back to its source?

16. How would a Project Management Information System differ from an ordinary Management Information System?

17. What type of general purpose software might project managers find useful?

18. How should a PMIS be chosen?

19. Discuss the uses of a PMIS in the different stages of the project life cycle.

20. Is it unethical, in an attempt to avoid a "shoot-the-messenger" response, to simply not mention bad news?

projects. Is the author saying engineers don't make good project managers?

26. In terms of monitoring and tracking, which of the ten oversights is probably most critical?

Success through Earned Value at Texas Instruments

27. Isn't arbitrarily reducing the available budget for tasks dangerous? What was ViewStar's probable strategic thinking here?

28. What would be the motivation of a project team that immediately falls behind schedule?

29. How did the trade late in the project between ViewStar and Texas Instruments probably operate?

▪ PROBLEMS

1. Find the schedule and cost variances for a project that has an actual cost at month 22 of $540,000, a scheduled cost of $523,000, and an earned value of $535,000.

2. A project at month 5 had an actual cost of $34,000, a planned cost of $42,000, and a value completed of $39,000. Find the spending and schedule variances and the CPI and SPI.

3. A construction project at day 70 exhibits an actual cost of $78,000, and a scheduled cost of $84,000. The foreman estimates a value completed of $81,000. What are the spending and schedule variances and CSI? Estimate the time variance.

4. A project to develop a county park has an actual cost in month 17 of $350,000, a planned cost of $475,000, and a value completed of $300,000. Find

the spending and schedule variances and the three indexes.

5. A regrading and surfacing project has an actual cost in month 10 of $23,000, a scheduled cost of $17,000, and a value completed of $20,000. Find the schedule and cost variances and the three indexes.

6. A project to develop a new type of telecommunications satellite at day 65 is 5 days behind schedule. It had a planned cost of $735,000 for this point in time, but the actual cost is only $550,000. Estimate the schedule and spending variances. Re-estimate the variances if the actual cost had been $750,000.

7. Given an activity in an advertising project whose planned cost was $12,000 but actual cost to date is $10,000 so far and the value completed is only 70%, calculate the spending and schedule variances. Will the client be pleased or angry?

8. For the following equipment installation project at week 6, calculate the cost, schedule, and time variances. Also calculate the CPI, SPI, CSI, and the ECT and Total Work Unit Cost estimate.

Activity	Predecessors	Duration (Weeks)	Budget, $	Actual Cost, $	% Complete
a	—	2	300	400	100
b	—	3	200	180	100
c	a	2	250	300	100
d	a	5	600	400	20
e	b,c	4	400	200	20

9. At week 24 of the following project, shoot a television commercial, what should the expenditures be? If the earned value is right on schedule but the actual expenses are $9000, what are the cost and schedule variances? What are the three indexes, the ECT, and the estimated Total Work Unit Cost?

Activity	Predecessors	Duration (Weeks)	Budget, $
a	—	6	900
b	—	6	1200
c	a	6	1200
d	a	12	1800
e	b,c	14	1400
f	b,c,d	10	1500
g	d,e	16	800

 INCIDENTS FOR DISCUSSION

Jackson Excavating Company

Mark Suturana joined Jackson Excavating Company six months ago. He is an experienced management information systems executive who has been given the task of improving the responsiveness of Jackson's data processing group to the end user. After several months of investigation, Mark felt certain he understood the current situation clearly enough to proceed. First, approximately 90 percent of all end user requests came to data processing (DP) in the form of a project, with the DP output either the final product of the project, or, more commonly, one step of a project. Accordingly, Mark felt he should initially direct his efforts toward integrating DP's approach to projects with the company's formal project management system.

It has been Mark's experience that most problems associated with DP projects revolve around poor project definition and inadequate participation by the end user during the system design phase. Typically, the end user does not become heavily involved in the project until the new system is ready to install. At that point, a great deal of work is required to adapt the system to meet end-user requirements. Mark decided to institute a procedure that put end-user cooperation and participation on the front end of the project. The idea was to define the objective and design of the system so thoroughly that implementation would become almost mechanical in nature rather than an introduction to the end user of "his or her new system."

Mark also recognized that something had to be done to control the programming quality of DP's out put. A more effective front-end approach to DP projects would subject DP managers to more intense pressure to produce results within user's needs, including time constraints. Mark was concerned that the quality of the DP output would deteriorate under those conditions, especially given the lack of technical expertise on the part of end users and outside project managers. To solve this problem, Mark recommended the creation of a DP quality assurance (QA) manager who would approve the initial steps of the projects and review each additional step. The QA manager would have the authority to declare any step or portion of the output inadequate and to send it back to be reworked.

Questions: Is this a good control system for DP? Why or why not? Does it also represent a good control point for company projects using DP to accomplish one portion of the project objective? What would your answer be if you were a non-DP project manager?

The U.S. Army Corps of Engineers

The U.S. Army Corps of Engineers has contracted with a medium-size excavation firm to construct a small series of three earthen dams as part of a flood control project in North Carolina. For economic reasons, dams #1 and #2 have to be constructed at the same time and dam #3 can only be built after #1 and #2 are completed. There is also a very important scheduled completion date that has to be met (relating to next year's flood season). The project is being handled by Bryan Johnson, who has been with the company for about a year.

This is a new job for Bryan in that he had never before headed more than one project at a time. About three months into the building of dams #1 and #2, he began to notice an information problem. He had supervisors from dams #1 and #2 reporting to him, but he never knew how far along they were in relation to each other. Since dam #3 cannot be built until both dams are fully complete, he cannot tell if it will be started on time and therefore completed on time. Realizing the situation was becoming serious, he began to wonder about how he could coordinate the projects. How could he tell where the projects were in relation to each other? How far were they *jointly* behind? Bryan's major problem was his inability to monitor and record the dual projects effectively.

Questions: What would you recommend to Bryan?

BIBLIOGRAPHY

1. AVOTS, I. "How Useful Are the Mass Market Project Management Systems?" *Project Management Journal,* August 1987.
2. BARR, Z. "Earned Value Analysis: A Case Study." *PM Network,* December 1996.
3. BOBROWSKI, P. M. "Project Management Control Problems: An Information Systems Focus." *Project Management Journal,* June. 1989.
4. BRACKETT, S. W., and A. M. ISBELL. "PMIS-An Integrated Approach for the Management and Distribution of Project Information." *Project Management Journal,* September 1989.
5. BRANDON, D. M., Jr. "Implementing Earned Value Easily and Effectively." *Project Management Journal,* June 1998.
6. CHRISTENSEN, D. S. "A Review of Cost/Schedule Control Systems Criterion Literature." *Project Management Journal,* September 1994.
7. CLELAND, D. I., and W. R. KING. *Systems Analysis and Project Management,* 3rd ed. New York: McGraw-Hill, 1983.
8. DEAN, B. V. *Evaluating, Selecting, and Controlling R & D Projects.* New York: American Management Association Research Study 89, 1968.
9. EVANS, J. R., and W. M. LINDSAY. *The Management and Control of Quality,* 2nd ed. Minneapolis: West, 1993.
10. FARID, F., and KANGARI, R. "A Knowledge-Based System for Selecting Project Management Microsoftware Packages." *Project Management Journal,* September 1991.
11. FERSKO-WEISS, H. "Project Management Software

Gets A Grip on Usability." *PC Magazine*, July 1992.

12. FLEMMING, Q. W., and J. M. KOPPELMAN. *Earned Value Project Management*. Upper Darby, PA: Project Management Institute, 1996.

13. FLEMMING, Q. W., and J. M. KOPPELMAN. "The Earned Value Body of Knowledge." *PM Network*, May 1996.

14. FLEMMING, Q. W., and J. M. KOPPELMAN. "Forecasting the Final Cost and Schedule Results." *PM Network*, January 1996.

15. FLEMMING, Q. W., and J. M. KOPPELMAN. "Taking Step Four With Earned Value: Establish the Project Baseline. *PM Network*, May 1995.

16. FLEMMING, Q. W., and J. M. KOPPELMAN. "Taking Step Three With Earned Value: Estimate and Budget Resources." *PM Network*, January 1995.

17. FLEMMING, Q. W., and J. M. KOPPELMAN "The 'Earned Value' " Concept: Back to The Basics." *PM Network*, January 1994.

18. FORD, R. C., and F. S. MCLAUGHLIN. "Ten Questions and Answers on Managing MIS Projects." *Project Management Journal*, September 1992.

19. FOX, T. L., and J. W. SPENCE. "Tools of the Trade: A Survey of Project Management Tools." *Project Management Journal*, September 1998.

20. GARREHY, P. J. "Project Managers Need Real-Time Data—and a Couple of ERP Modules of Their Own." *PM Network*, February 1999.

21. HATFIELD, M. A. "The Case for Earned Value." *PM Network*, December 1996.

22. JAY, A. "How to Run a Meeting." *IEEE Engineering Management Review*, Winter 1995 reprinted from the *Harvard Business Review*, March–April 1976.

23. JENSEN, C. A. "A Project Manager's On-Ramp to the Information Superhighway." *PM Network*, October 1996.

24. JOHNSON, R. V. "Resource Constrained Scheduling Capabilities of Commercial Project Management Software." *Project Management Journal*, December 1992.

25. KIDDER, T. *The Soul of a New Machine*. Boston: Little, Brown, 1981.

26. KNUTSON, J. "How to Prepare and Conduct a Project Review." *PM Network*, October 1996.

27. LAMBERT, L. R. "Cost/Schedule Control System Criteria (C/SCSC): An Integrated Project Management Approach Using Earned Value Techniques." In P. C. Dinsmore, ed., *The AMA Handbook of Project Management*. New York: AMACOM, 1993.

28. LEE, T. "Project Management for the Rest of Us." *Datamation*, January 1, 1993.

29. LEVINE, H. A. "PMI '97: A Report on the Exhibits." *PM Network*, January 1998.

30. LEVINE, H. A. "The Usability Factor: A Follow-Up." *PM Network*, January 1994.

31. LEVINE, H. A. "PM Software Forum." *Project Management Journal*, 1987 in (all issues). See "Hints for Software Selection," June and December 1987.

32. LEVINE, H. A. *Project Management Using Microcomputers*. Berkeley, CA: Osborne/McGraw-Hill, 1986.

33. LIBRATORE, M. J. "A Decision Support System Linking Research and Development." *Project Management Journal*, November 1988.

34. MANDAKOVIC, T., and L. A. SMITH. "Defining Project Management Software." *Proceedings*, Decision Sciences Institute, November 1986.

35. MATTHEWS, M. D. "A Conceptual Framework for Project Management Software." *Project Management Journal*, August 1987.

36. MCFARLAN, W. "Portfolio Approach to Information Systems." *Journal of Systems Management*, January 1982.

37. National Software Testing Laboratories, Inc. "Ratings Report." *Software Digest*, October 1991.

38. NEVISON, J. M. "Creative Time Wasting." *PM Network*, November 1995.

39. PALLA, R. W. "Introduction to Microcomputer Software Tools for Project Information Management." *Project Management Journal*, August 1987.

40. PARTOVI, F. Y., and J. BURTON. "Timing of Monitoring and Control of CPM Projects." *IEEE Transactions on Engineering Management*, February 1993.

41. POSPISIL, C. J. "A PC-Based Scheduling System for a Transmission and Distribution Construction Department." *Project Management Journal*, September 1990.

42. Project Management Institute Standards Committee. *A Guide to the Project Management Body of*

Knowledge. Upper Darby, PA: Project Management Institute, 1996.

43. "Project Management—Editor's Choice." *PC Magazine,* June 30, 1998.

44. "Project Management Software." *Federal Computer Week,* October 6, 1997. (Refer to http://www.few.com/pubs/gbb/1997/1006/gbbprojman-10-06-1997.html)

45. RAKOS, J. J. *Software Project Management.* Englewood Cliffs, NJ: Prentice Hall, 1990.

46. RANDALL, P. *Lotus Guide to One-Two-Three: Release 2.2.* New York: Lotus Books,1990.

47. REINGOLD, J. "Project Management in the Information Age." *PM Network,* May 1996.

48. SHAFER, S. M., and J. R. MEREDITH. *Operations Management: A Process Approach with Spreadsheets.* New York: Wiley, 1998.

49. SINGLETARY, N. "What's the Value of Earned Value?" *PM Network,* December 1996.

50. Software Survey, *Project Management Institute,* April 1999.

51. SPINNER, M. *Elements of Project Management: Plan, Schedule, and Control.* Englewood Cliffs, NJ: Prentice Hall, 1981.

52. THAMHAIN, H. J. "The New Product Management Software and Its Impact on Management Style." *Project Management Journal,* August 1987.

53. YAHDAV, D. "Project Spotlight: Project Management Gets Easier." *Computerworld,* October 19, 1992.

The following reading reports the results of a survey of PMI members concerning the computer tools they employ. The results identify the tools they use, their level of use, what they are used for, satisfaction with the tools, training received on the tools, and the adequacy of the tools. Software beyond project management packages are included in the survey.

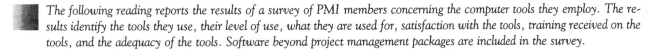

DIRECTED READING

SURVEY OF PROJECT MANAGEMENT TOOLS

T. L. Fox and J. W. Spence: Tools of the Trade: A Survey of Project Management Tools.
Project Management Journal, September 1998.
©1998 by the Project Management Institute. Reprinted by permission.

For carpenters, it is a hammer. For pilots, it is an instrument panel. For surgeons, it is a scalpel. These devices represent a primary tool of the trade for their users. Tools of the trade are those vital instruments without which completion of the tasks required for the job would be very difficult. In attempts to better serve the users of the tool, new features or enhancements are introduced periodically. However, sometimes these "improvements" can have unanticipated consequences, either negative or positive. For example, several versions of ergonomically improved hammers have been produced, but without successful adoption. When digital capabilities with specific, numeric displays were introduced into the cockpit of airplanes, pilots, who were accustomed to simply being able to scan their analog instruments, had to rethink the way in which they assessed their environment and physically "lock on" to the digital information. On the other hand, the introduction of lasers as surgical instruments has revolutionized the surgeons' job.

Virtually every profession has what would generally be regarded as special "tools of the trade," and project management is certainly no exception. A number of individuals have stated that the key to effective project management is the ability to track and control the progress of system projects (Rook, 1986; Zmud, 1980). Considering that many, if not most, projects are composed of hundreds of interrelated tasks, trying to track and control all those tasks effectively turns into a management nightmare. Therefore, using a computerized project management tool has become essential to achieving the requirements of effective project management (Moder, 1994; Shenhar & Laufer, 1995; Weil, 1986). Yet, we must be ever mindful that "improvements" in these tools should yield positive consequences for project managers, and therefore such "improvements" should be reevaluated periodically.

This paper presents the results of a nationwide survey (see Appendix) of project managers who provided insight into their "tools of the trade," along with assessments of satisfaction, training, and use made of these tools. A discussion of each element is presented, followed by a conclusion regarding the current state of project managers' tools of the trade.

The Survey

A nationwide survey was sent to almost 1,000 project managers. These individuals were randomly selected from the membership of the Project Management Institute (PMI) and represented a cross-section of the entire United States, many different industries and varying company sizes. The accompanying cover letter asked the participants to complete the survey only if their primary job responsibilities included project management. A total of 159 responses were received, representing a response rate of 16.3%

The participants were first asked to provide various demographic information. The respondents averaged 10.4 years of project management experience and 12.4 years of experience in the field of information systems. The vast majority of participants worked for companies described as focusing either on engineering or software development, while a much smaller percentage worked for companies that focused on hardware, or were either retailers or wholesalers. The types of projects these participants either participated in or managed within the past three years were primarily for in-house use, commercially contracted, or directly marketed to external customers. The participants also indicated that a larger number of projects were worked on in the past three years with a calendar duration of six months or less, but considerably more time was expended managing those projects having a duration of greater than six months.

Next, the respondents were asked to identify as many as three computerized project management tools that they were currently using or had used within the past three years. For each of these tools the respondents were asked to list the primary use made of these tools and their level of satisfaction with the tools. The respondents were also asked to indicate (1) how much training, if any, they had received on the use of the tools, and (2) what was the perceived adequacy of this training. Lastly, the respondents were asked to indicate how much use they actually make of the tools, both with respect to the number of months the tools had been used and the number of hours per week each of the tools was used. The respondents also provided an indication of the perceived adequacy of this amount of use.

The Tools

A quick review of both the literature and the market indicates that there are many computerized project management tools available and the survey conducted confirmed those findings. The respondents generated a listing of 70 unique computerized project management tools that they were currently using or had used within the past three years. Ten of these tools were identified by almost 75% of the respondents, and therefore, subsequent analysis was limited to these top 10 choices. The top 10 most frequently listed tools and their relative percentage of respondents using those tools are shown in Table 1.

Table 1. Top 10 Project Management Tools

PM Tool (Developer)	Percentage of Respondents Listing Tool
Microsoft Project (*Microsoft Corporation*)	48.4%
Primavera Project Planner (*Primavera Systems*)	13.8%
Microsoft Excel (*Microsoft Corporation*)	8.5%
Project Workbench (*Applied Business Technology*)	8.1%
Time Line (*Time Line Solutions*)	6.1%
SureTrak (*Primavera Systems*)	5.3%
CA-SuperProject (*Computer Associates, Int'l.*)	2.8%
Project Scheduler (*Scitor*)	2.8%
Artemis Prestige (*Lucas Management Systems*)	2.0%
FasTracs (*Applied Microsystems*)	2.0%

Table 2 Project Management Software by Type of Company

Type of Company		Artemis Prestige	CA-Super Project	FasTracs	MS Excel	MS Project	Primavera Project Planner	Project Workbench	Project Scheduler	SureTrak	Time Line	Total
Software	#	2	3	1	4	36	4	11	1	2	2	66
	%	3.0	4.5	1.5	6.1	54.5	6.1	16.7	1.5	3.0	3.0	100%
Hardware	#		1		2	11		3		1	1	19
	%		5.3		10.5	57.9		15.8		5.3	5.3	100%
Engineering	#	2	3	4	16	52	22	1	5	11	11	127
	%	1.6	2.4	3.1	12.6	40.9	17.3	0.8	3.9	8.7	8.7	100%
Retail	#				2	9	2	6		2	3	24
	%				8.3	37.5	8.3	25.0		8.3	12.5	100%
Wholesale	#		1		1	8	1	2			1	14
	%		7.1		7.1	57.1	7.1	14.3			7.1	100%
Legend	1st											
	2nd											

Clearly, Microsoft Project is by far the most frequently used computerized project management tool on the market today. This is consistent with previous surveys of project management tools (Levine, 1995). Levine contributed this leap to the top of the project management software sales to Microsoft Corporation's marketing and leveraging skills rather than the superb nature of the product, and comments that Microsoft Project is "far from being the perfect project management software package." Regardless, it remains the most widely used tool.

The second most widely used project management tool, as indicated by the survey, is Primavera Project Planning (also known as "P3") from Primavera Systems. This is considered to be a high-end tool, retailing for several thousand dollars and providing significantly more capability than a low-end tool such as Microsoft Project.

It is interesting to note that the next most widely used tool marketed specifically as a project management tool, ABT Project Workbench, was actually listed by fewer respondents than Microsoft Excel. Evidently, project managers do not rely solely on software packages specifically designated as project management tools, but consider a variety of other general-purpose software tools such as spreadsheets as part of their menagerie. Other nontraditional project management tools that were mentioned by the respondents include word processing packages such as Microsoft Word and WordPerfect, presentation packages such as Microsoft PowerPoint, and database packages such as Microsoft Access.

A cross-tabulation of these top 10 project management tools in relation to the types of companies for which the participants work is shown in Table 2.

Table 2 shows both the number of users and relative percentage by tool and company type and indicates that Microsoft Project consistently is the tool of choice across company types. The second most frequently selected tool is Project Workbench for all types of companies except engineering. Engineering firms prefer Primavera Project Planner considerably more often than Project Workbench, and actually rank Project Workbench as the least used tool.

A further analysis compared which project management tools were used with respect to both the number of projects worked on having a calendar duration of either less than six months or greater than six months, and the relative percentage of time spent working on the projects. This cross-tabulation is depicted in Table 3.

Table 3. Project Management Tools by Project Duration

Type of Company		Artemis Prestige	CA-Super Project	FasTracs	MS Excel	MS Project	Primavera Project Planner	Project Workbench	Project Scheduler	SureTrak	Time Line	Total
< 6 mos.	#	1	4.9	2.4	6.9	8.5	5.1	4.2	5.7	7.4	7.4	6.85
	%	12.4	51.7	13.0	31.7	21.7	27.2	28.3	16.3	40.8	40.8	25.9%
> 6 mos.	#	3.4	2.3	2.0	5.8	5.4	6.3	3.1	22.5	5.0	5	5.65
	%	87.6	48.3	87.0	68.3	78.3	72.8	71.7	83.7	59.2	59.2	74.1%

Note: Average number of projects and average percentage of time worked on projects.

Table 4. Exclusivity of Project Management Tool Use

PM Tool	Exclusivity
Project Workbench	72.3%
Microsoft Project	58.6%
Project Scheduler	50.1%
Microsoft Excel	47.5%
Artemis Prestige	45.0%
Primavera Project Planner	37.4%
SureTrak	32.7%
Time Line	29.9%
CA-SuperProject	28.7%
FasTracs	11.0%

As indicated in Table 3, it is interesting to note that three tools—Artemis Prestige, Primavera Project Planner, and Project Scheduler—are used more often for long-term projects (greater than six calendar months duration) than short-term projects. The other seven tools are chosen more often for smaller-scale projects.

The respondents also were asked to indicate the percentage of time they used each tool compared to all tools listed. This is essentially a measure of exclusivity of use. This measure is listed in Table 4, in descending order of exclusivity. These results show that project managers who listed that they used Project Workbench, for example, use that particular tool 72.3% of the time, and use other project management tools 27.7% of the time.

In an open-ended question, the respondents were asked to indicate the primary use(s) for which they used each project management tool they had listed. A variety of responses were provided, which are summarized in Table 5.

It appears that project managers use all of the project management tools for essentially the same basic functions: planning, scheduling, tracking, and controlling their projects. Project managers also use the tools to varying degrees for budgeting and analysis.

Satisfaction With the Tools

The respondents were asked to rate, on a 5-point Likert scale, their satisfaction with each of the project management tools listed (a rating of "1" indicates a lack of satisfaction and a rating of "5" indicates excellent satisfaction). Satisfaction was measured using Doll and Torkzadeh's (1988) 12-item User Satisfaction Instrument. This instrument provides a measure of overall satisfaction, as well as a measure of satisfaction pertaining to each of five specific elements: content, accuracy, format, ease of use, and timeliness. The average satisfaction scores for each of the top 10 most fre-

Table 5. Primary Use(s) Made of Project Management Tools

PM Tool	Primary Use(s)
Artemis Prestige	Multiproject planning and tracking; scheduling resources; cost analysis
CA-SuperProject	Small and large projects; scheduling; tracking and planning; training
FasTracs	Small projects; presentations; quick Gantt charts; scheduling analysis
Microsoft Excel	Budgeting; cost analysis; variance analysis; tracking and reporting; work breakdown structures (WBS)
Microsoft Project	Small, medium, and large projects; control and tracking; detailed scheduling; early project planning; communication; high-level planning; Gantt, CPM and PERT; planning, analyzing, tracking, reporting; total project management; "everything"
Primavera Project Planner	Large, complex multiproject environments; planning, scheduling, resource allocation, control; build overall detailed project plan; critical path analysis; client requested, corporate standard
Primavera SureTrak	Single and multiple projects—small, medium, and large; project scheduling, resource allocation, control
Project Scheduler	Multiproject; scheduling, resource management, budgeting, tracking
Project Workbench	Small, medium, and large projects; planning, estimating, scheduling, analyzing, tracking, reporting; WBS, Gantt, resource utilization
Time Line	Small-to medium-sized projects; planning, tracking, and scheduling

Table 6. Satisfaction With Project Management Tools

PM Tool	Overall	Content	Accuracy	Format	Ease of Use	Timeliness
Project Scheduler	3.93	3.9	4.3	3.9	3.2	4.4
Primavera Project Planner	3.91	4.1	4.3	4.0	3.2	3.9
Project Workbench	3.90	3.9	4.3	3.8	3.5	4.1
Microsoft Excel	3.88	3.8	4.3	4.0	3.8	3.6
Primavera SureTrak	3.79	3.7	4.1	3.8	3.2	4.1
CA-SuperProject	3.75	3.8	4.3	3.8	3.0	3.8
Microsoft Project	3.64	3.5	3.9	3.6	3.6	3.8
Artemis Prestige	3.33	3.6	4.0	3.3	2.0	3.5
FasTracs	3.33	3.3	3.5	3.6	3.4	3.0
Time Line	3.24	3.0	3.5	3.2	3.2	3.6
Total	3.70	3.6	4.0	3.7	3.4	3.8

quently listed project management tools are shown in Table 6, in descending order of overall satisfaction.

Clearly, the most widely used project management tools are rated above average (an average rating is 3.0) both in overall satisfaction and for each of the five elements (the one exception being the ease-of-use rating for Artemis Prestige). Therefore, it appears that project managers are reasonably satisfied with the currently available selection of project management tools.

Training on the Tools

The respondents also provided in indication of how much training they received on the tools that they listed, as well as a measure of the perceived adequacy of this training. The measure of perceived adequacy of training on the project management tools was based on a 5-point Likert scale, with a "1" indicating totally inadequate and a "5" indicating totally adequate. Table 7 shows, in descending order, the average number of hours of training received on the 10 most frequently listed project management tools and the respective measure of perceived adequacy of this training.

Several respondents reported that they had received no training on the use of a particular tool and subsequently did not report a measure of perceived adequacy of that training. Other respondents reported that they had received no training on the use of a particular tool,

Table 7. Training on Project Management Tools

PM Tool	Hours Reported		
	Excluded		Included
	Average # of Hrs	Average Adequacy	Average Adequacy
Primavera Project Planner	31.00	3.53	3.60
Project Workbench	28.92	4.08	3.82
Project Scheduler	24.00	4.33	3.50
CA-SuperProject	16.00	3.00	2.50
Microsoft Project	13.61	3.41	3.13
Artemis Prestige	12.80	2.80	2.80
Microsoft Excel	11.43	3.29	3.20
Primavera SureTrak	9.71	3.29	2.82
Time Line	4.00	3.75	3.13
FasTracs	0.00	NA	3.00
Total	18.02	3.48	3.21

Table 8. Amount and Adequacy of the Use of Project Management Tools

PM Tool	# of Mos.	# of Hrs/Wek	Adequacy
FasTracs	39.80	1.25	5.00
Artemis Prestige	45.40	6.50	4.40
Microsoft Excel	43.78	13.00	4.39
Project Workbench	38.05	9.35	4.35
Primavera Project Planner	42.62	11.63	4.14
CA-SuperProject	31.29	5.80	4.00
Project Scheduler	24.14	11.83	4.00
Primavera SureTrak	13.23	4.15	3.85
Microsoft Project	24.49	6.06	3.83
Time Line	43.54	5.10	2.90
Total	30.81	7.51	3.96

but subsequently did provide a measure of adequacy on the training, or lack thereof, on the tool. For example, every respondent who listed FasTracs reported that they had received no training on the use of the tool. However, several of these respondents rated the adequacy of the training, or lack thereof, which resulted in a mean score of 3.0. Overall, both measures of the perceived adequacy of training were above an average rating of 3.0, and thus it appears that project managers consider the training they receive on the use of the project management tools to be reasonably adequate.

Considering that several project managers reported a measure of perceived adequacy of training even if they had not received any training, a further analysis was conducted comparing the adequacy of training scores on those participants receiving training, regardless of how little, to those participants who did not receive training. Levene's (1960) test for equality of variance indicated that the variances were significantly different ($s_{training} = 3.48$, $s_{no\ training} = 2.67$, $F = 25.09$, $p = .000$). A t-test assuming unequal variances resulted in a significant t value of -3.65 (df $= 86.42$, $p = .000$), which confirmed this finding. Thus, obtaining even minimal training on the use of project management tools has a significant impact on perceived adequacy of training. Not surprisingly, the number of hours of training received and the perceived adequacy of this training were found to be significantly related and positively correlated. In other words, the more training, the better.

Additionally, the relationship between the measure of satisfaction with the project management tools and both the number of hours of training received and the perceived adequacy of this training was examined. Strong relationships were found in each case, and thus it appears that by obtaining training on the use of a project management tool, the project manager's overall satisfaction with that tool is increased.

Use of the Tools

As a final measure of the perceived adequacy of the project management tools, the project managers were asked to provide an indication of how much use is made of the tools and the perceived adequacy of this use. The respondents provided both a measure of duration (how many months the tool had been used) and intensity (how many hours each week the tool is used). This information, along with the measure of perceived adequacy of use, is summarized in Table 8. The project management tools are listed in descending order of the measure of perceived adequacy of use.

As Table 8 indicates, the project managers provided an above-average rating of the adequacy of use made of the tools. Additionally, a significant and positive correlation was found between the number of hours per week the tools were used and the perceived adequacy of this use. In other words, the more time spent using a project management tool, the higher the perceived adequacy of this use. Thus, it appears that project managers are indeed quite comfortable with the perceived adequacy of the use being made of the currently available project management tools. Generally, project managers had used the tools for at least one year, and often for several years. On average, project managers use the tools for the equivalent of almost an entire eight-hour workday each week.

Conclusion

This survey of project managers provides important insight into the project management tools currently being used by the profession. The survey confirms that there are literally dozens of project management tools on the market. However, the majority of project managers surveyed tend to use only a small subset of these tools, the most widely used being Microsoft Project. It is also interesting to note that project managers rely on nontraditional project management tools, such as Microsoft Excel, as readily as they do more project-focused tools. Although each project management tool is marketed and advertised as providing various features that other tools may not have, the uses made of all the tools are quite similar and focus on the basic project management tasks of planning, scheduling, tracking, and controlling. With respect to the perceived adequacy of this collection of project management tools, over-all the survey respondents indicated above-average ratings of satisfaction, adequacy of training, and adequacy of the use of the tools. It was confirmed that not only does receiving training on the use of a project management tool influence the perceived adequacy of the tool but also the overall satisfaction that a project manager has with respect to the tool.

Thus, it appears that project managers have quite a collection of project management tools at their disposal, and that they are relatively pleased with the adequacy of these tools. Considering that a computerized project management tool is an invaluable resource—the primary "tool of the trade"—for project managers, it is useful to periodically confirm that the tools are, in fact, meeting the needs of the professional.

References

DOLL, WILLIAM J., & TORKZADEH, GHOLAMREZA. (1988, June). The measurement of end-user computing satisfaction. *MIS Quarterly*, 259–274.

LEVENE, H. (1960). Robust tests for equality of variances. *Contributions to Probability and Statistics*. Palo Alto, CA: Stanford University Press.

LEVINE, HARVEY A. (1995, July). Innovators? Or tripping over their egos? Winners and losers in the PM software industry. *PM Network*, 22–25.

MODER, JOSEPH J. (1994). Conjecture on the future direction of MPM. *Project Management Journal*, 25 (3), 6–7.

ROOK, PAUL. (1986, January). Controlling software projects. *Software Engineering Journal*, 7–16.

SHENHAR, AARON J., & LAUFER, ALEXANDER. (1995, September). Integrating product and project management—A new synergistic approach. *Engineering Management Journal*, 7 (3), 11–15.

WEIL, DAVID E. (1986). Retrospective application of project management software as a planning tool: A case study examining the preparation of a U.S. Environmental Protection Agency air quality criteria document. *Project Management Journal*, 17 (2), 65–69.

ZMUD, ROBERT W. (1980, June). Management of large software development efforts. *MIS Quarterly*, 45–55.

Questions

1. According to Tables 6 and 8, Microsoft Project is below the average of all the packages surveyed in overall satisfaction and adequacy, yet is number one in terms of use in Table 1. How can this be?

2. Of the factors listed in Table 6, which would be most important to you in selecting a project management package to use in planning a project? Which PM package rated tops on this category?

3. Based on the number of projects in Table 3 for which various software packages were used, what package was used the most for short projects? For long projects? What might you conclude from this?

4. For project managers trying to manage several projects at once, which package would probably be best, based on Table 5 and the other tables?

5. Based on these survey results, what would you predict will be the future of project management software packages?

Appendix: A Survey of Project Management Tools

The purpose of this questionnaire is to gain an understanding and appreciation of the perspective that project managers have regarding the available tools they use in performing their job-related tasks.

1. Please indicate the number of years of experience you have working
   a. as a project manager _____   b. in information systems (if any) _____

2. Please indicate which of the following types of software development efforts (if any) you have worked on, as a project manager, during the past three years:
   _____ Personal/Home Use   _____ Direct Marketed to External Customers
   _____ In-house Use   _____ Commercially Contracted
   _____ Public Domain   _____ Government Contracted

3. Considering projects you have worked on during the past three years, please indicate the number of projects in each category and the amount of time spent working on each category of project, as a percentage of all categories. The categories represent *total project size* measured in calendar months:

	< 3 mths	3–6 mths	6–12 mths	12–18 mths	>18 mths
# of projects	_____	_____	_____	_____	_____
amount of time	_____ % +	_____ % +	_____ % +	_____ % +	_____ % = 100%

4. Please indicate which of the following best describes the type of work your company is primarily involved in:
   _____ Software Development   _____ Wholesale   _____ Engineering
   _____ Hardware Development   _____ Retail

Project Management Tools

5. Please list as many as three project management software tools you have used or are currently using. For this survey, an example of a project management tool could be Microsoft Project.
   Tool A _____   Tool B _____   Tool C _____
   _____   _____   _____

6. Please indicate the amount of time you use each tool, as a percentage of all project management tools listed in question 5.
   Tool A _____% + Tool B _____% + Tool C _____% = 100%

7. Please indicate the primary uses for which you might normally choose each of the project management tools listed in question 5.
   Tool A _____
   Tool B _____
   Tool C _____

8. For each of the project management tools listed in question 5, please respond to the following questions by drawing a circle around the appropriate ranking in the space provided.
   The possible rankings for each question and each project management tool are:

Nonexistent	Poor	Fair	Good	Excellent
1	2	3	4	5

	Tool A	Tool B	Tool C
a. Does the project management tool provide the precise information you need?	1 2 3 4 5	1 2 3 4 5	1 2 3 4 5
b. Does the information content meet your needs?	1 2 3 4 5	1 2 3 4 5	1 2 3 4 5

    c. Does the project management tool provide reports   1 2 3 4 5   1 2 3 4 5   1 2 3 4 5
       that seem to be just about exactly what you need?

    d. Does the project management tool provide sufficient   1 2 3 4 5   1 2 3 4 5   1 2 3 4 5
       information for you to perform your job?

    e. Is the project management tool accurate?   1 2 3 4 5   1 2 3 4 5   1 2 3 4 5

    f. Are you satisfied with the accuracy of the project   1 2 3 4 5   1 2 3 4 5   1 2 3 4 5
       management tool?

    g. Do you think the output is presented in a   1 2 3 4 5   1 2 3 4 5   1 2 3 4 5
       useful format?

    h. Is the output information clear?   1 2 3 4 5   1 2 3 4 5   1 2 3 4 5

    i. Is the project management tool user friendly?   1 2 3 4 5   1 2 3 4 5   1 2 3 4 5

    j. Is the project management tool easy to use?   1 2 3 4 5   1 2 3 4 5   1 2 3 4 5

    k. Do you get the information you need in a   1 2 3 4 5   1 2 3 4 5   1 2 3 4 5
       timely manner?

    l. Does the project management tool provide up-to-date   1 2 3 4 5   1 2 3 4 5   1 2 3 4 5
       information?

9. a. Please indicate the *number of hours* of formal training you received on the use of each of the project management tools listed in question 5:

      Tool A _____   Tool B _____   Tool C _____

    b. Please indicate whether you consider the training you received, if any, to be adequate for you to use the project management tool.
       Use a scale of 1–5 with 1 = totally inadequate and 5 = totally adequate:

      Tool A _____   Tool B _____   Tool C _____

10. a. Please indicate the *number of hours* each week you spend using each of the project management tools listed in question 5:

      Tool A _____   Tool B _____   Tool C _____

    b. Please indicate the *number of months* that you have used each of the project management tools listed in question 5:

      Tool A _____   Tool B _____   Tool C _____

    c. Please indicate whether you consider the amount of time you spend using the project management tool to be adequate for you.
       Use a scale of 1–5 with 1 = totally inadequate and 5 = totally adequate:

      Tool A _____   Tool B _____   Tool C _____

11

Project Control

In the previous chapter, we described the monitoring and information gathering process that would help the PM control the project. Control is the last element in the implementation cycle of planning–monitoring–controlling. Information is collected about system performance, compared with the desired (or planned) level, and action taken if actual and desired performance differ enough that the controller (manager) wishes to decrease the difference. Note that reporting performance, comparing the differences between desired and actual performance levels, and accounting for why such differences exist are all parts of the control process. In essence, control is the *act* of reducing the difference between plan and reality.

As has been emphasized throughout this book, control is focused on three elements of a project—performance, cost, and time. The PM is constantly concerned with these three aspects of the project. Is the project delivering what it promised to deliver or more? Is it making delivery at or below the promised cost? Is it making delivery at or before the promised time? It is strangely easy to lose sight of these fundamental targets, especially in large projects with a wealth of detail and a great number of subprojects. Large projects develop their own momentum and tend to get out of hand, going their own way independent of the wishes of the PM and the intent of the proposal.

Think, for a moment, of a few of the things that can cause a project to require the control of performance, costs, or time.

Performance

Unexpected technical problems arise.

Insufficient resources are available when needed.

Insurmountable technical difficulties are present.

Quality or reliability problems occur.

Client requires changes in system specifications.

Interfunctional complications arise.

Technological breakthroughs affect the project.

Cost

Technical difficulties require more resources.

The scope of the work increases.

Initial bids or estimates were too low.

Reporting was poor or untimely.

Budgeting was inadequate.

Corrective control was not exercised in time.

Input price changes occurred.

Time

Technical difficulties took longer than planned to solve.

Initial time estimates were optimistic.

Task sequencing was incorrect.

Required inputs of material, personnel, or equipment were unavailable when needed.

Necessary preceding tasks were incomplete.

Customer-generated change orders required rework.

Governmental regulations were altered.

And these are only a few of the relatively "mechanistic" problems that can occur. Actually, there are no purely mechanistic problems on projects. All problems have a human element, too. For example, humans, by action or inaction, set in motion a chain of events that leads to a failure to budget adequately, creates a quality problem, leads the project down a technically difficult path, or fails to note a change in government regulations. If, by chance, some of these or other things happen (as a result of human action or not), humans are affected by them. Frustration, pleasure, determination, hopelessness, anger, and many other emotions arise during the course of a project. They affect the work of the individuals who feel them—for better or worse. It is over this welter of confusion, emotion, fallibility, and general cussedness that the PM tries to exert control.

All of these problems, always combinations of the human and mechanistic, call for intervention and control by the project manager. There are infinite "slips 'twixt cup and lip," especially in projects where the technology or the deliverables are new and unfamiliar, and PMs, like most managers, find control is a difficult function to perform. There are several reasons why this is so. One of the main reasons is that PMs, again like most managers, do not discover problems. Managers discover what Russell Ackoff once described as a "mess" [1]. A "mess" is a general condition of a system that, when viewed by a manager, leads to a statement that begins, "%#^@*&+#!" and goes downhill from there. It is the discovery of a mess that leads the PM to the conclusion that there is a problem(s) lurking somewhere around. In systems as complex as projects, the task of defining the problem(s) is formidable, and thus knowing what to control is not a simple task. Another reason control is difficult is because, in spite of an almost universal need to blame some person for any trouble, it is often almost impossible to know if a problem resulted from human error or from the random random application of Murphy's Law.

PMs also find it tough to exercise control because the project team, even on large projects, is an "in-group." It is "we," while outsiders are "they." It is usually hard to criticize friends, to subject them to control. Further, many PMs see control as an ad hoc process. Each need to exercise control is seen as a unique event, rather than as one instance of an ongoing and recurring process. Whitten [39] offers the observation that projects are drifting out of control if the achievement of milestones is being threatened. He also offers some guidelines on how to resolve this problem and bring the project back in control.

Because control of projects is such a mixture of feeling and fact, of human and mechanism, of causation and random chance, we must approach the subject in an extremely orderly way. In this chapter, we start by examining the general purposes of control. Then we consider the basic structure of the process of control. We do this by describing control theory in the form of a cybernetic control loop. While most projects offer little opportunity for the actual application of automatic feedback loops, this system provides us with a comprehensive but reasonably simple illustration of all the elements necessary to control any system. From this model, we then turn to the types of control that are most often applied to projects. The design of control systems is discussed as are the impacts that various types of controls tend to have on the humans being controlled. The specific requirement of "balance" in a control system is also covered, as are two special control problems: control of creative activities, and control of change.

11.1 THE FUNDAMENTAL PURPOSES OF CONTROL

The two fundamental objectives of control are:

1. The regulation of results through the alteration of activities.
2. The stewardship of organizational assets.

Most discussions of the control function are focused on regulation. The PM needs to be equally attentive to both regulation and conservation. Because the main body of this chapter (and much of the next) concerns the PM as regulator, let us emphasize the conservationist role here. The PM must guard the physical assets of the organization, its human resources, and its financial resources. The processes for conserving these three different kinds of assets are different.

Physical Asset Control

Physical asset control requires control of the *use* of physical assets. It is concerned with asset maintenance, whether preventive or corrective. At issue also is the timing of maintenance or replacement as well as the quality of maintenance. Some years ago, a New England brewery purchased the abandoned and obsolete brewing plant of a newly defunct competitor. A PM was put in charge of this old facility with the instruction that the plant should be completely "worn out" over the next five-year period, but that it should be fully operational in the meantime. This presented an interesting problem: the controlled deterioration of a plant while at the same time maintaining as much of its productive capability as possible. Clearly, both objectives could not be achieved simultaneously, but the PM met the spirit of the project quite well.

If the project uses considerable amounts of physical equipment, the PM also has the problem of setting up maintenance schedules in such a way as to keep the equipment in operating condition while minimizing interference with ongoing work. It is critical to accomplish preventive maintenance prior to the start of that final section of the project life cycle known as the Last Minute Panic (LMP). (Admittedly, the timing of the LMP is not known, which makes the planning of pre-LMP preventive maintenance somewhat difficult.)

Physical inventory, whether equipment or material, must also be controlled. It must be received, inspected (or certified), and possibly stored prior to use. Records of all incoming shipments must be carefully validated so that payment to suppliers can be authorized. The same precautions applied to goods from external suppliers must also be applied to suppliers from inside the organization. Even such details as the project library, project coffee maker, project office furniture, and all the other minor bits and pieces must be counted, maintained, and conserved.

Human Resource Control

Stewardship of human resources requires controlling and maintaining the growth and development of people. Projects provide particularly fertile ground for cultivating people. Because projects are unique, differing one from another in many ways, it is possible for people working on projects to gain a wide range of experience in a reasonably short time.

Measurement of physical resource conservation is accomplished through the familiar audit procedures. The measurement of human resource conservation is far more difficult. Such devices as employee appraisals, personnel performance indices, and screening methods for appointment, promotion, and retention are not particularly satisfactory devices for ensuring that the conservation function is being properly handled. The accounting profession has worked for some years on the development of *human resource accounting*, and while the effort has produced some interesting ideas, human resource accounting is not well accepted by the accounting profession.

Financial Resource Control

Though accountants have not succeeded in developing acceptable methods for human resource accounting, their work on techniques for the conservation (and regulation) of financial resources has most certainly resulted in excellent tools for financial control.

It is difficult to separate the control mechanisms aimed at conservation of financial resources from those focused on regulating resource use. Most financial controls do both. Capital investment controls work to conserve the organization's assets by insisting that certain conditions be met before capital can be expended, and those same conditions usually regulate the use of capital to achieve the organization goal of a high return on investments.

The techniques of financial control, both conservation and regulation, are well known. They include current asset controls, and project budgets as well as capital investment controls. These controls are exercised through a series of analyses and audits conducted by the accounting/controller function for the most part. Representation of this function on the project team is mandatory. The structure of the techniques applied to projects does not differ appreciably from those applied to the general operation of the firm, but the context within which they are applied is quite different. One reason for the differences is that the project is accountable to an outsider—an external client, or another division of the parent firm, or both at the same time.

The importance of proper conformance to both organizational and client control standards in financial practice and recordkeeping cannot be overemphasized. The parent organization, through its agent, the project manager, is responsible for the conservation and proper *use of* resources owned by the client or owned by the parent and charged to the client. Clients will insist on, and the courts will require the practice of, *due diligence* in the exercise of such responsibility. While some clients may not be aware of this responsibility on the part of firms with whom they contract, the government is most certainly aware of it. In essence, due diligence requires that the organization proposing a project conduct a reasonable investigation, verification, and disclosure, in language that is understandable, of every material fact relevant to the firm's ability to conduct the project, and to omit nothing where such omission might ethically mislead the client. It is not possible to define, in some general way, precisely what might be required for any given project. The firm should, however, make sure that it has legal counsel competent to aid it in meeting this responsibility.

One final note on the conservationist role of the controller. The attitude or mind-set of the conservationist is often antithetical to the mind-set of the PM, whose attention is naturally on the use of resources rather than their conservation. The conservationist reminds one of the fabled librarian who is happiest when all the books are ordered neatly on the library shelves. The PM, often the manager and controller at one and the same time, is subject to this conflict and has no choice but to live with it. The warring attitudes must be merged and compromised as best they can. For an excellent work on the role of the manager as steward, see [4].

Project Management in Practice
Extensive Controls for San Francisco's Metro Turnback Project

By the late 1980s, transportation in San Francisco's financial district, an area built over loose fill which had once been part of the bay, had become a serious problem. The recent addition of the Bay Area Rapid Transit (BART), plus the usual busses, metro, cabs, and commuting traffic made for severe congestion in the district. To provide relief, the city launched the MUNI

Location of the MMT Project

Metro Turnback Project to increase capacity and provide for future expansion. The 11-year planned project consisted of building a pair of twin tunnels 18 feet in diameter and a sixth of a mile long under the busiest street in San Francisco, connected to a concrete box 23 feet high by 55 feet wide by a fifth of a mile long under the second busiest street, opening onto a 386 foot retaining wall and emerging surface track (see exhibit).

In addition to the inherent difficulties implied in the scope of the project as just described, the project was fraught with multiple challenges beyond just the disruption of traffic, business, events, and tourism:

1. The tunnels would pass directly over the BART tunnels, in places only 4.5 feet away, in loose fill and mud below the Bay water table.

2. Wooden pilings that had supported wharves and piers in bygone years would be encountered and would require major force to cut, further endangering the BART tunnels.

3. The excavation work would pass near many high valued buildings, some of historic designation.

4. The below-water table tunnels would run very close to the actual waters of San Francisco Bay, with the potential of a breakthrough.

5. Seismic activity was likely and there had been a recent major earthquake in the area which elevated the safety requirements.

Clearly, very careful controls were needed to manage the project in terms of not only the above risks but also in terms of schedule and costs. This was achieved by the overarching Management Plan and Control system and its multiple subsidiary control systems based on the detailed work breakdown structure.

• The Project Code of Accounts included the work breakdown structure and Cost Code of Accounts which gave the appropriate schedule and cost codes for reporting and monitoring.

- The Control Budget included the quantities, costs, and job-hour allocations for the Project Code of Accounts plus any approved scope changes.

- The Trend Program tracked scope changes and identified any potential cost impact due to new changes, ideas, directions, or requirements. Project managers used this tool to make cost/benefit decisions to keep costs under control.

- The Scope Change Log listed any changes identified from the Trend Program which then had to either be approved or deleted.

- A Monthly Contract Cash Flow Schedule reflected expenditures so contractor invoices could be compared with the expenditure schedule.

- The Contractual Milestone Summary Schedule (CMSS) was the overall plan for the total construction scope. The schedule was issued monthly for comparison of actual with planned progress. Analyses were made of critical and near-critical paths, areas of high risk, opportunities for schedule improvement, and so on.

- The Construction Schedule was derived from the CMSS above and was for coordination with the general contractor.

- The Three-Week Rolling Construction Schedule showed completed activities the previous week and those planned for the current and coming weeks. It was used to monitor progress against the baseline Construction Schedule.

- Quality Control and Quality Assurance responsibilities were segregated and partitioned between the contractor and construction management.

- A system of Contractor's Nonconformance Reports and Corrective Action Reports was established. By the end of the project, only 30 of these reports had been issued over the 11-year duration.

Opening ceremonies for the project were held in December 1996. Over the 11-year period, the project came in only two month's late (due to 17 new fire code requirements late in the project) and $22 million under budget.

Source: C. Wu and G. Harwell, "The MUNI Metro Turnback Project," *PM Network*, May 1998, pp. 49–55.

11.2 THREE TYPES OF CONTROL PROCESSES

The process of controlling a project (or any system) is far more complex than simply waiting for something to go wrong and then, if possible, fixing it. We must decide at what points in the project we will try to exert control, what is to be controlled, how it will be measured, how much deviation from plan will be tolerated before we act, what kinds of interventions should be used, and how to spot and correct potential deviations before they occur. In order to keep these and other such issues sorted out, it is helpful to begin a consideration of control with a brief exposition on the theory of control.

No matter what our purpose in controlling a project, there are three basic types of control mechanisms we can use: cybernetic control, go/no-go control, and post-control. In this section we will describe these three types and briefly discuss the information requirements of each. While few cybernetic control systems are used for project control, we will describe them here because they clearly delineate the elements that must be present in any control system, as well as the information requirements of control systems.

Cybernetic Control

Cybernetic, or steering, control is by far the most common type of control system. (*Cyber* is the Greek word for "helmsman.") The key feature of cybernetic control is its automatic operation. Consider the diagrammatic model of a cybernetic control system shown in Figure 11-1.

As Figure 11-1 shows, a system is operating with inputs being subjected to a process that transforms them into outputs. It is this system that we wish to control. In order to do so, we must monitor the system output. This function is performed by sensors that measure one or more aspects of the output, presumably those aspects one wishes to control. Measurements taken by a sensor are transmitted to the comparator, which compares them with a set of predetermined standards. The difference between actual and standard is sent to the decision maker, which determines whether or not the difference is of sufficient size to deserve correction. If the difference is large enough to warrant action, a signal is sent to the effector, which acts on the process or on the inputs to produce outputs that conform more closely to the standard.

A cybernetic control system that acts to reduce deviations from standard is called a *negative feedback loop*. If the system output moves away from standard in one direction, the control mechanism acts to move it in the opposite direction. The speed or force with which the control operates is, in general, proportional to the size of the deviation from standard. (Mathematical descriptions of the action of negative feedback loops are widely available. See, for example, [37].) The precise way in which the deviation is corrected depends on the nature of the operating system and the design of the controller. Figure 11-2 illustrates three different response patterns. Response path A is direct and rapid, while path B is more gradual. Path C shows oscillations of decreasing amplitude. An aircraft suddenly deflected from a stable flight path would tend to recover by following pattern C.

Types of Cybernetic Control Systems Cybernetic controls come in three varieties, or *orders*, differing in the sophistication with which standards are set. Figure 11-1 shows a simple *first-order* control system, a goal-seeking device. The standard is set and there is no provision made for altering it except by intervention from the

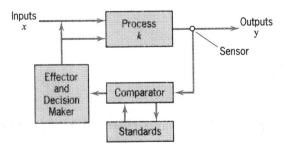

Figure 11-1 A cybernetic control system.

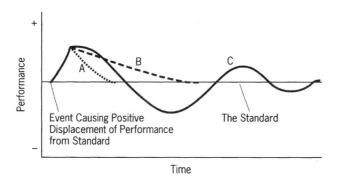

Event Causing Positive
Displacement of Performance
from Standard

The Standard

Time

Figure 11-2 Typical paths for correction of deviation of performance from standard.

outside. The common thermostat is a time-worn example of a *first-order* controller. One sets the standard temperature and the heating and air-conditioning systems operate to maintain it.

Figure 11-3 shows a *second-order* control system. This device can alter the system standards according to some predetermined set of rules or program. The complexity of second-order systems can vary widely. The addition of a clock to the thermostat to allow it to maintain different standards during day and night makes the thermostat a second-order controller. An interactive computer program may alter its responses according to a complex set of preprogrammed rules, but it is still only a second-order system. Many industrial projects involve second-order controllers—for example, robot installations, flexible manufacturing systems, and automated record-keeping or inventory systems.

A *third-order* control system (Figure 11-4) can change its goals without specific preprogramming. It can reflect on system performance and decide to act in ways that are not contained in its instructions. Third-order systems have reflective consciousness and, thus, must contain humans. Note that a second-order controller can be programmed to recognize patterns, and to react to patterns in specific ways. Such systems are said to "learn." Third-order systems can learn without explicit preprogramming, and therefore can alter their actions on the basis of thought or whim. An advantage of third-order controllers is that they can deal with the unforeseen and unexpected. A disadvantage is that, because they contain human elements, they may lack pre-

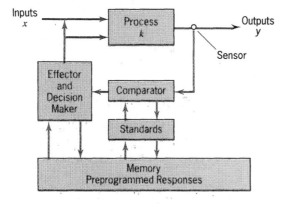

Figure 11-3 A second-order feedback system—preprogrammed goal changer.

Figure 11-4 A third-order feedback system—reflective goal changer.

dictability and reliability. Third-order systems are of great interest to the PM, for reasons we now discuss.

Information Requirements for Cybernetic Controllers In order to establish total control over a system, the controller must be able to take a counteraction for every action the system can take. This statement is a rough paraphrase of Ashby's Law of Requisite Variety [30]. This implies that the PM/controller is aware of the system's full capabilities. For complex systems, particularly those containing a human element, this is simply not possible. Thus, we need a strategy to aid the PM in developing a control system. One such strategy is to use a cost/benefit approach to control—to control those aspects of the system for which the expected benefits of control are greater than the expected costs. We are reminded of a firm that manufactured saw blades. It set up a project to reduce scrap losses for the high-cost steel from which the blades were made. At the end of the one-year project, the firm had completed the project—cost $9700, savings $4240. (Of course, if the savings were to be repeated for several years, the rate of return on the project would be acceptable. The president of the firm, however, thought that the savings would decline and disappear when the project ended.)

Relatively few elements of a project (as opposed to the elements of a system that operates more or less continuously) are subject to automatic control. An examination of the WBS or the details of an action plan will reveal which of the project's tasks are largely mechanistic and represent continuous types of systems. If such systems exist, and if they operate across a sufficient time period to justify the initial expense of creating an automatic control, then a cybernetic controller is useful.

Given the decisions about what to control, the information requirements of a cybernetic controller are easy to describe, if not to meet. First, the PM must define precisely what characteristics of an output (interim output or final output) are to be controlled. Second, standards must be set for each characteristic. Third, sensors must be acquired that will measure those characteristics at the desired level of precision. Fourth, these measurements must be transformed into a signal that can be compared to a "standard" signal. Fifth, the difference between the two is sent to the decision maker, which detects it, if it is sufficiently large, and sixth, transmits a signal to the effector that causes the operating system to react in a way that will counteract the deviation from standard. If the control system is designed to allow the effector to take one or more of several actions, an additional piece of information is needed. There must be built-in criteria that instruct the effector on which action(s) to take.

Knowledge of cybernetic control is important because all control systems are merely variants, extensions, or nonautomatic modifications of such controls. Because most projects have relatively few mechanistic elements that can be subjected to classic cybernetic controls, this concept of control is best applied to tracking the system and automatically notifying the PM when things threaten to get out of control.

Go/No-go Controls

Go/no-go controls take the form of testing to see if some specific precondition has been met. Most of the control in project management falls into this category. This type of control can be used on almost every aspect of a project. For many facets of performance, it is sufficient to know that the predetermined specifications for project output have been met. The same is often true of the cost and time elements of the project plan.

It is, of course, necessary to exercise judgment in the use of go/no-go controls. Certain characteristics of output may be required to fall within precisely determined limits if the output is to be accepted by the client. Other characteristics may be less precisely defined. In regard to time and cost, there may be penalties associated with nonconformance with the approved plans. Penalty clauses that make late delivery costly for the producer are often included in the project contract. At times, early delivery can also carry a penalty (e.g., when a just-in-time supply system is involved). Cost overruns may be shared with the client or borne by the project. Some contracts arrange for the first $X of cost overrun to be shared by client and producer, with any further overrun being the producer's responsibility. The number and type of go/no-go controls on a project is limited only by the imagination and desire of the contracting parties.

The project plan, budget, and schedule are all control documents, so the PM has a predesigned control system complete with prespecified milestones as control checkpoints. Control can be exercised at any level of detail that is supported by detail in the plans, budgets, and schedules. The parts of a new jet engine, for instance, are individually checked for quality conformance. These are go/no-go controls. The part passes or it does not, and every part must pass its own go/no-go test before being used in an engine. Similarly, computer programs are tested for bugs. The program passes its tests or it does not.

Go/no-go controls operate only when and if the controller uses them. In many cases, go/no-go controls function periodically, at regular, preset intervals. The intervals are usually determined by clock, calendar, or the operating cycles of some machine system. Such periodicity makes it easy to administer a control system, but it often allows errors to be compounded before they are detected. Things begin to go awry just after a quarterly progress check, for instance, and by the time the next quarterly check is made, some items may be seriously out of control.

Project milestones do not occur at neat, periodic intervals; thus, *controls should be linked to the actual plans and to the occurrence of real events, not simply to the calendar.* Senior management should review all projects at reasonably frequent intervals. We will discuss such reports shortly, but the PM cannot control the project properly with a strictly periodic reporting system.

The PM must keep abreast of all aspects of the project, directly or through deputies. Competent functional managers understand the importance of *follow-up*, and the project manager's work provides no exception. Control is best exerted while there is still time for corrective action. To this end, the PM should establish an *early warning system* so that potential problems can be exposed and dealt with before they turn into full-fledged disasters. One way to construct such an early warning system is to set up a project forecast data sheet. On this sheet, outputs or progress are forecast by period. Actual output or progress is then checked against the forecast, period by period.

For an early warning system to work, it must be clear that the messenger who brings bad news will not be shot, and that anyone caught sweeping problems and mistakes under the rug will be. As we have said before, the most important rule for any subordinate is the Prime Law of Life on a project: Never let the boss be surprised!

Controls have a tendency to terrorize the insecure and to induce high anxiety in everyone else. The result is avoidance, and avoidance is exactly what the PM cannot tolerate. Unless deviation from plan is discovered, it cannot be corrected. Therefore, a spirit of trust between superior and subordinate at all levels of the project is a prime requisite for the effective application of control.

Information Requirements for Go/No-Go Controls

Most of the input information needed to operate go/no-go project control has already been referenced directly or implied by the previous discussion. The project proposal, plans, specifications, schedules, and budgets (complete with approved change orders) contain all the information needed to apply go/no-go controls to the project. Milestones are the key events that serve as a focus for ongoing control activity. These milestones are the project's deliverables in the form of in-process output or final output. If the milestones occur on time, on budget, and at the planned level of quality, the PM can take comfort from the fact that things are proceeding properly. Perhaps just as important to the PM, senior management can be equally comfortable with the project—and with the project manager as well.

Except for a few important projects, senior management usually cannot keep up with the day-to-day or week-to-week progress of work; nor should they try. Senior management does, however, need a monthly or quarterly status review for all projects. The project status report contains a list of the important milestones for each project together with the status of each. If many of the projects are similar—such as construction projects or marketing projects, for example—the milestones will be of similar type, and one table can show the status of several projects in spite of the fact that each milestone may not be applicable to each and every project. The Elanco Products Company (the agricultural products division of Eli Lilly and Company, now DowElanco) uses such a report. A generalized version of Elanco's Project Status Report is shown in Figure 11-5. The Gantt chart (see Chapter 8) is also a convenient way to present senior managers with information on project status.

Either of these report forms can be altered to contain almost any additional information that might be requested. For example, the Gantt chart can be annotated

Task	Project #1	Project #2	Project #3
Priorities set	C	C	C
PM selected	C	C	C
Key members briefed on RFP	C	C	C
Proposal sent	C	C	C
Proposal accepted as negotiated	C	C	C
Preliminary design developed	C	W/10	C
Design accepted	C	W/12	C
Software developed	C	NS/NR	N/A
Product test design	C	W/30	W/15
Manufacturing scheduled	C	NS/HR	W/8
Tools, jigs, fixtures designed	W/1	NS/HR	W/2
Tools, jigs, fixtures delivered	W/2	NS/HR	W/8
Production complete	NS/HR	NS/HR	NS/HR
Product test complete	NS/HR	NS/HR	NS/HR
Marketing sign-off on product	NS/HR	NS/HR	NS/HR

Notes:

N/A—Not applicable
C—Completed

W—Work in progress (number refers to month required)

NS—Not started
NR—Need resources
HR—Have resources

Figure 11-5 Sample project status report.

with footnotes indicating such matters of interest as the resources required to get a late milestone back on schedule, or a statement of how an activity must be changed if it is to be approved by a regulatory agency. The information requirements for such extensions of standard reports must be set on an ad hoc basis. For the most part, such information will be readily available within the project, but occasionally, external sources must be utilized. If the PM ensures that the status reports given to senior management contain information that is current enough to be actionable (and always as accurate as required for control), little else can be done to furnish the decision makers with the proper data for them to exercise control. Some firms are now putting such control information on the Internet to make it instantly available to all parties on a worldwide basis. Some guidelines for this approach are given in [31].

The PM is well advised to insist that status reports make clear the implications of specific conditions where those implications might be overlooked—or not understood—by senior managers. If meetings between senior management and project managers are used to report project status and progress, it is critical to remember that the process employed in such meetings should not be punitive or intimidating. As we pointed out in Chapter 10, punitive meetings do far more damage than good.

Postcontrol

Postcontrols (also known as postperformance controls or reviews, or postproject controls or reviews) are applied after the fact. One might draw parallels between postcontrol and "locking the barn after the horse has been stolen," but postcontrol is not a vain attempt to alter what has already occurred. Instead, it is a full recognition of George Santayana's observation that "Those who cannot remember the past are condemned to repeat it." Cybernetic and go/no-go controls are directed toward accomplishing the goals of an ongoing project. Postcontrol is directed toward improving the chances for future projects to meet their goals.

Postcontrol is applied through a relatively formal document that is usually constructed with four distinct sections.

The Project Objectives The postcontrol report will contain a description of the objectives of the project. Usually, this description is taken from the project proposal, and the entire proposal often appears as an appendix to the postcontrol report. As reported here, project objectives include the effects of all change orders issued and approved during the project.

Because actual project performance depends in part on uncontrollable events (strikes, weather, failure of trusted suppliers, sudden loss of key employees, and other acts of God), the key initial assumptions made during preparation of the project budget and schedule should be noted in this section. A certain amount of care must be taken in reporting these assumptions. They should not be written with a tone that makes them appear to be excuses for poor performance. While it is clearly the prerogative, if not the duty, of every PM to protect himself politically, he or she should do so in moderation to be effective.

Milestones, Checkpoints, and Budgets This section of the postcontrol document starts with a full report of project performance against the planned schedule and budget. This can be prepared by combining and editing the various project status reports made during the project's life. Significant deviations of actual schedule and budget from planned schedule and budget should be highlighted. Explanations of why these deviations occurred will be offered in the next section of the postcontrol report. Each deviation can be identified with a letter or number to index it to the explanations. Where the same explanation is associated with both a schedule and budget deviation, as will often be the case, the same identifier can be used.

The Final Report on Project Results When significant variations of actual from planned project performance are indicated, no distinction is made between favorable and unfavorable variations. Like the tongue that invariably goes to the sore tooth, project managers focus their attention on trouble. While this is quite natural, it leads to complete documentation on why some things went wrong and little or no documentation on why some things went particularly well. Both sides, the good and the bad, should be chronicled here.

Not only do most projects result in outputs that are more or less acceptable, most projects operate with a process that is more or less acceptable. The concern here is not on what the project did but rather on how it did it. Basically descriptive, this part of the final report should cover project organization, an explanation of the methods used to plan and direct the project, and a review of the communication networks, monitoring systems, and control methods, as well as a discussion of intraproject interactions between the various working groups.

Recommendations for Performance and Process Improvement
The culmination of the postcontrol report is a set of recommendations covering the ways that future projects can be improved. Many of the explanations appearing in the

previous section are related to one-time happenings—sickness, weather, strikes, or the appearance of a new technology—that themselves are not apt to affect future projects, although other, different one-time events may affect them. But some of the deviations from plan were caused by happenings that are very likely to recur. Examples of recurring problems might be a chronically late supplier, a generally noncooperative functional department, a habitually optimistic cost estimator, or a highly negative project team member. Provision for such things can be factored into future project plans, thereby adding to predictability and control.

Just as important, the process of organizing and conducting projects can be improved by recommending the continuation of managerial methods and organizational systems that appear to be effective, together with the alteration of practices and procedures that do not. In this way, the conduct of projects will become smoother, just as the likelihood of achieving good results, on time and on cost, is increased.

Postcontrol can have a considerable impact on the way projects are run. A large, market-driven company in consumer household products developed new products through projects that were organized in matrix form, but had a functional tie to the marketing division. PMs were almost always chosen from the marketing area. Members of the project team who represented R & D had argued that they should be given a leadership role, particularly early in the project's life. Marketing resisted this suggestion on the grounds that R & D people were not market-oriented, did not know what would sell, and were mainly interested in pursuing their own "academic" interests. After reading the perennial R & D request in a postcontrol report, the program manager of one product line decided to reorganize a project as requested by R & D. The result was not merely a successful project, but was the first in a series of related projects based on extensions of ideas generated by an R & D group not restricted to work on the specific product sought by marketing. Following this successful experiment, project organization was modified to include more input from R & D at an earlier stage of the project.

There is no need to repeat the information requirements for postcontrol here. It should be noted, however, that we have not discussed the postcontrol audit, a full review and audit of all aspects of the project. This is covered in Chapter 12.

■ 11.3 COMMENTS ON THE DESIGN OF CONTROL SYSTEMS

Irrespective of the type of control used, there are some important questions to be answered when designing any control system: Who sets the standards? How realistic are the standards? How clear are they? Will they achieve the project's goals? What output, activities, behaviors should be monitored? Should we monitor people? What kinds of sensors should be used? Where should they be placed? How timely must the monitoring be? How rapidly must it be reported? How accurate must the sensors be? How great must a difference between standard and actual be before it becomes actionable? What corrective actions are available? Are they ethical? What are the most appropriate actions for each situation? What rewards and penalties can be used? Who should take what action?

If the control system is to be acceptable to those who will use it and those who will be controlled by it, the system must be designed so that it appears to be sensible.

Standards must be achievable by the mechanical systems used. Control limits must be appropriate to the needs of the client—that is, not merely set to show "how good we are." Like punishment, rewards and penalties should "fit the crime."

In addition to being sensible, a good control system should also possess some other characteristics.

- The system should be flexible. Where possible, it should be able to react to and report unforeseen changes in system performance.

- The system should be cost effective. The cost of control should never exceed the value of control. As we noted above, control is not always less expensive than scrap. One study [14] has found that the cost of control in projects ranges from as much as 5 percent of total project costs for small projects to less than one percent for very large projects.

- The control system must be truly useful. It must satisfy the real needs of the project, not the whims of the PM.

- The system must operate in an ethical manner.

- The system must operate in a timely manner. Problems must be reported while there is still time to do something about them, and before they become large enough to destroy the project.

- Sensors and monitors should be sufficiently accurate and precise to control the project within limits that are truly functional for the client and the parent organization.

- The system should be as simple to operate as possible.

- The control system should be easy to maintain. Further, the control system should signal the overall controller if it goes out of order.

- The system should be capable of being extended or otherwise altered.

- Control systems should be fully documented when installed and the documentation should include a complete training program in system operation.

No matter how designed, all control systems we have described use feedback as a control process. Let us now consider some more specific aspects of control. To a large extent, the PM is trying to anticipate problems or catch them just as they begin to occur. The PM wants to keep the project out of trouble because upper management often bases an incremental funding decision on a review of the project. This review typically follows some particular milestone and, if acceptable, leads to a follow-on authorization to proceed to the next review point. If all is not going well, other technological alternatives may be recommended; or if things are going badly, the project may be terminated. Thus, the PM must monitor and control the project quite closely.

The control of performance, cost, and time usually requires different input data. To control performance, the PM may need such specific documentation as engineering change notices, test results, quality checks, rework tickets, scrap rates, and maintenance activities. Of particular importance here is carefully controlling any changes, usually increases, in performance due to "scope creep," the natural inclination of the customer to change the deliverables as they obtain better information about their needs over time. Scope creep is not always the fault of the customer however; sometimes the team members themselves, in an effort to do their best work, unwittingly increase the scope of the project. The PM must be constantly on guard to identify such changes. We will have more to say about this shortly.

For cost control, the manager compares budgets to actual cash flows, purchase orders, labor hour charges, amount of overtime worked, absenteeism, accounting variance reports, accounting projections, income reports, cost exception reports, and the like. To control the schedule, the PM examines benchmark reports, periodic activity and status reports, exception reports, PERT/CPM networks, Gantt charts, the master project schedule, earned value graphs, and probably reviews the WBS and action plans.

Auditing will be discussed in Chapter 12, but it needs a brief mention here. It is basically an investigation and count to identify and locate all elements of a project. The PM may find a particular activity perplexing or not understand why it is taking longer than it should or costing more than expected. An audit would provide the data to explain the unusual nature of the discrepancy. The PM may choose to do the audit or have the organization's accountant perform the work.

A large variety of new tools have recently become available for the control of projects such as benchmarking (discussed briefly in Chapter 8 and again later in this chapter in more detail), quality function deployment, stage-gate processing, self-directed teams, the design-build approach, and so on. Thamhein [34] describes these tools and offers suggestions for selecting and implementing them according to individual circumstances of the project.

Some of the most important analytic tools available for the project manager to use in controlling the project are variance analysis and trend projection, both of which have been discussed earlier in this book. The essence of these tools is shown in Figure 11-6. A budget, plan, or expected growth curve of time or cost for some task is plotted. Then actual values are plotted as a dashed line as the work is actually finished. At each point in time a new projection from the actual data is used to forecast what will occur in the future if the PM does not intervene. Based on this projection, the manager can decide if there is a problem, what action alternatives exist, what they will cost and require, and what they will achieve. Based on this analysis, the PM will decide what to do. Trend projection charts can even be used for combined per-

Figure 11-6   Trend projection.

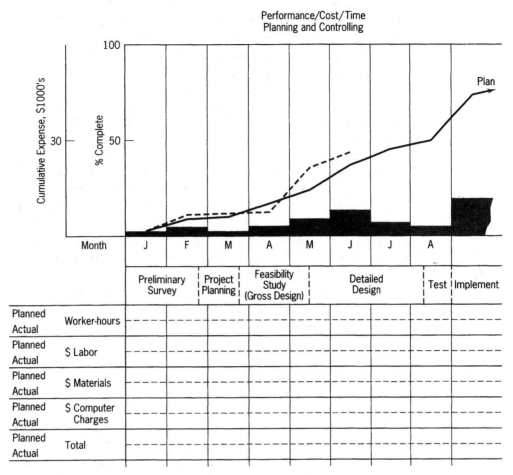

Figure 11-7 Integrated performance cost/time chart. *Source:* [22]

formance/cost/time charts, as illustrated in Figure 11-7. Earned value analysis was also described earlier.

Critical Ratio Control Charts

On occasion it may be worthwhile, particularly on large projects, for the PM to calculate a set of critical ratios for all project activities. The critical ratio is

(actual progress/scheduled progress) X (budgeted cost/actual cost)

The critical ratio is made up of two parts—the ratio of actual progress to scheduled progress, and the ratio of budgeted cost to actual cost. (In the language of C/SCSC, the budgeted cost is the BCWP and the actual cost is the ACWP.) *Cæteris paribus*, to quote any economist who ever lived,* a ratio of actual to scheduled

---

*For those who have never been blessed with a course in economics, this Latin phrase means "other things being equal." The phrase is the economist's equivalent of the physicist's frictionless plane. It does not and cannot exist in fact.

progress greater than one is "good." If the ratio is less than one, it is "bad." Similarly with the ratio of budgeted to actual cost—never forgetting *cæteris paribus*. Assuming moderately accurate measures for each element of each ratio (an assumption that rivals *cæteris paribus* for its *chutzpa*), the critical ratio is a good measure of the general health of the project. Note that the critical ratio is the product of the two separate ratios. This way of combining the two underlying ratios weights them equally, allowing a "bad" ratio for one part to be offset by an equally "good" ratio in the other. The PM may or may not agree that this results in a valid measure of project "health."

Consider Table 11-1. We can see that the first task is behind schedule but also below budget. If lateness is no problem for this activity, the PM need take no action. The second task is on budget but its physical progress is lagging. Even if there is slack in the activity, the budget will probably be overrun. The third task is on schedule but cost is running higher than budget, creating another probable cost overrun. The fourth task is on budget but ahead of schedule. A cost saving may result. Finally, the fifth task is on schedule and is running under budget, another probable cost saving.

Tasks 4 and 5 have critical ratios greater than 1 and might not concern some PMs, but the thoughtful manager wants to know why they are doing so well (and the PM may also want to check the information system to validate the unexpectedly favorable findings). The second and third activities need attention, and the first task may need attention also. The PM may set some critical-ratio control limits intuitively. The PM may also wish to set different control limits on different activities, controlling progress in the critical path more closely than on paths with high slack.

Charts can be used to monitor and control the project through the use of these ratios. Figure 11-8 shows an example. Note that the PM will ignore critical ratios in some ranges, and that the ranges are not necessarily symmetric around 1.0. Different types of tasks may have different control limits. Control charts can also be used to aid in controlling costs (Figure 11-9), work force levels, and other project parameters.

Benchmarking

Another recent addition to the arsenal of project control tools is *benchmarking*, or making comparisons to "best in class" practices across organizations. This concept is explained and demonstrated in many recent publications (see, for example, [7, 12, 16,

Table 11.1 (Actual Progress/Scheduled Progress) × (Budgeted Cost/Actual Cost)

Task Number	Actual Progress		Scheduled Progress		Budgeted Cost		Actual Cost		Critical Ratio
1	(2	/	3)	×	(6	/	4)	=	1.0
2	(2	/	3)	×	(6	/	6)	=	.67
3	(3	/	3)	×	(4	/	6)	=	.67
4	(3	/	2)	×	(6	/	6)	=	1.5
5	(3	/	3)	×	(6	/	4)	=	1.5

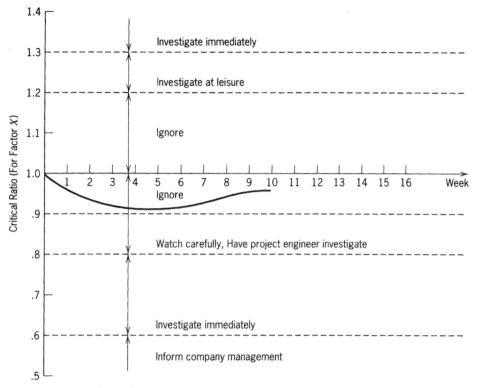

Figure 11-8 Critical ratio control limits.

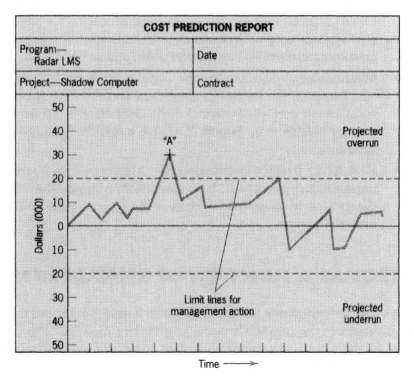

Figure 11-9 Cost control chart. *Source:* [13]

34, 36]). One case study [12] points out the importance of including the customer's perceptions in the benchmarking study or else the data may be accurate but not give the firm any insight into why customers don't recognize their top-level quality. A recent benchmarking study [16] to generate input for the Project Management Maturity Model measured project processes, tools, techniques, and practices across a range of industries, the six life-cycle phases, and the eight knowledge areas of the PMBOK. Graphs were then generated to show the distribution of scores in these industries across the various factors.

Another recent study [36] benchmarked Fortune 500 firms in terms of best practices and key success factors for projects being conducted in functional organizations. The conclusions of the study were reported in four major areas, as described below.

- *Promoting the benefits of project management* Have the project manager report to a top executive with multifunctional authority. Identify and nurture senior officers who champion project management. Conduct training in project management. Participate in project management benchmarking forums. Partner with educational and professional project management organizations. Use a variety of sources to communicate the benefits of project management to senior management.

- *Personnel* Pay for project management skills and high-risk projects through bonuses, stock options, and other incentives. Employ team-based pay. Create job descriptions and career paths for project managers. Develop a checklist for project manager selection and evaluation criteria. Offer project manager development programs. Design project manager retention programs. Offer advanced training and continuing education for project managers. Design a broad-based project manager evaluation process based on project skills, customer satisfaction, negotiation skills, and so on.

- *Methodology* Standardize the organization's project management methods. Integrate the project management processes. Develop project management into a core competence of the organization. Develop a standard process for change management. Develop a standard process for conflict management.

- *Results of project management* Measure project performance and the impact of the project on the organization. Measure the value received from the project. Measure the riskiness of the project. Identify the lessons learned from the project.

11.4 CONTROL AS A FUNCTION OF MANAGEMENT

With a few rare exceptions, control of projects is always exercised through people. Senior managers in the organization are governed by the CEO who is directed by such groups as the executive committee and/or board of directors/trustees. Senior managers, in turn, try to exercise governance of project managers, and project managers

Project Management in Practice
Schedule and Cost Control for Australia's New Parliament House

Over seven years in the making, Australia's new Parliament House at Canberra is actually a suite of buildings costing about $982 million! Meant to be an enduring symbol of the values and expectations of Australia and a source of pride for its citizens, the complex will consist of 5000 rooms, 40,000 items of furniture, 50,000 square meters of stonework, 7350 doors, and 170,000 square meters of drywall. To excavate the site, over one million cubic meters of rock was moved, and 170,000 cubic meters of concrete was poured to form the foundation. At its busiest point,

the complex was costing $1.2 million per working day.

Given the immensity of the project, the information systems to control its design, construction, and furnishing were equally extensive. Procedures were devised for planning, cost control, tendering, contract commencement, drawing and samples, purchasing, stores control, contracts administration, accounts, general administration, and accident prevention. In the area of contracts alone, 540 separate contracts were awarded. And 20,000 drawings were prepared, with 750,000

Project Control Process

The old parliament house (foreground) and the complex of buildings that comprise the new parliament house (background) in Canberra, Australia.

prints issued. Thus, computerized systems were developed for the data associated with contracts and bids, drawings, information requests, site instructions, change proposals, shop drawings, asset registers, time reporting, cost reporting, budgetary control, contracts payments, consultants' fees, and reimbursables.

Time control is based on monitoring at four levels of detail giving progressively more programming detail on aspects of the project. Special purpose programs are included for specific problems or requirements. In addition to exception reports, progress review and coordination

Source: T. R. Nixon, "Project Management at the New Parliament House, Canberra," *Project Management Journal,* September 1987.

meetings help management focus attention on the areas of concern. The overall control system is illustrated in the previous figure.

Cost control is based on the philosophy that 80 percent of the cost is designed in and only 20 percent is due to construction variations. Thus, attention was focused on three points during the design process: early on, to identify allocations and deviations; halfway through to check costs again; and at the completion. Still, ongoing cost control is necessary and performance against budget is measured monthly. Forecasts are also revised every six months to check for any problems ahead.

With such attention to control, the citizens of Australia are looking forward to the completion of their new "house."

try to exert control over the project team and others representing functions that are involved with the project. The purpose is always the same—to bring the actual schedule, budget, and deliverables of the project into reasonably close congruence with the planned schedule, budget, and deliverables. In this and the following sections of this chapter, we discuss the design and use of control systems with some emphasis on the ways in which people respond to various types of control. A number of the points we cover in these sections are discussed at greater length in William Newman's excellent classic, *Constructive Control* [23]. Its insights are as fresh today as they were when the book was written.

Finally, it should be noted that much of the literature on total quality management (TQM), ISO 9000 standards, employee involvement (EI), and the functioning of teams is devoted to techniques for developing creativity and synergistic problem solving through effective teamwork. What is almost never discussed is the implicit assumption that teams have a sense of direction, and are attempting to achieve some specified objectives. All of this implies control. Even the most chaotic brainstorming session is aimed at the solution of specific problems. Control is a necessary and inherent part of life in any organization. It is not helpful to think of control as coercive, though, at times, it may be. We prefer to think of control as the maintenance of ethical goal-directed behavior.

The PM is always subject to such eternal verities as the law of gravity, the laws of thermodynamics, and the brute fact that the exercise of managerial control will result in distorting the behavior of subordinates. The job of the PM/controller is to set controls that will encourage those behaviors/results that are deemed desirable and discourage those that are not. The unspoken assumption here is that control systems motivate individuals to behave in certain ways. While this may seem obvious, it is not the bland assertion it appears. The entire subject of motivation is a complex and rich field for research and there are several theories about the nature of motivation. Each has its supporters and critics. We adopt no particular theory here; we do, however, argue that the control mechanisms described in this chapter provide a context within which motivation takes place. Thus, while control does not provide a good explanation for the presence or absence of motivation, control does indicate the direction toward which the motivated person will move [21].

Though control does not ensure motivated behavior, individual reactions to the various types of control systems do affect levels of motivation. By and large, people respond to the goal-directedness of control systems in one of three general ways: (1) by active and positive participation and goal seeking, (2) by passive participation in order to avoid loss, and (3) by active but negative participation and resistance—usually not active resistance to the goal, but failure to undertake those activities that will result in goal achievement. Which of the three resemble a given individual's reaction to control depends on several variables, including such things as the specific control mechanism used, the nature of the goal being sought, the individual's self-image, assessment of the value of the goal, expectation of being able to achieve the goal, and basic tolerance for being controlled.

While human response to specific types of control is typified by its variety, some generalizations are possible.

Cybernetic Controls   Human response to steering controls tends to be positive. Steering controls are usually viewed as helpful rather than as a source of unwelcome pressure if the controllees perceive themselves as able to perform inside the prescribed limits. Contrary to the popular song, it is not the "impossible dream" that motivates goal-seeking behavior, but rather a moderately good chance of success.

Of course, response to steering control is dependent on the individual's acceptance of the goal as appropriate. Indeed, no control system is acceptable if the objective of control is not acceptable. Further, the source of control must be seen as legitimate for the control mechanism to be accepted.

While it appears to be true that humans respond positively to steering controls, they may not be so positive about the monitoring systems that drive the control mechanisms. Grant, et al. [11] have shown that computerized performance monitoring and control systems are viewed as mixed blessings and have both functional and dysfunctional effects. These monitoring systems, though not used for true cybernetic controls, are fairly common in software projects.

Go/No-go Controls   Response to go/no-go controls tends to be neutral or negative. The reason appears to be related to the inherent nature of this type of control system. With go/no-go control systems, "barely good enough" results are just as acceptable as "perfect" results. The control system itself makes it difficult for the worker to take pride in high-quality work because the system does not recognize gradations of quality. In addition, it is all too common to be rather casual about setting the control limits for a go/no-go control; the limits should be very carefully set. The fact that this kind of control emphasizes "good enough" performance is no excuse for the nonchalant application of careless standards.

While go/no-go control is the most frequent type of control exercised on projects, the impact of such control on the project team seems, to us, to be less negative than Newman suggests [23, pp. 41–42]. Perhaps this is because *project team performance* is the primary focus of control rather than specific items of work performed by individuals. The quality of the project taken as a whole serves as the source of satisfaction to the group, not the quality of bits and pieces. It also appears clear that the quality of the project also serves as a source of satisfaction with the process of doing projects. The entire subject of human response to control in a project environment is a prime area for additional research.

Postcontrols   Postcontrols are seen as much the same as a report card. They may serve as a basis for reward or punishment, but they are received too late to change current performance. Whether reaction to postcontrol is positive, neutral, or negative seems to depend on the "grade" received. In cases where a series of similar projects must be undertaken, postcontrols are regarded as helpful in planning for future work, but considerable care must be devoted to ensuring that controls are consistent with changing environmental conditions. To be effective, management must provide an incentive for project managers to study postcontrol reports, and to determine corrective procedures for problems exposed by the reports, as well as procedures that will replicate the techniques and systems that appear particularly helpful.

Because postcontrols are placed on the process of conducting a project, as well as on the usual time, cost, and performance standards, they may be applied to such areas as interproject communications, cooperation between the groups working on related task elements, the quality of project management, and the nature of interaction with the client. Application of control to such matters presents severe measurement problems. Often it is difficult to detect gross differences in the quality of intergroup communications, for example, or to relate these differences, if detected, to aspects of the project that can be controlled. To say that these matters are difficult to measure and control is not, of course, to obviate the need for control. The soft side of project performance is no less important in the longer run than the easier-to-measure hard side.

11.5 BALANCE IN A CONTROL SYSTEM

When developing a control system, it is important that the system be *well balanced.* Unfortunately, the concept of balance is fuzzy—difficult to explain, difficult to achieve, and difficult to recognize. Though precise definition is impossible, we can describe some general features of a balanced control system, and also indicate some of the things a controller can do to achieve good balance in a system.

- A balanced control system is built with cognizance of the fact that investment in control is subject to sharply diminishing returns. Costs increase exponentially as the degree of control increases linearly and the optimal level of control varies with project size [14].

- A balanced control system recognizes that as control increases past some point, innovative activity is more and more damped, and then finally shut off completely.

- A balanced control system is directed toward the correction of error rather than toward punishment. This requires a clear understanding of the fact that the past cannot be changed, no matter how loudly the manager yells.

- A balanced system exerts control only to the degree required to achieve its objectives. It rarely pays to spend dollars to find lost pennies, nor is it sensible to machine a part to the ten-thousandth if the client's requirements are to the tenth.

- A balanced system utilizes the lowest degree of hassle consistent with accomplishing its goals. The controller should avoid annoying those people whose cooperation is required to reach system objectives.

> My sister passed away, and her funeral was scheduled for Monday. When I told my boss, he said she died so that I would have to miss work on the busiest day of the year. He then asked if we could change her burial to Friday. He said, "That would be better for me."

To sum up, a balanced control system is cost-effective, well geared for the end results sought, and not overdone. The causes of imbalance are legion. For example, the application of across-the-board controls is usually not a good idea. Treating everyone alike appeals to a naive sense of equity, but better results are usually achieved by treating everyone individually.

Across-the-board freezes on expenditures or on hiring tend to reward those who have already overspent or overhired and to penalize the frugal and efficient. The side effects of this are often quite odd. Several years ago, Procter & Gamble put a freeze on hiring into effect for an engineering development laboratory. Project managers who were shorthanded hired temporary labor, including highly skilled technicians, from Manpower and similar firms. P & G's accounting system allowed temporary labor to be charged to material accounts rather than to the salary account. The lesson to be learned is that results-oriented, creative project managers tend to see across-the-board controls as a challenge and a barrier to be circumvented.

Other common causes of imbalance are these:

1. Placing too much weight on easy-to-measure factors and too little weight on difficult-to-measure, soft factors (the so-called "intangibles").

2. Emphasizing short-run results at the expense of longer-run objectives.

3. Ignoring the changes in the structure of organizational goals that result from the passage of time or changes in the firm's circumstances. For example, high quality and strict adherence to delivery schedules might be extremely important to a new firm. Later, perhaps, expense control might be more important.

4. Overcontrol by an aggressive executive often causes trouble. In an attempt to create a reputation for on-time delivery, one overly zealous PM put so much pressure on the project team that on-time shipments took precedence over proper test procedures. The result was serious malfunctions of the product and its subsequent recall.

5. Monitoring and controlling items may lead some people to ignore anything that is not measured. "If it isn't counted, it doesn't count," is the attitude. This factor was responsible for the failure of many attempts at Management-by-Objectives.

Achieving balance in a control system is rather easy to discuss but quite difficult to accomplish. Several principles must be simultaneously upheld. Perhaps most important is the need to tie controls directly to project objectives. Occasionally, firms establish tortuous, indirect linkages between control and objective, apparently on the theory that people should not be aware of or understand the controls under which they must operate. It is as if the firm were trying to trap employees unethically. Such control systems rarely work because they rest on two fallacious assumptions: (1) that people are generally perverse and will avoid trying to accomplish a known objective, and (2) that people are too stupid to see through the misdirection.

In addition to linking controls to objectives, controls should be closely and directly related to specific performance outcomes. Start by defining the desired results as precisely as possible. System actions that can cause deviation from the desired results are then examined and controls are designed for these actions, beginning with those that can be the source of serious deviation, particularly those that cause trouble with high frequency or without advance notice, such as scope creep.

The PM should also examine all controls in terms of the probable reactions of individuals to the proposed controls. One asks, "How will the various members of the project team react to this control?" If negative reaction is likely, the control should be redesigned.

The problem of developing a good balance between long-run and short-run control objectives is delicate, not because the blending is inherently difficult, but because the PM is often preoccupied with urgent short-run problems rather than longer-run problems that can always be "temporarily" set aside no matter how important the results may be at some later date. Even the timing and sequences of monitoring and controlling can affect the likelihood of time and cost overruns [24].

A good rule for the controller is to place the control as close as possible to the work being controlled and to design the simplest possible mechanism to achieve control. Giving the worker direct control over quality has had impressive results in Japanese production processes as well as at the Lincoln Electric Company in the United States. Similar results were achieved by a major producer of housing units. Carpenters, masons, electricians, and other workers were given considerable discretion over specific production methods. Projects on which this approach was employed showed significantly improved quality when compared to projects built by standard methods.

The most important step in constructing a balanced control system must be taken far in advance of the time when control systems are usually designed. Every step of project planning must be undertaken with the understanding that *whatever work is planned will also have to be controlled*. As we have emphasized, planning and control are opposite sides of the same coin. No amount of planning can solve the current crisis, but planning combined with the design and installation of appropriate control mechanisms can go a long way toward crisis prevention.

An excellent example of integrating the planning and control functions is provided by Mead Data Central, a producer of large-scale database systems and a subsidiary of Mead Corporation. In its *Project Management Development Guide*, Mead describes six stages of the project life cycle as seen from its point of view. For each stage, the purpose is carefully explained and the deliverables for that stage are listed. For example, the list of deliverables for the feasibility stage contains these items: project description, project number, preliminary business case, project requirements document, and so forth. For each deliverable, the individual(s) and/or groups responsible are noted.

An extensive glossary of terms is included in the document so that inexperienced project workers can understand what is meant by such diverse terms as "escalation document," "functional audit," "milestone," "not-to-do list," "project cost tracking," and "release readiness statement." In addition, the *Development Guide* summarizes the tasks that must be performed by each of the functional areas or individuals during each stage of the life cycle. The work of the Idea Champion, the Market Managers, the Business Management Process Director, the Project Review Committee, and so on is well defined. The result is an effective integration of planning and control that is available to anyone working on the organization's projects.

A senior executive at a large industrial firm that carries out many projects each year sees control in a slightly different light. Noting that differences between plan and reality usually represent problems for project managers, he remarked: "If you are solving problems faster than they are arriving to be solved, you have the project under control. If not, you haven't."

11.6 CONTROL OF CREATIVE ACTIVITIES

Some brief attention should be paid to the special case of controlling research and development projects, design projects, and similar processes that depend intimately on the creativity of individuals and teams. First, the more creativity involved, the greater the degree of uncertainty surrounding outcomes. Second, too much control tends to inhibit creativity. But neither of these dicta can be taken without reservation. Control is not necessarily the enemy of creativity; nor, popular myth to the contrary, does creative activity imply complete uncertainty. While the exact outcomes of creative activity may be more or less uncertain, the process of getting the outcome is usually not uncertain.

In order to control creative projects, the PM must adopt one or some combination of three general approaches to the problem: (1) progress review, (2) personnel reassignment, and (3) control of input resources.

Progress Review

The progress review focuses on the process of reaching outcomes rather than on the outcomes *per se*. Because the outcomes are partially dependent on the process used to achieve them, uncertain though they may be, the process is subjected to control. For example, in research projects the researcher cannot be held responsible for the outcome of the research, but can most certainly be held responsible for adherence to the research proposal, the budget, and the schedule. The process is controllable even if the precise results are not.

Control should be instituted at each project milestone. If research results are not as expected or desired, milestones provide a convenient opportunity to assess the state of progress, the value of accomplishment to date, the probability of valuable results in the future, and the desirability of changes in the research design. Again, the object of control is to ensure that the research design is sound and is being carried out as planned or amended. The review process should be participative. Unilateral judgments from the superior are not apt to be accepted or effective. Care must be taken not to overstress method as opposed to result. Method is controllable, and should be controlled, but results are still what count.

Personnel Reassignment

This type of control is straightforward—individuals who are productive are kept. Those who are not are moved, to other jobs or to other organizations. Problems with this technique can arise because it is easy to create an elite group. While the favored few are highly motivated to further achievement, everyone else tends to be demotivated. It is also important not to apply control with too fine an edge. While it is not particularly difficult to identify those who fall in the top and bottom quartiles of productivity, it is usually quite hard to make clear distinctions between people in the middle quartiles.

Control of Input Resources

In this case, the focus is on efficiency. The ability to manipulate input resources carries with it considerable control over output. Obviously, efficiency is not synonymous with creativity, but the converse is equally untrue. Creativity is not synonomous with extravagant use of resources.

The results flowing from creative activity tend to arrive in batches. Considerable resource expenditure may occur with no visible results, but then, seemingly all of a sudden, many outcomes may be delivered. The milestones for application of resource control must therefore be chosen with great care. The controller who decides to withhold resources just before the fruition of a research project is apt to become an ex-controller.

Sound judgment argues for some blend of these three approaches when controlling creative projects. The first and third approaches concentrate on process because process is observable and can be affected. But process is not the matter of moment; results are. The second approach requires us to measure (or at least to recognize) output when it occurs. This is often quite difficult. Thus, the wise PM will use all three approaches: checking process and method, manipulating resources, and culling those who cannot or do not produce.

11.7 CONTROL OF CHANGE AND SCOPE CREEP

In Chapter 6, we discussed the fact that the original plans for projects are almost certain to be changed before the projects are completed. The changes, we noted, result from three basic causes: uncertainty about the technology on which the work of the project or its output is based, an increase in the knowledge base or sophistication of the client/user leading to scope creep, or a modification of the rules applying to the process of carrying out the project or to its output. All three of these causes are especially common in software projects, where scope creep is legendary. When either the process or output of a project is changed, there is almost always a concomitant change in the budget and/or schedule.

Conversations in recent years with more than 500 project managers have convinced us that coping with changes and changing priorities is perceived as the most important single problem facing the PM—or if not the most important, certainly the most irritating. When a senior financial officer of a toy manufacturing firm makes an offhand, negative comment about the color of a toy, and triggers a "total redesign" of the toy, thereby invalidating an already approved design, schedule, and budget, the project manager and the design artist may consider murder. (It is probable that a knowledgeable jury would find their action justifiable.)

The most common changes, however, are due to the natural tendency of the client and project team members to try to improve the product or service. New demands and performance requirements become apparent to the client which were not realized at the time of project initiation. New technologies become available or better ideas occur to the team as work progresses. As noted earlier, the later these changes are made in the project, the more difficult and costly they are to complete.

Without control, a continuing accumulation of little changes can have a major negative impact on the project's schedule and cost.

Leffingwell suggests that interaction between the project team and the customer should be regularized by partnering. The customer may then take some official responsibility for helping to manage project scope [19]. When the client is a part of the parent organization, the problem is often more difficult. Jealousy, mistrust, and conflict between departments (e.g., the traditional battle between marketing and engineering) leads to uncontrolled scope creep and to inevitable delays and budget overruns [10].

There is, however, no insurance against the risks associated with project changes. Total quality management and employee involvement will help if both the deliverable and the process by which it is to be produced are carefully studied by thoughtful teams that represent the interests of the major stakeholders in any project, the client, senior management, the project team, and the community. Also, a thorough knowledge of production processes will help avoid some manufacturability-related engineering changes [27]. Since prevention of change is not possible, the PM's best hope seems to lie in controlling the process by which change is introduced and accomplished.

This is accomplished with a formal *change control system* which, in some industries, is a part of their *configuration management system* responsible for integrating and coordinating changes throughout the systems development cycle. The purpose of the formal change control system is to:

- review all requested changes to the project (both content and procedures)
- identify all task impacts
- translate these impacts into project performance, cost, and schedule
- evaluate the benefits and costs of the requested changes
- identify alternative changes that might accomplish the same ends
- accept or reject the requested changes
- communicate the changes to all concerned parties
- ensure that the changes are implemented properly
- prepare monthly reports that summarize all changes to date and their project impacts.

The following simple guidelines, applied with reasonable rigor, can be used to establish an effective change control procedure.

1. All project contracts or agreements must include a description of how requests for a change in the project's plan, budget, schedule, and/or deliverables, will be introduced and processed.

2. Any change in a project will be in the form of a *change order* that will include a description of the agreed-upon change together with any changes in the plan, budget, schedule, and/or deliverables that result from the change.

3. Changes must be approved, in writing, by the client's agent as well as by an appropriate representative of senior management of the firm responsible for carrying out the project.

4. The project manager must be consulted on all desired changes prior to the preparation and approval of the change order. The project manager's approval, however, is not required.

5. Once the change order has been completed and approved, the project master plan should be amended to reflect the change, and the change order becomes a part of the master plan.

The process of controlling change is not complicated. If the project is large, Roman suggests a change control board [26, p. 274], a group representing all interested parties that processes all requests for change. For the typical small- or medium-sized project, however, the problem of handling change need not be complex. The main source of trouble is that too many project managers, in an attempt to avoid anything that smacks of bureaucracy, adopt an informal process of handling requests for change. Misunderstanding often arises from this informality, and the PM finds that the project becomes committed to deliver a changed output of extended scope, but will have to swallow the additional cost involved, and will have to scramble to meet the old, unchanged schedule.

The problems associated with dealing with change orders informally are particularly severe in the case of software and information system projects. We resist the notion that computer-oriented projects are significantly different from other types of projects in this regard. (For a diametric view, see [25].) Nonetheless, the precise techniques of managing projects are not independent of the technology applied on the project. Service sector projects often require different planning and control methods than do construction projects or R & D projects.

The severity of the problem of dealing with change in software projects, it seems to us, is caused by two, interrelated factors. First, software and information systems experts too often fail to explain adequately to the client the real nature of the systems they develop. Second, clients too often fail to make an adequate effort to understand the systems that become the lifeblood for their organizations. All too often, the systems developer is preoccupied by the technical demands of the systems and ignorant of the user's needs. And all too often, the user views the systems developer as a practitioner of some arcane art that cannot be penetrated by normal minds.

Given this basic failure to communicate, the client has no real idea of what is involved in changing a software project in order to provide another useful feature not specified in the original project requirements. The software technician, eager to please the customer, agrees to provide the utility, but does not make clear to the client the level of effort and time that will be required. The project is late, over budget, and the customer is angry. This scenario is played out again and again with neither side profiting from the experience. The formal process for change suggested above tends to reduce the degree of misunderstanding and disappointment.

Difficult as it may be, control is an important part of the PM's job on every project. Perhaps the most helpful advice we can give the PM is, in the language of the 1970s, to "hang loose." One effective project manager of our acquaintance tells his project team, "I will not accept crises after 4:30 P.M. You are limited to one crisis per day. Crises are not cumulative. If you don't get yours in today, you do not get two tomorrow." All this is said, of course, with good humor. Team members understand that the PM is not serious, but his projects seem to progress with exceptional smoothness. Crises do occur from time to time, but everyone on the team works to prevent them by applying control in an effective and timely manner.

Project Management in Practice
Better Control of Development Projects at Johnson Controls

The Automotive Systems Group of Johnson Controls was having trouble controlling their product development programs with each project being managed differently, disagreements about who was responsible for what, projects failing because of rapid company growth, and new employees having trouble fitting into the culture. For a solution, they went to their most experienced and successful project managers and condensed their knowledge into four detailed procedures for managing projects. Because these procedures are now common to all projects, they can be used to train new employees, standardize practices, create a common language, tie together different company functions, create common experiences, act as implicit job descriptions, and create a positive overall project management culture.

The first procedure is project approval for authorizing the expenditure of funds and use of resources. The sales department must first provide a set of product/market information, including financial data, project scope, critical dates, and engineering resource requirements before management will approve the project. Thus, projects are now scrutinized much more closely before work is started and money spent—when more questions are asked and more people are involved, better decisions tend to be made.

The second procedure is the statement-of-work, identifying agreements and assumptions for the project. Here, both the customer and top management must sign off before product design

work begins, thereby reducing misunderstandings regarding not only product specifications, prices, and milestones but also intangible product requirements, explicit exclusions, and generic performance targets. Maintaining this documentation over the life of the project has helped avoid problems caused by late product changes from the customer, particularly for 3–5 year projects where the personnel rotate off the project. Customers have, however, been slow to agree to this level of documentation because it limits their ability to change timing, prices, and specifications late in the program when they are more knowledgeable about their needs.

The third procedure is the work breakdown structure, consisting of nine critical life-cycle phases running from definition through production. Included in each of these nine phases are four key elements: the tasks, the timing of each task, the responsible individuals, and the meeting dates for simultaneous engineering (a formalized procedure at Johnson Controls).

The fourth procedure is a set of management reviews, crucial to successful project completion. Both the content and timing of these reviews are specified in advance and progression to the next phase of a project cannot occur until senior management has approved the prespecified requirements, objectives, and quality criteria for that phase. The procedure also specifies questions that must be answered and work that must be reviewed by senior management.

Through the use of these procedures, which are updated and improved with each new project experience, the learning that occurs in the organization is captured and made useful for future projects.

Source: W. D. Reith and D. B. Kandt, "Project Management at a Major Automotive Seating Supplier," *Project Management Journal*, September 1991.

SUMMARY

As the final subject in the project implementation part of the text, this chapter described the project control process in the planning-monitoring-controling cycle. The need for control was discussed and the three types available were described. Then the design of control systems was addressed, including management's role, achieving the proper balance, and attaining control of creative activity as well as handling changes.

- Control is directed to performance, cost, and time.

- The two fundamental purposes of control are to regulate results through altering activity and to conserve the organization's physical, human, and financial assets.

- The three main types of control processes are cybernetic (either first-, second-, or third-order), go/no-go, and postcontrol.

- The postcontrol report contains four sections:
  –Project objectives

  –Milestones and budgets
  –Final project results
  –Recommendations for improvement

- The trend projection curve, critical ratios, and the control chart are useful control tools.

- Control systems have a close relationship to motivation and should be well-balanced; that is, cost-effective, appropriate to the desired end results, and not overdone.

- Three approaches to the control of creativity are progress review, personnel reassignment, and control of inputs.

- The most irritating problem facing a PM is the control of change.

In the next chapter, we initiate the project termination part of the text, beginning with evaluation and auditing. This topic is closely related to the postcontrol topics in this chapter.

GLOSSARY

Champion A person with organizational clout who takes on personal responsibility (though not usually day-to-day management) for the successful completion of a project for the organization.

Control Assuring that reality meets expectations or plans. Usually involves the process of keeping actions within limits to assure that certain outcomes will in fact happen.

Control Chart A chart of a measure of performance—commonly a quality characteristic—over time, showing how it changes compared to a desired mean and upper and lower limits.

Critical Ratio A ratio of progress (actual/scheduled) times a cost ratio (budgeted/actual).

Cybernetic An automatic control system containing a negative feedback loop.

Early Warning System A monitoring system that forewarns the project manager if trouble arises.

Go/No-Go Initially, a type of gauge that quickly tells an inspector if an object's dimension is within certain limits. In the case of project management, this can be any measure that allows a manager to decide whether to continue, change, or terminate an activity or a project.

QUESTIONS

Material Review Questions

1. What is the purpose of control? To what is it directed?

2. What are the three main types of control system? What questions should a control system answer?

3. What tools are available to the project manager to use in controlling a project? Identify some characteristics of a good control system.

4. What is the mathematical expression for the critical ratio? What does it tell a manager?

5. Describe the relationship between motivation and control.

Class Discussion Questions

12. How might the project manager integrate the various control tools into a project control system?

13. How could a negative feedback control system be implemented in project management to anticipate client problems?

14. Compare the trend projection curve and the earned value chart. Could they be combined to aid the PM's control?

15. What other project parameters might a control chart be used for? How would their limits be set?

16. Control systems are sometimes classified into two categories, preventive and feedback. How do the three types of systems described in the chapter relate to these two categories?

Questions for Project Management in Practice

Extensive Controls for San Francisco's Metro Turnback Project

24. Draw a hierarchy/organization chart illustrating your interpretation of the various control systems/programs described in the writeup.

25. How do you think Quality Control and Quality Assurance were divided? Who was responsible for each and what did the responsibilities of each entail?

26. This project was critically aware of the possibility of "scope creep" over the 11-year duration of the project. How did they propose to control this danger?

Schedule and Cost Control for Australia's New Parliament House

27. Compare the construction look-ahead schedules for this project and the SF Metro Turnback project.

6. How is creativity controlled?

7. What are go/no-go gauges?

8. What is a champion?

9. Describe a cybernetic control system.

10. What should the postcontrol report include?

11. How should change be controlled?

17. How do internal and external controls differ?

18. What are some difficulties encountered when attempting project control?

19. How might the information required for control systems be collected?

20. How might the information collected through the control system be used on subsequent projects?

21. How does the control of creative projects differ from the control of ordinary projects?

22. Where might ethical issues arise for a PM in the stewardship of the company's resources?

23. Why is the control of change such a difficult problem for a PM?

28. How did they control costs in this project?

29. Where in the contracting process was "scope creep" controlled?

Better Control of Development Projects at Johnson Controls

30. Summarize the unique way Johnson achieved control over their projects.

31. How did "scope creep" enter the projects in the past? Which procedure is now directed at controlling this effect?

32. Which of the four procedures is probably most critical to successful projects?

33. What is the term used in the chapter for the senior management review described in the fourth procedure?

▩ PROBLEMS

1. Given the following information, calculate the critical ratios and indicate which activities are on target and which need to be investigated. Comment on the situation for each of the activities.

Activity	Actual Progress	Scheduled Progress	Budgeted Cost	Actual Cost
A	2 days	2 days	$40	$35
B	4 days	6 days	$30	$40
C	1 day	3 days	$50	$70
D	3 days	2 days	$25	$25

2. Calculate the critical ratios for the following activities and indicate which activities are probably on target and which need to be investigated. Comment on each activity.

Activity	Actual Progress	Scheduled Progress	Budgeted Cost	Actual Cost
A	4 days	4 days	$60	$40
B	3 days	2 days	$50	$50
C	2 days	3 days	$30	$20
D	1 day	1 day	$20	$30
E	2 days	4 days	$25	$25

3. Given the following information about a showroom renovation, which activities are on time, which are early, and which are behind schedule?

Activity	Budgeted Cost	Actual Cost	Critical Ratio
A	$60	$40	1.0
B	$25	$50	0.5
C	$45	$30	1.5
D	$20	$20	1.5
E	$50	$50	0.67

4. Design and plot a critical ratio for a computer installation project that had planned constant, linear progress from 0 to an earned value of 200 over a 100 day duration. In fact, progress for the first 20 days has been: 2, 3, 4, 6, 7, 9, 12, 14, 15, 17, 20, 21, 21, 22, 24, 26, 27, 29, 31, 33. What can you conclude about this project?

5. Design and plot a critical ratio for a Web site project that has planned constant, linear spending from 0 to a total of 1000 over a 100 day duration. In fact, daily spending for the first 15 days has been: 11, 10, 9, 10, 11, 12, 11, 9, 8, 9, 10, 12, 14, 11, 7. What can you conclude about this project?

6. Empire State Building, Inc., has two project teams installing virtually identical buildings for a customer in two separate cities. Both projects have a planned daily cost of 100 and a planned daily earned value of 100. The first six days for each team have progressed as follows:

Day	Team A: Earned Value	Team B: Earned Value	A: Cost	B: Cost
1	90	90	95	95
2	92	88	98	94
3	94	95	101	102
4	98	101	106	109
5	104	89	116	99
6	112	105	126	118

Compare the two projects in terms of general progress and according to critical ratios.

7. World Trade Building, Ltd., is also constructing an identical building for the same customer as in Problem 6 and has the following earned values and costs for the first six days: EV: 90, 88, 95, 101, 89, 105; Cost: 92, 88, 93, 98, 85, 100. Compare this project to the two in Problem 6.

8. The following information concerns progress at day 40 of an equipment installation project. Determine if the project is in control based on time and cost to date and, if not, what is the cost overage or underage?

Activity	Duration	Budget	Actual Cost	% Completed
1-2	10	300	250	100
2-3	8	400	450	100
2-4	12	350	380	100
4-3	0	0	0	
3-5	18	405	400	70
5-6	16	450	—	0

INCIDENTS FOR DISCUSSION

Speciality Pak, Inc.

Speciality Pak, Inc., is a custom packing operation serving the chemical industry in seven states. Speciality Pak has one operation in each state, and they vary in size from 50 to 240 employees. A disturbing trend has been developing for the last couple of years that Speciality Pak management wishes to stop. The incidence of tardiness and absenteeism is on the increase. Both are extremely disruptive in a custom packing operation. Speciality Pak is nonunion in all seven locations, and since management wants to keep this situation, it wants a careful, low-key approach to the problem. Jason Horn, assistant personnel manager, has been appointed project manager to recommend a solution. All seven operations managers have been assigned to work with him on this problem.

Jason has had no problem interfacing with the operations managers. They have very quickly agreed that three steps must be taken to solve the problem:

1. Institute a uniform daily attendance report that is summarized weekly and forwarded to the main office. (Current practice varies from location to location, but comments on attendance are normally included in monthly operations reports.)

2. Institute a uniform disciplinary policy, enforced in a uniform manner.

3. Initiate an intensive employee education program to emphasize the importance of good attendance.

The team has further decided that the three-point program should be tested before a final recommendation is presented. They have decided to test the program at one location for two months. Jason wishes to control and evaluate the test by having the daily attendance report transmitted to him directly at headquarters, from which he will make the final decision on whether to present the program in its current format or not.

Questions: Does this monitoring and control method appear adequate? What are the potential problems?

Night Tran Construction Company

Night Tran Construction Company specializes in building small power plants, mostly for utility companies. The company was awarded a contract approximately two years ago to build such a power plant. The contract stated a project duration of three years, after which a 1 percent penalty would be invoked for each additional month of construction. Project records indicate the utility plan is only 50 percent completed and is encountering continuing problems. The owner of Night Tran Company, concerned over the potential losses, investigated the project and found the following: There were an excessive number of engineering design changes; there was a high work rejection rate; and the project was generally understaffed. As a result, she directed the project manager to develop a better system of project control and present this method to the board members in one week.

Questions: If you were the project manager, what characteristics would you be looking for in the new control system? Will a new control system be adequate for the problem? Explain.

 BIBLIOGRAPHY

1. ACKOFF, R. L. "Beyond Problem Solving." *Decision Sciences,* April 1974.

2. AMRINE, H. T., J. A. RITCHEY, and O. S. HULLEY. *Manufacturing Organization and Management,* 5th ed. Englewood Cliffs, NJ: Prentice Hall, 1987.

3. ARCHIBALD, R. D. *Managing High Technology Programs and Projects.* New York: Wiley, 1992.

4. BLOCK, P. *Stewardship.* San Francisco: Berrett-Koehler, 1993.

5. BOBROWSKI, P. M. "Project Management Control Problems: An Information Systems Focus." *Project Management Journal,* June 1989.

6. BRAZ, E. F. "Project Management Oversight: A Control Tool of Owners of Engineering and Con-

struction Projects." *Project Management Journal,* March 1989.

7. BYRNE, J. "Project Management: How Much is Enough?" *PM Network,* February 1999.

8. CAMMANN, C., and D. A. NADLER. "Fit Control Systems to Your Management Style." *Harvard Business Review,* January–February 1976.

9. CESTIN, A. A. "What Makes Large Projects Go Wrong." *Project Management Quarterly,* March 1980.

10. GIBSON, L. "Project Scope Creep." *Today's Engineer,* Spring 1998.

11. GRANT, R. A., C. A. HIGGINS, and R. H. IRVING. "Computerized Performance Monitors: Are They Costing You Customers?" *Sloan Management Review,* Spring 1988.

12. GUPTA, V. K., and D. J. GRAHAM. "A Customer-Driven Quality Improvement and Management Project at Diamond Offshore Drilling." *Project Management Journal,* September 1997.

13. HAJEK, V. G. *Management of Engineering Projects.* New York: McGraw Hill, 1977.

14. HEYWOOD, G. E., and T. J. ALLEN. "Project Controls: How Much is Enough." *PM Network,* November, 1996.

15. HOWARD, D. C. "Cost Schedule Control Systems." *Management Accounting,* October 1976.

16. IBBS, C. W. and Y. -H. KWAK. "Benchmarking Project Management Organizations." *PM Network,* February 1998.

17. KARAA, F. A., and B. ABDALLAH. "Coordination Mechanisms During the Construction Project Life Cycle." *Project Management Journal,* September 1991.

18. KERZNER, H. "Evaluation Techniques in Project Management." *Journal of Systems Management,* February 1980.

19. LEFFINGWELL, D. "Engage! Involve the Customer to Manage Scope." *PM Network,* August 1997.

20. LIKIERMAN, A. "Avoiding Cost Escalation on Major Projects." *Management Accounting,* February 1980.

21. LIVINGSTON, J. L., and R. RONEN. "Motivation and Management Control Systems." *Decision Sciences,* April 1975.

22. MURDICK, R. G. et al. *Information Systems for Modern Management,* 3rd ed. Englewood Cliffs, NJ: Prentice Hall, 1984.

23. NEWMAN, W. H. *Constructive Control.* Englewood Cliffs, NJ: Prentice Hall, 1975.

24. PARTOVI, F. Y., and J. BURTON. "Timing of Monitoring and Control of CPM Projects." *IEEE Transactions on Engineering Management,* February 1993.

25. ROETZHEIM, W. H. "Managing Software Projects: Unique Problems and Requirements." in P. C. Dinsmore, ed., *The AMA Handbook of Project Management.* New York: AMACOM, 1993.

26. ROMAN, D. D. *Managing Projects: A Systems Approach.* New York: Elsevier, 1986.

27. SAEED, B. I., D. M. BOWEN, and V. S. SOHONI. "Avoiding Engineering Changes through Focused Manufacturing Knowledge." *IEEE Transactions on Engineering Management,* February 1993.

28. SAITOW, A. R. "CSPC: Reporting Project Progress to the Top." In E. W. Davis, ed., *Project Management: Techniques, Applications and Managerial Issues.* Norcross, GA: American Institute of Industrial Engineers, 1976.

29. SANDERS, J. "Effective Estimating Process Outlined." *Computer World,* April 7, 14, and 21, 1980.

30. SCHODERBEK, C. G., P. P. SCHODERBEK, and A. G. KEFALAS. *Management Systems,* 4th ed. Homewood, IL: Irwin, 1989.

31. SEESING, P R. "Distributing Project Control Database Information on the World Wide Web." *PM Network,* October 1996.

32. SETHI, N. K. "Project Management." *Industrial Management,* January–February. 1980.

33. SNOWDON, M. "Measuring Performance in Capital Project Management." *Long Range Planning,* August 1980.

34. THAMHAIN, H. J. "Best Practices for Controlling Technology-Based Projects." *Project Management Journal,* December 1996.

35. TIONG, R. L. K. "Effective Controls for Large Scale Construction Projects." *Project Management Journal,* March 1990.

36. TONEY, F. "What the Fortune 500 Know about PM Best Practices." *PM Network,* February 1997.

37. VAN GIGCH, J. P. *Applied General Systems Theory*, 2nd ed. New York: Harper & Row, 1978.

38. WEBER, F. M. "Ways to Improve Performance on Projects." *Project Management Quarterly*, September 1981.

39. WHITTEN, N. "Managing Priorities Effectively." *PM Network*, July 1995.

40. YUNUS, N. B., D. L. BABCOCK, and C. BENJAMIN. "Development of a Knowledge-Based Schedule Planning System." *Project Management Journal*, December 1990.

The following article reports on a study of hundreds of project managers and the challenges and barriers they perceived in successfully controlling projects. The potential problems leading to schedule slips and budget overruns are identified and compared to the directly observed reasons. Also, the general managers' reasons for the slips and overruns are compared to the project managers' reasons and significant differences are noted. Last, the criteria that seem to be important to control are listed and discussed.

The value of this article for managers is the insight it gives concerning what needs to be controlled to bring about successful projects. The major factors are defining a detailed project plan that includes all key project personnel, reaching agreement on the plan among the project team members and the customer, obtaining the commitment of management, defining measurable milestones, and detecting problems early.

DIRECTED READING

CONTROLLING PROJECTS ACCORDING TO PLAN

H. J. Thamhain and D. L. Wilemon: Criteria for Controlling Projects According to Plan.
***Project Management Journal*, June 1986.**
©1986 by the Project Management Institute. Reprinted by permission.

Few project managers would argue the need for controlling their projects according to established plans. The challenge is to apply the available tools and techniques effectively. That is, to manage the effort by leading the multifunctional personnel toward the agreed-on objectives within the given time and resource constraints. Even the most experienced practitioners often find it difficult to control programs in spite of apparent detail in the plan, personnel involvement, and even commitment. As summarized in Table 1, effective program management is a function of properly defining the work, budgets, and schedules and then monitoring progress. Equally important, it is related to the ability to keep personnel involved and interested in the work, to obtain and refuel commitment from the team as well as from upper management, and to resolve some of the enormous complexities on the technical, human, and organizational side.

Responding to this interest, a field study was initiated to investigate the practices of project managers re-

garding their project control experiences. Specifically, the study investigates:

1. Type of project control problems experienced by project managers.

2. Project management practices and performance.

3. Criteria for effective project control.

Method of Investigation

Data were collected over a period of three years from a sample of over 400 project leaders in predominantly technical undertakings, such as electronics, petrochemical, construction, and pharmaceutical projects. The data were collected mostly by questionnaires from attendees of project management workshops and seminars, as well as during in-plant consulting work conducted by the authors. Selectively, questionnaires were followed up by personal interviews. All data were checked for relevant sourcing to assure that the peo-

Table 1 Challenges of Managing Projects According to Plan

Rank	Challenge	Frequency (Mentioned by % of PMs)
1	Coping with End-Date Driven Schedules	85%
2	Coping with Resource Limitations	83%
3	Communicating Effectively among Task Groups	80%
4	Gaining Commitment from Team Members	74%
5	Establishing Measurable Milestones	70%
6	Coping with Changes	60%
7	Working Out Project Plan Agreement with Team	57%
8	Gaining Commitment from Management	45%
9	Dealing with Conflict	42%
10	Managing Vendors and Subcontractors	38%
11	Other Challenges	35%

ple who filled in the questionnaire had the minimum project leadership qualifications we established. These included: two years of experience in managing multidisciplinary projects, leading a minimum of three other project professionals, and being formally accountable for final results.

Sample Characteristics

The final qualifying sample included 304 project leaders from 183 technical projects. The leaders had an average of 5.2 years of project management experience. As shown by the sigma/standard deviation* the sample data are distributed widely:

---

*The distribution of the sample data is skewed. The sigma/standard deviation listed in parentheses corresponds to the positive side only.

Number of Project Leaders in Sample	304
Number of Projects in Sample	183
Number of Project Leaders per Project	1.66 ($\sigma = 1$)
Project Size (Average)	$850K ($\sigma = 310K$)
Project Duration (Average)	12 Months ($\sigma = 4$)
Multidisciplinary Nature (Average)	8 Team Members ($\sigma = 5$)
Project Management Experience/PM	5.2 Years ($\sigma = 2.5$)
Number of Previous Projects/PM	6 ($\sigma = 4.5$)

Data were collected in three specific modes: (1) Open-ended questions leading to a broad set of data, such as condensed in Table 2, and used for broad classifications and further, more detailed investigations; (2) Specific questions, requested to be answered on a tested five-point scale, such as shown in Figure 1. The scores enabled subsequent data ranking and correlation analysis; and (3) Interviews leading to a discussion of the previous findings and further qualitative investigations into the practices and experiences of project managers and their superiors.

All associations were measured by utilizing Kendall's Tau rank-order correlation. The agreement between project managers and their superiors on the reason for project control problems was tested by using the nonparametric Kruskal-Wallis one-way analysis of variance by ranks, setting the null-hypothesis for agreement at various confidence levels depending on the strength of the agreement or disagreement as specified in the write-up.

Discussion of Results

The results of this study are being presented in four parts. First, the reasons for poor project control are analyzed as they relate to budget overruns and schedule slips. Second, the less tangible criteria for these control problems are discussed. This part shows that many of the reasons blamed for poor project performance, such as insufficient front-end planning and underestimating the complexities and scope, are really rooted in some less obvious organizational, managerial, and interpersonal problems. Third, the relationship between project performance and project management problems is

Rank by		Reason or Problem	Rarely	Sometimes	Often	Most Likely	Always	Agreement Between GM & PM
General Managers	Project Managers		1	2	3	4	5	
1	10	Insufficient Front-End Planning		PM			GM	Disagree
2	3	Unrealistic Project Plan						Strongly Agree
3	8	Project Scope Underestimated						Disagree
4	1	Customer/Management Changes						Disagree
5	14	Insufficient Contingency Planning						Disagree
6	13	Inability to Track Progress		PM	GM			Disagree
7	5	Inability to Detect Problems Early						Agree
8	9	Insufficient Number of Checkpoints						Agree
9	4	Staffing Problems						Disagree
10	2	Technical Complexities						Disagree
11	6	Priority Shifts						Disagree
12	10	No Commitment by Personnel to Plan						Agree
13	12	Uncooperative Support Groups						Agree
14	7	Sinking Team Spirit						Disagree
15	15	Unqualified Project Personnel						Agree

Figure 1 Directly observed reasons for schedule slips and budget overruns.

discussed, and fourth, the criteria for effective project controls are summarized.

The Reasons for Poor Project Control Figure 1 summarizes an investigation into 15 problem areas regarding their effects on poor project performance. Specifically, project managers and their superiors (such as senior functional managers and general managers) indicate on a five-point scale their perception of how frequently certain problems are responsible for schedule slips and budget overruns. The data indicate that project leaders perceive these problem areas in a somewhat different order than their superiors.

While *project leaders* most frequently blame the following reasons as being responsible for poor project performance:

1. Customer and Management Changes
2. Technical Complexities
3. Unrealistic Project Plans
4. Staffing Problems
5. Inability to Detect Problems Early

Senior management ranks these reasons somewhat differently:

1. Insufficient Front-End Planning
2. Unrealistic Project Plans
3. Underestimated Project Scope
4. Customer and Management Changes
5. Insufficient Contingency Planning.

On balance, the data support the findings of subsequent interviews that project leaders are more concerned with external influences such as changes, complexities, staffing, and priorities while senior managers focus more on what should and can be done to avoid problems.

In fact, the differences between project leaders' and senior/superior management's perceptions were measured statistically by using a Kruskal-Wallis analysis of variance by ranks, based on the following test statistics:

Strong Agreement: If acceptable at > 99% confidence

Agreement: If acceptable at > 90% confidence

Weak Agreement: If acceptable at > 80% confidence

Disagreement: If rejected at 80% confidence

Project leaders disagree with their superiors on the ranking of importance for all but six reasons. What this means is that while both groups of management actually agree on the basic reasons behind schedule slips and budget overruns, they attach different weights. The practical implication of this finding is that senior management expects proper project planning, organizing, and tracking from project leaders. They further believe that the "external" criteria, such as customer changes and project complexities, impact project performance only if the project had not been defined properly and sound management practices were ignored. On the other side, management's view that some of the subtle problems, such as sinking team spirit, priority shifts, and staffing, are of lesser importance might point to a potential problem area. Management might be less sensitive to these struggles, get less involved, and provide less assistance in solving these problems.

Less Obvious and Less Visible Reasons for Poor Performance Managers at all levels have long lists of "real" reasons why the problems identified in Figure 1 occur. They point out, for instance, that while insufficient front-end planning eventually got the project into trouble, the real culprits are much less obvious and visible. These subtle reasons, summarized in Table 2, strike a common theme. They relate strongly to organizational, managerial, and human aspects. In fact, the most frequently mentioned reasons for poor project performance can be classified in five categories:

1. Problems with organizing project team
2. Weak project leadership
3. Communication problems
4. Conflict and confusion
5. Insufficient upper management involvement

Most of the problems in Table 2 relate to the manager's ability to foster a work environment conducive

Table 2 Potential Problems* (subtle reasons) Leading to Schedule Slips and Budget Overruns

01	Difficulty of Defining Work in Sufficient Detail
02	Little Involvement of Project Personnel During Planning
03	Problems with Organizing and Building Project Team
04	No Firm Agreement to Project Plan by Functional Management
05	No Clear Charter for Key Project Personnel
06	Insufficiently Defined Project Team Organization
07	No Clear Role/Responsibility Definition for P-Personnel
08	Rush into Project Kick-off
09	Project Perceived as Not Important or Exciting
10	No Contingency Provisions
11	Inability to Measure True Project Performance
12	Poor Communications with Upper Management
13	Poor Communications with Customer or Sponsor
14	Poor Understanding of Organizational Interfaces
15	Difficulty in Working across Functional Lines
16	No Ties between Project Performance and Reward System
17	Poor Project Leadership
18	Weak Assistance and Help from Upper Management
19	Project Leader Not Involved with Team
20	Ignorance of Early Warning Signals and Feedback
21	Poor Ability to Manage Conflict
22	Credibility Problems with Task Leaders
23	Difficulties in Assessing Risks
24	Insensitivity or Organizational Culture/Value System
25	Insufficient Formal Procedural Project Guidelines
26	Apathy or Indifference by Project Team or Management
27	No Mutual Trust among Team Members
28	Too Much Unresolved/Dysfunctional Conflict
29	Power Struggles
30	Too Much Reliance on Established Cost Accounting System

*The tabulated potential problems represent summaries of data compiled during interviews with project personnel and management.

to multidisciplinary teamwork, rich in professionally stimulating and interesting activities, involvement, and mutual trust. The ability to foster such a high-performance project environment requires sophisticated skills in leadership, technical, interpersonal, and administrative areas. To be effective, project managers must consider all facets of the job. They must consider the task, the people, the tools, and the organization. The days of the manager who gets by with technical expertise or pure administrative skills alone, are gone. Today the project manager must relate socially as well as technically. He or she must understand the culture and value system of the organization. Research* and experience show that effective project management is directly related to the level of proficiency at which these skills are mastered. This is also reflected in the 30 potential problems of our study (see Table 2) and the rank-order correlations summarized in Table 3. As indicated by the correlation figure of $\tau = -.45$, the stronger managers felt about the reasons in Figure 1, the stronger they also felt about the problems in Table 2 as reasons for poor project performance. This correlation is statistically significant at a confidence level of 99 percent and supports the conclusion that both sets of problem areas are related and require similar skills for effective management.

Management Practice and Project Performance Managers appear very confident in citing actual and potential problems. These managers are sure in their own mind that these problems, summarized in Figure 1 and Table 2, are indeed related to poor project performance. However, no such conclusion could be drawn without additional data and the specific statistical test shown in Table 3. As indicated by the strongly negative correlations between project performance and (1) potential problems ($\tau = -.55$) and (2) actual problems ($\tau = -.40$), the presence of either problem will indeed result in lower performance. Specifically, the stronger and more frequently project managers experience these problems, the lower was the manager judged

*For a detailed discussion of skill requirements of project managers and their impact on project performance see H. J. Thamhain & D. L. Wilemon, "Skill Requirements of Project Managers," *Convention Record, IEEE Joint Engineering Management Conference*, October 1978. and H. J. Thamhain, "Developing Engineering Management Skills" in *Management of R & D and Engineering*, North Holland Publishing Company, 1986.

Table 3 Correlation of Project Management Practices to Performance

Potential Problems vs. Actual	Correlation of (1) Potential Problems (Table 2) and (2) Directly Observed Reasons for Budget and Schedule Slips (Figure 1)	$\tau = -.45^*$
Potential Problems vs. Performance	Correlation of (1) Potential Problems Leading for Budget and Schedule Slips (Table 2) and (2) Project Performance (Top Management Judgment)	$\tau = -.55^*$
Actual Problems vs. Performance	Correlation of (1) Directly Observed Reasons for Budget and Schedule Slips (Figure 1) and (2) Project Performance	$\tau = -.40^*$

*99% Confidence Level (p = .01)
All Tau values are Kendall Tau Rank-Order Correlation

by superior managers regarding overall on-time and on-budget performance.

Furthermore, it is interesting to note that the more subtle potential problems correlate most strongly to poor performance ($\tau = -.55$). In fact, special insight has been gained by analyzing the association of each problem to project performance separately. Taken together, it shows that the following problems seem to be some of the most crucial *barriers* to high project performance:

- Team organization and staffing problems
- Work perceived as not important, challenging, having growth potential
- Little team and management involvement during planning
- Conflict, confusion, power struggle
- Lacking commitment by team and management
- Poor project definition

- Difficulty in understanding and working across organizational interfaces
- Weak project leadership
- Measurability problems
- Changes, contingencies, and priority problems
- Poor communications, management involvement and support.

To be effective, project leaders must not only recognize the potential barriers to performance, but also know where in the life cycle of the project they most likely occur. The effective project leader takes preventive actions early in the project life cycle and fosters a work environment that is conducive to active participation, interesting work, good communications, management involvement, and low conflict.

Criteria for Effective Project Control

The results presented so far focused on the reasons for poor project performance. That is, what went wrong and why were analyzed. This section concentrates on the lessons learned from the study and extensive interviews investigating the forces driving high project performance. Accordingly, this section summarizes the criteria which seem to be important for controlling projects according to plan. The write-up follows a recommendations format and flows with the project through its life cycle wherever possible.

1. *Detailed Project Planning.* Develop a detailed project plan, involving all key personnel, defining the specific work to be performed, the timing, the resources, and the responsibilities.
2. *Break the Overall Program into Phases and Subsystems.* Use Work Breakdown Structure (WBS) as a planning tool.
3. *Results and Deliverables.* Define the program objectives and requirements in terms of specifications, schedule, resources and deliverable items for the total program and its subsystems.
4. *Measurable Milestones.* Define measurable milestones and checkpoints throughout the program. Measurability can be enhanced by defining specific results, deliverables, technical performance measures against schedule and budget.
5. *Commitment.* Obtain commitment from all key personnel regarding the problem plan, its measures and results. This commitment can be enhanced

and maintained by involving the team members early in the project planning, including the definition of results, measurable milestones, schedules, and budgets. It is through this involvement that the team members gain a detailed understanding of the work to be performed, develop professional interests in the project and desires to succeed, and eventually make a firm commitment toward the specific task and the overall project objectives.

6. *Intra-Program Involvement.* Assure that the interfacing project teams, such as engineering and manufacturing, work together, not only during the task transfer, but during the total life of the project. Such interphase involvement is necessary to assure effective implementation of the developments and to simply assure "doability" and responsiveness to the realities of the various functions supporting the project. It is enhanced by clearly defining the results/deliverables for each interphase point, agreed upon by both parties. In addition, a simple sign-off procedure, which defines who has to sign off on what items, is useful in establishing clear checkpoints for completion and to enhance involvement and cooperation of the interphasing team members.
7. *Project Tracking.* Define and implement a proper project tracking system which captures and processes project performance data conveniently summarized for reviews and management actions.
8. *Measurability.* Assure accurate measurements of project performance data, especially technical progress against schedule and budget.
9. *Regular Reviews.* Project should be reviewed regularly, both on a work package (subsystem) level and total project level.
10. *Signing-On.* The process of "signing-on" project personnel during the initial phases of the project or each task seems to be very important to a proper understanding of the project objectives, the specific tasks, and personal commitment. The sign-on process that is so well described in Tracy Kidder's book, *The Soul of a New Machine,* is greatly facilitated by sitting down with each team member and discussing the specific assignments, overall project objectives, as well as professional interests and support needs.
11. *Interesting Work.* The project leader should try to accommodate the professional interests and de-

sires of supporting personnel when negotiating their tasks. Project effectiveness depends on the manager's ability to provide professionally stimulating and interesting work. This leads to increased project involvement, better communications, lower conflict, and stronger commitment. This is an environment where people work toward established objectives in a self-enforcing mode requiring a minimum of managerial controls. Although the scope of a project may be fixed, the project manager usually has a degree of flexibility in allocating task assignments among various contributors.

12. *Communication.* Good communication is essential for effective project work. It is the responsibility of the task leaders and ultimately the project manager to provide the appropriate communication tools, techniques, and systems. These tools are not only the status meetings, reviews, schedules, and reporting systems, but also the objective statements, specifications, list of deliverables, the sign-off procedure and critical path analysis. It is up to the project leaders to orchestrate the various tools and systems, and to use them effectively.

13. *Leadership.* Assure proper program direction and leadership throughout the project life cycle. This includes project definition, team organization, task coordination, problem identification and a search for solutions.

14. *Minimize Threats.* Project managers must foster a work environment that is low on personal conflict, power struggles, surprises, and unrealistic demands. An atmosphere of mutual trust is necessary for project personnel to communicate problems and concerns candidly and at an early point in time.

15. *Design a Personnel Appraisal and Reward System.* This should be consistent with the responsibilities of the people.

16. *Assure Continuous Senior Management Involvement, Endorsement, and Support of the Project.* This will surround the project with a priority image, enhance its visibility, and refuel over all commitment to the project and its objectives.

17. *Personal Drive.* Project managers can influence the climate of the work environment by their own actions. Concern for project team members, ability to integrate personal goals and needs of project personnel with project goals, and ability to create personal enthusiasm for the project itself can foster a climate of high motivation, work involvement, open communication, and ultimately high project performance.

A Final Note

Managing engineering programs toward established performance, schedule, and cost targets requires more than just another plan. It requires the total commitment of the performing organization plus the involvement and help of the sponsor/customer community. Successful program managers stress the importance of carefully designing the project planning and control system as well as the structural and authority relationships. All are critical to the implementation of an effective project control system. Other organizational issues, such as management style, personnel appraisals and compensation, and intraproject communication, must be carefully considered to make the system self-forcing; that is, project personnel throughout the organization must feel that participation in the project is desirable regarding the fulfillment of their professional needs and wants. Furthermore, project personnel must be convinced that management involvement is helpful in their work. Personnel must be convinced that identifying the true project status and communicating potential problems early will provide them with more assistance to problem solving, more cross-functional support, and in the end will lead to project success and the desired recognition for their accomplishments.

In summary, effective control of engineering programs or projects involves the ability to:

- Work out a detailed project plan, involving all key personnel
- Reach agreement on the plan among the project team members and the customer/sponsor
- Obtain commitment from the project team members
- Obtain commitment from management
- Define measurable milestones
- Attract and hold quality people
- Establish a controlling authority for each work package
- Detect problems early

References

1. ADAMS, J. R., & S. E. BARNDT. "Behavioral Implications of the Project Life Cycle," Chapter 12 in D. I. Cleland and W. R. King, *Project Management Handbook*. New York: Van Nostrand Reinhold, 1983.

2. ARCHIBALD, RUSSEL C. "Planning the Project." In *Managing High-Technology Programs and Projects*. New York: Wiley, 1976.

3. CASHER, J. D. "How to Control Project Risks and Effectively Reduce the Chance of Failure." *Management Review*, June, 1984.

4. DELANEY, W. A. "Management by Phases." *Advanced Management Journal*, Winter, 1984.

5. KING, W. R., & D. I. CLELAND. Life Cycle Management. Chapter 11 in D. I. Cleland and W. R. King, *Project Management Handbook*. New York: Van Nostrand Reinhold, 1983.

6. MCDOUNOUGH, E. F., & R. M. KINNUNEN. "Management Control of a New Product Development Project." *IEEE Transactions on Engineering Management*, February 1984.

7. PESSEMIER, E. A. *Product Management*. New York: Wiley, 1982.

8. SPIRER, H. F. "Phasing Out the Project." Chapter 13 in D. I. Cleland and W. R. King, *Project Management Handbook*. New York: Van Nostrand Reinhold, 1983.

9. STUCKENBRUCK, L. C. "Interface Management." Chapter 20 in *Matrix Management Systems Handbook*. New York: Van Nostrand Reinhold, 1984.

10. THAMHAIN, H. J. *Engineering Program Management*. New York: Wiley, 1984.

11. THAMHAIN, H. J., & D. L. WILEMON. "Project Performance Measurement, The Keystone to Engineering Project Control." *Project Management Quarterly*, January 1982.

12. THAMHAIN, H. J., & D. L. WILEMON. "Conflict Management in Project Lifecycles." *Sloan Management* Review, Summer 1975.

13. TUMINELLO, J. A. "Case Study of Information/KnowHow Transfer." *IEEE Engineering Management* Review, June 1984.

14. URBAN, G. L., & J. R. HAUSER. *Design and Marketing of New Products*. Englewood Cliffs, NJ: Prentice-Hall, 1980.

15. U.S. Air Force. *Systems Management–System Program Office Manual*, AFSCM 375-3, Washington DC, 1964.

Questions

1. Why do project managers and senior general managers see the reasons for project difficulty differently?

2. Why do the potential problems correlate more strongly with poor performance than the actual problems?

3. Overall, what do you conclude are the reasons for poor project performance?

4. Relate the findings in this article to the PM in Practice SF Turnback project control process and the PM in Practice Johnson Controls project management procedures.

5. Of the types of control discussed in the chapter, which type(s) is this article referring to?

13

Project Termination

As it must to all things, termination comes to every project. At times, project death is quick and clean, but more often it is a long process; and there are times when it is practically impossible to establish that death has occurred. The skill with which termination, or a condition we might call "near termination," is managed has a great deal to do with the quality of life after the project. The termination stage of the project rarely has much impact on technical success or failure, but it has a great deal to do with residual attitudes toward the project—the "taste left in the mouth" of the client, senior management, and the project team. It also has a great deal to do with learning about the things that lead to success—or failure.

At this point, the joy of discovery is past. Problems have been solved, bypassed, lived with, or ignored. Implementation plans have been carried out. The client is delighted, angry, or reasonably satisfied. In construction-type projects where the project cadre remains intact, the termination issue is eased because the team moves on to another challenge. For nonrecurring projects, the issue is far more akin to the breakup of a family. While the members of the family may be on the best of terms, they must now separate, go their individual ways, divide or dispose of the family property, and make plans for individual survival. Unless the project life was only a few weeks or a few months, the change is stressful. For projects organized as weak matrices, there will be only a few individuals, perhaps only the project manager, who "belong" to the project. This may represent an even more stressful situation than the breakup of a large project family because there is less peer group support and few or no sympathetic colleagues with whom to share the anxieties associated with transfer to a new project or back to a functional group.

The process of termination is never easy, always complicated, and, as much as we might wish to avoid it, almost always inevitable. The problem is how to accomplish one of the several levels of what is meant by project termination with a minimum of trouble and administrative dislocation.

Source: DILBERT reprinted by permission of United Feature Syndicate, Inc.

In this chapter, we examine the variety of conditions that may be generally re-ferred to as *project termination.* As indicated above, some projects are not actually ter-minated, but rather are severely slowed down. We then view some decision-aiding models that can assist an organization in making the termination decision. This re-quires us to return to the subject of evaluation and discuss indicators of success and failure in projects. We also discuss some procedures that decrease the pain of termi-nation, and others that reduce the administrative problems that often arise after projects have been terminated. We look into the typical causes of termination, and finally note that the preparation of a project history is an integral part of the termi-nation process.

13.1 THE VARIETIES OF PROJECT TERMINATION

For our purposes, a project can be said to be terminated when work on the substance of the project has ceased or slowed to the point that further progress on the project is no longer possible, when the project has been indefinitely delayed, when its resources have been deployed to other projects, or when project personnel (especially the PM) become personae non gratae with senior management and in the company lunch-room. There may seem to be a spark of life left, but resuscitation to a healthy state is most unlikely. On rare occasions, projects are reborn to a new, glorious existence [2]. But such rebirth is not expected, and project team members who "hang on to the bit-ter end" have allowed optimism to overcome wisdom. The PM must understand that the ancient naval tradition that the captain should go down with the ship does not serve the best interests of the Navy, the crew, the ship, and most certainly not the captain.

On the other hand, the captain must not, ratlike, flee the "ship" at the first sign of trouble. In the next section of this chapter, we note many of the signs and signals that indicate that the project may be in real trouble. At this point, it is appropriate to consider the ways in which a project can be terminated. There are four fundamentally different ways to close out a project: extinction, addition, integration, and starvation.

Termination by Extinction

The project is stopped. It may end because it has been successful and achieved its goals: The new product has been developed and handed over to the client; the building has been completed and accepted by the purchaser; or the software has been installed and is running.

The project may also be stopped because it is unsuccessful or has been superseded: The new drug failed its efficacy tests; the yield of the chemical reaction was too low; there are better/faster/cheaper/prettier alternatives available; or it will cost too much and take too long to get the desired performance. Changes in the external environment can kill projects, too. The explosion of the Challenger stopped a number of space shuttle projects overnight. More recently, extraordinary cost escalation in the technology and materials associated with automotive racing caused the ruling bodies of both Formula 1 and Indy-car racing to stop (and even repeal) technological change in their respective venues.

A special case of termination by extinction is "termination by murder."* There are all sorts of murders. They range from political assassination to accidental projecticide. When senior executives vie for promotion, projects for which the loser is champion are apt to suffer. Corporate mergers often make certain projects redundant or irrelevant. NCR was forced to cancel several projects following its merger into AT&T, and probably several more when NCR was more recently unmerged.

Two important characteristics of termination by murder, premeditated or not, are the suddenness of project demise and the lack of obvious signals that death is imminent.

When a decision is made to terminate a project by extinction, the most noticeable event is that all activity on the *substance* of the project ceases. A great deal of organizational activity, however, remains to be done. Arrangements must be made for the orderly release of project team members and their reassignment to other activities if they are to remain in the parent organization. The property, equipment, and materials belonging to the project must be disbursed according to the dictates of the project contract or in accord with the established procedures of the parent organization. Finally, the Project Final Report, also known as the *project history*, must be prepared. These subjects will be covered in greater detail later in this chapter.

Termination by Addition

Most projects are "in-house," that is, carried out by the project team for use in the parent organization. If a project is a major success, it may be terminated by institutionalizing it as a formal part of the parent organization. NCR Corporation (prior to its merger and demerger with AT&T), for example, used this method of transforming a project into a division of the firm and then, if real economic stability seems assured, into an independent subsidiary. Essentially the same process occurs when a university creates an academic department out of what originally was a few courses in an exist-

---

*The authors thank Professor Samuel G. Taylor (University of Wyoming) for noting this special case of termination by extinction.

ing department. For example, most software engineering and/or information systems departments began by reorganizing an engineering or business school "sub-specialty" into a full-fledged department.

When the project is made a more or less full-fledged member of the parent, it lives its first years in a protected status—much as any child is protected by the adults in the family. As the years pass, however, the child is expected gradually to assume the economic responsibilities of full adulthood.

When project success results in termination by addition, the transition is strikingly different from termination by extinction. In both cases the project ceases to exist, but there the similarity stops. Project personnel, property, and equipment are often simply transferred from the dying project to the newly born division. The metamorphosis from project to department, to division, and even to subsidiary is accompanied by budgets and administrative practices that conform to standard procedure in the parent firm, by demands for contribution profits, by the probable decline of political protection from the project's corporate "champion," indeed by a greater exposure to all the usual stresses and strains of regular, routine, day-to-day operations.

It is not uncommon, however, for some of the more adventurous members of the project team to request transfers to other projects or to seek the chance to start new projects. Project life is exciting, and some team members are uncomfortable with what they perceive to be the staid, regulated existence of the parent organization. The change from project to division brings with it a sharply diminished sense of freedom.

This transition poses a difficult time for the PM, who must see to it that the shift is made smoothly. In Part I of this book, and especially in Chapter 3, we referred repeatedly to the indispensable requirement of political sensitivity in the PM. The transition from project to division demands a superior level of political sensitivity for successful accomplishment. Projects lead a sheltered life, for all the risks they run. The regular operating divisions of a firm are subjected to the daily infighting that seems, in most firms, to be a normal result of competition between executives.

Project Management in Practice
Nucor's Approach to Termination by Addition

Nucor, one of the early steel "minimills," is a highly entrepreneurial firm with a compound growth rate of 23 percent per year. In 1987, its sales were $851 million with an executive staff of only 19 monitoring the operations of 23 plants and 4600 employees. As part of its strategy, Nucor in 1983 decided to move into the flat rolled steel market, the largest market for steel products. They thus initiated the construction of a major plant in Crawfordsville, Indiana, which would comprise over 20 percent of their total assets.

As another part of its strategy, Nucor does its own construction management, with most of the construction team then transitioning into permanent positions in the newly constructed plant. In this case, four managers started the conceptual team for the new facility and then brought in 19 other people from outside the company to form the rest of the construction team, none of them ever having built a steel mill before. The manager on the conceptual team for the new plant was the lead person on the site determination team and became the general manager of the facility. The field shift superintendents on the construction project will have permanent managerial responsibility for the melt shop, the hot mill, and the cold mill. The engineers will become super-

visors in the mill. Even the secretary/clerk will have a position in the new facility.

Nucor also relies heavily on the services and capabilities of its suppliers in the construction process, since they are such a small firm. But it also reflects Nucor's "lean and mean" philosophy. In this case, the only error the construction team made was underestimating the engineering time required from suppliers, the time coming in at about double the estimate. Even so, the engineering costs (and probably most other labor costs, too) apparently only ran about 20 percent of what it historically costs to build this type of steel facility!

Source: R. Kimball, "Nucor's Strategic Project," *Project Management Journal,* September 1988.

Termination by Integration

This method of terminating a project is the most common way of dealing with successful projects, and the most complex. The property, equipment, material, personnel, and functions of the project are distributed among the existing elements of the parent organization. The output of the project becomes a standard part of the operating systems of the parent, or client.

In some cases, the problems of integration are relatively minor. The project team that installed a new machining center, instructed the client in its operation and maintenance, and then departed probably left only minor problems behind it, problems familiar to experienced operations managers. If the installation was an entire flexible manufacturing system, however, or a minicomputer complete with multiple terminals and many different pieces of software, then the complexities of integration are apt to be much more severe. In general, the problems of integration are inversely related to the level of experience that the parent organization (or client) has had with: (1) the technology being integrated and (2) the successful integration of other projects, regardless of technology.

Most of the problems of termination by addition are also present when the project is integrated. In the case of integration, the project may not be viewed as a competitive interloper, but the project personnel being moved into established units of the parent organization will be so viewed. Also, the project, which flourished so well in its protected existence as a project, may not be quite so healthy in the chill atmosphere of the "real world." The individuals who nurtured the project may have returned to their respective organizational divisions, and may have new responsibilities. They tend to lose their fervid interest in the "old" project.

Following is a list of a few of the more important aspects of the transition from project to integrated operation that must be considered when the project functions are distributed.

1. *Personnel* Where will the project team go? Will it remain a team? If the functions that the team performed are still needed, who will do them? If ex-team members are assigned to a new project, under what conditions or circumstances might they be temporarily available for help on the old project?

2. *Manufacturing* Is training complete? Are input materials and the required facilities available? Does the production system layout have to be replanned? Did the change create new bottlenecks or line-of-balance problems? Are new operating or control procedures needed? Is the new operation integrated into the firm's computer systems?

3. *Accounting/Finance* Have the project accounts been closed and audited? Do the new department budgets include the additional work needed by the project? Have the new accounts been created and account numbers been distributed? Has all project property and equipment been distributed according to the contract or established agreements?

4. *Engineering* Are all drawings complete and on file? Are operating manuals and change procedures understood? Have training programs been altered appropriately for new employees? Have maintenance schedules been adjusted for the change? Do we have a proper level of "spares" in stock?

5. *Information Systems/Software* Has the new system been thoroughly tested? Is the software properly documented and are "comments" complete? Is the new system fully integrated with current systems? Have the potential users been properly trained to use the new system?

6. *Marketing* Is the sales department aware of the change? Is marketing in agreement about lead times? Is marketing comfortable with the new line? Is the marketing strategy ready for implementation?

7. *Purchasing, Distribution, Legal, etc.* Are all these and other functional areas aware of the change? Has each made sure that the transition from project to standard operation has been accomplished within standard organizational guidelines and that standard administrative procedures have been installed?

Termination by Starvation

There is a fourth type of project termination, although strictly speaking, it is not a "termination" at all. It is "slow starvation by budget decrement."Almost anyone who has been involved with projects over a sufficient period of time to have covered a business recession has had to cope with budget cuts. Budget cuts, or decrements, are not rare. Because they are common, they are sometimes used to mask a project termination.

There may be a number of reasons why senior management does not wish to terminate an unsuccessful or obsolete project. In some firms, for example, it is politically dangerous to admit that one has championed a failure, and terminating a project that has not accomplished its goals is an admission of failure. In such a case, the project budget might receive a deep cut—or a series of small cuts—large enough to prevent further progress on the project and to force the reassignment of many project team members. In effect, the project is terminated, but the project still exists as a legal entity complete with sufficient staff to maintain some sort of presence such as a secretary who issues a project "no-progress" report each year. In general, it is considered bad manners to inquire into such projects or to ask why they are still "on the books."

13.2 WHEN TO TERMINATE A PROJECT

The decision to terminate a project early, by whatever method, is difficult. As we emphasized in Chapter 4, projects tend to develop a life of their own—a life seemingly independent of whether or not the project is successful. In an early article [8] on the subject of terminating R & D projects, Buell suspected that the main reason so little information was available on the subject was that it was hard to spell out specific guidelines and standards for the decision. He expressed strong doubts about the ability to "wrap everything up in a neat set of quantitative mathematical expressions," and then went on to develop an extensive set of questions that, if answered, should lead management to a decision. While these questions were aimed at R & D projects, they have wide, general applicability. Paraphrased and slightly modified to broaden and extend them beyond R&D projects, they are:

- Is the project still consistent with organizational goals?
- Is it practical? Useful?
- Is management sufficiently enthusiastic about the project to support its implementation?
- Is the scope of the project consistent with the organization's financial strength?
- Is the project consistent with the notion of a "balanced" program in all areas of the organization's technical interests? In "age"? In cost?
- Does the project have the support of all the departments (e.g., finance, manufacturing, marketing, etc.) needed to implement it?
- Is organizational project support being spread too thin?
- Is support of this individual project sufficient for success?
- Does this project represent too great an advance over current technology? Too small an advance?
- Is the project team still innovative, or has it gone stale?
- Can the new knowledge be protected by patent, copyright, or trade secret?
- Could the project be farmed out without loss of quality?
- Is the current project team properly qualified to continue the project?
- Does the organization have the required skills to achieve full implementation or exploitation of the project?
- Has the subject area of the project already been "thoroughly plowed"?
- Has the project lost its key person or champion?
- Is the project team enthusiastic about success?

- Can the potential results be purchased or subcontracted more efficiently than developed in-house?
- Does it seem likely that the project will achieve the minimum goals set for it? Is it still profitable? timely?

We could add many other such questions to Buell's list. For instance:

- Has the project been obviated by technical advances or new products/services developed elsewhere?
- Is the output of the product still cost-effective?
- Is it time to integrate or add the project as a part of the regular, ongoing operation of the parent organization?
- Would we support the project if it were proposed today at the time and cost required to complete it?
- Are there better alternative uses for the funds, time, and personnel devoted to the project?
- Has a change in the environment altered the need for the project's output?

Such questions clearly overlap, and the list could easily be extended further. Dean [10] reports that the probabilities of technical and/or commerical failure are the two most important reasons for terminating projects (see Table 13-1), according to

Table 13-1. Rank-Order of Important Factors Considered in Terminating R&D Projects (36 Companies)

Factors	No. of Companies Reporting the Factor as Being Important
Technical	
Low probability of achieving technical objectives or commercializing results	34
Technical or manufacturing problems cannot be solved with available R&D skills	11
Higher priority of other projects requiring R&D labor or funds	10
Economic	
Low profitability or return on investment	23
Too costly to develop as individual product	18
Market	
Low market potential	16
Change in competitive factors or market needs	10
Others	
Too long a time required to achieve commerical results	6
Negative effects on other projects or products	3
Patent problems	1

Source: [10]

the executives he surveyed. Balachandra and Raelin [5, 28] performed a discriminant analysis on 23 factors involved in terminating projects, not as a decision model, but as a way of highlighting the various factors involved and their relevance to the termination problem, as related to projects in general.

Compared to the great level of research and thought concerning the project selection decision before the 1980s (see also Chapter 2), there was relatively little research published on the termination decision. But even this bit was more than the work devoted to defining project success. As interest in project termination increased in the mid-1980s, interest in understanding project success also rose. Baker et al. [3] looked at factors associated with R & D project success and failure. Pinto and Slevin [25, 26] surveyed experienced PMs and found ten factors that the managers felt to be critical to successful project implementation (see Table 13-2). Jiang et al., surveyed information system "business professionals" on the relative importance of the Pinto and Slevin critical success factors and came to roughly similar conclusions [15].

Ingram studied 62 client/server and open systems projects and found, among several other conclusions, that "effective project management is directly linked to positive project outcomes while technical elegance shows only a minor correlation" [14, p.33]. Shenhar, et al. surveyed project managers and found four "dimensions of project success:" the efficiency with which the project is carried out, the customer's satisfaction and willingness to use (and repurchase) the product, the impact of the project on the organization carrying it out, and the degree to which the project contributes to the firm's future [32]. Many other researchers also attacked the problem of defining project success or delineating the path to it [see 11, 20, and 21, for example]. Balachandra and Friar have done an extensive review of the relevant literature and

Table 13-2. Critical Success Factors in Order of Importance

1. *Project Mission*—Initial clearly defined goals and general directions.
2. *Top-Management Support*—Willingness of top management to provide the necessary resources and authority/power for project success.
3. *Project Schedule/Plan*—A detailed specification of the individual action steps for project implementation.
4. *Client Consultation*—Communication, consultation, and active listening to all impacted parties.
5. *Personnel*—Recruitment, selection, and training of the necessary personnel for the project team.
6. *Technical Tasks*—Availability of the required technology and expertise to accomplish the specific technical action steps.
7. *Client Acceptance*—The act of "selling" the final project to its ultimate intended users.
8. *Monitoring and Feedback*—Timely provision of comprehensive control information at each stage in the implementation process.
9. *Communication*—The provision of an appropriate network and necessary data to all key actors in the project implementation.
10. *Trouble-shooting*—Ability to handle unexpected crises and deviations from plan.

Source: [25]

concluded that market, technological, and organizational factors are associated with success in R&D and new product development projects depending on whether the innovation is incremental or radical, the technology is low or high, and the market is new or existing [4].

A particularly important finding of Baker et al. [3] is that the *factors associated with project success are different for different industries*. Baker's work was restricted to R&D projects, but the Pinto and Slevin study covered many different types of projects. They found that the success-related factors differed between fundamentally different types of projects—between R&D and construction projects, for example. At the very least, the factors and their relative importance are idiosyncratic to the industry, to the project type, and, we suggest, possibly to the firm.

Out of this work came some models that could be used to predict project success or failure, based on certain project characteristics or practices. Pinto and Mantel [24], using Pinto's work cited above, reported on factors that were associated with project failure. The factors differed for the type of project involved (R&D vs. construction), for the project's position in the life cycle, as well as for the precise way in which "failure" was defined. Green, Welsh, and Dehler found that a poor fit with the firm's existing technological expertise and/or with its existing marketing area and channels was a good early predictor of project termination [12]. Kloppenborg and Plath [17] described precursors to success and failure for projects intended to implement expert systems, and Beale and Freeman [6] modeled project success, differentiating between factors exogenous and endogenous to the project and the project team.

In the face of this diversity of success factors, it is interesting to note that there are relatively few fundamental reasons why some projects fail to produce satisfactory answers to Buell's questions.

1. **A Project Organization Is Not Required**   The use of the project form of organization was inappropriate for this particular task or in this particular environment. The parent organization must understand the conditions that require instituting a project.

2. **Insufficient Support from Senior Management**   Projects invariably develop needs for resources that were not originally allocated. Arguments between functional departments over the command of such resources are very common. Without the direct support of a champion in senior management, the project is almost certain to lose the resource battle.

3. **Naming the Wrong Person as Project Manager**   This book is testimony to the importance of the PM. A common mistake is to appoint as PM an individual with excellent technical skills but weak managerial skills or training.

4. **Poor Planning**   This is a very common cause of project failure. In the rush to get the substance of the project under way, competent planning is neglected. In such cases, crisis management becomes a way of life, difficulties and errors are compounded, and the project slowly gets farther behind schedule and over budget. Indeed, careful planning is associated with success in almost all empirical research

on project success—Tom Peter's "Ready, Fire, Aim" to the contrary notwithstanding. Not only is proper planning often cited as a *success factor*, lack of planning is cited as a *cause of failure* [7].

These, and a few other reasons, are the base causes of most project failures. The specific causes of failure, for the most part, derive from these fundamental items. For example,

- No use was made of earlier project Final Reports that contained a number of recommendations for operating projects in the future.

- Time/cost estimates were not prepared by those who had responsibility for doing the work.

- Starting late, the PM jumped into the tasks without adequate planning.

- Project personnel were moved without adjusting the schedule, or were reassigned during slow periods and then were unavailable when needed.

- Project auditors/evaluators were reluctant to conduct careful, detailed meaningful evaluations.

- The project was allowed to continue in existence long after it had ceased to make cost-effective progress.

- Evaluations failed to determine why problems were arising during the early phases of the project life cycle.

All these causes of failure underline the need for careful evaluation at all stages of the project. But at the same time, it is most important for the reader to note that the lion's share of the attention given to the termination issue is focused on the failing project. It is equally or more important to terminate successful projects at the right time and by proper methods. One rarely mentioned problem affecting many organizations is the inability or unwillingness of successful project managers working on successful projects to "let their projects go." This is a particularly difficult problem for in-house projects. The PM (and team) simply will not release the project to the tender care of the client department. An outstanding technical specialist and manager conducting communications projects was released from employment simply because she insisted on maintaining semipermanent control of projects that had essentially been completed, but which were not released to the users because they "needed further testing" or "fine-tuning."

Also, little consideration has been given to *how* the termination decision is made and *who* makes it. We feel that a broadly based committee of reasonably senior executives is probably best. The broad organizational base of the committee is needed to diffuse and withstand the political pressure that accompanies all terminations—successes and failures alike. To the extent possible, the criteria used by the termination committee should be written and explained in some detail. It is, however, important to write the criteria in such a way that the committee is not frozen into a mechanistic approach to a decision. There are times when hunches should be followed (or rejected) and blind faith should be respected (or ignored). It depends on whose hunches and faith are under consideration [2].

On October 19, 1993, Congress pulled the plug on the Superconducting Super Collider (SSC) project, ending 11 years of work costing over $2 billion dollars and throwing 2000 people out of work. The objective of the planned $11 billion SSC was to accelerate subatomic particles within a 54-mile underground circular chamber to almost the speed of light and smash them together at energies of 40 trillion electronic volts. The benefits to society of these experiments were unclear, some maintaining they could have been

Source: B. Baker and R. Menon, "Politics and Project Performance: The Fourth Dimension of Project Management," *PM Network*, November 1995, pp. 16–21.

enormous, but others including congressmen were less sure.

The project also suffered from an identify crisis. It was not clear if this was to be a U.S. "first" in basic science or a "world" science project, funded in its early stages by a $1 billion commitment from other nations. Although the costs of the SSC had ballooned, the main reason it was terminated was that it lost its political support. Although the SSC scientists and backers had rallied good will among universities, schools, and scientific meetings, the potential benefits of the project never reached the Clinton administration, where it only enjoyed lukewarm support at best. When a $4 trillion budget deficit appeared likely, the SSC project was sacrificed.

The gigantic tunnels for the supercollider are prepared first.

13.3 THE TERMINATION PROCESS

The termination process has two distinct parts. First is the decision whether or not to terminate. Second, if the decision is to terminate the project, the decision must be carried out.

The Decision Process

Decision-aiding models for the termination decision fall into two generic categories. First, there are models that base the decision on the degree to which the project qualifies against a set of factors generally held to be associated with successful (or failed) projects. Second, there are models that base the decision on the degree to which the project meets the goals and objectives set for it.

Most of the research on factors associated with success and failure can be used to "predict" project success. Pinto's work with Slevin and others [particularly 24 and 26] can be used in that way. Tadisina [34], working with a set of factors associated with project success found by Baker, et al. [3], suggested a variety of termination-decision models that could be used if the success-related factors were monitored and used as input data in the models. Freeman and Beale [11] focused their decision model on the net present value of the project, which is determined by transforming a number of success-related factors (from the sponsor's and the project manager's points of view) into NPV equivalents. Riggs et al. [30] determined a set of success-related factors pertaining to government (NASA) projects by polling experienced managers using the Delphi method. From this, they developed statistically-generated "success predictor models" for manned and unmanned space projects. Finally, Chi and his colleagues developed a model for the termination decision on the projects that have an uncertain completion time and have some salvage value [9].

The use of models that measure project success or failure based on its achievement of present goals is subject to debate.

Balachandra and Raelin [5, 28] state that project selection models are not appropriate for the project termination decision. Others agree, but cite [5 and 28] as the reason [18, p. 277]. The argument is that the data requirements for selection models are too large and costly. They also argue that the evaluation of factors in project selection models may change as projects are evaluated at different stages in their life cycles. They note that the probability of technical success of a project is usually estimated to be close to 1.0 early in the life cycle, but lower during later stages when the technical problems are known. This, they say, would bias decisions in favor of new projects and against ongoing ones.

We think [19] that the first argument is generally untrue of those selection models actually being used, which are typically of modest size. As we have remarked elsewhere in this book, the uncertainty associated with most projects is not concerned with whether or not the project objective is technically achievable, but rather with the time and cost required to achieve it. The fact that selection criteria may change between the time that the project is started and the time it is judged for possible termination is not a relevant criticism of the use of a selection model. Indeed, whatever the source of the criteria for termination, they should be determined by the organization's policy at the time the decision is made—not judged by the policy of some prior time.

Adopting the position that sunk costs are not relevant to current investment decisions, we hold that the primary criterion for project continuance or termination is *whether or not the organization is willing to invest the estimated time and cost required to complete the project, given the project's current status and current expected outcome.* We emphasize that this criterion can be applied to any project. While we maintain the position that sunk costs are irrelevant, not everyone agrees [16].

Shafer and Mantel [31] developed a project termination decision support system (DSS) based on a constrained weighted factor scoring model (see Chapter 2). The capabilities of most popular spreadsheets allow direct modeling of the scoring model, allow customized menus, and allow decision makers to adapt and enhance the model as they gain experience in the use of the DSS. The database requirements include data on the project, on the parent organization, and on the environment. The criteria on which projects are rated, the specifics of the scores, and the relative weights of the criteria are often developed by organizational executives using the Delphi method. For a description of the use of the Delphi method to develop criteria weights, see the Web site for this book. If it seems desirable, the weights may be determined through discriminant analysis, as in [5, 28, 34].

Just as decision criteria, constraints, weights, and environmental data are unique to each organization, so are the specifics of using this (or any) decision model. A detailed discussion of various potential decision rules that might be useful with such a model can be found in [31]. Figure 13-1 illustrates the structure of this model.

The Implementation Process

Once it has been decided to terminate a project, the process by which it will be terminated must be implemented. The actual termination can be planned and orderly, or a simple hatchet job. The former is apt to have significantly better results, and so we suggest that the termination process be planned, budgeted, and scheduled just as is done for any other phase of the project life cycle. Such a project is illustrated in Figure 13-2. Archibald [1] has prepared an extensive checklist of items covering the closeout of both the administrative and substantive parts of the project (see Figures 13-3a and b).

In some organizations, the processing of the project closeout is conducted under the direct supervision of the PM, but this often raises dilemmas. For many PMs, termination signals the end of their reign as project leader. If the PM has another project to lead, the issue may not be serious; but if there is no other project and if the PM faces a return to a staid life in a functional division, there may be a great temptation to stretch out the termination process.

An examination of Figures 13-2 and 13-3a and 13-3b shows that implementing termination is a complex process. Note that in Figure 13-3b such items as A-4, B-4, C-3, and G-2, among many others, are actually small projects. It is all too easy, at this final stage of the game, to give this mountain of paperwork a "lick and a promise"—easy, but foolish. Someone must handle all the bureaucratic tasks, and if the PM

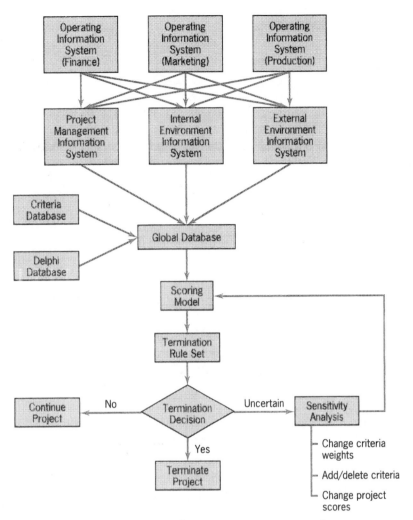

Figure 13-1 DSS structure for a project termination decision.

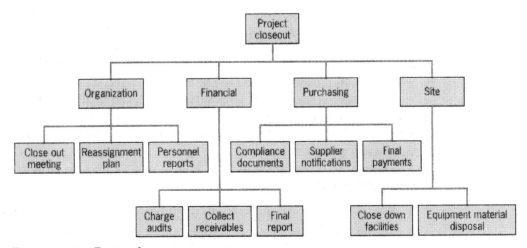

Figure 13-2 Design for project termination.

PROJECT TITLE _____ COMPLETION DATE _____

CONTRACT NO. _____ COST TYPE _____

CUSTOMER _____ PROJECT MGR. _____

The project close-out check lists are designed for use in the following manner:
Column I—Item No.: Each task listed is identified by a specific number and grouped into
   categories. Categories are based on functions, not on organizations or equipment.
Column II—Task Description: Task descriptions are brief tasks that could apply to more than
   one category but are listed only in the most appropriate category.
Column III—Required, Yes or No: Check whether the item listed applies to the project.
Column IV—Date Required: Insert the required date for accomplishment of the task.
Column V—Assigned Responsibility: Insert the name of the person responsible to see that
   the task is accomplished on schedule. This may be a member of the Project Office or an
   individual within a functional department.
Column VI—Priority (PR): A priority system established by the Project Manager may be
   used here, e.g., Priority #1 may be all tasks that must be accomplished before the
   contractual completion date, Priority #2 within 2 weeks after the completion date, etc.
Column VII—Notes, Reference: Refer in this column to any applicable Procedures, a
   government specification that may apply to that task, etc.

Figure 13-3a Instructions for project termination checklist. *Source:* [1]

leaves many loose ends, he or she will rapidly get a reputation for being slipshod, a characterization not associated with career success.

The PM also has another option, to ignore the termination process entirely. The evaluation has already been conducted and praise or censure has been delivered. Rather than deal with termination, the PM may let the project administrator handle things. Project team members may well have similar feelings and reactions, and may seek new jobs or affiliations before the project actually ends, thereby dragging out some final tasks interminably.

Special *termination managers* are sometimes useful in completing the long and involved process of shutting down a project. In such cases, the PM is transferred to another project or reassigned to a functional "home." The termination manager does not have to deal with substantive project tasks and therefore may be a person familiar with the administrative requirements of termination and the environment within which the project will be operating (if it continues to live).

If technical knowledge is required during the termination process, a member of the project team may be upgraded and assigned responsibility for the termination. This "promotion" is often a motivator and will provide development experience for the team member.

The primary duties of the termination manager are encompassed in the following nine general tasks:

1. Ensure completion of the work, including tasks performed by subcontractors.

2. Notify the client of project completion and ensure that delivery (and installation) is accomplished. Acceptance of the project must be acknowledged by the client.

Item No.	Task Description	Required		Required Date	Assigned Responsibility	PR.	Notes Reference
		Yes	No				
A.	*Project office (PO) and Project Team (PT) Organization*						
1.	Conduct project close-out meeting						
2.	Establish PO and PT release and reassignment plan						
3.	Carry out necessary personnel actions						
4.	Prepare personal performance evaluation on each PO and PT member						
B.	*Instructions and Procedures* issue instructions for:						
1.	Termination of PO and PT						
2.	Close-out of all work orders and contracts						
3.	Termination of reporting procedures						
4.	Preparation of final report(s)						
5.	Completion and disposition of project file						
C.	*Financial*						
1.	Close out financial documents and records						
2.	Audit final charges and costs						
3.	Prepare final project financial report(s)						
4.	Collect receivables						
D.	*Project Definition*						
1.	Document final approved project scope						
2.	Prepare final project breakdown structure and enter into project file						
E.	*Plans, Budgets, and Schedules*						
1.	Document actual delivery dates of all contractual deliverable end items						
2.	Document actual completion dates of all other contractual obligations						
3.	Prepare final project and task status reports						
F.	*Work Authorization and Control*						
1.	Close out all work orders and contracts						
G.	*Project Evaluation and Control*						
1.	Assure completion of all action assignments						
2.	Prepare final evaluation report(s)						
3.	Conduct final review meeting						
4.	Terminate financial, manpower, and progress reporting procedures						
H.	*Management and Customer Reporting*						
1.	Submit final report to customer						
2.	Submit final report to management						
I.	*Marketing and Contract Administration*						
1.	Compile all final contract documents with revision, waivers, and related correspondence						
2.	Verify and document compliance with all contractual terms						
3.	Compile required proof of shipment and customer acceptance documents						
4.	Officially notify customer of contract completion						
5.	Initiate and pursue any claims against customer						
6.	Prepare and conduct defense against claims by customer						
7.	Initiate public relations announcements re. contract completion						
8.	Prepare final contract status report						
J.	*Extension-New Business*						
1.	Document possibilities for project or contract extensions, or other related new business						
2.	Obtain commitment for extension						
K.	*Project Records Control*						
1.	Complete project file and transmit to designated manager						
2.	Dispose of other project records as required by established procedures						
L.	*Purchasing and Subcontracting*						
	For each Purchase Order and Subcontract:						
1.	Document compliance and completion						
2.	Verify final payment and proper accounting to project						
3.	Notify vendor/contractor of final completion						
M.	*Engineering Documentation*						
1.	Compile and store all engineering documentation						
2.	Prepare final technical report						
N.	*Site Operations*						
1.	Close down site operations						
2.	Dispose of equipment and material						

Figure 13-3b   Checklist for project termination. *Source:* [1]

3. Ensure that documentation is complete, including a terminal evaluation of the project deliverables and preparation of the project's Final Report.

4. Clear for final billings and oversee preparation of the final invoices sent to the client.

5. Redistribute personnel, materials, equipment, and any other resources to the appropriate places.

6. Clear project with legal counsel or consultant. File for patents if appropriate. Record and archive all "nondisclosure" documents.

7. Determine what records (manuals, reports, and other paperwork) to keep. Ensure that such documents are stored in the proper places and that responsibility for document retention is turned over to the parent organization's archivist.

8. Ascertain any product support requirements (e.g., spares, service), decide how such support will be delivered, and assign responsibility.

9. Oversee the closing of the project's books.

It is likely that tasks 1 to 3 will be handled by the regular PM immediately before the project termination process is started. If the termination manager must handle these tasks, technical support will almost certainly be needed. Of course, many of the tasks on this list will be quite simple if the project is not large, but even with small- or medium-sized projects, the PM should make sure all items are covered.

Item 5 on this list deserves some amplification. The PM can do a great deal to reduce the problems of termination by dealing with these issues well before the actual termination process begins. As we noted in Chapter 2, arrangements for the distribution and disposal of property and equipment belonging to the project should be included in the proposal and/or in the contract with the client. Obviously, this does not stop all arguments, but it does soften the conflicts. Dealing with project personnel is more difficult.

Most PMs delay the personnel reassignment/release issue as long as possible for three main reasons: a strong reluctance to face the interpersonal conflicts that might arise when new assignments and layoffs are announced; worry that people will lose interest and stop work on the project as soon as it becomes known that termination is being considered; or concern—particularly in the case of a pure project organization—that team members will try to avoid death by stretching out the work as far as possible.

As long as the PM has access to the functional managers' ears, any team member who "quits work" before the project is completed or stalls by stretching out tasks or creating task extensions would be subject to the usual sanctions of the workplace. The PM should make it quite clear that on-the-job resignations and tenure-for-life are equally unacceptable.

The first problem results when project leadership is held by a managerially weak PM. The height of weakness is demonstrated when the PM posts a written list of reassignments and layoffs on the project's bulletin board late Friday afternoon and then leaves for a long weekend. A more useful course of action is to speak with project members individually or in small groups, let them know about plans for termination, and offer to consult with each in order to aid in the reassignment process or to assist in finding new work. (A preliminary announcement to the entire project team is in order because the interviews may cover several weeks or months.) It is almost impossible to keep termination plans a secret, and to confront the matter immediately tends to minimize rumors.

In a large project, of course, the PM will not be able to conduct personal interviews except with a few senior assistants. The project's personnel officer, or a representative from the parent firm's personnel department, can serve instead. This may seem like an unnecessary service to the team members, but a reputation of "taking care of one's people" is an invaluable aid to the PM when recruiting for the next project.

Termination by murder makes it very difficult to follow these suggestions about dealing with project personnel. The project's death often occurs with so little warning that the PM learns of the fact at the same time as the project team—or, as sometimes happens, learns about it from a member of the project team.

There is little the PM can do in such a case except to try to minimize the damage. The team should be assembled as rapidly as possible and informed, to the best of the PM's ability, about what has happened. At this point the PM should start the reassignment/release process.

13.4 THE FINAL REPORT—A PROJECT HISTORY

Good project management systems have a memory. The embodiment of this memory is the Project Final Report. The final report is not another evaluation; rather, it is the history of the project. It is a chronicle of the life and times of the project, a compendium of what went right and what went wrong, of who served the project in what capacity, of what was done to create the substance of the project, of how it was managed. We learn from experience only if the experience is preserved and studied [35].

The elements that should be covered in the final report are listed below. When considering these elements it is also beneficial to consider where the source materials can be found. For the most part, the required information is contained in the project master plan, a document that includes the proposal, all action plans, budgets, schedules, change orders, and updates of the above. In addition to the master plan, all project audits and evaluations also contain required input data. Almost everything else required by the final report is reflective, based on the thoughts of the PM and others involved in the project. There is little problem in knowing where the needed documents should be kept—in the project's files. Making sure that they are, in fact, there and that they are, in fact, up to date is a serious concern.

The precise organization of the final report is not a matter of great concern; the content is. Some are organized chronologically, while others feature sections on the technical and administrative aspects of the project. Some are written in a narrative style and some contain copies of all project reports strung together with short commentaries. What matters is that several subjects should be addressed, one way or another, in the final report.

1. *Project Performance* A key element of the report is a comparison of what the project achieved (the terminal evaluation) with what the project tried to achieve (the project proposal). This comparison may be quite extensive and should include explanations of all significant deviations of actual from plan. A final earned value discussion can also be helpful. Because the final report is not a formal evaluation, it can reflect the best judgment of the PM on why the triumphs and failures occurred. This comparison should be followed with a set of recommendations for future projects dealing with like or similar technical matters.

2. *Administrative Performance* The substantive side of the project usually gets a great deal of attention, while the administrative side is often ignored until administrative problems occur. There is also a strong tendency on the part of almost everyone to treat the "pencil pushers" with grudging tolerance, at best. The administration of a project cannot solve technical problems, but it can enable good technology to be implemented (or prevent it). Administrative practices should be reviewed, and those that worked particularly well or poorly should be highlighted. It is important, when possible, to report the reasons why some specific practice was effective or ineffective. If poor administration is to be avoided and good practices adopted, it is necessary to understand why some things work well and others do not in the environment of a particular organization. This becomes the basis for the recommendations that accompany the discussion.

3. *Organizational Structure* Each of the organizational forms used for projects has its own, unique set of advantages and disadvantages. The final report should include comments on the ways the structure aided or impeded the progress of the project. If it appears that a modification to the accepted form of project organization—or a change to a different basic organizational form—might be helpful for project management, such a recommendation should be made. Obviously, recommendations should be accompanied by detailed explanations and rationales.

4. *Project and Administrative Teams* On occasion, individuals who are competent and likable as individuals do not perform well as members of a team when a high level of interpersonal communication and cooperation is required. A confidential section of the final report may be directed to a senior personnel officer of the parent organization, recommending that such individuals not be assigned to future projects. Similarly, the PM may recommend that individuals or groups who are particularly effective when operating as a team be kept together on future projects or when reassigned to the firm's regular operations.

5. *Techniques of Project Management* The outcome of the project is so dependent on the skill with which the forecasting, planning, budgeting, scheduling, resource allocation, and control are handled that attention must be given to checking on the way these tasks were accomplished. If the forecasts, budgets, and schedules were not reasonably accurate, recommendations for improved methods should be made. The techniques used for planning, control, and risk management should also be subject to scrutiny.

For each element covered in the final report, recommendations for changing current practice should be made and defended. Insofar as is possible, the implications of each potential change should be noted. Commonly ignored, but equally important, are comments and recommendations about those aspects of the project that worked unusually well. Most projects, project teams, and PMs develop informal procedures that speed budget preparation, ease the tasks of scheduling, improve forecasts, and the like. The final report is an appropriate repository for such knowledge. Once reported, they can be tested and, if generally useful, can be added to the parent organization's list of approved project management methods.

The fundamental purpose of the final report is to improve future projects. It is ultimately focused on the project itself and on the process by which the project was conducted. Data on the project and its outcomes are available in the many interim reports, audits, and evaluations conducted during the project's life. But data on the process come largely from the PM's recollections. To ensure that significant issues are included, the PM should keep a diary. The PM's diary is not an official project document, but rather an informal collection of thoughts, reflections, and commentaries on project happenings. Such a diary tends to be a rich source of unconventional wisdom when written by a thoughtful PM. It may also be a great source of learning for a young, aspiring PM. Above all, it keeps ideas from "getting lost" amid the welter of activity on the project.

Occasionally, the project diary serves a purpose not originally intended. A PM working for a Minnesota highway construction company made a habit of keeping a project diary, mostly for his own interest and amusement. The firm was sued as the result of an accident on a road under construction. The plaintiff alleged that the highway shoulder was not complete nor was it marked "Under Construction" at the time of the accident. The PM's diary noted daily progress on the road, and it showed that the relevant piece of the road had been completed several days prior to the accident. The company successfully defended its position. All company PMs keep diaries now. A vice-president of the firm mentioned that they are the same type of diary his high-school-aged daughter uses.

▌SUMMARY

At last, we come to the completion of our project—termination. In this chapter we looked at the ways in which projects can be terminated, how to decide if a project should be terminated, the termination process, and the preparation of the Project Final Report.

Specific points made in the chapter were these:

- A project can be terminated in one of four ways: by extinction, addition, integration, or starvation.

- Making a decision to terminate a project before its completion is difficult, but a number of factors can be of help in reaching a conclusion.

- Most projects fail because of one or more of the following reasons:

  Inappropriate use of the project form of organization
  Insufficient top-management support
  Naming the wrong project manager
  Poor planning

- Studies have shown that the factors associated with project success are different for different industries and the various types of projects.

- Success-related factors, or any factors management wishes, can be used in termination decision models.

- Special termination managers are often used, and needed, for closing out projects. This task, consisting of eight major duties, is a project in itself.

- The Project Final Report incorporates the process knowledge gained from the project. In addition to preservation of project records, the Final Report embodies the experience from which we learn. It should include:

Project performance comments
Administrative performance comments
Organizational structure comments
Personnel suggestions, possibly a confidential section

 GLOSSARY

Termination by Addition   Bringing the project into the organization as a separate, ongoing entity.

Budget Decrement   A reduction in the amount of funds for an activity. Termination by

Extinction   The end of all activity on a project without extending it in some form, such as by inclusion or integration.

Termination by Integration   Bringing the project activities into the organization and distributing them among existing functions.

Termination by Murder   Terminating a project suddenly and without warning, usually for a cause not related to the project's purpose.

Termination by Starvation   Cutting a project's budget sufficiently to stop progress without actually killing the project.

Termination Manager   An administrator responsible for wrapping-up the administrative details of a project.

 QUESTIONS

Material Review Questions

1. List and briefly describe the ways projects may be terminated.

2. What problems may occur if the project manager does not have a follow-on project when the current project nears termination?

3. What are the primary duties of a termination manager?

4. On termination of a project, what happens to the information gathered throughout the course of the project?

5. What is a budget decrement?

6. Identify the four reasons for project termination.

7. What does the Project Final Report include?

8. What factors are considered most important in the decision to terminate a project?

9. What issues should be considered when using the termination-by-integration method?

Class Discussion Questions

10. Discuss the impact, both positive and negative, of termination on the project team members. How might the negative impact be lessened?

11. If the actual termination of a project becomes a project in itself, what are the characteristics of this project? How is it different from other projects?

12. Discuss some reasons why a Project Final Report, when completed, should be permanently retained by the firm.

13. What elements of the termination process may be responsible for making a project unsuccessful?

14. How is discriminant analysis used in project management?

15. What are some characteristics of a good termination manager?

16. How might one choose which termination method to use?

17. Why might a failing project not be terminated?

18. How can termination for reasons other than achievement of project goals be avoided?

Questions for Project Management in Practice

Nucor's Approach to Termination by Addition

20. Why would Nucor have thought they could build a new steel mill with one-tenth the engineering resources it normally requires?

21. What characteristics of this project termination made it a termination by addition?

22. What other ways could Nucor have terminated this project? What terms would you give these approaches?

19. What must the project manager do in planning, scheduling, monitoring, and closing out the project?

Terminating the Superconducting Super Collider Project

23. Which of the various forms of termination was this?

24. How does the reading at the back of this chapter relate to this termination decision?

25. The authors of this article maintain that politics is an important element of project implementation. Do you agree? Was this project terminated through "political" means?

 INCIDENTS FOR DISCUSSION

Industrial Mop and Supply Co.

IMSCO began manufacturing and distributing mops and brooms to industrial customers 43 years ago. Mr. Bretting, president of IMSCO, has been toying with the idea of using IMSCO's manufacturing and distribution expertise to begin making and selling consumer products. He has already decided that he cannot sell any of his current products to consumers. Also, if IMSCO is going to go to the trouble of developing consumer markets, Mr. Bretting feels very strongly that their first product should be something new and innovative that will help establish their reputation.

He thinks that the expertise required to develop a new product exists within the company, but no one has any real experience in organizing or managing such a project. Fortunately, Mr. Bretting is familiar with a local consulting firm that has a good reputation and track record of leading companies through projects such as this, so he contacted them.

Three months into the project, Mr. Bretting contacted the program manager/consultant and mentioned that he was worried about the amount of risk involved in trying to introduce such an innovative consumer product with his current organization. He was worried that the project was oriented too strongly towards R&D and did not consider related business problems in enough depth. (This was a complete about-face from his feelings three months earlier, when he had approved the first plan submitted with no changes.)

Mr. Bretting suggested that the consultant modify the existing project to include the introduction of a "me-too" consumer product before IMSCO's new product was defined and tested. Mr. Bretting thought that some experience with a "me-too" product would provide IMSCO management with valuable experience and would improve later performance with the new product. He allowed the R&D portion of the project to continue concurrently, but the "me-too" phase would have top priority as far as resources were concerned. The consultant said she would think about it and contact him next week.

Questions: If you were the consultant, what would you recommend to Mr. Bretting? Would you continue the relationship?

Excel Electronics

Excel Electronics is nearing completion of a three-year project to develop and produce a new pocket computer. The computer is no larger than a cigarette pack but has all the power and features of a $5000 microcomputer. The assembly line and all the production facilities will be completed in six months and the first units will begin production in seven months. The plant manager believes it is time to begin winding the project down. He has three methods in mind for terminating the project: extinction, addition, and integration, but he is not sure which method would be best.

Question: Which of the three methods would you recommend, and why?

▧ BIBLIOGRAPHY

1. ARCHIBALD, R. D. *Managing High Technology Programs and Projects, 4th ed.* New York: Wiley, 1992.

2. BAKER, B. "Great Expectations." *PM Network*, May 1997.

3. BAKER, N. R., S. G. GREEN, A. S. BEAN, W. BLANK, and S. K. TADISINA. "Sources of First Suggestion and Project Success/Failure in Industrial Research." *Proceedings, Conference on the Management of Technological Innovation*, Washington, D.C., 1983.

4. BALACHANDRA, R., and J. H. FRIAR. "Factors for Success in R&D and New Product Innovation: A Contextual Framework." *IEEE Transactions on Engineering Management*, August 1997.

5. BALACHANDRA, R., and A. J. RAELIN. "How to Decide When to Abandon a Project." *Research Management*, July 1980.

6. BEALE, P., and M. FREEMAN. "Successful Project Execution: A Model." *Project Management Journal*, December 1991.

7. BLACK, K. "Causes of Project Failure: A Survey of Professional Engineers." *PM Network*, November 1996.

8. BUELL, C. K. When to Terminate a Research and Development Project. *Research Management*, July 1967.

9. CHI, T., J. LIU, and H. CHEN. "Optimal Stopping Rule for a Project with Uncertain Completion Time and Partial Salvageability." *IEEE Transactions on Engineering Management*, February 1997.

10. DEAN, B. V. *Evaluating, Selecting, & Controlling R & D Projects.* New York: American Management Association, 1968.

11. FREEMAN, M., and P. BEALE. "Measuring *Project Success.*" *Project Management Journal*, March 1992.

12. GREEN, S. G., M. A. WELSH, and G. E. DEHLER. "Red Flags at Dawn or Predicting Project Termi-

nations at Start Up." *Research-Technology Management*, May–June 1993.

13. HOCKNEY, J. W., and K. HUMPHREYS. *Control and Management of Capital Projects, 2nd ed.* New York: McGraw-Hill, 1991.

14. INGRAM, T. "Managing Client/Server and Open Systems Projects: A 10-Year Study of 62 Mission-Critical Projects." *Project Management Journal*, June 1994.

15. JIANG, J. J., G. KLEIN, and J. BALLOUN. "Ranking of System Implementation Success Factors." *Project Management Journal*, December 1996.

16. KEIL, M., D. P. TRUEX, III, and R. MIXON. "The Effects of Sunk Cost and Project Completion on Information Technology Project Escalation." *IEEE Transactions on Engineering Management*, November 1995.

17. KLOPPENBORG, T. J., and D. A. PLATH. "Effective Project Management Practices during Expert Systems Implementation." *Project Management Journal*, December 1991.

18. KUMAR, V., A. N. S. PERSAUD, and U. KUMAR. "To Terminate or Not an Ongoing R&D Project: A Managerial Dilemma." *IEEE Transactions on Engineering Management*, August 1996.

19. LEE, W., and S. J. MANTEL, JR. "An Expert System for Project Termination." *Proceedings, First International Conference on Engineering Management*, Arlington, VA, September 1986.

20. MATZLER, K., and H. H. HINTERHUBER. "How to make product development projects more successful by integrating Kano's model of customer satisfaction into quality function deployment." *Technovation*, January 1998.

21. MIGHT, R., and W. A. FISCHER. "The Role of Structural Factors in Determining Project Management Success." *IEEE Transactions on Engineering Management*, Vol. 32, 1985.

22. NORTHCRAFT, G. B., and M. A. NEALE. "Opportunity Costs and the Framing of Resource Allocation Decisions." *Organizational Behavior and Human Decision Processes*, 1986, pp. 348–356.

23. NORTHCRAFT, G. B., and G. WOLF. "Dollars, Sense, and Sunk Costs: A Life Cycle Model of Resource Allocation Decisions." *Academy of Management Review*, No. 2 1984.

24. PINTO, J. K., and S. J. MANTEL, JR. "The Causes of Project Failure." *IEEE Transactions on Engineering Management*, November 1990.

25. PINTO, J. K., and D. P. SLEVIN. "Critical Factors in Successful Project Implementation." *IEEE Transactions on Engineering Management*, February 1987.

26. PINTO, J. K., and D. P. SLEVIN. "Project Success: Definitions and Measurement Techniques." *Project Management Journal*, February 1988.

27. "Project Management Tasks: Wrap Up." *Design News*, April 19, 1982.

28. RAELIN, J. A., and R. BALACHANDRA. "R&D Project Termination in High-Tech Industries." *IEEE Transactions on Engineering Management*, February 1985.

29. RAMAMURTHY, K. "The Influence of Planning on Implementation Success of Advanced Manufacturing Technologies." *IEEE Transactions on Engineering Management*, February 1995

30. RIGGS, J. L., M. GOODMAN, R. FINLEY, and T. MILLER. "A Decision Support System for Predicting Project Success." *Project Management Journal*, September 1992.

31. SHAFER, S. M., and S. J. MANTEL, JR. "A Decision Support System for the Project Termination Decision." *Project Management Journal*, June 1989.

32. SHENHAR, A. J., O. LEVY, and D. DVIR. "Mapping the Dimensions of Project Success." *Project Management Journal*, June 1997.

33. STAW, B. M., and J. ROSS. "Knowing When to Pull the Plug." *Harvard Business Review*, March–April, 1987.

34. TADISINA, S. K. "Support System for the Termination Decision in R&D Management." *Project Management Journal*, November 1986.

35. WHITTEN, N. "Are You Learning From Project to Project?" *PM Network*, March 1999.

36. WOLFF, M. F. "Knowing When the Horse Is Dead." *Research Management*, November 1981.

This article has already become a classic on the psychological basis for continuing a project invariably headed for disaster. The authors clearly point out the dangers of certain personality types in project managers matching the needs profile of certain organizations. In these all-too-frequent situations, projects are continued way past the point where common sense would have called for their termination.

DIRECTED READING

KNOWING WHEN TO PULL THE PLUG

Last year you authorized the expenditure of $500,000 for what you thought was a promising new project for the company. So far, the results have been disappointing. The people running the project say that with an additional $300,000 they can turn things around. Without extra funding, they cry, there is little hope. Do you spend the extra money and risk further losses, or do you cut off the project and accept the half-million-dollar write-off?

Managers face such quandaries daily. They range from developing and placing employees to choosing plant sites and making important strategic moves. Additional investment could either remedy the situation or lead to greater loss. In many situations, a decision to persevere only escalates the risks, and good management consists of knowing when to pull the plug.

These escalation situations are trouble. Most of us can think of times when we should have bailed out of a course of action. The Lockheed L-1011 fiasco and the Washington Public Supply System debacle (commonly referred to as WHOOPS) are spectacular examples of organizational failure to do so. Decisions to persist with these crippled ventures caused enormous losses.

Of course, all managers will make some mistakes and stick with some decisions longer than they ought to. Recent research has shown, however, that the tendency to pursue a failing course of action is not a random thing. Indeed, at times some managers and even entire organizations, seem almost programmed to follow a dying cause.[1]

What leads executives to act so foolishly? Are they people who should never have been selected for responsible positions? Are these organizations simply inept? Or are they generally competent managers and companies that find themselves drawn into decisional quicksand, with many forces driving them deeper? Though we think this last description is probably the right one, we don't think the tendency is uncheckable. Managers and organizations that often fall into escalation traps can take steps to avoid them.

Why Projects Go Out of Control

As a start to understanding why people get locked into losing courses of action, let's look first at what a purely rational decision-making approach would be. Consider, for example, the decision to pursue or scuttle an R&D or a marketing project. On the basis of future prospects, you'd have made the initial decision to pursue the project, and enough time would have passed to see how things were going. Ideally, you'd then reassess the situation and decide on future action. If you were following a fully rational approach, whatever losses might have occurred before this decision point would be irrelevant for your reassessment. With a cold clear eye, you'd view the prospects for the future as well as your available options. Would the company be better off if it got out, continued with the project, or decided to invest more resources in it? You'd treat any previous expenses or losses as sunk costs, things that had happened in the past, not to be considered when you viewed the future.

In theory, pure rationality is great, but how many managers and organizations actually follow it? Not many. Instead, several factors encourage decision makers to become locked into losing courses of action.

The Project Itself The first set of factors have to do with the project itself. "Is the project not doing well because we omitted an important factor from our calculations, or are we simply experiencing the downside of problems that we knew could occur?" "Are the problems temporary (bad weather or a soon-to-be-settled supplier strike) or more permanent (a steep downturn in demand)?" Expected or short-term problems are likely to encourage you to continue a project. You may even view them as necessary costs or investments for achieving large, long-term gains. If you expect problems to arise, when they do, they may convince you that things are going as planned.

A project's salvage value and closing costs can also impede withdrawal. An executive could simply terminate an ineffective advertising campaign in midstream, but stopping work on a half-completed facility is another story. A project that has very little salvage value and high closing costs—payments to terminated employees, penalties for breached contracts, and losses from the closing of facilities—will be much more difficult to abandon than a project in which expenditures are recoverable and exit is easy. It's understandable why so many financially questionable construction projects are pursued beyond what seems to be a rational point of withdrawal.[2]

Consider the Deep Tunnel project in Chicago, a plan to make a major addition to the city's sewer system that will eventually improve its capacity to handle major storms. Although the project has absorbed millions of dollars, it won't deliver any benefits until the entire new system is completed. Unfortunately, as each year passes, the expected date of completion recedes into the future while the bill for work to be finished grows exponentially. Of course, no one would have advocated the project if the true costs had been known at the outset. Yet, once begun, few have argued to kill the project.

The problem is that the project was structured in ways that ensured commitment. First, the project managers viewed each setback as a temporary situation that was correctable over time with more money. Second, they perceived all moneys spent as investments toward a large payoff they'd reap when the project was complete. Third, expenditures were irretrievable: the laid pipe in the ground has no value unless the entire project is completed, and it would probably cost more to take the pipe out of the ground than it's worth. Thus, like many other large construction and R&D projects, investors in the Deep Tunnel have been trapped in the course of action. Even though what they receive in the end may not measure up to the cost of attaining it, they have to hang on until the end if they hope to recoup any of their investment.

Managers' Motivations   Most of the factors concerning projects that discourage hanging on are evident to managers. They may not fully factor closing costs and salvage value into their initial decisions to pursue certain courses of action (since new ventures are supposed to succeed rather than fail), but when deciding whether to continue a project or not, executives are usually aware of these factors. Less obvious to managers, however, are the psychological factors that influence the way information about courses of action are gathered, interpreted, and acted on.

We are all familiar with the idea that people tend to repeat behavior if they are rewarded and to stop it if they are punished. According to the theory of reinforcement, managers will withdraw from a course of action in the face of bad news. This interpretation, however, ignores people's history of rewards. Managers have often been rewarded for ignoring short-run disaster, for sticking it out through tough times. Successful executives—people whose decisions have turned out to be winners even when the outlook had appeared grim—are particularly susceptible. It's tough for managers with good track records to recognize that a certain course isn't a satisfactory risk, that things aren't once again going to turn their way.

Reinforcement theory also tells us that when people receive rewards intermittently (as from slot machines), they can become quite persistent. If a decline in rewards has been slow and irregular, a person can go on and on even after rewards have disappeared. Unfortunately, many business situations that escalate to disaster involve precisely this type of reinforcement pattern. Sales may fall slowly in fits and starts, all the while offering enough hope that things will eventually return to normal. The hope makes it difficult to see that the market may have changed in fundamental ways. Revenues that slowly sour or costs that creep upward are just the kind of pattern that can cause managers to hang on beyond an economically rational point.

Research has also shown other reasons that executives fail to recognize when a project is beyond hope. People have an almost uncanny ability to see only what accords with their beliefs. Much like sports fans who concentrate on their own team's great plays and the other team's fouls, managers tend to see only what confirms their preferences. For example, an executive who is convinced that a project will be profitable will probably slant estimates of sales and costs to support the view. If the facts challenge this opinion, the manager may work hard to find reasons to discredit the source of information or the quality of the data. And if the data are ambiguous, the manager may seize on just those facts that support the opinion. Thus information biasing can be a major roadblock to sensible withdrawal from losing courses of action.

In addition to the effects of rewards and biased information, a third psychological mechanism may be at work. Sometimes even when managers recognize that they have suffered losses, they may choose to invest further resources in a project rather than accept failure. What may be fostering escalation in these cases is a need for self-justification. Managers may interpret bad news about a project as a personal failure. And, like most of us who are protective of our self-esteem, managers may hang on or even invest further resources to "prove" the project a success.

A number of experiments have verified this effect of self-justification. Those who are responsible for previous losses, for example, have generally been found to view projects more positively and to be more likely to commit additional resources to them than are people who have taken over projects in midstream. Managers who are not responsible for previous losses are less likely to "throw good money after bad" since they have less reason to justify previous mistakes.[3]

Reinforcement, information biasing and self-justification—three psychological factors that we're all subject to—can keep us committed to projects or actions we have started. Most managerial decisions, however, involve some additional factors that come into play when other people are around to observe our actions. These are social determinants.

Social Pressures   Managers may persist in a project not only because they don't want to admit error to themselves but also because they don't wish to expose their mistakes to others. No one wants to appear incompetent. Though persistence may be irrational from the organization's point of view, from the point of view of the beleaguered manager seeking to justify past behavior, it can be quite understandable. When a person's fate is tied to demands for performance and when accepting failure means loss of power or loss of a job, hanging on in the face of losses makes sense. Research has shown, for example, that job insecurity and lack of managerial support only heighten the need for external justification.[4] Thus when a manager becomes closely identified with a project ("that's Jim's baby"), he can be essentially forced to defend the venture despite mounting losses and doubts about its feasibility.

Beyond the personal risks of accepting losses, our ideas of how a leader should act can also foster foolish persistence. Culturally, we associate persistence—"staying the course," "sticking to your guns," and "weathering the storm"—with strong leadership. Persistence that happens to turn out successfully is especially rewarded. For example, when we think about the people who have become heroes in business and politics (Iacocca and Churchill, for examples), we see leaders who have faced difficult and apparently failing situations but who have hung tough until they were successful. If people see persistence as a sign of leadership and withdrawal as a sign of weakness, why would they expect managers to back off from losing courses of action? Recent research demonstrates that even though it may not add to the welfare of the organization, persistence does make a manager look like a leader.[5]

In short, the need to justify one's actions to others and to appear strong as a leader can combine with the three psychological factors to push managers into staying with a decision too long. This combination of forces does not, however, account for all debacles in which organizations suffer enormous losses through excessive commitment. In many of these cases structural factors also play a role.

Organizational Pushes & Pulls Probably the simplest element impeding withdrawal from losing projects is administrative inertia. Just as individuals do not always act on their beliefs, organizations do not always base their practices on their preferences. All the rules, procedures, and routines of an organization as well as the sheer trouble it takes for managers to give up day-to-day activities in favor of a serious operational disruption can cause administrative inertia. Dropping a line of business may mean changing corporate layoff policies, and moving people to other projects may violate seniority and hiring procedures. Sometimes it's just easier not to rock the boat.

Beyond such simple inertia, the politics of a situation can prevent a bailout. British Columbia's decision to stage the world's fair Expo '86 is one of the most re-

cent public examples of the power of political forces to sustain a costly course of action. Expo '86 was supposed to operate close to the financial break-even point. But as plans for the fair got under way, the expected losses burgeoned. At first, the planners tried to minimize the financial hazards by providing heartening but biased estimates of revenues and costs. When they finally accepted the more dire financial projections, however, and even the director recommended cancellation, the planners still went ahead with the fair. Politically it was too late: the fortunes of too many businesses in the province were tied to Expo, it was popular with the voters, and the future of the premier and his political party were aligned with it. The province created a lottery to cope with the expected $300 million deficit, and the fair opened as scheduled.

Though the Expo example comes from the public sector, political force may also sustain costly business projects. As a venture withers, not only those directly involved with it may work to maintain it, but other interdependent or politically aligned units may support it as well. If the project's advocates sit on governing bodies or budget committees, efforts to stop it will meet further resistance. If a review finally does occur, the estimates of the costs and benefits of containing the venture will very likely be biased.

On occasion, support for a project can go even deeper than administrative inertia and politics. When a project such as a long-standing line of business is closely identified with a company, to consider its discontinuation is to consider killing the very purpose of the company. (Imagine Hershey without chocolate bars or Kimberly-Clark without Kleenex.) A project or a division can become institutionalized in an organization.

Consider the plight of Lockheed with its L-1011 Tri-Star Jet program. Although every outside analysis of the program found the venture unlikely to earn a profit, Lockheed persisted with it for more than a decade and accumulated enormous losses. The problem was not ending the project per se but what it symbolized. The L-1011 was Lockheed's major entry in the commerical aviation market (in which it had been a pioneer), and Lockheed shrank from being identified as simply a defense contractor.

Pan American World Airways has recently gone through a similar institutional process. More than most airlines, Pan Am suffered huge losses after deregulation of the industry, it was even in danger of not meeting its debt obligations. Although the prospects for large profits in the airline industry were dim, Pan Am chose to sell off most of its other more profitable assets—first the Pan Am building in New York and then the Intercontinental Hotels Corporation—so as to remain in its core business. Finally, as losses continued, Pan Am sold its valuable Pacific routes to United Air Lines. Following these divestitures, the company was left with only U.S. and international routes in corridors where competition is heavy. Apparently, management didn't seriously consider the possibility of selling or closing the airline and keeping most of the other profitable subsidiaries. Pan Am is, after all, in the airline and not the real estate or hotel business.

Not all the forces we've described are relevant to every case, and not all are of equal influence in the situations where they operate. In many instances, commitment to a course of action builds slowly. Psychological and social forces come into play first, and only later does the structure make its impact. And, in a few cases, because the rational point of withdrawal has long passed, even the economic aspects of a project can cry out for continuation.

Still, some executives do manage to get themselves and entire organizations out of escalating situations. There are solutions.

Steps Executives Can Take Themselves

Executives can do many things to prevent becoming overcommitted to a course of action. Some of these solutions they can take care of on their own. Others involve getting the organization to do things differently. Let's look first at the remedies that excutives themselves can apply.

Recognize Overcommitment   The most important thing for managers to realize is that they may be biased toward escalation. For all the reasons we have mentioned, executives may delude themselves into thinking that a project will pull through—that success is around the corner. Recognizing overcommitment is, however, easier to preach than to practice. It usually takes enthusiasm, effort, and even passion to get projects off the ground and running in bureaucratic organizations. The organization depends on these responses for vitality. Consequently, the line between an optimistic, can-do attitude and overcommitment is very thin and often difficult to distinguish.

See Escalation for What It Is   How, then, can managers know whether they have crossed the threshold

between the determination to get things done and overcommitment? Although the distinction is often subtle, they can clarify matters by asking themselves the following questions:

1. Do I have trouble defining what would constitute failure for this project or decision? Is my definition of failure ambiguous, or does it shift as the project evolves?

2. Would failure on this project radically change the way I think of myself as a manager or as a person? Have I bet the ranch on this venture for my career or for my own satisfaction?

3. Do I have trouble hearing other people's concerns about the project, and do I sometimes evaluate others' competence on the basis of their support for the project?

4. Do I generally evaluate how various events and actions will affect the project before I think about how they'll affect other areas of the organization or the company as a whole?

5. Do I sometimes feel that if this project ends, there will be no tomorrow?

If a manager has answered yes to one or more of these questions, the person is probably overcommitted to a project.

Back Off   Just knowing that one is under the sway of escalation can help. But knowing is not enough. It is also necessary to take some steps to avoid overcommitment. One way is to schedule regular times to step back and look at a project from an outsider's perspective. A good question to ask oneself at these times is, "If I took over this job for the first time today and found this project going on, would I support it or get rid of it?" Managers could take their cues from bankers. When they take over others' portfolios, bankers usually try to clean up any troubled loans since they want to maximize the future returns associated with their own loan activity. Managers can also encourage their subordinates to reevaluate decisions. Most critical here is establishing a climate in which, regardless of whether the data are supportive or critical of the ongoing project, people convey accurate information. Just stating a "nothing but the truth" policy, however, is usually not enough to change the pattern of information reporting. The messenger with extremely critical but important information needs an explicit reward.

One forum for getting objective and candid feedback is a variant of the currently popular quality circle. Managers could regularly convene key staff members for "decision circles," in which fellow employees would offer honest evaluations of the hurdles a project faces and its prospects. Managers from other departments or sections might also attend or even chair such sessions to ensure an objective look at the problems. Managers might also hold regular "exchanges of perspective" in which colleagues could help each other see the truth about their operations.

Change the Organization Though it is possible to come up with an array of decision aids to help managers gain an objective perspective about the projects they run, one could argue that the problem of escalation is larger than any one person, that it's organizational in scope. Unfortunately, such a pessimistic view is at least partially correct. Much of what causes escalation is in the nature of organizations, not people.

If organizational action is called for, what can the system do to minimize escalation?

Turn Over Administrators One way to reduce the commitment to a losing course of action is to replace those associated with the original policy or project. If overcommitment stems from psychological and social forces facing the originators of the action, then their removal eliminates some of the sources of commitment.

Turning over project managers can of course be both disruptive and costly. Moreover, because people who were once associated with the discontinued venture may still be committed to it, management may find it difficult to draw the appropriate line for making a purge. Nonetheless, to make a clean break with the past, many organizations do make occasional personnel sweeps, sometimes more for their symbolic value than because of any real differences in decision making.

Still, we don't recommend turnover as the way to make changes. Like treating the disease by killing the patient, taking committed decision makers off a project may produce nothing but a demoralized staff and disaffected managers hesitant to try again.

Separate Decision Makers One technique for reducing commitment that is far less drastic than turnover is to separate initial from subsequent decisions concerning a course of action. In some banks, for example, a "workout group" handles problem loans rather than the people who originally funded and serviced the loans. The idea is not only that specialists should be in-

volved in recouping bank funds but also that these officers are able to handle the loans in a more objective way than those who made the first decisions about the accounts.[6] Industrial companies could also make use of such procedures. They could separate funding from new-product development decisions and hiring from promotion decisions. They could keep deliberations on whether to discontinue lines of business apart from day-to-day management decisions.

Reduce the Risk of Failure Another way to reduce commitment is to lessen the risk of failure. Because project failure can spell the end to an otherwise promising career, an administrator may be forced to defend a losing course of action. In a no-win dilemma, the trapped manager may think, "Things look bleak now, but there's no point in my suggesting that the company withdraw. If the project doesn't succeed, I have no future here anyway."

In some companies, management has reduced the costs of failure by providing rationalizations for losing courses of action and excuses for their managers. People are told that the losses are beyond anyone's control or that the fault lies with more general economic conditions, government regulation, or foreign competition. Although this route takes managers off the hook, it doesn't help them see a losing course for what it is or how they may avoid making the mistakes again.

Most companies do not want to take the pressure off their managers to perform as winners. Yet because a strong fear of failure can cause overcommitment, management is better off setting only a moderate cost for failure, something to avoid but not to fear intensely. A large computer company, for example, puts managers who have made big mistakes in a "penalty box." It makes them ineligible for major assignments for up to a year. After the penalty period, the managers are restored to full status in the organization and are again eligible to run major projects. Organizations trying to cope with escalation situations may find such a compromise between support for failure and demand for competence helpful.

Improve the Information System Several laboratory experiments have shown that people will withdraw from escalating situations when they see the high costs of persisting.[7] The presentation of such negative data is more difficult in organizations, however. Because no one wants to be the conveyer of bad news, information is filtered as it goes up the hierarchy. Furthermore, because those intimately involved with a project are not likely to distribute unflattering and less-than-optimistic forecasts, information is also biased at the source.

What, then, can organizations do to improve their information reporting? The most common solution is to increase their use of outside experts and consultants. The problem with consultants, however, is that they are no more likely to hear the truth than anyone else in the organization, and they also may not find it easy to tell management what it doesn't want to hear.

A better solution is to try to improve the honesty of reporting throughout the organization. By rewarding process as highly as product, managers can encourage candid reporting. The purpose of rewarding managers for the way a process is carried out is to make them attend as much to the quality of analysis and decision making as to the final results. Instead of acting as champions who inflate the prospects of their own projects and minimize their risks, managers offered process rewards are motivated to recognize problems and deal with them.

At the outset of projects, companies should encourage the creation of fail-safe options, ways to segment projects into small, achievable parts, and analyses of the costs of withdrawal. Later in the life of projects, companies should reward honest recognition of problems and clear examination of the alternatives, including withdrawal.

This kind of reward system is quite different from the usual practice of giving people recognition for success on their projects and punishing them for failure on their undertakings. Yet it is a system that should reduce many of the forces for escalation.

Boosting Experimentation

As we noted earlier in our discussion, an entire organization can be so caught up in supporting a project—especially an institutionalized one—that it ignores the cost of persistence.

Rather than trying to discredit an institutionalized project on economic grounds, a good strategy for withdrawal from it is to reduce its links with the central purposes of the organization. A useful tactic is to label the project peripheral or experimental so that managers can treat it on its own merits rather than as a symbol of the organization's central goal or mission.

Ideally, managers should consider all ventures imperfect and subject to question in an "experimenting organization." [8] Every program should be subject to

regular reconsideration (à la zero-based budgeting), and every line of business should be for sale at the right price. In such an experimenting organization, projects wouldn't become institutionalized to the point where mangement couldn't judge them on their own costs and benefits. And because managers in such a system would be judged as much for recognition of problems facing their units and how they cope with them as for success and failure, experimenting organizations should be extremely flexible.

When a market or a technology changes, the experimenting organization would not simply try to patch up the old product or plant but would be quick to see when it is best to pull the plug and start anew.

References

1. For more complete reviews and escalation research, see BARRY M. STAW and JERRY ROSS, "Understanding Escalation Situations: Antecedents, Prototypes, and Solutions" in *Research in Organizational Behavior*, ed. L. L. Cummings and Barry M. Staw (Greenwich, CO: JAI Press, 1987); and Joel Brockner and Jeffrey Z. Rubin, *Entrapment in Escalating Conflict.* (New York: Springer Verlag, 1985).

2. See GREGORY B. NORTHCRAFT and GERRIT WOLF, "Dollars, Sense, and Sunk Costs: A Lifecycle Model of Resource Allocation," *Academy of Management Review*, April 1984, p. 22.

3. For experiment results, see BARRY M. STAW, "Knee-deep in the Big Muddy: A Study of Escalating Commitment to a Chosen Course of Action," in *Organizational Behavior and Human Performance*, June 1976, p. 27; Alan Tegar. *Too Much Invested to Quit* (New York: Pergamon Press, 1980); and Max H. Bazerman, R. I. Beekum, and F. David Schoorman, "Performance Evaluation in a Dynamic Context: A Laboratory Study of the Impact of Prior Commitment to the Ratee," *Journal of Applied Psychology*, December 1982, p. 873.

4. FREDERICK V. FOX and BARRY M. STAW, "The Trapped Administrator. The Effects of Job Insecurity and Policy Resistance upon Commitment to a Course of Action," *Administrative Science Quarterly*, September 1979, p. 449.

5. BARRY M. STAW and JERRY ROSS, "Commitment in an Experimenting Society: An Experiment on the Attribution of Leadership from Administrative Sce-

narios," *Journal of Applied Technology*, June 1980, p. 249.

6. See Roy J. Lewicki, "Bad Loan Psychology, Entrapment and Commitment in Financial Lending," Graduate School of Business Administration Working Paper No. 80-25 (Durham, NC: Duke University, 1980).

7. Bruce E. McCain, "Continuing Investment Under Conditions of Failure: A Laboratory Study of the Limits to Escalation," *Journal of Applied Psychology*, May 1986, p. 280; and Edward G. Conlon and Gerrit Wolf, "The Moderating Effects of Strategy, Visibility, and Involvement on Allocation Behavior: An Extension of Staw's Escalation Paradigm," *Organizational Behavior and Human Performance*, October 1980, p. 172.

8. Donald T. Campbell, "Reforms as Experiments," *American Psychologist*, April 1969, p. 409.

Questions

1. Of the reasons why projects go out of control, which do you believe are major ones? Why?

2. Of the "Steps Executives Can Take Themselves," which would be the easiest?

3. What is the "bottom-line" insight this article provides?

Photo Credits

Pages 8, 11, 18, 52, 61, 71, 93, 104, 116, 121, 134, 144, 159, 168, 175, 190, 202, 217, 228, 242, 263, 274, 290, 295, 304, 333, 362, 387, 399, 411, 421, 433, 453, 466, 483, 494, 500, 515, 542, 550

Chapter 1: *Page 13:* DILBERT reprinted by permission of United Feature Syndicate, Inc. **Chapter 2:** *Page 72:* Derek Hudson/Sygma. **Chapter 3:** *Page 112:* DILBERT reprinted by permission of United Feature Syndicate, Inc. **Chapter 5:** *Page 186:* DILBERT reprinted by permission of United Feature Syndicate, Inc. **Chapter 7:** *Page 262:* Courtesy NASA. **Chapter 8:** *Page 303:* By permission of Johnny Hart and Creators Syndicate, Inc. **Chapter 10:** *Page 439:* DILBERT reprinted by permission of United Feature Syndicate, Inc. **Chapter 11:** *Page 487:* Courtesy Australian Consulate. **Chapter 13:** *Page 542:* DILBERT reprinted by permission of United Feature Syndicate, Inc. *Page 552:* ©John Bird Photography.

Author Index

Aaron, J. M., 191, 192, 215
Abdallah, B., 499
Abernathy, W. J., 77
Abudayyeh, O. Y., 19
Ackoff, R. L., 77, 120, 463, 498
Adams, C., 190
Adams, J. R., 173, 175, 235, 250, 507
Adams, L. L., 173, 175
Adler, P. S., 175, 241, 251, 391, 405
Afzalur, R. M., 250
Aggarwal, R., 294
Aho, C. M., 120, 131
Al-Hammad, A., 357
Allen, T. J., 499
Amor, J. P., 294
Amrine, H. T., 498
Anderson, D. R., 405, 589
Anthony, W. P., 174
Antonioni, D., 215
Aquilano, N., xi, 294
Archibald, R. D., 24, 77, 131, 137, 175, 215, 498, 507, 554, 564

Argyris, C., 164
Arnoff, E. L., 77
Asahi, M., 115, 132
Assaf, S., 357
Atkins, W., 131
Avots, I., 440, 451
Azani, H., 77

Babcock, D. L., 400
Badaway, M., 134, 137
Badiru, A. B., 215, 279, 294, 357, 386, 405
Bailetti, A. J., 210, 212, 215
Bailey, D. E., 164, 173
Baker, B., 77, 552, 564
Baker, B. N., 34
Baker, K. R., 250
Baker, N. R., 549, 550, 553, 564
Baker, S. T., 250
Balachandra, R., 535, 549, 553, 564, 565
Balloun, J., 564
Barndt, S. E., 235, 250, 507

Barr, Z., 431, 451
Barry, D., 425
Barry, V., 131
Baumgardner, C. R., 132
Baxter, J. B., 363
Bazerman, M. H., 571
Beale, P., 77, 535, 550, 553, 564
Bean, A. S., 564
Beecham, M. A., 231, 250
Beekum, R. I., 571
Beer, S., 88, 131
Benjamin, C., 500
Benningson, L. A., 24, 208, 216
Berger, R. J., xi
Bhattacharyya, G., 589
Bierce, A., 285, 519, 535
Bierman, H., 294
Bigelow, D., 216
Black, K., 564
Blake, R. R., 252, 253, 256, 257
Blanchard, B. S., 216
Blanchard, K., 165
Blank, W., 564
Block, T. R., 173, 498
Bobrowski, P. M., 131, 451, 498
Boehm, B. W., 216
Boggon, I., 169
Bolles, D., 173
Boquist, J. A., 294
Boulding, K. E., 131, 257, 258
Bowen, D. M., 499
Boznak, R. G., 173
Bracey, R., 523, 535
Bracker, J. S., 217
Brackett, S. W., 451
Bradford, M., 219
Brandon, D. M., Jr., 451
Bratta, C. P., 215

Braz, E. F., 498
Brimson, J. A., 272, 294
Brizola, J. O., 122
Brockner, J., 571
Brocks, E., 250
Brooks, F. P., 283, 294
Brown, B., 55
Bruce, R. A., 133
Bubshait, K. A., 345, 357
Buell, C. K., 547, 550, 564
Burke, R. J., 241, 252, 253, 256, 257
Burton, J., 250, 416, 452, 499
Byrne, J., 499

Cabanis, J., 357
Cadbury, G. A. H., 249, 250
Callahan, J. R., 215
Camm, J., xi, 294
Cammann, C., 499
Campanis, N. A., 357
Campbell, D. T., 572
Cantanese, A. J., 388
Carland, J. C., 78, 358
Carland, J. W., 78
Carlisle, A. S., 165, 173
Case, J., 294
Casher, J. D., 507
Ceniceros, R., 220, 224
Cestin, A. A., 499
Chalfin, N., 264
Chamberlain, H., xi
Chambers, G. J., 173
Champy, J., 174
Chang, L., 358
Chase, R. B., 294
Chen, H., 564
Chi, T., 553, 564
Childs, P. D., 294

Chittenden, R. A., 160
Chopra, K. J., 131
Chrichton, M., 115, 131
Christensen, D. S., 294, 451
Churchman, C. W., 77, 131
Clarke, K., 33, 34
Cleland, D. I., 24, 29, 34, 173, 174, 216, 451, 507
Coburn, S., 294
Codas, M. M. B., 126, 131
Cohen, H., 229, 245, 250
Combe, M. W., 357
Conlon, E. G., 572
Conrath, D. W., 77
Cook, D., xi
Cooke, V. G., 77
Cooke-Davis, T., 131
Cooper, R., 294
Cordey-Hayes, M., 231, 250
Corwin, B. D., 394, 405
Cowen, C., 231, 250
Cowdrey, W., 77
Cox, J., 405
Cummings, L. L., 571

Dalkey, N. C., 55, 77
Darnell, R., 24
Davis, E. W., xii, 24, 357, 358, 405, 406, 499
Davis, J. C., 34
Dean, B. V., xii, 24, 294, 357, 451, 548, 564
Dean, J. W., Jr., 173
Dehler, G. E., 550, 564
de Laat, P. B., 173, 216, 241, 250
Delaney, W. A., 507
de Macedo-Soares, T. D. L. v. A., 131
Desbiens, R., 243
Dettbarn, A. A., 72

Devaux, S. A., 535
Dewhirst, H. D., 167, 173
DeYoung-Currey, J., 357
Diab, P., 8
Digman, L. A., 345, 357
Dinsmore, P. C., 122, 126, 131, 132, 173, 174, 216, 217, 452, 499
Di Pietro, P., 215
Dodson, W. R., 121, 132, 250
Doll, W. J., 456, 459
Drexler, J. A., Jr., 251
Drucker, P., 164, 174, 182
Duncan, W. R., 216
Dvir, D., 25, 535, 565
Dyer, W. G., 174, 242, 251

Edison, T. A., 8
Eichhorn, B. R., 327, 357
Einsiedel, A. A., 26, 34
Estes, W. E., 535
Evans, J. R., xi, 77, 78, 173, 174, 294, 451

Fabrycky, W., 216
Farid, F., 405, 451
Fedor, K. J., 132
Fendley, L. G., 390, 405
Fersko-Weiss, H., 451
Finley, R., 565
Fischer, W. A., 564
Fisher, D., 34
Fisher, R., 244, 245, 251
Fleming, Q. W., 452
Ford, R. C., 132, 174, 216, 452
Fox, F. V., 571
Fox, T. L., 452, 453
Frame, J. D., 26, 34, 174, 294, 357
Freeman, M., 77, 535, 550, 553
Friar, J. H., 549, 564

Fulton, J. C., 53
Fusco, J. C., 141, 174

Gaddis, P. O., 132
Gagne, M., 145
Gagnon, R. J., 132, 267, 269, 294
Gales, L. M., 174
Gallagher, C., 316, 357
Ganesh, L. S., 406
Gantt, H. L., 332
Garcia, A., 77
Garrehy, P. J., 452
Gemmill, D. D., 405
Gemmill, G. R., 132
Gershanov, K. M., 221, 224
Gibson, L., 499
Gido, J., 357
Gilyutin, I., 405
Githens, G., 51, 77
Glass, G. W., 294
Glauber, L. W., 405
Globerson, S., 391, 406
Gobell, D. H., 174
Gogal, H. C., 125, 132
Goldratt, E. M., 302, 340, 357, 391, 405
Gonzalez, R. F., 216
Goodman, L. J., 24
Goodman, M., 565
Gordon, J. A., 294
Gosselin, T., 32, 34
Gotzis, T. P., 275
Gousty, Y., 77
Graham, D. J., 357, 499
Graham, R. G., 125, 132
Graham, R. J., 24, 34
Grant, K. P., 132
Grant, R. A., 486, 499
Gray, C., 231, 250

Green, G. I., 345, 357
Green, S. G., 132, 550, 564
Greiner, L. E., 174, 574
Grinbergs, A., 125, 132
Grod, M. C., 24
Grossman, J., 251
Grove, C., 114
Gulliver, F. R., 536
Gupta, V. K., 357, 499

Haar, J., 133
Hajek, V. G., 251, 499
Hallowell, W., 114, 115
Hamburger, D. H., 132, 295
Hammer, M., 174
Hare, L. B., 357
Harris, R. D., 216
Harrison, F. L., 24, 294, 405
Harwell, G., 468
Hatfield, M. A., 452
Hauptman, O., 115, 132, 210, 216
Hauser, J. R., 507
Hayes, C. C., 210, 217, 251
Hayes, R., 77
Heady, R. B., 358
Helin, A. F., 77
Helpern, A., 251
Hertenstein, J. H., 291
Hertz, D. B, 77
Herzberg, F. H., 97, 132, 163
Heywood, G. E., 499
Higgins, C. A., 499
Hill, R., 167, 174
Hinterhuber, H. H., 78, 564
Hirji, K. K., 115, 132, 210, 216
Hitchcock, L., 135, 137
Hjelman, T. A., 174
Hobbs, B., 174

Hockney, J. W., 24, 564
Hodge, B. J., 174
Hoerl, R. W., 357
Hoffman, L. R., 256, 258
Holland, R. G., 412
Holt, D. H., 174
Horner, M., 33, 35
Houde, R., 243
Howard, D. C., 499
Hromi, J. D., 357
Hubbard, D. G., 216
Huber, G. P., 66, 77
Huber, W. D., 387, 406
Hughes, T. P., 6, 7, 24, 87, 98, 113, 132,
    174, 241, 251
Hulett, D. T., 325, 357
Hulley, O. S., 498
Humble, J. E., xi
Humphreys, K. K., 24, 564

Ibbs, C. W., 24, 345, 357, 405, 499
Ingram, T., 433, 517, 549, 564
Ireland, L. R., 125, 132
Irving, R. H., xii, 77, 499
Isbell, A. M., 451
Isgar, T., 174

Jackson, B., 535
Jandt, F. E., 251
Jay, A., 426, 452
Jensen, C. A., 452
Jergeas, G. F., 77
Jiang, J. J., 132, 564
Johannessen, O., 174
Johnson, J. R., 406
Johnson, R. A., 589
Johnson, R. V., 405, 452
Johnson, S., 165

Jones, D. P., 295
Jordan, B. D., 78
Jung, J. R., 358

Kahn, R. I., 257, 258
Kalu, T. Ch. U., 132, 150, 174, 210, 216,
    575
Kamburowski, J., 317, 357
Kandt, D. B., 497
Kangari, R., 451
Karaa, F. A., 499
Kast, F. E., 176
Kata, D., 257
Katzenbach, J. R., 165, 174
Keefer, D. L., 317, 357, 589
Kefalas, A. G., 499
Keil, M., 564
Kelton, W., 77
Kerzner, H., 24, 137, 174, 216, 357, 499,
    535
Ketcham, L., 174
Kharbanda, O. P., 25, 35, 242, 251
Khorramshahgol, R., 77
Khumawala, B., 406
Kidder, T., 452, 505
Kimball, R. K., 216, 544
King, W. R., 34, 173, 451, 507
Kinnunen, R. M., 507
Klein, G., 132, 564
Kloppenborg, T. J., 100, 132, 550, 564
Knutson, J., 69, 77, 174, 216, 358, 452
Koppelman, J. M., 452
Kostner, J., 176
Kotter, J. P., 92, 132, 141, 174
Kretlow, W. J., 78
Kruse, C., 219, 224
Kumar, P., 131
Kumar, U., 564

Kumar, V. K., 406, 564
Kurstedt, H. A., Jr., 217, 221, 224, 225
Kurtulus, I., 406
Kwak, Y-H., 24, 345, 357, 499

Lagadec, P., 218, 225
Lambert, L. R., 452
Langley, A., 182, 216
Larsen, M., 406
Larson, E. W., 174, 231, 250, 251
Laufer, A., 183, 216, 453, 459
Lavold, G. D., 216
Law, A. M., 77
Lawrence, A. O., 294
Lawrence, P. R., 35, 256, 257, 258
Layard, P. R. G., 294
Lee, S. A., 405
Lee, T., 452
Lee, W., 564
Leffingwell, D., 492, 499
Leonard, J. B., 220, 225
Levene, H., 458, 459
Levine, H. A., 174, 358, 438, 441, 452, 455, 459
Levinson, N. S., 115, 132
Levy, F. K., 358
Levy, M., xi
Levy, N. S., 391, 406
Levy, O., 25, 535, 565
Lewicki, R. J., 572
Li, M. I., 405
Liberatore, M. J., 60, 61, 78, 216, 358, 452
Likert, J. G., 167, 174
Likert, R., 164, 167, 174
Likierman, A., 499
Lindsay, W. M., 174, 451
Littlefield, T. K., Jr., 316, 358
Liu, J., 564

Livingston, J. L., 499
Lloyd, J., 223, 225
Lock, D., 25
Long, A., 251
Long, B. G., 251
Lorenz, C., 358
Lorsch, J. W., 35, 256, 257, 258
Love, S. F., 216, 251
Lucas, D., 131
Luehrman, T. A., 294
Lynn, L. H., 132

Maes, J. D., 251
Maier, N. R. F., 256, 258
Mallak, L. M., 217, 221, 224, 225
Mallon, J. C., 358
Mandakovic, T., 452
Mandelbaum, A., 405
Mann, G. A., 78
Manoharan, S., 405
Mantel, S. J., Jr., 77, 78, 132, 133, 294, 550, 554, 564, 565
Margulis, S., 132
Martin, J. E., 294
Martin, M. D., 118, 132
Martin, M. G., 216
Martin, P. K., 216, 358
Martinez, E. V., 216
Massarick, F., 133
Matson, E., 132
Matthews, M. D., 452
Matzler, K., 78, 564
McCahon, C. S., 358
McCain, B. E., 572
McCollum, J. K., 174
McDounough, E. F., 507
McFarlan, W., 452
McGregor, D., 174, 258

McGuigan, J. R., 78
McIntosh, J. O., 406
McKeown, T. J., 132
McKinney, J. M., xi
McLaughlin, F. S., 132, 174, 216, 452
McLuhan, M., 124
Menard, P., 174
Mendenhall, W., 589
Ménon, R., 77, 552
Meredith, J. R., 55, 78, 79, 294, 325, 358, 359, 406, 453, 524
Meyers, W. R., xi, 535
Middleman, L. I., 223, 225
Might, R., 564
Miller, T., 565
Mills, N. L., 358, 406
Milosevic, D. Z., 117
Minghe, S., 125, 132
Mintzberg, H., 132
Mixon, R., 564
Moder, J. J., 358, 406, 453, 459
Moolman, G. C., 294
Moore, C. C., 251
Moravec, M., 174
Morris, W. T., 216
Morse, L. C., 386, 406
Moshman, J., 406
Mouton, J. S., 252, 253, 256, 257
Moyer, R. C., 78
Murdick, R. G., 499
Murphy, P. C., 34
Myers, C. L., 535

Nacco, S., 104
Nadler, D. A., 499
Naik, B., 358
Narula, S. C., 406
Navarre, C., 406

Neale, M. A., 565
Nelson, B., 175
Neter, J., 589
Nevison, J. M., 452
Newman, W. H., 485, 486, 499
Newton, J. K., 535
Nguyen, V., 405
Nicholas, J. M., 406
Nichols, M., 35
Nierenberg, G. I., 251
Nixon, M. A., 109, 133
Nixon, T. R., 484
Normandeau, P., 243
Northcraft, G. B., 565, 571

Obrodovitch, M. M., 251
O'Connor, L., 32, 35
O'Connor, P. J., 221, 225
Odiorne, G. S., 175, 250
Ono, D., 93
Orczyk, J. J., 358
Ott, S. H., 294
Overbye, D. L., xii

Pacifici, L. C., 221, 225
Padgham, H. F., 175
Paley, A. I., 216
Palla, R. W., 452
Partovi, F. Y., 416, 452, 499
Pascal, B., 88
Pascale, S. J., 60, 78, 358
Pastin, M., 133
Patterson, J. H., 387, 405, 406
Patterson, N., 133
Patzak, G. A., 217, 224, 225
Pawar, K. S., 175
Peale, N. V., 131
Pearson, R., 400

Pelled, L. H., 175, 241, 251
Pells, D. L., 216
Persaud, A. N. S., 564
Pessemier, E. A., 507
Peters, T. J., 182, 551
Petters, J. F., 165, 175
Pettersen, N., 26, 35
Phillips, C. R., 358, 406
Phillips, R. C., 133
Pike, W. J., 132
Pill, J., 98, 133, 241, 251
Pinto, J. K., xi, 25, 35, 96, 133, 175, 198, 216, 242, 251, 549, 550, 553, 565
Pinto, M. B., 133, 175
Plath, D. A., 550, 564
Posner, B. Z., 26, 35, 134
Pospisil, C. J., 452
Powers, J. R., 358
Prentis, E. L., 183, 216
Pritsker, A. A. B., 342, 358

Raelin, J. A., 535, 549, 553, 564, 565
Raiffa, H., 229, 251
Rakos, J. J., 217, 453
Ramamurthy, K., 565
Randall, P., 453
Randolph, P. H., 316, 358
Randolph, W. A., 35
Ray, A., 294
Raynal, W., 175
Raz, T., 60, 78
Reck, R., 251
Reif, W. E., 217
Reimus, B., 294
Reingold, J., 453
Reith, W. D., 494
Remy, R., 358
Riggs, J. L., 553, 565

Riley, R. T., xi
Ritchey, J. A., 498
Robb, D. J., xii, 133
Robinson, P. B., 358
Robinson, T., 251
Roepcke, L. A., 294
Roetzheim, W. H., 499
Rogers, B., 61
Roman, D. D., 25, 69, 78, 134, 137, 183, 217, 493, 499
Ronen, R., 499
Rook, P., 453, 459
Rosegger, G., xi, 133
Rosenau, M. D., Jr., 25, 78
Rosensweig, J. E., 176
Ross, J., 565, 571
Ross, S. A., 78
Rossy, G. L., 175
Rubenstein, A. H., 125, 132
Rubin, J. Z., 571
Ruffenach, G., 11
Ruskin, A. M., 535

Saaty, T. S., 55, 66, 78
Saeed, B. I., 499
Sahlin, J. P., 133
Saitow, A. R., 499
Sanders, J., 499
Sangameswaran, A., 535
Santayana, G., 474
Santell, M. P., 358
Sasieni, M. W., 316, 317, 358
Sawle, W. S., 217, 225
Schaan, J., 406
Schaefer, A. G., 133, 535
Schaeffer, R. L., 589
Schlicter, J., 358
Schmidt, R. L., 78

Schoderbek, C. G., 499
Schoderbek, P. P., 499
Schoorman, F. D., 571
Schrock, J. L., 132
Schultz, R. L., 217
Schuyler, J. R., 78
Schwerer, E., 405
Scott, S. G., 133
Seesing, P. R., 499
Selen, W. J., 345, 357
Sethi, N. K., 499
Shafer, S. M., xi, 294, 325, 358, 453, 554, 565
Sharifi, S., 175
Shaw, M., 210, 217, 251
Shaw, M. E., 175
Shearer, R. A., 251
Shenhar, A., 16, 25, 110, 133, 453, 459, 535, 549, 565
Shepard, H. A., 256, 257, 258
Sherman, J. D., 174
Sholes, C., 264
Sigurdsen, A., 273, 294, 295
Silverberg, E. C., 358
Simon, H. A., 78
Singletary, N., 453
Sivak, J., 422
Slack, C., 219, 225
Slevin, D. P., 35, 112, 133, 198, 215, 549, 550, 553, 565
Smith, D. K., 165, 174
Smith, D. P., 216
Smith, L. A., 133, 452
Smith, M. B., 251
Smith, R. P., 215
Snee, R. D., 357
Snow, H., 175
Snowdon, M., 499

Sohoni, V. S., 499
Solow, R., 120
Souder, W. E., 41, 77, 78, 97, 133
Spence, J. W., 452, 453
Spinner, M., 453
Spirer, H. F., xii, 24, 407, 507
Starr, M. K., 133
Staw, B. M., 565, 571
Stephenou, S. E., 251
Stewart, J. M., 25
Stinson, J. P., 406
Stone, G. S., 132
Strickland, M. W., 229
Stuckenbruck, L. C., 137, 507, 535
Sun, M., 25
Sutton, M. M., xi
Sweeney, D. J., 405, 589
Sweet, P., 33, 35

Tadisina, S. K., 553, 564, 565
Talbot, F. B., 387, 406
Tan, G. W., 210, 217, 252
Tannenbaum, R., 133
Tate, K., 216, 358
Taylor, S., xii, 543
Tegar, A., 571
Teplitz, C. J., 294
Thamhain, H. J., 35, 132, 137, 165, 175, 235, 237, 239, 241, 251, 358, 439, 453, 478, 499, 500, 504, 507
Thomas, H., 77
Tiong, R. L. K., 499
Tipnis, V. A., 78
Tippet, D. D., 165, 175
Titus, G. J., 60, 62, 78, 358
Todryk, L., 175
Toelle, R. A., 358
Toney, F., 358, 499

Torfason, G., 202
Torkzadeh, G., 456, 459
Town, C., 295
Townsend, H. W. R., 78
Triantis, A. J., 294
Trist, E., 174
Truex, D. P., III, 564
Tsai, Y. W., 405
Tukel, O. I., 358, 386, 406
Tuminello, J. A., 507
Turban, E., 55, 78, 359, 406
Turner, R., 33, 35
Turner, W. S., III, 535

Umapathy, S., 295
Urban, G. L., 507
Ury, W., 244, 245, 251

Vallancourt, K. A., 291
Vandament, W. F., 295
van Gigch, J. P., 78, 88, 133, 500
Vazsonyi, A., 196, 358
Verdini, W. A., 317, 357, 589
Voich, D., Jr., 175

Wackerly, D., 589
Walker, J. A., 223, 225
Walker, M. G., 523, 535
Wall, J. A., Jr., 229, 245, 251
Walles, T. K., 251
Warner, J. C., 358
Wasserman, W., 589
Weaver, J., 406
Weber, F. M., 500
Webster, J. L., 217

Weil, D. E., 453, 459
Weist, J. D., xii, 358, 394, 395, 406
Welsh, M. A., 550, 564
Werther, W. B., Jr., 132
Westerfield, R. W., 78
Westney, R. E., 217
White, B. J., 167, 174
Whitehouse, G. E., 78, 406
Whitmore, G. A., 589
Whitten, N., 133, 464, 500, 565
Wilemon, D. L., 137, 165, 175, 235, 237,
    239, 241, 251, 500, 504, 507
Wilkens, T. T., 358
Williams, G., 175
Williams, T. A., 405, 589
Williams, T. M., 358
Willie, C. T., 386, 406
Willman, J., xii
Witherspoon, J., 358
Wolf, G., 565, 571, 572
Wolff, M. F., 565
Womer, N. K., 294
Woodworth, B. M., 386, 406
Wren, D. A., 175
Wu, C., 468
Wynter, L. E., 133

Yahdav, D., 453
Yasin, M. M., 133
Yunus, N. B., 500

Zaller, A. J., 133, 535
Zhu, Z., 358
Zimmerer, T. W., 133
Zmud, R., 453, 459

Subject Index

Accounting data assumptions and problems, 66–67, 266

Action plan, 165, 310–311, 471
  form of, 195–201
  hierarchical planning, 194–195
  as information source, 434
  monitoring system design, 414

Activity. *See also* Activity times
  definition, 308
  dummy, 310, 312–313, 394
  earliest finish time (EFT), 392
  earliest start time (EST), 317–318
  latest start time (LST), 319–320, 392
  pseudoactivity, 394

Activity-on-arrow, on-node (AOA, AON), 309–310, 328, 331–332, 340, 345, 366

Activity times, 307–328
  deterministic, 307, 364
  estimate at 95% and 90% levels, 325–328, 585–586
  expected time, 315–316
  normal, crash, 307, 363–369
  optimistic/pessimistic, 312–314
  probabilistic, stochastic, 307, 364
  standard deviation of, 316–317, 321–325
  variance of, 316, 321–325

Addition rule, 580–581

Airbus Industries, 118

Allison Engine Co., 149

American Automobile Association (AAA), 57

American Telephone and Telegraph Co., 114–115, 416, 541

Analytical approach, 88

Analytic hierarchy process, 55

AOA, AON, see Activity-on-arrow, on-node

ARPANET (Department of Defense Advanced Research Projects Agency's Internet), 7

Ashby's Law of Requisite Variety, 471

Ashland Oil Co., 41

Atlas Intercontinental Ballistic Missile project, 7, 87
Audits, 478, 511
  audit costs, 517
  baseline, data base, 523–524
  depth, 518
  ethics, 109
  evaluation, 189, 511–528
    goals, 512–515. *See also* Project goals
    purposes of, 512–515
  life cycle, 523–526
  measurement, 528–529
    difficulties, 528–529
    permission to enter system, 531
  reports, 519–522, 525–526
    contents, 515–516, 519–521
    style, 519, 527
  team, 526–527
    access to personnel, 527–528
    access to records, 527
  timing, 518
  types, 516–517
Auditor/evaluator, 530–531
  responsibilities, 521–522
  trust building, 530–531
Authority conflicts, 235–238
Automotive Composites Consortium, 118

Baseline plan, *see* Master plan
Bell Labs, 7
Benefit/cost, 95, 372, 471
Beta distribution, 315, 325–328, 586
Bill of materials, 196
Booz-Allen Hamilton, 307
Boston Central Artery/Tunnel, 7
Branch and bound, *see* Resource allocation
British Petroleum, 41

Budget, 188, 261, 475
  activity vs. program, 272–274
  baseline, 261, 428
  contingency allowance, 269
  control mechanism, 261–262
  cost estimation, *see* Cost estimation
  decrement, 544–545
  negotiation process, 269–271
    life cycle, 270–271
  policy, 271–272
  process, 271–272
  program budgeting, 272–273
  stability, 264–266, 267
  top-down/bottom-up, 266–268
  work element costing, 268–269
Bureau of Labor Statistics, 281

Capability Maturity Model, 347
Career ladders, 93, 93fn
CFM International, 118
Change, 102
  causes for, 232–233, 491
  of scope, 232–234
  technical change procedure, 163
Change control system, 492–493
Change orders, 185–186
Chartering, 232, 234, 238–239
China, 125
Chiquita Brands International Inc., 109
Chrysler Corporation, 41, 118, 150, 210
Communications, 90
  breadth of, 102–104
  multicultural, 124–126
Compadre system, 114, 114n, 118
Comparative benefit model, 46–47
Competitive necessity model, 46
Concurrent engineering, 187, 210, 571

Conflict, 10, 165–168, 226–248
  avoidance of, 167, 239
  categories, 235–238
  definition, 226
  intensity, 168, 238
  interpersonal, 236–237
  interproject, 237–238, 239
  intraproject, 229–230
  life cycle, 165–168, 235–242
  parties-at-interest, 90, 226–227,
      235–238
  partnering/chartering, 230–232, 234
  project manager vs. functional manager,
      89–90, 96–97, 237, 238
  reduction/resolution, 226–230
    in matrix management, 573
    Pareto optimal solution, 230
  scope change, 232–234
  sources, 165–168, 186
  successful, 227
Contingency planning, 70, 102
Control, 462–493
  balance, 487–489
    causes of imbalance, 488
    elements of, 487
  control of change and scope creep,
    491–493
    causes for, 491
    change control system, 491–493
    guidelines and process, 492–493
    purpose, 492
  control of creativity, 490–491
    methods of, 490–491
  critical ratio, 479–481
  cybernetic control, 469–472
    1st order, 2nd order, 3rd order,
      470–471
    information requirements, 471

go/no-go control, 472–474
    information requirements, 473–475
  human response to, 482, 484–487
    cybernetic control, 485–486
    go/no-go control, 484
    postcontrol, 486–487
  need for, 462–464
  postcontrol, 474–476
    elements of, 474–476
  postcontrol report, 475
    milestones, checkpoints, budgets,
      475
    project objectives, 475
    project results, 475
    recommendations, 475–476
  purposes of, 464–466
    financial resource control, 465–466
    human resource control, 465
    physical assets control, 464–465
  system design, 476–482
    benchmarking, 480–482
    characteristics of, 477
    critical ratio control charts,
      479–480
  timing, 472–473, 489
    early warning system, 473
  types, 468–476
Cost
  cost shifting, 376
  direct costs, 276
Cost estimation, 264–291
  allowance for waste and spoilage, 282
  contingency allowance, 282
  errors, 284–285
  ethical problems, 282
  improving process, 276–290, 284–290
    tracking signal, 285–289
  learning curve, 278–280

Cost estimation (*continued*)
  methods, 282–283
  price changes, 281–282
  technological shock, 280–281
Cost/schedule control systems criteria
        (C/SCSC), 428, 434, 479
Cost/time slope, 365
Creativity management, 91
Critical path method (CPM), *see* Resource
        allocation; Scheduling
Critical ratio, 479–481
C/SCSC, *see* Cost/schedule control
        systems criteria

Data, *see* Monitoring
Decision-making, 62–63
Decision support system (DSS), 45, 552
Delphi method, 55, 57, 61, 551, 552
Department of Defense, 69, 434
Department of General Services, 344–345
Direct costs, 276
DSS, *see* Decision support system
Due diligence, 466, 517
Dummy activities, 310, 312–313, 394
DuPont, Inc., 307

Earliest finish time (EFT), 392
Earliest start time (EST), 317–318
Earned value, *see* Monitoring
EFT (earliest finish time), 392
EI, *see* Employee Involvement
Elanco Products Co., 473
Eli Lilly Co., 93n, 307, 473
Employee Involvement (EI), 164, 485
Environmental impact on project
        management, 117–120
  business cycle environment, 119–120
  definition, 117

legal environment, 118–119
  socioeconomic environment, 117–118
  technological environment, 120–121
EST, *see* Earliest start time
Ethics, 282, 420
  code of, 109–111
  of negotiation, 230
Evaluation, *see* Audits
Evaluator, *see* Auditor/evaluator
Even planning process, 193–195
Event, node
  definition, 308
  earliest occurrence time (EOT),
        317–318, 333
  latest occurrence time (LOT),
        319–320
Excel[reg. symbol] (Microsoft), 42,
        285–287, 325, 328
Expected time, 315–316
Expected value, 62
Expediting projects, 363–369
Experimental probability, 578

Facilitator, *see* Project manager
Factor scoring models, *see* Scoring models
Fast-tracking, 369–371
Fiat, 118
Float, *see* Slack scheduling
Ford Motor Co., 118
Fortune 500, 61
Functional project organization, *see*
        Organization

Gantt chart, 332–335
  advantages/disadvantages, 332–335
  examples of, 443–444, 446–447
  hierarchy of, 394

PERT/CPM diagram vs., 374
relation to PERT/CPM, 332–333
updating, 419
General Electric Co., 9, 118
General Motors Corp., 118
GERT, *see* Graphical Evaluation and
Review Technique
Goddard Space Flight Center, 344
Goodyear Aircraft Co., 265
Gozinto chart, 196, 198
Graphical evaluation and review
technique (GERT), 340–344
comparison with PERT/CPM, 340–342
definition of symbols, 343
methods, 342
Q-GERT, VERT, 342
Grumman Aircraft Co., 389

Harvard negotiation project, 245
Hierarchical planning, 193–195, 266
Holistic approach, 144, 146. *See also*
Systems approach

IBM, 7, 41
Inferential statistics, 584–586
Information system, *see* Project
Management Information
System
Integration management, 208–212
Interdependencies, 10
Interface coordination, 208
Interfaces, 240
International Aero Engines, 118
Internet, 422–423, 474
Interpersonal conflict, 236–237
Interproject conflict, 237–238
Intraproject conflict, 229–230
ISO 9000, 485

J. C. Penney Co., 518
Japan Aero Engines, 118

Latest start time (LST), 319–320, 392
Learning curves, 278–280
Life cycle, 9
alternate cycle, 270–271
conflict, 235–242
project goals, 14–17, 100–101
stages, 14–18
Lincoln Electric Co., 489
Linear responsibility charts, 205–207
Lockheed Corp., 146, 307
Logical probability, 578
Lotus 1–2–3® (Lotus Development
Corp.), 42, 56
LST, *see* Latest start time
LTV Corp., 46
Lucent Technologies, 7

MAD, *see* Mean absolute deviation
Management by exception, 420
Management by objectives (MBO), 164,
315–316
Management of change, *see* Change
Management style, 110, 125
Manhattan Project, 7, 9
Manpower Temporary Services, 448
MAR, *see* Mean absolute ratio
Massachusetts Department of Highways, 7
Massachusetts Institute of Technology
(MIT), 7
Master plan, 262, 434
Materials requirements planning (MRP),
196
Matrix organization, 147–152
advantages/disadvantages, 151–152
authority conflicts, 235–238

Matrix organization (*continued*)
    conflict in, 150, 573
    strong/weak, 147–149, 162–163, 239
Maturity level, 345, 347
MBO, *see* Management by objectives
Mead Corp., 489
    Mead Data Corp. project development
        guide, 489
Mean absolute deviation (MAD),
    285–288
Mean absolute ratio (MAR), 288–290
Measurement, 67–68
    difficulties, 528–529
    quantitative/qualitative, 67
    reliable/unreliable, 67
    subjective/objective, 67, 414–415
    valid/invalid, 67–68
Meetings, 425–426
Merge bias, 324
Micromanagement, 89–90, 201
Microsoft, 571–572
Microsoft Project®, 21, 203
Microsoft Project 98®, 373, 428, 431, 433,
    438, 442–446
Milestones, 70, 310, 333, 414, 423–424,
    472–475, 528
    reports, 435–437
MIT (Massachusetts Institute of
    Technology), 7
Models, 40. *See also* Project selection;
    Scoring models
Monitoring, 410–437, 469
    accounting data, 66–67
    data collection procedures, 414–416,
        416–421
    definition, 410
    earned value, 416–417, 479
        value completed, 428–430

        variances, 428–434
        of work performed, 428–430
    ethical issues, 420
    human factors, 419
    measurement problems and issues,
        414–415, 415–416
    planning, monitoring, controlling cycle,
        412–421
        closed loop information flow, 413
    purpose of, 411
    reports, 418–425
        benefits of, 424
        common problems, 427
        final report, 475
        frequency, 419
        milestone reports, 435–437, 475
        project status or progress, 418–425,
            473–474, 475–476
        timing of, 419, 423
        types of, 424–425
    schedule, 302–303
    standards and criteria, 414–416
        changes in, 415
    system design, 414–416
    types of data, 417
Motivation, 96–97, 144, 146,
    163–167
MRP (materials requirements planning),
    196
MTU, 118
Multicultural project management,
    112–126
    compadre system, 114, 114n, 118
    culture impact on project, 113–115
    definitions of culture, 113
    elements of culture, 113
    managerial behavior, 125–126
    microcultures, 115

multicultural communication, 124–126
  managerial and personal behavior, 125–126
  structure and style of communications, 124–125
psychosocial needs of project team, 126
Multicultural projects, 86
Multifunctional teams, 187, 208
  and project risk, 193
  structuring, 210–212
Multiplication rule, 579–580
Multiproject scheduling/allocation, 388–398
  effectiveness measures, 389–390
  heuristic methods, 392–398
    descheduling/borrowing, 396–397
    effect of alternate life cycles, 395–398
    RAMPS, 393
    SPAR-1, 395–398
    Walt-capacity, 399
  manufacturing process models, 390–391
  mathematical programming, 391–392
  optimizing methods, 390

NAFTA (North American Free trade Agreement), 119
Name-Only-Teams (NOTs), 167
NASA, 1, 97, 344, 551
National Cooperative Research Act of 1984, 118
NCR Corp., 541
Negotiation, 104, 121, 152, 162, 163, 201, 226–248
  budget, 269–271
  definition, 229
  ethics of, 230
  nature of, 243
  partnering/chartering, 230–232, 234
  positional, 244
  principled, 244–245
  requirements, 243–244
  style, 243–246
  win-win, 227, 244–246, 269
Networks, 303, 306–332, 419, 440–441, 443
  activity-on-arrow, on-node, see Activity-on-arrow, on-node (AOA, AON)
  benefits, 303, 306
  construction of, 309–314
  definition, 303
  terminology, 308–310
New York State Bar Association, 227
Non-projects, 10–11
Normal probability distribution, 322–323, 575–576
North American Free trade Agreement (NAFTA), 119
Northrup Corp., 389
NOTs (Name-Only-Teams), 167

Objective/subjective measures, 67
Office of Naval Research, 148
Operating necessity model, 46
Organization, 139–169
  choosing form, 154–156
  functional, 141–145
    advantages/disadvantages, 141–144
  matrix, see Matrix organization
  mixed form, 152–154
    advantages/disadvantages, 153–154
  project-oriented, 139–141, 571
  pure project, 145–147
    advantages/disadvantages, 145–147

Parties-at-interest, 10, 90, 102–103, 113, 226–227, 235–238

Partnering, 230–231, 234, 238

Pentagon, 7

Personnel, acquiring and motivating, *see* Motivation

PERT, *see* Program evaluation and review technique

Peter Principle, 574

Planning, 182–184. *See also* Action plan
  contingency plan, 70, 102
  effectiveness, 192
  elements of, 187–189
  even planning process, 193–195
  importance of, 198
  master plan, 262, 434
  phases, 183
  post-planning review, 186
  project launch meeting, 184–185
  project plan, 183–185, 302
  sign-offs, 201, 232
  systems integration, 192–193
  work breakdown structure, 203–208

PMBOK, *see* Project management body of knowledge

PMI, *see* Project Management Institute

PMIS, *see* Project management information system

Political tactics, 96

Pratt & Whitney, 9, 118

Precedence diagramming, 340–341

Primavera Project Planner®, 438

Priorities, 233–234, 237–238, 239–241, 382

Probability and statistics, 577–586
  event relationships and probability laws, 578–581
    addition rule, 580–581
    definitions, 578–579
    multiplication rule, 579–580

  probability, 577–578
    experimental probability, 578
    logical probability, 578
    subjective probability, 578
  standard probability distributions, 586
  statistics, 581–586
    definitions, 581–587
    descriptive vs. inferential statistics, 583
    inferential statistics, 584–586
    measures of central tendency, 582–583
    measures of dispersion, 583–584

Procter & Gamble, 59, 92, 488

Product line extension model, 46

Profit/profitability models, 48–52
  advantages/disadvantages, 51
  average rate of return, 48
  discounted cash flow, 48–49
  internal rate of return, 50
  payback period, 48
  profitability index, 50

Program budgeting, 272–273

Program evaluation and review technique (PERT), 307–308, 328–330, 374

Project
  champion, 96, 542
  coordination, 184–192
  definition, 8–9
  deliverables, objectives, 3, 186, 473, 475, 512–515
  evaluation, 39–73
  failure, 103
    effect on morale, 102
    fear of, 101–102
    reasons for, 102
  final report, 541. *See also* Termination
  goals, 3, 14–17, 42–44, 512–515
    ancillary, 512–515

direct, 513
    threshold values, 44
master schedule, 188, 205–206, 475
meetings, 425–426
nonproject vs., 10–11
objectives, 3–4, 183
portfolio, 39
predicting success or failure,
    548–549
    causes of failure, 548–549
project plan, 183
proposals, 40, 46, 68–71, 475
    executive summary, 69
    implementation plan, 70
    logistic support, 70–71
    technical approach, 69–70
purpose, 9, 12, 103
Project budgeting, *see* Budget
Project charter, 189
Project goals, 14–17, 100–101
Projectitis, 147, 154
Project launch meeting, 184–185
Project management
    advantages/disadvantages, 12
    definition, 6
    forces for, 1–2
    limitations, 13
    professionalization of, 5, 15
Project management body of knowledge
    (PMBOK), 5, 92, 434
Project management information system
    (PMIS), 437–447, 572–573
    desirable capabilities, 440–441
    management errors, 439–440
    selection process, 441–442
    typical software output, 442–447
Project Management Institute (PMI), 5, 8,
    92, 109, 397, 571–572

Project manager, 85–128
    authority, 12, 235–238
    career, 6, 13, 91–93
    credibility, 107–108
    demands on, 95–104
    diary, 559
    ethics, 109–111, 420
    facilitator vs. functional manager, 87–89
    firefighting, 99
    information network, 103–104
    initial tasks, 85–87
    institutional environments, 117–121
    interpersonal sensitivity, 167–168
    leadership, 108–111
    management style of, 110
    multicultural issues, 124–127
    orientation, problem vs. discipline, 87, 98
    political sensitivity, 98, 103, 108
    responsibilities, 90–91
        in balanced matrix organization, 149
        conflict resolution, 241
        control of creative activities, 490
        control systems, 477–478, 485
        early warning system, 473
        in functional organizations, 145–146,
            152
        institutional environment, 117–118
        linear responsibility chart, 208
        managerial/personal behavior, 126
        in matrix-organized projects, 152
        monitoring, 419–421
        project termination, 556
        resource loading, 373
        scheduling, 389
    rewarding excellence of, 574
    role of, 87–90
    selection of, 107–112
    stress, 111–112

Project office, war room, 160, 161, 419, 514–515
Project-oriented organization, 139–141, 571. *See also* Organization
Project planning, *see* Planning
Project review committee, 426
Project scheduling, *see* Scheduling
Project selection, 39–73, 237
   information base, 66–68
   models
      choice, 60–61
      criteria, 40–42
      nature of, 40, 42–45
      nonnumerical models, 45–48
      numerical models, 48–60
      types, 40, 42–43, 48–52
   under uncertainty, 62–66
Project team, 91, 160–169, 486. *See also* Multifunctional teams
   characteristics, 97–98
   composition, 161–162
   human factors, 163–168
   interpersonal conflict, 165–168. *See also* Conflict
   morale, 102
   motivation, 146, 163–167
   psychosocial needs in multicultural project, 127
   team building, 165
Project termination, *see* Termination
Proposals, *see* Project, proposals
Pseudoactivity, 394

Q-sort, 47
Quattro Pro® (Borland), 42

RAND Corporation, 7, 55
Raz's iterative rating process, 60

Reliance Electric Co., 68
Reports, *see* Audits; Monitoring
Republic Steel Corp., 46
Request for Proposal (RFP), 39, 69, 282
Request for Quotation (RFQ), 69
Resource acquisition, 95–96
Resource allocation, 361–401. *See also* Trade–offs
   constrained resource allocation, 378–388
      branch and bound approach, 383, 387
      Burgess's method, 386
      heuristic methods, 379–386
      optimizing methods, 386–387
   critical path method (CPM), 363–369
      cost/time slope, 365
      fast-tracking, 369–371
   multiproject scheduling/ allocation, *see* Multiproject scheduling/allocation
Resource allocation for multiple project scheduling (RAMPS), 393
Resource contouring, 384–386
Resource leveling, 375–381
Resource loading, 372–375
Resource scarcity, 371–372, 397–398
Responsibility matrix, 205–207
RFQ (Request for Quotation), 69
Risk
   analysis, 64
   uncertainty vs., 62–63
Risk+[reg. symbol], 325
Rolls Royce, 118, 149

Sacred cow model, 45
SAGE (Semiautomatic Ground Environment) air defense system, 7, 87

Scheduling. *See also* Activity
  control mechanism, 302–303
  critical path, 307, 308, 317–319
    reverse critical path, 340
  critical path method (CPM), 307–310,
      361, 374
  critical time, 317–319
  distinction between PERT and CMP,
      307, 310, 363
  Gantt chart, *see* Gantt chart
  GERT, *see* Graphical Evaluation and
      Review Technique
  master schedule, 188, 205–206, 475
  networks, *see* Networks
  other scheduling methods, 344
  program evaluation and review
      technique (PERT), 307–308,
      328–330, 374
  project completion time, 321–325
  slack, 307, 319–321, 333, 375
Scheduling program for allocation of
      resources (SPAR–1), 395–398
Scope change, 232–234. *See also* change
Scope creep, 477–478, 491–492
Scoring models, 53–60, 529
  advantages/disadvantages, 60
  constrained weighted factor, 59
  Raz's iterative rating process, 60
  unweighted factor, 53–55
  unweighted 0–1 factor, 53
  weighted factor, 55–58
Selection, *see* Project selection
Self–directed work teams (SDWTs), 164,
      165
SEMATECH, 118
Semiautomatic Ground Environment
      (SAGE) air defense system,
      7, 87

Simulation, 64–65, 324–325, 339
  Crystal Ball[reg. symbol], 325
  Monte Carlo, 63
  risk analysis, 64
  Risk+®, 325
  At Risk®, 325
  software, 65
Slack scheduling, 307, 319–321, 333, 375
Snecma, 118
Software Engineering Institute, 347
Stakeholders, *see* Parties-at-interest
Standard probability distributions, 586
Statistical bias, 284–290
Statistics, *see* Probability and statistics
Subjective measures, 67
Subjective probabilities, 63
Subjective probability, 578
Suboptimize, 12, 144
Success, 512, 547–549
Support from senior management, 103,
      187, 198, 261
Systems approach, 88, 150
Systems integration, engineering, 192–193

Tactics, political, 96
Task, 9
Team building, *see* Project team
Teams, multifunctional, *see*
      Multifunctional teams
Technical change procedure, 163
Technical proposal requirements
      (TPR), 69
Technological shock, 68, 280–281
Termination, 539–560
  decision, 545–551
    major questions, 545–546
    mathematical/statistical models,
      551–552

Termination (*continued*)
  decision support system (DSS), 552
  process, 551–557
    implementation, 552–557
    project final report, history, 541, 549,
      557–559
      content, 557–559
    special considerations, 543–544
    termination manager, 554, 556
      duties, 554, 556
    types of termination, 540–545
      by addition, 541–543
      by extinction, 541
      by integration, 543–544
      by starvation, 544–545
Texas Instruments, 153
Top management support, *see* Support
      from senior management
Total quality management (TQM), 164,
      231, 234, 270, 485
TPR (technical proposal requirements), 69
TQM, *see* Total quality management
Tracking signal, 285–289
  as ratio, 285–289
Trade-offs, 4, 100–101, 230, 240, 307,
      361–366, 372, 389–390

and life cycle, 100–101, 240
  time/cost trade-offs, 363–369
    cost shifting, 376
Transdisciplinary projects, 7, 7fn
TREND, 208–212, 339
Tweed coat management, 91

Uncertainty, 17–18, 44, 208, 232, 264–265
  project completion time, 321–325
  risk vs., 62–63
United Way, 46
University of California, 2
University of Cincinnati, 141–143
U.S. Air Force, 9
U.S. Navy, 1, 307, 316

Value engineering, 193, 270
Virtual positions, 150
Virtual projects, 422

War room, 160, 419, 514–515
Window-of-opportunity analysis, 65–66
Work breakdown structure (WBS),
      161–162, 203–208, 262, 266,
      267, 303, 423, 443, 471
  design of, 203–209
Work packages, units, 9, 201